Western Civilization

Beyond Boundaries

Western Civilization

Beyond Boundaries

Fifth Edition

VOLUME C
since 1789

Thomas F. X. Noble
University of Notre Dame

Barry Strauss
Cornell University

Duane J. Osheim
University of Virginia

Kristen B. Neuschel
Duke University

Elinor A. Accampo
University of Southern California

David D. Roberts
University of Georgia

William B. Cohen
Late of Indiana University

Houghton Mifflin Company   Boston   New York

Publisher: Suzanne Jeans
Senior Sponsoring Editor: Nancy Blaine
Marketing Manager: Katherine Bates
Marketing Assistant: Lauren Bussard
Senior Development Editor: Julie Swasey
Editorial Assistant: Adrienne Zicht
Senior Project Editor: Christina Horn
Editorial Assistant: Carrie Parker
Art and Design Coordinator: Jill Haber
Cover Design Director: Tony Saizon
Senior Photo Editor: Jennifer Meyer Dare
Composition Buyer: Chuck Dutton
New Title Project Manager: James Lonergan

Volume C cover image: Umberto Boccioni (1882–1916), *Unique Forms of Continuity in Space.*
Photograph: Tate Gallery, London/Art Resource, NY.

Text credits: Page 831: Excerpts from *A Room of One's Own* by Virginia Woolf. Copyright
© 1929 by Harcourt, Inc., and renewed 1957 by Leonard Woolf. Reprinted by permission
of the publisher.

Printed in the U.S.A.

Library of Congress Control Number: 2006935032

ISBN-13: 978-0-618-79429-4
ISBN-10: 0-618-79429-8

123456789-VH-10 09 08 07

Brief Contents

CONTENTS

MAPS

Documents

The Visual Record

PREFACE

An old adage says that each generation must write history for itself. If the adage is true, then it would also be true that each generation must teach and learn history for itself. The history, of course, does not change, although new discoveries come to light all the time. What does change is us, each succeeding generation of us. What causes us to change, and thus to experience and understand history in ever new ways, are the great developments of our own times. Think of the world-changing events of the last century: two world wars, the Great Depression, the cold war, nuclear weapons, the civil rights movement, the women's movement, the explosion in scientific knowledge, and the media revolutions involving radio and television, the computer, and the Internet. The pace of change has accelerated in our time, but the process of change always affects people's view of their world.

As we launch the fifth edition for this book we are once again acutely aware of the need to address big questions in ways that make sense to teachers and students right now, in the world we live in today. As these words are being written, the news is full of reports from Afghanistan, Iraq, Iran, and Darfur. In such circumstances we might well ask, What is the West; what is Western? Some believe that we are engaged in a "Clash of Civilizations." Is one of these Western Civilization? If so, who or what is its adversary? The West is sometimes understood geographically and sometimes culturally. For most people, the West means western Europe. And yet western Europe itself is the heir of the peoples and cultures of antiquity, including the Sumerians, Egyptians, Persians, Greeks, Romans, Jews, Christians, and Muslims. In fact, Europe is the heir of even earlier civilizations in Asia and Africa. As a cultural phenomenon, "Western" implies many things: freedom and free, participatory political institutions; economic initiative and opportunity; monotheistic religious faiths (Judaism, Christianity, and Islam); rationalism and ordered thought in the social, political, and philosophical realms; an aesthetic sensibility that aspires to a universal sense of beauty. But the West has felt free to evoke tradition as its guiding light and also to innovate brilliantly, to accommodate slavery and freedom simultaneously, and to esteem original thought and persecute people who deviate from the norm. "Western" indeed has meant many things in various places at different times. This book constantly and explicitly attempts to situate its readers in place, time, and tradition.

Another big question is this: What exactly is civilization? No definition can win universal acceptance, but certain elements of a definition are widely accepted.

Cities are crucial; with cities emerge complex social organizations that involve at least a minimal division of labor. Some people work in the fields, some in the home. Soldiers defend the city, and artisans provide its daily goods. Governing institutions have a wide measure of acceptance and have the ability to enforce their will. Complex cultures also develop religious ideas and authorities; a literature and law that may be oral or written; monumental architecture, especially fortifications, palaces, and temples; and arts such as music, painting, and sculpture.

Western Civilization has had an influence on almost every person alive today. The West deserves to be studied because its tale is compelling, but it demands to be studied because its story has been so central to the development of the world in which we live. Many of the world's dominant institutions are Western in their origin and in their contemporary manifestations—most notably parliamentary democracy. Commercial capitalism, a Western construct, is the world's dominant form of economic organization, and even its greatest rival, communism, is fundamentally Western: its theoreticians were Europeans who drew on utopian ideals, classical economics, Enlightenment doctrines, and the ideologies of the French Revolution.

Until a generation or so ago, Western Civilization was a staple of college and university curricula and was generally studied in isolation. Although it was, and is, important for us to know who we are, it is also important for us to see that we have changed in dramatic ways and that we can no longer understand ourselves in isolation from the world around us. Accordingly, this book repeatedly sets the experience of the West into its global context. This is not a World History book. But it is a book that sees Western Civilization as one significant segment of the world's history.

BASIC APPROACH

Nearly two decades ago the six original authors of *Western Civilization: Beyond Boundaries* set out to create a textbook for a course that would, as a total effort, inform students about essential developments within a tradition that has powerfully, though not always positively, affected everyone in the contemporary world. Although each of us found something to admire in all of the existing textbooks, none of us was fully happy with any of them. We were disappointed with books that claimed "balance," but actually stressed a single kind of history. We regretted that so many texts were uneven in their command of recent scholarship. Although we were convinced of both the inherent interest of Western Civilization and the importance of teaching the subject, we were disconcerted by the celebratory tone of some books, which portrayed the West as resting on its laurels instead of creatively facing its future.

We decided to produce a book that is balanced and coherent; that addresses the full range of subjects that a Western Civilization book needs to address; that provides the student reader with interesting, timely material; that is up-to-date in terms of scholarship and approach; and that is handsome to look at—in short, a book that helps the instructor to teach and the student to learn. We have kept our common vision fresh through frequent meetings, correspondence, critical mutual readings, and expert editorial guidance. The misfortune of the untimely death of one member of our team has brought us the fortune of a new colleague who has inspired and challenged the rest of us in new ways. Because each of us has focused on his or her own area of specialization, we believe that we have attained a rare blend of competence, confidence, and enthusiasm. Moreover, in moving from plans for a first edition to the preparation of a fifth, we have been able to profit from the experience of using the book, the advice and criticism of dozens of colleagues, and the reactions of thousands of students.

Western Civilization is a story. Therefore, we aimed at a strong chronological narrative line. Our experience as teachers tells us that students appreciate this clear but gentle orientation. Our experience tells us, too, that an approach that is broadly chronological will leave instructors plenty of room to adapt our narrative to their preferred organization, or to supplement our narrative with one of their own.

Although we maintain the familiar, large-scale divisions of a Western Civilization book, we also present some innovative adjustments in arrangement. For instance, Chapter 2 treats early Greece together with the whole eastern Mediterranean region in the period from about 1500 to 750 B.C. This approach both links kindred cultures and respects chronological flow better than customary treatments, which take western Asia to a certain point and then backtrack to deal with early Greece. We incorporate a single chapter on Late Antiquity, the tumultuous and fascinating period from about A.D. 300 to 600 that witnessed the transformation of the Roman Empire into three successors: Byzantine, Islamic, and European. One chapter studies those three successors, thereby permitting careful comparisons. But we also assign chapters to some of the greatest issues in Western Civilization, such as the Renaissance, the age of European exploration and conquest, the Scientific Revolution, and the industrial transformation. Our twentieth-century chapters reflect an understanding of the last century formed in its clos-

ing years rather than in its middle decades. What is new in our organization represents adjustments grounded in the best scholarship, and what is old represents time-tested approaches.

In fashioning our picture of the West, we took two unusual steps. First, our West is itself bigger than the one found in most textbooks. We treat the Celtic world, Scandinavia, and the Slavic world as integral parts of the story. We look often at the lands that border the West—Anatolia/Turkey, western Asia, North Africa, the Eurasian steppes—in order to show the to-and-fro of peoples, ideas, technologies, and products. Second, we continually situate the West in its global context. Just as we recognize that the West has influenced the rest of the world, we also carefully acknowledge how the rest of the world has influenced the West. We begin this story of mutual interaction with the Greeks and Romans, carry it through the European Middle Ages, focus on it in the age of European exploration and conquest, and analyze it closely in the modern world of industry, diplomacy, empire, immigration, and questions of citizenship and identity.

Another approach that runs like a ribbon throughout this textbook involves balance and integration. Teachers and students, just like the authors of this book, have their particular interests and emphases. In the large and diverse American academy, that is as it should be. But a textbook, if it is to be helpful and useful, should incorporate as many interests and emphases as possible. For a long time, some said, Western Civilization books devoted excessive coverage to high politics—"the public deeds of great men," as an ancient Greek writer defined the historian's subject. Others felt that high culture—all the Aristotles and Mozarts—were included to the exclusion of supposedly lesser figures and ordinary men and women. In the 1970s books began to emphasize social history. Some applauded this new emphasis even as they debated fiercely over what to include under this heading.

In this book, we attempt to capture the Western tradition in its full contours, to hear the voices of all those who have made durable contributions. But because we cannot say everything about everybody at every moment, we have had to make choices about how and where to array key topics within our narrative. Above all, we have tried to be integrative. For example, when we talk about government and politics, we present the institutional structures through which power was exercised, the people who possessed power as well as the people who did not, the ideological foundations for the use of power, and the material conditions that fostered or hindered the real or the would-be powerful. In other words, instead of treating old-fashioned "high politics" in abstract and descriptive ways, we take an approach that is organic and analytical: How did things work? Our approach to the history of women is another example. A glance at this book's table of contents and then at its index is revealing. The former reveals very few sections devoted explicitly and exclusively to women. The latter shows that women appear constantly in every section of this book. Is there a contradiction here? Not at all. Women and men have not been historical actors in isolation from one another. Yet gender, which is relational, reciprocal, and mutual, is an important variable that has shaped individual and collective experience. Hence we seek to explain why certain political, economic, or social circumstances had differing impacts on men and women, and how such conditions led them to make different choices.

Similarly, when we talk of great ideas, we describe the antecedent ideas from which seemingly new ones were built up, and we ask about the consequences of those ideas. We explore the social positions of the authors of those ideas to see if this helps us explain the ideas themselves or gauge their influence. We try to understand how ideas in one field of human endeavor prove to be influential in other fields. For instance, gender is viewed as connected to and part of the larger fabric of ideas including power, culture, and piety.

We invite the reader to look at our narrative as if it were a mosaic. Taken as a whole, our narrative contains a coherent picture. Viewed more closely, it is made up of countless tiny bits that may have their individual interest but do not even hint at the larger picture of which they are parts. Finally, just as the viewer of a mosaic may find his or her eye drawn especially to one area, feature, color, or style, so too the reader of this book will find some parts more engaging or compelling than others. But it is only because there is, in this book as in a mosaic, a complete picture that the individual sections make sense, command our attention, excite our interest.

One word sums up our approach in this book: "balance." We tell a good story, but we pause often to reflect on that story, to analyze it. We devote substantial coverage to the typical areas of Greece, Rome, Italy, France, Great Britain, and so forth, but we say more about western Europe's frontiers than any other book. We do not try to disguise our Western Civilization book as a World History book, but we take great pains to locate the West within its global context. And we always assume that context means mutuality and reciprocity. We have high politics and big ideas alongside household management and popular culture. We think that part of the fascination of the past lies in its capacity to suggest understandings of the present and possibilities for the future.

Our subtitle, "Beyond Boundaries," is intended to suggest growth, challenge, and opportunity. The West began in Mesopotamia but soon spread to all of western Asia. Gradually the Greeks entered the scene and disseminated their ideas throughout the Mediterranean world. The Romans, always heirs of the Greeks, carried ideas and institutions from Britain to Mesopotamia. As the Roman order collapsed, Rome's imprint was left on a small segment of Europe lying west of the Rhine and south of the Danube. Europeans then crashed through those boundaries to create a culture that extended from Iceland to the Russian steppes. At the dawn of the modern age Europe entered into a complex set of commercial, colonial, military, and political relations with the rest of the globe. Our contemporary world sees Western influences everywhere. No western "boundary" has ever been more than temporary, provisional.

DISTINCTIVE FEATURES

To make this book as accessible as possible to students, we have constantly been aware of its place in a program of teaching and learning. In the preceding paragraphs something has been said about this book's distinctive substantive features and how, we believe, they will contribute to the attainment of a deeper understanding of Western Civilization, as well as of its importance and place in the wider history of the earth's peoples. Teaching and learning also involves pedagogical techniques and innovations. We have attended conscientiously to pedagogical issues from the start, and we have made some significant changes in this edition.

Our chapters have always begun with a vignette that is directly tied to an accompanying picture. These vignettes alert the reader to one or more of the key aspects of the chapter. Thus the readers have encountered a thematic introduction that evokes interest while pointing clearly and in some detail to what follows.

To make our chapter introductions more effective, which means to give students greater confidence as they proceed through the book, we have taken numerous steps. First, as in past editions, we reviewed and revised our opening vignettes to connect text and picture more closely and to use both to invite the reader into the chapter.

Second, the first page of each chapter contains a succinct Outline that immediately and dramatically tells the reader what he or she is going to encounter in the following pages. Third, a list of Key Terms is designed to work with the introduction and Outline to give the student a clear orientation to what will follow. Fourth, the chapter introductions conclude with a list of Focus Questions that both echo the introduction and set the reader off on the right path into the following pages. Fifth, as the student begins to read the chapter proper, a Chronology serves as yet another orientation to the material contained in the chapter. Subject-specific chronologies still appear in various parts of the book, but we felt readers would benefit from a chronological guide at the beginning of each chapter.

In this edition we have repeated each Focus Question at the head of the section to which it pertains. At the end of each major section, we provide succinct Section Summaries. Each chapter concludes with a Chapter Summary that reiterates the Focus Questions and then briefly answers them once again.

As a complement to text coverage, a ready reference, and a potential study guide, all of the Key Terms have always been gathered into a Glossary at the back of the book. For this edition, we have also placed definitions on the pages where the Key Terms first appear.

In addition to this fundamental attention to chapter themes and contents, we have sought to improve the book's teachability by adding a pronunciation guide. Whenever we use an unfamiliar name or term, we show the reader how to pronounce it. Instead of using the intricate rules of phonetics, we provide commonsense guides to pronunciation in parentheses directly following the word.

This edition is a bit shorter than its predecessors. Relevance, "teachability," and "learnability" were our guides in streamlining our coverage at many points. Virtually every chapter experienced some slimming in the interest of keeping major points and themes front and center.

We have been conscious of how the book *looks* to the reader from the very beginning. Attractively laid-out pages, a handsome full-color design, engaging maps, and beautifully reproduced pictures enhance the book's appearance. In keeping with our desire to integrate the components of the book into a coherent whole, we carefully anchor the maps and pictures into the volume. The authors designed the content of the maps in this book, labeled them to complement its text, and captioned them to advance its teaching role. The same is true of the pictures: the authors selected them, worked with the book's designers to place them advantageously (and not just decoratively), and wrote all the captions. For this edition, we paid particular attention to reviewing all the captions and to revising many of them. All of the maps are cross-referenced in the text, some of them several times, and the text often refers directly to the pictures.

From the start, every chapter in this book has had boxed documents, one of which treated a "global" theme, as well as a two-page feature entitled "Weighing the Evidence." For this edition, we thought hard about our features and decided to take some decisive steps to make them work better for teachers and students. First, we reduced the number of features to three per chapter. Second, we introduced a uniform structure and format. One feature, entitled "The Global Record," presents a significant document that sets some aspect of Western Civilization within the global perspective.

These documents are substantial, are carefully introduced, and conclude with study questions. Another feature is called "The Written Record." This feature contains a significant document relevant to the text materials then under discussion with a careful introduction and study questions. The third feature is called "The Visual Record." This feature represents a reconceptualization of our former "Weighing the Evidence" feature. Most of those features did focus on visual evidence, but now the Visual Record features all do so. As with the Global Record and Written Record features, the Visual Records have helpful questions. Whereas the Weighing the Evidence features always concluded our chapters, now the Visual Records are placed into the chapters at the most appropriate position. For this edition, we cast a careful eye over all the Visual Record features and prepared eight new ones.

ORGANIZATION AND CONTENT CHANGES

As always, we have paid close attention to how our chapters "work." Accordingly, Chapter 1 contains new material on ancient treaty making, Chapter 2 incorporates new archaeological findings, Chapter 3 has fresh material on Greek politics, and Chapter 5 includes revised material on Roman politics and the conflict of the orders, as well as material on the Roman household and the connection between family and government. Chapter 7 has reorganized material on the Catholic Church, and Chapter 9 has expanded coverage of the Crusades. Chapters 9 and 10 have been shortened and streamlined. Chapter 13 has new material, as do Chapters 15 and 17, both of which were significantly reorganized. The material on the Thirty Years' War in Chapter 15 has been fully reworked and now includes a section on the developments in eastern and central Europe. New material on the slave trade has been added to Chapter 18. The treatment of industrialization in Chapter 20 has been recast. In Chapter 23, a new discussion of women and charity has been added, focusing on Josephine Grey Butler, Annie Wood Besant, and others. Chapter 24 has exciting new material on communications and propaganda. Chapter 28 incorporates new scholarship on the role of Pope Pius XII during the Holocaust, as well as an expanded account of the Warsaw uprising. Finally, in light of the drastic changes in the world since this book was last revised, Chapter 30 has been thoroughly rewritten to include coverage of the Iraq War, recent environmental issues, the expanding European Union, the changing demographics of Europe, the issues of unilateralism and Western responsibility in an increasingly global community, and the outrage provoked in the Muslim world over certain Danish political cartoons.

ANCILLARIES

A wide array of supplements accompany this text to help students better master the material and to help instructors in teaching from the book:

▶ *Online Study Center student website* Online Study Center

▶ *Online Teaching Center instructor website* Online Teaching Center

▶ *HM Testing CD-ROM (powered by Diploma)*

▶ *Online Instructor's Resource Manual*

▶ *PowerPoint maps, images, and lecture outlines*

▶ *PowerPoint questions for personal response systems*

▶ *Blackboard™ and WebCT™ course cartridges*

▶ *Eduspace™ (powered by Blackboard™)*

▶ *Interactive ebook*

The *Online Study Center* is a companion website for students that features a wide assortment of resources to help students master the subject matter. The website, prepared by Jacqueline Cavalier of Community College of Allegheny County and Douglas Keith, is divided into three major sections:

▶ **"Prepare for Class"** includes material such as learning objectives, chapter outlines, and pre-class quizzes for a student to consult before going to class.

▶ **"Improve Your Grade"** includes practice review material like interactive flashcards, chronological ordering exercises, primary sources, and interactive map exercises.

▶ **"ACE the Test"** features our successful ACE brand of practice tests as well as other self-testing materials.

Students can find additional text resources such as an online glossary, audio MP3 files of chapter summaries, and material on how to study more effectively in the **"General Resources"** section. Throughout the text, icons direct students to relevant exercises and self-testing material located on the *Online Study Center*. Access the *Online Study Center* for this text by visiting **college.hmco.com/pic/noble5e.**

The *Online Teaching Center* is a companion website for instructors. It features all of the material on the student site plus additional password-protected resources that help instructors teach the course, such as an electronic version of the *Instructor's Resource Manual* and *PowerPoint* slides. Access the *Online Teaching Center* for this text by visiting **college.hmco.com/pic/noble5e.**

The *Instructor's Resource Manual,* prepared by William A. Paquette of Tidewater Community College, contains instructional objectives, chapter outlines and summaries, lecture suggestions, suggested debate and research topics, cooperative learning activities, and suggested readings and resources.

HM Testing (powered by *Diploma*) offers instructors a flexible and powerful tool for test generation and test management. Now supported by the Brownstone Research Group's market-leading *Diploma* software, this new version of *HM Testing* significantly improves on functionality and ease of use by offering all the tools needed to create, author, deliver, and customize multiple types of tests. *Diploma* is currently in use at thousands of college and university campuses throughout the United States and Canada. The *HM Testing* content for this text was developed by Janusz Duzinkiewicz of Purdue University North Central and offers key term identification, multiple-choice questions (with page references to the correct response), short answer, essay questions (with sample answers), and map questions that refer to maps in the text, as well as final exams for both volumes.

We are pleased to offer a collection of Western Civilization *PowerPoint* lecture outlines, maps, and images for use in classroom presentations. Detailed lecture outlines correspond to the book's chapters and make it easier for instructors to cover the major topics in class. The art collection includes all of the photos and maps in the text, as well as numerous other images from our Western Civilization titles. *PowerPoint* questions and answers for use with personal response system software are also offered to adopters free of charge.

A variety of assignable homework and testing material has been developed to work with the *Blackboard™* and *WebCT™* course management systems, as well as with *Eduspace™*, Houghton Mifflin's Online Learning Tool (powered by Blackboard™). *Eduspace™* is a web-based online learning environment that provides instructors with a gradebook and communication capabilities, such as synchronous and asynchronous chats and announcement postings. It offers access to assignments such as over 650 gradable homework exercises, writing assignments, interactive maps with questions, primary sources, discussion questions for online discussion boards, and tests, which all come ready-to-use. Instructors can choose to use the content as is, modify it, or even add their own material. *Eduspace™* also contains an interactive ebook, which contains in-text links to interactive maps, primary sources, and audio pronunciation files, as well as review and self-testing material for students.

ACKNOWLEDGMENTS

The authors have benefited throughout the process of revision from the acute and helpful criticisms of numerous colleagues. We thank in particular: **Daniel Brown,** Moorpark College; **Elizabeth Carney,** Clemson University; **Jacqueline Cavalier,** Community College of Allegheny County; **Janusz Duzinkiewicz,** Purdue University North Central; **Lisa Lane,** Mira Costa College; **Clementine Oliver,** California State Northridge; **William Paquette,** Tidewater Community College; **Rick Parrish,** Brevard Community College; and **Stuart Smyth,** SUNY Albany.

Each of us has benefited from the close readings and careful criticisms of our coauthors, although we all assume responsibility for our own chapters. Barry Strauss has written Chapters 1–6; Thomas Noble, 7–10; Duane Osheim, 11–14; Kristen Neuschel, 15–19; and David Roberts, 25–30. William Cohen originally wrote Chapters 20–24, and these have now been thoroughly reviewed by Elinor Accampo.

Many colleagues, friends, and family members have helped us develop this work as well. Thomas Noble continues to be grateful for Linda Noble's patience and good humor. He is also grateful to John Contreni, Thomas Head, Elizabeth Meyer, Julia Smith, the late Richard E. Sullivan, John Van Engen, and Robert Wilken. He also thanks some two dozen teaching assistants who have helped him to think through the Western Civilization experience.

Barry Strauss is grateful to colleagues at Cornell and at other universities who offered advice and encouragement and responded to scholarly questions. He would also like to thank the people at Cornell who provided technical assistance and support. Most important have been the support and forbearance of his family. His daughter, Sylvie; his son, Michael; and, above all, his wife, Marcia, have truly been sources of inspiration.

Duane Osheim thanks family and friends who continue to support and comment on the text. He would especially like to thank colleagues at the University of Virginia who have engaged him in a long and fruitful discussion of Western Civilization and its relationship to other cultures. They make clear the mutual interdependence of the cultures of the wider world. He particularly wishes to thank H. C. Erik Midelfort, Arthur Field, Brian Owensby, Joseph C. Miller, Chris Carlsmith, Beth Plummer, and David D'Andrea for information and clarification on a host of topics.

Kristen Neuschel thanks her colleagues at Duke University for sharing their expertise. She is especially grateful to Sy Mauskopf, Bill Reddy, John Richards, Tom Robisheaux, Alex Roland, Barry Gaspar, and Peter Wood. She also thanks her husband and fellow historian, Alan Williams, for his wisdom about Western Civilization and his support throughout the project, and her children, Jesse and Rachel, for their patience, joy, and curiosity.

Elinor Accampo is deeply indebted to the late Bill Cohen, whose work she edited, revised, and added to. His original chapters offered a model of expertise and prose, and it is with great pride, respect, and humility that she carries on what he originated. She also wishes to thank the coauthors—Thomas Noble, Barry Strauss, Duane Osheim, Kristen Neuschel, and David Roberts for their warm welcome to the team, and for the advice and expertise they offered. She owes special thanks to Kristen Neuschel and Rachel Fuchs (who contributed to an earlier edition) for friendship, support, and advice, as well as to Nancy Blaine and Julie Swasey for graciously responding to the persistent questions of a novice on this long-standing project.

David Roberts wishes to thank Bonnie Cary, Vici Payne, and Brenda Luke for their able assistance and Walter Adamson, Timothy Cleaveland, Karl Friday, Michael Kwass, John Morrow, Miranda Pollard, Judith Rohrer, William Steuck, and Kirk Willis for sharing their expertise in response to questions. He also thanks Beth Roberts for her constant support and interest and her exceedingly critical eye.

The first plans for this book were laid in 1988, and over the course of eighteen years there has been remarkable stability in the core group of people responsible for its development. The author team lost a member, Bill Cohen, but Elinor Accampo stepped into Bill's place with such skill and grace that it seemed as though she had been with us from the start. Our original sponsoring editor, Jean Woy, moved up the corporate ladder but never missed an author meeting with us. Christina Horn, our senior project editor, has been the wizard behind the curtain for all five editions. More than anyone else, she has taught us how to *make* a book. Carole Frohlich, our picture researcher, has also been with us from the beginning, and she has been masterful at fulfilling and enhancing our picture requests. Our sponsoring editor for most of a decade, Nancy Blaine, has been a tower of strength. She believes in us, as we believe in her. We have been fortunate in our editors, Elizabeth Welch, Jennifer Sutherland, and Julie Swasey. All these kind and skillful people have elicited from us authors a level of achievement that fills us at once with pride and humility.

Thomas F. X. Noble

ABOUT THE AUTHORS

Thomas F. X. Noble   After receiving his Ph.D. from Michigan State University, Thomas Noble taught at Albion College, Michigan State University, Texas Tech University, and the University of Virginia. In 1999 he received the University of Virginia's highest award for teaching excellence. In 2001 he became Robert M. Conway Director of the Medieval Institute at the University of Notre Dame. He is the author of *The Republic of St. Peter: The Birth of the Papal State, 680–825; Religion, Culture and Society in the Early Middle Ages; Soldiers of Christ: Saints and Saints' Lives from Late Antiquity and the Early Middle Ages; Images and the Carolingians: Tradition, Order, and Worship;* and *From Roman Provinces to Medieval Kingdoms.* Noble's articles and reviews have appeared in many leading journals, including the *American Historical Review, Byzantinische Zeitschrift, Catholic Historical Review, Revue d'histoire ecclésiastique, Speculum,* and *Studi medievali.* He has also contributed chapters to several books and articles to three encyclopedias. He was a member of the Institute for Advanced Study in 1994 and the Netherlands Institute for Advanced Study in 1999–2000. He has been awarded fellowships by the National Endowment for the Humanities (twice) and the American Philosophical Society. He was elected a Fellow of the Medieval Academy of America in 2004.

Barry Strauss   Professor of history and Classics at Cornell University, Barry Strauss holds a Ph.D. from Yale. He has been awarded fellowships by the National Endowment for the Humanities, the American School of Classical Studies at Athens, the MacDowell Colony for the Arts, the Korea Foundation, and the Killam Foundation of Canada. He is the recipient of the Clark Award for excellence in teaching from Cornell. He served as Director of Cornell's Peace Studies Program. His many publications include *Athens After the Peloponnesian War: Class, Faction, and Policy, 403–386 B.C.; Fathers and Sons in Athens: Ideology and Society in the Era of the Peloponnesian War; The Anatomy of Error: Ancient Military Disasters and Their Lessons for Modern Strategists* (with Josiah Ober); *Hegemonic Rivalry from Thucydides to the Nuclear Age* (co-edited with R. Ned Lebow); *War and Democracy: A Comparative Study of the Korean War and the Peloponnesian War* (co-edited with David R. McCann); *Rowing Against the Current: On Learning to Scull at Forty; The Battle of Salamis, the Naval Encounter That Saved Greece—and Western Civilization;* and *The Trojan War: A New History.* His book *The Battle of Salamis* has been translated into five languages and was named one of the best books of 2004 by the Washington Post.

Duane J. Osheim   A Fellow of the American Academy in Rome with a Ph.D. in history from the University of California at Davis, Duane Osheim is department chair and professor of history at the University of Virginia. He is the author and editor of numerous books on the social and cultural history of late medieval and Renaissance Italy, including *A Tuscan Monastery and Its Social World; An Italian Lordship: The Bishopric of Lucca in the Late Middle Ages;* and *Beyond Florence: The Contours of Medieval and Early Modern Italy.* To appear shortly is *Chronicling History: Chroniclers and Historians in Medieval and Renaissance Italy.*

Kristen B. Neuschel   After receiving her Ph.D. from Brown University, Kristen Neuschel taught at Denison University and Duke University, where she is currently associate professor of history. She is a specialist in early modern French history and is the author of *Word of Honor: Interpreting Noble Culture in Sixteenth-Century France* and articles on French social history and European women's history. She has received grants from the National Endowment for the Humanities and the American Council of Learned Societies. She has also received the Alumni Distinguished Undergraduate Teaching Award, which is awarded annually on the basis of student nominations for excellence in teaching at Duke.

Elinor A. Accampo   Professor of history and gender studies at the University of Southern California, Elinor Accampo completed her Ph.D. at the University of California, Berkeley. Prior to her career at USC, she taught at Colorado College and Denison University. She specializes in modern France and is the author of *Blessed Motherhood; Bitter Fruit: Nelly Roussel and the Politics of Female Pain in Third Republic France;* and *Industrialization, Family, and Class Relations: Saint Chamond, 1815–1914.* She has also published *Gender and the Politics of Social Reform in France* (co-edited with Rachel Fuchs and Mary Lynn Stewart) and articles and book chapters on the history of reproductive rights and birth control movements. She has received fellowships and travel grants from the German Marshall Fund, the Haynes Foundation, the American

Council of Learned Societies, and the National Endowment for the Humanities, as well as an award for Innovative Undergraduate Teaching at USC.

David D. Roberts After taking his Ph.D. in modern European history at the University of California, Berkeley, David Roberts taught at the Universities of Virginia and Rochester before becoming professor of history at the University of Georgia in 1988. At Rochester he chaired the Humanities Department of the Eastman School of Music, and he chaired the History Department at Georgia from 1993 to 1998. A recipient of Woodrow Wilson and Rockefeller Foundation fellowships, he is the author of *The Syndicalist Tradition and Italian Fascism; Benedetto Croce and the Uses of Historicism; Nothing but History: Reconstruction and Extremity After Metaphysics;* and *The Totalitarian Experiment in Twentieth-Century Europe: Rethinking the Poverty of Great Politics,* as well as two books in Italian and numerous articles and reviews. He is currently the Albert Berry Saye Professor of History at Georgia.

19

AN AGE OF REVOLUTION, 1789–1815

A French Citizen Army
The National Guard of
Paris leaves to join the
army, September 1792
(detail). *(Photos12.com-ARJ)*

These militiamen marching off to defend France against the invader in September 1792 appear to be heroes already. Adoring women in the crowd hand them laurel wreaths as they pass; the men march by, resolute and triumphant. Symbols of the ongoing revolution stand out as well: the prominent tricolor flag, the tricolor cockade in each man's hat. In fact, that September France's citizen armies for the first time defeated the army of a foreign monarch poised to breach its borders and snuff out its revolution. The painting celebrates this triumph about to happen and thereby inspires confidence in the Revolution and pride in its citizen-soldiers.

Today the French Revolution is considered the initiation of modern European as well as modern French history. The most powerful monarch in Europe was forced to accept constitutional limits to his power by subjects convinced of their right to demand them. Eventually, the king was overthrown and executed, and the monarchy abolished. Events in France reverberated throughout Europe because the overthrow of one absolute monarchy threatened fellow royals elsewhere. Revolutionary fervor on the part of ordinary soldiers enabled France's armies unexpectedly to best many of their opponents. By the late 1790s the armies of France would be led in outright conquest of other European states by one of the most talented generals in European history: Napoleon Bonaparte. He brought to the continental European nations that his armies eventually conquered a mixture of imperial aggression and revolutionary change. Europe was transformed both by the shifting balance of power and by the spread of revolutionary ideas.

Understanding the French Revolution means understanding not only its origins but also its complicated course of events and their significance. Challenges to the power of the king were not new, but the Revolution overthrew his right to rule at all. The notion that the people constituted the nation, were responsible as citizens, and had some right to representation in government became irresistible. Louis XVI was transformed from the divinely appointed father of his people to an enemy of the people, worthy only of execution. Central to the Revolution was the complex process by which public opinion was shaped and, in turn, shaped events. Change was driven

CHAPTER OUTLINE

THE BEGINNINGS OF REVOLUTION, 1775–1789

THE PHASES OF THE REVOLUTION, 1789–1799

THE NAPOLEONIC ERA AND THE LEGACY OF REVOLUTION, 1799–1815

KEY TERMS

Third Estate

National Assembly

Tennis Court Oath

Declaration of the Rights of Man and the Citizen

sans-culottes

Jacobins

Maximilien Robespierre

the Terror

Society of Revolutionary Republican Women

Directory

Napoleon Bonaparte

Civil Code

François Toussaint-Louverture

Online Study Center
This icon will direct you to interactive map and primary source activities on the website **college.hmco.com/pic/noble5e**

in part by the power of symbols—flags, rallying cries, inspiring art—to challenge an old political order and legitimize a new one.

FOCUS QUESTIONS

What factors led to the beginning of revolution in France in 1789?

Why did several phases of revolutionary change occur after 1789 and what were the characteristics of each phase?

What impact did the Revolution and Napoleonic rule have on France, the rest of Europe, and the wider world?

THE BEGINNINGS OF REVOLUTION, 1775–1789

What factors led to the beginning of revolution in France in 1789?

"I am a citizen of the world," wrote John Paul Jones, captain in the fledgling U.S. Navy, in 1778. He was writing to a Scottish aristocrat, apologizing for raiding the lord's estate while marauding along the British coast during the American Revolution. Jones (1747–1792), born a Scotsman himself, was one of the thousands of cosmopolitan Europeans who were familiar with European cultures on both sides of the Atlantic. As a sailor, Jones literally knew his way around the Atlantic world, but he was a "citizen of the world" in another sense as well. The Scotsman replied to Jones, surprised by the raid, since he was sympathetic to the American colonists; he was a man of "liberal sentiments" like Jones himself.[1] Both Jones and the Scottish lord felt they belonged to an international society of gentlemen who recognized certain Enlightenment principles regarding just and rational government.

In the Atlantic world of the late eighteenth century, both practical links of commerce and shared ideals about "liberty" were important shaping forces. The strategic interests of the great European powers were also always involved. Thus when the American colonists actively resisted British rule and then in 1776 declared their independence from Britain, the consequences were widespread and varied: British trading interests were challenged, French appetites for gains at British expense were whetted, and illusive notions about "liberty" seemed more plausible. The victory of the American colonies in 1783, followed by the creation of the U.S. Constitution in 1787, further heightened the appeal of liberal ideas elsewhere. Attempts at liberal reform were mounted in several states, including Ireland, the Netherlands, and Poland. However, the American Revolution had the most direct impact on later events in France because the French had been directly involved in the American effort.

REVOLUTIONARY MOVEMENTS IN EUROPE

While the British government was facing the revolt of the American colonies, it also confronted trouble closer to home. Like many Americans, many Britons had divided loyalties, and many who did favor armed force to subdue the rebellion were convinced that the war was being mismanaged. The prosecution of the war against the American colonies proceeded amid calls for reform of the ministerial government. The American rebellion also had ripple effects in other parts of Europe.

Ireland   A reform movement also sprang up in Ireland in 1779. The reformers demanded greater autonomy from Britain. Like the Americans, Irish elites—mostly of English or Scottish origin—felt like disadvantaged junior partners in the British Empire. They objected to British policies that favored British imperial interests over those of the Irish ruling class: for example, the exclusion of Irish ports in favor of English and Scottish ones and the granting of political rights to Irish Catholics so that they might fight in Britain's overseas armies.

Protestant Irish landlords and elite families in towns, threatened by such policies, expressed their opposition not only in parliamentary debates but also in military defiance. Following the example of the American rebels, they set up a system of locally sponsored voluntary militia to resist British troops if necessary. The Volunteer Movement was neutralized when greater parliamentary autonomy for Ireland was granted in 1782, following the repeal of many restrictions on Irish commerce. Unlike the Americans, the Irish elites faced an internal challenge to their own authority—the Catholic population whom they had for centuries dominated. That challenge forced them to reach an accommodation with the British government.

The Netherlands Meanwhile, a political crisis with constitutional overtones was also brewing in the Netherlands. The United Provinces (the Netherlands) was governed by a narrow oligarchy of old merchant families, particularly in Amsterdam, and a military governor, the "stadtholder," from the princely House of Orange. The interests of the merchants and of the stadtholder frequently conflicted. Tensions between them deepened during the American Revolution, as merchants favored trade with the colonists and the prince favored maintaining an English alliance.

The conflict changed character when the representatives of the various cities, calling themselves the Dutch "Patriot" Party, defended their positions on the grounds of traditional balance of power within the Netherlands as well as with wider claims to American-style "liberty." The challenge to traditional political arrangements widened when middling urban dwellers, including newly wealthy traders and professionals, long disenfranchised by the closed merchant oligarchies, demanded "liberty," too—that is, political enfranchisement within the cities—and briefly took over the Patriot movement. Just as many Irish rebels accepted the concessions of 1782, the Patriot oligarchs in the Netherlands did nothing to resist an invasion in 1787 that restored the power of the stadtholder, the prince of Orange, and thereby ended the challenge to their own control of urban government.

Both the Irish volunteers and the Dutch Patriots, though members of very limited movements, echoed the American rebels in practical and ideological ways. Both were influenced by the economic and political consequences of Britain's relationship with its colonies. Both were inspired by the success of the American rebels and their thoroughgoing claims for political self-determination.

Poland Desire for political reform flared in Poland as well during this period. Reform along lines suggested by Enlightenment precepts was accepted as a necessity by Polish leaders after the first partition of Poland in 1772 had left the remnant state without some of its wealthiest territories (see Map 18.1 on page 570). Beginning in 1788, however, reforming gentry in the *Sejm* (representative assembly) went further; they established a commission to write a constitution, following the American example. The resulting document, known as the May 3 (1791) Constitution, was the first codified constitution in Europe; it was read and admired by George Washington.

Poles thus established a constitutional monarchy in which representatives of major towns as well as gentry and nobility could sit as deputies. The *liberum veto*, or individual veto power, which had allowed great nobles to obstruct royal authority, was abolished. However, Catherine the Great, empress of Russia, would not tolerate a constitutional government operating so close

to her own autocratic regime; she ordered an invasion of Poland in 1792. The unsuccessful defense of Poland was led by, among others, a Polish veteran of the American Revolution, Tadeusz Kosciuszko (tah-DAY-oosh kos-USE-ko) (1746–1817). The second, more extensive partition of Poland followed, to be answered in turn in 1794 by a widespread insurrection against Russian rule, spearheaded by Kosciuszko. The uprising was mercilessly suppressed by an alliance of Russian and Prussian troops. Unlike the U.S. Constitution from which they drew inspiration, the Poles' constitutional experiment was doomed by the power of its neighbors.

CHRONOLOGY

1775–1783	American Revolutionary War
1779–1782	Irish Volunteer Movement
1788	U.S. Constitution ratified; Reform movement begins in Poland; "Patriot" movement ends in the Netherlands
1789	French Estates General meets at Versailles (May); Third Estate declares itself the National Assembly (June); Storming of the Bastille (July)
1791	Polish constitution French king Louis XVI captured attempting to flee (June) Slave revolt begins in Saint Domingue
1792	France declares war on Austria; revolutionary wars begin (April); Louis XVI arrested; France declared a republic (August–September)
1793	Louis XVI guillotined
1793–1794	Reign of Terror in France
1799	Napoleon seizes power in France
1801	Concordat with pope
1804	Napoleon crowned emperor Napoleonic Civil Code Independence of Haiti (Saint Domingue) declared
1805	Battle of Trafalgar; Battle of Austerlitz
1806	Dissolution of Holy Roman Empire
1812	French invasion of Russia
1814	Napoleon abdicates and is exiled French monarchy restored
1815	Hundred Days (February–June) Battle of Waterloo

THE AMERICAN REVOLUTION AND THE KINGDOM OF FRANCE

As Britain's greatest commercial and political rival, France naturally was drawn into Britain's struggle with its North American colonies. In the Seven Years' War (1756–1763), the French had lost many of their colonial settlements and trading outposts to the English (see page 578). Stung by this outcome, certain French courtiers and ministers pressed for an aggressive colonial policy that would regain for France some of the riches in trade that Britain now threatened to monopolize. The American Revolution seemed to offer the perfect opportunity. The French extended covert aid to the Americans from the very beginning of the conflict in 1775. After the first major defeat of British troops by the Americans—at the Battle of Saratoga in 1777—France formally recognized the independent United States and committed troops as well as funds to the American cause. John Paul Jones's famous ship, the *Bonhomme Richard* (bon-OHM ree-SHARD), was purchased and outfitted by the French government, as were many other American naval vessels. French support was decisive. In 1781 the French fleet kept reinforcements from reaching the British force besieged by George Washington at Yorktown. The American victory at Yorktown effectively ended the war; the colonies' independence was formally recognized by the Treaty of Paris in 1783.

The consequences for France of its American alliance were momentous. Aid for the Americans saddled France with a debt of about 1 billion *livres* (pounds), which represented as much as one-quarter of the total debt that the French government was trying to service. A less tangible impact of the American Revolution came from the direct participation of about nine thousand French soldiers, sailors, and aristocrats. The best known is the Marquis de Lafayette, who became an aide to George Washington and helped command American troops. For many humble men, the war was simply employment. For others, it was a quest of sorts. For them, the promise of the Enlightenment—belief in human rationality, natural rights, and universal laws by which society should be organized—was brought to life in America.

Exposure to the American conflict occurred at the French court, too. Beginning in 1775, a permanent American mission to Versailles lobbied hard for aid and later managed the flow of that assistance. The chief emissary of the Americans was Benjamin Franklin (1706–1790), a philosophe by French standards whose writings and scientific experiments were already known to European elites. His talents—among them, a skillful exploitation of a simple, Quaker-like demeanor—succeeded in promoting the idealization of America at the French court.

The U.S. Constitution, the various state constitutions, and the debates surrounding their ratification were all published in Paris and much discussed in salons and at court, where lively debate about reform of French institutions had been going on for decades. America became the prototype of the rational republic—the embodiment of Enlightenment philosophy. It was hailed as the place where the irrationalities of inherited privilege did not prevail. A British observer, Arthur Young (1741–1820), believed that "the American revolution has laid the foundation of another in France, if [the French] government does not take care of itself."[2]

By the mid-1780s there was no longer a question of whether the French regime would experience reform but rather a question of what form the reform would take. The royal government was almost bankrupt. A significant minority of the politically active elite was convinced of the fundamental irrationality of France's system of government. Nevertheless, a dissatisfied elite and a financial crisis—even fanned by a successful revolt elsewhere—do not necessarily lead to revolution. Why did the French government—the *Ancien Régime* (ahn-SYEN ray-ZHEEM) or "Old Regime," as it became known after the Revolution—not "take care of itself"?

THE CRISIS OF THE OLD REGIME

The Old Regime was brought to the point of crisis in the late 1780s by three factors: (1) heavy debts that dwarfed an antiquated system for collecting revenue; (2) institutional constraints on the monarchy that defended privileged interests; and (3) public opinion that envisioned thoroughgoing reform and pushed the monarchy in that direction. Another factor was the ineptitude of the king, Louis XVI (r. 1774–1793).

Louis came to the throne in 1774, a year before the American Revolution began. He was a kind, well-meaning man better suited to be a petty bureaucrat than a king. The queen, the Austrian Marie Antoinette (1755–1793), was regarded with suspicion by the many who despised the "unnatural" alliance with Austria the marriage had sealed. She, too, was politically inept, unable to negotiate the complexities of court life and widely rumored to be selfishly wasteful of royal resources despite the realm's financial crises.

The fiscal crisis of the monarchy had been a long time in the making and was an outgrowth of the system by which the greatest wealth was protected by traditional privileges. At the top of the social and political pyramid were the nobles, a legal grouping that included warriors and royal officials. In France nobility conferred exemption from much taxation. Thus the royal government could not directly tax its wealthiest subjects.

This situation existed throughout much of Europe, a legacy of the individual contractual relation-

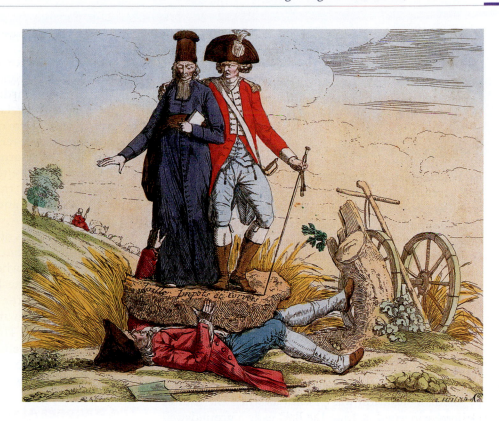

The Common People Crushed by Privilege
In this contemporary cartoon, a nobleman in military dress and a clergyman crush a commoner under the rock of burdensome taxes and forced labor *(corvées)*. The victim's situation reflects that of the peasantry, but his stylish clothes would allow affluent townspeople to identify with him. *(Musée Carnavalet, Paris/ Giraudon/Art Resource, NY)*

ships that had formed the political and economic framework of medieval Europe. Unique to France, however, was the strength of the institutions that defended this system. Of particular importance were the royal law courts, the parlements (par-luh-MAWHN), which claimed a right of judicial review over royal edicts. All the parlementaires—well-educated lawyers and judges— were noble and loudly defended the traditional privileges of all nobles. Louis XV (d. 1774), near the end of his life, had successfully undermined the power of the parlements by a bold series of moves. Louis XVI, immediately after coming to the throne, buckled under pressure and restored the parlements to full strength.

Deficit financing had been a way of life for the monarchy for centuries. After early efforts at reform, Louis XIV (d. 1715) had reverted to common fundraising expedients such as selling offices, which only added to the weight of privileged investment in the old order. England had established a national bank to free its government from the problem, but the comparable French effort early in the century had been undercapitalized and had failed. Late in the 1780s, under Louis XVI, one-fourth of the annual operating expenses of the government was borrowed, and half of all government expenditure went to paying interest on its debt. Short-term economic crises, such as disastrous harvests, added to the cumulative problem of government finance.

The king employed able finance ministers who tried to institute fundamental reforms, such as replacing the tangle of taxes with a simpler system in which all would pay and eliminating local tariffs, which were stifling commerce. The parlements and many courtiers and aristocrats, as well as ordinary people, resisted these policies. Peasants and townsfolk did not trust the "free market" (free from traditional trade controls) for grain; most feared that speculators would buy up the grain supply and people would starve. Trying to implement such reforms in times of grain shortage almost guaranteed their failure. Moreover, many supported the parlements simply because they were the only institution capable of standing up to the monarchy. Yet not all members of the elite joined the parlements in opposing reform. The imprint of "enlightened" public opinion was apparent in the thinking of some courtiers and thousands of educated commoners who believed that the government and the economy had to change and openly debated the nature and extent of reform needed.

In 1787 the king called an "Assembly of Notables"— an ad hoc group of elites—to support him in facing down the parlements and proceeding with some changes. He found little support even among men known to be sympathetic to reform. Some did not support particular proposals, and many were reluctant to allow the monarchy free rein. Others, reflecting the influence of the American Revolution, maintained that a "constitutional" body such as the Estates General, which had not been called since 1614, needed to make these decisions.

Ironically, nobles and clergy who were opposed to reform supported the call for the Estates General, too, confident they could control its deliberations. The three Estates met and voted separately by "order"—clergy (First Estate), nobles (Second Estate), and commoners (**Third Estate**). The combined votes of the clergy and nobles would presumably nullify whatever the Third Estate might propose.

THE ESTATES GENERAL

In 1788 mounting pressure from common people as well as courtiers led Louis to summon the Estates General. On Louis's orders, deputies were to be elected by local assemblies, which were chosen in turn by wide male suffrage. Louis mistakenly assumed he had widespread support in the provinces and wished to tap it by means of this grass-roots voting. Louis also agreed that the Third Estate should have twice as many deputies as the other two Estates, but he did not authorize voting by head rather than by order, which would have brought about the dominance of the Third Estate. Nevertheless, the king hoped that the specter of drastic proposals put forth by the Third Estate would frighten the aristocrats and clergy into accepting some of his reforms.

Louis's situation was precarious when the Estates General convened in May 1789. Already a groundswell of sentiment confirmed the legitimacy of the Estates General and the authority of the Third Estate to enact change. Political pamphlets abounded arguing that the Third Estate deserved enhanced power because it carried the mandate of the people. The most important of these was *What Is the Third Estate?* (1789) by Joseph Emmanuel Sieyès (1748–1836), a church official from the diocese of Chartres. The sympathies of Abbé Sieyès (say-EZ), as he was known, were with the Third Estate: his career had stalled because he was not noble. Sieyès argued that the Third Estate represented the nation because it did not reflect special privilege.

Among the deputies of the first two Estates—clergy and nobility—were men, such as the Marquis de Lafayette (1757–1834), who were sympathetic to reform. In the Third Estate, a large majority of deputies reflected the most radical political thought possible for men of their standing. Most were lawyers and other professionals who were functionaries in the government but, like Sieyès, of low social rank. They frequented provincial academies, salons, and political societies. They were convinced of the validity of their viewpoints and determined on reform, and they had little stake in the system as it was. When this group convened and met with resistance from the First and Second Estates and from Louis himself, they seized the reins of government and a revolution began.

1789: A REVOLUTION BEGINS

As soon as the three Estates convened at the royal palace at Versailles, conflicts surfaced. The ineptness of the Crown was immediately clear. On the first day of the meetings in May, Louis and his ministers failed to introduce a program of reforms for the deputies to consider. This failure raised doubt about the monarchy's commitment to reform. More important, it allowed the political initiative to pass to the Third Estate. The deputies challenged the Crown's insistence that the three Estates meet and vote separately. Deputies to the Third Estate refused to be certified (that is, to have their credentials officially recognized) as members of only the Third Estate rather than as members of the Estates General as a whole.

For six weeks the Estates General was unable to meet officially, and the king did nothing to break the impasse. During this interlude, the determination of the deputies of the Third Estate strengthened. More and more deputies were won over to the notion that the three Estates must begin in the most systematic way: France must have a written constitution.

The National Assembly   By the middle of June, more than thirty reformist members of the clergy were sitting jointly with the Third Estate, which had invited all deputies from all three Estates to meet and be certified together. On June 17 the Third Estate simply declared itself the **National Assembly** of France. At first the king did nothing, but when the deputies arrived to meet on the morning of June 20, they discovered they had been locked out of the hall. Undaunted, they assembled instead in a nearby indoor tennis court and produced the document that has come to be known as the **Tennis Court Oath.** It was a collective pledge to meet until a written constitution had been achieved. Only one deputy refused to support it. Sure of their mandate, the deputies had assumed the reins of government.

The king continued to handle the situation with both ill-timed self-assertion and feeble attempts at compromise. As more and more deputies from the First and Second Estates joined the National Assembly, Louis "ordered" the remaining loyal deputies to join it, too. Simultaneously, however, he ordered troops to come to Paris. He feared disorder in the wake of the recent disturbances throughout France and believed that any challenge to the legitimacy of arbitrary monarchical authority would be disastrous.

Third Estate   In France, the common people, as distinct from the nobles (First Estate) and clergy (Second Estate), in the representative body the Estates General.

National Assembly   Legislative body formed in France in June 1789, when members of the Third Estate in the Estates General, joined by some deputies from the clergy, declared themselves the representatives of the nation.

Tennis Court Oath   Pledge signed by all but one deputy of the National Assembly in France on June 20, 1789, to meet until a constitution was drafted.

The Tennis Court Oath

It was raining on June 20, 1789, when the deputies found themselves barred from their meeting hall and sought shelter in the royal tennis court. Their defiance created one of the turning points of the Revolution; the significance was recognized several years later by the creator of this painting. *(Réunion des Musées Nationaux/Art Resource, NY)*

Louis's appeal for armed assistance provoked unrest in the capital. Paris, with a population of about 600,000, was one of the largest cities in Europe. It was the political nerve center of the nation—the site of the publishing industry, salons, the homes of parlementaires and royal ministers. It was also a working city, with thousands of laborers of all trades plus thousands more—perhaps one-tenth of the inhabitants—jobless recent immigrants from the countryside. The city was both extremely volatile and extremely important to the stability of royal power. The king's call for troops aroused Parisians' suspicions. Some assumed a plot was afoot to starve Paris and destroy the National Assembly. Already they considered the Assembly to be a guarantor of acceptable government.

The Storming of the Bastille

It took little—the announcement of the dismissal of a reformist finance minister—for Paris to erupt in demonstrations and looting. Crowds besieged City Hall and the royal armory, where they seized thousands of weapons. A popular militia formed as citizens armed themselves. Armed crowds assailed other sites of royal authority, including the huge fortified prison, the Bastille, on the

morning of July 14. The Bastille now held only a handful of petty criminals, but it still remained a potent symbol of royal power and, it was assumed, held large supplies of arms. Like the troops at the armory, the garrison at the Bastille had received no firm orders to fire on the crowds if necessary. The garrison commander at first mounted a hesitant defense, then decided to surrender after citizens managed to secure cannon and drag them to face the prison. Most of the garrison were allowed to go free, although the commander and several officers were murdered by the crowd.

The citizens' victory was a great embarrassment to royal authority. The king immediately had to embrace the popular movement. He came to Paris and in front of crowds at City Hall donned the red and blue cockade worn by the militia and ordinary folk as a badge of resolve and defiance. This symbolic action signaled the reversal of the Old Regime—politics would now be based on new principles.

Encouraged by events in Paris, inhabitants of cities and towns around France staged similar uprisings. In many areas, the machinery of royal government completely broke down. City councils, officials, and even parlementaires were thrown out of office. Popular

Women's March on Versailles, October 1789

Parisian marketwomen marched the 12 miles to the king's palace at Versailles, some provisioning themselves with tools or weapons as they left the capital.

(Réunion des Musées Nationaux/Art Resource, NY)

militias took control of the streets. A simultaneous wave of uprisings shook the countryside. Most of them were the result of food shortages, but their timing added momentum to the more strictly political protests in cities.

Toward Constitutional Government   These events forced the members of the National Assembly to work energetically on the constitution and to pass legislation to satisfy popular protests against economic and political privileges. On August 4 the Assembly issued a set of decrees abolishing the remnants of powers that landlords had enjoyed since the Middle Ages, including the right to co-opt peasant labor and the bondage of serfdom itself. Although largely symbolic, because serfdom and forced labor had been eliminated in much of France, these changes represented a dramatic inroad into the property rights of the elite as they had been traditionally construed. The repeals were hailed as the "end of feudalism." A blow was also struck at established religion by eliminating the tithe, the forced payment of one-tenth of a person's income to the church. At the end of August, the Assembly issued the **Declaration of the Rights of Man and the Citizen.** It was a

bold assertion of the foundations of a newly conceived government, closely modeled on portions of the U.S. Constitution. Its preamble declared "that [since] the ignorance, neglect or contempt of the rights of man are the sole cause of public calamities and the corruption of governments," the deputies were "determined to set forth in a solemn declaration the natural, inalienable and sacred rights of man."[3]

In September the deputies debated the king's role in a new constitutional government. Monarchists favored a government rather like England's, with a two-house legislature, including an upper house representing the hereditary aristocracy and a royal right to veto legislation. More radical deputies favored a single legislative chamber and no veto power for the king. After deliberation, the Assembly reached a compromise. The king was given a three-year suspensive veto—the power to suspend legislation for the sitting of two legislatures. This was still a formidable amount of power but a drastic curtailment of his formerly absolute sovereignty.

The Women's March to Versailles   Again Louis resorted to troops. This time he called them directly to Versailles, where the Assembly sat. News of the troops' arrival provoked outrage, which heightened with the threat of another grain shortage. Early on the morning of October 5, women in the Paris street markets saw the empty grocers' stalls and took immediate collective action. "We want bread!" they shouted at the steps of City

Declaration of the Rights of Man and the Citizen   Document issued by the National Assembly of France in August 1789. Modeled on the U.S. Constitution, it asserted "the natural, inalienable and sacred rights of man."

Hall. Because they were responsible for procuring their families' food, women often led protests over bread shortages. This protest, however, went far beyond the ordinary. A crowd of thousands gathered and decided to walk all the way to Versailles, accompanied by the popular militia (now called the "National Guard"), to petition the king directly for sustenance.

Online Study Center **Improve Your Grade**
Primary Source: Popular Revolution: The Women of Paris March on Versailles

At Versailles, a joint delegation of the women and deputies from the National Assembly was dispatched to see the king. Some of the women fell at the feet of the king with their tales of hardship, certain that the "father of the people" would alleviate their suffering. He did order stored grain supplies distributed in Paris, and he agreed to accept the constitutional role that the Assembly had voted for him.

The king also agreed to return to Paris to reassure the people and was escorted back to the capital by both popular militia and bread protesters. The king was now in the hands of his people. Already, dramatic change had occurred as a result of a complex dynamic among the three Estates, the Crown, and the people of Paris. The king was still assumed to be the fatherly guardian of his people's well-being, but his powers were now limited and his authority badly shaken. The Assembly had begun to govern in the name of the "nation" and so far had the support of the people.

SECTION SUMMARY

- Inspired by events in America, elites in Ireland, the Netherlands, and Poland pushed for greater political liberty.

- France's support for the American colonies against Great Britain increased French government debt and exposed French soldiers and courtiers to revolutionary ideas.

- By the late 1780s, French royal government was in crisis owing to bankruptcy, institutions that impeded reform, and agitation for reform within elite society.

- The French Revolution began in 1789 when the Estates General convened and commoners in the Third Estate claimed a mandate to write a constitution and enact major changes in law.

- French citizens, led by the Parisians, formed popular militias, attacked royal fortresses, and marched to Versailles to confront the king.

THE PHASES OF THE REVOLUTION, 1789–1799

Why did several phases of revolutionary change occur after 1789 and what were the characteristics of each phase?

The French Revolution was a complicated affair. It was a series of changes, in a sense a series of revolutions, driven not by one group of people but by several groups. Even among elites convinced of the need for reform, the range of opinion was wide. The people of Paris continued to be an important force for change. Country people also became active, primarily in resisting changes forced on them by the central government.

All of the wrangling within France was complicated by foreign reaction to events there. Managing war to defend the revolution soon became a routine burden for the fragile revolutionary governments. In addition, they had to cope with the continuing problems that had precipitated the Revolution in the first place, including the government's chronic indebtedness and recurrent grain shortages. Finally, the Revolution itself was an issue in that, once the traditional arrangements of royal government had been altered, momentum for further change was unleashed.

THE FIRST PHASE COMPLETED, 1789–1791

At the end of 1789 Paris was in ferment, but for a time forward progress blunted the threat of disastrous divisions between king and Assembly and between either of them and the people of Paris. The capital continued to be the center of lively political debate. Salons continued to meet; academies and private societies proliferated. Deputies to the Assembly swelled the ranks of these societies or helped to found new ones. Several would be important throughout the Revolution—particularly the Jacobin (JACK-oh-bin) Club, named for the monastic order whose buildings the members used as a meeting hall.

These clubs represented the gamut of revolutionary opinion. Some, in which ordinary Parisians were well represented, focused on economic policies that would directly benefit common people. Women were active in a few of the more radical groups. Monarchists dominated other clubs. At first similar to the salons and debating societies of the Enlightenment era, the clubs quickly became sources of political pressure on the government. A bevy of popular newspapers also contributed to the vigorous political life in the capital.

The broad front of revolutionary consensus began to break apart as the Assembly forged ahead with decisions about the constitution and with policies necessary to remedy France's still-desperate financial situation. The largest portion of the untapped wealth of the nation lay with the Catholic Church, an obvious target of anticlerical reformers. The deputies did not propose to dismantle the church, but they did make sweeping changes: They kept church buildings intact and retained the clergy as salaried officials of the state. They abolished all monasteries and pensioned the monks and nuns to permit them to continue as nurses and teachers where possible. With the depleted treasury in mind, the Assembly seized most of the vast lands of the church and declared them national property (*biens nationaux*) to be sold for revenue.

However, revenue was needed faster than the property could be inventoried and sold, so government bonds (*assignats* [ah-see-NYAH]) were issued against the eventual sale of church lands. Unfortunately, in the cash-strapped economy, the bonds were treated like money, their value became inflated, and the government never realized the hoped-for profits. A greater problem was the political divisiveness generated by the restructuring of the church. Many members of the lower clergy, living as they did near ordinary citizens, were among the most reform-minded of the deputies. These clergy were willing to go along with many changes, but the required oath of loyalty to the state made a mockery of clerical independence.

The Civil Constitution of the Clergy, as these measures were called, was passed by the Assembly in July 1790 because the clerical deputies opposing it were outvoted. More than half of the churchmen did take the oath of loyalty. Those who refused, concentrated among the higher clergy, were in theory thrown out of their offices. A year later (April 1791) the pope declared that clergy who had taken the oath were suspended from their offices. Antirevolutionary sentiment grew among thousands of French people, particularly in outlying regions, to whom the church was still vital as a source of charity and a center of community life. This religious opposition worked to undermine the legitimacy of the new government.

Meanwhile, the Assembly proceeded with administrative and judicial reform. The deputies abolished the medieval provinces as administrative districts and replaced them with uniform *départements* (departments). They declared that local officials would be elected—a revolutionary dispersal of power that had previously belonged to the king.

As work on the constitution drew to a close in the spring of 1791, the king decided that he had had enough. Royal authority, as he knew it, had been virtually dismantled and Louis himself was now a virtual prisoner in the Tuileries (TWEE-lair-ee) Palace in central Paris. The king and a few loyal aides worked out a plan to flee France and on June 20, 1791, he and the members of his immediate family set out in disguise. However, the party was stopped—and recognized—in the town of Varennes (vah-REN) near the eastern border of the kingdom.

Louis and his family were returned to Paris and held under lightly disguised house arrest. The circumstances of his flight were quickly discovered. He and the queen had sent money abroad ahead of themselves. He had left behind a document that condemned the constitution and revealed his intention was to invade France with Austrian troops, if necessary. Thus, in July 1791, just as the Assembly was completing its proposal for a constitutional monarchy, the constitution it had created began to seem unworkable because the monarch was not to be trusted.

Editorials and protests against the monarchy increased. In one incident known as the Massacre of the Champ (Field) de Mars (SHOM duh MARSS), government troops led by Lafayette fired on citizens at an antimonarchy demonstration that certain Parisian clubs had organized; about fifty men and women died. This inflammatory incident heightened tensions between moderate reformers satisfied with the constitutional monarchy, such as Lafayette, and outspoken republicans who wanted to eliminate the monarchy altogether.

Nevertheless, on September 14 the king swore to uphold the constitution. He had no choice. The event became an occasion for celebration, but the tension between the interests of the Parisians and the provisions of the new constitution could not be glossed over. Though a liberal document for its day, the constitution reflected the views of the elite deputies who had created it. The right to vote, based on a minimal property qualification, was given to about half of all adult men. However, these men only chose electors, for whom the property qualifications were higher. The electors in turn chose deputies to national bodies as well as local officials. Although in theory any eligible voter could be an elected deputy or official, the fact that elite electors determined every officeholder meant that few ordinary citizens would become deputies or local administrators. A new Declaration of Rights accompanied the constitution that reflected a fear of the masses that had not existed when the Declaration of the Rights of Man and the Citizen was first promulgated in 1789. Freedom of the press and freedom of assembly, for example, were not fully guaranteed.

Further, the constitution granted neither political rights nor legal equality to women, nor did the Assembly pass laws beneficial to women, such as legalizing divorce or mandating female education. Educated women had joined some of the Parisian clubs and had attempted to influence the Assembly. A Declaration of the Rights of Woman was drafted by a woman named Olympe de Gouges (oh-LAMP duh GOOZH) to draw attention to the treatment of women in the new constitution.

Online Study Center **Improve Your Grade**
Primary Source: A French Woman Broadens the Revolution: Declaration of the Rights of Woman and Citizen

Very soon after the constitution was implemented, the fragility of the new system became clear. The National Assembly declared that its members could not serve in the first assembly to be elected under the constitution. Thus the members of the newly elected Legislative Assembly, which began to meet in October 1791, lacked any of the cohesiveness that would have come from collective experience. Also, unlike the previous National Assembly, they did not represent a broad range of opinion but were mostly republicans.

In fact, the Legislative Assembly was dominated by republican members of the Jacobin Club. They were known as Girondins (zhih-ron-DEHN), after the region in southwestern France from which many of the club's leaders came. The policies of these new deputies and continued pressure from the ordinary citizens of Paris would cause the constitutional monarchy to collapse in less than a year.

THE SECOND PHASE AND FOREIGN WAR, 1791–1793

An additional pressure on the new regime soon arose: a threat of foreign invasion and a war to respond to the threat. Aristocratic émigrés, including the king's brothers, had taken refuge in nearby German states and were planning to invade France. The emperor and other German rulers did little actively to aid the plotters. Austria and Prussia, however, in the Declaration of Pillnitz of August 1791, declared, as a concession to the émigrés, that they would intervene if necessary to support the monarchy in France.

The threat of invasion, when coupled with distrust of the royal family, seemed more real to the revolutionaries in Paris than it may actually have been. Indeed, many deputies hoped for war. They assumed that the outcome would be a French defeat, which would lead to a popular uprising that would rid them, at last, of the monarchy. In April 1792, under pressure from the

The French Revolution

May 5, 1789	Estates General meets in Versailles
June 17, 1789	Third Estate declares itself the National Assembly
June 20, 1789	Tennis Court Oath
July 14, 1789	Storming of the Bastille
August 27, 1789	Declaration of the Rights of Man and the Citizen
October 5–6, 1789	Women's march on Versailles Louis XVI returns to Paris
July 1790	Civil Constitution of the Clergy
June 1791	Louis XVI captured attempting to flee
August 1791	Declaration of Pillnitz
September 1791	New constitution implemented
October 1791	Legislative Assembly begins to meet
April 1792	France declares war on Austria
August 10, 1792	Storming of the Tuileries; Louis XVI arrested
September 21, 1792	National Convention declares France a republic
January 21, 1793	Louis XVI guillotined
May 1793	First Law of the Maximum
July 1793	Terror inaugurated
July 1794	Robespierre guillotined; Terror ends
October 1795	Directory established
November 1799	Napoleon seizes power

Assembly, Louis XVI declared war against Austria. From this point on, foreign war would be an ongoing factor in the Revolution.

At first the war was a disaster for France. The army had not been reorganized into an effective fighting force after the loss of many aristocratic officers and the addition of newly self-aware citizens. On one occasion troops insisted on putting an officer's command to a vote. Early defeats further emboldened critics of the monarchy. Under the direction of the Girondins, the Legislative Assembly began to press for the deportation of priests who had been leading demonstrations against the government. The Assembly abolished the personal guard of the king and summoned provincial National Guardsmen to Paris.

Louis XVI in 1792

The king, though a kindly man, had neither the character nor the convictions necessary to refashion royal authority symbolically as the Revolution proceeded. When Parisian crowds forced him to wear the "liberty cap," the monarchy was close to collapse.

(Metropolitan Museum of Art, The Elisha Whittelsey Collection, The Elisha Whittelsey Fund, 1962 [62.520.333]. Image © The Metropolitan Museum of Art)

The king's resistance to these measures, as well as fears of acute grain shortages owing to a poor harvest and the needs of the armies, created further unrest. Crowds staged boisterous marches near the royal palace, physically confronted the king, and forced him to don the "liberty cap," a symbol of republicanism. The king's authority and prestige were now thoroughly undermined.

By July 1792 tensions had become acute. The grain shortage was severe, Austrian and Prussian troops committed to saving the royal family were threatening to invade, and, most important, Parisian citizens were better organized and more determined than ever before. In each of the forty-eight "sections"—administrative wards—of Paris, a miniature popular assembly thrashed out all the events and issues of the day just as deputies in the nationwide Legislative Assembly did. Derisively

called **sans-culottes** (sahn–koo-LOT) ("without knee pants") because they could not afford elite fashions, the ordinary Parisians in the section assemblies included shopkeepers, artisans, and laborers. Their political organization enhanced their influence with the Assembly, the clubs, and Parisian newspapers. By late July most sections of the city had approved a petition calling for the exile of the king, the election of new city officials, the exemption of the poor from taxation, and other radical measures.

In August the sans-culottes took matters into their own hands. On the night of August 9, after careful preparations, representatives of the section assemblies constituted themselves as a new city government with the aim of "saving the state." The next day, August 10, they assaulted the Tuileries Palace, where the royal family was living. In the bloody confrontation, hundreds of royal guards and citizens died. The king and his family were imprisoned in one of the fortified towers in the city, under guard of the popularly controlled city government.

The storming of the Tuileries inaugurated the second major phase of the Revolution: the establishment of republican government in place of the monarchy. By their intimidating numbers, the people of Paris now controlled the Legislative Assembly. Some deputies fled. Those who remained agreed under pressure to dissolve the Assembly and make way for another body to be elected by universal manhood suffrage. On September 20 that assembly, known as the National Convention, began to meet. The next day the Convention declared the end of the monarchy and set to work crafting a constitution for the new republic.

Coincidentally, that same September day, French forces won their first genuine victory over the allied Austrian and Prussian invasion forces. Though not a decisive battle, it was a profound psychological triumph. A citizen army had defeated the professional force of a ruling prince. The victory bolstered the republican government and encouraged it to put more energy into the wars. Indeed, maintaining armies in the field became a weighty factor in the delicate equilibrium of revolutionary government. The new republican regime let it be known that its armies were not merely for self-defense but for the liberation of all peoples in the "name of the French Nation."

The Convention faced the divisive issue of what to do with the king. Some of the king's correspondence, discovered after the storming of the Tuileries, provided the pretext for charges of treason. The Convention held a trial for him, which lasted from December 11, 1792, to January 15, 1793. He was found guilty of treason by an overwhelming vote (683 to 39); the republican government would not compromise with monarchy. Less

sans-culottes Ordinary citizens of revolutionary Paris, whose derisive nickname referred to their inability to afford fashionable knee pants ("culottes").

lopsided was the sentence: Louis was condemned to death by a narrow majority, 387 to 334.

The consequences for the king were immediate. On January 21, 1793, Louis mounted the scaffold in a public square near the Tuileries and was beheaded. The execution split the ranks of the Convention and soon resulted in the breakdown of the institution itself.

THE FALTERING REPUBLIC AND THE TERROR, 1793–1794

In February 1793 the republic was at war with virtually every state in Europe; the only exceptions were the Scandinavian kingdoms and Russia. Moreover, the regime faced massive and widespread counterrevolutionary uprisings within France. Vigilance against internal and external enemies became a top priority. The Convention established an executive body, the Committee of Public Safety. In theory, this executive council was answerable to the Convention as a whole. As the months passed, however, it acted with greater and greater autonomy not only to institute policies but also to eradicate enemies. The broadly based republican government represented by the Convention began to disintegrate.

Robespierre and the Committee for Public Safety
In June 1793, pushed by the Parisian sections, a group of extreme **Jacobins** purged the Girondin deputies from the Convention, arresting many of them. The Girondins were republicans who favored an activist government in the people's behalf, but they were less radical than their fellow Jacobins who now moved against them, less insistent on central control of the Revolution, and less willing to share power with the citizens of Paris. After the purge, the Convention still met, but most authority lay with the Committee of Public Safety.

Now, new uprisings against the regime began as revolts by Girondin sympathizers added to counterrevolutionary revolts by peasants and aristocrats. As resistance to the government mounted and the foreign threat continued, a dramatic event in Paris led the Committee of Public Safety officially to adopt a policy of political repression. A well-known figure of the Revolution, Jean Paul Marat (1743–1793), publisher of a radical republican newspaper very popular with ordinary Parisians, was murdered on July 13 by Charlotte Corday (1768–1793), a young aristocratic woman who had asked to meet with him. Shortly afterward, a longtime member of the Jacobin Club, **Maximilien Robespierre** (ROBES-pee-air) (1758–1794), joined the

Committee and called for "Terror"—the systematic repression of internal enemies. He was not alone in his views. Members of the section assemblies of Paris led demonstrations to pressure the government into making Terror the order of the day.

Since the previous autumn the guillotine had been at work against identified enemies of the regime, but now a more energetic apparatus of Terror was instituted. A Law of Suspects was passed that allowed citizens to be arrested simply on vague suspicion of counterrevolutionary sympathies. Revolutionary tribunals and an oversight committee made arbitrary arrests and rendered summary judgments. In October a steady stream of executions began, beginning with the queen, imprisoned since the storming of the Tuileries the year before. The imprisoned Girondin deputies followed, and then the beheadings continued relentlessly. Paris witnessed about 2,600 executions from 1793 to 1794.

Around France the verdicts of revolutionary tribunals led to approximately 14,000 executions. Another 10,000 to 12,000 people died in prison. Ten thousand or more were killed, usually by summary execution, after the defeat of counterrevolutionary uprisings. For example, 2,000 people were summarily executed in Lyon when a Girondin revolt collapsed there in October. The aim of **the Terror** was not merely to stifle active resistance; it was also to silence simple dissent. The victims in Paris included not only aristocrats or former deputies but also sans-culottes. The radical Jacobins wanted to seize control of the Revolution from the Parisian citizens who had lifted them to power.

Robespierre embodied all the contradictions of the policy of Terror. He was an austere, almost prim man who lived very modestly—a model, of sorts, of the virtuous, disinterested citizen. His unbending loyalty to his political principles earned him the nickname "the Incorruptible." The policies followed by the government during the year of his greatest influence, from July 1793 to July 1794, included generous, rational, and humane actions to benefit ordinary citizens as well as the atrocities of official Terror. (See the box "The Written Record: Robespierre Justifies Terror Against Enemies of the Revolution.") Indeed, the Terror notwithstanding, the government of the Committee of Public Safety was effective in providing direction for the nation at a critical time. In August 1793 it instituted the first mass conscription of citizens into the army (levée en masse [leh-VAY ohn MAHSS]), and a consistently effective popular army came into existence. In the autumn of 1793 this army won impressive victories. In May the

Jacobins   In revolutionary France, a republican political club named for a monastic order.

Maximilien Robespierre   French lawyer and revolutionary leader, influential member of the Committee of Public Safety (1793–1794); advocated Terror to suppress internal dissent.

the Terror   Systematic repression of internal enemies undertaken by French revolutionary government from 1793 to 1794. Approximately fourteen thousand people were executed, including aristocrats, Girondins, and sans-culottes.

THE WRITTEN RECORD

ROBESPIERRE JUSTIFIES TERROR AGAINST ENEMIES OF THE REVOLUTION

In this excerpt from a speech before the National Convention in December 1793, Robespierre justifies the revolutionary government's need to act in a vigorous manner in order to defend itself from challenges within and without.

The defenders of the Republic must adopt Caesar's maxim, for they believe that "nothing has been done so long as anything remains to be done." Enough dangers still face us to engage all our efforts. It has not fully extended the valor of our Republican soldiers to conquer a few Englishmen and a few traitors. A task no less important, and one more difficult, now awaits us: to sustain an energy sufficient to defeat the constant intrigues of all the enemies of our freedom and to bring to a triumphant realization the principles that must be the cornerstone of public welfare.... Revolution is the war waged by liberty against its enemies; a constitution is that which crowns the edifice of freedom once victory has been won and the nation is at peace. The revolutionary government has to summon extraordinary activity to its aid precisely because it is at war. It is subjected to less binding and less uniform regulations, because the circumstances in which it finds itself are tempestuous and shifting, above all because it is compelled to deploy, swiftly and incessantly, new resources to meet new and pressing dangers. The principal concern of a constitutional government is civil liberty; that of a revolutionary government, public liberty. [A] revolutionary government is obliged to defend the state itself against the factions that assail it from every quarter. To good citizens revolutionary government owes the full protection of the state; to the enemies of the people it owes only death....

Is a revolutionary government the less just and the less legitimate because it must be more vigorous in its actions and freer in its movement than ordinary government? No! For it rests on the most sacred of all laws, the safety of the people, and on necessity, which is the most indisputable of all rights. It also has its rules, all based on justice and on public order. It has nothing in common with anarchy or disorder; on the contrary, its purpose is to repress them and to establish and consolidate the rule of law. It has nothing in common with arbitrary rule; it is public interest which governs it and not the whims of private individuals.

QUESTIONS

1. How does Robespierre describe the differences between constitutional and revolutionary government?

2. How does Robespierre defend the legitimacy of revolutionary government?

Source: Reprinted with permission of Scribner, an imprint of Simon & Schuster Adult Publishing Group, from *Robespierre,* edited by George Rudé. Copyright © 1967 by Prentice-Hall, Inc., copyright renewed © 1995 by George Rudé. All rights reserved.

Convention had instituted the Law of the Maximum, which controlled the price of grain so that city people could afford their staple food—bread. In September the Committee extended the law to apply to other necessary commodities. Extensive plans were made for a system of free and universal primary education. Slavery in the French colonies was abolished in February 1794. Divorce, first legalized in 1792, was made easier for women to obtain.

Social Reforms in the Name of Reason In the name of "reason," traditional rituals and rhythms of life were changed. One reform of long-term significance was the introduction of the metric system of weights and measures. Although people continued to use the old, familiar measures for a very long time, the change was eventually accomplished, leading the way for standardization throughout Europe. Equally "rational" but not as successful was the elimination of the traditional calendar; weeks and months were replaced by uniform thirty-day months and *decadi* (ten-day weeks with one day of rest), and all saints' days and Christian holidays were eliminated. The years had already been changed—Year I had been declared with the founding of the republic in the autumn of 1792.

Churches were rededicated as "temples of reason." Believing that outright atheism left people with no basis for personal or national morality, Robespierre sought instead to promote a cult of the Supreme Being. The new public festivals were solemn civic ceremonies intended to ritualize and legitimize the new political order. But the French people generally resented the elimination of the traditional calendar and the attacks on the church. In the countryside massive peasant uprisings protested the loss of poor relief, community life, and familiar ritual.

Divorce law and economic regulation were a boon, especially to urban women, but women's participation in section assemblies and in all organized political activity—which had been energetic and widespread—was banned in October 1793. The particular target of the regime was the **Society of Revolutionary Republican Women,** a powerful club representing the interests of female sans-culottes. By banning women from political life, the regime helped to ground its legitimacy, since the seemingly "natural" exclusion of women might make the new system of government appear part of the "natural" order. (See the feature "The Visual Record: Political Symbols.") Outlawing women's clubs and barring women from section assemblies also eliminated a source of popular power, from which the regime was now trying to distance itself.

The End of the Terror   The Committee and members of the Convention were divided over religious and other policies, but the main policy differences concerned economic matters: how far to go to assist the poor, the unemployed, and the landless. Several of the moderate critics of Robespierre and his allies were guillotined for disagreeing about policy and for doubting the continuing need for the Terror itself. Their deaths helped precipitate the end of the Terror by causing Robespierre's power base to shrink so much that it had no further legitimacy.

Deputies to the Convention finally dared to move against Robespierre in July 1794. French armies had scored a major victory over Austrian troops on June 26, so there was no longer any need for the emergency status that the Terror had thrived on. In late July the Convention voted to arrest Robespierre, the head of the revolutionary tribunal in Paris, and their closest associates and allies in the city government. On July 28 and 29 Robespierre and the others—about a hundred in all—were guillotined, and the Terror ended.

THE THERMIDORIAN REACTION AND THE DIRECTORY, 1794–1799

After the death of Robespierre, the Convention reclaimed the executive powers that the Committee of Public Safety had seized. It dismantled the apparatus of the Terror, repealed the Law of Suspects, and forced the revolutionary tribunals to adopt ordinary legal procedures. The Convention also passed into law some measures, such as expanded public education, that had been proposed the preceding year but not enacted. This post-Terror phase of the Revolution is called the "Thermidorian Reaction" because it began in the revolutionary month of Thermidor (July 19–August 17).

Lacking the weapons of the Terror, the Convention was unable to enforce controls on the supply and price of bread. Thus economic difficulties and a hard winter produced famine by the spring of 1795. The people of Paris tried to retain influence with the new government. In May crowds marched on the Convention chanting "Bread and the Constitution of '93," referring to the republican constitution drafted by the Convention but never implemented because of the Terror. The demonstrations were met with force and were dispersed.

Members of the Convention remained fearful of a renewed, popularly supported Terror, on the one hand, or a royalist uprising, on the other. Counterrevolutionary uprisings had erupted in the fall of 1794, and landings on French territory by émigré forces occurred the following spring. The Convention drafted a new constitution that limited popular participation in government, as had the first constitution of 1791. The new plan allowed fairly widespread (but not universal) male suffrage, but only for electors, who would choose deputies for the two houses of the legislature. The property qualifications for being an elector were very high, so all but elite citizens were effectively disenfranchised. The Convention also decreed, at the last minute, that two-thirds of its members must serve in the new legislature, regardless of the outcome of elections. Although this maneuver enhanced the stability of the new regime, it undermined the credibility of the new vote.

Governance under the provisions of the new constitution, beginning in the fall of 1795, was called the **Directory,** for the executive council of five men chosen by the upper house of the new legislature. To avoid the concentration of authority that had produced the Terror, the members of the Convention had tried to enshrine separation of powers in the new system. However, the governments under the Directory were never free from outside plots or from their own extraconstitutional maneuvering.

The most spectacular challenge was an attempted coup by the "Conspiracy of Equals," a group of extreme Jacobins who wanted to restore popular government and aggressive economic and social policy on behalf of the common people. The conspiracy ended with arrests and executions in 1797. When elections in 1797 and 1798 returned many royalist as well as Jacobin deputies, the Directory abrogated the constitution: many "undesirable" deputies were arrested, sent into exile, or denied seats.

The armies of the republic did enjoy some spectacular successes during these years, for the first time carrying the fighting—and the effects of the Revolution—onto foreign soil. French armies conquered the Dutch in 1795. In 1796–1797 French armies led by the

Society of Revolutionary Republican Women
In revolutionary Paris, a powerful political club that represented the interests of female sans-culottes.

Directory   French revolutionary government from 1795 to 1799, consisting of an executive council of five men chosen by the upper house of the legislature.

Political Symbols

During the French Revolution, thousands of illustrations in support of various revolutionary (or counterrevolutionary) ideas were reproduced on posters, on handbills, and in pamphlets. Some satirized their subjects, such as Marie Antoinette, or celebrated revolutionary milestones, such as the fall of the Bastille. The etching here of the woman armed with a pike, dating from 1792, falls into this category. Other pictures, such as the representation from 1795 of Liberty as a young woman wearing the liberty cap, symbolized or reinforced various revolutionary ideals.*

Political images like these are an invaluable though problematic source for historians. Let us examine these two images of women and consider how French people during the Revolution might have responded to them. To understand what they meant to contemporaries, we must know something about the other images that these would have been compared to. We must also view the images in the context of the events of the Revolution itself. Immediately, then, we are presented with an interpretive agenda. How ordinary and acceptable was this image of an armed woman? If women were not citizens coequal with men, how could a woman be a symbol of liberty? What, in short, do these political images reveal about the spectrum of political life in their society?

The woman holding the pike stares determinedly at the viewer. Many details confirm what the original caption announced: This is a French woman who has become free. In her hat she wears one of the symbols of revolutionary nationhood: the tricolor cockade. The badge around her waist celebrates a defining moment for the revolutionary nation: the fall of the Bastille. Her pike itself is inscribed with the words "Liberty or death."

The woman appears to be serving not merely as a symbol of free women. She comes close to being the generic image of a free citizen, willing and

An Armed Citizen, ca. 1792
(Bibliothèque nationale de France)

able to fight for liberty—an astonishing symbolic possibility in a time when women were not yet treated equally under the law or granted the same political rights as the men of their class. Other images prevalent at the time echo this possibility. Many contemporary representations of the women's march on Versailles in 1789 show women carrying arms, active in advancing the Revolution. By the time this image was created (most likely in 1792), many other demonstrations and violent

---

*This discussion draws on the work of Joan Landes, "Representing the Body Politic: The Paradox of Gender in the Graphic Politics of the French Revolution," and Darlene Gay Levy and Harriet B. Applewhite, "Women and Militant Citizenship in Revolutionary Paris," in Sara E. Melzer and Leslie W. Rabine, eds., *Rebel Daughters: Women and the French Revolution* (New York: Oxford University Press, 1992), pp. 15–37, 79–101.

confrontations by ordinary people had resulted in the creation of dozens of popular prints and engravings that showed women acting in the same ways as men.

Repeatedly during 1792, women proposed to the revolutionary government that they be granted the right to bear arms. Their request was denied, but it was not dismissed out of hand. There was debate, and the issue was in effect tabled. Nevertheless, women's actions in the Revolution had created at least the possibility of envisaging citizenship with a female face.

The image of Liberty from 1795 does not reflect the actions of women but rather represents their exclusion from political participation. It is one of a number of images of Liberty that portray this ideal as a passive, innocent woman, here garbed in ancient dress, surrounded by a glow that in the past had been reserved for saints. Liberty here is envisaged as a pure and lofty goal, symbolized as a pure young woman.

Late in 1793, during the Terror, women were excluded from formal participation in politics with the disbanding of women's organizations. Nor did they gain political rights under the Directory, which re-established some of the limited gains of the first phase of the Revolution. The justification offered for their exclusion in 1793 was borrowed from Jean-Jacques Rousseau: it is contrary to nature for women to be in public life (see page 557). Women "belong" in the private world of the family, where they will nurture male citizens. Women embody ideal qualities such as patience and self-sacrifice; they are not fully formed beings capable of action in their own right.

Such notions made it easy to use images of women to embody ideals for public purposes. A woman could represent liberty precisely because actual women were not able to be political players.

The two images shown here thus demonstrate that political symbols can have varying relationships to "reality." The pike-bearing citizen is the more "real." Her image reflects the way of thinking about politics that became possible for the first time because of their actions. The other woman reflects not the attributes of actual women but an ideal type spawned by the use of arbitrary gender distinctions to legitimize political power. In these images we can see modern political life taking

Liberty as a Young Woman, ca. 1795 *(S. P. Avery Collection, Miriam and Ira D. Wallach Division of Arts, Prints, and Photographs, The New York Public Library, Astor, Lenox, and Tilden Foundations/Art Resource, NY)*

shape: the sophistication of its symbolic language, the importance of abstract ideas such as liberty and nationhood—as well as the grounding of much political life in rigid distinctions between public and private, male and female.

QUESTIONS

1. What circumstances explain the 1792 image of a woman as an armed citizen?
2. How would an idealized image of a young woman be useful as a symbol of liberty?

Online Study Center
Improve Your Grade Visual Record Activities

young general **Napoleon Bonaparte** wrested control of northern Italy from the Austrians. Both regions were transformed into "sister" republics, governed by local revolutionaries but under French protection. By 1799, however, conditions had once again reached a critical juncture. The demands of the war effort, together with rising prices and the continued decline in the value of the assignats, brought the government again to the brink of bankruptcy. The government also seemed to be losing control of the French countryside; there were continued royalist uprisings, local political vendettas between moderates and Jacobins, and outright banditry.

Members of the Directory had often turned to sympathetic army commanders to suppress dissent and to carry out arrests and purges of the legislature. They now invited General Bonaparte to help them form a government that they could more strictly control. Two members of the Directory plotted with Napoleon and his brother, Lucien Bonaparte, to seize power on November 9, 1799.

=== S E C T I O N   S U M M A R Y ===

- The phases of the French Revolution were shaped by elites' desires for change, demands of common people, and the need to defend France against foreign monarchs.

- Between 1789 and 1791, the National Assembly wrote a constitution, seized and sold church property, ended traditional obligations of peasants, and reorganized local government.

- In 1791, the constitution was implemented and a Legislative Assembly elected.

- In 1792, Parisian citizens overthrew the monarchy; the Convention, elected by universal manhood suffrage, governed the republic.

- Control of the government passed to the Committee of Public Safety, which defended France from foreign invasion and gave economic assistance to common people but also implemented a policy of official Terror in which thousands of French people were killed.

- After the Terror, suffrage was again restricted, but the government of the Directory could not bring stability.

THE NAPOLEONIC ERA AND THE LEGACY OF REVOLUTION, 1799–1815

What impact did the Revolution and Napoleonic rule have on France, the rest of Europe, and the wider world?

Talented, charming, and ruthless, Napoleon Bonaparte (1769–1821) was the kind of person who gives rise to myths. His audacity, determination, and personal magnetism enabled him to profit from the political instability and confusion in France and to establish himself in power. Once in power, he temporarily stabilized the political scene by fixing in law the more conservative gains of the Revolution. He also used his power and his remarkable abilities as a general to continue wars of conquest against France's neighbors, which helped deflect political tensions at home.

Napoleon's troops in effect exported the Revolution as they conquered most of Europe. In most states that came under French control, law codes were reformed, governing elites were opened to talent, and public works were upgraded. Yet French conquest also meant domination, pure and simple, and involvement in France's rivalry with Britain. The Napoleonic era left Europe an ambiguous legacy—war and its enormous costs, yet also revolution and its impetus to positive change.

NAPOLEON: FROM SOLDIER TO EMPEROR, 1799–1804

Napoleon was from Corsica, a Mediterranean island that had passed from Genoese to French control in the eighteenth century. The second son of a large gentry family, he was educated at military academies in France, and he married the politically well-connected widow Joséphine de Beauharnais (1763–1814), whose aristocratic husband had been a victim of the Terror.

Napoleon steered a careful course through the political turmoil of the Revolution. By 1799 his military victories had won him much praise and fame. He had

Napoleon Bonaparte   French general who took part in a coup in 1799 against the Directory, Napoleon consolidated power as first consul and ruled as emperor from 1804 to 1815.

demonstrated his reliability and ruthlessness in 1795 when he ordered troops guarding the Convention to fire on a Parisian crowd. He had capped his successful Italian campaign of 1796–1797 with an invasion of Egypt in an attempt to strike at British influence and trade connections in the eastern Mediterranean. The Egyptian campaign failed in its goals, but individual spectacular victories during the campaign ensured Napoleon's military reputation. In addition, Napoleon had demonstrated his widening ambitions. He had taken leading scientists and skilled administrators with him to Egypt in order to export the seeming benefits of French civilization—and to install a more lasting bureaucratic authority.

Napoleon's partners in the new government after the November 1799 coup soon learned of his great political ambition and skill. In theory, the new system was to be a streamlined version of the Directory: Napoleon was to be first among equals in a three-man executive—"First Consul," according to borrowed Roman termi-nology. But Napoleon quickly asserted his primacy among them and began not only to dominate executive functions but also to bypass the authority of the regime's various legislative bodies.

Perhaps most important to the success of his increasingly authoritarian rule was his effort to include men of many political stripes—Jacobins, reforming liberals, even former Old Regime bureaucrats—among his ministers, advisers, and bureaucrats. He welcomed many exiles back to France, including all but the most ardent royalists. He thus stabilized his regime by healing some of the rifts among ruling elites. Napoleon combined toleration with ruthlessness, however. Between 1800 and 1804 he imprisoned, executed, or exiled dozens of individuals for alleged Jacobin agitation or royalist sympathies, including a prince of the royal family, whom he had kidnapped and coldly murdered.

Under Napoleon's regime, any semblance of free political life ended. Legislative bodies lost all initiative in the governing process, becoming rubber stamps for the

Napoleon Crossing the Alps

This stirring portrait by the great neoclassical painter Jacques-Louis David memorializes Napoleon's 1796 crossing of the Alps before his victorious Italian campaign, as a general under the Directory. In part because it was executed in 1801–1802, the painting depicts the moment heroically rather than realistically. (In truth, Napoleon wisely crossed the Alps on a sure-footed mule, not a stallion.) Napoleon, as First Consul, wanted images of himself that would justify his increasingly ambitious claims to power. *(Réunion des Musées Nationaux/ Art Resource, NY)*

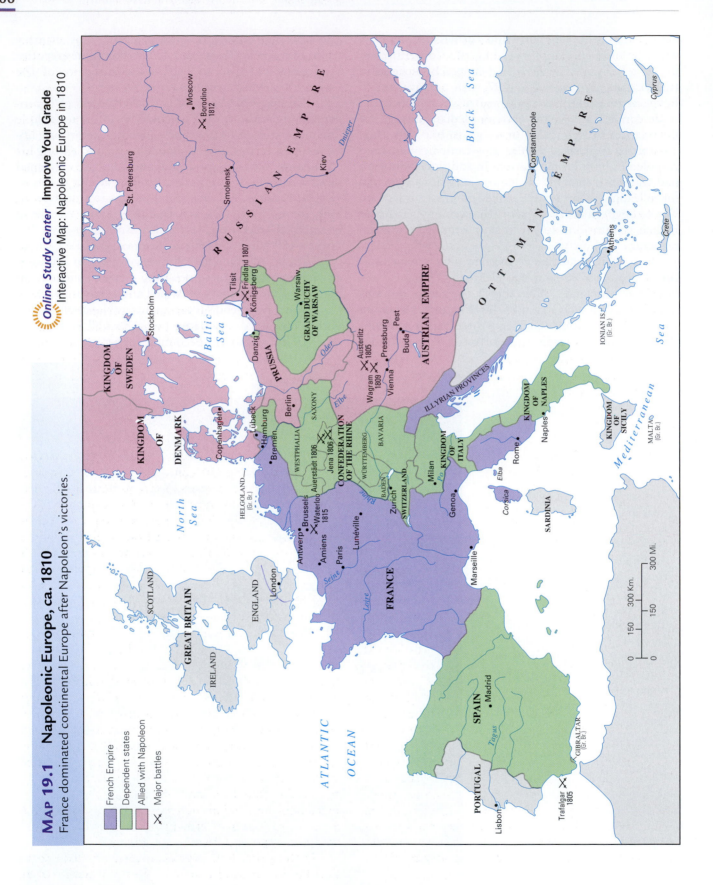

MAP 19.1 Napoleonic Europe, ca. 1810
France dominated continental Europe after Napoleon's victories.

Online Study Center Improve Your Grade
Interactive Map: Napoleonic Europe in 1810

Legend:
- French Empire
- Dependent states
- Allied with Napoleon
- ✕ Major battles

Labels on map:

RUSSIAN EMPIRE
OTTOMAN EMPIRE
AUSTRIAN EMPIRE
KINGDOM OF SWEDEN
KINGDOM OF DENMARK
PRUSSIA
GRAND DUCHY OF WARSAW
CONFEDERATION OF THE RHINE
WESTPHALIA
SAXONY
BAVARIA
WÜRTTEMBERG
BADEN
SWITZERLAND
KINGDOM OF ITALY
ILLYRIAN PROVINCES
KINGDOM OF NAPLES
KINGDOM OF SICILY
FRANCE
SPAIN
PORTUGAL
GREAT BRITAIN
SCOTLAND
ENGLAND
IRELAND
SARDINIA

Moscow
Borodino 1812
St. Petersburg
Smolensk
Kiev
Stockholm
Tilsit
Friedland 1807
Königsberg
Danzig
Warsaw
Pressburg
Pest
Buda
Vienna
Austerlitz 1805
Wagram 1809
Berlin
Hamburg
Bremen
Lübeck
Copenhagen
Jena 1806
Auerstädt 1806
Zurich
Milan
Genoa
Rome
Naples
Constantinople
Athens
Brussels
Antwerp
Amiens
Waterloo 1815
Paris
Lunéville
Marseille
Madrid
Lisbon
Trafalgar 1805
London
Gibraltar (Gr. Br.)
Malta (Gr. Br.)
Helgoland (Gr. Br.)
Ionian Is. (Gr. Br.)
Elba
Corsica
Cyprus
Crete

Black Sea
Baltic Sea
North Sea
Mediterranean Sea
ATLANTIC OCEAN
Oder
Elbe
Rhine
Seine
Loire
Po
Dnieper
Tagus

300 Mi.
300 Km.
150
0

consuls' policies. In any case, there were no meaningful elections. Voters chose only candidates for a kind of pool of potential legislators, from which occasional replacements were chosen by members of the Senate, an advisory body entirely appointed by Napoleon himself. Political clubs were banned; the vibrant press of the revolutionary years wilted under heavy censorship. Napoleon also further centralized the administrative system, set up by the first wave of revolutionaries in 1789, by establishing the office of prefect to govern the départements. All prefects and their subordinates were appointed by Napoleon, thus extending the range of his power and undermining autonomous local government.

Certain administrative changes that enhanced central control, such as for tax collection, were more uniformly positive in their effects. Napoleon oversaw the establishment of the Bank of France, modeled on the Bank of England. The bank provided capital for investment and helped the state stabilize the French currency. Perhaps the most important achievement early in his regime was the Concordat of 1801. The aim of this treaty with the pope was to solve the problem of church-state relations that for years had provoked counterrevolutionary rebellions. The agreement allowed for the resumption of Catholic worship and the continued support of the clergy by the state, but also accepted the more dramatic changes accomplished by the Revolution. Church lands that had been sold were guaranteed to their new owners. Although Catholicism was recognized as the "religion of the majority of Frenchmen," Protestant churches also were allowed, and their clergy were paid. Later, Napoleon granted new rights to Jews as well.

The law code that Napoleon established in 1804 was much like his accommodation with the church in its limited acceptance of revolutionary gains. His **Civil Code** (also known as the *code napoléon,* or Napoleonic Code) honored the revolutionary legacy in its guarantee of equality before the law and its requirement for the taxation of all social classes; it also enshrined modern forms of property ownership and civil contracts. Neither the code nor Napoleon's political regime fostered individual rights, especially for women. Fathers' control over their families was enhanced. Divorce was no longer permitted except in rare instances. Women lost all property rights when they married, and they generally faced legal domination by fathers and husbands.

Napoleon was careful, though, to avoid heavy-handed displays of power. He cleverly sought ratification of each stage of his assumption of power through national plebiscites (referendums in which all eligible voters could vote for or against proposals)—one plebiscite

for a new constitution in 1800 and another when he claimed consulship for life in 1802. He approached his final political coup—declaring himself emperor—with similar dexterity. Long before he claimed the imperial title, Napoleon had begun to sponsor an active court life appropriate to imperial pretensions. The empire was proclaimed in May 1804 with the approval of the Senate; it was also endorsed by another plebiscite. Napoleon rewarded members of his family and certain favorites with noble titles that carried no legal privilege but signaled social and political distinctions of great importance. Old nobles were allowed to use their titles on this basis.

Many members of the elite, whatever their persuasions, tolerated Napoleon's claims to power because he safeguarded fundamental revolutionary gains yet reconfirmed their status. War soon resumed against political and economic enemies—principally Britain, Austria, and Russia—and for a time Napoleon's success on the battlefield continued. Because military glory was central to the political purpose and self-esteem of elites, Napoleon's early successes as emperor further enhanced his power.

CONQUERING EUROPE, 1805–1810

Napoleon maintained relatively peaceful relations with other nations while he consolidated power at home, but the truces did not last. Tensions with the British quickly re-escalated when Britain resumed aggression against French shipping in 1803, and Napoleon countered by seizing Hanover, the ancestral German home of the English king. England was at war at sea with Spain and the Netherlands, which Napoleon had forced to enter the fray. Napoleon began to gather a large French force on the northern coast of France; his objective was to invade England.

The British fleet, commanded by Horatio Nelson (1758-1805), intercepted the combined French and Spanish fleets that were to have been the invasion flotilla and inflicted a devastating defeat off Cape Trafalgar in southern Spain (see **MAP 19.1**) on October 21, 1805. The victory ensured British mastery of the seas and, in the long run, contributed to Napoleon's demise. In the short run, the defeat at Trafalgar paled for the French beside Napoleon's impressive victories on land. Even as the French admirals were preparing for battle, Napoleon had abandoned the plans to invade England and in August had begun to march his army east through Germany to confront the great continental powers, Austria and Russia.

In December 1805, Napoleon's army routed a combined Austrian and Russian force near Austerlitz (AW-stir-lits), north of Vienna (see Map 19.1). The Battle of Austerlitz was Napoleon's most spectacular victory.

Civil Code Law code established under Napoleon in 1804 that included limited acceptance of revolutionary gains, such as a guarantee of equality before the law and taxation of all social classes.

Austria sued for peace. In further battles in 1806, French forces defeated Prussian as well as Russian armies once again. Prussia was virtually dismembered, but Napoleon tried to remake Russia into a contented ally. His hold on central Europe would not be secure with a hostile Russia, nor would the anti-British economic system that he envisioned—the Continental System (see page 609)—be workable without Russian participation.

French forces were still trying to prevail in Spain, which had been a client state since its defeat by revolutionary armies in 1795 but was resisting outright rule by a French-imposed king. In 1808, however, Napoleon turned his attention to more fully subduing Austria. After another loss to French forces in July 1809, Austria, like Russia, accepted French political and economic hegemony in a sort of alliance. By 1810 Napoleon had transformed most of Europe into allied or dependent states (see Map 19.1). The only exceptions were Britain and the parts of Spain and Portugal that continued, with British help, to resist France.

The states least affected by French hegemony were its reluctant allies: Austria, Russia, and the Scandinavian countries. Denmark allied with France in 1807 only for help in fending off British naval supremacy in the Baltic. Sweden reluctantly made peace in 1810 after losing control of Finland to Napoleon's ally, Russia, and only minimally participated in the Continental

System. At the other extreme were territories that had been incorporated into France. These included the Austrian Netherlands, territory along the Rhineland, and sections of Italy that bordered France. These regions were occupied by French troops and were treated as though they were départements of France itself.

In most other areas, some form of French-controlled government was in place, usually headed by a member of Napoleon's family. In both northern Italy and the Netherlands, where "sister" republics had been established after French conquests under the Directory, Napoleon imposed monarchies. Rulers were also installed in the kingdom of Naples and in Spain. Western German states of the Holy Roman Empire that had allied with Napoleon against Austria were organized into the Confederation of the Rhine, with Napoleon as its "Protector." After a thousand years, the Holy Roman Empire ceased to exist. Two further states were created, largely out of the defeated Prussia's territory: the kingdom of Westphalia in western Germany and the Grand Duchy of Warsaw in the east (see Map 19.1).

Napoleon's domination of these various regions had complex, and at times contradictory, consequences. On the one hand, Napoleonic armies essentially exported the French Revolution, in that French domination brought with it the Napoleonic Civil Code, and with it political and economic reform akin to that of the

"And It Cannot Be Changed"

This horrifying scene of an execution of rebels against French rule in Spain was one of a series of etchings by Madrid artist Francisco Goya. In the 1810 series, titled "The Disasters of War," Goya was severely critical of French actions, as well as of barbarities committed by the British-backed Spaniards.

(Foto Marburg/Art Resource, NY)

early phases of the Revolution. Equality before the law was decreed following the French example. This meant the end of noble exemption from taxation in the many areas where it existed. In general, the complex snarl of medieval taxes and tolls was replaced with straightforward property taxes that were universally applied. As a consequence, tax revenues rose dramatically—by 50 percent in the kingdom of Italy, for example. Serfdom and forced labor also were abolished, as they had been in France in August 1789.

In most Catholic regions the church was subjected to the terms of the Concordat of 1801. The tithe was abolished, church property was seized and sold, and religious orders were dissolved. Although Catholicism remained the state-supported religion in these areas, Protestantism was tolerated, and Jews were granted rights of citizenship. Secular education, at least for males, was encouraged.

On the other hand, Napoleon would allow in the empire only those aspects of France's revolutionary legacy that he tolerated in France itself. Just as he had suppressed any meaningful participatory government in France, so too did he suppress it in conquered regions. This came as a blow in states such as the Netherlands, which had experienced its own democratizing "Patriot" movement and which had enjoyed republican self-government after invasion by French armies during the Revolution itself. Throughout Napoleon's empire, many of the benefits of streamlined administration and taxation were offset by the drain of continual warfare. Deficits rose three- and fourfold, despite increased revenues. And throughout Europe Napoleon randomly allotted lands to reward his greatest generals and ministers, thereby exempting those lands from taxation and control by his own bureaucracy.

If true self-government was not allowed, a broad segment of the elite in all regions was nevertheless won over to cooperation with Napoleon by being welcomed into his bureaucracy or into the large multinational army, called the *Grande Armée* (grawnd are-MAY). Their loyalty was cemented when they bought confiscated church lands.

The impact of Napoleon's Continental System was equally mixed. Under this system the Continent was in theory closed to all British shipping and goods. The effects were widespread but uneven, and smuggling to evade controls on British goods became a major enterprise. Regions heavily involved in trade with Britain or its colonies or dependent on British shipping suffered in the new system, as did overseas trade in general when Britain gained dominance of the seas after Trafalgar. However, the closing of the Continent to British trade, combined with increases in demand to supply Napoleon's armies, spurred the development of continental industries, at least in the short run.

DEFEAT AND ABDICATION, 1812–1815

Whatever its achievements, Napoleon's empire was ultimately precarious because of the hostility of Austria and Russia, as well as the belligerence of Britain. Russia was a particularly weak link in the chain of alliances and subject states because Russian landowners and merchants were angered when their vital trade in timber for the British navy was interrupted and when supplies of luxury goods, brought in British ships, began to dwindle. A century of close alliances with German ruling houses made alliance with a French ruler an extremely difficult political option for Tsar Alexander I.

It was Napoleon, however, who ended the alliance by provoking a breach with Russia. He suddenly backed away from an arrangement to marry one of Alexander's sisters and accepted an Austrian princess instead. (He had reluctantly divorced Joséphine because their marriage had not produced an heir.) Also, he seized lands in Germany belonging to a member of Alexander's family. When Alexander threatened rupture of the alliance if the lands were not returned, Napoleon mounted an invasion. Advisers warned him about the magnitude of the task he seemed so eager to undertake—particularly about winter fighting in Russia—but their alarms went unheard.

Napoleon's previous military successes had stemmed from a combination of strategic innovations and pure audacity. Napoleon divided his forces into independent corps. Each corps included infantry, cavalry, and artillery. Organized in these workable units, his armies could travel quickly by several separate routes and converge in massive force to face the enemy. Leadership on the battlefield came from a loyal and extremely talented officer corps that had grown up since army commands had been thrown open to nonaristocrats during the Revolution. The final ingredient in the success formula was the high morale of French troops. Since the first victory of the revolutionary armies in September 1792, citizen-soldiers had proved their worth. Complicated troop movements and bravery on the battlefield were possible when troops felt they were fighting for their *nation*, not merely their ruling dynasty. Napoleon's reputation as a winning general added a further measure of self-confidence.

The campaign against Russia began in June 1812. It was a spectacular failure. Napoleon had gathered a force of about 700,000 men—about half from France and half from allied states—a force twice as large as Russia's. But the strategy of quickly moving independent corps and assembling massive forces could not be implemented: simply mustering so many men along the border was already the equivalent of gathering them for battle. Bold victories had often enabled Napoleon's troops to live off the countryside while they waited for supplies to catch up to the front line. But when the enemy attacked supply lines, the distances traveled were very great, the countryside was impoverished, or battles were not decisive, Napoleon's ambitious strategies proved futile. In varying degrees, these conditions prevailed in Russia.

By the time the French faced the Russians in the principal battle of the Russian campaign—at Borodino (bore-uh-DEE-no), west of Moscow (see Map 19.1)—the Grande Armée had been on the march for two and a half months and stood at less than half its original strength. After the indecisive but bloody battle, the French occupied and pillaged Moscow but found scarcely enough food and supplies to sustain them. When Napoleon finally retreated from Moscow late in October, the fate of the French forces was all but sealed. As they retreated, the soldiers who had not died in battle died of exposure or starvation or were picked off by Russian peasants when they wandered away from their units. Of the original 700,000 troops of the Grand Armée, fewer than 100,000 made it out of Russia.

Napoleon left his army before it was fully out of Russia to counter a coup attempt in Paris. The collapse of his reign had begun, spurred by a coincidental defeat in Spain. Since 1808 Spain had been largely under French domination, with Napoleon's brother, Joseph, as king. A rebel Cortes (national representative assembly), however, continued to meet in territory that the French did not control, and British troops supported resistance to the French. In 1812, as Napoleon was advancing against Russia, the collapse of French control accelerated. By the time Napoleon reached Paris at the turn of the new year, Joseph had been expelled from Spain, and an Anglo-Spanish force led by the duke of Wellington was poised to invade France.

Napoleon lost his last chance to stave off a coalition of all major powers against him when he refused an Austrian offer of peace for the return of conquered Austrian territories. With Britain willing to subsidize the allied armies, Tsar Alexander determined to destroy Napoleon, and the Austrians now anxious to share the spoils, Napoleon's empire began to crumble. Imperial forces—many now raw recruits—were crushed in the massive "Battle of Nations" in Germany in October 1813. The allies invaded France and forced Napoleon to abdicate on April 6, 1814.

Napoleon was exiled to the island of Elba, off France's Mediterranean coast. He was installed as the island's ruler and was given an income drawn on the French treasury. Meanwhile, however, the restored French king was having his own troubles. Louis XVIII (r. 1814–1824) was the brother of the executed Louis XVI (he took the number eighteen out of respect for Louis XVI's son, who had died in prison in 1795). The new monarch had been out of the country and out of touch with its circumstances since the beginning of the Revolution. In addition to the delicate task of establishing his own legitimacy, he faced enormous practical problems, including pensioning off thousands of soldiers now unemployed and still loyal to Napoleon.

Napoleon, bored and almost penniless in his island kingdom (the promised French pension never materialized), took advantage of the circumstances and returned surreptitiously to France on February 26, 1815. His small band of attendants was joined by the soldiers sent by the king to halt his progress. Louis XVIII abandoned Paris to the returned emperor.

Napoleon's triumphant return lasted only one hundred days, however. Though many soldiers welcomed his return, many members of the elite were reluctant to throw in their lot with Napoleon again, and many ordinary French citizens were disenchanted, especially since the defeat in Russia, with the high costs, in conscription and taxation, of his armies. In any case, Napoleon's reappearance galvanized the divided allies, who had been haggling over a peace settlement, into unity. Napoleon tried to strike first, but he lost against English and Prussian troops in his first major battle, at Waterloo (in modern Belgium; see Map 19.1) on June 18, 1815. When Napoleon arrived in Paris after the defeat, he discovered the government in the hands of an ad hoc committee that included the Marquis de Lafayette. Under pressure, he abdicated once again. This time he was exiled to the tiny, remote island of St. Helena in the South Atlantic, where he died in 1821.

THE LEGACY OF REVOLUTION FOR FRANCE AND THE WORLD

The process of change in France between 1789 and 1815 was so complex that it is easy to overlook the overall impact of the Revolution. Superficially, the changes seemed to come full circle—with first Louis XVI on the throne, then Napoleon as emperor, and then Louis XVIII on the throne. Even though the monarchy was restored, however, the Revolution had discredited absolute monarchy in theory and practice.

France Louis XVIII had to recognize the right of "the people," however narrowly defined, to participate in government and to enjoy due process of law. Another critical legacy of the Revolution and the Napoleonic era was a centralized political system of départements rather than a patchwork of provinces. For the first time, a single code of law applied to all French people. Most officials—from département administrators to city mayors—were appointed by the central government until the late twentieth century. The conscientious attention of the government, at various stages of the Revolution, to advances for France generally reflects the positive side of this centralization. The government sponsored national scientific societies, a national library and archives, and a system of teachers' colleges and universities. Particularly under Napoleon, canal- and road-building projects improved transport systems.

Napoleon's legacy, like that of the Revolution itself, was mixed. His self-serving reconciliation of aristocratic pretensions with the opening of careers to men of talent ensured the long-term success of revolutionary principles from which the elite as a whole profited. His reconciliation of the state with the Catholic Church helped to stabilize his regime and cemented some revolutionary gains. The restored monarchy could not renege on these gains. Yet whatever his achievements, Napoleon's overthrow of constitutional principles worsened the problem of political instability. His brief return to power in 1815 reflects the degree to which his power had always been rooted in military adventurism and in the loyalty of soldiers and officers. Similarly, the swiftness of his collapse suggests that although the empire under Napoleon may have seemed an enduring solution to the political instability of the late 1790s, it was no more secure than any of the other revolutionary governments.

Although Louis XVIII acknowledged the principle of constitutionalism at the end of the Revolution, his regime rested on fragile footing. Indeed, the fragility of new political systems was one of the most profound legacies of the Revolution. There was division over policies, but even greater division over legitimacy—that is, the acceptance by a significant portion of the politically active citizenry of a particular government's right to rule. Before the Revolution started, notions about political legitimacy had undergone a significant shift. The deputies who declared themselves to be the National Assembly in June 1789 already believed that they had a right to do so. In their view, they represented "the nation," and their voice had legitimacy for that reason. These deputies brought to Versailles not only their individual convictions that "reason" should be applied to the political system but also their experience in social settings where those ideas were well received. In their salons, clubs, and literary societies, they had experienced the familiarity, trust, and sense of community that are essential to effective political action.

The deputies' attempt to transplant their sense of community into national politics, however, was not wholly successful. The National Assembly had scarcely been inaugurated when its deputies guaranteed its failure by disqualifying themselves from standing for office under the new constitution. The king also actively undermined the system because he disagreed with it in principle. The British parliamentary system, by comparison, though every bit as elitist as the narrowest of the

representative systems during the French Revolution, had a long history as a workable institution for lords, wealthy commoners, and rulers. This shared experience was an important counterweight to differences over fundamental issues, so that Parliament as an institution both survived political crises and helped resolve them. The Revolution thus left a powerful yet ambiguous legacy for France. Politics was established on new principles, yet still lacking were the practical means to achieve the promise inherent in those principles.

Europe   France's continental conquests were the least enduring of the changes of the revolutionary era. Nevertheless, French domination of Europe had certain lasting effects: elites were exposed to modern bureaucratic management, and equality under the law transformed social and political relationships. The breaking down of ancient political divisions provided important practical grounding for later cooperation among elites in nationalist movements. In Napoleon's kingdom of Italy, for example, a tax collector from Florence for the first time worked side by side with one from Milan.

Naturally, the most important legacy of the French Revolution, as of the American, was the very success of the Revolution. The most powerful absolute monarchy in Europe had succumbed to the demands of its people for dramatic social and political reforms. Throughout Europe in the nineteenth century, ruling dynasties faced revolutionary movements that demanded constitutional government, among other changes, and resorted to force to achieve it.

The most important legacy of the revolutionary wars, however, was the change in warfare itself made possible by the citizen armies of the French. Citizen-soldiers who identified closely with their nation, even when conscripts, proved able to maneuver and attack on the battlefield in ways that the brutishly disciplined poor conscripts in royal armies would not. In response, other states tried to build competing armies; the mass national armies that fought the world wars of the twentieth century were the result.

Europe and Its Colonies   European colonies overseas felt the impact of the Revolution and subsequent European wars in several ways. The British tried to take advantage of Napoleon's preoccupation with continental affairs by seizing French colonies and the colonies of the French-dominated Dutch. In 1806 they seized the Dutch colony of Cape Town—crucial for support of trade around Africa—as well as French bases along the African coast. In 1811 they grabbed the island of Java. In the Caribbean, the French sugar-producing islands of Martinique and Guadeloupe were particularly vulnerable to English sea power. On the most

NAPOLEON'S LETTER TO TOUSSAINT-LOUVERTURE

In November 1801, Napoleon sent this letter to the governor of the colony of Saint Domingue, Toussaint-Louverture. Toussaint, a former slave, had commanded an army, composed largely of ex-slaves, which had restored order in Saint Domingue following a complicated civil war. As he mentions in the letter, Napoleon had dispatched a force to re-establish French control of the formerly profitable colony. Although Toussaint was captured and later died in a French prison, Napoleon's forces were not successful in re-establishing French control.

To Citizen General Toussaint Louverture, commander in chief of the armies of Saint-Domingue,

Peace with England and with other powers in Europe [now] enables France to pay attention to its colony of Saint-Domingue. We are sending General Leclerc, our brother-in-law, to serve as captain general and governor of the colony. He is accompanied by forces suitable to make the sovereignty of France respected. In these circumstances, it pleases us to hope that you will demonstrate to us and to all of France the sincerity of the sentiments that you have continually expressed in your letters to us. We hold you in very high esteem and it pleases us to acknowledge the great service you have rendered to the French people. . . . Called by your talents and by the force of circumstance to command, you have ended civil war. . . . The constitution you have made contains many good things but also things which are contrary to the dignity and the sovereignty of the French people, of which the people of Saint-Domingue form only a part. The circumstances in which you found yourself, surrounded on all sides by enemies, perhaps made some provisions of the constitution necessary and legitimate. But, happily, now that things have changed you will be able to render homage to the sovereignty of the Nation of which you are one of the most illustrious citizens. . . . Any contrary conduct . . . would lead you to lose the many rights you have earned to the recognition and the benefits of the Republic [and] would bring you to the edge of a precipice which, in swallowing you up, would contribute to the misery of the brave blacks, whose courage we admire and whose rebellion we would be sorry to have to punish.

Help the new captain general with your counsel, your influence and your talents. What could you want? The freedom of blacks? You know that in every country we have entered we have given liberty to the people who did not have it. Do you want respect, honors and fortune? . . . Given the services you have rendered and our esteem for you, you cannot be in doubt that respect, honors and fortune await you.

Make known to the peoples of Saint-Domingue that our concerns for their well-being were often impotent because of the demands of war that we faced. But now, peace and the force of our government will assure them prosperity and liberty. Tell them that if liberty is to them the most important right, that it cannot be enjoyed without the title of "French citizen" and that all acts contrary to the nation, and contrary to the obedience they owe its government and to its representative, the captain general, will be crimes against the national sovereignty. . . . And you, General, consider that if you are the first man of color to have arrived at such a pinnacle of power . . . you are also, before God and before us, responsible for their good conduct. . . .

QUESTIONS

1. What, in your opinion, was Napoleon trying to accomplish with this letter?

2. How would Toussaint-Louverture have interpreted Napoleon's words?

Source: Paul Rossier, ed., *Lettres du Général Leclerc* (Paris: Société de l'Histoire des Colonies Françaises, 1937). Translated by Kristen B. Neuschel.

productive of the French-controlled Caribbean islands, Saint Domingue (SAHN dome-ANGUE), the Revolution inspired a successful rebellion by the enslaved plantation workers.

The National Assembly in Paris had delayed abolishing slavery in French colonies, despite the moral appeal of such a move, because of pressure from the white planters and out of fear that the financially strapped French government would lose some of its profitable sugar trade. But the example of revolutionary daring in Paris and confusion about ruling authority as the Assembly and the king wrangled did not go unnoticed in the colonies—in either plantation mansions or slave quarters. White planters on Saint Domingue simply hoped for political and economic "liberty" from the French government and its mercantilist trade policies. White planter rule was challenged, in turn, by wealthy people of mixed European and African descent who wanted equal citizenship, hitherto denied them. A civil war broke out between these upper classes and was fol-

Haitian Leader Toussaint-Louverture

Son of an educated slave, Toussaint-Louverture had himself been freed in 1777 but took on a leadership role when the slave revolt began on Saint Domingue in 1791. His military skill and political acumen were vital to the success of the revolt and to ruling the island's diverse population afterward.   *(Stock Montage, Inc.)*

lowed by a full-fledged slave rebellion, beginning in 1791. Britain sent aid to the rebels when it went to war against the French revolutionary government in 1793. Only when the republic was declared in Paris and the Convention abolished slavery did the rebels abandon alliances with France's enemies and attempt to govern in concert with the mother country.

Although it recovered other colonies from the British, France never regained control of Saint Domingue. Led by a former slave, **François Dominique Toussaint-Louverture** (too-SAHN–loo-ver-TOUR) (1743–1803), the new government of the island tried to run its own affairs, though without formally declaring independence from France. (See the box

François Toussaint-Louverture   Former slave who governed the island of Saint Domingue (Haiti) as an independent state after the slave revolt of 1791.

"The Global Record: Napoleon's Letter to Toussaint-Louverture.") Napoleon decided to tighten control of the profitable colonies by reinstituting slavery and ousting the independent government of Saint Domingue. In 1802 French forces fought their way onto the island. They captured Toussaint-Louverture, who died shortly thereafter in prison. But in 1803 another rebellion, provoked by the threat of renewed slavery, expelled French forces for good. A former aide of Toussaint's declared the independence of the colony under the name Haiti—the island's Native American name—on January 1, 1804.

The French Revolution and Napoleonic rule, and the example of the Haitian revolution, had a notable impact on Spanish colonies in the Americas. Like other American colonies, the Spanish colonies wanted to loosen the closed economic relationships with the mother country. In addition, the liberal ideas that had helped spawn the French Revolution spurred moves toward independence in Spanish America. Because of the confusion of authority in Spain, some of these colonies were already governing themselves independently in all but name. Echoes of radical republican ideology and of the Haitian experience were present in two major rebellions in Mexico; participants espoused the end of slavery and championed the interests of the poor against local and Spanish elites. The leaders of these self-declared revolutions were executed (in 1811 and 1815), and their movements were crushed by local elites in alliance with Spanish troops. The efforts of local elites to become self-governing—the attempted liberal revolutions—were little more successful. Only Argentina and Paraguay broke away from Spain at this time.

But as in Europe, a legacy remained of both limited and more radical revolutionary activity. Slave rebellions rocked British Caribbean islands in subsequent decades. In some regions dominated by plantations, such as some British possessions and the Spanish island of Cuba, planters were reluctant to disturb the prevailing order with any liberal political demands on the mother country.

THE VIEW FROM BRITAIN

Today the city of Paris is dotted with public monuments that celebrate Napoleon's victories. In London another hero and other victories are celebrated. In Trafalgar Square stands a statue of Lord Nelson, the British naval commander whose fleet destroyed a combined French and Spanish navy in 1805. Horatio Nelson was a brilliant tactician, whose innovations in maneuvering ships in the battle line resulted in stunning victories at Trafalgar and, in 1798, at the Nile Delta, which limited French ambitions in Egypt and the eastern Mediterranean. Trafalgar looms large in British history because it ensured British mastery of

The Battle of Trafalgar

Admiral Nelson's bold strategy of dividing his fleet to break through the line of the French-Spanish fleet at Trafalgar resembled Napoleon's successful strategies in land warfare. Nelson's maneuver isolated portions of the enemy fleet, which could then be attacked in strength. Nelson's intense naval engagements, like Napoleon's battles, caused many casualties, even for the victorious side. *(The Bridgeman Art Library)*

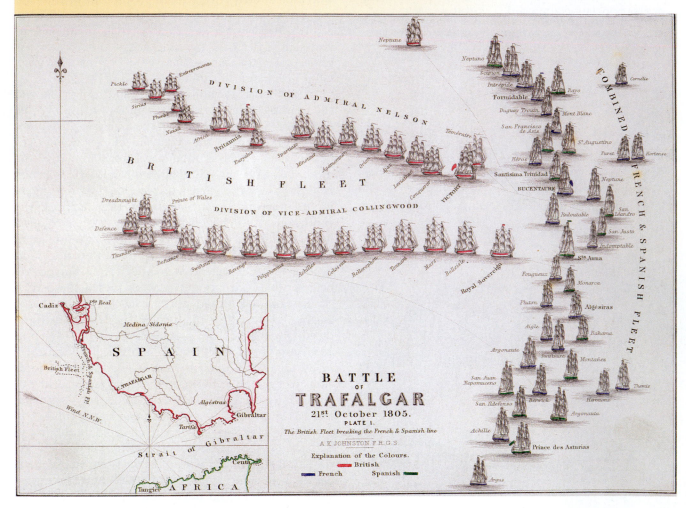

the seas, which then forced Napoleon into economic policies that strained French ties to France's allies and satellites. Virtually unchallenged sea power enabled the British to seize colonies formerly ruled by France and its allies.

Britain's maritime supremacy and seizure of French possessions expanded British trading networks overseas—though in some cases only temporarily—and closer to home, particularly in the Mediterranean. As long as the British had been involved in trade with India, the Mediterranean had been important for economic and strategic reasons because it lay at the end of the land route for trade from the Indian Ocean. Especially after Napoleon's aggression in Egypt in the 1790s, the British redoubled their efforts to control strategic outposts in the Mediterranean.

The British economy would expand dramatically in the nineteenth century as industrial production soared. The roots for growth were laid in this period in the countryside of Britain, where changes in agriculture and in production were occurring. These roots were also laid in Britain's overseas possessions as tighter control of foreign sources of raw materials, notably raw Indian cotton, meant rising fortunes back in Britain. In regions of India, the East India Company was increasing its political domination, and hence its economic stranglehold on Indian commodities. The export of Indian cotton rose significantly during the revolutionary period as part of an expanding trading system that included China, the source of tea.

However, economic expansion was not the sole motive for British aggression. In fact, economic expansion was often a byproduct of increased British control of particular regions or sea-lanes, and the reasons for it were as much strategic as economic. But British elites were sure that strategic domination was a desirable step, wherever it could be achieved, and whether or not every conquest had direct economic payoffs. One Scotsman spoke for many when he said that Britain needed an empire to ensure its greatness and that an empire of the sea was an effective counterweight to Napoleon's empire on land. Much as the French were at that mo-ment exporting features of their own political system, the British, he said, could export their constitution wherever they conquered territory.

Thus England and France were engaged in similar phases of expansion in this period. In both, desire for both power and profit drove policy. In each, myths about heroes and about the supposed benefits of domination masked the state's self-interest. For both, the effects of conquest would become a fundamental shaping force in the nineteenth century.

SECTION SUMMARY

- General Napoleon Bonaparte and two other men seized power from the Directory in a coup in 1799; Napoleon carefully expanded his power and finally declared himself emperor of France in 1804.

- Napoleon's law code and his agreement with the Catholic Church made permanent some of the key changes from the first phase of the Revolution.

- Napoleon recruited former royal officials, old nobility, and recent revolutionaries into his government, thereby resolving some of the political tensions that had resulted from the Revolution.

- The costs associated with Napoleon's foreign conquests resulted in the overthrow of his regime and contributed to the long-term problems of the French government.

- The export of revolution by French armies brought economic costs from war itself and from Napoleon's continental trading system but also political reform that led, in many cases, to further political liberty.

- In the Americas, the French Revolution inspired movements for independence from colonial rule; in Haiti, slaves and free persons without political rights allied to successfully overthrow French rule.

CHAPTER SUMMARY

Online Study Center **ACE the Test**

What factors led to the beginning of revolution in France in 1789?

Why did several phases of revolutionary change occur after 1789 and what were the characteristics of each phase?

What impact did the Revolution and Napoleonic rule have on France, the rest of Europe, and the wider world?

The French Revolution was a watershed in European history because it successfully challenged the principles of hereditary rule and political privilege by which all European states had hitherto been governed. The Revolution began when a financial crisis forced the monarchy to confront the desire for political reform by a segment of the French elite. Political philosophy emerging from the Enlightenment and the example of the American Revolution moved the French reformers to action. In its initial phase the French Revolution established the principle of constitutional government and ended many of the traditional political privileges of the Old Regime.

Then, because of the intransigence of the king, the threat of foreign invasion, and the actions of republican legislators and Parisian citizens, the Revolution moved in more radical directions. Its most extremist phase, the Terror, produced the most effective legislation for ordinary citizens but also the worst violence of the Revolution. A period of unstable conservative rule that followed the Terror ended when Napoleon seized power.

Although Napoleonic rule solidified some of the gains of the Revolution, it also subjected France and most of Europe to the great costs of wars of conquest. After Napoleon the French monarchy was restored, but henceforth its power would not be absolute—and the people would not be refused a voice in government—as a result of the Revolution. The impact of events in France also continued beyond its borders; political and legal reform had been imposed in many parts of Europe and even, in more limited ways, had been embraced in European colonies.

LOOKING AHEAD

Hereditary rule and traditional social hierarchies remained in place in much of Europe, but they would not be secure in the future. The legacy of revolutionary change would prove impossible to contain in France or anywhere else.

KEY TERMS

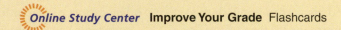 **Online Study Center** Improve Your Grade Flashcards

Third Estate (p. 592)

National Assembly (p. 592)

Tennis Court Oath (p. 592)

Declaration of the Rights of Man and the Citizen (p. 594)

sans-culottes (p. 598)

Jacobins (p. 599)

Maximilien Robespierre (p. 599)

the Terror (p. 599)

Society of Revolutionary Republican Women (p. 601)

Directory (p. 601)

Napoleon Bonaparte (p. 604)

Civil Code (p. 607)

François Toussaint-Louverture (p. 613)

SUGGESTED READING

Baker, Keith Michael. *Inventing the French Revolution.* 1990. A series of essays situating the Revolution amid the dramatic changes in eighteenth-century political culture.

Hunt, Lynn. *The French Revolution and Human Rights: A Brief Documentary History.* 1996. A well-presented short collection of documents, useful for a greater understanding of the impact of the Revolution on the development of human rights.

Jordan, D. P. *The King's Trial.* 1979. An engaging study of Louis XVI's trial and its importance for the Revolution.

Landes, Joan. *Women and the Public Sphere in the Age of the French Revolution.* 1988. An analysis of the uses of gender ideology to fashion the new political world of the revolutionaries.

Langley, Lester D. *The Americas in the Age of Revolution, 1750–1850.* 1996. A survey of all the American states and colonies and the impact of the Atlantic revolutions.

Popkin, Jeremy. *A Short History of the French Revolution.* 1995. A compact and readable recent synthesis of research.

NOTES

1. Quoted in Samuel Eliot Morrison, *John Paul Jones: A Sailor's Biography* (Boston: Little, Brown, 1959), pp. 149–154.

2. Quoted in Owen Connelly, *The French Revolution and the Napoleonic Era* (New York: Holt, Rinehart, and Winston, 1979), p. 32.

3. James Harvey Robinson, *Readings in European History* (Boston: Ginn, 1906), p. 409.

20

THE INDUSTRIAL TRANSFORMATION OF EUROPE, 1750–1850

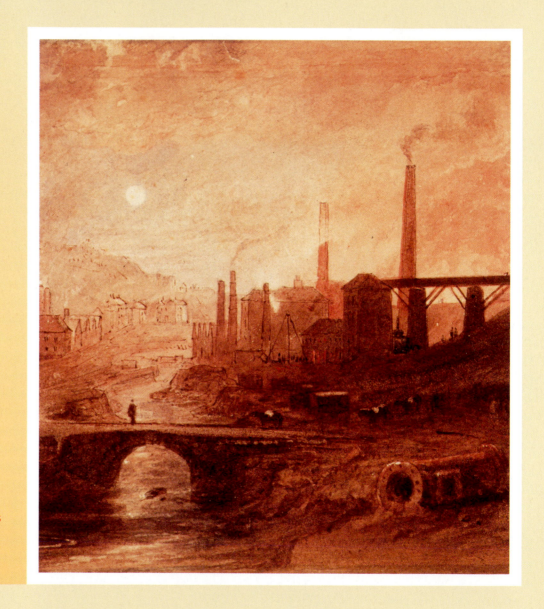

George Robertson: Nat-Y-Glo Iron Works

(National Museums & Galleries of Wales)

As the French Revolution gave way to the fires of war in continental Europe, across the Channel fires from factory chimneys in England's industrializing cities blurred the distinction between day and night with their constant flames, smoke, and smog. The painting on the left depicts Shropshire, England, in 1788, a region previously renowned for its natural beauty. Industrial activity had already transformed its landscape beyond recognition. Abraham Darby (1676–1717) and his descendants built one of the largest and most important concentrations of ironworks in Shropshire because it contained the ideal combination of coal and iron deposits. The dramatic rise in the use of new machinery throughout Britain, which led to previously unheard-of levels in the production of iron and textiles, struck contemporaries. In the 1830s the French socialist Louis Blanqui (blahn-KEE) (see page 661) proposed a descriptive term, suggesting that just as France had recently experienced a political revolution, so Britain was undergoing an "industrial revolution." Eventually, that expression entered the general vocabulary to describe the advances in production that occurred first in England and then dominated most of western Europe by the end of the nineteenth century. Many economic historians now emphasize how gradual and cumulative the changes were and question the appropriateness of the term *revolution*. Indeed, although mechanization transformed Europe, it did so unevenly. Great Britain offered a model of economic change because it was the first to industrialize; each nation subsequently took its own path and pace in a continuous process of economic transformation.

Industrial development left its mark on just about every sphere of human activity. Scientific and rational methods altered production processes, removing them from the home—where entire families had often participated—to less personal workshops and factories. Significant numbers of workers left farming to enter mining and manufacturing, and major portions of the population moved from rural to urban environments. Machines replaced or supplemented manual labor.[1]

Industrial development transformed Europe socially, culturally, physically. Mechanical production often meant that skilled artisans lost not only their livelihood, but their craft identity as well; it also drew women and children out of the home and into factories. New modes of production

CHAPTER OUTLINE

PRECONDITIONS FOR INDUSTRIALIZATION

NEW MODES OF PRODUCTION

SOCIAL, CULTURAL, AND ENVIRONMENTAL IMPACTS

RESPONSES TO INDUSTRIALIZATION

KEY TERMS

industrialization

mass production

steam engine

factories

entrepreneurs

primogeniture

urbanization

proletariat

friendly societies

Luddites

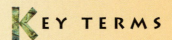

Online Study Center

This icon will direct you to interactive map and primary source activities on the website **college.hmco.com/pic/noble5e**

offered unprecedented opportunities for manufacturers, merchants, and entrepreneurs to create and amass wealth at levels previously unimaginable. Mechanization also caused pollution and environmental destruction. Miners in search of coal, iron ore, and other minerals cut deep gashes into the earth. The rapid growth of cities resulted in crowded slums, poor sanitation, filth, and visible poverty.

Industrialization simultaneously created unprecedented advancement and opportunity as well as unprecedented hardships and social problems. The social gap between the rich and the working poor increased. The latter, with a growing sense of solidarity, struggled to protect and advance their interests.

FOCUS QUESTIONS

What factors allowed Europe to industrialize before the rest of the world?

Which inventions appear to have been the most important in launching industrialization?

What impact did industrialization have on the environment and on social classes?

What did workers gain and lose as a result of industrialization, and how did they respond?

PRECONDITIONS FOR INDUSTRIALIZATION

What factors allowed Europe to industrialize before the rest of the world?

Industrialization—the substitution of human and animal power by mineral power—required a massive shift of labor and capital resources from agriculture to manufacturing and services. Europe, and especially Great Britain, were endowed with a unique combination of conditions—geographic, cultural, economic, demographic—that made this shift and its timing possible. Industrialization did not simply consist of mechanization. It consisted of, and required, simultaneous growth in commerce, population, and agricultural production. An entrepreneurial spirit and government support for banking and trading were required so that capital could be accumulated for investment in industry. Population growth increased pressure to supply manufactured goods at a faster pace. It also required more efficient food production. As farmers applied new scientific methods to cultivation, less labor was required for food production, thus allowing migration to towns and cities.

WHY EUROPE?

A unique set of circumstances in Europe favored its potential for rapid economic development. Centralized state power and the development of due legal process reduced the risks of highway robbery and the confiscation of wealth that merchants accumulated from trade. Such security was nonexistent in other parts of the world, such as the Ottoman Empire, where sultans and corrupt officials could grab wealth on a whim. Hence in the West, accumulating wealth was a worthwhile endeavor.

Compared with Asia, Europe exhibited far greater cultural, political, and social diversity. Challenges to dominant religious and political powers that had come from the Reformation, Counter-Reformation, and the Enlightenment promoted innovation. Toleration for such freedom was a rarity in Asia, where large territories tended to be dominated by a single ruler and faith. International competition among European states drove them to try to outdo one another. Governments actively encouraged industries and commerce to enrich their countries and make them more powerful than their neighbors. None of these factors alone explains why industrialization occurred, but their combination facilitated the process as well as its timing.[2] The industrialization of Europe radically transformed power relationships between the industrial West and nonindustrial Africa, Asia, and South America. By 1900 the West had overwhelmed the other regions with its economic and military power. (See the box "The Global Record: Alexis de Tocqueville's Thoughts on Colonization.")

industrialization A system of mass production of goods in which specialization and mechanization made manufacturing efficient and profitable.

TRANSFORMATIONS ACCOMPANYING INDUSTRIALIZATION

A number of other transformations favored economic innovation in Europe. Improved agricultural techniques dramatically increased food production. Rather than leaving a portion of their land fallow when crops depleted the soil, farmers learned to rotate them, use fertilizers, and plant new crops from the Americas—such as the potato and maize—that not only flourished in poor soil, but replenished the soil with nitrogen. New, more efficient plows enabled farmers to cultivate more land than ever before with less labor. Most important, the new crops and the more efficient cultivation of traditional ones increased the capacity to feed a growing population and freed many people to go to the city and work in the industries. Until these changes began occurring in the eighteenth century, food production required the work of 80 percent of the European population.

Population growth also helped promote industrialization. The first spurt in growth occurred in the mid-eighteenth century, before the effects of industrialization could be widely felt. Thereafter the population of Europe increased dramatically throughout the industrial era, doubling between 1750 and 1850. This growth was partly due to a lowering of the death rate. Infant mortality had been very high from illness and disease, such as gastrointestinal disorders from poor food, smallpox, diphtheria, and tuberculosis. Although none of these diseases had been medically conquered, slow improvement in sanitation and food intake after 1750 enabled children to better resist them. New employment opportunities led to earlier marriages and thus higher fertility. This growing population supplied the labor force for the new industries and provided the large surge in consumers of various industrial goods.

In the countryside industrialization was foreshadowed by a form of production that had developed beginning in the seventeenth century—the putting-out system, or cottage industry. During the winter and at other slack times, peasants took in handwork such as spinning, weaving, or dyeing. Often they were marginal agriculturists, frequently women, who on a part-time basis could augment the family income. Entrepreneurs discovered that some individuals were better than others at specific tasks. Rather than have one household process the wool through all the steps of production until it was a finished piece, the entrepreneur would buy wool produced by one family, then take it to another to spin, a third to dye, a fourth to weave, and so on. Although cottage industry, through its specialization, was an important contributor to industrialization in some regions, that was not the case everywhere.

1712	Newcomen invents steam-operated water pump
1733	Kay invents flying shuttle
1750–1800	Three million Africans are brought to the Americas as slaves
1753	First steam engine in the Americas
1760s	Hargreaves invents spinning jenny
1765	Watt improves steam engine with separate condenser
1769	Arkwright patents water frame for spinning
1785	Cartwright patents power loom
1793	Whitney invents cotton gin
1804	Jacquard invents automatic loom
1811–1812	Luddites organize
1825	Börsig builds first steam engine in Germany
1831, 1834	Workers' uprising in Lyon
1832	Cholera epidemic
1834	Creation of German customs union, the Zollverein
1844	Workers' uprising in Silesia
1851	Majority of Britain's population becomes urban

A less ambiguous prerequisite for industry was a good transportation network. Transportation improved significantly in the eighteenth century, particularly in response to expanding markets for agricultural and manufactured products. Better roads were built; new coaches and carriages could travel faster and carry heavier loads. Government and private companies built canals linking rivers to each other or to lakes. Road- and canal-building hastened and cheapened transportation, facilitating the movement of raw materials to factories and finished goods to local and distant markets. In Great Britain these transformations occurred simultaneously with industrialization; on the Continent they were actual precursors to economic change.

Britain, the first to industrialize, was the dominant political power throughout the nineteenth century. The rest of Europe admired Britain and regarded it not only as an economic model but also as a political and cultural one.

ALEXIS DE TOCQUEVILLE'S THOUGHTS ON COLONIZATION

The French military conquest of Algeria, beginning in 1830, provides an example of how economic modernization gave Europeans a sense of superiority and changed their relationship with the rest of the world. Charles X, king of France, sent the French military to the town of Algiers in response to a perceived insult from the dey (Algerian governor). The military conquest took seventeen years. Alexis de Tocqueville (1805–1859), member of the French parliament and author of the famous Democracy in America, *like many Europeans, thought that industrial progress not only enabled but legitimized the military and economic takeover of undeveloped regions inhabited by people of color. He also argued that white settlement would facilitate military conquest. In the first excerpt below, Tocqueville shares his awe at the vibrancy of urban culture in Algiers, and he describes how the French have begun to tear down and rebuild sections of the town. In the second excerpt, he portrays an example of what already had occurred in the French military occupation of Algeria and warns against it.*

From "Notes on the Voyage to Algeria in 1841"

First appearance of [Algiers]: I have never seen anything like it. Prodigious mix of races and costumes, Arab, Kabyle, Moor, Negro, Mahonais, . . . French. Each of these races, tossed together in a space much too tight to contain them, speaks its language, wears its attire, displays different mores. This whole world moves about with an activity that seems feverish. The entire lower town seems in a state of destruction and reconstruction. On all sides, one sees nothing but recent ruins, buildings going up; one hears nothing but the noise of the hammer. It is Cincinnati transported onto the soil of Africa.

The French are substituting broad arcaded streets for the Moors' tortuous little alleys. This is a necessity of our civilization. But they are also substituting their architecture for that of the Moors, and this is wrong; for the latter is very appropriate to the needs of the country, and besides, it is charming. . . .

From "First Report on Algeria," 1847

The indigenous towns were invaded, turned upside down, and sacked by our administration even more than by our arms. . . . In the vicinity of Algiers itself, the very fertile areas were torn from the hands of the Arabs and given to Europeans who, not being able or not wanting to cultivate them themselves, rented them to these same indigenous people, who thus became the mere farmers of the domains that had belonged to their fathers. Elsewhere, tribes or factions of tribes that were not hostile to us, or even more who had fought with us and sometimes without us,

were pushed off their territory. We accepted conditions we did not fulfill, we promised indemnities we did not pay, thus allowing our honor to suffer even more than the interests of these indigenous peoples. . . .

Muslim society in Africa was not uncivilized; it was merely a backward and imperfect civilization. There existed within it a large number of pious foundations, whose object was to provide for the needs of charity or for public instruction. We laid our hands on these revenues everywhere, partly diverting them from their former uses; we reduced the charitable establishments and let the schools decay, we disbanded seminaries. Around us knowledge has been extinguished, and recruitment of men of religion and men of law has ceased; that is to say, we have made Muslim society much more miserable, more disordered, more ignorant, and more barbarous than it had been before knowing us. . . .

It is not along the road of our European civilization that they must, for the present, be pushed, but in the direction proper to them; we must demand of them things that suit their ways, and not those contrary to them. Individual property, industry, and sedentary dwelling [as opposed to nomadic lifestyle] are in no way contrary to the religion of Muhammad. Arabs know or have known these things elsewhere; they are known and appreciated by some in Algeria itself. Why do we despair of making them familiar to a greater number? . . . Islam is not absolutely impenetrable to enlightenment.

. . . If our arms have decimated certain tribes, there are others whom our commerce has enriched and strengthened considerably, and who feel and understand this. Everywhere the prices that the indigenous people can get for their wares and their labor have increased greatly by our presence. In addition, our agriculturalists gladly make use of indigenous manpower. The European needs the Arab to make his lands valuable; the Arab needs the European to obtain a high salary.

QUESTIONS

1. How does Tocqueville react to Algerian culture? Why does he compare Algiers with Cincinnati? How are the French attempting to remake Algeria in their own image?

2. What are Tocqueville's assumptions about economic modernization in Algeria, and its appropriateness for indigenous culture?

Source: Alexis de Tocqueville, *Writings on Empire and Slavery,* ed. and trans. Jennifer Pitts (Baltimore: Johns Hopkins University Press), pp. 36, 140, 142, 145.

First Railroad, from Manchester to Liverpool, England

The engineer George Stephenson (1781–1848) first built engines that could pull coal at mines, then in 1821 he constructed the first "locomotive" for public transportation. Four years later the first regular railroad line, connecting Manchester with Liverpool, was erected. *(Private Collection/Bridgeman Art Libraryl)*

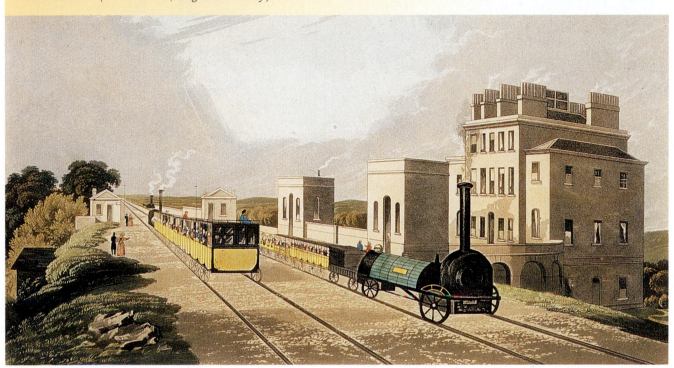

BRITAIN'S LEAD IN INDUSTRIAL INNOVATION

Britain led the way industrially for many reasons. It was the first European country to have a standard currency, tax, and tariff system. Although Britain was by no means an egalitarian society, it accommodated some movement between the classes. Ideas and experiments were readily communicated among entrepreneurs, workers, and scientists.

In addition, England had gained an increasing share of international trade since the seventeenth century. This trade provided capital for investment in industrial plants. The world trade network also ensured that Britain had a market beyond its borders, and because total demand was relatively high, mass manufacture was feasible. The international trade network also enabled Britain to import raw materials for its industry, the most important of which was cotton.

Earlier than its competitors, Britain had a national banking system that could finance industries in areas where private funding fell short. In addition to numerous London banks lending mainly in the capital, six hundred provincial banks serviced the economy by 1810. The banking system reflected the growth of the economy as much as it contributed to it. Banking could flourish because Britons had wide experience in trade, had accumulated considerable amounts of wealth, and had found a constant demand for credit.

Geographically, Britain was also fortunate. Coal and iron were located close to each other (see **MAP 20.1**). Because Britain is a relatively narrow island, virtually all of it has easy access to the sea—no part of the country is more than 70 miles from the coast. This was a strategic advantage, for water was by far the cheapest means of transportation. Compared with the Continent, Britain had few tolls, and moving goods was relatively easy and inexpensive.

On the whole, British workers were better off than their continental counterparts. They were more skilled, earned higher wages, and had discretionary income to spend on the manufactured goods now for sale. But because labor was more costly than on the Continent, British business owners had an incentive to find labor-saving devices and reduce the number of workers needed for production.

The population of Great Britain increased by 8 percent in each decade from 1750 to 1800, in part as a

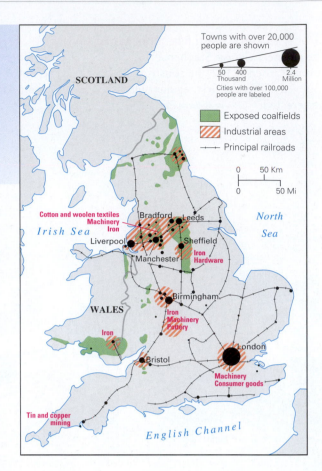

MAP 20.1 The Industrial Transformation in England, ca. 1850
Industry developed in the areas rich in coal and iron fields. Important cities sprang up nearby and were soon linked by a growing rail network.

Online Study Center **Improve Your Grade**
Interactive Map: Industrialization in England, ca. 1850

result of industrial growth. This swelling population, in turn, expanded the market for goods. The most rapid growth occurred in the countryside, causing a steady movement of people from rural to urban areas. The presence of this work force was another contributing factor in Britain's readiness for change.

Britain was far more open to dissent than were other European countries at the time. The lack of conformity was reflected in religion and also in a willingness to try new methods of production. In fact, the two often went together. A large proportion of British entrepreneurs was Quaker or belonged to one of the dissenting (non-Anglican) religious groups. Perhaps dissenters were accustomed to questioning authority and treading new paths. They were also well educated and, as a result of common religious bonds, inclined to provide mutual aid, including financial support.

Plentiful harvests in the years 1715 to 1750 also favored Britain and influenced the timing of industrial change. Farmers with good earnings could afford to

order the new manufactured iron plows, and demand for industrial goods generally rose with population growth, improvements to the transportation system, and the growing availability of capital for investment. Thus each change triggered more change; the cumulative effect was staggering.

SECTION SUMMARY

- Europe, and especially Great Britain, was endowed with rich iron and coal deposits, one of the most important factors that gave them the lead in industrialization.

- Population growth in the eighteenth century inspired greater efficiency in agricultural production, which in turn created a surplus labor force available for industrial production in urban areas and created a market for mass-produced goods.

- Toleration of religious diversity and dissent, especially in Great Britain, helped inspire innovation and an entrepreneurial spirit.

- The expansion of trade from the seventeenth century onward created new sources of raw materials for manufacture, such as cotton.

- Merchants brought raw materials to the countryside for processing, leading to the development of cottage industry (the putting-out system), the division of labor, and specialization of tasks.

- Centralized governments supported national banks and encouraged commerce, which in turn led to improved transportation.

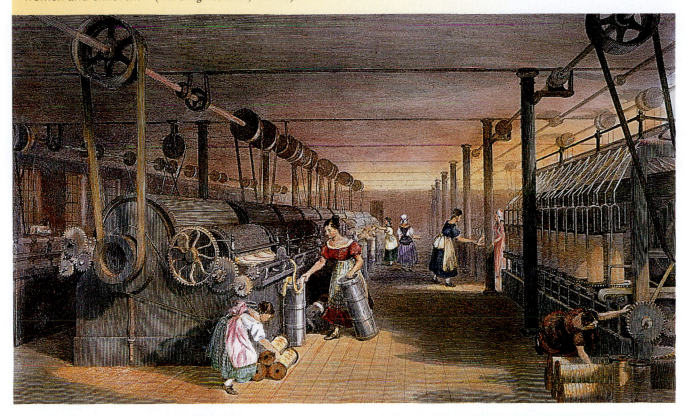

British Cotton Manufacture
Machines simultaneously performed various functions. The carding machine (*front left*) separated cotton fibers, readying them for spinning. The roving machine (*front right*) wound the cotton onto spools. The drawing machine (*rear left*) wove patterns into the cloth. Rich in machines, this factory needed relatively few employees; most were women and children.   (*The Granger Collection, New York*)

NEW MODES OF PRODUCTION

Which inventions appear to have been the most important in launching industrialization?

Several important technological advances powered European industry, and breakthroughs in one field often led to breakthroughs in others. Major technological innovations first transformed textiles and iron. At first limited to the British Isles, industry spread to the Continent, a development that occurred unevenly in various regions and at different times.

ADVANCES IN THE COTTON INDUSTRY

A series of inventions in the eighteenth century led to the **mass production** of textiles. One of the earliest was the flying shuttle, introduced in Britain in 1733 by John Kay (1704–1764). (A shuttle carries the thread back and forth on a loom.) Kay's flying shuttle accelerated the weaving process to such an extent that it increased the demand for thread. This need was met in the 1760s by James Hargreaves (1720–1778), who invented the spinning jenny, a device that spun thread from wool or cotton. Improvements in spinning thread, such as the mule of Samuel Crompton (1753–1827), made the spinning jenny increasingly efficient, and by 1812 one jenny could produce as much yarn as two hundred hand spinners. In 1769 Richard Arkwright (1732–1792), a barber and wigmaker, patented the water frame, a machine capable of simultaneously spinning many threads. It was installed in a single establishment with three hundred employees, forming the first modern factory. The frame was originally powered by waterfall, but in 1780s Arkwright began operating it with a steam engine. This mode of production created a glut of thread for hand weavers, which then

mass production   System in which great numbers of people work in centralized, mechanized factories to produce large quantities of goods. The steam engine led to mass-produced textiles.

THE WRITTEN RECORD

A FRENCH WOMAN GOES TO WORK

The new cotton mills presented several obstacles to women workers. They had to negotiate the machinery while wearing the petticoats and aprons that custom required. Such dress could catch in the machinery, causing broken limbs and loss of a job, if not of life. At work and on their way to and from work in the British mills or at the less mechanized garment workshops of France, women had to pass dangerous places, where some experienced sexual harassment. Suzanne Voilquin (ca. 1801–ca. 1876) went to work to help her family after her mother had died. She took a job not at a mill or a factory, as was common in England, but as an embroiderer in a small workshop in Paris. In this selection she writes of her experiences as a young woman from about 1823 to 1825.

We had to be at our looms at seven o'clock sharp and, even before setting out on the long race to get there on time, we had to carry out all our little household duties as quickly as we could. If certain details made us late, Mrs. Martin [her employer] would accept no excuses and offer no reprieve. We had to pay in kind, that is to say, make good those few minutes at the end of the day's work. When our days were prolonged in this way, I had a horrible fear of meeting on my return one of those contemptible men who make a game of accosting young working women and frightening them with disgraceful remarks. When this happened, my nerves were always on edge and I lacked all physical courage. It was quite otherwise with . . . Adrienne [her younger sister]. She would say to me, . . . "Dear Sister, aren't I here?" (She was barely fifteen.) "If the occasion arises, why then you'll see that *a person's worth is not measured in years!*" And indeed, one evening, she gave me positive proof. Around nine o'clock . . . we were stopped by the vulgar words and filthy gestures of some poor wretch. As always, I stood there trembling and unable to speak

before this reviler. Adrienne, on the contrary, experienced a moment of sublime energy. She managed to find such a tone of resolve, while brandishing an enormous key before his eyes, that he backed away, and, when we reached the corner of the main street, we were delivered from his insolent remarks.

Mrs. Martin seemed satisfied with our work, and we were accepted as regular employees. And so, at the end of the first week, we were very proud to deposit on our father's mantelpiece the eighteen francs we earned as wages. It was the same each week, for he had made himself the provisioner of our little group.

That cruel year was brought to an end by an accident that nearly caused my sister the loss of her right hand. My father's wail when he thought his child had been maimed for life was heart-rending. He cried!

. . . Around this time, my father wanted to marry us off. . . . The widower whom my father begged me to marry was fairly well established but neither handsome nor pleasant nor witty. Moreover, he came with a son twelve or thirteen years old, a charming Parisian street urchin who had been very badly raised. As a result, my mind, my senses, my whole being rebelled against the thought of such a match.

QUESTIONS

1. What is Suzanne Voilquin's attitude toward work? What hardships does she face?

2. What does this excerpt tell you about family relations? Why does Suzanne's father want to "marry her off"?

Source: Suzanne Voilquin, "Recollections of a Daughter of the People," in Mark Traugott, ed. and trans., The French Worker: Autobiographies from the Early Industrial Era, pp. 112–113. Copyright © 1993 The Regents of the University of California. Reprinted by permission of The University of California Press.

led to the development of the power loom by Richard Cartwright in 1785. These innovations in turn increased the demand for raw cotton, inspiring American Eli Whitney (1765–1825) to invent the cotton gin, which sped up the removal of seeds from raw cotton. These innovations mechanized cotton manufacturing, moving most production from the home to factories. The industry's output increased 130-fold between 1770 and 1841.

The cotton manufacturing industry in Great Britain was an important departure from traditional production. For the first time in history a staple industry was based on a natural resource that was not do-

mestically produced—Britain imported cotton from the U.S. South. Manufactured cotton became so cheap that it competed effectively with all handmade textiles. Comfortable and easy to wash, the popularity of cotton may have improved public health as well, for it enabled people to own several changes of clothing and keep them clean. Everyone was eager to buy British cottons. The higher demand for raw material put pressure on cotton growers in the U.S. South, who opened up new land. Whitney's cotton gin not only massively increased cotton production and the profitability of the United States' southern plantation economy; it also made slave labor more attractive.

Between 1750 and 1800 approximately three million Africans were forcibly transported to the New World, causing an enormous demographic loss to Africa. At least 10 percent of the captives died in the Middle Passage while being transported to the Americas, and an unknown number died in the wars triggered by slavers. Since predominantly young men were enslaved, villages were often left without their most productive workers and became vulnerable to famine, which also may have decimated the population.

The slave economy in the Americas influenced Britain's economy in several ways. Slave-produced sugar in the West Indies and cotton in the American South shifted Britain's trade patterns from Asia to the Atlantic. The sophisticated administrative skills that went into organizing and operating the slave trade provided invaluable management experience to the more conventional sectors of the British economy. It also benefited enormously from the sugar and cotton produced by slaves.

The cotton trade, and later, other products, linked the economies of various nations and peoples. No longer, as in preindustrial trade, were all goods locally made, nor did the consumers have personal contact with the producers of goods they purchased. Increasingly, specialization became the norm. Those most skilled performed a particular function efficiently and productively. The results were high production and low prices for finished textile products. Hand sewing and needlework, usually done by young women, completed the garment-making process. (See the box "The Written Record: A French Woman Goes to Work.")

Iron, Steam, and Factories

Coal, a new energy source, fueled industrial production. Traditionally, smelters used charcoal to extract iron from ore. Eventually, however, the source of charcoal—wood—became depleted in Britain. Coal offered an alternative fuel, and it was plentiful. But it contained impurities, particularly sulfur, which contaminated the materials with which it came into contact. In 1708 the English ironmaster Abraham Darby discovered that coal in a blast furnace could smelt iron without these attending complications. His discovery triggered the iron industry's use of coal. In 1777 the introduction of a steam engine to operate the blast furnace considerably increased efficiency. In 1783 a steam engine was first used to drive a forge hammer to shape the iron; three years later steam-driven rollers flattened the iron into sheets. With these innovations, the output of the English iron industry doubled between 1788 and 1796 and again in the following eight years.

The greater supply of iron stimulated other changes. Wooden machines, which wore out rapidly, were replaced by relatively cheap and durable iron machines.

The new machines opened the door to further advances. Improvements in manufacturing methods and techniques increased the production of a large variety of goods, usually at lower prices. Industrial change started with cotton, but breakthroughs in the use of iron and coal continued and sustained these changes.

Before the age of industry, humans, animals, wind, and water provided the power sources for production. Humans and animals were limited in their capacities to drive the large mills needed to grind grain or cut wood. Wind was unreliable because it was not constant. Water-driven mills depended on the seasons—streams dried up in the summer and froze in the winter. And water mills could be placed only where a strong current of water flowed downward. Clearly the infant industries needed a power source that was constant and not confined to riverbanks. The **steam engine,** invented and improved on in Britain, met that need and stoked Britain's industrial growth. As late as the 1860s, traditional sources of energy still supplied more than half of the manufacturing needs in Great Britain and the United States. But the steam engine was clearly the wave of the future.

The steam engine was first used to pump water out of coal mines. As mining shafts were dug ever deeper through groundwater, drainage became a critical factor. In 1712 Thomas Newcomen (1663–1729) invented a steam-operated water pump. Its use spread rapidly. James Watt (1736–1819) improved on the Newcomen engine, making it twice as efficient in energy output. Eventually, by developing a separate condenser, Watt devised an engine that could power a variety of machines. Thus steam engines could operate mills that had previously been powered by water or wind.

The steam engine made it practical and commonplace to organize work in a factory. Locating a manufacturing plant where it was most convenient eliminated the expense of transporting raw materials to be worked on at a natural but fixed power source such as a waterfall. The central factory also reinforced work discipline. These **factories** were large, austere edifices, sometimes inspired by military architecture and therefore resembling barracks. With the introduction of blast furnaces and other heat-producing manufacturing methods, the tall factory chimney became a common sight on the industrial landscape.

The steam engine powered a dramatic growth in production. It increased the force of blast furnaces and the mechanical power of machinery used to forge iron

steam engine   The steam engine provided mechanized power for manufacturing and made factories and mass production possible.

factories   Centralized workplaces where a number of people cooperate to mass-produce goods. The steam engine as a central power source in factories led to huge productivity increases.

The Jacquard Loom
Joseph-Marie Jacquard invented this loom in 1804. The pasteboard punch cards controlled the action of the loom to create complex designs automatically, making it possible for amateur weavers to produce highly prized fabrics. The punch card was an important precursor to computing hardware and programming. The looms' cards were interchangeable. They could also be stolen—an early instance of software piracy. *(Private Collection)*

and to produce equipment for spinning and weaving. Assisted by machines, workers were enormously more productive than when they depended solely on hand-operated tools. In 1700 spinning 100 pounds of cotton took 50,000 worker-hours; by 1825 it took only 135 worker-hours—a 370-fold increase in productivity capacity per worker.

INVENTORS AND ENTREPRENEURS

Inventions triggered the industrial age, and the continued flow of new ones sustained it. Rather than cling to traditional methods, many **entrepreneurs** persistently challenged tradition and attempted to find new ways of improving production. In this age of invention, innovation was prized as never before.

The early inventors and industrialists came from a variety of backgrounds. Many came from the merchant

entrepreneurs   People who assume the risks of organizing and investing in new business ventures, inventions, and innovations.

class, since the possession of capital was a distinct advantage in launching an industrial enterprise. In 1804, Frenchman Joseph-Marie Jacquard (1752–1834), the son of a weaver, invented the Jacquard loom, which used a punched-card system to automate complex silk weaving. Within his lifetime industrialists in France and England adopted his loom, which later became the model for early computers using punched cards.

Entrepreneurs such as Arkwright and Watt pioneered innovations and became famous, but most of those who advanced the cause of industrial production were not particularly inventive. They just replicated methods of production that had proved profitable to others. Truly successful entrepreneurs, however, seemed to share one attribute: they were driven by a nearly insatiable appetite for innovation, work, and profit.

Entrepreneurs took the financial risk of investing in new types of enterprises. Most industrialists ran a single plant by themselves or with a partner, but even in the early stages, some ran several plants. In 1788

Richard Arkwright and his partners ran eight mills. Some enterprises were vertically integrated, controlling production at many stages. The Peels in Britain owned operations ranging from spinning to printing and even banking. The entrepreneurs' dynamism and boldness fostered the growth of the British industrial system, making that small nation the workshop of the world.

THE SPREAD OF INDUSTRY TO THE CONTINENT

The ideas and methods that were changing industry in Britain spread to the Continent by direct contact and by emulation. Visitors came to Britain, studied local methods of production, and returned home to set up blast furnaces and spinning works inspired by British design. The German engineer August Börsig (BEUR-sick) (1804–1854), after studying steam engines in Britain, built the first German steam engine in 1825 and the first German locomotive in 1842. Some visitors even resorted to industrial espionage, smuggling blueprints of machines out of Britain. Despite a British law

that forbade local artisans to emigrate, some did leave, including entrepreneurs who helped set up industrial plants in France and Belgium. By the 1820s British technicians were all over Europe—in Belgium, France, Germany, and Austria.

France   In the eighteenth century, France had seemed a more likely candidate for economic growth than Britain. France's overseas trade was growing faster than Britain's, and in 1780 its industrial output was also greater. In the nineteenth century, however, British industry boomed and Britain became the workshop of the world. French production changed more slowly. Why?

Historians have suggested several reasons. The wars and revolutions of the late eighteenth century slowed economic growth and cut France off from the flow of information and new techniques from Britain. Moreover, in the 1790s, revolutionary legislation relieved some of the peasants' misery. Thus peasants were not forced off the land by poor conditions as they were in Britain, where they provided cheap and ready labor for industry. Further, the Napoleonic Code of 1804

The Börsig Ironworks in the 1840s
August Börsig, an artisan, founded these ironworks in Berlin. The factory expanded to meet the needs of the burgeoning German rail system. By the time of Börsig's death in 1854, his factory had built five hundred locomotives.   *(Bildarchiv Preussischer Kulturbesitz/Art Resource, NY)*

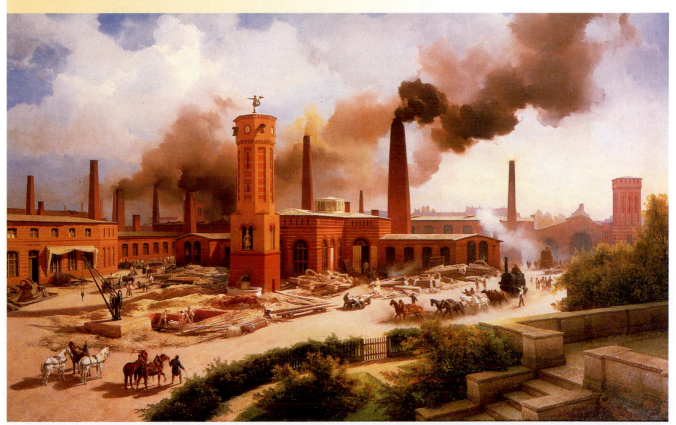

MAP 20.2 Continental Industrialization, ca. 1850

Industry was still sparse on the Continent, but important regions had developed near major coal deposits in Liège, the Ruhr, and Silesia.

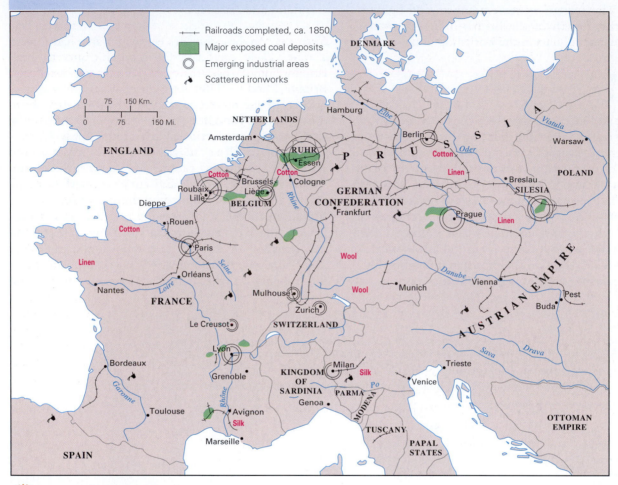

Online Study Center **Improve Your Grade** Interactive Map: Continental Industrialization, ca. 1850

abolished **primogeniture,** so that when a peasant died, all of his children, at least in principle, enjoyed equal inheritance.

Population figures suggest another reason for France's relatively slow economic growth. Between 1800 and 1914 the population of France grew at half the average rate experienced by the rest of the Continent. In Britain during this period, much of the labor that left the land and worked the factories and mills came from the rural population explosion. But no such phenomenon occurred in the French countryside, and thus the labor force in France was not poised for industrial growth.

Traditionally, France had produced high-quality luxury goods, and French entrepreneurs who sought to emulate British accomplishments faced serious difficulties. Iron and coal deposits in France were not close

together (see **MAP 20.2**). Because labor was still quite cheap, many goods could be manufactured inexpensively by hand; thus the incentive to invest in laborsaving devices was absent. Soon, however, French manufacturers found themselves facing British competition. By being the first to industrialize, the British had the advantage of being able to manufacture goods and to corner markets efficiently and relatively cheaply. The French were the first to feel the negative effects of being industrial latecomers.

German States The Napoleonic invasions of Germany caused considerable destruction, but they also brought some positive economic benefits. The example of revolutionary change in France led to important socioeconomic changes in the German states. Restrictive guilds declined. The French occupiers suppressed many tariffs and taxes that had hindered trade between German states; they also reduced the number of

primogeniture A legal inheritance system that provided the firstborn, usually the firstborn son, the right to inherit all the family land and farm.

separate states, established a single unified legal system, and introduced a single standard of measurement based on the metric system. These changes remained intact after 1815.

Government in the German states played an important role in the adoption of improved methods of manufacturing. Eager for industrial development, the Prussian state sent an official to Britain to observe the puddling process (the method by which iron is freed of carbon) and bring that expertise back home. The Prussian government promoted industrial growth by investing in a transportation network to carry raw materials for processing and finished goods to their markets. To spur both trade and industrial growth, Prussia took the lead in creating a customs union, the *Zollverein* (TZOLL-fair-eyn), which abolished tariffs among its members. By 1834 a German market embracing eighteen German states with a population of 23 million had been created. The Zollverein was an important step toward the later unification of Germany into a single nation-state.

German industrial growth accelerated dramatically in the 1850s. Massive expenditures on railways created a large demand for metal, which pressured German manufacturers to enlarge their plant capacities and increase efficiency. The German states were not yet politically unified, but the German middle classes saw economic growth as the means by which their country could win a prominent place among Europe's nation-states.

Germany's growth was phenomenal. It successfully emulated Britain and overtook France's rate of economic growth. Toward the end of the nineteenth century Germany pioneered in the electrical engineering and chemical industries. If France experienced the disadvantages of being a latecomer to industrialization, Germany reaped the benefits of that status. The Germans were able to avoid costly and inefficient early experimentation and adopted the latest, proven methods; moreover, Germany entered fields that Britain had neglected.

Eastern and Southern Europe   Even by the end of the century, however, progress remained slow in many areas of Europe. As long as Russia retained serfdom (until 1861), it would lack the mobile labor force needed for industrial growth. And until late in the century, the ruling Russian aristocracy hesitated to adopt an economic system in which wealth was not based on labor-intensive agriculture. In Austria, Bohemia was the only important industrial center; otherwise, Austria remained heavily agrarian (see Map 20.2).

The impoverished southern Mediterranean countries experienced little economic growth. With mostly poor soil, their agriculture yielded only a meager surplus. Spain, lacking coal and access to other energy sources, could not easily diversify its economic base. Some industry emerged in Catalonia, especially around Barcelona, but it was limited in scope and did not have much impact on the rest of the country. The Italian peninsula was still industrially underdeveloped in the middle of the nineteenth century. There were modest advances, but growth was too slow to have a measurable positive impact on the Italian economy. In 1871, 61 percent of the population of Italy was still agrarian.

Although by midcentury only a few European nations had experienced industrialization to any great extent, many more would do so by the end of the century, pressured by vigorous competition from their more advanced neighbors (see **FIGURE 20.1**). Economic

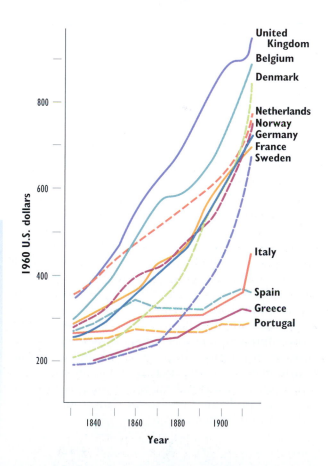

FIGURE 20.1   The Increase in Gross National Product per Capita in Principal European Countries, 1830–1913

The countries that industrialized rapidly—such as the United Kingdom in particular, and also Belgium, France, and Germany—experienced dramatic increases in per capita income during the nineteenth century. Other countries, such as Greece and Portugal, economically trailed the industrial leaders, and per capita income there remained essentially flat.   *(Source: Norman J. G. Pounds,* An Historical Geography of Europe, 1800–1914 *[New York: Cambridge University Press, 1985], p. 32. Used by permission of the publisher.)*

modernization had political and international implications as well, for industrialized nations had the backing of military might and superiority. Compared with the rest of the world, the European continent in the nineteenth century had acquired a distinct material culture that was increasingly based on machine manufacture or was in the process of becoming so. The possession of "skillful industry," one Victorian writer exulted, was "ever a proof of superior civilization." Although only some regions of Europe were industrialized, many Europeans came to view themselves as obviously "superior," while deeming all other races inferior (see the box on page 622).

SECTION SUMMARY

- The influx of raw cotton into Britain, innovations that sped up the processes of spinning and weaving, as well as the mechanical removal of cotton seeds, led the revolution in textile production.

- The introduction of the blast furnace and steam engine doubled iron production at the end of the eighteenth century, leading to the production of less expensive and more durable machines, such as those used for textiles. Steam-driven machines led to the centralization of production into factories.

- The innovations that came with industrial production also depended upon entrepreneurs who were hungry for profits and willing to take investment risks.

- The pace of industrialization varied among nations and changed the nature of competition among them; the material culture produced by machine manufacture led Europeans to view themselves as a superior civilization with the military capability for colonial conquest.

SOCIAL, CULTURAL, AND ENVIRONMENTAL IMPACTS

What impact did industrialization have on the environment and on social classes?

Industry changed the traditional methods of agriculture, commerce, trade, and manufacture. It also transformed people's lives, individually and collectively. It altered how they made a livelihood, where and how they lived, even how they thought of themselves. Because industry required new specialized skills, the range of occupations that people adopted expanded dramatically.

The advent of industry transformed the way society functioned. Until the eighteenth century, power and influence derived from hereditary privilege, which meant aristocratic birth and land. The aristocracy did not disappear overnight. From the late eighteenth century on, however, it was challenged by a rising class of people whose wealth was self-made and whose influence was based on economic contributions to society rather than on bloodlines. Increased social mobility opened opportunities even for some workers. Industrialization transformed both the social and the natural environment. Cities experienced extraordinary growth as a result of industrialization. Europeans faced not only urban problems but also the dangerous pollution of their air and water.

URBANIZATION AND ITS DISCONTENTS

A sociologist at the end of the nineteenth century observed, "The most remarkable social phenomenon of the present century is the concentration of population in cities."[3] The number and size of cities grew as never before. The major impetus for urban growth was the concentration of industry in cities and the resulting need of large numbers of urban workers and their families for goods and services (see **MAP 20.3**).

Industrialization was not the only catalyst. France provides many examples of urban growth with little industry. Increased commercial, trading, and administrative functions led to the growth of cities in countries that had not yet witnessed much industrialization, such as France, Holland, Italy, and Switzerland. Urban growth in some places was explosive. In the entire eighteenth century, London grew by only 200,000; but in the first half of the nineteenth century, it grew by 1.4 million, more than doubling its size. Census figures show that by 1851 Britain was a predominantly urban society, the first country to have as many people living in cities as in the countryside. For Germany that date

MAP 20.3   Cities Reaching Population Level of 100,000 by 1750, 1800, and 1850

In 1750 the largest cities owed their existence primarily to commerce, but industrialization caused populations to concentrate more in cities. England, the leading industrial nation, contained many of the largest cities.   *(Source: Data from Tertius Chandler,* Four Thousand Years of Urban Growth: An Historical Census *[Lewistown, N.Y.: St. David's University Press, 1987], pp. 22–24.)*

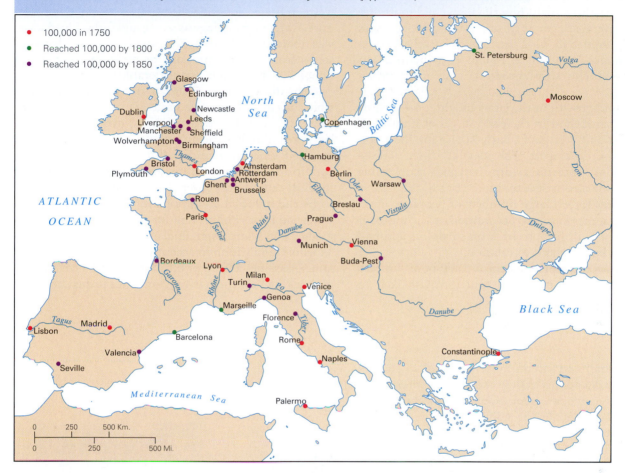

was 1891, and for France it was not until 1931. Although the proportion of people who were urban varied from place to place, the trend was clear and has continued.

As the pace of industry in part governed the growth of cities, **urbanization** in turn fueled it. Large cities provided convenient markets for goods and for a manufacturing labor pool. The concentration of people encouraged the exchange of ideas. A large city was likely to have scientific societies and laboratories where engineers and scientists could share new ideas and new inventions that would encourage industrial production. After midcentury, scientific and technological breakthroughs made in urban environments increasingly drove industrialization.

urbanization   Term related to the growth of cities, largely connected to the industrialization of the late eighteenth and nineteenth centuries.

Cities pulled in people from near and far; larger cities attracted migrants from great distances. The medium-sized French town of Saint-Etienne (sen-et-YEN) drew resettlers from the nearby mountains, whereas Paris drew from the entire country. Industrial centers even attracted people from beyond the nation's borders. The Irish arrived in large numbers to work in the factories of Lancashire, in northwestern England; Belgians came for mine work in northern France; and Poles sought employment in the Ruhr Valley of western Germany. Industrial activity stimulated the growth of world trade and shipping across the seas, taking merchant sailors far from home. Many large cities were marked by heterogeneous populations, which included people with different native languages, religions, and national origins, and increasingly, of different races. Africans and Asians inhabited port cities such as Amsterdam, Marseille, and Liverpool.

With the growth of cities came a multitude of urban ills, causing mortality rates to climb in cities. In the 1840s Britain as a whole had a death rate of 22 per thousand, but Liverpool averaged 39.2 and Manchester 33.1. In France national mortality rates were around 22 per thousand, but in some French cities the rate was as high as 35 per thousand. Social inequality in the face of death was startling. Including the high child mortality rate, the average age at death among upper-class Liverpool families in 1842 was 35; for members of laborers' families it was 15. In 1800 boys living in urban slums were 8 inches shorter than the sons of rich urban dwellers.

The rapid growth of the cities caught local authorities unprepared, and in the early stages of industrialization, city life was particularly severe for the poor. Urban slums developed. The squalor of St. Giles—London's most notorious slum—had such shock value that it became a tourist attraction. Housing shortages in many cities forced large numbers of people to cram into small areas. Houses to accommodate the influx of workers were built back to back on small lots and had insufficient lighting and ventilation.

Overcrowding worsened the already poor sanitary conditions. A single privy in a courtyard was likely to serve dozens of tenants—in some notorious cases in Britain and France, a few hundred. Waste from the privy might contaminate nearby wells, or drain through open sewers to a nearby river, which was likely to be the local source of drinking water. Some tenants lacked toilets and relieved themselves in the streets. In the 1830s people living in the poorest sections of Glasgow stored human waste in heaps alongside their houses and sold it as manure. Water in the cities was scarce and filthy. Piped water was reserved for the rich. The poor had to supply themselves from public fountains or wells and were often obliged to carry water a considerable distance.

The dizzying pace of urban growth made it impossible for cities to provide basic sanitary facilities. The causes of many diseases, such as typhus and tuberculosis, were unknown; the dirt, dampness, and darkness of crowded tenements and polluted streets created the conditions that fostered disease. Social reformers and medical experts, moreover, decried what they perceived to be the immoral conditions in which families lived. Physician James Philips Kay, for example, who practiced medicine in Manchester, England, wrote in 1832 of how "A whole family is often accommodated on a single bed, and sometimes a heap of filthy straw and a covering of old sacking hide them in one undistinguished heap, de-

St. Giles

This neighborhood was the most notorious London slum. Visual portrayals such as this one did not necessarily exaggerate slum conditions, but did help create negative images of the poor. Note the implied promiscuousness of the disheveled couple, and the indifferent attitude of the mother (who might be single) toward her infant. Note as well the class differences this image portrays: the disapproving middle-class women standing off to the side on the right often ventured into slums for charitable works, one of the few excuses respectable women had to be in public.

(From Thomas Beames, The Rookeries of London. *Photo: Harvard Imaging Service)*

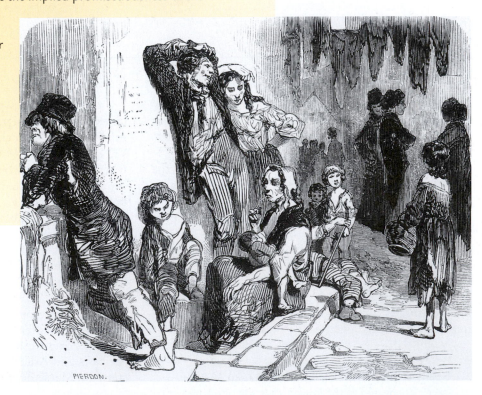

PIERDON.

based alike by penury, want of economy and dissolute habits. Frequently, the inspectors found [that] . . . more than one family lived in a damp cellar, containing only one room, in whose pestilential atmosphere from twelve to sixteen persons were crowded. To these fertile sources of disease were sometimes added the keeping of pigs and other animals in the house, with other nuisances of the most revolting character."[4] Such descriptions contributed to the growing perceptions, as well as material reality, of class differences.

In manufacturing towns factory chimneys spewed soot, and everything was covered with dirt and grime. Smoke was a major ingredient of the famous London fog, which not only reduced visibility but posed serious health risks. Refuse, including the rotting corpses of dogs and horses, littered city streets. In 1858 the stench from sewage and other rot was so putrid that the British House of Commons was forced to suspend its sessions.

It is not surprising that cholera, a highly infectious disease transmitted through contaminated water, swept London and other European urban centers. In the 1830s one of the first epidemics of modern times struck Europe, killing 100,000 in France, 50,000 in Britain, and 238,000 in Russia. Typhoid fever, also an acute infectious disease, struck mostly the poor but did not spare the privileged. Queen Victoria of Great Britain nearly died of it; her husband, Prince Albert, did.

THE WORKING CLASSES AND THEIR LOT

In 1842 a middle-class observer traveling in industrial Lancashire noted that around the mills and factories there had developed a "population [that] like the system to which it belongs is NEW . . . hourly increasing in breadth and strength."[5] A French countess, using the pen name Daniel Stern, wrote in the 1830s and 1840s about the emergence of "a class apart, as if it were a nation within the nation," working in factories and mines, called "by a new name: the industrial **proletariat.**"[6] Originally used to designate the poorest propertyless wretches in Roman society, the term *proletariat* became synonymous with the class of workers developing in the burgeoning factories. What distinguished this growing class throughout the nineteenth century was that it was relatively unskilled and totally dependent on the factory owners for its livelihood. Even lowly apprentices of earlier eras never occupied such a precarious status because guild rules and traditions protected them from arbitrariness; the guild system also made it possible for apprentices to become journeymen and then master artisans, owning their own tools and working on their own time and on their own premises. Improvement in

proletariat   Karl Marx's term for the new class of industrial workers who owned none of the means of production and were dependent on factory owners for their livelihoods.

status and owning the means of production would never be a possibility for the new proletariat.

As industry advanced and spread, more and more people depended on it for a livelihood. In the putting-out system, during an agricultural downturn, a cottager could spend more time on hand labor; when demand for piecework slacked off, the cottager could devote more time to cultivating the land. But people living in industrial cities had no such backup. And neither skilled nor unskilled workers were assured of regular employment: any downturn in the economy translated into layoffs or job losses. In addition, the introduction of new industries often devastated laborers in older forms of production. The mechanization of cotton production reduced the earning power of weavers. Cheap cotton production also drove down workers' wages in other textiles with higher production costs, such as linen, because of competition.

Most factory work was dirty and laborious and took place in grim plants with heavy, noisy machinery. Sixteen-hour workdays were common. Child labor was widespread. With no safety provisions, the workers were prone to accidents. Few factory owners protected their workers against dangerous substances or circumstances. Mercury used in hat manufacturing gradually poisoned the hatmakers and often led to dementia, hence the term *mad hatters*. Lead used in paints and pottery also had a devastating impact on workers' health.

Smaller than boys, and often underfed, young girls especially suffered poor health from heavy labor. In 1842, 18-year-old Ann Eggley, a mineworker since the age of 7, hauled carriages loaded with ore weighing 800 pounds for twelve hours a day. She testified to a parliamentary commission that, so worn out from her work, upon coming home, she often fell asleep before even going to bed. Isabel Wilson, another mineworker, testified that she had given birth to ten children and had suffered five miscarriages. These women were overworked, exhausted, and vulnerable to disease, and they faced premature death.

Did industrialization improve the workers' lot? Until the mid-nineteenth century, information about workers' standard of living, measured by income and expenses, is incomplete. The best evidence comes from Britain, where an average family of five needed at least 21 shillings a week to fend off poverty. Skilled workers, who were in demand, might earn as much as 30 shillings a week, but most workers were unskilled. And even skilled workers enjoyed little security: if they became less productive because of illness or old age, their wages fell. Women and children usually had to pitch in. Even when women were the main breadwinners, they almost never received wages sufficient to meet the needs of their own subsistence, let alone those of an entire family. Regardless of what work they performed,

Children Toiling in Mines

Able to crawl in narrow mine shafts, many children were employed underground. In this woodcut, a woman joins a child in his labor. Often whole families worked together and were paid a fixed price for the amount of coal extracted.

(Hulton Archive/Getty Images)

women always earned a fraction of men's wages. Employers based women's wages on the assumption that they supplemented the income of a husband or father.

Incomes were so low that workers normally spent between two-thirds and three-fourths of their budget on food. Those who lived in rural areas might raise chickens or pigs or have a plot of potatoes. Bread was the largest single item consumed, varying between one and two pounds a day per person. A little bacon or other meat gave flavor to the soup in which people dipped their bread or potatoes, but meat was rarely consumed as a main course. Because men were the chief breadwinners and tended to have the most strenuous occupations, they received the choice piece of meat and the largest amount of food. Women and children ate what remained.

From the beginning, industrialization increased society's wealth, but historians continue to debate whether and at what point it benefited workers. "Optimist" historians argue that some of the new wealth trickled down to the lower levels of society. "Pessimist" historians say that a downward flow did not necessarily occur. Statistics suggest that by the 1840s workers' lives in Britain did improve. Their real income rose by 40 percent between 1800 and 1850 because of relatively low prices of many basic goods. As the cost of cloth declined, the dress of working-class people noticeably improved. On the Continent, the lot of workers improved a little later than in Britain, but the process followed the same pattern. Nonetheless, the general trend in real wages meant little when workers were unemployed and when they lived in crowded conditions, or during a major economic downturn such as occurred in the 1840s.

INDUSTRIALIZATION AND THE FAMILY

Industrialization dramatically changed the character of family and household among both the working and middle classes. Mechanization and removal of work from the home created job segregation on the basis of gender and age. The best-paying jobs went to men; they became factory supervisors and ran machinery such as the jenny. The textile industries especially employed children and women in the lowliest positions, where they tended machines, tied broken threads, and performed menial tasks. Women generally received from 30 to 50 percent of men's wages, children from 5 to 25 percent.

Factory work often undermined the ability of working women to take care of their children. As farmers or cottagers, women had been able to work and supervise their children simultaneously. The factory, however, often separated mothers from their children. It was not uncommon for an older child, sometimes only 5 or 6 years old, to be entrusted with the care of younger siblings.

Urban and rural women sometimes resorted to more dangerous methods of child-care. In both England and on the Continent many mothers sent their children to wet nurses in the countryside, where—if they survived—they stayed for up to two years. The mortality of these babies was high, as they were often neglected. In France and Italy, the poorest of mothers—especially single mothers—abandoned their infants at foundling homes, which in turn sent them out to be wet nursed. In many cases baby-farming was no more than a camouflaged form of infanticide. Mothers who kept their children, but were obliged to leave them unwatched at home during factory hours, sometimes pacified them with mixtures of opium, readily available from the local apothecary.

Because of the many demands on them, women often had sporadic work patterns. Young women might work before marriage or before giving birth, stay home until the children were older, and then return to work. Factory work had a harsh impact on women's lives, but it should be remembered that relatively few women were in the wage market—by 1850 only about a quarter in both Britain and France. Of that quarter, few worked in factories; far more were in agriculture, crafts industries (which still flourished despite poor working conditions), and domestic service. Some sectors of industry, such as textiles, employed a large proportion of women. Other sectors, such as the metal and mining industries, were heavily male-dominated.

Online Study Center **Improve Your Grade**
Primary Source: "Sweated Labor": A Poor
  Woman's Fate

The textile industry found employment for children once they were over the age of 5 or 6. Their size and agility made them useful for certain jobs, such as reaching under machines to pick up loose cotton. Because of their small hands they were also hired as "doffers," taking bobbins off frames and replacing them. Elizabeth Bentley began work as a doffer in 1815 at the age of 6. At the age of 23, when she testified before a parliamentary commission, she was "considerably

The Iron Forge

This painting from the late eighteenth century by Joseph Wright of Derby suggests the pride, dignity, and independence of the preindustrial forger, whose work not only allowed him to support his family but also blended with his unregimented everyday life. This romanticized portrayal starkly contrasts with the factory labor that would replace small-scale iron forgery.
(*Broadlands Trust, Hampshire, UK/The Bridgeman Art Library*)

deformed . . . in consequence of this labor." She normally worked from 6:00 A.M. to 7:00 P.M., but for six months worked sixteen-hour days, beginning at 5:00 A.M. She told the commission that children were strapped if they arrived late. She had only forty minutes at noon to eat, but said "I had not much to eat, and the little I had I could not eat it, my appetite was so poor, and being covered with dust; and it was no use taking it home, I could not eat it. . . ."[7] Child labor certainly did not start with the industrial transformation; it had always existed. The stern industrial discipline imposed on the very young, however, was new. Children were subject to the clock, closely supervised and prevented from taking long breaks or mixing work and play—as had been possible in an earlier era. Although children commonly worked in British textile industries, overall less than 10 percent of working children were employed in industrial work. Most were in agriculture or the service sector.

In some cases industrialization meant a transformation in the authority structure of workers' households; women's wage-earning capacity outside the home might undermine the influence of the male as head of the household. Most women did not, however, experience emancipation in factory or mine work because their low wages were not sufficient to support their independence. Even young women who left the countryside for factory work in towns and cities usually sent their wages back to their families. Moreover, as in the putting-out system, whole families were often hired as a group to perform a specific function. Contemporaries sometimes denounced industry for dissolving family bonds, but the family often remained an effective work unit.

If not participating in the wage market, wives and children contributed in other ways to the household budget—by making clothes, raising a pig, tending a potato patch, and performing daily household chores. Grandparents often moved from the country to live with the family and take care of the children. When industrial workers married, they frequently settled with their spouses on the same street or in the same neighborhood as their own parents. Thus although industry had the potential to break up traditional family structures, the historical evidence shows that the family generally adjusted and survived the challenges posed by the new economic system.

Industrial capitalism also gave rise to a new middle class or bourgeoisie, whose wealth derived from the capitalistic activities of trade, finance, and manufacturing. Previously the wives and daughters of small shopkeepers readily performed tasks such as bookkeeping or serving customers because the businesses were in or near the home. But as small businesses became public companies, women ceased participating. Family life came to reflect these new economic realities, justified and reinforced by a new set of cultural values. In more than any other social class, new family values based on gender distinctions became just as important a signifier of class identity as wealth itself. As Catherine Hall has noted in the history of middle-class private life in the nineteenth century, "A man's dignity lay in his occupation; a woman's gentility was destroyed if she had one."[8] The nineteenth-century world of market capitalism made wealth—rather than aristocratic bloodlines—the sign of success and power. Conspicuous consumption on homes, home furnishings, and clothing offered visible proof of success.

With business affairs removed from the home and enough wealth that women's employment was not required, motherhood and women's devotion to it became more idealized in the middle class than it ever had been in the past. Women developed a "cult of domesticity" in which they devoted themselves to their children and to home décor—or supervised servants who did—as men became preoccupied with work and with male sociability. While bourgeois men and women did not always live up to these ideals, they did generally embrace them as a prescription appropriate for family life in the new industrial world. These ideals also became a basis for judgment of those who did not live up to them—the lower classes and errant women of all classes.

THE LAND, THE WATER, AND THE AIR

Industrialization seriously disturbed the environment, transforming the surface of the earth, the water, and the air. To run the new machinery, coal was mined in increasing amounts (see **TABLE 20.1**). Iron and other minerals were also in great demand. The exploitation of coal ushered in the modern age of energy use, in which massive amounts of nonrenewable resources are consumed.

TABLE 20.1
Coal Production in Industrializing Nations

	Millions of Tons	Kilograms per Inhabitant
1700	4	26
1750	7	16
1800	16	76
1830	30	120
1860	129	390

Source: Based on B. R. Mitchell, "Statistical Appendix, 1700–1914," in *The Fontana Economic History of Europe,* ed. Carlo Cippola, vol. 4 (London: Collins, 1973), pp. 747, 770; and Norman J. G. Pounds, *An Historical Geography of Europe, 1500–1840* (New York: Cambridge University Press, 1979), pp. 268–269.

To extract coal and other minerals, miners dug deep tunnels, removing millions of tons of earth, rock, and other debris. This material, plus slag and other waste from the factories, was heaped up in mounds that at times covered acres of land, creating new geological formations.

With axes and saws people cut down trees, depleting forests to supply the wood needed to build shafts for coal, iron, and tin mines, or to make the charcoal necessary for glassmaking. Between 1750 and 1900 industrial and agricultural needs led to the clearing of 50 percent of all the forests ever cleared. Many of Europe's major forests disappeared or were seriously diminished. Deforestation in turn sped up soil erosion.

Industry changed the physical environment in which people lived. Forests, lakes, rivers, and air—as well as people themselves—showed the harmful effects of industry. Centrifugal pumps drained large marshes in the Fenland in eastern England. A contemporary lamented, "The wind which, in the autumn of 1851 was curling the blue water of the lake, in the autumn of 1853 was blowing in the same place over fields of yellow corn." Smoke and soot darkened the skies, intensifying the fog over London and other cities. Foul odors from factories could be detected at several miles' distance. Alkali, used for making glass, when released into the atmosphere killed trees for several miles around. Factories dumped waste ash into rivers, changing their channels and making them considerably shallower. Because of pollution from industrial and human waste, by 1850 no fish could survive in the lower Thames River. The Calder River in northern England was so thickly polluted that an irate Englishman used its water as ink when he wrote to the health board in 1868 to make his point about the river's condition. He also noted that readers of his letter would miss one dimension of the situation—the river's stench. Not merely unpleasant, these various pollutants caused cancer and lung diseases, though the connection between pollutants and disease was not yet understood.

A CHANGING SENSE OF TIME

In agrarian societies time was measured in terms of natural occurrences, such as sunrise and sunset, or the time it might take to milk a cow. With industrialization, punctuality became essential. Shifts of labor had to be rotated to keep the smelters going; they could not stop, or the molten iron would harden at the bottom of the hearths. The interactive nature of industrial production, in which workers with differing specialties each performed a particular task in finishing a product, made it necessary for employees to be at the factory at an appointed time. Factory rules often reflected an obsession with the efficient use of time. In some workplaces, those arriving two minutes late lost an hour's wages, and after more than two minutes they were locked out until the first break. Idleness, and even conversation between workers, could be cause for dismissal.

Clocks were installed in church towers and municipal buildings as early as the fourteenth century, but they were not very reliable until the eighteenth century. Watches were commonly owned by men of property and even by some artisans. By the mid-nineteenth century, at least in Britain, as the price of watches dropped, many workers could afford them. And even when workers did not own timepieces, they were intensely aware of time. Those who ignored time were fined or fired from their jobs. People listened for the church bell or factory whistle or asked a neighbor or passerby for the time. Western societies increasingly regularized and internalized the sense of time.

S E C T I O N   S U M M A R Y

- Industrialization, as well as commerce and the growth of administrative bureaucracy, caused urbanization; rapid growth of cities created overcrowding and unsanitary conditions, facilitating the spread of infectious diseases.

- Industrialization ultimately raised living standards, but its early stages disrupted workers' lives by mechanizing traditional forms of production, which rendered some artisanal skills obsolete and caused systematic poverty.

- By removing production from the home, industrialization often forced women and children into low-paying factory jobs; it also reshaped middle-class families by making gender roles more distinct.

- Industrial production, particularly the consumption of nonrenewable resources such as coal, transformed the environment and polluted the earth, water, and air.

- Mechanical modes of production transformed the sense of time; they allowed work to be organized in long shifts that required discipline and rigid punctuality.

RESPONSES TO INDUSTRIALIZATION

What did workers gain and lose as a result of industrialization, and how did they respond?

People living at subsistence levels in urban slums offered visible and disquieting evidence of industrialization's social consequences. As middle-class reformers wondered how to contend with social ills, the working classes developed their own sense of a common interest and fate. The result was a resounding cry for political and social democracy that began in the first half of the nineteenth century and became increasingly insistent—and sometimes violent.

THE GROWTH OF WORKING-CLASS SOLIDARITY

Hardest hit by economic changes, workers sought to improve their conditions by organizing and articulating their needs. In the preindustrial economy, artisans and craftsmen lived in an accepted hierarchy with prescribed rules. They began by serving for a certain number of years as apprentices to a master, next became journeymen, and finally with hard work and good fortune became masters of their trades. As tradesmen with common interests, they tended to band together into brotherhoods, promising one another help and trying to improve their working conditions.

With industrialization, guilds declined. Unlike the skilled handicrafts that required years of apprenticeship, few aspects of industrial production demanded extensive training. The system of dependence between apprentice and master became irrelevant. Guilds trying to protect their members often resisted new technologies and came to be seen as a hindrance to economic development. Liberals viewed guilds as constraints on trade and on the free flow of labor. For this reason, the French abolished guilds and all workers' coalitions during the Revolution of 1789. Throughout the eighteenth century, the British Parliament passed various acts against "combinations" by workmen.

While guilds faded in importance, the solidarity and language born of the guild continued to shape workers' attitudes throughout much of the nineteenth century. New experiences also reinforced the sense of belonging to a group and sharing common aspirations.

Cultural forces such as shared religious practice further fostered workers' sense of solidarity. Religious sects flourished in an environment of despair punctuated by hopes of deliverance. Some historians believe that the growth of Methodism in England in the 1790s

(see page 654) was a response to grim economic conditions. Emphasis on equality before God fueled the sense of injustice in a world where a privileged few lived in luxury while others were condemned to work along with their children for a pittance. Joanna, a self-proclaimed prophet active in the 1810s in England, announced both salvation and the coming of a new world of material well-being. In France workers believed the new society would come about by their martyrdom; like Jesus, the workers would suffer, and from their suffering would emerge a new, better society. Ideas of social justice were linked in the countryside with religious broadsides speaking of "Jesus the worker." Religious themes and language continued to be important in labor organization for many years.

Other cultural and social factors created bonds among workers. Housing became increasingly segregated by class. Thus urban workers lived close together, in similar conditions of squalor and hardship, either in the center of cities or in the outlying areas near factories. They grew close by spending their leisure time together, drinking in pubs, attending theaters and new forms of popular entertainment such as the circus, or watching traditional blood sports such as boxing or cockfights. Sports became popular as both spectator and participatory events in the 1880s. Soccer, which developed in England at this time, drew players and fans overwhelmingly from the working classes.

Social institutions also encouraged class unity. In the eighteenth century, both husband and wife were usually in the same craft. By 1900 it became more common for workers to marry across their crafts, thereby strengthening the sense of solidarity that encompassed the working classes as a whole.

Faced with the uncertainties of unemployment and job-related accidents, in addition to disease and other natural catastrophes, workers formed so-called **friendly societies** in which they pooled their resources to provide mutual aid. These societies, descendants of benefit organizations of the Middle Ages and Renaissance, combined business activity with feasts, drinking bouts, and other social functions.

Friendly societies had existed as early as the seventeenth century, but they became increasingly popular and important after industrialization. Their strength in a region often reflected the degree to which the area

friendly societies   Nineteenth-century organizations formed by workers; members pooled their resources to provide mutual aid.

Leisure Activity for the Working Poor
Some harsh forms of entertainment turned up in the industrial period. Scores of working-class spectators came to see the celebrated dog "Billy" kill a hundred rats at one time at the Westminster Pit in London in 1822. *(The British Library)*

was industrialized. Initially organized to provide aid for workers in a particular trade, they soon included members from several crafts. In time they federated into national organizations, so that a worker who moved to a new town could continue membership in the new locale. Connected by common membership in friendly societies, workers expressed a feeling of group solidarity beyond their individual occupations. Though far from solidified, a self-conscious working class was in the making.

COLLECTIVE ACTION

Militant and in some cases violent action strengthened workers' solidarity. Since they did not have the vote, they could not express their grievances through official political channels, and their frustrated efforts to improve their own work and living conditions underscored their common plight.

In the face of hardships, artisans organized for collective action. In 1811 and 1812 British hand weavers, in reaction against mechanized looms, organized in groups claiming to be led by a mythical General Ned Ludd. In the name of economic justice and to protect their livelihood, the **Luddites,** as the general's followers were called, smashed machines or threatened to do so. German weavers went on machine-crushing campaigns in the 1830s and 1840s.

Online Study Center **Improve Your Grade**
Primary Source: Yorkshire Luddites Threaten the Owner of a Mechanized Factory

In Lyon, France, in 1831 and 1834, workers led insurrections to demand fair wages for piecework. Angered when the silk merchants lowered the amount they would pay, the workers marched in the streets bearing banners proclaiming "Live Working or Die Fighting." The government sent troops to restore order to the riot-torn city. Although conditions of the silk trade had been the immediate impetus for the uprising, the workers appealed for help to their fellow workers in other trades, who joined in the protests.

Labor agitation in much of Europe increased in the 1840s. A major strike wave involving twenty thousand workers broke out in Paris in 1840. In the summer of

Luddites   Organized groups of British workers who smashed machines that threatened their livelihood. The name comes from their mythical leader, General Ned Ludd.

THE VISUAL RECORD

Union Membership Certificates

Though for the most part illegal, trade unions, often in the form of "brotherhoods" and mutual aid societies, existed in Europe from the beginning of the nineteenth century. But governments greatly restricted their power. The British Parliament, for example, gave unions legal status in 1825. However, it prohibited them from interfering with production, thus crippling their power to bargain effectively for improved wages or working conditions. Workers in other countries faced more severe restrictions.

In Britain, local unions of engineers began forming in the 1780s. In 1826, the Journeymen Steam Engine Makers' Society (JSEMS) organized and became one of the important early British unions. But to exert effective power, unions needed to organize on the national rather than on a local level, and to include more than one craft or trade. In 1851, William Allan, general secretary of the JSEMS, formed the national Amalgamated Society of Engineers, Machinists, Millwrights, Smiths, and Pattern Makers. By 1852, it had almost 11,000 members, and by 1866 its membership tripled.

This union represented skilled workers and professionals, a "labor aristocracy" that earned high enough wages to be able to afford the mem-

Unionization Certificate: Membership in the Amalgamated Society of Engineers *(The Art Archive)*

642

bership dues. It did not include those who worked at unskilled jobs for low wages, who could have most benefited from membership. The Amalgamated Society of Engineers provided various forms of relief to its members, such as insurance for unemployment, sickness, disability, and accidents, and benefits for funerals.

Pictured here is an elaborate membership certificate for the Society. Note the wide array of symbolism and allegory on which it draws, with images of classical antiquity, Greek mythology, and the modern material culture of the nineteenth century. What do these symbols represent, and what did they mean to the union members? Surely they imbued a sense of pride, dignity, and an assured place in the industrial progress of Great Britain—all reinforced and justified by the timeless ideals of the classical past and of contemporary religion.

The angelic winged figure hovering above the symmetrical structure is the "Goddess of Fame." The dove, with the olive branch of peace in its beak, represents the Holy Spirit. Together these otherworldly beings connect the works of this professional union to the heavens. The goddess stands upon a Cornucopia of Plenty, which connotes the fruit of honest and industrious labor. With heavenly authority, she simultaneously crowns an iron smith (left) and an engineer (right) each with a laurel wreath. The iron smith represents the body and the physical strength of manual labor, while the engineer represents the mind and its capacity for innovation.

Mars, the god of war, asks the smith to repair his sword—but, as a further sign of the peaceful intent of the union's production, the latter refuses. Clio, the Muse of history, presents a design to the engineer, which he willingly accepts, perhaps signifying the historical progress of innovation. Between Mars and Clio are the portraits of three inventors: Samuel Crompton (left), inventor of the mule jenny; James Watt (middle), whose improvement to the steam engine allowed its use for machines; and Richard Arkwright (right), who invented the spinning frame. The two kneeling figures next to Mars and Clio illustrate Aesop's fable, "The Bundle of Sticks," in which a father teaches his sons that sticks cannot be broken when tied together; they are breakable only when separated. The fable

thus represents the strength that unity brings to workers.

Below the portrait is a large bird with majestic red and gold plumage—the phoenix of classical mythology rising from its ashes. After living for hundreds of years, it burned to ashes on a funeral pyre in a flame ignited by the sun and fanned by its flapping wings. But it rises from the ashes, reborn to live through another cycle.

The base of this altar-like structure houses five branches of the iron trade that surround, at the bottom center, James Watt's rotating engine. Note how the labor performed here is very different from that of the unskilled industrial work in large factories, such as that portrayed in the background on the left. The train calls to mind the modern age of industry and transport, while the ship on the right conjures up commerce and trade. The rose, thistle, and shamrock symbolize the United Kingdom, as they are the emblems, respectively, of England, Scotland, and Ireland.

QUESTIONS

1. Which types of workers are depicted on this certificate and which workers are excluded?

2. How are religion, science, and industry combined here? How do these symbols evoke Christianity as well as classical antiquity?

3. In what ways would these symbols and allegories inspire pride, dignity, and a sense of unity among the workers who held membership certificates? How is gender represented in this image, and what is its significance?

Online Study Center

Improve Your Grade Visual Record Activities

1842 an industrial downturn in England led to massive unemployment and rioting. During the summer of 1844 in Silesia, in eastern Prussia, linen hand-loom weavers, desperate because of worsening conditions brought on by competition from machine-made cotton fabrics, attacked the homes of the wealthy. In 1855 in Barcelona, the government tried to dissolve unions, and fifty thousand workers went on strike, carrying placards that warned "Association or Death."

Workers had to conform to severe discipline and rigid rules not only in the workplace but also away from it. Workers in some factories were forbidden to read certain newspapers, had to attend religious services, and could marry only with the owners' permission. Workers resisted these attempts at control and resented employers' intrusiveness.

Workers' actions in the early nineteenth century clearly showed that they wanted both freedom from intrusive regulation by their employers and the security of employment at a decent wage. Unions provided a means to these goals. (See the feature "The Visual Record: Union Membership Certificates.")

Many of the friendly societies struggled to improve their members' working conditions, acting very much as labor unions would. They organized strikes and provided support to members during work stoppages. The advantages offered by unions were well understood—by both sides. Unions were illegal in Britain until 1825, in Prussia until 1859, and in France until the 1860s. As a French workers' paper declared in 1847, "If workers came together and organized . . . nothing would be able to stop them." An organized force could threaten to withhold labor if the employer did not grant decent wages and acceptable conditions. Unions made workers a countervailing force to factory owners.

The process of unionization was difficult. By 1850 many countries had passed laws supporting employers against workers. Censorship and the use of force against organized strikes were not uncommon. Population growth made it difficult for workers to withhold labor lest they be replaced by others only too willing to take their places. Foreign workers—for example, the Irish who streamed into England and the Belgians and Italians who migrated to France—were often desperate for work and not well informed about local conditions.

In many countries workers formed unions illegally. Although there were early attempts in Britain to organize unions on a national basis, most were centered on a single craft or a single industry. Because labor unions originated in the crafts tradition, the earliest members were skilled craftsmen who organized to protect their livelihoods from the challenge that industrialization posed. These craftsmen were usually literate and long-time residents of their communities. They provided the labor movement with much of its leadership and organization. Skilled craft workers also played a strong role

in developing a sense of class-consciousness. The language and institutions that they had developed over decades, and sometimes over centuries, became the common heritage of workers in general.

Workers looked to political action as the means to improve their situations. In the 1830s and 1840s British and French workers agitated for the right to vote; they saw voting as a way to put themselves on equal footing with the privileged and to win better conditions. Their disappointment at their failure to win political representation strengthened their class solidarity against the wealthy, privileged upper classes. Politically, organized workers played a major role in the revolutions that would rock Europe in 1848 (see pages 671–677), sometimes helping to instigate the uprisings, often influencing their course. However vague their ideas, European workers showed that their organizations were legitimate representatives of the people and that the lot of the worker should be the concern of government. In general, workers upheld the ideal of a moral economy—one in which all who labored got a just wage and every person was assured a minimum level of well-being.

The working classes were never a monolithic group. They consisted of people with varying skills, responsibilities, and incomes. Artisans with valuable skills were the segment that employers most respected and favored in pay and in working conditions. In contrast, unskilled workers were poorly paid, harshly treated, and often given only temporary work. Many skilled workers looked with contempt on the unskilled.

The industrial workplace usually segregated men and women, but when they did work side by side, it created little solidarity between them. Men worried that women were undermining their earning power by accepting lower wages. They often excluded women from their unions. Men even went on strike to force employers to discharge women.

Nor was there solidarity across nationalities. Foreign workers were heartily despised. British workers were hostile toward the Irish, the French toward the Belgian and Italian immigrants. The hostility often led to anti-immigrant riots. Many forces fostered dissension among the working classes in the nineteenth century. Nevertheless, shared economic, material, and cultural experiences broadened and deepened workers' sense of a shared fate and common goals.

By the mid-nineteenth century, the middle classes had developed a clear fear of workers and viewed them as a single class that threatened society. It was not unusual for members of the elite to refer to workers as "the swinish multitude" or, as the title of a popular English book put it, *The Great Unwashed* (1868). In France reference was alternately made to "the dangerous classes" and "the laboring classes." Not just workers but even the privileged seemed to see relations between the groups as a form of class war.

=== S E C T I O N   S U M M A R Y ===

- As guilds declined (or were prohibited), new worker solidarities based on religion, language, a sense of social justice, and shared experiences provided the foundation for the emergence of trade unions.

- Workers at times resorted to violence in their effort to preserve more traditional modes of production and protect their right to work.

- Friendly societies and unions sought to provide health, accident, unemployment, and funeral benefits.

- Professional unionization faced the obstacles of government repression as well as the diversity of the labor force itself: skilled workers versus the unskilled; men versus women; nationals versus foreigners.

C H A P T E R   S U M M A R Y

Online Study Center **ACE the Test**

What factors allowed Europe to industrialize before the rest of the world?

Which inventions appear to have been the most important in launching industrialization?

What impact did industrialization have on the environment and on social classes?

What did workers gain and lose as a result of industrialization, and how did they respond?

Industrial transformation altered the face of Europe. This process, which started around 1750 in parts of England, spread by 1850 to the Continent. The proximity of coal and iron, the relative ease of domestic transportation, a culture open to innovation and entrepreneurship, and the existence of an already relatively dynamic economy help explain why Britain was the first nation to industrialize, and why industrialization spread to much of Europe. The new industrial economy changed power relations within Europe and altered the relationship of Europe to the rest of the world.

A number of key inventions gave impetus to industrialization. The desire for more efficient cotton production led to John Kay's flying shuttle, which so increased the production of weaving that it created a shortage of thread. James Hargreave's spinning jenny and Samuel Crompton's mule more than met the need for thread production, further inspiring the invention of power looms. The use of coal to process iron made possible the creation of iron machinery that could be powered by James Watt's steam engine, as well as stronger blast furnaces that could, in turn, improve iron processing.

The extraction and use of energy resources such as coal transformed the landscape and polluted the air and water. Industry also changed the nature of work for large numbers of Europeans. A decreasing number of people worked in agriculture, and more entered manufacturing, where machines replaced human energy. For the first time European cities grew to more than one million inhabitants.

Industrialization ultimately raised the standard of living across social classes, but in the short term a large portion of the lower classes suffered low wages, geographical displacement, periodic unemployment, and overcrowding in the cramped, unsanitary housing of fast-growing towns and cities. The amassing of workers in factories and urban areas called attention to their potential power. Eager to improve their lives, workers began to organize into associations that were more broadly based and therefore more powerful than those of the past. As workers began to think of themselves as a class, the dominant elites within society began to perceive them as such. The new proletarian class, shaped by industrialization, was a growing force that would challenge the existing order throughout the nineteenth century and much of the next.

OOKING AHEAD

Industrialization began in England prior to the French Revolution of 1789 and the Napoleonic Wars that ensued. As industrialization spread to the Continent in the first half of the nineteenth century, its impacts unfolded in a distinct political context: the effort to return to and uphold the stable monarchical and hierarchical order that existed prior to 1789. But economic change and the new ideologies it produced, coupled with the persistent memory of eighteenth-century revolution, thwarted that effort. The new social classes to which industrial capitalism gave rise—the proletariat and bourgeoisie—promoted social reform and revolution, making a complete return to the past impossible. To these reactionary, reformist, and revolutionary efforts we now turn.

KEY TERMS

industrialization (p. 620)   **primogeniture** (p. 630)

mass production (p. 625)   **urbanization** (p. 633)

steam engine (p. 627)   **friendly societies** (p. 640)

factories (p. 627)   **proletariat** (p. 635)

entrepreneurs (p. 628)   **Luddites** (p. 641)

Online Study Center **Improve Your Grade** Flashcards

SUGGESTED READING

Clark, Anna. *The Struggle for the Breeches: Gender and the Making of the British Working Class.* 1995. An examination of the role of working women and gender conflicts in domestic life, work, and politics.

Fuchs, Rachel. *Gender and Poverty in Nineteenth Century Europe.* 2005. A fascinating study of the challenges facing women in daily experiences of birth, sex, and death in this era of enduring change.

Hopkins, Eric. *Industrialisation and Society.* 2000. A survey that considers the social and political impact of industry on British society.

Landes, David S. *The Wealth and Poverty of Nations.* 1999. Explores why Europe industrialized as compared with the rest of the world.

Mokyr, Joel. *The Lever of Riches: Technological Creativity and Economic Progress.* 1990. A comparative study of Western and Chinese technology, emphasizing cultural elements as explanations for the industrialization of the West.

Sylla, Richard, and Gianni Toniolo, eds. *Patterns of European Industrialization.* 1991. A comparative perspective on the patterns of industrialization.

Thompson, E. P. *The Making of the English Working Class.* 1963. Emphasizes the cultural factors that encouraged the development of working-class consciousness in England.

NOTES

1. Phyllis Deane, *The First Industrial Revolution* (Cambridge: Cambridge University Press, 1965), p. 1.

2. These ideas are provocatively developed in E. L. Jones, *The European Miracle: Environments, Economies and Geopolitics of Europe and Asia* (Cambridge: Cambridge University Press, 1981).

3. Adna Ferrin Weber, *The Growth of Cities in the Nineteenth Century: A Study in Statistics* (New York: Macmillan, 1899; repr., Ithaca, N.Y.: Cornell University Press, 1963), p. 1.

4. J. P. Kay, *The Moral and Physical Condition of the Working Classes Employed in the Cotton Manufacture in Manchester* (London: James Ridgway, 1832), pp. 6, 14–15, 19.

5. Cooke Taylor, *Notes of a Tour in the Manufacturing Districts of Lancashire, in a Series of Letters to His Grace the Archbishop of Dublin* (London, 1842), pp. 4–6, quoted in E. P. Thompson, *The Making of the English Working Class* (New York: Vintage, 1963), p. 191.

6. Marie de Flavigny d'Agoult [Daniel Stern], *Histoire de la Révolution de 1848,* 2d ed., vol. 1 (Paris, 1862), p. 7, quoted in Theodore S. Hamerow, *The Birth of a New Europe: State and Society in the Nineteenth Century* (Chapel Hill: University of North Carolina Press, 1983), pp. 206–207.

7. House of Commons, *Sessional Papers, 1831–32,* hearing of 4 June 1932, vol. 15, pp. 195–197.

8. Catherine Hall, "The Sweet Delights of Home," in *A History of Private Life: From the Fires of Revolution to the Great War,* ed. Michelle Perrot (Cambridge: Belknap Press, 1990), p. 74.

21

RESTORATION, REFORM, AND REVOLUTION, 1814–1848

Barricades in Vienna, Austria, May 1848
(Historical Museum Vienna/The Art Archive)

n 1848 Europe experienced a revolutionary wave, unprecedented in over a half century since the heady days of the French Revolution. These revolutions erupted in protest against the reactionary regimes established after the fall of Napoleon.

Workers, artisans, and even members of the middle classes poured into the streets to challenge authoritarian rulers and the militaries that tried to repress rebellion. They built street barricades to defend themselves and to trap and attack military troops. Barricades, long a part of urban insurrectionary history, had almost become an art form. Revolutionaries systematically tore the paving stones from streets and beams from the façades of houses. To build the barricade, they confiscated passing omnibuses, carriages, and carts to pile rubble, along with empty barrels and casks. The barricades they built sometimes rose as high as nine feet.

In addition to its material reality, the painting at the left represents the spirit present at the barricades, as well as in the revolutions as a whole. Its mixture of social classes and genders shows the inclusive camaraderie in conquering the streets, as even fraternizing soldiers listen attentively to the speaker atop the rubble. The neatly piled shovels and signs of meal preparation suggest a systematic order in the midst of a chaos that is only apparent. The figure hung in effigy reminds the viewer of the seriousness of the event. Scenes such as this burst forth in major cities throughout western and eastern Europe.

The revolutions of 1848 had their ideological origins in the irrepressible forces unleashed in the Revolution of 1789. With the end of the Napoleonic Wars in 1815, the victorious Great Powers—Austria, Great Britain, Prussia, and Russia—tried to re-establish as much of the old European state system as possible. The international arrangements they carved out at the Congress of Vienna were soon shaken by outbreaks of nationalist fervor. Nationalists aimed either to create larger political units, as in Italy and Germany, or to win independence from foreign rule, as in Greece. In addition to nationalism, which had in part been sparked by Napoleonic reforms, other new ideologies such as romanticism, liberalism, and socialism, born of the French Revolution, prevented a complete restoration of the old order. (An ideology is a structured, organized set of ideas that reflects a group's thinking about life or society.) Even after the success of counterrevolution in 1848, the

CHAPTER OUTLINE

THE CONGRESS OF VIENNA, 1814–1815
IDEOLOGICAL CONFRONTATIONS
RESTORATION, REFORM, AND REACTION
THE REVOLUTIONS OF 1848

KEY TERMS

Congress of Vienna
conservatism
romanticism
nationalism
liberalism
laissez faire
utilitarianism

socialism
Marxism
July Revolution
Great Reform Bill
Chartism
Decembrists
Frankfurt Assembly

Online Study Center

This icon will direct you to interactive map and primary source activities on the website **college.hmco.com/ pic/noble5e**

ideologies that helped promote revolution continued to shape development in the second half of the century.

The conservatism of European rulers and their opposition to change after 1815 were also at odds with the new dynamism of European society. Between 1800 and 1850 Europe's population increased by nearly 50 percent, from around 190 million to 280 million. Population growth and surging industrialization had turned small towns into large cities. The rapid growth of factory manufacturing reshaped class structures and the lives of workers. Romanticism, liberalism, and other systems of thought were redefining the relationship of the individual to society and the concept of human rights. Sporadic outbreaks of collective violence reached a crescendo when the revolutions of 1848 swept most of Europe, undermining the established order in state after state.

As revolution swept through Europe, a similar pattern took place: after the first exhilarating mo-

ments of emancipation from authoritarian monarchies, conflict, disappointment, and failure allowed the forces of reaction and repression to take control. Revolutionaries did not win all their goals, and in many cases the forces of order crushed them. Yet by midcentury major intellectual, social, and political changes had occurred.

FOCUS QUESTIONS

What were the goals and results of the Congress of Vienna?

What major ideologies developed in the first half of the nineteenth century?

How did the restorations that followed the Napoleonic era give way to reform?

What were the main causes of the revolutions of 1848, and what roles did nationalism, liberalism, and socialism play in inciting and sustaining revolution?

THE CONGRESS OF VIENNA, 1814–1815

What were the goals and results of the Congress of Vienna?

The defeat of Napoleon put an end to French dominance in Europe. In September 1814 the victorious Great Powers—Austria, Great Britain, Prussia, and Russia—convened an international conference, the **Congress of Vienna,** to negotiate the terms of peace. The victors sought to draw territorial boundaries advantageous to themselves and to provide long-term stability on the European continent. Having faced a powerful France, which had mobilized popular forces with revolutionary principles, the victors decided to erect an international system that would remove such threats. One method was to restore the European order that had existed before the French Revolution. Thus, following principles of "legitimacy and compensation," they redrew the map of Europe (see **MAP 21.1**). Rulers who had been overthrown were restored to their thrones. The eldest surviving brother of Louis XVI of France became King Louis XVIII. In

Spain Ferdinand VII was restored to the throne from which Napoleon had toppled him and his father. The restoration, however, was not so complete as its proponents claimed. After the French Revolution certain new realities had to be recognized. For example, Napoleon had consolidated the German and Italian states; the process was acknowledged in the former with the creation of a loose German Confederation. In Italy the number of independent states had shrunk to nine. Also, unlike earlier French kings, Louis XVIII could not rule as an absolute monarch.

Negotiations at the Congress of Vienna strengthened the territories bordering France, enlarged Prussia and created the kingdom of Piedmont-Sardinia, joined Belgium to Holland, and provided the victors with spoils and compensation for territories bartered away. Austria received Venetia and Lombardy in northern Italy to strengthen its position and to compensate for the loss of Belgium (to the Netherlands) and parts of Poland (to Russia). Prussia was also allowed annexations in compensation for giving up parts of Poland. England acquired a number of colonies and naval out-

Congress of Vienna Conference called by the Great Powers after Napoleon's defeat. They sought long-term stability as they drew new territorial boundaries and restored some of the rulers who had been overthrown.

Metternich
A consummate statesman and aristocrat, the Austrian prince Metternich tried to quell revolution at home and abroad. Some called his era the Metternichean age. *(The Royal Collection © 2006 Her Majesty Queen Elizabeth II)*

CHRONOLOGY

1808	Beethoven, *Pastoral* Symphony
1814–1815	Congress of Vienna
1819	Peterloo Massacre
	Carlsbad Decrees
1821	Spanish revolt
	Greek Revolution
1821–1825	Spanish colonies in the Americas win independence
1823	Monroe Doctrine
1824	Owen establishes New Harmony
1825	Decembrists in Russia
1830	July Revolution in France
	Ottoman Empire recognizes Serbian autonomy
1832	Great Reform Bill in Britain
1833	Abolition of slavery in British colonies
1834	Turner, *Fire at Sea*
1838	"People's charter" in Great Britain
1839	Anti-Corn Law League
1845–1848	Hungry '40s
1848	Marx and Engels, *Communist Manifesto*
	Revolutions of 1848

posts. Thus with one hand these conservative statesmen swore their loyalty to the prerevolutionary past, and with the other they redrew national boundaries with no consideration for the inhabitants whose territories changed.

The leading personality at the Congress of Vienna was the Austrian foreign minister, Prince Clemens von Metternich (MEH-ter-nick) (1773–1859). An aristocrat in exile from the Rhineland, which had been annexed by revolutionary France, he had gone into the service of the Habsburg empire and risen to become its highest official. Personal charm, tact, and representation of a state that for the time being was satisfied with its territories made Metternich seem a disinterested statesman. His influence at the congress was great.

Because it was Napoleon's belligerent imperialism that had brought the powers together in Vienna, France was at first treated as an enemy at the conference. By the end, however, France was included as one of the five Great Powers jointly known as the "Concert of Europe." The Concert continued to function for nearly forty years, meeting and resolving international crises and preventing any major European war from breaking out. Underlying the states' cooperation was the principle of a common European destiny.

SECTION SUMMARY

- At the Congress of Vienna (1814–1815), Austria, Great Britain, Prussia, and Russia, having defeated Napoleon, redrew territorial boundaries for their own advantage and to create stability.

- Rulers who had been overthrown by Napoleon were restored to their thrones.

- France, with its monarchy restored, became one of the five Great Powers known as the "Concert of Europe."

- The principle of a common European destiny lay at the basis of international cooperation; stability was maintained for nearly forty years.

651

MAP 21.1   Europe in 1815
Intent on regaining the security and stability of prerevolutionary years, the Great Powers redrew the map of Europe at the Congress of Vienna.

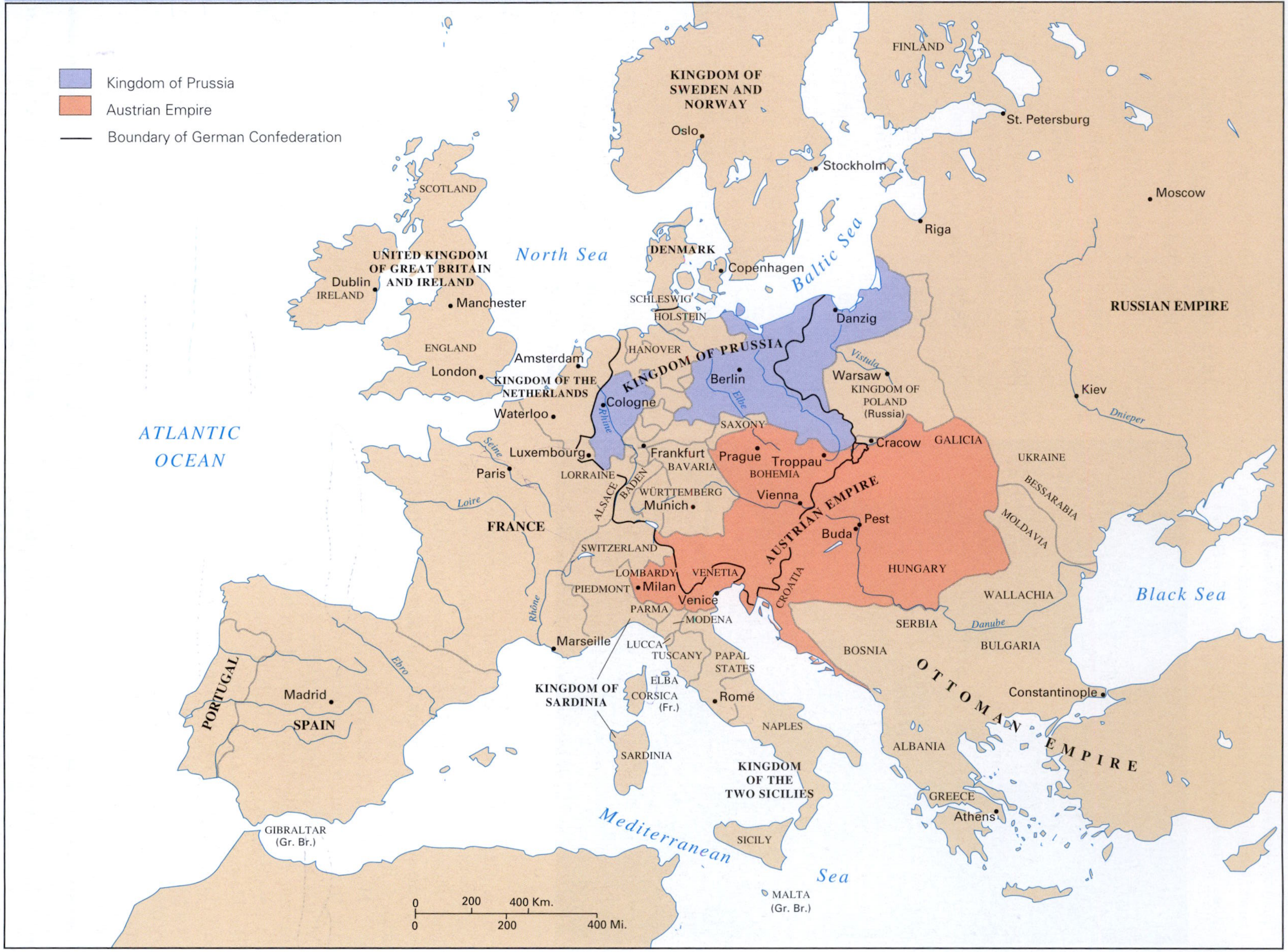

Kingdom of Prussia

Austrian Empire

Boundary of German Confederation

RUSSIAN EMPIRE

Moscow

St. Petersburg

FINLAND

Riga

Stockholm

KINGDOM OF SWEDEN AND NORWAY

Oslo

Copenhagen

DENMARK

SCHLESWIG

HOLSTEIN

Baltic Sea

Danzig

Vistula

Warsaw

KINGDOM OF POLAND (Russia)

Kiev

Dnieper

UKRAINE

BESSARABIA

MOLDAVIA

GALICIA

Cracow

HUNGARY

WALLACHIA

Danube

BULGARIA

SERBIA

BOSNIA

CROATIA

AUSTRIAN EMPIRE

Pest

Buda

Vienna

Prague

Troppau

BOHEMIA

Constantinople

OTTOMAN EMPIRE

ALBANIA

GREECE

Athens

Black Sea

North Sea

HANOVER

KINGDOM OF PRUSSIA

Berlin

Elbe

SAXONY

Frankfurt

BAVARIA

Munich

WÜRTTEMBERG

BADEN

Cologne

Rhine

VENETIA

Venice

Milan

LOMBARDY

PIEDMONT

PARMA

MODENA

LUCCA

TUSCANY

PAPAL STATES

Rome

ELBA

CORSICA (Fr.)

SARDINIA

KINGDOM OF SARDINIA

NAPLES

KINGDOM OF THE TWO SICILIES

SICILY

MALTA (Gr. Br.)

Mediterranean Sea

KINGDOM OF THE NETHERLANDS

Amsterdam

Luxembourg

Waterloo

Seine

Paris

FRANCE

LORRAINE

ALSACE

SWITZERLAND

Rhone

Marseille

Loire

Ebro

UNITED KINGDOM OF GREAT BRITAIN AND IRELAND

SCOTLAND

Manchester

ENGLAND

London

Dublin

IRELAND

ATLANTIC OCEAN

Madrid

SPAIN

PORTUGAL

GIBRALTAR (Gr. Br.)

0   200   400 Km.
0   200   400 Mi.

IDEOLOGICAL CONFRONTATIONS

What major ideologies developed in the first half of the nineteenth century?

The international and domestic political system established in 1815 was modified by a series of challenges, even revolts, culminating in revolutions throughout Europe in 1848. The order established in 1815 was inspired by conservatism. Its challengers advocated competing ideologies: romanticism, nationalism, liberalism, and socialism.

CONSERVATISM

The architects of the restoration justified their policies with doctrines based on the ideology of **conservatism,** emphasizing the need to preserve the existing order of monarchies, aristocracy, and an established church. As a coherent movement, conservatism sprang up during and after the French Revolution to resist the forces of change. Before the American and French Revolutions, the existing political institutions appeared to be permanent. When the old order faced serious challenges in the late eighteenth and early nineteenth centuries, an ideology justifying traditional authority emerged.

Edmund Burke (1729–1797), a British statesman and political theorist, launched one of the first intellectual assaults on the French Revolution. The revolutionary National Assembly had asserted that ancient prerogatives were superseded by the rights of man and principles of human equality based on appeals to natural law. In *Reflections on the Revolution in France* (1790), Burke countered that such claims were abstract and dangerous and that the belief in human equality undermined the social order. Government should be anchored in tradition, he argued. No matter how poorly the French monarchy and its institutions had served the nation, they should be preserved; their very longevity proved their usefulness. Burke's writings were widely read and influential on the Continent.

Reaction against the French Revolution also inspired a moral and religious conservatism. One of the most popular authors of this new morality was Hannah More (1745–1833), who with her four sisters ran a prosperous school. More saw piety as a rampart against rebellion. In a series of pamphlets titled *Cheap Repository Tracts,* she advocated the acceptance of the existing order and the solace of religious faith. Costing but a penny, the moral tracts were often handed out by the rich together with alms or food to the poor. More was the first writer in history to sell over a million copies; within three years her sales doubled. Conservative values thus spread to a very large audience in both Britain and the United States, where one of her works appeared in thirty editions.

A more extreme version of conservatism was the counterrevolutionary or "ultraroyalist" ideology. Unlike Burke, who was willing to tolerate some change, counterrevolutionaries wanted to restore society to its prerevolutionary condition. The most extreme counterrevolutionaries were those who personally experienced the revolutionary upheavals. Count Joseph de Maistre (MESS-treh) (1753–1821), a Savoyard (from the Franco-Italian border region) nobleman whose estates were occupied by the invading French, described monarchy as a God-given form of government in his *Considerations on France* (1796). Any attempt to abolish or even limit it was a violation of divine law. According to de Maistre and his fellow reactionaries, only the authority of church and state could prevent human beings from falling into evil ways. De Maistre advocated stern government control, including the generous use of the death penalty, to keep people loyal to throne and altar.

Conservative ideas were not limited to intellectual circles; at times they had mass appeal, even for the peasantry. Especially in bourgeois and aristocratic circles, conservatism extended to private life, and placed priority on family stability, with a strict separation of gender roles and a strong sense of patriarchy, in which the husband and father held exclusive authority. Conservatism was also influenced by **romanticism,** with its glorification of the past, taste for pageantry, and belief in the organic unity of society.

ROMANTICISM

The long-lived romantic movement had emerged in the 1760s as a rebellion against rationalism and persisted until the 1840s. It was primarily a movement in the arts. Writers, painters, composers, and others consciously rebelled against the Enlightenment and its rationalist values. In contrast to the philosophes and their emphasis on reason (see Chapter 18), the romantics praised

conservatism   Ideology underlying the order established in Europe in 1815, which afterward emphasized support for the existing order of monarchy, aristocracy, and an established church.

romanticism   Cultural movement, prevalent from the 1760s to 1840s, that rebelled against rationalism and its Enlightenment values and prized sentiment.

Lord Byron in Albanian Costume

The British romantic poet had himself painted in exotic garb. Romantics were attracted to what were believed to be the mysteries of the East, representing a truer, more authentic existence. *(Courtesy of the National Portrait Gallery, London)*

emotion and feeling. Jean-Jacques Rousseau's strong appeal to sentiment was taken up by the German writer Johann Wolfgang von Goethe (GOE-teh) (1749–1832), who declared, "Feeling is everything." Goethe's *Sorrows of Young Werther* (1774), the most widely read book of the era—Napoleon had a copy by his bedside—depicted the passions of the hero, who, depressed over unrequited love, kills himself. Many young men dressed in "Werther clothes"—tight black pants, long blue jacket, and buff yellow leather vest—which exemplified the clothing of tradesmen and provided a visual protest by young intellectuals against the frivolous dress of the upper classes. In some cases they emulated the tragic hero by committing suicide.

Whereas the Enlightenment had studied nature for the principles it could impart, the romantics worshiped nature for its inherent beauty. The German composer Ludwig van Beethoven (1770–1827) wrote his *Pastoral* Symphony in praise of idyllic nature, depicting the passions one might feel in contemplating its loveliness and serenity. The English poets William Wordsworth (1770–1850) and Samuel Taylor Coleridge (1772–1834)

treated untamed wilderness as a particular subject of wonder. Fellow Englishman Joseph Mallord William Turner (1775–1851) displayed the raw passions of the sea in such paintings as *Fire at Sea* (1834) and *Snowstorm: Steamboat off a Harbour's Mouth* (1842). Before painting the latter, Turner is said to have tied himself to a ship's mast and braved a snowstorm for four hours.

In pursuit of the authentic and the ancient, of feeling rather than rationality, many romantics rediscovered religion. In some areas of Europe, popular religion had anticipated the artists' and intellectuals' romantic sensibilities. France experienced a revival of Catholicism. In the German states, pietism, which had emerged in the seventeenth and eighteenth centuries, stressed the personal relationship between the individual and God, unimpeded by theological formalities or religious authorities. The influence of pietism, with its emphasis on spirituality and emotion, spread throughout central Europe in schools and churches.

In England emotionalism in religion expressed itself in the popularity of Methodism. Founded in the 1730s by the English preacher John Wesley (1703–1791), this movement emphasized salvation by a faith made active in one's life, a method of living. Appealing especially to the poor and desperate, Methodism by the 1790s had gained seventy thousand members; within a generation it quadrupled its flock.

The classicism of the Enlightenment had required an audience well versed in the traditional texts. Since the mid-eighteenth century, however, the reading public had grown to include people without access to elite culture. Appeals to emotion and sentiment were congenial to these new audiences, and a new interest developed in folklore and rustic life. Franz Schubert (1797–1828) composed over 600 songs that echo the simplicity of folk tunes, and Frédéric Chopin (1810–1849) composed works influenced by the peasant music of his native Poland.

Whereas the philosophes had decried the Middle Ages, the romantics celebrated the medieval period. Painters frequently took Gothic buildings or ruins as their theme. Architects imitated the Gothic style in both private and public buildings. Sir Walter Scott (1771–1832) in Scotland and Victor Hugo (U-go) (1802–1885) in France recaptured chivalry and the age of faith in such popular works as *Ivanhoe* (1819) and *The Hunchback of Notre Dame* (1831). Thus romanticism also had a liberal and nationalistic appeal.

The romantics sought displacement not only in time but also in place. The exotic had great appeal to them. Recently conquered Algeria in North Africa provided exotic scenes for French painters, among them Eugène Delacroix (de-la-KRWAH) (1798–1863) and Jean Ingres (AENG-reh) (1780–1867). Senegal, in West Africa, which the French recovered from the British in 1815, offered the setting for Théodore Géricault's powerful *Raft of the "Medusa."* (See the feature "The Visual Record: Raft of the 'Medusa.'")

Romanticism exalted mythical figures as embodiments of human energy and passion. In the dramatic poem *Faust,* Goethe retold the legend of a man who sells his soul to the Devil in exchange for worldly success. Several composers set that story to powerful music. In the poetic drama *Prometheus Unbound,* the English romantic poet Percy Bysshe Shelley (1792–1822) celebrated Prometheus, who, according to Greek mythology stole fire from the gods and gave it to human beings. In much the same spirit, many romantics lionized Napoleon, who had overthrown kings and states. Delacroix, who witnessed the July Revolution of 1830 in Paris (see page 663), celebrated the heroism and passion of the revolutionaries in his huge canvas *Liberty Leading the People* (1830).

Romantics often challenged existing power relations, including relations between the sexes. The French writer Amandine-Aurore Dupin (1804–1876), better known by her pen name, George Sand (SAN), spoke for the emancipation of women from the oppressive supervision of their husbands, fathers, and brothers. In her personal life Sand practiced the freedom she preached, dressing like a man, smoking cigars, and openly pursuing affairs with a number of well-known artists. The English writer Mary Ann Evans (1819–1892), like George Sand, adopted a male pseudonym, George Eliot. She conducted her life in a nonconformist manner, living with a married man. The use of male pen names by both writers attests to the hostility that intellectual women still faced.

After the French Revolution nobles and monarchs ceased sponsoring art on a grand scale and were expected to conduct their lives soberly. Cut off from royal patronage, artists had to depend on members of the new middle classes to buy paintings and books and attend plays and musical performances. If earning a livelihood had often been difficult for artists in the past, it now became even more so. Forced to live marginally, they cultivated the image of the artist as unconventional. In their lifestyles and their work, they deliberately rejected the norms of society. The romantic period gave rise to the notion of the starving genius, alienated from society and loyal only to his all-consuming art.

Romantics of many stripes declared their determination to overthrow the smug present and create a new world. Victor Hugo called for "no more rules, no more models" to constrain the human imagination. Romantic painters and musicians consciously turned their backs on the classical tradition in both subject matter and style. The English poet George Gordon, Lord Byron (1788–1824), declared war on kings, on established religion, and on the international order. A nationalist as well as a romantic, he died while fighting for the independence of Greece.

NATIONALISM

The ideology of nationalism emerged in, and partly shaped, this era. **Nationalism** is the belief that people derive their identity from their nation and owe it their primary loyalty. A list of criteria for nationhood is likely to include a common language, religion, and political authority, as well as common traditions and shared historical experiences. Some nineteenth-century nationalists found any one of those criteria sufficient. Others insisted that all of them had to be present before a group could consider itself a nation.

In an era that saw the undermining of traditional religious values, nationalism offered a new locus of faith. To people who experienced the social turmoil brought about by the erosion of the old order, nationalism held out the promise of a new community. Nationalism became an ideal espoused as strongly as religion. The Italian nationalist Giuseppe Mazzini (mat-SEE-nee) (1805–1872) declared that nationalism was "a faith and mission" ordained by God. The Polish romantic poet and nationalist Adam Mickiewicz (MISS-kyev-ich) (1798–1855) compared perpetually carved-up Poland to the crucified Christ. The religious intensity of nationalism helps explain its widespread appeal.

Many forces shaped nationalism. Its earliest manifestation, cultural nationalism, had its origins in Rousseau's concept of the "general will" constituting the sovereign nation, greater than the sum of its parts. Johann Gottfried Herder (1744–1833), Rousseau's German disciple, elaborated on his mentor's ideas, declaring that every people has a "national spirit." To explore the unique nature of this spirit, intellectuals all over Europe began collecting local folk poems, songs, and tales. In an effort to document the spirit of the German people, the Grimm brothers, Jacob (1785–1863) and Wilhelm (1786–1859), compiled fairy tales and published them between 1812 and 1818; among the better known are "Little Red Riding Hood" and "Snow White."

Political nationalism, born in the era of the French Revolution, injected urgency and passion into the new ideology. French aristocrats resisted taxation by claiming that they embodied the rights of "the nation" and could not be taxed without its consent. Thus the concept of nation was given general currency. When revolutionary France was attacked by neighboring countries, which were ruled by kings and dukes, the Legislative Assembly called on the French people to rise and save the nation. The kingdom of France had become a nation of citizens who had a stake in its destiny. In reaction to the French threat, intellectuals in Germany and Italy embraced the

nationalism   Belief that people derive their identity from their nation and owe it their primary loyalty. The criteria for nationhood typically included a common language, religion, and political authority, as well as common traditions and shared historical experiences.

Raft of the "Medusa"

In September 1816 the French were shocked at the news of the disaster that had befallen the government ship *Méduse* (Medusa) as it headed for Senegal in West Africa the previous July. Including the ship's crew, 400 passengers had boarded the vessel.

The captain of the ship was a nobleman, Duroys de Chaumareys (du-RWAH duh sho-mah-RAY), whom the restoration government had appointed solely on the basis of his family and political connections. Inexperienced as a seaman, the captain clumsily ran his ship aground on the Mauritanian coast, off West Africa, on July 2. The *Medusa* had only 6 lifeboats, capable of carrying a total of 250 people. For the rest of the passengers, a raft was rigged with planks, beams, and ropes. The captain and his officers forcibly took over the lifeboats, abandoning 150 passengers, including one woman, to the less secure raft. With no navigational tools and insufficient food and water, the passengers of the raft were at the mercy of stormy seas and a brutal sun. Anger at officers for having abandoned them led seamen on the raft to murder some of their superiors. By the third day, driven by thirst and hunger, some passengers ate their dead companions—killed by exposure or drowned by huge waves. On the sixth day the strongest among the survivors, fearing that their rations were dwindling, banded together and murdered the weaker ones. On the thirteenth day the French frigate *Argus* spotted the raft and rescued 15 survivors. Five died soon after, leaving only 10 survivors out of the raft's original 150 passengers.

Although the government tried to suppress information about the event, the French press exposed the incompetence and cowardice of Captain de Chaumareys. The event was understood to reflect the weakness of the regime that had appointed him. The selfish act of the captain and his fellow officers suggested the narrow class interest of the restoration government, favoring aristocracy at the cost of the common people.

The French painter Théodore Géricault (1791–1824) befriended the ship's surgeon, Henri Savigny, one of the lucky ten who survived the harrowing experience on the raft. In addition to press reports, Géricault (jair-ih-KO) thus had a direct eyewitness account of the event. The painter shared Savigny's sense of outrage against the government for having appointed the incompetent captain and for having treated the survivors callously. (At one point the government arrested Savigny for publicizing the tragedy.) The light prison sentence imposed on the captain was another source of grievance.

Since 1815 the French government had sought to bring distinction to itself by displaying art in salon expositions. That of 1819 was intended to be larger and more glorious than any previous one. Among its paintings was Géricault's huge canvas—the largest in that year's exposition—measuring 16 feet high by 24 feet wide and innocently titled "Scene of Shipwreck." Carelessly, the regime had wanted to gain glory for itself by exhibiting this impressive artwork while at the same time keeping hidden its real subject. But the stratagem failed; everyone recognized the painting to be the *Raft of the "Medusa"* and an attack on the Bourbon regime.

The painting, reproduced here, depicts the moment the survivors spotted the frigate *Argus*, barely visible on the horizon. Notice the figure of an African standing at the fore of the raft, waving a red and white cloth to attract the ship's attention. In this painting the nobility and symbol of hope the African symbolizes is an attack on the slave trade, which Britain had abolished but which France was still engaged in. By including the African, the artist was implicitly criticizing the restoration regime for sanctioning commerce in humans. Just as the *Argus* is coming to the rescue of the shipwrecked, the painting appears to suggest, so Africans will see the day when their enslavement will be ended.

Historians often regard the *Raft of the "Medusa"* as the most important painting of French romanticism, and it includes nearly all the major themes of the movement. By locating the scene off the coast of Africa, Géricault incorporated an element of exoticism. Nature—cruel and unforgiving—is central to the scene, reflected in the turbulent sea, dark clouds, and imperiled raft. The canvas includes an extraordinary range of passions. Observe, for example, the inconsolable grief of the figure at the bottom left, a father cradling the dead body of his son. Other figures express despair and terror, and still others limitless hope. The painting evokes the dark passions lurking in the human heart. Although it does not show the scenes of insanity,

Géricault: Raft of the "Medusa"   *(Erich Lessing/Art Resource, NY)*

murder, and cannibalism that the survivors had witnessed, they undoubtedly came to the minds of the viewers, who were familiar with the tragic events. The painting is a powerful indictment of Enlightenment faith in humans as creatures of reason and balance.

Romantic artists wanted to engage the passions of those viewing, reading, or hearing their works. *Raft of the "Medusa"* purposely stages the events in the foreground in order to pull viewers into the picture and make them participants in the drama. They thus share in the alternating feelings of terror and hope that swept the raft.

The fate of the painting and the artist followed a romantic script. When Géricault started the painting, he intended it as an indictment of the restoration government. He poured energy into it in an effort to take his mind off a disastrous love affair. As his work proceeded, he came to see the painting as an allegory of larger human passions and concerns. Yet when it was displayed, much to his disappointment, the painting was understood mainly in political terms. Disillusioned by this reaction, Géricault thereafter painted no major works. He grew sickly, rarely bestirred himself, and died of bone tuberculosis in 1824 at age 33. He illustrates the romantics' view of a heroic life—the genius who performs a major feat and then dies young, before realizing his potential. To the romantics, human intent and effort often appeared thwarted by larger forces. This painting, originally meant to criticize the regime, was purchased after Géricault's death by the restoration government and hung in France's national museum, the Louvre.

QUESTIONS

1. What elements in the subject matter and style of this painting typify romanticism?

2. Why was this painting seen as a brutal critique of the French restoration government? What had been the artist's intent?

Online Study Center
Improve Your Grade Visual Record Activities

spirit of nationalism. In Germany the philosopher Johann Gottlieb Fichte (FISH-te) (1762–1814) delivered his series of *Addresses to the German Nation* after the Prussian defeat at Jena, calling on all Germans to stand firm against Napoleon. He argued that Germans were endowed with a special genius that had to be safeguarded for the well-being of all humankind. Italian writer Vittorio Alfieri (1749–1803) insisted that, as the descendants and heirs of ancient Rome, Italians, not France, should lead the peoples of Europe.

For the most part, however, after the French Revolution and the Napoleonic era, early-nineteenth-century nationalism was generous and cosmopolitan in its outlook. Herder and Mazzini believed that each of Europe's peoples was destined to achieve nationhood by forming its own political identity and that the nations of Europe would then live peacefully side by side. The members of dedicated nationalist groups such as Young Germany and Young Italy were also members of Young Europe. Many nationalists in the 1830s and 1840s were likewise committed to the ideal of a "Europe of free peoples." Victor Hugo even envisioned a "European republic" with its own parliament.

It is important to remember, however, that although many intellectuals found nationalism attractive, in the first half of the nineteenth century most people felt stronger local and regional affinities than national identities. Only after several decades of propaganda by nationalists and governments did Europeans begin to imagine themselves as part of a national rather than local community, and only then could they think of dying for their nations.

LIBERALISM

Liberalism was a direct descendant of the Enlightenment's critique of eighteenth-century absolutism. Nineteenth-century liberals believed that individual freedom was best safeguarded by reducing government powers to a minimum. They wanted to impose constitutional limits on government, to establish the rule of law, to sweep away all restrictions on individual enterprise—specifically, state regulation of the economy—and to ensure a voice in government for men of property and education. Liberalism was influenced by romanticism, with its emphasis on individual freedom and the imperative of the human personality to develop to its full potential. Liberalism was also affected by nationalism, especially in multinational autocratic states such as Austria, Russia, and the Ottoman Empire, in which free institutions could be established only if political inde-

pendence were wrested from, respectively, Vienna, St. Petersburg, and Istanbul. (Nationalism challenged the established order in the first half of the century, but in the second half conservatives were to use nationalism as a means to stabilize their rule.)

Economic Liberalism Liberalism was both an economic and a political theory. In 1776 Adam Smith (1723–1790), the influential Scottish economist, published *An Inquiry into the Nature and Causes of the Wealth of Nations*. Smith advocated freeing national economies from the fetters of the state. Under the mercantilist system, prevalent throughout Europe until about 1800, the state regulated the prices and conditions of manufacture. Smith argued for letting the free forces of the marketplace shape economic decisions. He believed that economics was subject to basic unalterable laws that could be discerned and applied in the same fashion as natural laws. Chief among them, in Smith's view, was the compatibility of economic self-interest and the general good. He argued that entrepreneurs who lower prices sell more products, thus increasing their own profits *and* providing the community with affordable wares. In this way an individual's drive for profit benefits society as a whole. The economy is driven as if "by an invisible hand." This competitive drive for profits, Smith predicted, would expand the "wealth of nations." In France advocates of nonintervention by government in the economy were called supporters of *laissez faire* (meaning "to leave alone, to let run on its own").

Smith and his disciples formed what came to be known as the school of classical economy, emphasizing the importance of laissez faire. Smith had been relatively optimistic about the capacities of the free market. Those who followed him, and who witnessed the negative results of industrial capitalism, developed gloomier views. Thomas Malthus (1766–1834), a parson, published in 1798 *An Essay on the Principle of Population,* which suggested that the rate of population growth was much higher than the rate of food production. Unless people had fewer children, they would suffer starvation. By their failure to exercise sexual restraint, the poor, Malthus declared, "are themselves the cause of their own poverty." The laws of economics suggested to Malthus that factory owners could not improve their workers' lot by increasing wages or providing charity because higher living standards would lead to more births, which in turn would depress wages and bring greater misery. He therefore advocated abstinence (birth control was considered sinful and unnatural) and thought couples

liberalism Nineteenth-century economic and political theory that called for reducing government powers to a minimum. Liberals sought to eliminate state regulation of the economy and ensure a voice in government for men of property and education.

laissez faire French term meaning "to leave alone," to advocate freeing national economies from the fetters of the state and allowing supply and demand to shape the marketplace.

should marry only when they could afford to raise children. Malthus himself had twelve.

David Ricardo (1772–1823) made his fortune in the stock market, retired young, and wrote on economics; his best-known work was *Principles of Political Economy* (1817). Ricardo argued that the only way capitalists could make profits in a competitive market would be to pay the lowest wages possible. The "iron law of wages" seemed to provide, as had Malthus, scientific justification for the exploitation of workers.

Even supporters of laissez faire had some reservations about the market economy. In France in the first half of the nineteenth century, commentators on the factory system, including industrialists, expressed fear that factory work would undermine the stability of family life and hence of society itself. Contrary to Malthus, they hoped philanthropic intervention would resolve the problems they had identified.

Even some of the British classical economists doubted the wisdom of allowing the market economy to operate entirely without regulation and of trusting it to provide for human happiness. Smith warned that the market tended to form monopolies, and he suggested that government intervene to prevent this occurrence. According to Smith, the marketplace could not provide for all human needs; the government needed to supply education, road systems, and an equitable system of justice.

Political Liberalism   John Stuart Mill (1806–1873), the leading British economic and political thinker at midcentury, initially voiced strong support for laissez-faire economics in the first edition of his *Principles of Political Economy* (1848). In subsequent editions, however, he noted that the free market could not address every human need, and he argued that the state had an obligation to relieve human misery. Toward the end of his life, Mill seemed to be leaning toward socialism.

Mill's about-face reflected and presaged changing attitudes among the proponents of laissez faire. In the face of unsanitary urban conditions, child labor, stark inequities in wealth, and other alarming results of industrialization, at least some liberals around midcentury called on the state to intervene in areas of concern that would have been unthinkable a half century earlier. In the tradition of the Enlightenment and the French Revolution, French liberals in the nineteenth century continued to see human liberty—the freedom to pursue happiness—as founded on natural law. Their English counterparts were less theoretical in outlook. Jeremy Bentham (1748–1832) argued that the purpose of government is to provide "the greatest happiness of the greatest number" and that governments should be judged on that basis. Bentham and his disciples

believed that the test of government is its usefulness; thus his theory is known as **utilitarianism.**

John Stuart Mill, a disciple of Bentham, was the foremost proponent of political liberalism, seeing it as guaranteeing the development of a free society. In his essay *On Liberty,* one of the fundamental documents of nineteenth-century liberalism, Mill argued for the free circulation of ideas—even false ideas. For in the free marketplace of ideas, false ideas will be defeated, and truth vindicated, in open debate. Mill also asserted that all members of society should have equal access to freedom. Influenced by his wife, Harriet Taylor Mill (1807–1856), he wrote in *On the Subjection of Women* (1861) that women should be permitted to vote and should have access to equal educational opportunities and the professions. Such equality not only would be just but also would have the advantage of "doubling the mass of mental faculties available for the higher service of humanity." Mill, the foremost male proponent of women's rights in his generation, helped win a broader audience for the principle of equality between the sexes.

Despite Mill's influence, many liberals, especially in the early nineteenth century, feared the masses and therefore vigorously opposed democracy. They feared that the common people, uneducated and supposedly gullible, would easily be swayed by demagogues who might become despotic or who, in a desire to curry favor with the poor, might attack the privileges of the wealthy. The French liberal Benjamin Constant denounced democracy as "the vulgarization of despotism"; the vote, he declared, should be reserved for the affluent and educated. When less fortunate Frenchmen denounced the property requirements that prevented them from voting, the liberal statesman François Guizot (1787–1874) smugly replied, "Get rich."

Guizot's comment reflects attitudes associated with the bourgeoisie, a social class that came of age in the nineteenth century. The word *bourgeois* derives from *burgers,* a term that referred to a group of people who gained wealth and civic identity from urban occupations beginning in the twelfth and thirteenth centuries. This class fully developed in the nineteenth century. If unsympathetic to extending suffrage to the lower classes, the *bourgeoisie* championed liberalism because it justified its own right to participate in governance. Economic liberalism was also attractive to merchants and manufacturers, who wished to gather wealth without state interference. The basic tenets of liberalism—the belief in the sanctity of human rights, of the freedoms of speech and of association, and of the rule of law and equality before the law—eventually

utilitarianism   Political theory of Jeremy Bentham, who argued that the purpose of government is to provide "the greatest happiness of the greatest number" and that the test of government is its usefulness.

became widely accepted, even among conservatives and socialists who originally opposed them.

SOCIALISM

A fundamental element in the pursuit of happiness according to liberals was the ability to accumulate property. Socialists, on the other hand, believed that the "social" ownership of property, unlike private ownership, would benefit society as a whole. The notion that human happiness can best be ensured by the common ownership of property had been suggested in earlier times by individuals as different as the Greek philosopher Plato (427?–347 B.C.) and Sir Thomas More (1478–1535), the English author of *Utopia*. In the 1820s, troubled by the harsh condition of the working classes, thinkers in Britain and France began to espouse new theories to address the social ills produced by industrial capitalism. During the first half of the nineteenth century, most workers were still artisans, even in industrializing England, where manufacturing was increasingly large scale. Only in a later era would **socialism** address the issues raised by industry.

Early Socialist Thinkers In 1796, during the French Revolution, Gracchus Babeuf (GRAH-kus bah-BOEF) (1760–1797), a minor civil servant, participated in the Conspiracy of Equals (see page 601). He believed political equality was meaningless without economic equality. Babeuf advocated revolution to bring about a "communist" society—a society in which all property would be owned in common and private property would be abolished. Work would be provided for everyone; medical services and education would be free to all. Upon the discovery of his plot, Babeuf was guillotined, but his theories and his example of conspiratorial revolutionary action would influence later socialists.

Several other important French thinkers made contributions to European socialism. Henri de Saint-Simon (saen-see-MON) (1760–1825), a French aristocrat, emphasized the need "to ameliorate as promptly and as quickly as possible the moral and physical existence of the most numerous class." The state, he declared, should ensure the welfare of the masses. He argued, furthermore, that technical experts rather than an elite derived from birth should govern the state and formulate economic policies.

Another vital contribution to socialist thought came from thinkers who tried to imagine an ideal world. They were later derisively dismissed as builders of utopias, fantasy worlds (the Greek word *utopia* means "nowhere"). Their schemes varied, but they shared the view that property should be owned in common and used for the common good. They also believed that society should rest on principles of cooperation rather than on competitive individualism.

One of the earliest and most notable utopians was the Welsh mill owner Robert Owen (1771–1859). Beginning in 1800 he ran a prosperous cotton mill in New Lanark, Scotland. He also provided generously for his workers, guaranteeing them jobs and their children a decent education. In his writings Owen suggested the establishment of self-governing communities owning the means of production. Essentials would be distributed to all members according to their needs. His ideas for the new society also included equal rights for women. Owen received little support from fellow manufacturers and political leaders, and his own attempt in 1824 to establish an ideal society in the United States at New Harmony, Indiana, ended in failure after four years.

Another influential contributor to early socialist theory was the Frenchman Charles Fourier (foor-YAY) (1772–1837). A clerk and salesman, Fourier wrote out in great detail his vision of the ideal future society. It would consist of cooperative organizations called "phalansteries," each with sixteen hundred inhabitants who would live in harmony with nature and with one another. Everyone would be assured gainful employment, which would be made enjoyable by rotating jobs. Because cooperative communes often faced the issue of who would carry out the distasteful tasks, everyone would share the pleasant *and* unpleasant work.

Fourier had an important female following because of his belief in the equality of the sexes, and some of these women tried to put his ideas into action. In Belgium the activist Zoé Gatti de Gamond (1806–1854) cofounded a phalanstery for women. She believed that if women could be assured of economic well-being, other rights would follow. Also inspired by Fourier, Flora Tristan (1801–1844) was an effective advocate for workers' rights. In her book *Union Ouvrière* (*Workers' Union*), she suggested that all workers should contribute funds to establish a "Workers' Palace" in every town. In the palace, the sick and disabled would have shelter, and the workers' children could receive a free education. Crossing France on foot, she spread the word of workers' solidarity and self-help.

There were other approaches. The French socialist journalist Louis Blanc (BLAHN) (1811–1882) thought that by securing the vote, the common people could win control over the state and require it to serve their needs. Once the workers controlled the state by the ballot, the state in turn would establish social workshops in which the workers would be responsible for produc-

socialism Nineteenth-century economic and social doctrine and political movement that advocated the "social" or state ownership of property in order to create a more just system.

Karl Marx
Through his writings and agitation, Marx transformed the socialism of his day and created an ideology that helped shape the nineteenth and twentieth centuries.
(Corbis)

tion and for supervision of business matters. Society should be established according to the maxim, "Let each produce according to his aptitudes and strength; let each consume according to his need."

Blanc's contemporary Louis Blanqui (1805–1882) suggested a more violent mode of action. He advocated seizure of the state by a small, dedicated band of men who would establish equality for all through communism. His ideas strengthened the notion of class warfare. The thought and example of Blanqui and the other socialists would have a major influence on the thinking of the most important socialist of the nineteenth century, Karl Marx.

Marxism   Karl Marx (1818–1883), the son of a lawyer, grew up in the Rhineland, in western Germany, an industrializing area that was particularly open to political ideas and agitation. As a young man, Marx studied philosophy at the University of Berlin and joined a group known as the "Young Hegelians," self-declared disciples of the idealist philosopher G. W. F. Hegel (1770–1831). Hegel taught that reality is mainly based on the ability of the mind to conceive of it. Marx, by contrast, was a materialist, believing that material realities impose themselves on the mind.

In 1842–1843 Marx edited a newspaper that spoke out for freedom and democracy in Germany. The following year, in Paris, he met several of the French socialist writers.

Because of his radical journalism, Marx was exiled from the Rhineland and lived briefly in Paris, then Brussels. In 1849 he settled in London, where he lived for the rest of his life, dedicated to establishing his ideas on what he viewed as scientific bases. In 1848 Marx and Friedrich Engels (1820–1895) published the *Communist Manifesto*. A pamphlet written for the Communist League, a group of Germans living in exile, the Manifesto made an appeal to the working classes of the world. The league deliberately called itself "Communist" rather than "Socialist." Communism was a revolutionary program, bent on changing property relations by violence; socialism was associated with more peaceful means of transformation. The pamphlet laid out Marx's basic ideas. "The history of all hitherto existing society," he said, "is the history of class struggles." In this pamphlet, Marx and Engels called on the proletariat to rise—"You have nothing to lose but your chains"—and create a society that would end the exploitation of man by man. The idea of an international workers' movement contrasted with the dominant currents of capitalism and nationalism.

A number of political and polemical works flowed from Marx's pen, but most of them remained unpublished during his lifetime. The first volume of his major work, *Capital*, was published in 1867; subsequent volumes appeared posthumously. **Marxism,** the body of Marx's thought, is complex and sometimes contradictory, but certain basic concepts resound throughout and were embraced by Marx's followers.

Marx agreed with Hegel and many of his contemporaries that human history has a direction and a goal. Hegel believed that the goal was the realization of the

Marxism   The "scientific socialism" of Karl Marx and Friedrich Engels, which stated that the working class inevitably would rebel against the capitalist owners and build a communist society.

world spirit. Marx believed that it was the abolition of capitalism, the victory of the proletariat, the disappearance of the state, and the ultimate liberation of all humankind.

Whereas Hegel thought that ideas govern the world, Marx insisted that material conditions determine it. Hegel said that history evolves by the "dialectic": a principle, say despotism, has within it ideas that oppose it; in the struggle between despotism and its opposite, a higher ideal emerges—freedom, the ultimate goal of history. Following Hegel, Marx posited a world of change but insisted that it was embedded in material conditions, not in a clash of ideas. Hence the process of history was grounded on the notion of "dialectical materialism." Ideas, to Marx, were but a reflection of the material world.

Marx grouped human beings into classes based on their relationship to the means of production. Capitalists constituted a class because they owned the means of production. Workers were a separate class—the proletariat—because they did not own any of the means of production and their income came only from wage labor. Because these two classes had different relationships to the means of production, they had different—in fact, antagonistic—interests and were destined (Marx believed) to engage in a class struggle.

Online Study Center **Improve Your Grade**
Primary Source: Working Men of All Countries Unite!

Some of Marx's contemporaries lamented the increasing hostility between workers and capitalists. Marx, however, saw the conflict as necessary to advance human history, and he sought to validate his thesis by the study of the past. In the Middle Ages, he pointed out, the feudal class dominated society but eventually lost the struggle to the commercial classes. Now, in turn, the capitalists were destined to be defeated by the rising proletariat. Thus industrial capitalism, he argued, was a necessary, if painful, economic stage through which humankind had to traverse on its way to liberation.

In his study of history and economics, Marx found not only justification for but irrefutable proof of the "scientific" basis of his ideas. Capitalism was itself creating the forces that would supplant it. The large industrial plants necessitated an ever greater work force with a growing sense of class interest. The inherently competitive nature of capitalism would inevitably drive an increasing number of enterprises out of business, and a form of monopoly capitalism would emerge, abusive of both consumers and workers. Ever more savage competition would force businesses to fail, creating widespread unemployment. Angered and frustrated by their lot, workers would overthrow the system that had abused them for so long: "The knell of private property has sounded. The expropriators will be expropriated." Workers would take power and, to solidify their rule, would temporarily exercise the "dictatorship of the proletariat." Once that had taken place, the state would wither away. With the coming to power of the proletariat, the history of class war would end and the ideal society would prevail. In the absences of classes and struggles between them, history would end.

Marx's study of economics and history proved to him that the coming of socialism was not only desirable, but inevitable. The laws of history dictated that capitalism, having created the rising proletariat, would collapse. By labeling his brand of socialism as scientific, Marx gave it the aura it needed to become the faith of millions of people. To declare ideas scientific in the nineteenth century, when science was held in such high esteem, was to ensure their popularity.

═══════════ S E C T I O N   S U M M A R Y ═══════════

- From 1815 to 1848, conservatism provided the ideological foundations for restored monarchies and social hierarchy; the ideologies of romanticism, nationalism, liberalism, and socialism challenged that order.

- Romanticism was based on feeling and passion rather than on reason; it inspired the arts, but also revived religion and challenged the existing political order through its influence on nationalism.

- Nationalism—the identification with one's nation based on shared language, culture, political author- ity, and historical past—began to emerge in the first half of the nineteenth century.

- The economic and political theory of liberalism originated with and justified middle-class interests and stressed individual freedoms.

- Socialist ideologies—"utopian" and "scientific"— emerged in response to the harsh conditions of the working classes and offered an alternative to capitalism.

RESTORATION, REFORM, AND REACTION

How did the restorations that followed the Napoleonic era give way to reform?

Despite the new ideologies that emerged to challenge the existing order, efforts at restoration appeared successful until at least 1830. Indeed, in central and eastern Europe, from the German states to Russia and the Ottoman Empire, the political systems established in 1815 would persist virtually unchanged until midcentury. In western Europe, however, important transformations would occur by the 1830s as reaction gave way to reform. Then in 1848 widespread revolutions would break out on much of the Continent. The language of liberalism and nationalism, and even the newer idiom of socialism, would be heard on the barricades, in popular assemblies, and in parliamentary halls.

WESTERN EUROPE: FROM REACTION TO LIBERALISM, 1815–1830

Most of Europe until the 1830s experienced the heavy hand of reaction. Then western Europe saw more liberal regimes come into their own. Revolution and the threat of revolution helped dismantle the worst features of the restored regimes. The more liberal western European states faced continuing discontents of various sorts—mainly social and political—which they managed to negotiate with varying degrees of success.

France   The most dramatic restoration of the older order occurred in France. The restored Bourbons turned the clock back, not to 1789 but closer to 1791, when the country had briefly enjoyed a constitutional monarchy. Moreover, it maintained the Napoleonic Code with its provisions of legal equality. The Bourbon constitution provided for a parliament with an elected lower house, the Chamber of Deputies, and an appointed upper house, the Chamber of Peers. Although suffrage to the Chamber of Deputies was limited to a small elite of men with landed property—only 100,000 voters, about 0.2 percent of the population—this constitution was a concession to representative government that had not existed in the Old Regime (see page 590). Louis XVIII (r. 1814–1824) stands out among European rulers because he realized that it would be necessary to compromise on the principles of popular sovereignty proclaimed by the French Revolution. He intended to "popularize the monarchy" and "royalize the nation."

A moderate, Louis was succeeded by his ultrareactionary brother, Charles X (r. 1824–1830), who alienated the middle classes. More general disenchantment came with an economic downturn in 1827, marked by poor harvests and increased unemployment in the cities. Discontent brought to Parliament a liberal majority that refused to accept the reactionary ministers the king appointed. On July 26, 1830, after the humiliating defeat of his party at the polls, the king issued a set of decrees suspending freedom of the press, dissolving the Chamber of Deputies, and stiffening property qualifications for voters in subsequent elections. The king appeared to be engineering a coup against the existing political system.

The first to protest were the Parisian journalists and typesetters, directly threatened by the censorship laws. On July 28 others joined the protest and began erecting barricades across many streets. After killing several hundred protesters, the king's forces lost control of the city. This **July Revolution,** also known as "the three glorious days," drove the king into exile.

Alarmed by the crowds' clamor for a republic, the liberal opposition—consisting of some of the leading newspaper editors and sympathetic deputies—quickly drafted the duke of Orléans, Louis Philippe (r. 1830–1848), known for his liberal opinions, to occupy the throne.

Great Britain   Compared with the rest of Europe, Great Britain enjoyed considerable constitutional guarantees and a parliamentary regime. Yet liberals and radicals found their government retrograde and repressive. Traumatized by the French Revolution, the ruling class clung to the past, certain that advocates for change were Jacobins in disguise. Change seemed to invite revolution.

Social unrest beset Britain as it faced serious economic dislocation. The arrival of peace in 1815 led to a sudden drop in government expenditures, the return into the economy of several hundred thousand men who had been away at war, financial disarray, and plummeting prices. The poor and the middle classes were especially incensed over the clear economic advantages that the landed classes, dominating Parliament, had secured for themselves. In 1815 the Parliament passed legislation—known as the Corn Laws—that imposed high tariffs on various forms of imported grain. These

July Revolution   Uprising in Paris in July 1830 that forced King Charles X to abdicate and signaled a victory for constitutional reform over an absolute monarchy.

"Peterloo" Massacre
In August 1819 at St. Peter's Fields in Manchester, England, a crowd demanding parliamentary reform was charged by government troops, leading to bloodshed. Many English people derided the event and called it "Peterloo." (*The National Archives, Public Record Office*)

laws shielded landowning grain producers from international competition and allowed them to reap huge profits at the expense of consumers. All these issues caused various forms of protest.

In August 1819, sixty thousand people gathered in St. Peter's Fields in Manchester to demand universal suffrage for men and women alike, an annual Parliament, and other democratic reforms. The crowd was peaceful and unarmed, yet mounted soldiers charged, killing eleven and wounding four hundred. Using military force against the people as if against the French at Waterloo was seen as wrong, and the confrontation was branded "the battle of Peterloo," or more often "the Peterloo Massacre." The British public was shocked by this use of violence against peaceful demonstrators; Parliament responded by passing the so-called Six Acts, which outlawed freedom of assembly and effectively imposed censorship. Through much of the 1820s Britain appeared resistant to reform until news of revolution across the Channel in 1830 brought about change.

Spain and Its Colonies   Spain, under the Napoleonic occupation, had in 1812 elected a national parliament, the Cortes. It issued a democratic constitution that provided for universal manhood suffrage and a unicameral legislature with control over government policy. Supporters and admirers of the constitution in Spain were known as "friends of liberty," and the term *liberal* was coined. But in 1814, Ferdinand VII (r. 1808, 1814–1833), the Bourbon king of Spain whom Napoleon had ousted, returned to power. Though he promised to respect the liberal 1812 constitution, Ferdinand believed in the divine right of kings and was hostile to the new order. With support from the aristocracy and from segments of the general population still loyal to the call of throne and altar, Ferdinand had liberals arrested or driven into exile.

Ferdinand's plan to restore Spain to its earlier prominence included a reassertion of control over its American colonies. The Spanish dominions had grown restless in the eighteenth century, for they had witnessed the advent of an independent United States and the French occupation of Spain itself. Spain's emboldened colonies had refused to recognize the Napoleonic regime in Madrid and became increasingly self-reliant. Their attitude did not change when French control of Spain ended. Ferdinand refused to compromise with the overseas territories. Instead, he gathered an army to subdue them. Some liberal junior officers, declaring the army's loyalty to the constitution of 1812, won support from the rank and file, who balked at going overseas. This military mutiny coincided with a sympathetic provincial uprising to produce the "revolution of 1820," the first major assault on the European order established in 1815 at the Congress of Vienna. Ferdinand appealed to the European powers for help. France intervened on his behalf and crushed the uprising.

Ferdinand restored his reactionary regime but could not regain Spain's American colonies. The British, sympathetic to the cause of Latin American independence and eager for commercial access to the region, opposed reconquest, and their naval dominance of the seas kept Spain in its place. The United States, meanwhile, had recognized the independence of the Latin American republics and wished to see their independence maintained. In 1823 President James Monroe issued the statement known as the Monroe Doctrine, prohibiting European colonization or intervention in the affairs of independent republics in the Americas. Of course, the United States had no military muscle to back this proclamation, but the British navy effectively enforced it. By 1825 all of Spain's colonies on the mainland in Central and South America had won their freedom.

The newly independent states patterned their regimes on models of Spanish liberalism; all had constitutions stipulating separation of powers and guaranteeing human rights. Brazil, the Portuguese empire in the Americas, was a monarchy for most of the rest of the nineteenth century, as was Mexico for a short time, but all the other states became republics, opting for what was then an unusual form of government. Although most of the Latin regimes eventually became dictatorships, they continued to pay lip service to liberal values.

WESTERN EUROPE, 1830–1848

For the political systems of western Europe, the 1830s marked a time of modification. The threat, and occasionally the sting, of revolt produced more liberal regimes, but except for Britain and Spain, most governments were unable to stem the tide of discontent, which became revolution in 1848.

France and the July Monarchy

As a result of the 1830 revolution in Paris, a more liberal regime was installed in France. Louis Philippe proclaimed himself "King of the French," thus acknowledging that he reigned at the behest of the people. Freedom of the press was reinstated. Suffrage was extended to twice as many voters as before, 200,000 men. The July Monarchy, named after the month in which it was established by revolution, justified itself by celebrating the great Revolution of 1789. On the site where the Bastille had been razed in 1789, the government erected a large column with the names of the victims of the July 1830 revolution, thus suggesting a continuity between those who had fought tyranny in 1789 and 1830.

Identification with the Revolution appeared to legitimize the regime but also had the potential to subvert it. Fearful that the cult of revolution would encourage violence against the new monarchy, the regime censored artistic production, promoting only works that extolled the period from 1789 to 1791, when the revolutionaries had attempted to found a constitutional monarchy. Now that the revolution of 1830 had established a constitutional monarchy, the regime was suggesting, any further uprisings were illegitimate. If the July Monarchy turned out not to be as liberal as its founders had hoped, foreign visitors coming from more authoritarian societies were nonetheless impressed by France's apparently liberal institutions. (See the box "The Global Record: A Moroccan Describes French Freedom of the Press.") Many French liberals, however, saw the regime as a travesty of the hopes and promises it had represented on coming to power in 1830.

British Reforms

The major political problem facing Britain in the early nineteenth century was the composition of Parliament, which did not reflect the dramatic population shifts that had occurred since the seventeenth century. Industrialization had transformed mere villages into major cities—Manchester, Birmingham, Leeds, Sheffield—but those cities had no representation in Parliament. Localities that had lost population, however, were still represented. In districts known as "pocket boroughs," single individuals owned the right to a seat in Parliament. In districts known as "rotten boroughs," a handful of voters elected a representative.

News of the July 1830 revolution in Paris encouraged British liberals to push for reform. Fearing the same fate as the hapless Charles X, some conservatives silently yielded. The government introduced a reform bill abolishing or reducing representation for sparsely populated areas while granting seats for the populous and unrepresented cities. The bill also widened the franchise by lowering property qualifications to include many middle-class men. Following a prolonged, bitter political battle between the government and middle classes on one side and the aristocracy on the other, the House of Lords finally passed what came to be known as the **Great Reform Bill** of 1832.

The reform was not particularly radical. Only the upper layers of the male middle class were enfranchised, or one in seven adult men. Yet despite its shortcomings, the reform demonstrated the willingness of the political leaders to acknowledge the increasing economic importance of manufacturing. Parliament became a more representative forum whose makeup better reflected the shift of economic power from agricultural landowners to the industrial and commercial classes. The bill passed as a result of nationwide agitation, evidence that the

Great Reform Bill   British law that broadened the franchise and provided parliamentary seats for new urban areas that had not previously been represented.

THE GLOBAL RECORD

A MOROCCAN DESCRIBES FRENCH FREEDOM OF THE PRESS

In 1845–1846 a Moroccan diplomatic mission visited Paris. The ambassador's secretary, Muhammad as-Saffar (d. 1881), wrote an account of the visit. Impressed by many aspects of French society, he praises France's press in the following passage. The "Sultan" as-Saffar refers to is King Louis Philippe. To this Moroccan observer, the extent to which the French enjoyed constitutional government was striking.

The people of Paris, like all the French indeed, like all of [Europe] are eager to know the latest news and events that are taking place in other parts [of the world]. For this purpose they have the gazette.[In] these papers . . . they write all the news that has reached them that day about events in their own country and in other lands both near and far.

This is the way it is done. The owner of a newspaper dispatches his people to collect everything they see or hear in the way of important events or unusual happenings. Among the places where they collect the news are the two Chambers, the Great and the Small, where they come together to make their laws. When the members of the Chamber meet to deliberate, the men of the gazette sit nearby and write down everything that is said, for all debating and ratifying of laws is matter for the gazette and is known to everyone. No one can prevent them from doing this. . . .

. . . [I]f someone has an idea about a subject but he is not a member of the press, he may write about it in the gazette and make it known to others, so that the leaders of opinion learn about it. If the idea is worthy they may follow it, and if its author was out of favor it may bring him recognition.

No person in France is prohibited from expressing his opinion or from writing it and printing it, on condition that he does not violate the law. . . .

In the newspapers they write rejoinders to the men of the two Chambers about the laws they are making. If their Sultan demands gifts from the notables or goes against the law in any way, they write about that too, saying that he is a tyrant and in the wrong. He cannot confront them or cause them harm. Also, if someone behaves out of the ordinary, they write about that too, making it common knowledge among people of every rank. If his deeds were admirable, they praise and delight in him, lauding his example; but if he behaved badly, they revile him to discourage the like.

Moreover, if someone is being oppressed by another, they write about that too, so that everyone will know the story from both sides just as it happened, until it is decided in court. One can also read in it what their courts have decided.

QUESTIONS

1. Based on the diplomat's reaction to the French system, what can you deduce about freedom of the press and the expression of public opinion in Morocco?

2. Do you think this observer has a positive opinion of the French press? Why or why not?

Source: Susan Gilson Miller, ed. and trans., *Disorienting Encounters: Travels of a Moroccan Scholar in France in 1845–1846; The Voyage of Muhammad as-Saffar.* Copyright © 1992 Regents of the University of California. Reprinted by permission of the University of California Press Books in the format Textbook via Copyright Clearance Center.

---

political system could respond to grievances and bring about reform peacefully.

A series of colonial reforms also showed Parliament's willingness to adapt to changing circumstances. Opposition to slavery had been voiced since the 1780s. (See the box "The Written Record: A Plea to Abolish Slavery in the British Colonies.") Slavery, the very opposite of human freedom, was an affront to liberal principles. Moreover, its persistence threatened the empire—in 1831 sixty thousand slaves rebelled in Jamaica. Parliament heeded the call for change and in 1833 abolished slavery throughout the British Empire.

In addition, the British began to review their imperial administration. Their control over Canada had been challenged in an uprising in 1837. London sent out a fact-finding mission headed by Lord Durham (1806–1848). As a result of the *Durham Report,* the British government promulgated self-government for Canada in 1839 and 1841. Eventually all the British colonies with a majority of white settlers were given similar rights of self-rule. The idea of self-government for nonwhites in the colonies was not yet imagined.

Reforms solidified Britain's influence overseas. In Canada they reduced opposition to British rule. The antislavery campaign led to the extension of British power into Africa. Having abolished the slave trade in 1807, the British worked to compel other nations to end the trade. With the largest navy in the world, Britain was well equipped to patrol the coast of West Africa to suppress the traffic in humans and hinder its

THE WRITTEN RECORD

A PLEA TO ABOLISH SLAVERY IN THE BRITISH COLONIES

Among the causes that British reformers embraced was the abolition of slavery. The slave trade had been abolished in 1807; one more step was left—ending in the colonies the institution of slavery itself. In this petition to Parliament in 1823, the Society for the Mitigation and Gradual Abolition of Slavery Throughout the British Dominions explains the harsh and degrading nature of the institution. Trading in slaves had been abolished as immoral and unnatural; here the petitioners remind Parliament that holding slaves is no less abhorrent. Under the pressure of this type of agitation, Parliament in 1833 abolished slavery in the British Empire.

In the colonies of Great Britain there are at this moment upwards of 800,000 human beings in a state of degrading personal slavery.

These unhappy persons, whether young or old, male or female, are the absolute property of their master, who may sell or transfer them at his pleasure, and who may also regulate according to his discretion (within certain limits) the measure of their labour, their food, and their punishment.

Many of the slaves are (and all may be) branded like cattle, by means of a hot iron, on the shoulder or other conspicuous part of the body, with the initials of their master's name; and thus bear about them in indelible characters the proof of their debased and servile state. . . .

It can hardly be alleged that any man can have a right to obtain his fellow creatures in a state so miserable and degrading as has been described. And the absence of such right will be still more apparent, if we consider how these slaves were originally obtained.

They, or their parents, were the victims of the Slave Trade. They were obtained, not by lawful means, or under any colourable pretext, but by the most undisguised rapine, and the most atrocious fraud. Torn from their homes and from every dear relation in life, barbarously manacled, driven like herds of cattle to the sea-shore, crowded into the potential holds of slaveships, they were transported to our colonies and there sold in bondage. . . .

The Government and Legislature of this country have on various occasions, and in the most solemn and unequivocal terms denounced the Slave Trade as immoral, inhuman, and unjust; but the legal perpetuation of that state of slavery, which has been produced by it, is surely, in its principle, no less immoral, inhuman and unjust, than the trade itself. . . .

QUESTIONS

1. Why would the British Parliament abolish the slave trade but allow slavery to continue in its colonies?

2. Why did it take ten years from the time of this petition for slavery to be abolished? What changes occurred in the British Parliament that might explain the timing of abolition?

Source: Reprinted in *Circular Letters of the Society for the Mitigation and Gradual Abolition of Slavery Throughout the British Dominions* (April 1823).

---

colonial rivals from benefiting from the trade. Needing bases for these patrols, the British established a number of minor settlements in West Africa, and thereby became the predominant European power along the coast. Although unimportant when acquired, these possessions foreshadowed the increasing European intrusion into African affairs.

Parliament's reforming zeal stimulated support for **Chartism,** a movement for political democracy as a means for social change. In 1838 political radicals with working-class support drew up a "people's charter," a petition calling for universal male suffrage, electoral districts with equal population, salaries and the abolition of property qualifications for members of Parliament, the secret ballot, and annual general elections. The Chartists hoped that giving workers the vote would end the dominance of the much smaller upper classes in Parliament and ensure an improvement in the workers' lot.

Chartism won wide support among men and women in the working classes, sparking demonstrations and petition drives of unprecedented size—millions signed the petition. Women participated to a larger extent than in any other political movement of the day, founding over a hundred female Chartist chapters. Some Chartists, especially female members, asked

Chartism Nineteenth-century British political movement calling for universal male suffrage, electoral districts with equal population, salaries and the abolition of property qualifications for members of Parliament, the secret ballot, and annual general elections.

for women's suffrage, but this demand failed to gain overall adherence from the membership. Winning mass support during particularly hard economic years, Chartism lost followers during a temporary economic upswing. The movement also fell under the sway of advocates of violence, who scared off many artisans and potential middle-class supporters. Chartism failed as a political movement; yet it drew public attention to an integrated democratic program whose main provisions (except for yearly elections) would be adopted piecemeal over the next half century.

In 1839 urban businessmen founded the Anti–Corn Law League for the purpose of abolishing the Corn Law of 1815, which kept the price of grain high. The Corn Law was unpopular with manufacturers, who knew that low food prices would allow them to pay low wages. It was also unpopular with workers, who wanted bread at a price they could afford. The anti–Corn Law movement proved more effective than Chartism because it had the support of the middle classes. Alarmed by the threat of famine after the poor harvest of 1845, Parliament repealed the Corn Law in 1846.

In the end this action did not affect the price of grain. Nevertheless, repeal of the Corn Law was a milestone in British history, demonstrating the extent to which organized groups could bring about economic improvements. A popular, mass organization had been able to shape public policy—a far cry from the days of Peterloo, when the government had not only ignored the public but attacked it with bayonets fixed.

THE ABSOLUTIST STATES OF CENTRAL AND EASTERN EUROPE, 1815–1848

Having seen the turmoil unleashed by the French Revolution and suffered at the hands of the Grande Armée, the states of central and eastern Europe were particularly committed to maintaining absolute government. In contrast to many parts of western Europe, which saw important political changes in the 1830s, the absolutist states were able to preserve themselves essentially unchanged until 1848—and in some cases even beyond.

The Austrian Empire The Austrian Empire's far-flung territories seemed to its Habsburg rulers to require a firm hand (see Map 21.1). Liberalism, which challenged imperial power, could not be countenanced. Nor, in this multinational empire, could nationalism be tolerated. The emperor, Francis I (r. 1792–1835), was opposed to any change; his motto was "Rule and change nothing." Prince Metternich, Francis's chief minister, viewed the French Revolution of 1789 and its aftermath as a disaster and believed his task was to hold the line against the threat of revolution. Quick to in-

terpret protests or the desire for change as a threat to the fundamental order, Metternich established a network of secret police and informers to spy on the imperial subjects and keep them in check.

The German States In most of the German states, the political order was authoritarian and inflexible. The states of Baden, Württemberg, and Bavaria had granted their subjects constitutions, although effective power remained in the hands of the ruling houses. The king of Prussia had repeatedly promised a constitution, but none had materialized. A representative Diet would not meet there until 1847. Prussia was ruled by an alliance of the king and the *Junkers* (YUNG-kurz), the landowning aristocrats who staffed the officer corps and the bureaucracy. The efficiency of the officer corps and the bureaucracy earned admiration throughout Europe. But by liberal standards, Prussia's political institutions seemed outdated.

Throughout the German states, the urban middle classes, intellectuals, journalists, university professors, and students were frustrated with the existing system. They were disappointed by the lack of free institutions and the failure of the patriotic wars against Napoleon to create a united Germany. University students formed *Burschenschaften* (BOOR-shen-shaft-en), or brotherhoods, whose slogan was "Honor, Liberty, Fatherland." Metternich reacted swiftly in July 1819 with the Carlsbad Decrees; these decrees established close supervision over the universities, censorship of the press, and dissolution of the youth groups. Wholesale persecution of liberals and nationalists followed. The Prussian king dismissed his more enlightened officials.

Renewed nationalist agitation swept the German states in the 1840s. A mass outpouring of patriotic sentiment erupted in response to possible French ambitions on the Rhine during a diplomatic crisis in 1840. Two patriotic songs were penned: "The Watch on the Rhine" and *"Deutschland, Deutschland über alles"* ("Germany, Germany Above All"); the latter became Germany's national anthem half a century later. German rulers, who in the past had been reluctant to support the national idea, now attempted to co-opt it. Cologne's unfinished cathedral, for example, became a symbol of German enthusiasm; from all over Germany donations poured in to finish it. These events suggested a broadening base for nationhood, which potentially could replace the existing system of a fragmented Germany. But with minor exceptions, the system established in 1815 prevailed until 1848.

Italian States By the end of Napoleon's reign, Italy consisted of eight political states. Austria exercised considerable power over Italy through its possession of its northern territories, Lombardy and Venetia.

Austria also had dynastic ties to several ruling houses in the central part of the peninsula, and had political alliances with the papacy. The only ruling house free of Austrian ties—and hence eventually looked to by nationalists as a possible rallying point for the independence of the peninsula—was the Savoy dynasty of Piedmont-Sardinia. But it was in Austria's interest to maintain disunity.

Many Italian governments—notably the papacy, the kingdom of Naples, and the central Italian duchies—imposed repressive policies, knowing that they could count on Austrian assistance to squelch any uprising. Indeed, Metternich did crush rebellions that were intended to bring about freer institutions and a unified Italy. His interventions generated hatred of Austria among Italian liberals and nationalists.

Russia   By far the most autocratic of the European states was tsarist Russia. Alexander I (r. 1801–1825) was an enigmatic character who puzzled his contemporaries. His domestic policy vacillated between liberalism and reaction; his foreign policy wavered between brutal power politics and apparently selfless idealism. When the Congress of Vienna gave additional Polish lands to the tsar, establishing the kingdom of Poland, he demonstrated his liberalism to the world (and curried favor with his new subjects) by granting Poland a liberal constitution. But he offered no such constitution to his own people. Within a few years, moreover, he violated the same Polish constitution he had approved, by refusing to call the Diet into session. His planned efforts to abolish serfdom between 1803 and 1812 also failed. As much as he desired freedom for them, he was unwilling to impose the necessary policies toward that end because they would be detrimental to the interests and privileges of the landed gentry.

Toward the end of his rule, Alexander became increasingly authoritarian and repressive, probably in response to growing opposition. Myriad groups—Russian military officers who had served in western Europe, Russian Freemasons who had corresponded with Masonic lodges in western Europe, and Russian intellectuals who read Western liberal political tracts—had warmed to the ideals of individual freedom and constitutionalism. These groups formed secret societies with varying agendas. Some envisioned Russia as a republic, others as a constitutional monarchy, but all shared a commitment to the abolition of serfdom and the establishment of a freer society.

Alexander died in December 1825, without designating which of his brothers would succeed him. Taking advantage of the confusion, the military conspirators declared in favor of the older brother, Constantine, in the belief that he favored a constitutional government. The younger brother, Nicholas, claimed to be the legal heir. The St. Petersburg garrison rallied to the conspirators' cause. Taking their cue from the Spanish uprising of 1820, the officers believed that the military could bring about change on its own.

The "Decembrist uprising," as it is known, quickly failed. The military revolt in the Russian capital was badly coordinated with uprisings planned in the countryside, and Nicholas moved quickly to crush the rebellion. He had the leaders, called the **Decembrists**, executed, sent to Siberia, or exiled. In spite of its tragic end, throughout the nineteenth century the Decembrist uprising served as an inspiration to Russians resisting tsarist oppression.

Coming to the throne under such circumstances, Nicholas I (r. 1825–1855) was obsessed with the danger of revolution and determined to suppress all challenges to his authority. The declared goal of his rule was to uphold "orthodoxy, autocracy, and nationality." Nicholas created a stern, centralized bureaucracy to control all facets of Russian life. He originated the modern Russian secret police, called the "Third Section"; a state within the state, it was above the law. Believing in the divine right of monarchs, Nicholas refused to accept limits to his imperial powers. The tsar supported the primacy of the Russian Orthodox Church within Russian society; the church in turn upheld the powers of the state. Nicholas also used nationalism to strengthen the state, exalting the country's past and trying to "Russify" non-Russian peoples. After a nationalist rebellion in 1831 in Poland attempted to shake loose Russian control, Nicholas abrogated the kingdom's constitution and tried to impose the Russian language on its Polish subjects.

Russia's single most overwhelming problem was serfdom. Economically, serfdom had little to recommend it; free labor was far more efficient. Moreover, the serfs' dissatisfaction with their lot threatened public safety. Nicholas's thirty-year reign was checkered with over six hundred peasant uprisings, half of them put down by the military. Nicholas understood that serfdom had to be abolished for Russia's own good, but also he believed emancipation would only sow further disorder. Except for a few minor reforms, he did nothing. Nicholas's death, followed by Russia's defeat in the Crimean War (see pages 682–684), eventually brought to an end the institution that had held nearly half of the Russian people in bondage.

Ottoman Empire and Greek Independence

In its sheer mass, the Ottoman Empire continued to be a world empire. It extended over three continents. In Africa it ran across the whole North African coast. In

Decembrists   Group of Russian military officers, later viewed as martyrs, who led the unsuccessful December 1825 rebellion seeking to install a constitutional monarchy.

Europe it stretched from Dalmatia (on the Adriatic coast) to Istanbul. In Asia it extended from Mesopotamia (present-day Iraq) to Anatolia (present-day Turkey). But it was an empire in decline, seriously challenged from inside by nationalist movements and from outside by foreign threats.

The Ottoman bureaucracy, once the mainstay of the government, had fallen into decay. In the past officials had been recruited and advanced by merit; now lacking funds, Constantinople sold government offices. Tax collectors ruthlessly squeezed the peasantry. By the eighteenth century, the Janissaries, formerly an elite military force, had become an undisciplined band that menaced the peoples of the Ottoman Empire—especially those located at great distances from the close control of the capital. The reform-minded Sultan Selim III (r. 1789–1807) sought to curb the army, but rebellious Janissaries killed him. They then forced the new ruler, Mahmud II (r. 1808–1839), to retract most of the previous improvements. The worst features of the declining empire were restored.

Mehemet Ali
Painted by the famed British artist Sir David Wilkie, this portrait depicts the Egyptian leader at the height of his powers. Mehemet challenged the Ottoman Empire, winning for Egypt virtual independence and bringing Syria under his control.
(Tate Gallery, London/Art Resource, NY)

The ideas of nationalism and liberty that triggered changes in western Europe also stirred the peoples of the Balkans. Most of the Ottoman Empire was inhabited by Muslims, but in the Balkans Christians were in the majority. Ottoman officials usually treated religious minorities such as Jews and Orthodox Christians with tolerance. But the Christian subject peoples found in their religion a means of collectively resisting a harsh and at times capricious rule. Some Christian peoples in the Balkans looked back nostalgically to earlier eras—the Greeks to their great Classical civilization or the Serbs to their era of self-rule.

The Serbs were the first people to revolt successfully against Ottoman rule. A poor, mountainous region, Serbia suffered greatly from the rapaciousness of the Janissaries. In protest, a revolt broke out in 1804. At first the Ottomans were able to contain the insurrection, but in 1815 they had to recognize one of its leaders, Milosh Obrenovich (r. 1815–1839), as governor and allow the formation of a national assembly. In 1830, under pressure from Russia, which took an interest in fellow Slavs and members of the Orthodox faith, Constantinople recognized Milosh as hereditary ruler over an autonomous Serbia.

The Greeks' struggle led to complete independence from Ottoman rule. Greeks served as administrators throughout the Ottoman lands and, as merchants and seafarers, traveled widely throughout the Mediterranean world and beyond. They had encountered the ideas of the French Revolution and, in the 1790s, were affected by the nationalism spreading in Europe. Adamantios Koraïs (KOOR-ay-iss) (1748–1833), an educator living in revolutionary Paris, reformed written Greek to make it more consonant with ancient Greek by removing foreign accretions. Koraïs created a new, more elegant Greek and edited Greek classics to connect his fellow countrymen with their ancient and illustrious past. Greek cultural nationalism found an echo among some intellectuals. The *Philike Hetairia* (Society of Friends), a conspiratorial group founded in 1814, dedicated itself to restoring Greek independence by political means.

Greek peasants were not particularly interested in politics, but they were hostile to the Ottoman Turks, who had accumulated vast landholdings at their expense. This in part motivated Greek peasants to join the anti-Turkish revolt that began in 1821 and lasted several years. By 1827 the Ottomans, aided by their vassal Mehemet Ali (1769–1849) of Egypt, controlled most of the Balkan peninsula. The rest of Europe, excited by the idea of an independent Greece restored to its past greatness, widely supported the Greek movement for freedom. The Great Powers intervened in 1827, sending their navies to intercept supplies intended for the Ottoman forces. At Navarino Bay, in the southwest of the Peloponnesus, the Ottoman navy fired on the allies, who returned fire and sank the Turkish ships. The destruction of Ottoman power ensured the independence of Greece. In 1830 an international agreement spelled out Greek independence.

Losing influence in the Balkans, the Ottoman Empire also faced challenges elsewhere. In Egypt Mehemet Ali, nominally subordinate to Constantinople, actually ruled Egypt as if it were independent. He wrested Syria away in 1831 and threatened to march against his overlord, the sultan. Britain and Russia, concerned that an Ottoman collapse would upset the region's balance of power, intervened on the empire's behalf. Constantinople won back Syria but in 1841 had to acknowledge Mehemet Ali as the hereditary ruler of Egypt. The survival of the Ottoman Empire was beginning to depend on the goodwill—or self-interest—of the Great Powers.

S E C T I O N ━ S U M M A R Y

- Between 1815 and 1830, the restored governments in western Europe encountered periodic social discontent, which they managed to negotiate with various degrees of success, often through repressive measures.

- In July 1830, the French responded to reactionary measures taken by their king with revolution, which marked the beginning of more serious opposition to other regimes.

- British liberals responded to France's July Revolution by redrawing the voting districts to reflect the growth of cities, widening the franchise to include the middle classes, and loosening colonial rule over white settler populations.

- Having suffered more directly from Napoleonic invasions, rulers in central and eastern Europe remained determined to preserve absolute political power from 1815 to 1848.

- The 1825 "Decembrist uprising" in Russia challenged the power of Nicholas I; the memory of its brutal repression would inspire resistance to tsarist oppression throughout the nineteenth century.

- National movements from within and foreign threats from without challenged the religiously diverse Ottoman Empire, already in decay because of its corrupt bureaucracy; Serbs and Greeks successfully revolted against Ottoman rule.

THE REVOLUTIONS OF 1848

What were the main causes of the revolutions of 1848, and what roles did nationalism, liberalism, and socialism play in inciting and sustaining revolution?

From France in the west to Poland in the east, at least fifty separate revolts and uprisings shook the Continent in 1848, the most extensive outbreak of popular violence in nineteenth-century Europe (see **MAP 21.2**). The revolt had an impact far beyond Europe's borders. Inspired by the example of the European revolutions, Brazilians rose up against their government. In Bogota, Colombia, church bells rang, and in New York public demonstrations enthusiastically greeted the announcement of a republic in France. And as a result of the Parisian revolution, slaves in French colonies were finally emancipated.

The revolutions of 1848 also brought women into the political arena, creating new opportunities to criticize their legal status. In France, feminist clubs and newspapers proliferated as they never had before. In central, eastern, and southeastern Europe, revolution gave women political experience that promoted an emancipatory consciousness among them. The revolutions produced a long list of eloquent feminists throughout Europe who made various demands through their newspapers, magazines, and in their political participation. But just as had happened in the French Revolution of 1789, revolutionary governments eventually excluded women from politics, censored their newspapers, and disbanded their clubs.

ROOTS OF REBELLION

At no time since 1800 had so many Europeans been involved in collective action. Many reasons account for this widespread outbreak of discontent. In the countryside, restrictions in access to land such as enclosure frustrated peasants. Although in the past many had enjoyed free access to village commons, these were coming increasingly under private control, or the peasants faced competition for their use. Formerly a peasant might have grazed sheep in the commons, but now a

MAP 21.2   Major Uprisings and Reforms, 1848–1849

In no other year had as many revolts broken out simultaneously. In many cases the revolutions led to reforms and new constitutions.

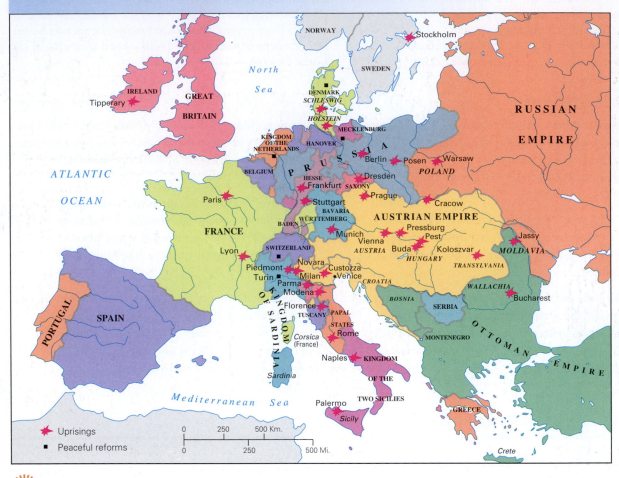

Uprisings
Peaceful reforms

Online Study Center **Improve Your Grade** Interactive Map: Major Uprisings and Reforms, 1848–1849

peasant's two or three animals competed with herds of sometimes hundreds of sheep owned by a rich farmer. Also, the poor once had relatively free access to forests to forage for firewood, but the limitation of this right also now led to frequent conflicts.

Points of friction were made worse by growing populations that put pressure on available resources. In the urban environment a crisis erupted in the handicrafts industry, which dominated city economies. Urban artisans were being undercut by the putting-out system or cottage industry, in which capitalists had goods produced in the countryside by cottagers—part-time artisans who supported themselves as well through agriculture and were thus willing to work for lower wages. Crises in the crafts hurt the journeymen who wanted to be masters; they had to serve far longer apprenticeships and in many cases could never expect promotion. Where the guild system still existed, it was in decline, unable to protect the economic interests of artisans anxious about their futures.

These developing concerns came to a crisis point as a result of the economic depression of 1845–1846. In 1845 a crop disaster, including the spread of potato blight, destroyed the basic food of the poor in northern Europe. The Irish suffered the most catastrophically from this blight: one million starved to death between 1844 and 1851. The poor harvests doubled the price of food from the 1840 level. An industrial downturn accompanied these agricultural disasters, creating massive unemployment. Municipal and national governments seemed unable to deal with the crowding, disease, and unsanitary conditions that were worsening already high tensions in the cities, the sites of national governments. The call to overthrow the existing regimes resonated not only because of discontent, but because new ideologies had created hope for change, as well as a vision for what it should be. The insurrections disoriented the established political and administrative elites, and they found they could not count on their traditional sources of support.

The revolutions of 1848 were sparked by the revolution in Paris in February. News of the fall of Louis Philippe triggered a ripple effect, spreading turbulence to over fifty localities in Europe. In France the revolution was for political and social rights, particularly the right to work. In several other countries, another issue was added to the combustible situation—nationalism. Once revolution in the German states broke out, the demands arose for national unification. National unity also became a goal throughout the Italian peninsula; northern Italians also desired independence from the Habsburg empire. In other Habsburg lands the cry went out for national independence: the Hungarians, Poles, and Czechs all wanted to be masters of their own destinies and free from Vienna's control.

LIBERALS: FROM SUCCESS TO DEFEAT

The revolutions of 1848 went through a number of stages. In the first stage liberal demands for more political freedoms such as the right to vote joined with popular demands for social and economic justice. In France the victors declared a republic, which provided basic constitutional freedoms and granted universal male suffrage (the first European regime to do so). The provisional government attempted to solve the problem of widespread unemployment by creating jobs through a system of "national workshops." Inspired by the example of Paris, crowds in Vienna demonstrated and petitioned the emperor. Having lost control over the capital, Metternich resigned and fled to England. On March 15, 1848, the Austrian imperial court, faced with continued agitation by students and

workers, announced its willingness to issue a constitution. Even more important was Austria's decision to abolish serfdom. Some had feared a serf uprising, but the relatively generous terms of the emancipation mollified the peasantry.

News of the February uprising in Paris also acted as a catalyst for change in the German states. The forces of change seemed irresistible. As the king of Württemberg observed, "I cannot mount on horseback against ideas." The wisest course appeared to be compromise. He and many of his fellow dukes and princes changed their governments by dismissing their cabinets and instituting constitutions.

Up to this point Prussia was conspicuous for being untouched by the revolutionary wave. But when news of Metternich's fall in Vienna reached Berlin on March 16, middle-class liberals and artisans demonstrated for reforms. King Friedrich Wilhelm IV (r. 1840–1861), who initially opposed the revolutionaries' demands for political liberties and a unified nation, chose appeasement. The king surprised his subjects on March 21 by announcing support for a united, free, constitutional Germany. He appointed as chief minister a liberal

King Friedrich Wilhelm IV Announcing His Devotion to German Unity
This print, distributed by the thousands, shows the grateful people—well-dressed middle-class citizens and humble artisans united in their purpose—acclaiming the king (*center*) on horseback. The black, red, and gold flags, the symbol of German unity since the Napoleonic Wars, are prominently displayed. (*Germanisches National Museum Nuremberg*)

Rhenish businessman, who in a ceremonial march through Berlin symbolically walked ahead of the king (see illustration on page 673). Representative government was introduced, and suffrage was extended, though it was still restricted to men of property. No longer the exclusive preserve of the aristocracy, the government was opened to men from the liberal professions and the business classes. As in Austria, the German countryside was appeased by reducing some of the feudal arrangements that still existed in many areas.

The second stage of the revolution marked a breakdown in the unity that had initially formed against the old regimes. With the enemy defeated or compliant, the middle classes, peasants, and workers discovered that they no longer shared a common goal. In France the peasants, who at least had not opposed the revolution, by April 1848 were hostile to the new republic. They decried the additional taxes that had to be levied to pay for the national workshops supporting unemployed urban workers. Armed with the vote, the peasants elected conservative landowners, lawyers, and notaries—a group nearly identical to the pre-1848 deputies. In June the new parliament decided to terminate the costly national workshops. The workers, in despair, revolted. The government carried out a bloody repression, killing 3,000 and arresting 15,000. The re-election of conservative forces revealed that universal suffrage could serve as a means to mobilize moderate public opinion against radicalism in Paris. The advent of railroads allowed the government to muster military support from outside the city. Thereafter it would be far more difficult for radical Parisian crowds to dictate policies to the rest of the country.

The propertied classes, feeling menaced by the poor, looked to authority for security. Of the several candidates for president in 1848, Louis Napoleon (1808–1873), a nephew of Napoleon Bonaparte, appealed to the largest cross section of the population.

Ballots, Not Bullets
This print from 1848 encourages the revolutionary on the barricades to put away his rifle and trust the democratic process. Pointing to the rifle, our French revolutionary announces, "This is for the external enemy." "As for the internal ones," he says, indicating the election urn, "this is how one fights them loyally."
(Harlingue-Viollet/Getty Images)

The middle class was attracted by the promise of authority and order. Peasants, disillusioned by the tax policies of the republic, remained loyal to the memory of Napoleonic glory. Workers embittered by the government's repression of the June uprisings were impressed by Louis Napoleon's vaguely socialistic program. Louis Napoleon was elected president. Three years later he dissolved the National Assembly by force and established a personal dictatorship. In 1852 he declared himself Emperor Napoleon III.

In Austria and Germany the middle classes became wary of the lower classes; the class conflict in Paris intensified their concern. Once the peasants had won their freedom from feudal dues in Germany and from serfdom in the Austrian Empire, they were no longer interested in what was occurring in the capital. Thus the alliance in favor of change disappeared, and it could not even serve as a bulwark against the return of conservative forces. In Austria the reactionary forces around the court, led by General Windischgrätz, reconquered Vienna in October 1848 for the emperor and suspended the liberals' constitution. In December the king of Prussia, who had appeared to bow to liberal opinion, regained his courage and dismissed the elected assembly. Most of the liberal forces were spent and overcome by the end of the year.

THE NATIONALIST IMPULSE

The revolutions did not break out because of nationalism, but once they erupted, the nationalist cause helped shape the outcome in several regions. Faced with internal turmoil, Prussia and Austria—which both opposed German unification lest it undermine their power—could not prevent the question of a united Germany from coming to the fore. In March 1848 a self-appointed national committee invited five hundred prominent German liberals to convene in Frankfurt to begin the process of unifying the German states into a single nation. In addition to fulfilling a long-standing liberal dream, a united Germany would consolidate the liberal victory over absolutism. The gathering called for suffrage based on property qualifications, thus excluding most Germans from the political process and alienating them from the evolving new order. The first all-German elected legislature met in May 1848 in Frankfurt to pursue unification. It faced the thorny issue of which regions should be included and which excluded in this new Germany. The most ambitious plan envisioned a *Grossdeutschland* (Grose-doyt-shlant), or large Germany, consisting of all the members of the German Confederation, including the German-speaking parts of Austria and the German parts of Bohemia. Such a solution would include many non-Germans, including Poles, Czechs, and Danes. The

proponents of *Kleindeutschland* (Kline-doyt-shlant), or small Germany, which would exclude Austria and its possessions, saw their solution as a more likely scenario, although it would exclude many Germans. The proposal of a small Germany succeeded in the end, largely because the reassertion of Austrian imperial power in the fall of 1848 put the non-German areas under Vienna's control out of reach.

The Prussian reassertion of royal power, though partial, was a signal for other German rulers in late 1848 to dismiss their liberal ministers. The moment for liberalism and national unification to triumph had passed by the time the **Frankfurt Assembly** drew up a constitution in the spring of 1849. Having opted for the *Kleindeutsch* solution, the parliament offered the throne to Friedrich Wilhelm IV, king of Prussia. Although the king was not a liberal, he ruled the largest state within the designated empire. If power could promote and protect German unity, he possessed it in the form of the Prussian army. But Friedrich Wilhelm feared that accepting the throne would lead to war with Austria. Believing in the principle of monarchy, he also did not want an office offered by representatives of the people, and so he refused the offer. Lacking an alternative plan, most members of the Frankfurt Assembly went home. A rump parliament and a series of uprisings in favor of German unity were crushed by the Prussian army. So German unification failed. Liberalism alone was unable to bring about German unity; other means would be required to do so.

In Italy, too, nationalist aspirations emerged once a revolt triggered by social and economic grievances had broken out. In the years before 1848 nationalists and liberals hoped somehow to see their program of a united and free Italy implemented. News of the Paris uprising in February galvanized revolutions in Italy. Italians under Austrian rule forced the Austrians to evacuate their Italian possessions. Revolts and mass protests in several Italian states led rulers to grant, or at least promise, a constitution. The king of Piedmont, Charles Albert (r. 1831–1849), granted his people a constitution, the Statuto. Charles Albert hoped to play a major part in unifying Italy. In Austrian Italy the middle classes, although eager to be free of foreign rule, feared radical elements among the laborers. They believed that annexation to nearby Piedmont would provide security from both Austria and the troublesome lower classes. The king of Piedmont decided to unite Italy under his throne if doing so would prevent the spread of radicalism to his kingdom. On March 24, 1848, he declared war on Austria but was defeated in July and had to sue for an armistice. The continued spread of nationalist and revolutionary sentiment

Frankfurt Assembly   Popularly elected national assembly that attempted to create a unified German state.

Constitutional Government in Denmark

On March 21, 1848, fifteen thousand Danes, inspired by the example of Paris, marched on the palace to demand constitutional rights. Unlike the protests at the French capital, however, this event was peaceful and led to the establishment of a constitutional government. This painting honors the new parliament that came into being after the liberal constitution was adopted in 1849.   *(Photo, Statens Museum for Kunst, Copenhagen)*

tempted Charles Albert to declare war on Austria once again, in March 1849. The outcome for Piedmont was even worse than it had been a year earlier. Within six days its army was defeated. Humiliated, Charles Albert resigned his throne to his son, Victor Emmanuel II (r. 1849–1878). The Austrians quickly reconquered their lost provinces and reinstated their puppet governments. The dream of a united Italy was dashed.

In the multinational empire of the Habsburgs, nationalism manifested itself in the form of demands for national independence from foreign rule. With Austria's power temporarily weakened as a result of revolution in Vienna, nationalist revolts broke out not only in Italy, but simultaneously in Hungary, the Czech lands, and Croatia. The Austrian emperor yielded in Hungary, giving it virtual independence; it was joined to the empire solely by personal union to the ruler.

Constitutional government was established in Hungary, but participation in the political process was limited to Magyars, who were the single largest ethnic group, constituting 40 percent of the population. The other nationalities in Hungary—Romanians, Slovaks, Croats, and Slovenes—preferred the more distant rule of Austrian Vienna to Magyar authority. The Czech lands also witnessed agitation, but there and elsewhere the tide favoring the nationalists turned. The revolt against the empire was not coordinated, and the nationalisms were often in conflict with one another. Once the emperor re-established his power in Vienna, he could move against his rebellious subjects. The Austrian Empire practiced a policy of divide and rule; it re-established its authority in Italy, bombarded Prague into submission, and with Russian help brought Hungary to heel. If the nationalist fires had been quenched, the dangers nationalism posed to the survival of the Habsburg empire were also revealed.

Three major countries escaped the large sweep of revolutions that washed across Europe. In Great Britain the government had proven capable of adjusting to some of the major popular demands, averting the need for revolution. In Russia the repressive tsarist system prevented any defiance from escalating into an opposition mass movement. Spain was also spared. General Ramón Narváez (Nar-va-yes) (1799–1868) brutally ran the country from 1844 to 1851. When he was on his deathbed, the priest asked him whether he forgave his enemies. He answered, "I have no enemies. I have shot them all!"

SECTION SUMMARY

- Across the Continent, the roots for revolution lay in increasingly restricted resources among rural peasants and urban workers; the economic depression of 1845–1846 made this situation into a crisis.

- The liberal impulse to revolution at first united middle classes, peasants, and workers in demands for political freedoms and economic justice.

- Once regimes gave into the challenge or were overturned, the goals of different social classes conflicted; the divisions between them opened the path to reaction and repression.

- Liberal revolution in eastern and central Europe inspired movements of national unification in the German states and in Italy, Hungary, the Czech lands, and Croatia, all at the expense of the Austrian Empire.

- Although counterrevolutionary forces temporarily defeated both the liberal and nationalistic impulses behind the revolutions of 1848, experiments born of these events suggested new modes of political organization that would later come to fruition.

CHAPTER SUMMARY

Online Study Center ACE the Test

What were the goals and results of the Congress of Vienna?

What major ideologies developed in the first half of the nineteenth century?

How did the restorations that followed the Napoleonic era give way to reform?

What were the main causes of the revolutions of 1848, and what roles did nationalism, liberalism, and socialism play in inciting and sustaining revolution?

In 1814 and 1815, after more than twenty-two years of war, the powers that finally defeated Napoleon—Great Britain, Austria, Prussia, and Russia—sought to restore the prerevolutionary Old Regime to Europe. The Congress of Vienna sought to establish international stability by creating a balance of power. To that end, the Great Powers even brought the vanquished nation of France—with its Bourbon monarchy restored—into the Concert of Europe on equal footing.

In reaction to the revolutionary challenges of the past, a conservative ideology developed that asserted human beings were neither equal nor rational and were incapable of governing themselves. The artistic and literary movement of romanticism also rejected the Enlightenment past, by privileging passion and emotion over human reason, and helped fuel a religious revival. But romanticism also increased the appeal of nationalism, a new awareness of one's cultural past and national identity—a sentiment that would ultimately destabilize the restored order. The legacy of the Enlightenment and French Revolution, moreover, could not be extinguished completely, particularly as industrial capitalism developed. Liberalism, which advocated individual freedom in laissez-faire economics and in political rights, advanced middle-class interests. Socialism, in both its "utopian" and "scientific" varieties, addressed the social injustices wrought by capitalism.

By 1830, the restored order had already shown cracks that led to revolution and reform. The July Revolution of 1830 in France replaced its reactionary king with a more liberal one. That event sparked reform in Britain, which extended the vote to the middle classes. Eastern European regimes remained more autocratic, but nationalist and liberal sentiments developed nonetheless between 1820 and 1848.

The main causes of the 1848 revolutions were economic and ideological. By the 1840s, even though industrialization had only begun on the Continent, capitalist development had already transformed modes of production and displaced, or threatened to displace, many workers. The growing middle classes, still disenfranchised in most of Europe, sought more political freedom. In February 1848, revolutionaries in France demanded universal manhood suffrage and solutions to unemployment, setting off by their example revolutions elsewhere. Central and eastern Europeans demanded representative governments; but nationalism also raised the issue of *which* peoples the governments would represent. Most of the aspirations of the 1848 revolutions failed to be realized as authoritarian regimes regained the upper hand by 1851.

 OOKING AHEAD

Although the revolutionary and nationalistic movements of 1848–1849 were crushed, and the republics proclaimed in France, Germany, Hungary, and Italy did not last, this time, as opposed to 1815, the re-established monarchs knew that they could not simply return to the past. Rulers could no longer govern without considering public opinion; constitutions would become the norm in the second half of the century. Nationalism, too, would become a permanent feature in European politics, one that rulers of nation-states and empires could no longer ignore. In the next chapter, we will turn to these nationalist movements.

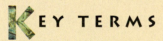 EY TERMS

Congress of Vienna (p. 650)	**socialism** (p. 660)
conservatism (p. 653)	**Marxism** (p. 661)
romanticism (p. 653)	**July Revolution** (p. 663)
nationalism (p. 655)	**Great Reform Bill** (p. 665)
liberalism (p. 658)	**Chartism** (p. 667)
laissez faire (p. 658)	**Decembrists** (p. 669)
utilitarianism (p. 659)	**Frankfurt Assembly** (p. 675)

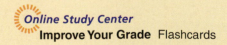
Online Study Center
Improve Your Grade Flashcards

SUGGESTED READING

Broers, Michael. *Europe After Napoleon: Revolution, Reaction, and Romanticism, 1815–1848.* 1996. Evaluates the era from the point of view of the participants.

Harsin, Jill. *Barricades: The War on the Streets in Revolutionary Paris, 1830–1848.* 2002. An insightful account

of how the optimism for reform in 1830 helped produce the disillusion and anger of 1848.

Hobsbawm, E. J. *The Age of Revolution, 1789–1848.* 1962. Presents compelling arguments that the era was dominated by two simultaneous revolutions, the French Revolution and the industrial transformation.

Johnson, Paul. *The Birth of the Modern World Society, 1815–1830*. 1991. A weighty but readable book providing a panoramic view of the era; includes biographical sketches of some of the major figures of the time.

Laven, David, and Lucy Riall, eds. *Napoleon's Legacy: Problems of Government in Restoration Europe*. 2000. Essays on the restoration experience in different European countries.

Sperber, Jonathan. *The European Revolutions, 1848–1851*. 1994. The best up-to-date synthesis, which includes some new emphases, such as the role of rural and religious discontent in shaping the revolts.

Wheen, Francis. *Karl Marx: A Life*. 2000. A lively biography that, in addition to discussing Marxian thought, emphasizes the man's personal life.

22

NATIONALISM AND POLITICAL REFORM, 1850–1880

Wilhelm I at Versailles
Wilhelm is proclaimed ruler of the German Empire, 1871. *(Bismarck Museum/akg-images)*

The ceremonial occasion depicted in the painting on the left is a monumental one for European and world history: the crowned heads of different German states, without the benefit of a parliament or popular vote, proclaim the unification of all their states under one nation. On the podium, standing just behind the newly declared kaiser, Wilhelm I, is Crown Prince Friedrich Wilhelm (later Kaiser Friedrich III). To the kaiser's left, with his arm upraised, is the grand duke of Baden. In the middle of the scene, resplendent in his white uniform, is Bismarck, the political architect of German unification. On the right nearby is Field Marshal Helmuth von Moltke (fon molt-KEH), the military genius who provided the series of military victories allowing Prussia to unify Germany under its aegis. The location of this ceremony also has profound symbolism as well as irony: four months after delivering a humiliating defeat to France, a unified Germany was proclaimed in the famed Hall of Mirrors in the grandiose palace of Versailles, the former seat of French kings and royal court.

Germany had become a united nation by war. In the generation after 1850 the contours of European politics changed—new states appeared on the map, and within their national borders a good number of states reformed their political institutions. To meet the demand for popular participation in government so forcefully expressed in 1848, every European state except the Ottoman and Russian Empires found it necessary to have a parliament. Rare before midcentury, such institutions became common thereafter. No longer was the demand for popular participation seen as a threat to the existing political and social order. In fact, popular participation, or the appearance of it, gave the existing order a legitimacy it had not enjoyed since before the French Revolution. Nationalism flourished during this period, emerging as a decisive force throughout the West—in European affairs as well as in the United States, where it promoted territorial expansion and fired a determination to preserve the Union.

These political transformations occurred in an era of unprecedented economic growth and prosperity. Industrial production expanded the economy; the discovery of gold in California in 1848 led to the expansion of credit (since currencies were backed by gold), which in turn led to the

KEY TERMS

Realpolitik

congress system

risorgimento

trasformismo

Otto von Bismarck

February Patent

Compromise of 1867

Young Turks

mir

manifest destiny

Second Reform Bill

Paris Commune

Online Study Center

This icon will direct you to interactive map and primary source activities on the website **college.hmco.com/pic/noble5e**

founding of new banks and mass investments in growing industries. The standard of living rose significantly in industrializing nations. Between 1850 and 1880 industrial production increased by 90 percent in Great Britain and by 50 percent in France. The middle classes expanded dramatically.

In the first half of the century, international relations had been dominated by the congress system, in which representatives of the major European states met periodically to refine and preserve the balance of power. This system collapsed in the second half of the century, as political leaders pursued the narrow nationalist interests of their respective states. Instead of negotiating with one another, a new generation of leaders employed brute military force—or the threat of its use—to resolve international conflicts. The new age was dominated not by ideals but by force, announced Bismarck, the main practitioner of what became known as *Realpolitik,* a policy in which war became a regular instrument of statecraft.

FOCUS QUESTIONS

How did the Crimean War affect international relations?

How did political leaders in Piedmont harness the forces of nationalism to achieve Italian national unity?

What events led to the unification of Germany and what was the character of the new German nation?

How did the Austrian, Ottoman, and Russian Empires deal with the challenges they faced?

How were the United States and Canada transformed during this period?

How did western European states create democracies?

THE CHANGING NATURE OF INTERNATIONAL RELATIONS

How did the Crimean War affect international relations?

The Crimean War and its aftermath shaped European international relations for several decades. Following the 1815 Congress of Vienna (see Chapter 21), European states attempted, through the **congress system,** to work out their differences by negotiation, avoiding situations in which one state triumphed at the cost of another. The Crimean War and subsequent realignments raised mutual suspicions, leading nations to act in their own self-interests and to ignore the concerns of the other major players in the international system. This reorientation facilitated the emergence of nation-states at the expense of traditional empires.

Realpolitik Style of governing that uses all means, including war, to expand the influence and power of a state.

congress system System of European international relations in the first half of the nineteenth century in which the major European states cooperated to preserve the balance of power.

THE CRIMEAN WAR, 1854–1856

The Crimean War had many causes. Principally, however, it had to do with Russia claiming the right to protect Orthodox Christians within the predominantly Muslim Ottoman Empire. This claim led to war between Russia and the Ottoman Empire in 1853, resulting in a Russian victory. The defeat of the Ottoman Empire made it more vulnerable to further Russian incursions.

British and French statesmen had considerable interest in the conflict. Britain had long feared that the collapse of the Ottoman Empire would lead Russia to seek territorial gains in the Mediterranean. Such a move would challenge Britain's naval supremacy in that region. An explosion of public sentiment against Russia's aggressiveness also obliged the British government to consider military action. Meanwhile, the French emperor, Napoleon III, believed that successful war against Russia would provide the opportunity to redraw European borders. He hoped that a new order would lead to increased French power and influence. Napoleon also imagined that fighting side by side with Britain could lay the foundation for Anglo-French friendship. And so England and France rushed to defend the Ottoman Empire and declared war on Russia in March 1854.

The war was poorly fought on all sides. Leadership was woefully inadequate, and five times more casualties resulted from disease than from enemy fire. Although the Russians had a standing army of a million men, their poor communications and supply systems prevented them from ever fielding more than a quarter of their forces. In Britain, the press and members of Parliament denounced their side's inadequate materiel and incompetent leadership. For the first time, the press played an active role in reporting war; the new technologies of the telegraph and photography brought to readers at home the gruesome realities of battle. One of the few heroic figures to emerge from this conflict was the English nurse Florence Nightingale (1820–1910), who organized a nursing service to care for the British sick and wounded. Later her wartime experience allowed her to pioneer nursing as a professional calling. (See the box "The Written Record: Florence Nightingale in the Crimean War.")

Florence Nightingale
This photograph was taken in 1856, shortly after Nightingale returned to England from the Crimean War. Her privileged background provided the official connections that helped her nursing services succeed.
(Courtesy, Florence Nightingale Museum, St. Thomas' Hospital, London. Photo: London Metropolitan Archives)

CHRONOLOGY

1851	Louis Napoleon's coup d'état
1854–1856	Crimean War
1860	Italy united under Piedmontese rule
1861	Great Reforms in Russia
1861–1865	U.S. Civil War
1862	Bismarck appointed minister president of Prussia
1864	Austria and Prussia attack Denmark and occupy Schleswig-Holstein
1866	Austro-Prussian War
	Abolition of estate system in Sweden
1867	Second Reform Bill in England
	North America Act creates Canadian federation
	Austro-Hungarian compromise
1870	Franco-Prussian War
	Rome, joined to Italy, becomes its capital
	Declaration of French Third Republic
1871	Unification of German Empire
	Paris Commune
1876	Bulgarian horrors
1878	Congress of Berlin

After almost two years of fighting in the Balkans and the Crimean peninsula, Russia abandoned the key fortress of Sevastopol in September 1855. Militarily defeated, the Russians also were alarmed at Austria's posture. Tsar Nicholas I had expected Austrian assistance in the war in return for his help in crushing the Hungarian rebellion in 1849. Instead, Austria's leaders not only withheld aid but even threatened to join the Western alliance.

The Crimean conflict killed three-quarters of a million people—more than any European war between the

Crimean War
This photograph shows the interior of the Sevastopol fortress after it had been battered into surrender. The Crimean War was the first conflict to be documented by photographers. *(Courtesy of the Board of Trustees of the Victoria & Albert Museum)*

end of the Napoleonic Wars and World War I. It was a particularly futile, senseless war whose most important consequence was political: it unleashed dramatic new changes in the international order that allowed for the emergence of the new nation-states.

THE CONGRESS OF PARIS, 1856

The former combatants met in Paris in February 1856 to work out a peace treaty. Their decisions—which pleased no one—shaped relations among European states for the next half century. Russian statesmen were especially discontented, as their country was forbidden to have a fleet in the Black Sea. Nor did French leaders feel that their nation had benefited, other than the prestige of holding the congress in Paris. The north Italian state of Piedmont, which had joined the allies, only gained a vague statement about the unsatisfactory nature of Italy's existing situation. Prussia was invited to attend the congress only as an afterthought and hence also felt slighted.

Although the war seemed to have sustained the integrity of the Ottoman Empire, the peace settlement weakened it indirectly by dictating reforms in the treatment of its Christian populations. These reforms impaired the empire's ability to repress the growing nationalist movements in the Balkans. British political leaders, galled by the heavy sacrifices of the war, moved toward isolationism in foreign policy. Austrian policymakers had hoped Britain and France would aid them in preserving the Habsburg empire; instead, these powers, angry that Austria had not helped in the war, offered no assistance—a stance that would further weaken Habsburg imperial hegemony. At the time the peace treaty was signed, few people foresaw the enormous results that would flow from it.

By and large, the decisions reached in Paris would be disregarded or unilaterally revised as competition and rivalry between the major powers destabilized the international system. This new international climate also allowed new states to take shape without international sanction.

THE WRITTEN RECORD

FLORENCE NIGHTINGALE IN THE CRIMEAN WAR

Florence Nightingale used her influential family connections to win an appointment to the Crimean battlefield. Once there, she organized nursing for the wounded and was able to secure additional personnel and medical supplies for her hospital. Women were supposed to be sheltered from the harsh realities of the outside world, but as this letter indicates, Nightingale was not spared war in its cruelest aspects.

We have no room for corpses in the wards. The Surgeons pass on to the next, an excision of the shoulder-joint—beautifully performed and going on well—[cannon] ball lodged just in the head of the joint, and fracture starred all round. The next poor fellow has two stumps for arms—and the next has lost an arm and leg. As for the balls, they go in where they like, and do as much harm as they can in passing. That is the only rule they have. The next case has one eye put out, and paralysis of the iris of the other. He can neither see nor understand. But all who can walk come into us for Tobacco, but I tell them that we have not a bit to put into our own mouths. Not a sponge, nor a rag of linen, not anything have I left. Everything is gone to make slings and stump pillows and shirts. These poor fellows have not had a clean shirt nor been washed for two months before they came here, and the state in which they arrive from the transport is literally crawl-ing. I hope in a few days we shall establish a little cleanliness. But we have not a basin nor a towel nor a bit of soap nor a broom—I have ordered 300 scrubbing brushes. But one half the Barrack is so sadly out of repair that it is impossible to use a drop of water on the stone floors, which are all laid upon rotten wood, and would give our men fever in no time. . . .

I am getting a screen now for the Amputations, for when one poor fellow, who is to be amputated tomorrow, sees his comrade today die under the knife it makes an impression—and diminishes his chance. But, anyway, among these exhausted frames the mortality of the operations is frightful.

QUESTIONS

1. How did Florence Nightingale's presence on the Crimean battlefield defy Victorian middle-class gender roles? How did it reaffirm them?

2. What does her description convey about the impact that modern technology had on warfare by 1854?

Source: Letter to Dr. William Bowman, November 14, 1854, in *"I Have Done My Duty": Florence Nightingale in the Crimean War, 1854–56,* ed. Sue M. Goldie (Iowa City: University of Iowa Press, 1987), pp. 37–38.

SECTION SUMMARY

- The Crimean War of 1854–1856 marked the end the spirit of cooperation that had resulted from the Congress of Vienna in 1815.

- The Crimean War was caused by the Russian defeat of the Ottomans in 1853, British fear of Russian influence in the Mediterranean, and Napoleon III's desire to increase French influence.

- The 1856 Congress of Paris humiliated Russia and restricted its military access to the Black Sea. The postwar settlement dictated reforms in the treatment of Christians in the Ottoman Empire, which, in turn, impaired the Ottoman ability to repress nationalist movements in the Balkans.

ITALIAN UNIFICATION, 1859–1870

How did political leaders in Piedmont harness the forces of nationalism to achieve Italian national unity?

n Metternich's memorable phrase, Italy at midcentury was nothing but a "geographic expression." The revolution of 1848 (see pages 671–677) had revealed an interest in national unification, but the attempt had failed. Within a dozen years, however, what many believed to be impossible would come to pass. Idealists such as Giuseppe Mazzini (see page 655) had preached that Italy would be unified not by its rulers but by its people, who would rise and establish a free republic. Instead, the deed was done by royalty, by war, and with the help of a foreign state. Although ideals were not absent from the process of unification, cynical manipulation and scheming also came into play.

Since the late eighteenth century, some Italians had been calling for a *risorgimento* (ree-sor-djee-MEN-toe), a political and cultural renewal of Italy. By the mid-nineteenth century, the idea was actively supported by a small, elite group consisting of the educated middle class, urban property owners, and members of the professions. For merchants, industrialists, and professionals, a unified state would provide a larger stage on which to pursue their ambitions.

CAVOUR PLOTS UNIFICATION

After the failed 1848 revolution, most Italian rulers resorted to repression. Only the northern Italian kingdom of Piedmont kept the liberal constitution adopted during the 1848 revolution, and it welcomed political refugees from other Italian states. Not only politically but economically, it was a beacon to the rest of Italy, establishing modern banks and laying half the rail lines on the peninsula.

The statesman who was to catapult Piedmont into a position of leadership in the dramatic events leading to Italian unification was Count Camillo di Cavour (1810–1861). The son of a Piedmontese nobleman and high government official, he grew up speaking French, the language of the royal court and formal education in Piedmont, and mastered Italian only as an adult. Cosmopolitan in his interests, Cavour knew more about Britain and France than about Italy. He was sympathetic to the aspirations of the middle class and saw in Britain and France models of what Italy ought to become, a liberal and economically advanced society.

Short, fat, and nearsighted, Cavour hardly cut a heroic figure. Yet he was ambitious, hard-working, and driven to succeed. A well-known journalist and the editor of the newspaper *Risorgimento,* he joined the government in 1850. Two years later King Victor Emmanuel appointed him prime minister. Cavour shared the enthusiasm of the middle classes for an Italian nation, but his vision did not include the entire Italian peninsula, only its north and center, which then could dominate the rest of Italy in a loose federation. Unifying the north and center would first require ousting Austria from the northern provinces. The failures of 1848 had taught Cavour that this task would require foreign help, especially French assistance.

When the Crimean War broke out in 1854, Cavour steered Piedmont to the allied side, hoping to advance his cause. He sent twenty thousand troops to the Crimea,

one-tenth of whom died. This act gained him a seat at the Congress of Paris, where his presence boosted the kingdom's prestige—and where he and Napoleon III had an opportunity to meet and size up each other.

Napoleon III favored the cause of Italian liberation from Austrian rule and some form of unification of the peninsula. Austria had been France's traditional opponent; destroying Austria's power in Italy might strengthen France. Thus in July 1858 the French emperor and the Piedmontese prime minister met secretly at Plombières (plom-bee-YAIR), a French spa, to discuss how Italian unity could be achieved. They agreed that Piedmont would stir up trouble in one of Austria's Italian territories in an effort to goad the Austrians into war. France would help the Piedmontese expel Austria from the northern provinces of Lombardy and Venetia, and the new Piedmont, doubled in size, would become part of a confederation under the papacy. In exchange, the French emperor demanded the Piedmontese provinces of Nice and Savoy, which bordered France.

War between Austria and Piedmont broke out in April 1859. By June the combined Piedmontese and French forces had routed the Austrians at Magenta and Solferino (see **MAP 22.1**). So bloody were these battles that the color magenta was named after the deep red of the soaked battlefield. The horrors of this war also inspired the founding of the Red Cross.

Shocked by the bloodshed he had witnessed, Napoleon III decided to end the fighting instead of pressing on. Prussian mobilization on behalf of Austria also alarmed him. In addition, his plan for Italy began to unravel. Several states in central Italy expressed a desire to be annexed to Piedmont, which would have resulted in an independent state much larger than Napoleon III had anticipated. These factors led him to betray Cavour; he made an agreement with the Austrians, which gave Lombardy to Piedmont, but allowed Venetia to remain within the Austrian Empire.

UNIFICATION ACHIEVED, 1860

Napoleon's betrayal outraged Cavour, but unexpected events in the south also changed his vision of national unification. The centuries-old misgovernment of the kingdom of Naples led to an uprising in Sicily in April 1860. The revolutionary firebrand Giuseppe Garibaldi (1807–1882), a rival of Cavour, set sail for Sicily in May 1860 with but a thousand poorly armed, red-shirted followers to help the island overthrow its Bourbon ruler. Winning that struggle, Garibaldi's forces crossed to the mainland in August. Victory followed victory, and enthusiasm for Garibaldi grew. His army swelled to 57,000 men, and he won the entire kingdom of Naples.

Threatened by the advance of Garibaldi's power and fearing its reach into the Papal States, Cavour sent his army into the area in September 1860. Although

risorgimento   Italian term, beginning in the late eighteenth century, for the political and cultural renewal of Italy. It later came to be associated with Italian unification.

MAP 22.1   The Unification of Italy, 1859–1870

Piedmontese leadership under Cavour in the north, and nationalist fervor inspired by Garibaldi in the south, united Italy.

Garibaldi was a republican, he was convinced that Italy could best achieve unity under the king of Piedmont, and he willingly submitted the southern part of Italy, which he controlled, to the king, Victor Emmanuel II (r. 1849–1878). Thus by November 1860 Italy had been united under Piedmontese rule (see Map 22.1). The territories that had come under Piedmont's control affirmed their desire to be part of the new Italy through plebiscites based on universal male suffrage. The 1848 constitution of Piedmont became the constitution of the newly united Italy. Cavour lived to relish his handiwork for only a few months, as he died of an undiagnosed illness in May 1861. His last words were "Italy is made—all is safe."

Still to be joined to the new state were Austrian-held Venetia in the northeast and Rome and its environs, held

Garibaldi Leading His "Red Shirts" to Victory over the Neapolitan Army, May 1860
Garibaldi's conquests in the south and Cavour's in the north opened the way for Italian unification.   *(Museo di Risorgimento, Milan/Scala/Art Resource, NY)*

by the pope with the support of a French garrison. But within a decade, a favorable international situation enabled the fledgling country to acquire both key areas. Upon its defeat in the Austro-Prussian War in 1866, Austria ceded Venetia to Italy. Then the Franco-Prussian War forced the French to evacuate Rome, which they had occupied since 1849. Rome was joined to Italy and became its capital in 1870. With that event unification was complete.

THE PROBLEMS OF A UNIFIED ITALY

National unity had been achieved, but it was frail. The uprisings that Garibaldi had led in the south were motivated more by hatred of the Bourbons than by fervor for national unification. And once the union was achieved, the north behaved like a conquering state—sending its officials to the south, raising taxes, and imposing its laws. In 1861, rebellion broke out among disbanded Neapolitan soldiers and brigands. Civil war ensued for five years, producing more casualties than the entire effort of unification.

Other major divisions remained. In 1861 only 2.5 percent of the population spoke the national language, Florentine Italian. Economics also divided the country. The north was far more industrialized than the rural south. In the south child mortality was higher, life expectancy was lower, and illiteracy was close to 90 percent. The two regions seemed to belong to two different nations. Piedmont imposed strong central control, resolutely refusing a federal system of government, which many Italians in an earlier era had hoped for. This choice reflected Piedmont's fear that any other form of government might lead to disintegration of the new state. Piedmont wanted to save the new Italian state from a fate similar to that of the United States, whose federal system of government led to secessionism and the Civil War in early 1861 (see page 700).

Piedmont imposed its constitution on unified Italy, which limited suffrage to men of property and education—less than 2 percent of the population. Further, as prime minister, Cavour created and manipulated parliamentary majorities in favor of his cabinet, reversing the logic behind the parliamentary system in which cabinets were supposed to represent, and answer to, freely elected legislative bodies. He cajoled and bribed parliamentarians, transforming previous foes into supporters. This system of manipulation, known as *trasformismo* (trass-for-MEES-mo), would characterize Italian government for the next several decades. Nevertheless, the new unified Italy was a liberal state that guaranteed legal equality and freedom of association, and provided more freedom for its citizens than the Italian people had seen for centuries.

The Catholic Church remained hostile to the new Italian state. The popes, left to rule a tiny domain—a few square blocks around the papal palace known as the Vatican—considered themselves prisoners. They denounced anyone who participated in elections. Thus many Italian Catholics refused to recognize the new state for decades, thwarting its legitimacy. With its 27 million people in 1870, Italy was the sixth most populous European nation. It was too small to be a great power and too large to accept being a small state. Italian statesmen found it difficult to define their country's role in international politics, and they lacked a firm consensus on Italy's future.

= S E C T I O N   S U M M A R Y =

- As prime minister of the northern Italian kingdom of Piedmont, Cavour plotted with Napoleon III to wage war against Austria so that he could unify northern and central Italy.

- Napoleon, betraying Cavour, ended the war before the Austrians were completely expelled from northern Italy.

- When rebellion broke out in the south, Giuseppe Garibaldi and his army overthrew the kingdom of Naples and then willingly submitted the southern part of Italy to Piedmont. Complete unification was achieved by 1870.

- The newly unified Italy was a liberal state that guaranteed freedom and equality; but stark economic and cultural differences between north and south, opposition of the Catholic Church, and the imposition of central control from Piedmont made national unity frail.

GERMAN UNIFICATION, 1850–1871

What events led to the unification of Germany and what was the character of the new German nation?

Like Italy, Germany had long been a collection of states. Since 1815 the thirty-eight German states had been loosely organized in the German Confederation. Like Piedmont in Italy, one German state, powerful Prussia, led the unification movement. And just as Italy had in Cavour a strong leader who imposed his will, so did German unification have a ruthless and cunning champion: **Otto von Bismarck,** minister president of Prussia. But whereas Cavour, for all his wiliness, was committed to establishing a liberal state, Bismarck was wedded to autocratic rule.

The revolutionaries of 1848 had failed in their attempt to achieve German unification when the king of Prussia refused to accept a throne offered by the elected Frankfurt Assembly. As the painting at the beginning of this chapter illustrates, German unification was ratified not by the ballot, as it was in Italy, but by the acclamation of the crowned heads of Germany. The nation was united by the use of military force and the imposition of Prussian absolutism over the whole country.

THE RISE OF BISMARCK

Austria under Metternich had always treated Prussia as a privileged junior partner. After Metternich's fall in 1848, however, rivalry erupted between the two German states. Each tried to manipulate for its own benefit the desire for national unity that had become manifest during the revolution of 1848.

In March 1850 representatives from a number of German states met to consider unification under Prussian sponsorship. Austria opposed such a union and, with Russian support, threatened war. Since the

trasformismo System of political manipulation used by Count Camillo di Cavour (1810–1861), Piedmont's prime minister, to create majorities in parliament to support his cabinet.

Otto von Bismarck Nineteenth-century German statesman who, through a series of aggressive wars, united Germany. Germany became the dominant power in Europe under his administration.

Prussian military was not strong enough to challenge Austria, Prussia agreed to abandon the plan for unification and to accept Austrian leadership in Germany. But a decade later, the new Prussian king, Wilhelm I (r. 1861–1888), was determined to strengthen Prussia by expanding the size and effectiveness of the army. The parliament, however, refused to approve funding for a military build-up. The conflict was not simply about the budget; it was an issue of who should govern the country—the king or the elected representatives. To get his way, the king appointed Count Otto von Bismarck as minister president.

Bismarck was a Junker, a Prussian aristocrat known for his reactionary views, who had opposed the liberal movement in 1848. As Prussian emissary to the German Confederation, he had challenged Austrian primacy. Devoted to his monarch, Bismarck sought to heighten Prussian power in Germany and throughout Europe. He faced down the parliament, telling the Budget Commission in 1862, "The position of Prussia in Germany will be decided not by its liberalism but by its power . . . not through speeches and majority decisions are the great questions of the day decided—that was the mistake of 1848 and 1849—but by iron and blood."[1]

Bismarck tried to win over the liberals by suggesting that with military force at its disposal, Prussia could lead German unification. But the liberals continued to resist, and the parliament voted against the military reforms. Unfazed, Bismarck carried out the military measures anyway and ordered the collection of the necessary taxes. The citizens acquiesced and paid to upgrade their army. Prussia would not yield to parliamentarism as Britain had.

German liberals faced a dilemma: which did they value more—the goal of nationhood or the principles of liberty? Fellow liberals elsewhere lived in existing nation-states in which statehood had preceded the development of liberalism. In Italy unification had been led by the liberal state of Piedmont. That was not the case in Germany, where the natural leader, Prussia, had a long tradition of militarism and authoritarianism. To oppose Bismarck effectively, German liberals knew they would have to join with the working classes, but they feared the workers and forestalled such an alliance. Germany appeared embarked on an illiberal course.

Bismarck ingeniously exploited the weakness of the liberals and the growing desire for German unification. During the Franco-Austrian War of 1859, which launched Italian unification, Germans had feared that the French would attack across the Rhine River. Many came to believe that only a strong, united Germany could give its inhabitants security. Prussia had already led the important move toward economic unification with the *Zollverein,* a customs union that included most German states, but excluded Austria. Founded in 1834, the customs union had become more extensive with the passage of time; even states that were politically hostile to Prussia joined the union to protect their economic interests. Economic unity led to all-German professional and cultural associations that surpassed state boundaries; it was an indispensable stage in the process toward political unity. By 1860, the idea of a united Germany had gained a substantial appeal.

PRUSSIAN WARS AND GERMAN UNITY

Having built up the military and established the supremacy of royal power in Prussia, Bismarck was ready to enlarge its role in Germany—and he believed that war against Austria was the only means to do so. Conflicts over the provinces of Schleswig (SHLES-vik) and Holstein (HOLL-shteyn) served as a pretext (see **MAP 22.2**). In 1864, Prussia and Austria had successfully gone to war against Denmark to secure the independence of these two German-speaking provinces. Bismarck then used disputes over their joint administration as an excuse for war against Austria. Prussia attacked Austrian-administered Holstein in June 1866, launching the Austro-Prussian War. After a scant seven weeks, the newly reformed Prussian army won a decisive victory in the Battle of Sadowa (SAH-doe-wah). Prussia's industrial superiority had enabled it to equip its soldiers with the new breech-loading rifles. These "needle guns" allowed troops to fire from a prone position, while the Austrians, with their muzzle loaders, had to stand up to shoot. With military victory, Prussia annexed its smaller neighbors, which had supported Austria. In Bismarck's scheme this enlarged Prussia would dominate the newly formed North German Confederation, comprising all the states north of the Main (MINE) River. From now on, Austria was excluded from German affairs.

The triumph of Sadowa made Bismarck a popular hero. Elections held on the day of the battle returned a conservative pro-Bismarck majority to the Prussian parliament. The legislature, including a large number of liberals mesmerized by the military victory, voted to legalize retroactively the illegal taxes that had been levied since 1862 to upgrade the military. In compromising their principles, liberals rationalized that national unity ought to be gained first, with liberal constitutional institutions secured later. Their optimism proved to be a miscalculation.

The unification of Germany, like that of Italy, was facilitated by a favorable international situation. The Crimean War had estranged Russia from Austria, once allies. Although it would have been opportune for France to intervene on the Austrian side, the French emperor had been lulled into inaction by vague Prussian promises of support for French plans to annex Luxembourg. Once the war was won, Bismarck reneged on these promises. France was left with the problem of a strong,

MAP 22.2   The Unification of Germany, 1866–1871
A series of military victories made it possible for Prussia to unite the German states under its domain.

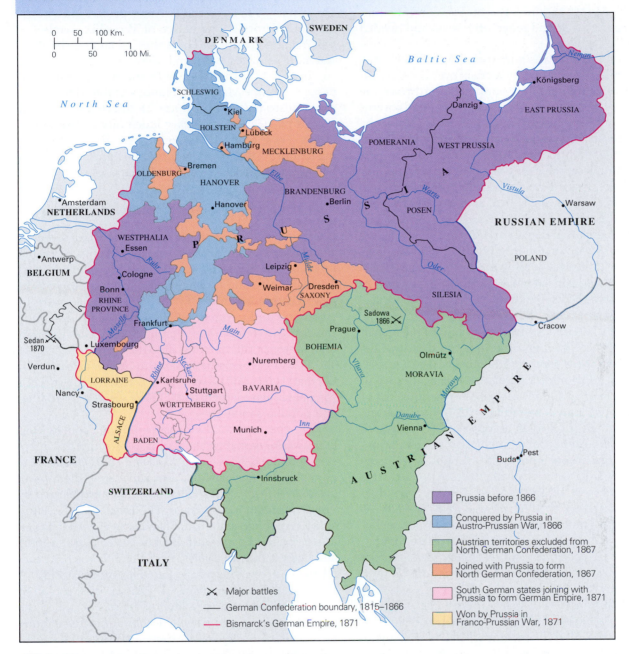

Prussia before 1866

Conquered by Prussia in Austro-Prussian War, 1866

Austrian territories excluded from North German Confederation, 1867

Joined with Prussia to form North German Confederation, 1867

South German states joining with Prussia to form German Empire, 1871

Won by Prussia in Franco-Prussian War, 1871

✕ Major battles

— German Confederation boundary, 1815–1866

— Bismarck's German Empire, 1871

Online Study Center **Improve Your Grade**   Interactive Map: The Unification of Germany, 1866–1871

enlarged Prussia on its eastern border, which threatened France's position as a Great Power. British leaders likewise did not intervene in the unification process. Disillusioned by the results of the Crimean War, they were in an isolationist mood. Moreover, Britain's government was sympathetic to the rise of a fellow Protestant power.

Bismarck's design was almost complete. Only the southern German states remained outside the North

German Confederation. He obliged them to sign a military treaty with Prussia and established a customs parliament for all the members of the Zollverein (the customs union), including the southern German states. The southern states, which were Catholic and sympathetic to Austria, were reluctant to see German unity advance any further. Only some dramatic event could remove their resistance.

THE FRANCO-PRUSSIAN WAR AND UNIFICATION, 1870–1871

French leaders were also determined to prevent German unity. Moreover, since the mid-seventeenth century, French security had relied on a weak and divided Germany.

Both Berlin and Paris anticipated war, which came soon enough, precipitated by a crisis over the Spanish succession. In 1868 a military coup had overthrown the Spanish queen Isabella, and the provisional government offered the throne to a Catholic member of the Hohenzollerns (HO-en-tsoll-ernz), the reigning Prussian monarch's family. The French viewed this candidacy as an unacceptable expansion of Prussian power and influence. Fearing a two-front war with Prussia in the east and Spain in the south, they insisted that the Hohenzollerns refuse the proffered throne. As passions heated, Bismarck was elated at the prospect of war, but King Wilhelm was not. On July 12, 1870, Wilhelm engineered the withdrawal of the young prince's candidacy for the Spanish throne, removing the cause for war. Bismarck was bitterly disappointed.

Not content with this diplomatic victory, the French pushed their luck further. On July 13 the French ambassador met the king of Prussia at Ems and demanded guarantees that no Hohenzollern would ever again be a candidate for the Spanish throne. Unable to provide any more concessions without a serious loss of prestige, the Prussian king refused the French petition.

Wilhelm telegraphed an account of his meeting to Bismarck. The chancellor immediately seized the opportunity this message provided. He edited what became known as the Ems dispatch, making the exchange between king and ambassador seem more curt than it actually had been; then he released it to the press. As he hoped, the French interpreted the report as a deliberate snub to their ambassador and overreacted. Napoleon III was deluged with emotional demands that he avenge the imagined slight to French national honor. On July 15 he declared war.

The Prussians led a well-planned campaign. An army of 384,000 Prussians was rushed by rail to confront a force of 270,000 Frenchmen. The French had the advantage of better rifles, but the Prussians were equipped with heavier cannon, which could pulverize French positions from a distance. Within a few weeks Prussia won a decisive victory at Sedan (seh-DAEN), taking the French emperor prisoner on September 2. The French continued the struggle, despite difficult odds. Infuriated by the continuation of the war, the Prussians resorted to extreme measures. They took hostages and burned down whole villages, and then laid siege to Paris, starving and bombarding its beleaguered population.

Throughout Germany the outbreak of the war aroused general enthusiasm for the Prussian cause. Exploiting this popular feeling, Bismarck called on leaders of the southern German states to accept the unification of Germany under the Prussian king. Reluctant princes, such as the king of Bavaria, were bought off with bribes. On January 18, 1871, the German princes met in the Hall of Mirrors at the palace of Versailles, symbol of past French greatness. There they acclaimed the Prussian king as Kaiser Wilhelm I, German emperor.

In May 1871 the Treaty of Frankfurt established the peace terms (see Map 22.1). France was forced to give up the industrially rich provinces of Alsace and Lorraine and to pay Germany a heavy indemnity of five billion francs. These harsh terms embittered the French, leading many to desire revenge and establishing a formidable barrier to future Franco-German relations.

THE CHARACTER OF THE NEW GERMANY

German unity had been won through a series of wars—against Denmark in 1864, Austria in 1866, and France in 1870. The military had played a key role in forging German unity, and it remained a dominant force in the new nation. Italian unity had been sanctioned by plebiscites and a vote by an elected assembly accepting the popular verdict. The founding act of the new German state, as the opening illustration to this chapter shows, was the acclamation of the German emperor by German rulers on the soil of a defeated neighbor. Thus the rulers placed themselves above elected assemblies and popular sanction.

On the surface, the constitution of the new Germany was remarkably democratic. It provided for an upper, appointed house, the *Bundesrat* (BOON-tes-raht), representing the individual German states, and a lower house, the *Reichstag* (RYSH-stak), which was elected by universal manhood suffrage. The latter might seem a surprising concession from Bismarck, the authoritarian aristocrat. But he knew the liberals lacked mass support and had confidence that he would be able to create majorities that could be manipulated for his purposes.

The authoritarianism of Prussia was projected onto all of Germany. The king of Prussia occupied the post of emperor, and the chancellor and other cabinet members were responsible only to him, and not to parliament. Only the emperor could make foreign policy and war, command the army, and interpret the constitution.

The emergence of a strong, united Germany shattered the European balance of power. In February 1871 the British political leader Benjamin Disraeli observed that the unification of Germany was a "greater political event than the French revolution of last century.... There is not a diplomatic tradition which has not been swept away. You have a new world. . . . The balance of power has been entirely destroyed."[2] Germany had become the dominant power on the Continent.

SECTION SUMMARY

- German unity resulted from a series of wars—against Denmark in 1864, Austria in 1866, and France in 1870.

- Under the leadership of Otto von Bismarck, Prussia reformed and expanded its army, leading to victory in war. To build up the army, Bismarck levied taxes and recruited troops without the approval of parliament.

- The Zollverein, a customs union that included most German states, but excluded Austria, helped

advance support for national unification under Prussia.

- Despite a liberal constitution that granted universal manhood suffrage, Prussian authoritarianism dominated Germany.

- With unification, Germany became the dominant power on the Continent, shattering the European balance of power.

PRECARIOUS EMPIRES

How did the Austrian, Ottoman, and Russian Empires deal with the challenges they faced?

The three large empires of central and eastern Europe, battered by aggressive behavior from other European states and challenged by internal tensions, attempted to weather the endless crises they confronted. The Austrian, Ottoman, and Russian Empires labored to fortify their regimes with political reforms, but only Austria tried to accommodate democratic impulses by establishing a parliament. The Ottoman sultans and the Russian tsars clung tenaciously to their autocratic traditions.

THE DUAL MONARCHY IN AUSTRIA-HUNGARY

Emperor Franz Joseph (r. 1848–1916) had come to the Austrian throne as an 18-year-old in that year of crisis, 1848. He was a well-meaning monarch who took his duties seriously. His upbringing was German, he lived in German-speaking Vienna, and he headed an army and a bureaucracy that was mostly German. But Franz Joseph was markedly cosmopolitan. He spoke several of his subjects' languages and thought of himself as the emperor of all his peoples. A much-loved, regal figure, Franz Joseph provided a visible symbol of the state. He lacked imagination, however, and did little more than try to conserve a disintegrating empire coping with the modern forces of liberalism and nationalism.

After the war with Piedmont and France (see page 686), Austrian statesmen sensed the vulnerability of their empire. To give the government credibility, in February 1861 Franz Joseph issued what became known as the **February Patent,** which guaranteed civil

liberties and provided for local self-government and a parliament elected by eligible males.

The need to safeguard the remaining territories was clear. By 1866 the Austrian Habsburgs were no longer a German or an Italian power (Venetia had been handed over to a united Italy). The strongest challenge to Habsburg rule came from Hungary, where the Magyars insisted on self-rule, a claim based on age-old rights and Vienna's initial acceptance of autonomy in 1848. Since Magyar cooperation was crucial for the well-being of the Habsburg empire, the government entered into lengthy negotiations with Magyar leaders in 1867. The outcome was the **Compromise of 1867.** The agreement divided the Habsburg holdings into Austria in the west and Hungary in the east (see **MAP 22.3**). Each was independent, but they were linked by the person of the emperor of Austria, Franz Joseph, who was also king of Hungary. Hungary had full internal autonomy and participated jointly in imperial affairs—state finance, defense, and foreign relations. The new state created in 1867 was known as the dual monarchy of Austria-Hungary.

Online Study Center **Improve Your Grade**
Primary Source: The Dual Monarchy Is Born: The Austro-Hungarian Augleich

The compromise confirmed Magyar dominance in Hungary. Although numerically a minority, the Magyars controlled the Hungarian parliament, the army, the bureaucracy, and other state institutions. They opposed self-rule of other ethnic groups in the kingdom who spoke different languages: the Croats, Serbs,

February Patent   Enactment issued in 1861 by the Austrian emperor Franz Joseph that established a constitutional monarchy in the old Austrian Empire.

Compromise of 1867   Agreement that divided the Habsburg empire into Austria in the west and Hungary in the east, a dual monarchy under Emperor Franz Joseph called Austria-Hungary.

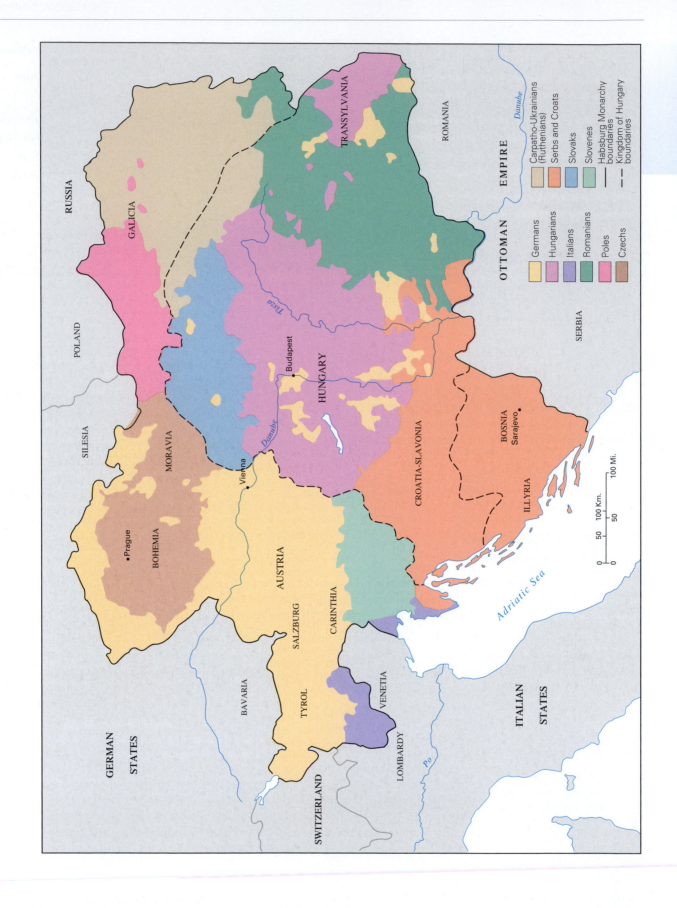

RUSSIA

GALICIA

POLAND

SILESIA

Tisza

TRANSYLVANIA

ROMANIA

Danube

OTTOMAN

EMPIRE

Budapest

HUNGARY

SERBIA

MORAVIA

Vienna

Prague

BOHEMIA

Danube

CROATIA-SLAVONIA

BOSNIA
Sarajevo

AUSTRIA

GERMAN
STATES

SALZBURG

CARINTHIA

ILLYRIA

BAVARIA

TYROL

VENETIA

LOMBARDY

Po

ITALIAN
STATES

SWITZERLAND

Adriatic Sea

Germans
Hungarians
Italians
Romanians
Poles
Czechs

Carpatho-Ukrainians
(Ruthenians)
Serbs and Croats
Slovaks
Slovenes
Habsburg Monarchy
boundaries
Kingdom of Hungary
boundaries

50   100 Km.
0
0   50   100 Mi.

MAP 22.3 Austria-Hungary in 1878
The Compromise of 1867 produced the dual monarchy of Austria-Hungary. A state of many languages and ethnicities, the Austro-Hungarian Empire occupied Bosnia in 1878, bringing more dissatisfied peoples under its rule. Tensions in the Balkans would lead to the outbreak of world war in 1914.

Slovaks, Romanians. They also attempted a policy of Magyarization—teaching only Magyar in the schools, conducting all government business in Magyar, and giving access to government positions only to those fully assimilated in Magyar culture. This arrangement created frustrations and resistance among the various nationalities under their rule.

The terms of the compromise also gave the Hungarians a voice in imperial foreign policy. The Magyars feared that Slavic groups outside the empire, who planned to form independent states or had already done so, would inspire fellow Slavs in Austria-Hungary to revolt. To prevent that, the Hungarians favored an expansionist foreign policy in the Balkans, which the monarchy embraced (see Map 22.3). Having lost its influence in Germany, Austria-Hungary saw the Balkans as an area in which it could assert itself. The policy was fraught with risks and, by bringing more discontented Slavs into the empire, led to hostilities with other states.

THE AILING OTTOMAN EMPIRE

At midcentury the Ottoman Empire was still one of the largest European powers, but it faced unrest within its borders and threats from the expansionist designs of its neighbors. The ailing empire was commonly referred to as "the sick man of Europe." Over the next twenty-five years the empire shed some of its territory and modernized its government, but nothing could save it from decline in the face of nationalist uprisings in its Balkan possessions.

Western-Style Reform As early as the 1840s, the Ottoman Empire had begun various reform movements to bring more security to its subjects. Emulating Western institutions, the reforms introduced security of property, equity in taxation, and equality before the law regardless of religion. Government officials—who previously had been free to collect taxes arbitrarily, sending the required amount to the central government and keeping the rest—were given fixed salaries and subjected to regular inspections.

These reforms were strengthened after the Crimean War by further imperial edicts. Many young intellectu-

als were impatient with the pace of change, however, and critical of the sultan. Unable freely to express their opinions at home, some went into exile in Paris and London in the late 1860s. Their hosts called them the **Young Turks,** an expression that became synonymous with activists for change and improvement.

The failure to hold on to its empire caused further dissatisfaction with Ottoman rule among its people, and in the spring of 1876 rioters demanded and won the establishment of constitutional government. Within a year, however, the new sultan, Abdul Hamid II (r. 1876–1909), dismissed the constitutional government and reverted to personal rule. Part of the administration's problem was financial. The easy terms of foreign credit lured the sultan into taking out huge loans to finance extravagant projects. In spite of drought and famine, the authorities raised taxes to pay debts, fostering widespread discontent.

Balkan Nationalism Nationalist fervor further intensified opposition to the government. The central administration had lost control over its provincial officials, who were often corrupt and tyrannical. Christians, the majority population in the Balkans, blamed their suffering on Islamic rule, and many were inspired by the 1821 Greek war of independence and the revolutions of 1848 to seek their own independence.

The Romanians, who lived mainly in the adjoining provinces of Moldavia in the north and Wallachia (vall-AK-yah) in the south, began to express nationalist sentiments in the late eighteenth century. These sentiments were nurtured by Western-educated students, who claimed for their countrymen illustrious descent from Roman settlers of antiquity. News of the 1848 revolution in Paris helped trigger a revolt in both provinces by those demanding unification and independence. This uprising was quickly crushed by the Turks.

Upon Russia's defeat in the Crimean War, the Congress of Paris in 1856 removed Russia's right of protection over Moldavia and Wallachia and provided for a referendum to determine their future. In 1859 the two provinces chose a local military officer, Alexander Cuza (r. 1859–1866), as the ruler of each territory. In 1862 the Ottoman Empire recognized the union of the two principalities in the single, autonomous state of Romania. The Congress of Berlin in 1878 recognized Romania's full independence. Thus, in less than a quarter century, two provinces of the Ottoman Empire had gained full sovereignty.

The path to independence was much more violent for the Bulgarians. Revolutionary committees—

Young Turks Young intellectuals who wanted to transform the Ottoman Empire into a more modern, Westernized state. The expression has subsequently come to designate any group of activists pushing for political change.

encouraged by Serbia and Russia—spread propaganda and agitated against Ottoman rule. An uprising in Bulgaria broke out in May 1876. The Christian rebels attacked not only symbols of Ottoman authority but also peaceable Muslim Turks living in their midst. The imperial army, aided by local Turkish volunteers, quickly re-established Ottoman authority. Incensed by the massacre of fellow Muslims, the volunteers resorted to mass killing, looting, and burning of Christian villages. The "Bulgarian horrors" shocked Europe and made the continuation of Turkish rule unacceptable.

Russia, which saw itself as the protector of the Slavic peoples, reacted to the Bulgarian horrors by declaring war on the Ottoman Empire in April 1877. At first progress was slow; then the Russians broke through the Turkish lines and forced the sultan to sue for peace. The resulting Treaty of San Stefano, signed in March 1878, created a huge, independent Bulgaria as essentially a Russian protectorate.

Nationalistic Uprising in Bulgaria
In this 1879 lithograph, Bulgaria is depicted in the form of a maiden—protected by the Russian eagle, breaking her chains, and winning liberty from the Ottoman Empire. *(St. Cyril and Methodius National Library, Sofia)*

The Congress of Berlin, 1878   The British, Austrians, and French were shocked at the extent to which the San Stefano treaty favored Russia. Under their pressure, the European Great Powers met in Berlin in 1878 to reconsider the treaty and re-establish a balance of power. The Congress of Berlin returned part of the Bulgarian territory to the Ottomans. It also removed Bosnia and Herzegovina from Ottoman rule. Henceforth Austria-Hungary administered these provinces (see Map 24.4 on page 765). The sultan was forced to acknowledge the legal independence of Serbia, Montenegro, and Romania and the autonomy of Bulgaria.

Thus Turkey was plundered not only by its enemies but also by powers that had intervened on its behalf. When France complained that it received no compensation, it was given the chance to grab Tunisia, another land under Ottoman rule. Russia was given the Bessarabian provinces that Romania had acquired in 1856. The devious work of the Congress of Berlin reflected the power politics that now characterized international affairs. Statesmen shamelessly used force against both foe and friend for the aggrandizement of their own states. Neither morality nor international law restrained ambition. While the Great Powers attempted to appease one another to maintain peace in the short run, the settlement of 1878 led to further instability in the Balkans, which ultimately became the principal cause of the First World War.

RUSSIA AND THE GREAT REFORMS

Russia's defeat in the Crimean War and its distrust of the Western powers forced the tsar to consider ways of strengthening Russia by restructuring its institutions. Beginning in 1861, a series of measures known collectively as the Great Reforms began to change the face of Russia.

The Abolition of Serfdom   Already by the 1840s concern about the archaic nature and structure of Russian government was mounting. Many officials lamented the tendency of a timid bureaucracy to lie to and mislead the public. Defeat in the Crimean War widened the critique of Russian institutions. The chief problem that needed resolution was serfdom. Educated opinion had long denounced serfdom as immoral, but it also presented clear disadvantages in both the domestic and international domains.

Serfdom held Russia back in its competition with the rest of the world. Defeat in the Crimean War by Britain and France suggested that soldiers with a stake in their society fought harder than men bound to lifetime servitude. In addition, the victorious Western states had won in part because their industrial might translated into more and better guns, ammunition, and transportation. Industrial progress required a mobile labor force, not one tied to the soil by serfdom.

A Critique of Russian Serfdom

The French artist Gustave Doré reveals how landowners inhumanely viewed their serfs as mere property that could be won and lost with a draw of the cards.
(Miriam and Ira D. Wallach Division of Art, Prints and Photographs, The New York Public Library, Astor, Lenox and Tilden Foundations/Art Resource, NY)

With a free labor force, rural populations, as in the West, could become the abundant labor supply that drove industrial production. Many educated Russians felt that the defeat in the Crimea had revealed Russia's general backwardness. To catch up with the West, they argued, Russia needed to shed its timeworn institutions, particularly serfdom.

The new tsar, Alexander II (r. 1855–1881), feared that if serfdom were not abolished from above, it would be overthrown by a serf rebellion that would destroy the aristocracy itself. In April 1861 he issued a decree freeing the serfs. With one stroke of a pen, he emancipated 22 million people from a system that allowed them to be bought and sold, separated from their families, and treated in the cruelest ways imaginable. Emancipation represented a compromise with the gentry, who had reluctantly agreed to liberate its serfs. They nonetheless insisted on compensation. As a result, the newly liberated peasants had to reimburse the government with mortgage payments lasting fifty years. The peasants received some land, but its value was vastly overrated and its quantity insufficient for peasant families. To make ends meet, most freed peasants continued working for their former masters.

The local commune, or **mir** (also the name of the Russian space station first launched in 1986), handled the mortgage payments and taxes that the central government imposed on the peasants. The mir (MEER) determined how the land was to be used, and it paid collectively for the mortgages and taxes on the land. As a consequence, the commune was reluctant for the peasants to leave the land, and they could do so only with its permission. Freed from serfdom, the peasants still suffered many constraints. In fact, the emancipation declaration was accompanied by massive peasant uprisings that had to be put down by force.

Online Study Center **Improve Your Grade**
Primary Source: Post-Emancipation Problems for Russian Peasants

The tsar and his advisers feared the large mass of uneducated peasants as a potential source of anarchy and rebellion. They depended on the mir to preserve control even though the commune system had some inherent economic disadvantages. Since increased productivity benefited the commune as much as the

mir Russian peasant commune. After Tsar Alexander II freed the serfs in 1861, the mir determined land use and paid the government mortgages and taxes.

individual peasant, there was little incentive for peasants to improve their land, and agricultural yields remained low. The mir system of organization also, however, helped promote the collective consciousness that later contributed to peasant revolutionary mentality.

Alexander remained wedded to the principles of autocracy. His aim in abolishing serfdom and introducing other reforms was to modernize and strengthen Russia and stabilize his divinely mandated rule. Like most Russians, Alexander believed that only the firm hand of autocracy could hold together a large, ethnically diverse country. The peasant uprisings that accompanied emancipation only confirmed his beliefs. Clearly, however, the sudden freedom of 22 million illiterate peasants threatened to overwhelm existing institutions, and some changes had to be made. Although he surrendered no powers, Alexander did institute a number of reforms, altering the government and the judicial and military systems so they could deal more effectively with the totally remodeled Russian society.

Government Reform Government reform had paramount importance. Between 1800 and 1850 the Russian population had increased from 36 million to 59 million, and administering this vast country had become more and more difficult. Overcentralized, with a poorly trained civil service, the government was unable to cope effectively with the problems of its people. Emancipation of the serfs greatly exacerbated this situation. To address these problems, an 1864 law created village or regional governments, or *zemstvos* (SEMST-vose), which gave Russians the authority and the opportunity to use initiative in local matters.

The zemstvos were largely controlled by the gentry and not particularly democratic. They were forbidden to debate political issues, and their decisions could be overridden or ignored by local officials appointed by the tsar. Some hoped that zemstvos could become the basis for self-government at the national level and looked for the creation of an all-Russian zemstvo, but the tsar firmly squelched such hopes. He jealously continued to insist and depend on an undivided and undiminished autocracy. Nonetheless, the zemstvos were a viable attempt to modernize an overburdened central government and created an important precedent for self-government.

The tsar also created an independent judiciary that ensured equality before the law, public jury trials, and uniform sentences. Russian political leaders recognized that growth in commerce and industry required public confidence in the judiciary and the rule of law. Businessmen would no longer fear arbitrary intervention by capricious officials and could develop enterprises in greater security.

In addition, censorship of the press was abolished. Under the previous tsar, Nicholas I, all ideas that did not conform to government policy were censored. Such censorship prevented the central government from being well informed about public opinion or about the effects of its policies on the country. Under Alexander openness in the press was viewed as a remedy for corruption and misuse of power.

Reform also extended to the Russian army. Its structure and methods became more Western. Military service, previously limited to peasants, became the obligation of all Russian men, who submitted to a lottery. Those with an "unlucky" number entered the service. In an effort to make military service more attractive, the length of service was drastically cut and corporal punishment was abolished. Access to the officer corps was to be by merit rather than by social connection. The Ministry of War also improved the system of reserves, enabling Russia to mobilize a larger army with more modern weapons in case of war.

The Great Reforms represented considerable change for Russia. They abolished serfdom, created local self-government, established the rule of law, and made army service more humane. But above the change, the tsarist regime remained autocratic and repressive, flexible only to the degree that its rulers had the will and wisdom to be.

SECTION SUMMARY

- Internal tensions and aggressive behavior of the European powers, as well as nationalist aspirations in the Balkan provinces, forced the Austrian, Ottoman, and Russian Empires to reform.

- Loss of the Italian territories and Magyar desire for self-rule in Hungary resulted in the Compromise of 1867, which divided Habsburg territories into the dual monarchy of Austria-Hungary.

- The Ottoman Empire became weakened by nationalist uprisings in its Balkan possessions, making it prey to Western imperialistic ambitions.

- The Congress of Berlin in 1878 reduced Russia's influence in Bulgaria. It also became the occasion for a feeding frenzy on the ailing Ottoman Empire. Territorial shifts such as the transfer of Bosnia and Herzegovina to Austrian administration created conditions for further instability and war in the Balkans.

- Russia undertook a series of reforms beginning in 1861: the abolition of serfdom, establishment of local governments, equality before the law, abolition of press censorship, and improvements in military service.

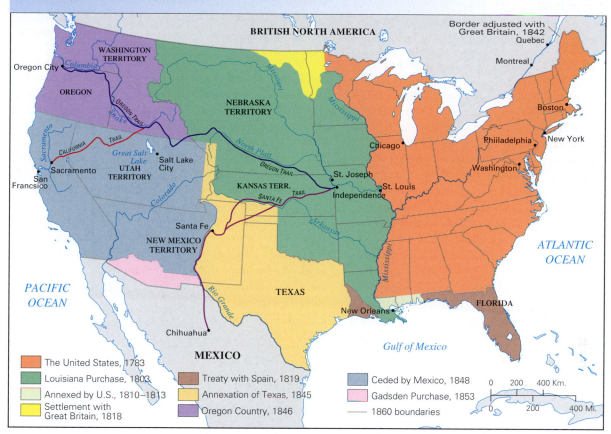

MAP 22.4   U.S. Expansion Through 1853
In just eight years, from 1845 to 1853, the United States increased its territory by a third. The principle of manifest destiny appeared to be fulfilled, as the United States now stretched from the Atlantic to the Pacific.

Legend:
- The United States, 1783
- Louisiana Purchase, 1803
- Annexed by U.S., 1810–1813
- Settlement with Great Britain, 1818
- Treaty with Spain, 1819
- Annexation of Texas, 1845
- Oregon Country, 1846
- Ceded by Mexico, 1848
- Gadsden Purchase, 1853
- 1860 boundaries

THE EMERGENCE OF NEW POLITICAL FORMS IN THE UNITED STATES AND CANADA, 1840–1880

How were the United States and Canada transformed during this period?

Across the sea, a new power emerged in these years, the United States. It enlarged its territories, strengthened its national government, and broadened its democracy by including a large category of people previously excluded from the political process—African Americans. But these achievements were the result of the bloodiest conflict in U.S. history, the Civil War.

TERRITORIAL EXPANSION AND SLAVERY

In the early years of its existence, the United States was confined to the land east of the Mississippi River, but in the nineteenth century it gained much territory through westward expansion (see **MAP 22.4**). In 1803 President Thomas Jefferson secured the Louisiana Pur-

chase from the French, which nearly doubled the size of the United States. In 1819 Florida was acquired from Spain. Some Americans looked even farther west and began to insist that the United States had a **manifest destiny** to occupy the whole North American continent from coast to coast.

The U.S. government used the settlements of American citizens in Mexican- and British-held territories as pretexts for expansion. In 1845 Congress voted to annex Texas, which had gained independence from Mexico in 1836. As a result of negotiation with Britain,

manifest destiny   Coined in 1845 for the belief that the United States was destined to occupy the North American continent from coast to coast. It justified war with Mexico and the U.S. acquisition of California and the Southwest.

the United States in 1846 acquired the Oregon Country south of the forty-ninth parallel. Declaring war on Mexico that same year, and quickly winning, the United States added California and the Southwest in 1848. Manifest destiny or not, the United States now spanned the continent from the Atlantic to the Pacific.

Serious sectional clashes began in the 1820s, especially between the North and the South. Many issues divided the two regions, notably a conflict between the industrial interests of the North and the agrarian interests of the South. The issue of slavery sharpened the divide. As the United States annexed new territories, the question of whether they would be slave or free divided the nation. The North opposed the extension of the "peculiar institution," while much of the South favored it. Southerners believed that if the new areas were closed to slavery, the institution would weaken in the South; slaveholding would eventually disappear, and with it Southern prosperity. They would then be unable to withstand the political and economic pressure of an economically richer and more populous North.

Americans passionately debated the issue of slavery for decades. In November 1860 Illinois Republican Abraham Lincoln (1809–1865) was elected president in a highly contested four-way race. Lincoln opposed the spread of slavery beyond its existing borders and hence appeared to threaten its future in the South. For many Southerners his election to the highest office was the final straw.

Beginning in December 1860, most Southern state legislatures voted to secede from the Union, forming in February 1861 the Confederate States of America. The South defined its cause as defending states' rights, claiming that the people of each state had the right to determine their destiny, free from what they viewed as the tyranny of the national government. The Southern states seized federal funds and property, and in April 1861 the Confederates bombarded federally held Fort Sumter, South Carolina. Lincoln was determined to preserve the Union and to put down the insurrection. The long-dreaded Civil War had begun.

CIVIL WAR AND NATIONAL UNITY, 1861–1865

The North had many advantages. It had nearly three times as many people as the South, a strong industrial base that could supply an endless stream of weapons, and a far more extensive rail system for transporting men and materiel to the front. Although blue and gray armies clashed in a number of important military engagements, the North effectively blockaded the South, leading it, toward the end of the war, to be desperately short of men, money, and supplies.

During the war, Lincoln's government took measures that centralized power in Washington, changing the nation from a loose federation of states to a more centrally governed entity. The federal government intruded into areas of life from which it had before been absent, establishing, for example, national banking and railroad systems. The word *national* came into increasing use.

When the main Confederate army surrendered in 1865, the principle of state sovereignty, proclaimed by the South, was roundly defeated. With the passage of the Thirteenth Amendment to the U.S. Constitution the same year, slaves, previously considered property, were declared to be free. The North occupied the South in an attempt to "reconstruct" it. Reconstruction included efforts to root out the Confederate leadership and ensure full civil and political rights for the newly emancipated African Americans. The government also embarked on a short-lived campaign to provide freed slaves with enough land to ensure them a livelihood—another example of federal authority at work. At the end of Reconstruction, federal power retreated and many states denied African Americans their rights. But certainly the nation was more centralized and its citizens were more enfranchised after the Civil War than before.

THE CREATION OF A CANADIAN NATION

Just north of the United States, in Canada, some similar processes unfolded during the 1800s that also resulted in a larger, freer, and more centralized society. Though Canada was spared a civil war, a popular uprising did occur as citizens chafed under the oligarchical grip of British colonial rule, in which authority was in the hands of a few families. Lord Durham, the new governor, suggested in 1839 a series of reforms (see page 666) that in the end were implemented, uniting Upper and Lower Canada and providing for an elected assembly and a government responsible to it. The British North America Act in 1867 created a federal system of government, with each province exercising considerable autonomy. With the purchase of the Northwest Territories from the private Hudson's Bay Company in 1869 and the gradual attachment of other provinces, Canada gained in size. By 1871 the country stretched from the Maritime Provinces in the east to the Pacific Ocean in the west (see **MAP 22.5**). The building of a transcontinental railroad in the 1880s helped unite the huge nation. By the end of the nineteenth century, Canada was virtually self-governing, having full control over all its affairs, except for defense and foreign affairs.

MAP 22.5   Dominion of Canada, 1873

By 1873 Canada had become a vast nation with the addition of the western territories. Like the United States, Canada reached from the Atlantic to the Pacific.

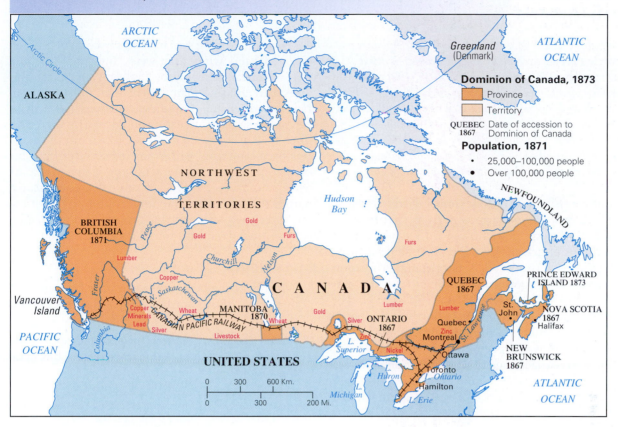

S E C T I O N   S U M M A R Y

- Through war and land purchases, by 1848 the United States spanned the North American continent.

- The United States experienced a civil war between North and South from 1861 to 1865, resulting in the abolition of slavery and an extension of federal powers at the expense of states' rights.

- By 1871 Canada also spanned the continent from east to west. The British North America Act of 1867 created a federal system of government that gave significant autonomy to each province, yet maintained Canada's unity as a nation.

THE DEVELOPMENT OF WESTERN DEMOCRACIES

How did western European states create democracies?

In the generation after 1850 Britain, France, and several smaller states in northern Europe made major strides forward in creating democratic political systems and cultures. Although universal manhood suffrage had been instituted only in France, all these countries' governments were responsible to elected representatives of the voters. Lincoln had spoken of the United States enjoying "government of the people, by the people, for the people." As a result of a series of political reforms, many European countries took up the process of attaining these goals.

VICTORIAN BRITAIN

The mid-nineteenth century was a period of exceptional wealth and security for Britain, as the population as a whole began to share in the economic benefits of industrialization. Britain enjoyed both social and political peace. The political system was not challenged as it had been in the generation after the Napoleonic Wars. A self-assured, even smug, elite—merchants, industrialists, and landowners—developed a political system reflecting liberal values.

A JAPANESE VIEW OF THE BRITISH PARLIAMENT

In 1862 the Japanese government sent its first diplomatic mission to Europe. Accompanying the delegation was a young translator, Fukuzawa Yukichi (1835–1901). Intrigued by what he saw and eager to interest his fellow Japanese in the West, Fukuzawa published several books. In fact, all books about the West in Japan came to be known as "Fukuzawa-bon." Toward the end of his life, in his Autobiography, *he described how, while in London, he had tried to understand the workings of the British Parliament.*

Of political situations at that time, I tried to learn as much as I could from various persons that I met in London . . . though it was often difficult to understand things clearly as I was as yet unfamiliar with the history of Europe. . . . A perplexing institution was representative government. When I asked a gentleman what the "election law" was and what kind of an institution the Parliament really was, he simply replied with a smile, meaning I suppose that no intelligent person was expected to ask such questions. But these were the things most difficult of all for me to understand. In this connection, I learned that there were different political parties—the Liberal and the Conservative—who were always "fighting" against each other in the government.

For some time it was beyond my comprehension to understand what they were "fighting" for, and what was meant, anyway, by "fighting" in peace time. "This man and that man are 'enemies' in the House," they would tell me. But these "enemies" were to be seen at the same table, eating and drinking with each other. I felt as if I could not make much out of this. It took me a long time, with some tedious thinking, before I could gather a general notion of these separate mysterious facts. In some of the more complicated matters, I might achieve an understanding five or ten days after they were explained to me. But all in all, I learned much from this initial tour of Europe.

QUESTIONS

1. Why might the Japanese visitor have been puzzled by the use of the words *fighting* and *enemies* in this context?

2. Would Japanese readers have obtained a good idea of the British parliamentary system based on this report?

Source: The Autobiography of Fukuzawa Yukichi, trans. Eiichi Kiyooka (Tokyo: Hokuseida Press, 1948), pp. 138, 143–144.

Although suffrage was still restricted to propertied Christian men before the 1850s, the parliamentary system was firmly established, with government clearly responsible to the electorate. The importance of Parliament was symbolized by the new building in which it met, finished in 1850 and of unprecedented splendor and size. The form of government developed in its halls after midcentury aroused the curiosity and envy of much of the world. (See the box "The Global Record: A Japanese View of the British Parliament.")

In the twenty years after 1846 five different political parties vied for power. Depending on the issue, parties and factions coalesced to support particular policies. After 1867, however, a clear two-party system emerged: Liberal and Conservative (Tory), both with strong leadership. This development gave the electorate a distinct choice. The Conservatives were committed to preserving traditional institutions and practices, whereas the Liberals were more open to change.

Two strong-minded individuals headed these parties and dominated British political life for over a generation: William E. Gladstone (1809–1898), a Liberal, and Benjamin Disraeli (1804–1881), a Conservative. Gladstone came from a family of industrialists and married into the aristocracy; Disraeli was the son of a Jewish man of letters who had converted to Christianity. His father's conversion made his career possible—before the 1850s Jews were barred from Parliament. Both Gladstone and Disraeli were master debaters; Parliament and the press hung on their every word. Each was capable of making speeches lasting five hours or more and of conducting debates that kept the house in session until 4:00 A.M. The rivalry between the two men thrilled the nation and made politics a popular pastime.

The Conservatives' electoral base came from the landed classes, from Anglicans, and from England, rather than the rest of the United Kingdom (consisting of Scotland, Wales, and Ireland). The Liberals' base came from the middle classes, from Christian groups other than the Church of England, and from Scotland and Wales. In the House of Commons both parties had a large number of members from the landed aristocracy, but cabinet members were increasingly chosen for political competence rather than family background. Aristocratic birth was no longer a requirement for reaching the pinnacle of power, as Gladstone and Disraeli so clearly illustrated.

Disraeli and Gladstone: Victorian Political Rivals

This 1868 cartoon from *Punch* magazine captures the politicians' personalities. Disraeli was known as vain and theatrical, while Gladstone was dour and moralistic.   *(Mary Evans Picture Library)*

The competition for power between the Liberals and the Conservatives led to an extension of suffrage in 1867. The **Second Reform Bill** lowered property qualifications for the vote, thus extending it from 1.4 million to 2.5 million people out of a population of 22 million. The bill also equalized electoral districts, which gave new urban areas better representation. Although some in Parliament feared that these changes would lead to the masses capturing political power—"a leap into the dark," one member called it—in fact no radical change ensued. Extending the vote to clerks, artisans, and other skilled workers made them feel more a part of society and thus bolstered the existing system rather than undermining it. John Stuart Mill, then a member of Parliament, along with his colleague and wife, Harriet Taylor Mill (1807–1856), championed the cause of women's suffrage, but he had few allies in Parliament, and that effort failed.

Second Reform Bill   British legislation that extended suffrage to clerks, artisans, and other skilled workers by lowering property qualifications.

As the extension of voting rights increased the size of the electorate, parties became larger and stronger. Strong party systems meant alternation of power between the Liberals and the Conservatives. With an obvious majority and minority party, the monarch could no longer play favorites in choosing a prime minister. The leader of the majority party had to be asked to form a government. Thus even though Queen Victoria (r. 1837–1901) detested Gladstone, she had to ask him to form governments when the Liberals won parliamentary elections. (See the feature "The Visual Record: An Engraving of the British Royal Family.")

The creation of a broad-based electorate also meant that politicians had to make clear appeals to the public and its interests. In the past, oratory had been limited to the halls of Parliament, but after the electoral reforms, it occurred in the public arena as well. Public election campaigns became part of the political scene in Britain as they increasingly had to appeal to the common man. The adoption of the secret ballot in 1872 protected lower-class voters from intimidation by their employers, landowners, or other social superiors. In 1874 the first two working-class members of Parliament were elected, sitting as Liberals. Although their victory represented a very modest gain for workers' representation, it presaged the increasingly democratic turn England was to take.

FRANCE: FROM EMPIRE TO REPUBLIC

France took a more tumultuous path to parliamentary democracy than Britain. Revolutions and wars overthrew existing political systems and inaugurated new ones. Each time the French seemed to have democracy within reach, the opportunity slipped away.

The constitution of the Second French Republic provided for a single four-year presidential term. Frustrated by this limitation of power, Louis Napoleon engineered a coup d'état in 1851 to extend his presidency to a ten-year term. The following year he called for a plebiscite to confirm him as Napoleon III (r. 1852–1870), emperor of the French. Both of these moves were resisted in the countryside, particularly in the south, but massive repression defeated all opposition.

In the rest of the country huge majorities of voters endorsed first the prolonged presidency and then the imperial title. The new emperor seemed different from his predecessors. He believed in the principle of popular sovereignty (he maintained universal male suffrage, introduced in 1848), he did not pretend to reign by divine right, and he repeatedly tested his right to rule by an appeal to the popular vote. He seemed to combine order and authority with the promises of the Revolution—equality before the law, careers open to talent, and the abolition of hereditary rights.

An Engraving of the British Royal Family

This illustration of the British royal family might have been that of any upper-middle-class family. Queen Victoria is plainly dressed; her husband, Prince Albert, wears a dark business suit; the children are clothed in simple outfits. The simplicity conveyed by the family extends to the image of the rest of England, depicted as a quaint farm with a grouping of common people. Notice the crown hovering over this idyllic pastoral scene.

Illustrations of this type familiarized the British with their monarch. Surrounded by her husband and children, the queen focuses her gaze not on the viewer—a British subject—but on her children. It is her husband, the prince, who, protective of his family, gazes outward. In the past, representations of the monarchy had suggested power and intimidation. The aura of the close-knit, nuclear royal family suggested a serenity that was reassuring to British subjects. It also offered a model for the family and gender very much like those to which middle-class families aspired.

Victoria cultivated the image of herself as contented mother, but in reality she resented much about motherhood. She complained of the extent to which her pregnancies interfered with her daily routines and prevented her from traveling and from being with her beloved Albert. She lamented, "I think our sex a most unenviable one." She described childbearing as an "annoyance" that made her feel "so pinned down—one's wings clipped." She also refused to romanticize birthing, seeing it as an animal-like act that reduced a woman to "a cow or a dog." For the births of her seventh and eighth children, she resorted to the uncommon practice of using chloroform to alleviate the pain of labor—the first public figure to do so openly. Even after their infancy, Victoria continued to describe her children as "an awful plague and anxiety" who showed no gratitude. But such views were expressed privately, and the public never suspected Victoria's ambivalence about motherhood.

Despite her complaints, the highly moral image of Victoria's family life contrasted with that of her predecessors. Her grandfather George III (r. 1760–1820) had been plagued with bouts of insanity. Her uncle George IV (r. 1820–1830) was a notorious philanderer. George IV and his brothers, the duke of Clarence (later to be William IV [r. 1830–1837]) and the duke of Kent (Victoria's father), were bigamists. They fathered a large brood of children out of wedlock and were implicated in numerous public scandals.

Public outrage at the excesses of Victoria's predecessors had produced a call to abolish the institution of monarchy. Given the disrepute into which the monarchy had fallen and the rise of republican sentiment, the crowning of a woman in 1837 may have substantially lessened antimonarchical sentiment. Victoria, as a young, seemingly frail woman coming to the throne at age 18, lent a certain gallantry to the royal household. Moreover, as a female monarch, she was seen as less of a threat to constitutional liberties.

The image of Victoria shown here intentionally contrasts her reign with those of her predecessors. The simple terms in which she and her family are depicted appealed to the growing middle class of the second half of the nineteenth century. The portrayal also fit the emerging democratic spirit—and electoral power—of the lower classes. Henceforth, monarchs would not be able to ignore public opinion. This image marks a historical departure in other ways. Victoria is surrounded by four of her children (eventually she would have nine). Her royal predecessors had died without leaving any legitimate direct heirs, thus endangering the regular succession to the throne. This engraving sent the message that the royal line was assured. British people wary of a female ruler could find solace, not only from her husband's confident gaze outward, but in knowing that Victoria would be succeeded by one of her sons.

Unlike Victoria's uncles and father who were wastrels and bankrupts, the queen and her husband lived frugally by royal standards and conducted an exemplary family life. Royal wealth increased under Prince Albert's careful administration. Instead of being subject to various debtors, the British royal house became one of the wealthiest and most prominent landowners in Great Britain. It is most telling that by the time of her death in 1901, Victoria had considerably strengthened the institution of monarchy, having restored confidence in and respect for it.

Under Victoria's rule, Britain completed the process of becoming a constitutional monarchy.

ILLUSTRATED BOOK OF BRITISH SONG.

THY CHOICEST GIFTS IN STORE. ON HE BE PLEASED TO POUR.

GOD SAVE THE QUEEN.

Illustration from the *Illustrated Book of British Song*

The queen cultivated the image of being above politics and a symbol of national unity. Fellow monarchs in central and eastern Europe exercised greater power, but after World War I they were all toppled. In Britain, monarchy in its constitutional form endured. Victoria established a pattern of public and private behavior by which members of subsequent generations of the British royal family were to be judged. This portrayal of the royal family also suggests the important role that visual imagery played in creating public support for state power in the nineteenth century.

QUESTIONS

1. Why did it make sense for the British royal family to have itself portrayed so simplistically? What values does this engraving communicate to British subjects?

2. How does this engraving exemplify the importance of visual imagery in conveying the meaning of monarchy to British subjects?

Online Study Center
Improve Your Grade Visual Record Activities

705

Most Frenchmen, including urban workers and peasants, generally enjoyed better living standards as a result of economic growth in the 1850s and 1860s. Louis Napoleon, in his youth the author of a book on pauperism, introduced measures congenial to labor. Workers won limited rights to strike, and labor unions were virtually legalized. The emperor expressed his desire to improve the workers' lot, and the government initiated a few concrete measures, such as providing some public housing. Although slum clearance during the rebuilding of Paris drove many from their homes to the outskirts of the city, it did provide healthier conditions for those who stayed behind, and the ambitious urban projects provided work for many (see page 723). Other public works projects, such as ports, roads, railroads, and monumental public buildings, also created jobs. Railroad mileage in France increased tenfold, enabling peasants to market their harvests more widely. If some peasants had initially opposed Louis Napoleon, most supported him once he was in power. Not only were they a cautious group, preferring stable authority, but they saw in the emperor—the heir to the great Napoleon—an incarnation of national glory.

Not all the French supported the emperor; many republicans could not forget that he had usurped the constitution of 1848. In protest, some had gone into exile, including the poet Victor Hugo. In an attempt to win over the opposition, Napoleon made some concessions in 1860, easing censorship and making his government more accountable to the parliament. But instead of winning him new support, liberalization allowed the expression of mounting opposition.

A number of issues—including opposition to policies of free trade, widespread hostility toward the influence of the Catholic Church, and the desire for more extensive freedom of expression and assembly—helped forge a republican alliance of the middle classes and workers. This alliance was strongest in the large cities and in some southern regions notorious for their opposition to central government control. Republicanism was better organized than in earlier years and had a more explicit program. Moreover, its proponents were now better prepared to take over the government, if the opportunity arose.

By 1869 the regime of Napoleon III, which declared itself a "liberal empire," had evolved into a constitutional monarchy, responsible to the parliament. In a plebiscite in May 1870, Frenchmen supported the liberal empire by a vote of five to one. It might have endured had Napoleon III not rashly declared war against Prussia two months later in a huff over the supposedly insulting Ems dispatch (see page 692). Rapid defeat at the hands of Bismarck brought down the empire. In September, at news of the emperor's capture, the republican opposition in the parliament declared a republic. It continued the war but had to sign an armistice in January 1871.

The leader of the new government was an old prime minister of Louis Philippe, Adolphe Thiers (tee-YAIR) (1797–1877). Before signing a definitive peace, the provisional government held elections. The liberals, known as republicans since they favored a republic, were identified with continuing the war; the conservatives, mostly royalists, favored peace. Mainly because of their position on this issue, the royalists won a majority from a country discouraged by defeat.

The new regime had no time to establish itself before a workers' uprising in the spring of 1871 shook France, while reminding the rest of Europe of revolutionary dangers. The uprising was called the **Paris Commune**—a name referring to the municipal government that harked back to 1792 to 1794, when the Paris crowds had dictated to the national government. The Commune insisted on its right to local rule. Radicals and conservatives greeted the Commune as a workers' revolt intended to establish a workers' government. Marx described it as the "bold champion of the emancipation of labor." Women took an active part, fighting on the barricades, pouring scalding water on soldiers, posting revolutionary broadsides. Louise Michel (1830–1905) was a schoolteacher who became famous for her leadership in active fighting and for her agitation for socialism and women's rights.

Online Study Center **Improve Your Grade**
Primary Source: An Eyewitness Account of the Paris Commune

Although labor discontent played a role in the Paris Commune, other forces also contributed, notably the earlier Prussian siege of Paris during the Franco-Prussian War. Paris had become radicalized during the siege: the rich had evacuated the city, leaving a power vacuum quickly filled by the lower classes. Parisians suffered much because of the siege, and angered that their economic needs went unmet and their courage against the Prussians unnoticed, they rose up against the new French government. Food was the paramount issue sparking the massive women's participation in the uprising. The Commune, composed largely of artisans, now governed the city.

In March 1871 the Commune declared itself free to carry out policies independent of the central government, temporarily located in Versailles. Its goals were quite moderate: it sought free universal education, a fairer taxation system, a minimum wage, and disestablishment of the official Catholic Church. But this was too radical for the conservative French government, which sent in the army. It suppressed the Commune,

Paris Commune   Parisian workers' uprising intended to establish a workers' government under home rule. It was violently suppressed by the army of the conservative French government.

massacring 25,000 people, arresting 40,000, and deporting several thousand more.

The crushing of the Paris Commune and some of its sister communes in southern France, which had also asserted local autonomy, signified the increasing power of centralized government. One mark of the emerging modern state was its capacity to squelch popular revolts that, in the past, had constituted serious threats. Western Europe would not again witness a popular uprising of this magnitude.

Despite its brutality, the suppression of the Commune reassured many Frenchmen. The question now at hand was what form the new government would take. The monarchist majority in the democratically elected parliament offered the throne to the Bourbon pretender. However, he insisted he would become king only if the *tricouleur*—the blue, white, and red flag of the Revolution, which long since had become a cherished national symbol—were discarded and replaced by the white flag of the house of Bourbon. This was unacceptable, so France remained a republic. The republic, as Thiers put it, "is the regime which divides us the least."

By 1875 the parliament had approved a set of basic laws that became the constitution of the Third Republic. Ironically, a monarchist parliament had created a liberal, democratic parliamentary regime. A century after the French Revolution, the republican system of government in France was firmly launched.

SCANDINAVIA AND THE LOW COUNTRIES

France and especially Britain served as models of parliamentary democracy for the smaller states in northern Europe. Denmark, Sweden, Norway, Holland, and Belgium recast their political institutions at midcentury. Several of the states were affected by the revolutions of 1848. That year Denmark saw a peaceful protest demanding enlarged political participation (see page 676), Sweden saw minor riots, and the king of the Netherlands (after 1830 Holland and the Netherlands refer to the same country) feared that his country would be affected by revolution as in the neighboring German states. In Copenhagen King Frederick VII (r. 1848–1863), who had no stomach for a confrontation, yielded and accepted a constitution providing for parliamentary government. "Now I can sleep as long as I like," he is reputed to have said.

Sweden's parliamentary system, established in the Middle Ages, had representation by estates—noble, clergy, burgher, and peasant. The 11,000 nobles were given the same weight as the 2.5 million to 3 million peasants. After the riots of 1848 liberal aristocrats recognized that abolition of the estates system would best preserve their privileges, removing the major issue that had provoked popular resentments. With some delays, this conviction was finally carried out in 1866. The estates were replaced by a parliament with two houses. The upper house was restricted to the wealthiest landowners and the lower house to men of property, providing the vote to 20 percent of adult men. Although the king was not constitutionally obligated to choose a government reflecting parliamentary currents, he usually did so in an effort to avoid conflict.

Norway had been joined to Sweden in 1814 under the Swedish king, but it had a separate parliament and made its own laws. Swedish rule rankled the Norwegians, however, and in the 1850s the Norwegian Liberal Party began to insist that the king should not have the final word in governance. Instead, they argued, the parliament, representative of the Norwegian people, should be supreme. In 1883 the principle that government officials are responsible to parliament won out. In 1905 Norway peacefully separated from Sweden and became an independent state.

In the Netherlands, as a result of the revolutions of 1848, the king recognized the need to strengthen support for his crown by acceding to liberals' demands for parliamentary government. By midcentury, government officials in the Netherlands were responsible to the parliament rather than to the king. A new constitution guaranteed the principles of freedom of speech, assembly, and religion.

Belgium had enjoyed a liberal constitution from the time it became an independent state after its revolution in 1830, but because no strong party system materialized, the king was able to appoint to government whomever he pleased. In the 1840s the liberals organized, and the king, reluctantly, had to invite them to govern in 1848. The new government reduced property qualifications for voting, thus increasing the electorate. Contrary to the conservative backlashes that rescinded reform following the revolutions of 1848 elsewhere, the sweeping reforms in northern European states became the basis for their evolution into full democracies. For full democracy to take hold, the electorate had to be broadened. These years witnessed much agitation for universal male suffrage. Property qualifications, wherever they were instituted, were questioned and resisted. For instance, in Sweden the stipulation that a man had to earn 800 crowns a year to be a voter unleashed a pamphlet war: What if a man earned only 799 crowns? Did that make him less qualified? What if a man qualified one year but, through no fault of his own—for instance, because of a natural disaster—did not earn that much the following year? Should he then be barred from voting? In the 1880s Belgium saw a mass movement in favor of universal suffrage. The letters "SU," standing for universal suffrage in French, became emblematic of the masses' hope for a better life. Although suffrage still remained limited in these countries, it was only a matter of time before democracy would be achieved.

SECTION SUMMARY

- By the late 1860s, a two-party system emerged in Britain: Conservative (Tory) and Liberal.

- The Second Reform Bill (1867) in Britain extended the vote and equalized voting districts, giving significantly more representation to urban areas.

- War and revolution continued to shape France's path to democracy. The French Second Republic, born of revolution, gave way to the authoritarian rule of Louis Napoleon, who became Napoleon III in 1852.

- The Franco-Prussian War of 1870–1871 ended the Second Empire of Napoleon III and gave birth to the French Third Republic.

- France and Britain provided both positive and negative models for change in northern Europe. Denmark, Sweden, Norway, the Netherlands, and Belgium peacefully established governments responsible to parliaments rather than to their kings, providing the basis for their evolution toward full democracies.

CHAPTER SUMMARY

Online Study Center **ACE the Test**

How did the Crimean War affect international relations?

How did political leaders in Piedmont harness the forces of nationalism to achieve Italian national unity?

What events led to the unification of Germany and what was the character of the new German nation?

How did the Austrian, Ottoman, and Russian Empires deal with the challenges they faced?

How were the United States and Canada transformed during this period?

How did western European states create democracies?

 iberal nationalists in the early nineteenth century had believed that Europe would be freer and more peaceful if each people had a separate nation, if the power between those nations could be balanced. The Crimean War proved them wrong. The Great Powers became rival states in pursuit of their own self-interests, largely at the expense of the Ottoman Empire. The postwar peace settlement impaired Ottoman efforts to repress nationalist movements in the Balkans.

The Crimean War and its aftermath also created an international climate that permitted the emergence of two newly unified nation-states, Italy and Germany. In the case of Italy, unification occurred through the leadership of Cavour in Piedmont. After waging war against Austria to acquire the northern provinces (with partial success), Cavour brought the revolutionary national movement of the south, led by Garibaldi, under the centralized control of Piedmont. Plebiscites and an elected assembly sanctioned Italian unification.

Germany, through a series of wars, became unified under the authoritarian, centralized control of Prussia. Bismarck annexed the northern German states after defeating Austria. After Prussia's victory in war against France, Bismarck was able to press the southern states into unity with the north. This process lent the German state, even with parliamentary rule, an authoritarian and militaristic character. The rulers of the German states accepted unification by acclamation rather than through consent from the German people.

The Austrian and Ottoman Empires faced the daunting challenges of nationalistic movements seeking to break away from their rule. In the effort to keep their empires intact, rulers offered various reforms from above, modeled on the West; but at the same time they attempted to exert centralized rule to suppress breakaway movements. Austria compromised by establishing a dual monarchy with Hungary. But the empire then turned its aggressive ambitions toward the Balkans in order to exert control over Slavic people. These ambitions further challenged the Ottoman Empire, already weakened by defeat in war against Russia in 1853. The 1856 Congress of Paris and subsequent Balkan wars led to the creation of the independent and sovereign states of Romania and Bulgaria, formerly Ottoman provinces.

Russia, considering itself a protector of Slavic peoples, took advantage of the Ottoman Empire's weakness to wage war against it, further fueling Balkan nationalism and extending its influence there. In the face of its own domestic ills, Russia instituted major reforms on a Western model; nonetheless it remained autocratic, repressive, and inflexible.

Canada and the United States also faced challenges in the effort to govern vast expanses of territory with divergent regional needs under the auspices of representative government. The crisis of the American Civil War restored a federal government, albeit with tightened central control, and at the same time extended political participation. Canada more peacefully achieved a federalized government that permitted provincial autonomy and fostered democracy.

Britain, France, and several northern European states became increasingly democratic, answerable to a growing electorate. Britain successfully and peacefully extended suffrage and maintained its monarchy. In France the crushing of the Paris Commune spelled doom for those who wanted a nation of decentralized self-governing units. Indeed, strong, centralized governments increasingly became the norm. In other states, parliaments had only limited powers; but once they were in place, they gradually gained more power and expanded the electorate. Parliaments gave governments the appearance of legitimacy through the consent of their peoples. Hence all European rulers, except those of the Ottoman and Russian Empires, found it necessary to have a parliament.

LOOKING AHEAD

Two major changes that liberals had agitated for in 1848 had become a reality: freer political institutions and the organization of nation-states. Although neither of these changes was fully implemented everywhere, both appeared to have been generally established. Many Europeans—at least those who embraced these ideals as progress—could easily believe that they were living in an age of optimism.

KEY TERMS

Realpolitik (p. 682)

congress system (p. 682)

risorgimento (p. 686)

trasformismo (p. 689)

Otto von Bismarck (p. 689)

February Patent (p. 693)

Compromise of 1867 (p. 693)

Young Turks (p. 695)

mir (p. 697)

manifest destiny (p. 699)

Second Reform Bill (p. 703)

Paris Commune (p. 706)

Online Study Center
Improve Your Grade Flashcards

SUGGESTED READING

Alter, Peter. *The German Question and Europe: A History.* 2000. Explains the international context within which German unity was possible and its impact on European diplomacy.

Blackbourn, David. *The Long Nineteenth Century: A History of Germany, 1780–1918.* 1998. Particularly strong on the social aspects and consequences of German unification.

Eichner, Carolyn J. *Surmounting the Barricades: Women in the Paris Commune.* 2004. A study of three important revolutionary leaders and the intersection of feminism with social and political events.

Lewis, Bernard. *The Emergence of Modern Turkey.* 2001. The foremost historian on Turkey and the modern Middle East provides an important survey of the Ottoman Empire.

Lincoln, W. Bruce. *Great Reforms.* 1990. Shows the reforms to be part of a general program of modernization.

Matthew, Colin, ed. *The Nineteenth Century: The British Isles, 1815–1901.* 2000. An up-to-date collection of articles on major themes in British history.

NOTES

1. Quoted in Otto Pflanze, *Bismarck and the Development of Germany,* vol. 1 (Princeton, N.J.: Princeton University Press, 1990), p. 184.

2. Quoted in William Flavelle Monypenny and George Earle Buckle, *The Life of Benjamin Disraeli: Earl of Beaconsfield,* vol. 2 (London: John Murray, 1929), pp. 473–474.

23

THE AGE OF OPTIMISM, 1850–1880

Felix Valloton:
Le bon marché
(Private Collection)

The first department store in Paris, which served as a model for others in France and abroad, Le bon marché (the "good buy") opened its doors in the 1850s. The store bought goods in mass quantities and thus could sell them at low prices. Constructed of glass and iron, Le bon marché represented the new, modern age. It combined under one roof a large range of products that previously had been available only in separate specialty shops—a timesaving convenience in an increasingly harried age. The store also had a large catalog sales department for customers too busy or distant to shop in person. Filled with toys, bed linens, furniture, crystal, and other items, the department store was a symbol of the new opulence of the middle classes.

This new type of store would not have been possible in an earlier age. It serves as a summary of the various technological and social changes that the more prosperous regions of the West experienced as industrialization advanced in the second half of the nineteenth century. Industrial innovation had lowered the price of glass and steel, so that these new, huge commercial emporiums could be built at reasonable cost. Railroads brought into the city large quantities of increasingly mass-produced goods, as well as out-of-town customers. In town, trams and omnibuses transported shoppers to the store. The penny press provided advertising for the department store, which in turn supported the emergence of this new medium. The expansion of the postal system facilitated catalog sales and the mailing of parcels to customers. And the higher incomes available to many people allowed them to purchase more than just the necessities. A phenomenon began that would become predominant in the West a century later—the consumer society.

As industrialization spread throughout western Europe, rising productivity brought greater wealth to more social groups and nations. This wealth not only led to more consumer spending; it also changed attitudes. The second half of the nineteenth century was an era shaped to a large extent by the growing middle classes, who were filled with optimism and convinced they were living in an age of progress. John Stuart Mill proclaimed that in his era "the general tendency is and will continue to be . . . one of improvement—a tendency towards a better and happier state." Across the Channel in France, the social thinker Auguste Comte (1798–1857) concurred, confidently stating,

CHAPTER OUTLINE

INDUSTRIAL GROWTH AND ACCELERATION

SOCIAL IMPACTS OF ECONOMIC GROWTH

URBAN PROBLEMS AND SOLUTIONS

SOCIAL AND POLITICAL INITIATIVES

CULTURE IN AN AGE OF OPTIMISM

KEY TERMS

second industrial revolution

bourgeois century

professionalization

Victorian morality

separate spheres

solidarism

social Catholics

positivism

Darwinism

Social Darwinism

impressionist

Online Study Center
This icon will direct you to interactive map and primary source activities on the website **college.hmco.com/ pic/noble5e**

"Human development brings . . . an ever growing amelioration." The successful application of science and technology to social problems gave many men and women confidence in the human ability to improve the world. People controlled their environments to a degree never before possible. On farms they increased the fertility of the soil; to the burgeoning cities they brought greater order. Scientists used new methods to study and combat disease. Public authorities founded schools, trained teachers, and reduced illiteracy. Transportation and communication rapidly improved.

Not all of society benefited from the fruits of progress. The new wealth was far from equally shared. Eastern and southern Europe changed little, and even in the western regions a large part of the population still lived in great misery. If some cities carried out ambitious programs of urban renewal, others continued to neglect slums. Public sanitation programs did not affect the majority of Europeans who lived in rural areas. Despite spectacular advances in science, much of the population maintained a traditional belief in divine intervention. Many intellectuals strongly denounced the materialism and smugness of the age, stressing the meanness and ignorance that lay just beneath the surface.

It was the ascendant middle classes in western Europe who set the tone of the age. Their optimism was all the greater because the ultimate effects of the social and technological changes taking place in Europe were not yet known. Of the major processes that unfolded between 1850 and 1880, many were still in their infancy in 1880. What lay beyond the horizon would certainly be even more wonderful, or so many believed.

FOCUS QUESTIONS

What technological changes led to the expansion of the European economy after the mid-nineteenth century?

How did the economic expansion affect the various social classes, and city versus rural areas, differently?

What problems did urbanization create, and what were the solutions?

How and why did the state increasingly intervene in people's everyday lives?

What new scientific, intellectual, and cultural trends emerged in this period, and what impact did they have on systems of belief?

INDUSTRIAL GROWTH AND ACCELERATION

What technological changes led to the expansion of the European economy after the mid-nineteenth century?

Beginning in the 1850s, western Europe experienced an unprecedented level of economic expansion. Manufacturers created new products and harnessed new sources of energy. An enlarged banking system provided more abundant credit to fund this expansion. Scientific research was systematically employed to improve methods of manufacture. A revolution in transportation speedily delivered goods and services to distant places. Technological innovation profoundly changed the daily lives of many Europeans.

THE "SECOND INDUSTRIAL REVOLUTION"

The interrelated cluster of economic changes that began in the generation after 1850 is often called the **second industrial revolution.** It was characterized by a significant speedup in production and by the introduction of new materials such as mass-produced steel, synthetic dyes, and aluminum. Manufacturers replaced the traditional steam engine with stronger

second industrial revolution Interrelated economic changes after 1850 that included new products, new methods of manufacture, and new materials such as mass-produced steel, synthetic dyes, and aluminum.

steam-powered turbines or with machines powered by new forms of energy—petroleum and electricity.

The invention of new products and methods of manufacture spurred this industrial expansion. The second half of the nineteenth century has often been called the "age of steel." In 1856 Sir Henry Bessemer (1813–1898) discovered a method that produced in twenty minutes the same amount of steel previously produced in twenty-four hours. In the next two decades, further advances in England and France made steel production even more efficient. The results were dramatic. In Great Britain steel production increased fourfold, and by the 1880s, its price fell by 50 percent. Greater steel production made possible the expansion of the rail system, the creation of a steamship fleet, and an explosive growth in the building industry. Steel, once a rare alloy used only for the finest swords and knives, became the material that defined the age.

Significant changes in the supply of credit further stimulated economic expansion. Discovery of gold in California and Australia led to the inflow of huge amounts of the precious metal to Europe, expanding the supply of money and credit. This led to the establishment of the modern banking system.

Each advance made possible additional changes. Increased wealth and credit accelerated further expansion of industrial plants and the financing of an ambitious infrastructure of roads, railroads, and steamships, which in turn boosted trade. Between 1850 and 1870 the value of world trade increased by 260 percent.

By the 1880s important scientific discoveries fueled industrial improvements. Electricity began to be more widely used, replacing coal as a source of energy. Synthetic dyes revolutionized the textile industry, as did alkali in the manufacture of soap and glass. Dynamite, invented by the Swedish chemist Alfred Nobel (no-BELL) (1833–1896) in the 1860s, made it possible to level hills and blast tunnels through mountains, facilitating construction. Nobel's will established a prestigious prize in his name to honor significant contributions to science and peace.

TRANSPORTATION AND COMMUNICATION

The rail system grew dramatically in the middle decades of the nineteenth century. By 1880 total European railroad mileage reached 102,000 (see **MAP 23.1**). In 1888 the Orient Express line opened, linking Constantinople to Vienna and thus to the rest of Europe. Speed also conquered distance. By midcentury trains ran 50 miles per hour, ten times as fast as when they were invented. The cost of rail transport steadily decreased, allowing for its greater use. Between 1850 and 1880 in Germany, the number of rail passengers increased tenfold and the volume of goods eightyfold. In France and Great Britain the increases were nearly as impressive.

CHRONOLOGY

1813	Gas streetlamps in London
1820s	Omnibuses introduced in France
1830	Lyell founds the principles of modern geology
1831	Faraday discovers electromagnetic induction
1833	Telegraph invented
1840	Penny stamp introduced
1848	England adopts first national health legislation
1850s	Age of clipper ships
	Trams added to public transportation systems
1851	Crystal Palace
1852–1870	Rebuilding of Paris
1859	Darwin, *On the Origin of Species*
1863	Europe's first underground railroad, in London
1864	Pope Pius IX issues *Syllabus of Errors*
1865	Transoceanic telegraph cable installed
	Lister initiates antiseptic surgery
	University of Zurich admits women
1869	Opening of Suez Canal
	Mendeleev produces periodic table of elements
1874	Impressionist exhibition
1875	Bell invents telephone
	Electric lights in Paris
1881	Pasteur proposes germ theory of disease
1891	Pope Leo XIII issues *Rerum novarum*

Ocean transportation was also revolutionized. In 1869 the French built the Suez Canal across Egyptian territory, linking the Mediterranean to the Red Sea and the Indian Ocean. The canal reduced by 40 percent the thirty-five-day journey between London and Bombay. More efficient carriers—such as the clipper ship and the steamship—were developed. By 1880 European shipping carried nearly three times the cargo it had thirty years earlier.

The optimism born of conquering vast distances was reflected in a popular novel by the French writer Jules Verne (DJOOL VAIRN) (1828–1905), *Around the*

The Suez Canal

Opened in 1869, the canal cut through one hundred miles of Egyptian desert to enable passage between the Mediterranean and the Red Seas. It reduced by half the voyage from Europe to India and the rest of Asia, and particularly benefited Britain. The Suez Canal exemplified the speeding up of transportation and communication in the second half of the nineteenth century.   *(akg-images)*

World in Eighty Days (1873). The hero, Phineas Fogg, travels by balloon, llama, and ostrich, as well as by the modern steam locomotive and steamship, to accomplish in eighty days a feat that, only thirty years earlier, would have taken at least eleven months. In 1889 the New York newspaper the *World,* in a publicity gambit to increase readership, sent its reporter Nellie Bly (1867–1922) on an around-the-world trip to see if she could beat Phineas Fogg's record. Readers breathlessly kept up with reports of her progress. She circled the globe in 72 days, 6 hours, 11 minutes, and 14 seconds. Such was the impact of the steamship, the locomotive, the Suez Canal—and the newspaper.

Along with the new speed, advances in refrigeration changed food transport. Formerly, refrigeration could be achieved only with natural ice, cut from frozen ponds and lakes, but this changed in the 1870s with the introduction of mechanical ice-making machines. By the 1880s dairy products and meat were being transported vast distances by rail and even across the seas by ship. Thanks to these advances, the surplus food of the Americas and Australia, rich in grasslands, could offer Europe a cheaper and far more varied diet.

Regular postal service was also a child of the new era of improved transportation. In 1840 Britain instituted a postage system based on standard rates. Replacing the earlier practice in which the recipient paid for the delivery of a letter, the British system enabled the sender to buy a stamp—priced at just one penny—and drop the letter into a mailbox. It was collected, transported speedily by the new railroads, and delivered. The efficiency and low cost of mail led to a huge increase in use.

The reformed postal service and transoceanic telegraphs revolutionized the exchange of information. The telegraph was invented in the early 1830s, and by the 1860s, telegraph wire had been laid on both the European and North American continents; the two continents were then connected via the transatlantic cable. By the 1870s, telegraph lines extended 650,000 miles, connecting twenty thousand towns and villages around the world.

MAP 23.1   **European Rails, 1850 and 1880**
During the mid-nineteenth century, European states built railroads at an increasing
rate, creating a dense network by the 1880s.   *(Adapted from Norman J. G. Pounds,* An Historical
Geography of Europe, 1800–1914 *[New York: Cambridge University Press, 1985]. Used by permission of the publisher.)*

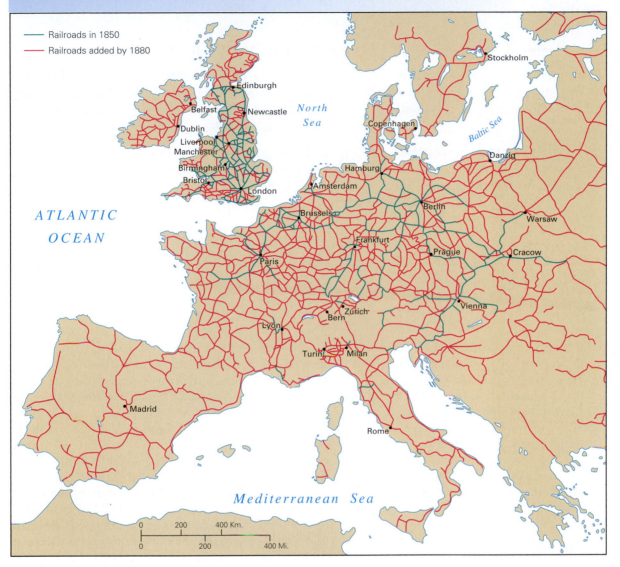

Online Study Center   **Improve Your Grade**   Interactive Map: European Rails, 1850–1880

The telegraph had many uses. Newspapers prided themselves on being "wired" and so able to give their readers the latest news. Governments found the telegraph useful in collecting information and issuing orders to subordinates, better assuring imperial authority over distant territories. In the 1840s it took ten weeks for a message and a reply to go from London to Bombay and back. Thirty years later the exchange took four minutes.

The telegraph was also a tool of warfare. The first conflict in which it played a crucial role was the Crimean War. The British and French high commands in London and Paris were able to communicate with their officers in the Crimea, directing operations from afar. It was also the first war whose unfolding events could be communicated immediately through the telegraph to newspapers at home. Charles Dickens described the telegraph as "of all our modern wonders the most wonderful." Even more than improved transportation, it transformed the world into an instant, global village. As the governor of New York said at a commemorative event, "Men speak to one another now, though separated by the width of the earth, with light-ning's speed and as if standing face to face."

To the telegraph was added another instant form of communication. In 1875 the American Alexander Graham Bell (1847–1922) invented a machine capable of transmitting the human voice by electrical impulses;

in 1879 the first telephones were installed in Germany; two years later they appeared in France. At first a cu-riosity, used to listen to a musical or theatrical pro-duction at a distance, the phone entered the homes of the elite and became a new form of interpersonal communication.

S E C T I O N   S U M M A R Y

- After 1850, steam-powered turbines and new sources of energy, such as petroleum and electricity, increased the pace and quantity of industrial production.

- New methods of steel production made possible the expansion of railroads, the construction of steam-ships, and explosive growth in the building industry.

- Built by the French in 1869, the Suez Canal helped revolutionize ocean transportation by cutting travel time to India and other parts of Asia nearly in half, while ships as well became more efficient.

- The telegraph, telephone, and standardized mail systems sped up communications and collapsed global distances of time and space.

SOCIAL IMPACTS OF ECONOMIC GROWTH

How did the economic expansion affect the various social classes, and city versus rural areas, differently?

Industrial advances transformed the traditional structure of European society. Fewer people worked the land; more worked in manufacturing and services. The social and political influence of the aris-tocracy waned as wealth became far less dependent on landed property ownership. To varying degrees, this in-fluence now had to be shared with the growing middle classes. Generally, life for both industrial and farm workers improved in this period. However, great dis-parities persisted, and many people continued to suffer from profound deprivation.

THE DECLINING ARISTOCRACY

Always a small, exclusive group, the European aristoc-racy in the nineteenth century represented less than 1 percent of the population. Many of noble birth were quite poor and economically indistinguishable from their non-noble neighbors. Others owned vast estates and were fabulously wealthy.

Distinctions between aristocrats and members of the upper middle class became increasingly blurred. Noble families in financial straits often married their children to the offspring of wealthy merchants. And many nobles who previously had shunned manufac-ture participated in the new economy by becoming in-dustrialists and bankers. Idle members of the nobility were now somewhat rare. Although many aristocrats still enjoyed a lavish lifestyle, others had adopted the habits of successful business people.

The power of the aristocracy had surprisingly per-sisted through much of the nineteenth century despite the theories of egalitarianism sweeping Europe in the aftermath of the French Revolution and the rapidly changing social structure engendered by industrializa-tion. In Prussia some of the wealthiest industrialists came from the highest aristocracy. The heavily aristo-cratic officer corps played an important role in running the Prussian state and unified Germany. In France about 20 to 25 percent of officers and many diplomats were aristocrats. In Britain officers, diplomats, and high-ranking civil servants were usually of noble birth. In Austria and Russia, aristocratic origin was the norm for government service.

Nonetheless, nobles no longer asserted privileges based exclusively on birth. In most European states, such claims had become anachronisms.

THE EXPANDING MIDDLE CLASSES

Up to the eighteenth century, society had been di-vided into legally separate orders on the basis of birth. In the nineteenth century, it became more customary to classify people by their economic functions. The "middle class" belonged neither to the nobility nor to the peasantry nor to the industrial working class. It included such people as wealthy manufacturers, country physicians, and bank tellers. Given this di-versity, it has become common to use the plural and think of all these people as forming the "middle classes." Another term frequently used to describe these people is *bourgeois*.

The nineteenth century has often been described as the **bourgeois century,** because, especially in western Europe, the middle classes expanded dramatically and had an enormous social and cultural influence. More trade and manufacture meant more entrepreneurs and managers, while the increasingly complex society called for more engineers, lawyers, accountants, and bankers. New standards of comfort and health demanded more merchants and doctors. Urban improvements in the generation after 1850 created a need for architects and contractors, among other professionals.

The middle and lower levels of middle-class society grew most rapidly. In the 1870s about 10 percent of urban working-class people reached lower-middle-class status by becoming storekeepers, lower civil servants, clerks, or salespeople. Faster growth occurred for white-collar workers than for their blue-collar counterparts. As industries matured, the increasing use of machinery and better industrial organization created a greater need for clerks and bureaucrats rather than laborers. Large import-export businesses, insurance companies, and department stores provided opportunities of this kind. So did the expansion of government services.

The social impact of job growth was great. The men and women staffing these new positions often came from modest backgrounds. For the son or daughter of peasants to become village postmaster, schoolteacher, or clerk in a major firm signified social ascension, however modest. Accessibility to its ranks was certainly one of the strengths of the bourgeoisie, an ever growing group whose promise of social respectability and material comfort exercised a compelling force of attraction over the lower classes.

A widening subgroup of the middle classes consisted of members of the professions, those whose prestige rested on the claim of exclusive expertise in a particular field. In the early nineteenth century, requirements for exercising a profession, though they varied by country, became more stringent. Medical doctors, for instance, began requiring specialized education to distinguish themselves from herbalists, midwives, bonesetters, healers, and other competitors, and they insisted on their exclusive right to exercise their profession. Doctors controlled access to their ranks by establishing powerful professional associations.

Similarly other professions such as law, architecture, and engineering encouraged **professionalization**

Interior of a Danish Middle-Class Home
With its stuffed furniture, lace curtains and table-cloths, and gilt-edged framed paintings, this meticulously decorated living room contrasted sharply with the grimy exterior of the industrial city from which it provided a sheltered escape. *(National Museum of Denmark)*

through the adoption of common requirements and standards of expertise. By midcentury either professional associations or the state itself accredited members of the professions. Women had limited access to these professions; typically their opportunities were confined to lower teaching positions. After the Crimean War, as a result of Florence Nightingale's efforts (see page 683), nursing became an increasingly popular profession for women. Even so, the dominant culture generally opposed middle-class women's salaried employment outside the home.

The growing role of the state in society led to bureaucratic expansion. Civil servants were increasingly subjected to educational requirements and had to pass civil service exams, sharply reducing the role that patronage played in the assignment of government positions.

bourgeois century Characterization of the nineteenth century. Having expanded dramatically with industrialization, the bourgeoisie helped shape western European society.

professionalization Standardization of requirements and regulation of expertise, especially in medicine, law, architecture, and engineering.

MIDDLE-CLASS LIFESTYLES

The standard of living among the middle classes varied considerably, ranging from the wealthy entrepreneur who bought a château, or built one, to the low-level clerk who dwelled in a modest apartment. All lived in new standards of comfort. Their homes increasingly had running water, upholstered furniture, and enough space to provide separate sleeping and living quarters. They owned several changes of clothing and consumed a varied diet that included meat and dairy products, sugar, coffee, and tea. They read books and subscribed to newspapers and journals. Having at least one servant was a requisite for anyone who wished to be counted among the middle classes in the mid-nineteenth century.

By 1900 servants were still common among bourgeois households, but their number was declining in proportion to the population as a whole. As service industries developed, the need for servants decreased.

With the growth of cab services, for instance, a family could dispense with a coachman and groom. Toward the end of the century, domestics' wages rose as competing forms of employment vied for their service, and households below the upper layers of the bourgeoisie found it difficult to afford domestic help.

The need to escape the relentless stimulation of crowded cities gave rise to resort towns throughout Europe, devoted principally to the amusement of the well-off. Water cures—bathing in hot springs and drinking the mineral waters thought to have special attributes—became fashionable, as did gambling in resorts such as Baden-Baden in Germany and Vichy in France. For the first time, tourism became big business. Thomas Cook (1808–1892), an Englishman, organized tours to the Crystal Palace exhibition of 1851 in London, the largest world exposition, which highlighted industrial accomplishments. Discovering the large market for guided travel, Cook began running tours in England and on the Continent. Middle-class wealth and leisure time led

The Crystal Palace

Built in 1851, this building was the largest glass and steel structure of its time. Site of the first great international exposition, the Crystal Palace displayed the inventiveness and opulence of the age.   *(Courtesy of the Trustees of the British Museum)*

to the construction of more hotels, restaurants, and cafés.

The middle classes shared certain attitudes about the conduct of their lives. They believed their successes were due not to birth but to talent and effort. They wanted to be judged by their merits, and they expected their members to abide by strict moral principles. Their lives were supposed to be disciplined, especially with regard to sex and drink. The age was called "Victorian" because the middle classes in Britain saw in the queen who reigned for two-thirds of the century a reflection of their own values. (See the feature "The Visual Record: An Engraving of the British Royal Family" on pages 704–705 in Chapter 22.) **Victorian morality,** widely preached but not always practiced, was often viewed as hypocritical by social critics. Yet as the middle classes came to dominate society, their values became the social norms. Public drunkenness was discouraged, and anti-alcohol movements vigorously campaigned against drinking. Public festivals were regulated, making them more respectable and less rowdy.

In spite of their differences in education, wealth, and social standing, most of the bourgeoisie resembled one another in dress, habits of speech, and deportment. Bourgeois men dressed somberly, in dark colors, avoiding any outward signs of luxury. Their clothing fit closely and lacked decoration—a symbolic adjustment to the machine age, in which elaborate dress hampered activity. It also reflected a conscious attempt to emphasize achievement-oriented attitudes, and new standards for what constituted honorable manhood. Through dress and other fashionable tastes, middle classes distinguished themselves from what they viewed as a decadent and effeminate nobility.

Bourgeois conventions regarding women's dress were the opposite of men's, further reinforcing gender distinctions—women's dress became the material symbol of male success. Extravagant amounts of colorful fabrics used to fashion huge, beribboned hoop dresses reflected the newfound wealth of the middle classes and confirmed their view of women as ornaments whose lives were to be limited to the home and made easier by servants. The language and paraphernalia of idealized domesticity dominated this era. While the man was out in the secular world earning a living and advancing his career, the bourgeois woman was supposed to provide her family with an orderly, comfortable shelter from the storms of daily life. In 1861, London housewife Isabella Mary Mayson Beeton published *Mrs. Beeton's Book of Household Management,* which provided British middle-class women with advice on running their households. This book reflected middle-class values in fostering discipline, frugality, and cleanliness. The ideal woman decorated the rooms, changed the curtains with the seasons and styles, supervised the servants, kept the accounts, oversaw the children's homework and religious education, and involved herself in charitable works. In Britain this book was outsold only by the Bible. In the decades around mid-century, the notion of two **separate spheres**—one male and public, the other female and private—reached its height.

In spite of the relatively passive role assigned to bourgeois women, many were very active. Some helped their husbands or fathers in the office, the business, or the writing of scientific treatises. Others achieved success on their own terms, running their own businesses, writing, painting, or teaching. Though advice books prescribed a world of separate spheres, in practice the boundaries between them were not always rigid.

The expectation that middle-class women would be married and taken care of by their husbands led to the provision of inferior education for girls and young women, which sharply limited their options. Even bright and intellectually curious young girls most often could not receive as good an education as their brothers, nor as a consequence could they pursue as interesting a career.

Some liberals insisted that sexual difference should not constitute the basis for denying equal rights to women. Proponents of women's rights demanded equal access to education and the professions. Slowly, secondary and university education was made available to young women. On the European continent the University of Zurich was the first university to admit women, in 1865. Although British universities admitted women, they did not initially grant them degrees. Oxford and Cambridge did not grant degrees to women until after World War I. In spite of discriminatory laws, harassment by male students, and initial obstruction by professional and accrediting groups, a few female doctors and lawyers practiced in England by the 1870s and on the Continent in the following decades.

Women more easily penetrated the lower levels of middle-class occupations. Expanding school systems, civil services, and businesses provided new employment opportunities for them. By the 1890s two-thirds of primary school teachers in England and half the post office staff in France were women. By 1914 nearly half a million women worked as shop assistants in England. Some new technologies created jobs that became heavily feminized, such as the positions of typist and telephone operator.

Victorian morality   Nineteenth-century ethos wherein the strict moral principles of the dominant middle class became the social norm. The middle classes saw in Queen Victoria a reflection of their own values.

separate spheres   Notion of two distinct sets of roles—one male and public, the other female and private. While the man was out in the world advancing his career, the bourgeois woman was to run her home.

THE WORKERS' LOT

The increased prosperity and greater productivity of the period gradually improved the conditions of both female and male workers in the generation after 1850. Their wages and standards of living rose, and they enjoyed more job security. In Britain the earning power of the average worker rose by one-third between 1850 and 1875. For the first time, workers were able to put money aside to tide them over in hard times.

Legislation gradually reduced the length of the workweek. The British workweek, typically 73 hours in the 1840s, was reduced to 56 hours in 1874. In France it was reduced to 10 hours a day, in Germany to 11. But these improvements were accompanied by an increased emphasis on efficiency in the workplace. Fewer informal breaks were allowed as industrialists insisted on greater worker productivity. New machines increased the tempo of work, frequently leading to exhaustion and accidents.

As workers had more time and money, they had greater access to leisure activities that previously had been limited to the upper classes. Expanded rail connections enabled workers to visit resort towns. New music and dance halls, popular theaters, and other forms of public entertainment sprang up to claim workers' increased spending money.

Although most workers believed that their lot had improved, they were also aware that a vast gulf remained between them and the middle and upper classes. In the 1880s in the northern French industrial city of Lille, the combined property of twenty thousand workers equaled the estate of one average industrialist. Life expectancies still varied dramatically according to income. In Bordeaux in 1853, the life expectancy of a male bourgeois was twenty years greater than that of a male laborer.

The disparity between rich and poor was especially striking in the case of domestics, one of the most common sources of employment for women. Servants led tiring and restricted lives under the close supervision of their employers. Their hours were overly long, as they often worked six and a half days a week. Housed in either the basement or the attic, servants experienced extremes of cold, heat, and humidity. Sometimes they were subjected to physical or sexual abuse by the master of the house, his sons, or the head of the domestic staff. And yet, for impoverished rural women with little chance of finding better work, domestic service was a risky but often necessary option. It provided free housing, food, and clothing and sometimes allowed a servant to save an annual sum that might reach one-third to one-half of a worker's yearly wages. These savings often served as a dowry and could enable a young woman to marry advantageously.

Although a few members of the working class managed to enter the lower levels of the middle classes, most remained mired in the same occupations as their grandparents. Poverty was still pervasive. In the 1880s about one-third of Londoners were living at or below the subsistence level. Workers more commonly suffered from industrial and urban diseases, such as tuberculosis. Compared with the healthier, better-fed, and better-housed middle classes, the workers continued living in shabby and crowded conditions.

THE TRANSFORMATION OF THE COUNTRYSIDE

Before the nineteenth century, the countryside had hardly changed, but beginning at midcentury it transformed radically. Especially in western Europe, an increasing number of people left the land. In 1850, 20 percent of the British people worked in agriculture; by 1881 they constituted only 11 percent of the population. The decrease in the number of agricultural work-ers led in many places to labor shortages and therefore higher wages for farm hands.

The food supply grew significantly as agricultural methods became more efficient. Not only was more land cultivated, but the yield per acre increased. In 1760 an agricultural worker in England could feed himself and one other person; by 1841 he could feed himself and 2.7 others. The population of Europe nearly doubled between 1800 and 1880, and yet it was better nourished than ever before.

Higher yields were the result of an increased use of manure, augmented in the 1870s by saltpeter imported from Chile and, beginning in the 1880s, by chemical fertilizers manufactured in Europe. Innovations in tools also improved productivity. The sickle, which required the laborer to crouch to cut grass or wheat, was replaced by the long-handled scythe, which allowed the field hand to stand and use the full weight of the body to swing the instrument through the grain. This new method increased efficiency fourfold. In the 1850s steam-driven threshing machinery was introduced in some parts of western Europe. Organizational techniques borrowed from industrial labor, including specialization and regular schedules, also contributed to greater productivity on the land.

Steam-Powered Thresher
This image shows the thresher being operated in the French countryside in 1860. Its loud noise and relentlessly rhythmic speed changed the pace and sensibility of rural labor, and sometimes prolonged the hours demanded of workers. It would be decades before this kind of technology became a common sight in Europe, but it was a harbinger of the change coming to the rural world.   *(Bibliothèque nationale de France)*

Economic growth and new and expanded technologies began to break through the insularity of rural life. Improved roads and dramatically expanded rail lines enabled farmers to extend their markets nationally and internationally. They also brought teachers into the villages, making school systems national. Local dialects, and in some cases even distinct languages that peasants had spoken for generations, were replaced by a standardized national language. Local provincial costumes became less common as styles fashionable in the cities spread to the countryside via mail order catalogs. The farm girls who went to the cities to work as domestic servants returned to their villages with urban and middle-class ideals. The military draft brought the young men of the village into contact with urban folk and further spread urban values to the countryside.

Many rural regions, however, suffered from modernization. The growth of urban manufacturing caused rural cottage industry to decline, depriving agricultural

workers of the supplementary income on which they previously relied during slack seasons. In many cases railroads bringing goods made elsewhere wiped out some of the local markets on which cottage industries had depended. The steamship brought freight such as grain from distant Canada and Argentina, which often undersold wheat grown in Europe. The resultant crisis caused millions to emigrate; they left the land for towns and cities or even migrated across the seas to the Americas and Australia (see page 747).

These trends had a striking effect in the rural areas of western Europe. Eastern Europe, in contrast, was hardly touched by them. In Russia agriculture remained backward; the average yield per acre in 1880 was one-quarter that in Great Britain. The land sheltered a large surplus population that was underemployed and contributed little to the rural economy. In the Balkans, most peasants were landless and heavily indebted.

SECTION SUMMARY

- As landed wealth declined in economic importance during the second half of the nineteenth century, so too did the power and influence of the old aristocracy.

- New technologies of the second industrial revolution and the expansion of commerce, government bureaucracy, and the professions dramatically increased the size and influence of the middle classes.

- The middle class (bourgeoisie) helped instill the notion of separate spheres for men and women, but many women defied their prescribed role and sought

the right to higher education and entry into the professions.

- Standards of living rose among workers who generally had better diets and more leisure time; stark class disparities of wealth and living conditions nonetheless persisted.

- New agricultural methods and technologies greatly increased agricultural production. But modernization also created competition for agricultural and cottage industry products, forcing migration from the countryside.

URBAN PROBLEMS AND SOLUTIONS

What problems did urbanization create, and what were the solutions?

Epidemics, crowding, crime, and traffic jams were among the many problems that accompanied explosive urban growth in the nineteenth century. In the second half of the century, city governments more aggressively tackled these problems by developing public health measures and urban planning. They provided amenities such as streetlights, public transportation, and water and sewer systems, and they established large, more efficient police forces. Cities gradually became safer and more pleasant places to live, although for a long time city dwellers continued to suffer high mortality rates.

CITY PLANNING AND URBAN RENOVATION

Most of Europe's cities, originating in the Middle Ages as walled enclaves, had grown haphazardly into major industrial centers. Their narrow, crooked streets could not accommodate the increased trade and daily movement of goods and people, and traffic snarls were common. City officials began to recognize that broad, straight avenues would help relieve the congestion and also bring sunlight and fresh air into the narrow and

Pissarro: L'avenue de l'Opéra, Sunlight, Winter Morning
Camille Pissarro, one of the leading impressionists, portrayed the broad new Parisian avenue designed by Baron Haussmann. The avenue leads to the new opera in the background, also planned during the Second Empire. Note the active pedestrian as well as equestrian traffic.   *(Musée Saint-Denis, Reims/Giraudon/Art Resource, NY)*

perpetually dank lanes and alleys. (See the feature "The Visual Record: The Modern City and Photography" on pages 734–735.)

The most extensive program of urban rebuilding took place in midcentury Paris. Over a period of eighteen years Napoleon III and his aide Baron Georges Haussmann (1809–1891) transformed Paris from a dirty medieval city to a beautiful modern one (see **MAP 23.2**). Haussmann and his engineers carved broad, straight avenues through what had been overcrowded areas. They built visually elegant, if uniform, apartment houses on the new tree-lined avenues. Public monu-

ments and buildings, such as the new opera house, enhanced the city. The urban renewal program drove tens of thousands of the poorest Parisians to the outskirts of the city, leading to greater social segregation than had previously existed.

Haussmann's extensive work in Paris served as a model for other cities, and although none was rebuilt as extensively, many underwent significant improvements. The cities of Europe began to display an expansive grace and sense of order, supporting the belief of the middle classes that theirs was an age of progress.

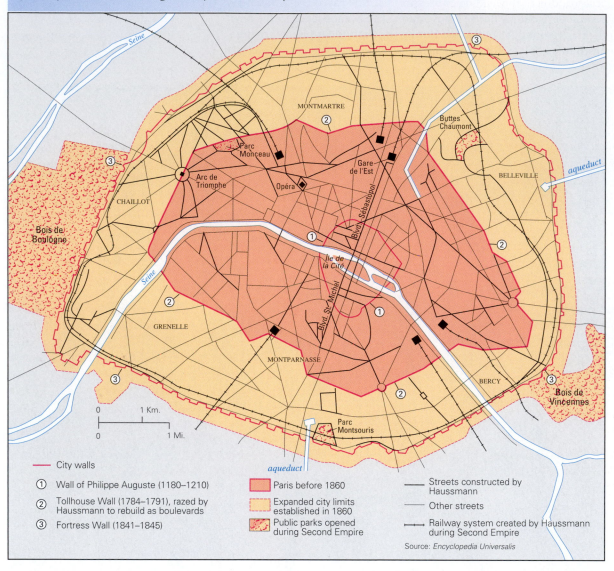

MAP 23.2 Haussmann's Paris, 1850–1870

During the reign of Napoleon III, Baron Georges Haussmann reshaped the city of Paris, replacing its narrow medieval streets with a system of broad avenues and public parks and encircling the city with a railway.

Map labels: Seine, MONTMARTRE, Buttes Chaumont, Parc Monceau, Gare de l'Est, BELLEVILLE, aqueduct, Arc de Triomphe, Opéra, CHAILLOT, Blvd. Sébastopol, Bois de Boulogne, Ile de la Cité, Blvd. St. Michel, Seine, GRENELLE, MONTPARNASSE, BERCY, Bois de Vincennes, Parc Montsouris, aqueduct

Scale: 0 — 1 Km., 0 — 1 Mi.

Legend:
- ——— City walls
- ① Wall of Philippe Auguste (1180–1210)
- ② Tollhouse Wall (1784–1791), razed by Haussmann to rebuild as boulevards
- ③ Fortress Wall (1841–1845)
- Paris before 1860
- Expanded city limits established in 1860
- Public parks opened during Second Empire
- ——— Streets constructed by Haussmann
- ——— Other streets
- +—+—+ Railway system created by Haussmann during Second Empire

Source: *Encyclopedia Universalis*

THE INTRODUCTION OF PUBLIC SERVICES

Beginning at midcentury, government at the central and local levels helped make cities more livable by legislating sanitary reforms and providing public transportation and lighting. Medical practitioners in the 1820s had observed that disease and higher mortality were related to dirt and lack of clean air, water, and sunshine. Since diseases spreading from the poorer quarters of town threatened the rich and powerful, there was a general interest in improving public health by clearing slums, broadening streets, and supplying clean air and water to the cities.

Reform began in England with the Public Health Bill of 1848. This legislation established national standards for urban sanitation and required cities to regulate the installation of sewers and the disposal of refuse.

The 1875 Health Act mandated certain basic health standards for water and drainage. Armed with these laws, cities and towns took the initiative: Birmingham cleared 50 acres of slums in the 1870s, for example.

London was also a leader in supplying public water, a service later adopted by Paris and many other cities. Berlin had a municipal water system in 1850, but it would be several decades before clean water was available in every household. In Paris, which typically led France in innovations, 60 percent of the houses had running water in 1882. The French capital did not have a unitary sewer system until the 1890s, however. As running water in the home became a standard rather than a luxury, bathing became more common. The English upper classes had learned the habit of frequent bathing from their colonial experience in India; on the

Continent it did not become the custom until about the third quarter of the nineteenth century.

All these changes had a direct impact on the lives of city dwellers. Between the 1840s and 1880, London's death rate fell from 26 per thousand to 20 per thousand. During the same period, the rate in Paris declined from 29.3 per thousand to 23.7 per thousand. The incidence of diseases associated with filthy living conditions also fell; improved water supplies sharply reduced the prevalence of waterborne diseases such as cholera and typhoid.

Other improvements also contributed to a better quality of life. With the introduction of urban transportation, city dwellers no longer had to live within walking distance of their workplaces. An early example of public transportation was the French omnibus service of the 1820s—a system of horse-drawn carriages available to the public on fixed routes. In the 1850s the tram was introduced. A carriage drawn on a rail line by horses, a tram could pull larger loads of passengers faster than the omnibus. Because of the many rail stations in London and the difficulty of getting from one station to another in time to make a connection, London built an underground railway in 1863, the predecessor of the subway system. Techno-

logical improvements made the bicycle a serious means of transportation. By the mid-1880s nearly 100,000 bicycles were being pedaled around Great Britain; by 1900 France had 1 million bicycles.

Improvements in public transportation and urban renewal projects led workers to move out of the inner city and into the less dense and less expensive suburbs. This trend in turn led to a decrease in urban population density and eventually helped make the city a healthier place to live.

Gaslights also improved city life, making it easier and safer to be outside at night. (Prior to gaslights, city dwellers depended mainly on moonlight or, rarely, expensive and time-consuming oil lamps—which had to be lit one at a time.) In 1813 London was the first city to be illuminated by gas; Berlin followed in 1816. Electrical lights were introduced in Paris in 1875, although they were not common until the end of the century.

Cities also significantly expanded police forces to impose order, control criminal activity, and discourage behavior deemed undesirable, such as dumping garbage on the street, relieving oneself in public, and carousing late at night. In 1850 London was the best-policed city in Europe, with a 5,000-man force. Paris had around 3,000 police officers.

SECTION SUMMARY

- Rapid population growth occurred in cities that had originally been constructed in haphazard fashion; to cope with the problems of growth, city officials began programs of urban rebuilding.

- The most notable example of urban renewal was that of Haussmann in Paris, which became a model in cities elsewhere.

- Central and local governments introduced sanitary reforms to combat disease, such as installing sewers, regulating the disposal of refuse, and supplying public water.

- Improvement in public transportation allowed workers to leave the overcrowded conditions in urban centers, further contributing to improved health.

SOCIAL AND POLITICAL INITIATIVES

How and why did the state increasingly intervene in people's everyday lives?

Several institutions and groups emerged to tackle the unequal distribution of wealth and critical urban problems that followed in the wake of economic growth. The state intervened in the economy in new ways. Private charitable groups, which had existed for decades, continued to administer to a few of the poor, and new charities developed. Socialist political parties, exclusively dedicated to improving the workers' lot, gained in numbers and strength.

STATE INTERVENTION IN WELFARE

The difficult conditions industry imposed on workers led to debates in several countries about the need for

the state to protect the workers. The growing militancy of organized labor also forced authorities to consider ways to meet the workers' needs. While some rejected government intervention in the free operation of market forces, others argued that the laws of supply and demand had caused the exploitation of many who ought to have been protected—especially very young children and pregnant women. Britain led the way with the Factory Acts, regulating child and female labor. Similar acts were passed later in Prussia and France. In much of Europe, however, the state did little to improve the welfare of the working class. In eastern Europe, where industry was still in its infancy, workers had no protection.

Fear of social upheaval, a desire to prevent depopulation, and the rising strength of socialist political parties prompted some governments to act. In France moderate bourgeois liberals attempted to defuse class war by advocating **solidarism.** Solidarism insisted on the mutual responsibility of classes and individuals for one another's well-being. Guided by such sentiments, French republicans passed a number of laws toward the end of the century that improved the lot of the working class. In newly unified Germany, the government wanted to impress workers with state benefits so they would abandon the growing Socialist Party and back the kaiser's authoritarian government. Thus in the 1880s the new German government, under the leadership of Chancellor Otto von Bismarck, provided a comprehensive welfare plan that included health insurance and old-age pensions.

Apart from state initiatives, upper- and middle-class individuals, inspired by pity and religious teachings, also became concerned about conditions among the poor. Women especially engaged in charity and social reform. In Sweden by the 1880s, women had founded shelters for the destitute, old-age homes, a children's hospital, an asylum for the mentally handicapped, and various societies to promote female industry. As many as half a million English women involved themselves in charities or efforts to enact social legislation. Among them was Josephine Grey Butler (1828–1906), who fought for the education of impoverished women. She also waged a fierce battle against the harsh laws directed against prostitutes. The Contagious Diseases Acts (beginning in 1864) empowered the police to arrest any woman suspected of prostitution and to force her to be examined for venereal disease. Largely as a result of Butler's efforts, these acts were repealed in 1886. Annie Wood Besant (1847–1933) became an active social reformer on behalf of the poor. Arguing that poor women suffered from excessive childbearing and that their children died too often because of their poverty, she and Charles Bradlaugh (1833–1891) republished a pamphlet that contained information on birth control. British authorities called the publication pornographic and brought Besant and Bradlaugh to trial in 1877. After being found guilty, Bradlaugh and Besant won the case on appeal. In 1888 Besant turned her attention to protecting the health of young women workers, and in 1893 she went to India to establish schools for girls, educate widows, and agitate for Indian home rule.

Religious sentiment in the second half of the century inspired a number of Christians, lay and clerical, to emphasize the church's need to address social issues. Pope Leo XIII (r. 1878–1903) reflected this trend and re-

inforced it among Catholics when in 1891 he issued his encyclical *Rerum novarum* (Of New Things), which defined the moral responsibility of Christians for the well-being of the poor. He declared, "Rich men and masters should remember this—that to exercise pressure for the sake of gain upon the indigent and the destitute and to make one's profit out of the need of another is condemned by all laws, human and divine." His message was taken up in France, Italy, and Spain among activists who became known as **social Catholics.** In England Protestants founded the Salvation Army to assist the poor in 1878. Religious groups also hoped to win converts to their faith through the assistance they provided.

Increasingly, municipalities, volunteer groups, and churches accepted responsibility for the well-being of others by providing cheap housing, advice, material assistance, and medical aid. In many cases these pioneering efforts were later taken over by the state—a first step toward the development of the twentieth-century welfare state.

EDUCATIONAL AND CULTURAL OPPORTUNITIES

At the beginning of the nineteenth century, governments took little responsibility for providing education. Some upper-class children were educated with private tutors, and others attended elite schools. All schools were segregated by social class and charged tuition. A few charity schools offered minimal education for the poor. In England the Second Reform Bill of 1867 made public education a national priority. This legislation reduced the tax-based voting qualification, extending suffrage to better-off workers, and prompted a movement to ensure that the new voters were educated. The English government provided significant subsidies for education, set educational standards, and established a national inspection system to enforce them. France joined England in establishing mandatory primary school education in the 1880s for boys and girls.

In addition to the skills of reading, writing, and arithmetic, public education also taught discipline. By insisting on punctuality and obliging students to carry out repetitive tasks, schools formed youth to fit into the emerging industrial society. The obedience and respect for authority learned at school shaped the soldiers and factory workers of the future. And regardless of political inclination, each regime took advantage of its control of the educational system to inculcate the love of one's country and of its form of government.

Secondary education was, on the whole, available only to the privileged few in the upper-middle classes, giving them access to the universities and the profes-

solidarism A policy that emphasized the mutual responsibility of classes and individuals for one another's well-being and led to the passage of laws and benefits to improve the lot of the working class.

social Catholics Catholics in western Europe who believed that society bore responsibility for the well-being of the poor.

sions. A small fraction of the lower middle class attended universities, and the children of workers and peasants were totally absent.

Other public institutions made culture available to the masses in new ways. Between 1840 and 1880 the number of large libraries in Europe increased from forty to five hundred. The French national public library, the *Bibliothèque nationale,* was established in Paris in the 1860s. This iron and glass building, radical for its time, was an impressive monument to the desire to make reading available to an expanded public. Many

provincial cities, as well as the glittering capitals of Europe, were endowed with new libraries. Traveling libraries allowed books to reach rural populations.

Museums and art galleries, which in the previous century had been open to only a select few, gradually became accessible to the general public. After the Revolution of 1789, the Louvre in Paris became the first museum to open to the public. Other European countries lagged behind in making their cultural heritages available to the masses, but even the poorer classes gained access to these temples of culture by the late nineteenth century.

═══════ S E C T I O N   S U M M A R Y ═══════

- Some European governments responded to the threat of growing worker militancy and socialist politics through measures of social reform, such as protective labor legislation for women and children, health insurance, and old-age pensions.

- Municipalities, churches, and other charitable groups offered numerous forms of assistance to the poor, some of which the state eventually took over.

- The extension of voting rights led, in France and England, to the establishment of free and mandatory primary education whose goal was to instill love of country, discipline, and obedience to authority, as well as basic skills.

- Public libraries, museums, and art galleries provided further access to education and helped build national cultures.

CULTURE IN AN AGE OF OPTIMISM

What new scientific, intellectual, and cultural trends emerged in this period, and what impact did they have on systems of belief?

The improving economic and material conditions of the second half of the nineteenth century buoyed European thinkers. Many believed that men and women were becoming more enlightened, and they expressed faith in humankind's ability to transform the world with a parade of scientific and technological breakthroughs. The world seemed knowable and perfectible. This faith advanced secularism while it undermined the certainties of traditional religion. The arts reflected these new values, emphasizing realism and science—as well as an underlying foreboding about the dark side of this "age of optimism."

DARWIN AND EVOLUTION

By midcentury most thinkers accepted the notion of the change and transformation of society—and, by analogy, of the natural environment. The French thinker Auguste Comte (oh-GOOST KONT) championed the notion that human development—human history—proceeded through distinct and irreversible stages. Human progress, inscribed in the laws of nature, leads inexorably upward to the final and highest stage of development, the "positive"—or scientific—

stage. Widely read throughout Europe and Latin America, Comte's writings helped bolster the era's faith in science, and the very progress science made seemed to confirm its precepts. Comte's philosophy, known as **positivism,** dominated the era. Whereas the romantics had emphasized feeling, the positivists upheld the significance of what could be measured and verified. They were confident that scientific methods would ensure the continued progress of humanity.

Although evolution in the biological realm had been suggested as early as the end of the eighteenth century, Charles Darwin (1809–1882) was the first to offer a systematic explanation of the process. As the naturalist on an official British scientific expedition in the 1830s, he had visited the Galápagos Islands off the western coast of South America. On these islands he found species similar to but very different from those on the mainland. Could they be the results of separate creations? Or was it more likely that in varying environments they had

positivism Philosophy of the French thinker Auguste Comte who asserted that human history progressed through distinct and irreversible stages, leading to the final and highest stage of development, the positive—or scientific—stage.

THE WRITTEN RECORD

DARWIN'S BASIC LAWS OF EVOLUTION

Writing in an age of vast transformations, Darwin could imagine the mutability of all nature, including species, over time. And like his contemporaries, he could imagine that evolution would lead to improvement, to increasing "perfection" of various species. A religious man who lost much of his faith as a result of his scientific investigations, Darwin was anxious to reassure Christians, hence his attempt to portray evolution as part of God's divine plan.

Nothing at first can appear more difficult to believe than that the more complex organs and instincts have been perfected, not by means superior to, though analogous with, human reason, but by the accumulation of innumerable slight variations, each good for the individual possessor. Nevertheless, this difficulty, though appearing to our imagination insuperably great, cannot be considered real if we admit the following propositions, namely, that all parts of the organisation and instincts offer, at least, individual differences—that there is a struggle for existence leading to the preservation of profitable deviations of structure or instinct—and, lastly, that gradations in the state of perfection of each organ may have existed, each good of its kind. The truth of these propositions cannot, I think, be disputed. . . .

As geology plainly proclaims that each land has undergone great physical changes, we might have expected to find that organic beings have varied under nature, in the same way as they have varied under domestication. And if there has been any variability under nature, it would be an unaccountable fact if natural selection had not come into play. . . .

There is grandeur in this view of life, with its several powers, having been originally breathed by the Creator into a few forms or into one; and that, whilst this planet has gone cycling on according to the fixed law of gravity, from so simple a beginning endless forms most beautiful and most wonderful have been, and are being evolved.

QUESTIONS

1. What role does natural selection play in Darwin's theory, and what is the logic behind it?
2. How and why does Darwin attempt to reconcile his theory with religion?

Source: Charles Darwin, *On the Origin of Species by Means of Natural Selection,* 6th ed., vol. 2 (1872; repr., New York: Appleton, 1923), pp. 267–268, 279, 305–306.

---

adapted differently? Darwin proposed that closely related species compete for food and living space. In this struggle, those in each species that are better adapted to the environment have the advantage over the others and hence are more likely to survive. In the "struggle for existence," only the fittest endure. Those surviving, Darwin surmised, pass on the positive traits to their offspring. He called the mechanism that explained the evolution and development of new species "natural selection," a process that he proposed was imperceptible but continuous. Darwin's observations in the Galápagos Islands became the basis for *On the Origin of Species by Means of Natural Selection* (1859), the most important scientific work of the nineteenth century. (See the box "The Written Record: Darwin's Basic Laws of Evolution.")

Darwin's theory that evolution in nature was inevitable echoes the nineteenth-century conviction that the present represented an ever more developed stage of the past. Many viewed his work as confirmation that societies—like species—were preordained to evolve toward progressively higher stages. Darwin at first avoided the question of whether human beings, too, are affected by the laws of evolution. The notion of human evolution would throw into question humanity's uniqueness and its separation from the rest of creation by its possession (in the Christian view) of a soul. But Darwin finally did confront the issue in *The Descent of Man* (1871), in which he presented evidence that humanity, too, is subject to these natural laws. The recognition that human beings are members of the animal kingdom like other species disturbed him, and the admission, he wrote, "is like confessing a murder." Nonetheless, for Darwin scientific evidence took precedence over all other considerations.

These assertions shocked Christians, and some denounced the new scientific findings. Some argued that science and faith belonged to two different worlds. Others claimed that there was no reason why God could not have created the world through natural forces. In the long run, however, **Darwinism** seemed to undermine

Darwinism   Influential theory of biological evolution, first put forth by Charles Darwin. He proposed that all forms of life continuously develop through natural selection, whereby those that are better adapted to the environment have the advantage and are more likely to survive and pass on their beneficial traits to their offspring.

the certainties of religious orthodoxies; many found them incompatible with scientific discovery.

Some contemporaries took Darwin's theories beyond biology and applied them to human social development. Social Darwinists argued that human societies evolve in the same way as plants and animals. According to their logic, human societies—races, classes, nations—like species, were destined to compete for survival, and some would be condemned to fade away. And from these harsh laws, a better humanity would evolve. The British social theorist Herbert Spencer (1820–1903), who coined the expression "survival of the fittest," believed that society should be established in such a way that the strongest and most resourceful would survive. The weak, poor, and improvident were not worthy of survival, and if the state helped them survive—for instance, by providing welfare—it would only perpetuate the unfit. Poverty was a sign of biological inferiority, wealth a sign of success in the struggle for survival. In Europe and the United States (where Spencer was extremely popular, selling hundreds of thousands of books), **Social Darwinism** was thus used to justify callousness toward the poor at home and toward imperial conquest abroad. The European subjugation of Africans and Asians through colonization offered confirmation for Social Darwinists of white racial superiority. People of color were seen as poorly endowed to compete in the race for survival (see Chapter 24).

PHYSICS, CHEMISTRY, AND MEDICINE

Dramatic scientific breakthroughs occurred in the nineteenth century, confirming the prevalent belief that human beings could understand and control nature. Since the seventeenth century, scientists had attempted to study nature by careful observation, seeking its regularities and developing theories to explain what they had observed. The scientific method of experimental testing yielded major breakthroughs. In physics, laws regarding electricity and magnetism were articulated by Michael Faraday (1791–1867) and James Clerk Maxwell (1831–1879) in the 1830s and 1850s, respectively. Their work established the field of electrical science. In the 1840s Hermann von Helmholtz (1821–1894) in Germany and James Joule (1818–1889) in Great Britain defined the nature of energy in the laws of thermodynamics. In chemistry, new elements were discovered almost every year. In 1869 Russian chemist Dmitri Mendeleev (men-del-LAY-ef) (1834–1907) developed the periodic table, in which the elements are arranged by their atomic weight. He left blank spaces

for elements still unknown but that he was confident existed. Within ten years, three of these elements were discovered, affirming the belief that scientific knowledge not only can be experimentally tested but also has predictive value. Such triumphs further enhanced science's prestige.

Science also became increasingly specialized. In the eighteenth century, the scientist had been a learned amateur practicing a hobby. In the nineteenth century, as the state and industry became more involved in promoting scientific research, the scientist became a professional employed by a university, a hospital, or some other institution. Scientific journals and meetings of scientific associations disseminated new discoveries and theories. Around midcentury a number of important breakthroughs occurred in medicine. Before the development of anesthesia, surgical intervention was limited. With only alcohol to dull the patient's pain, even the swiftest surgeons could perform only modest surgical procedures. In the 1840s, however, the introduction of ether and then chloroform allowed people to undergo more extensive surgery. It also was used to relieve pain in more routine procedures and in childbirth; Queen Victoria asked for chloroform when in labor.

Increasingly, physicians applied the scientific experimental method to medicine, and as a result they became concerned with discovering the origins of diseases and not just their treatment. Louis Pasteur (1822–1895) achieved notable breakthroughs when he discovered that microbes, small organisms invisible to the naked eye, cause various diseases. Pasteur found that heating milk to a certain temperature kills disease-carrying organisms. This process, called pasteurization, reduced the incidence of gastrointestinal illnesses that were particularly harmful to children. Pasteur initiated other advances as well in the prevention of disease. Vaccination against smallpox had started in England in the eighteenth century, but Pasteur invented vaccines for other diseases and was able to explain the process by which the body, inoculated with a weak form of bacilli, developed antibodies that successfully overcame more serious infections. In England the surgeon Joseph Lister (1827–1912) developed an effective disinfectant, carbolic acid, to kill the germs that cause gangrene and other infections in surgical patients. Lister's development of germ-free procedures transformed the science of surgery. By reducing the patient's risk, more ambitious surgery could be attempted. Eventually midwives and doctors, by washing their hands and sterilizing their instruments, began to reduce the incidence of the puerperal, or "childbed," fever that killed so many women after childbirth. The increasingly scientific base of medicine and its visible success in combating disease improved its reputation.

Social Darwinism Theory of social evolution that states that human societies evolve in the same way as plants and animals, and that the weak, poor, and improvident are not worthy of survival.

BIRTH OF THE SOCIAL SCIENCES

The scientific method, so dramatically effective in uncovering the mysteries of nature, could, it was thought, also be applied to the workings of society.

No field in the human sciences flourished as much in the nineteenth century as that of history. In an era undergoing vast transformations, many people became interested in change over time, particularly with regard to their own national histories. The father of modern historical writing is the German Leopold von Ranke (fon RANG-key) (1795–1886). Departing from the tradition of earlier historians, who explained the past as the ongoing fulfillment of an overarching purpose—divine will, the liberation of humanity, or some other goal—Ranke insisted that the role of the historian was to "show how things actually were." Like a scientist, the historian must be objective and dispassionate. By viewing humankind of all eras and environments on their own terms, and not those of others, historians could arrive at a better understanding of humanity.

This perspective transformed the study of history into a discipline with recognizable common standards of evidence. Historians studied and interpreted original (or "primary") sources; they collected and published their findings; they founded professional organizations and published major journals.

Other social sciences also developed in this period. Anthropology, the comparative study of people in different societies, had been the subject of speculative literature for hundreds of years. Increased contacts with non-European societies in the nineteenth century—the effect of burgeoning trade, exploration, and missionary activities—stimulated anthropological curiosity. In 1844 the Society of Ethnology was founded in Paris, followed by the Anthropological Society (1859). London, Berlin, and Vienna quickly followed suit, establishing similar societies in the 1860s. Anthropologists speculated on the causes of the perceived differences among human races, mainly attributing the variations to their physical structures. They offered apparent "scientific" backing to the era's racism, explaining that non-Europeans were condemned to an existence inferior to the white races.

The main anthropological theorist in Britain was Edward Tylor (1832–1917), the son of a brass manufacturer. Through his travels Tylor came into contact with non-European peoples, who aroused his curiosity. Strongly influenced by the evolutionary doctrines of his day, Tylor believed that the various societies of humankind were subject to discoverable scientific laws. Tylor posited that if one could travel back in time, one would find humankind increasingly unsophisticated. So, too, the farther one traveled from Europe, the more primitive humankind became. Thus, according to his view, the contemporary African was at a level of development similar to that of Europeans in an earlier era.

Tylor was not technically a racist, since he argued that the conditions of non-Europeans were not due to biology but rather were a function of their institutions. Eventually they would "evolve" and become akin to Europeans. Like racists, however, evolutionists believed in European superiority. Anthropology gave "scientific" sanction to the idea of a single European people, sharing either a similar biological structure or a common stage of social development, which distinguished them from non-Europeans.

The term *sociology* was coined by Auguste Comte. A number of ambitious thinkers, among them the English "social philosopher" Herbert Spencer (see page 729), had considered how individuals are affected by the society in which they live. In the 1840s various social reformers published detailed statistical investigations revealing relationships between, for instance, income, disease, and death rates. A few decades later the theoretical principles underlying sociology were spelled out. Among the first researchers to do so was Emile Durkheim (DIRK-hime) (1858–1917), who insisted that sociology was a verifiable science. His disciples, and the journal he founded, ensured the success of sociology as a professionalized discipline.

Whereas in the past history, anthropology, and sociology were the purview of amateurs, now professional historians, anthropologists, and sociologists were engaged full-time in research and teaching at universities or research institutes. Professionalization and specialization led to significant advances in several disciplines, but it also led to the fragmentation and compartmentalization of knowledge. People of broad learning and expertise became far less common.

THE CHALLENGE TO RELIGION

The scientific claims of the era clashed with some fundamental religious precepts. Although most Europeans continued to be strongly influenced by traditional religious beliefs, they appeared less confident than in earlier eras.

Religion had assumed increased importance as a bulwark of order in the wake of the 1848 revolutions. In France Napoleon III gave the Catholic Church new powers over education, and the bourgeoisie flocked to worship. In Spain moderates who had been anticlerical (opposed to the clergy) began to support the church, and in 1851 they signed a concordat (an agreement with the papacy) declaring Roman Catholicism "the only religion of the Spanish nation." In Austria in 1855, the state surrendered powers it had acquired in the 1780s, returning to bishops full control over the clergy, the seminaries, and the administration of marriage laws.

In 1848 the papacy had been nearly overthrown by revolution, and in 1860 it lost most of its domains to Italy. Thus Pope Pius IX became a sworn enemy of liberalism. In 1864, he issued the *Syllabus of Errors,* in which he condemned a long list of faults that included "progress," "liberalism," and "modern civilization." To establish full control over the clergy and believers, the Lateran Council in 1870 issued the controversial doctrine of papal infallibility, which declared that the pope, when speaking officially on matters of faith and morals, is incapable of error. This doctrine became a target of anticlerical opinion.

The political alliance the Catholic Church struck with reactionary forces meant that when new political groups came to power, they moved against the church. In Italy, since the church had discouraged national unification, conflict raged between the church and the new state. In Germany Catholics had either held on to their regional loyalties or favored unification under Austrian auspices. When Protestant Prussia unified Germany, Chancellor Bismarck viewed the Catholics with suspicion as unpatriotic and launched a campaign against them, the *Kulturkampf* (KOOL-toor-kampf) ("cultural struggle"). Bismarck expelled the Jesuits and attempted to establish state control over the Catholic schools and appointment of bishops. Not satisfied, he seized church property and imprisoned or exiled eighteen hundred priests.

In France the republicans, who finally won the upper hand over the monarchists in 1879, bitterly resented the church's support of the monarchist party. Strongly influenced by Comte's ideas of positivism, republicans believed that France would not be a free country until the power of the church was diminished and its nonscientific or antiscientific disposition was overcome. The republican regime reduced the role of the church in education as well as some other clerical privileges.

Greater tolerance, or perhaps indifference to religion in general, led to more acceptance of religious diversity. In 1854 and 1871 England opened university admission and teaching posts at all universities to non-Anglicans. In France, too, the position of religious minorities improved. Some of the highest officials of the Second Empire were Protestants, as were some early leaders of the Third Republic and some important business leaders and scientists.

Legal emancipation of Jews, started in France in 1791, subsequently spread to the rest of the Continent. The British allowed Jews to hold seats in the House of Commons in 1858, and in the House of Lords the following decade. In the 1860s Germany and Austria-Hungary granted Jews the rights of citizenship. Although some Jews occupied high office in France and Italy, they had to convert to Christianity before they could aspire to such positions in Germany and Austria-Hungary. In other fields such as banking and commerce, access was easier.

Social discrimination continued, however—most of European society refused to accept Jews as social equals.

In the expanding economy of western Europe, where the condition of most people was improving, the enhanced opportunity of a previously despised minority aroused relatively little attention. In other parts of Europe, Jews were not so fortunate. In eastern Europe, they incurred resentment when they moved into commerce, industry, and the professions. Outbreaks of violence against them, called *pogroms,* occurred in Bucharest, the capital of Romania, in 1866 and in the Russian seaport of Odessa in 1871. Although economic rivalries may have fueled anti-Jewish feelings, they do not completely explain it. In most cases anti-Jewish sentiment occurred in the areas of Europe least exposed to liberal ideas of human equality and human rights.

As the continued anti-Semitism demonstrates, science by no means always led to increased tolerance; nor did it necessarily weaken religious fervor. Church attendance continued to be high, especially in rural areas. French people reported frequent sightings of the Virgin Mary. In 1858 a shepherd girl claimed to have seen and spoken with her at Lourdes (LOORD), which became an especially important shrine whose waters were reputed to heal the lame and the sick. In 1872 construction of a rail line allowed 100,000 people a year to visit the town.

CULTURE IN THE AGE OF MATERIAL CHANGE

The era's admiration of technology and science and its idolization of progress were reflected in the arts. Some artists optimistically believed they could more accurately portray reality by adopting the methods of the scientist, objectively depicting their subjects. A minority, however, were disillusioned by the materialism of the age and warned against its loss of values.

Photography had a direct impact on painting. Various experiments in the late eighteenth century, plus the inventions of the Frenchman Louis Daguerre (dah-GAIR) (1789–1851), made the camera relatively usable by the 1830s. Its widespread use began in the 1890s with the introduction of celluloid film and American George Eastman's (1854–1932) invention of the Kodak camera, which became mass-produced. Unlike painting and sculpture, photography was affordable for the public. Photographic services were in high demand; by the 1860s, thirty thousand people in Paris made a living from photography and allied fields. (See "The Visual Record: The Modern City and Photography.")

The ability of photography to depict a scene with exactitude had a significant impact on art. On the one hand, it encouraged many artists to be true to reality, to reproduce on the canvas a visual image akin to that of a photograph. On the other hand, some artists felt that such realism was no longer necessary in their sphere.

Courbet: The Stone Breakers
This realistic 1849 painting depicts the rough existence of manual laborers. The bleak-
ness of the subject matter and the style in which it was carried out characterized
much of the realist school of art. *(Staatliche Kunstsammlungen, Dresden/The Bridgeman Art Library)*

However, the great majority of the public, which now had wide access to museum exhibitions, was accustomed to photographic accuracy and desired art that was representative and intelligible. Realistic works of art met this need, at least superficially.

Many artists discarded myths and symbols to portray the world as it actually was, or at least as it appeared to them—a world without illusions, everyday life in all its grimness. The realist painter Gustave Courbet (koor-BAY) (1819–1877) proclaimed himself "without ideals and without religion." His fellow Frenchman Jean-François Millet (mil-LAY) (1814–1875) held a similar opinion. Instead of romanticizing peasants in the manner of earlier artists, he painted the harsh physical conditions under which they labored. In England the so-called pre-Raphaelites took as their model those painters prior to Raphael in Renaissance Italy, who had depicted the realistic simplicity of nature. In painting historical scenes, these artists meticulously researched the landscape, architecture, fauna, and costumes of their subjects.

Photography and artistic realism also helped inspire their counterpoint in less realistic representations. On April 15, 1874, six French artists—Edgar Degas (1834–1917), Claude Monet (1840–1926), Camille Pissarro (1830–1903), Auguste Renoir (1840–1919), Alfred Sisley (1839–1899), and Berthe Morisot (1841–1895)— opened an exhibition in Paris that a critic disparagingly called **impressionist,** after the title of one of Monet's paintings, *Impression: Sunrise.* The impressionists were influenced by new theories of physics that claimed images were transmitted to the brain as small light particles that the brain then reconstituted. The impressionists wanted their paintings to capture what things looked like before the brain "distorted" them. Many of these painters unconventionally left their studios to paint objects exactly as they looked outdoors when light hit them at a certain angle. Monet, for example, emphasized outdoor painting and the need for spontaneity—for reproducing subjects without preconceptions about how earlier artists had depicted them— and seeking to show exactly how the colors and shapes struck the eye. Monet was particularly interested in creating multiple paintings of the same scene—from different viewpoints, under different weather conditions, at different times of day—to underscore that no single "correct" depiction could possibly capture a subject.

Online Study Center **Improve Your Grade**
Primary Source: Impressionism Defined

impressionist Late-nineteenth-century style of painting pioneered by the French artists Degas, Monet, Pissarro, Renoir, Sisley, and Morisot.

THE GLOBAL RECORD

A Chinese Official's Views of European Material Progress

Educated in European universities, Ku Hung-Ming rose to become a high official in the Chinese court. His essays were penned under the impact of the European military intervention in China during the Boxer Rebellion in 1900. Ku denounced European notions of superiority over Asia by arguing that material progress was not an appropriate measure of a civilization's value.

In order to estimate the value of a civilization, it seems to me, the question we must finally ask is not what great cities, what magnificent houses, what fine roads it has built and is able to build; what beautiful and comfortable furniture, what clever and useful implements, tools and instruments it has made and is able to make; no, not even what institutions, what arts and sciences it has invested: the question we must ask, in order to estimate the value of a civilization—is what type of humanity, what kind of men and women it has been able to produce. In fact, the man and woman,—the type of human beings—which a civilization produces, it is this which shows the essence, the personality, so to speak, the soul of that civilization. Now if the men and women of a civilization show the essence, the personality and soul of that civilization, the language which the men and women in that civilization speak, shows the essence, the personality, the soul of the men and women of that civilization. . . .

To Europeans, and especially to unthinking practical Englishmen, who are accustomed to take what modern political economists call "the standard of living" as the test of the moral culture of or civilization of a people, the actual life of the Chinese and of the people of the East at the present day, will no doubt appear very sordid and undesirable. But the standard of living by itself is not a proper test of the civilization of a people. The standard of living in America at the present day, is, I believe, much higher than it is in Germany. But although the son of an American millionaire, who regards the simple and comparatively low standard of living among the professors of a German University, may doubt the value of the education in such a University, yet no educated man, I believe, who has traveled in both countries, will admit that the Germans are a less civilized people than the Americans.

QUESTIONS

1. How does the Chinese official define civilization? How does his view differ from the European view?
2. What is Ku Hung-Ming's idea of a hierarchy of civilization?
3. According to the ideas in this reading, what is the connection between progress and civilization?

Source: Ku Hung-Ming, *The Spirit of the Chinese People*, 2d ed. (Beijing: Commercial Press, 1922), pp. 1, 144–145.

The school of realism also influenced literature, especially the novel. In realist novels, life was not glorified or infused with mythical elements; the stark existence of daily life was seen as a suitable subject. Charles Dickens (1812–1870), who came from a poor background and had personally experienced the inhumanity of the London underworld, wrote novels depicting the lot of the poor with humor and sympathy. The appalling social conditions he described helped educate his large middle-class audience on the state of the poor.

Another realist, the French novelist Gustave Flaubert (flo-BEAR) (1821–1880), consciously debunked the romanticism of his elders. His famous novel, *Madame Bovary,* describes middle-class life as bleak, boring, and meaningless. The heroine seeks to escape the narrow confines of provincial life by adulterous and disastrous affairs.

Emile Zola (1840–1902), another Frenchman, belonged to the naturalist school of literature. The writer, he declared, should record and represent human behavior scientifically. He described his own work as similar to "the analysis that surgeons make on cadavers." Zola's Rougon-Macquart (roo-ZHON–mah-KAR) series, which includes the novels *Nana* and *Germinal,* describes in detail the experience of several generations of a family. His major theme is the impact of environment and heredity on his characters' lives of degradation and vice, in which they seem locked in a Darwinian struggle for survival: some are doomed by the laws of biology to succeed, others to succumb.

The Russian novelist Leo Tolstoy (1828–1910) brought a new perspective to the historical novel in *War and Peace.* Instead of a heroic approach to battle, he showed individuals trapped by forces beyond their control. Small and insignificant events as well as major ones seemed to govern human destiny. Another Russian novelist often associated with the realist school, Feodor Dostoyevsky (1821–1881), aimed to portray realistically the psychological dimensions of his characters in novels such as *Crime and Punishment* (1866), *The Idiot* (1868), and *The Brothers Karamazov* (1879–1880).

THE VISUAL RECORD

The Modern City and Photography

This photo of Piccadilly Square in Manchester documents the modernization of the nineteenth-century city and at the same time conveys the sense of immediacy that photography provided as a new means of representation.

Taken in the 1880s, this photo* shows evidence of the great progress that had taken place in photography since its invention half a century earlier. In 1839 Louis Daguerre publicized the method of fixing an image on silvered copperplate. At first the cameras and equipment were so cumbersome that photography was confined to studios. Thus the only images were portraits of people and the occasional still life. As the camera became simpler, photographers could leave the studio and take pictures outdoors. The introduction of the dry plate method in the 1870s made film far more sensitive to light, reducing exposure time to a fraction of a second. Now a photograph could capture movement without reducing it to a blur, as in this bustling city scene.

Originally photography had been regarded as a more exact, and less expensive, form of illustration and so was influenced by the conventions of painting. Because of the slowness of taking pictures and the obvious presence of the photographer with bulky equipment, most early photographs, even outdoor shots, were staged. But soon thereafter, thanks to technical innovations, photographers could capture a scene even without the cooperation of the subject. None of the subjects in this photo has eye contact with the camera. In fact, they seem unaware of the photographer as they go about their daily business.

This photo also conveys important visual information about the emerging modern city. A vibrant textile city, Manchester had a population that more than doubled to 600,000 inhabitants between 1830 and 1900. Piccadilly was its commercial center. As the photo here shows, it had been built as a large open square intended for the easy movement of pedestrians and wagons. City planners of the nineteenth century created squares and broad, straight avenues feeding into them, such as suggested here. Replacing old slums and narrow alleys, broad avenues eased the flow of traffic and admitted fresh air and sunlight. The square contained fancy stores with dwellings situated on the upper floors behind the elegantly crafted façades.

*The advice of Thomas Prasch in the choice of this photo is gratefully acknowledged.

Piccadilly, the commercial center of Manchester, had warehouses and offices where buyers purchased textiles that they would in turn sell to retail consumers. As seen in this photo, Piccadilly Square, as a commercial center, required public transportation to move people quickly on the broad new avenues. Notice the rails for the horse-drawn tramway that had been introduced as early as the 1820s. They were the first means of mass transportation within the city. Trams on rails reduced friction and allowed a horse to pull a far greater load. In this case the tram, located in the center of the photo, is a double-decker.

The large modern city required ease of communication at night as well as in the daytime. Street lighting not only provided that convenience but also made the streets more secure by making potential crime more visible. Streetlamps became the norm in large cities, especially in the better neighborhoods. The elegant gaslights viewable in the photo of Piccadilly Square were replaced a few years later by electric lamps that were cheaper to operate and allowed for the spread of city lighting.

An industrial town, Manchester was not a particularly pleasant city to live in. Visitors complained of its grime, pollution, and foul smells. Many members of the commercial classes lived in wealthy suburbs and commuted by tram to work in the center. Sometime after this picture was taken, the horse-drawn tram was replaced by the electric tram, which could transport more people faster than its predecessor. Its lower cost also meant that it was accessible to most workers. With the advent of the electric tram, workers also began to move to the suburbs, making the center less crowded.

If the modern photograph was different from a painting, photography still adhered to some of the traditions of painting—notably composition. The photographer composed this image by making choices, for example, as to what to put in the foreground. Our eye centers on the harried merchant crossing the well-ordered street with its backdrop of amenities.

Compare this photograph with Camille Pissarro's *L'avenue de l'Opéra, Sunlight, Winter Morning* on page 723. Paris, known as the "city of light," was very different from Manchester, though like that industrial city, the new boulevards resulting from "Hausmannization" allowed for a larger and speedier flow of traffic and commerce. Pissarro also

Piccadilly Square, Manchester, ca. 1886 *(Topham Picturepoint/The Image Works)*

conveys in this painting the bustle—and perhaps alienation—some felt in modern life. Note the predominance of solitary figures in both the painting and the photograph. Wide boulevards meant that pedestrians did not "run into each other" and socialize as readily as they had on narrow streets. Indeed, Pissarro and other impressionist painters disdained the modernization of cities and turned instead to the suburbs and rural landscapes, leaving the documentation of urban change to photographers. Pissarro thought Paris had become "ill" from all of its changes.

The chemical and optical breakthroughs that made the camera such an effective new tool were implemented by inventors in cities such as London, Paris, and Berlin. Photographers in turn took pictures of some of the great technical feats of their era, such as the Eiffel Tower. The modern aspects of the city, such as the scene in this photo, were frequent subjects for the photographer's lens. Before

the end of the century, photographs such as this were commonly used on postcards. The producers and consumers of postcards were more fascinated by the reality of representation rather than the beauty of particular sites, as postcards geared toward tourism would later embrace.

QUESTIONS

1. How did modernization—urbanization, commercialization, the design of cities, and modern means of transportation—change people's sensual experience and perceptions?

2. In its replication of "reality," how did photography both record and create our understanding of the past? How did it both replicate traditional art and create new ways of seeing?

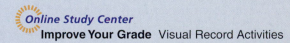

Online Study Center
Improve Your Grade Visual Record Activities

Although this era generally celebrated material progress, a number of intellectuals reacted against it. They were alarmed by the prospect of the popular masses achieving political power through winning the vote and by mass production and consumption. They denounced the smug and the self-satisfied, who saw happiness in acquisition and consumption. Some condemned the age in severe terms. Dostoyevsky railed against the materialism and egotism of the West, branding its civilization as driven by "trade, shipping, markets, factories." In Britain—the nation that seemed to embody progress—the historian Thomas Carlyle (1795–1881) berated his age as one not of progress but of selfishness. He saw parliamentarianism as a sham, and he called for a strong leader to save the nation from endless debates and compromises. Unlike most of his contemporaries, who saw in material plenty a sign of progress, Carlyle saw the era as one of decline, bereft of spiritual values.

Another Englishman, John Ruskin (1819–1900), looked back to the Middle Ages as an ideal era in which people exercised a fine sense of craftsmanship instead of producing with machines. People then supposedly had a better sense of community and labored for the common good rather than out of a sense of selfish individualism. Ruskin was one of the founders of the arts and crafts movement, which aimed to produce goods for daily use with an eye for beauty and originality. "Industry without art is brutality," Ruskin warned.

In France republicans saw in the ostentation of the Second Empire a sign of depravity and decline. The 1870–1871 defeat in war and the insurrection of the Paris Commune contributed to the mood of pessimism among many intellectuals. Flaubert detested his own age, seeing it as petty and mean. The characters in Zola's Rougon-Macquart novels slide steadily downward as each generation's mental faculties, social positions, and morals degenerate. Some people abroad also were unimpressed with developments in Europe. (See the box "The Global Record: A Chinese Official's Views of European Material Progress.")

Not all were optimistic in this age of optimism. If many people celebrated what they viewed as an age of progress, others claimed that under the outer trappings of material comfort lay a frightening ignorance of aesthetic, moral, and spiritual values.

S E C T I O N   S U M M A R Y

- Darwin's theory of evolution reinforced the belief among some of the inevitability of human progress; others found the placement of human beings in the same category as animal species profoundly disturbing.

- Social Darwinists applied Darwin's theories to human society in order to justify inequality, racial hierarchies, and "survival of the fittest."

- The application of the scientific method (experimentation) led to scientific breakthroughs, transforming fields such as physics (especially electrical science), chemistry, and medicine.

- The scientific method also transformed the study of human society, professionalizing the fields of history, anthropology, and sociology.

- Scientific discoveries and theories undermined religious belief among some people; others, however, reacted to the harshness of the material world by embracing religion more fervently.

- Science and technology infused the arts with a new emphasis on realism and on the importance of visual representations.

C H A P T E R   S U M M A R Y

Online Study Center   ACE the Test

What technological changes led to the expansion of the European economy after the mid-nineteenth century?

How did the economic expansion affect the various social classes, and city versus rural areas, differently?

What problems did urbanization create, and what were the solutions?

How and why did the state increasingly intervene in people's everyday lives?

What new scientific, intellectual, and cultural trends emerged in this period, and what impact did they have on systems of belief?

During the second half of the nineteenth century, the cluster of technological innovations known as the second industrial revolution—mass-produced steel, synthetic dyes, new forms of energy such as petroleum and electricity, and the speedup in production—created for many Westerners an era of unprecedented material plenty. The expansion of railroads, advances in shipping, the standardization of postal service, and the inventions of the telegraph and telephone collapsed distances of time and space, and brought Europe further into a global economy.

Economic changes transformed the class structure of many European countries: the middle classes expanded and their values and tastes defined the second half of the century, while the aristocracy declined in power. Many rural and urban laborers still lived in poverty. Agricultural workers left the countryside, and cities continued their rapid growth, giving rise to overcrowding, traffic jams, and pollution and facilitating the spread of contagious diseases.

To address problems of urban growth, local governments established services such as street lighting and public transportation. They, along with charities, also took measures to improve public health and provide advice and material assistance. In both the countryside and the cities, governments provided new services, such as public education and cultural institutions.

Intellectual and cultural currents reflected material changes and the confidence they inspired. In addition to new breakthroughs in the sciences, scientific methods were applied to the study of human behavior. Novelists and painters aimed to dissect like scientists the world around them, adopting realism in the arts. Some intellectuals, however, were repulsed by the crass self-satisfaction of the bourgeoisie, and they despised their age's worship of industry and materialism.

LOOKING AHEAD

Progress, as Europeans were to learn in a later era, was two-edged: the very forces that improved life for many also threatened it. The same breakthroughs in chemistry that led to the development of artificial fertilizers also provided more powerful military explosives. The expansion of education and the reduction of illiteracy lessened ignorance but created a public that could more easily absorb messages of hate against a rival nation or against religious or ethnic minorities at home. In the shadows of material progress lurked new forces that would ultimately undermine the comforts, self-assurance, and peace of this age.

KEY TERMS

second industrial revolution (p. 712)
bourgeois century (p. 717)
professionalization (p. 717)
Victorian morality (p. 719)
separate spheres (p. 719)
solidarism (p. 726)
social Catholics (p. 726)
positivism (p. 727)
Darwinism (p. 728)
Social Darwinism (p. 729)
impressionist (p. 732)

Online Study Center
Improve Your Grade Flashcards

SUGGESTED READING

Browne, Janet. *Charles Darwin: The Power of Place.* 2005. A highly readable biography that surveys debates between scientists and churchmen over evolutionary theory.

Cannadine, David. *The Rise and Fall of Class in Britain.* 1999. Reveals the importance of class in nineteenth-century British society.

Clark, Linda L. *The Rise of Professional Women in France.* 2000. A fine study delineating the increasing role of women in the professions, especially public administration.

Goodman, David, and Colin Chant, eds. *European Cities and Technology Reader.* 1999. Emphasizes the importance of technological breakthroughs in the modernization of cities.

Hobsbawm, Eric J. *The Age of Capital, 1848–1875.* 1979. Particularly strong on social and economic developments.

Nord, Philip. *Impressionists and Politics.* 2000. Sets the French impressionists in their political and social contexts.

Standage, Tom. *The Victorian Internet.* 1998. A brief, popular history of the telegraph.

24

Escalating Tensions, 1880–1914

The "Unsinkable" Titanic
The *Titanic* proudly announces its maiden voyage.
(Corbis)

n April 1912 the *Titanic,* the largest and most technologically advanced passenger ship ever built, sailed from Southampton, England, for New York. Its owners, the White Star Line, boasted that the building of this majestic vessel testified to "the progress of mankind" and would "rank high in the achievements of the twentieth century." Hailed as "virtually unsinkable," on the night of April 12 the *Titanic* struck an iceberg south of Newfoundland and rapidly sank. More than 1,500 of the 2,100 people aboard perished in the icy North Atlantic waters. The overconfident captain had not taken warnings of icebergs in the ship's path seriously enough.

Two years later European society was hit by a major disaster—the outbreak of a world war. That such a disaster would end the era called by contemporaries the *belle époque* (BELL eh-POK), or "beautiful epoch," was as unimaginable as the *Titanic*'s fate. The booming economy had been expanding opportunities for many. Parliamentary government continued to spread, and more nations seemed to be adapting to democracy as suffrage was extended. Yet hand in hand with these trends of apparent progress appeared troubling tendencies. Under the surface were forces threatening the stability of European society, which is why, in 1914, a lone assassin's bullet could set off a series of reactions that brought a whole era to a tragic close.

In the decades prior to 1914, governing became more complex as nations grew larger. The population of Europe jumped from 330 million in 1880 to 460 million by the outbreak of war. A larger population coupled with extended suffrage meant that more men participated in the political system, but it became harder to reach a consensus. The example of democracy in some countries led to discontent in the autocracies that failed to move toward freer institutions. Where freer institutions did exist, those excluded from them—women, ethnic minorities, and the poor—became ever more resentful.

Intellectuals revolted against what they viewed as the smug self-assuredness of earlier years. They no longer felt certain that the world was knowable, stable, or subject to mastery by rational human beings. Some jettisoned rationality and instead glorified emotion, irrationality, and in some

KEY TERMS

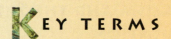

new imperialism

Second International

anti-Semitism

Zionism

Sigmund Freud

avant-garde

suffragists

Weltpolitik

Bolsheviks

Triple Alliance

Triple Entente

Online Study Center

This icon will direct you to interactive map and primary source activities on the website **college.hmco.com/pic/noble5e**

cases violence. The works of painters and writers seemed to anticipate the impending destruction of world order.

The anxieties and tensions that beset many Europeans took a variety of forms. Ethnic minorities became targets of hatred. European states embarked on a race for empire throughout the world, forcibly putting non-Europeans under white domination. On the Continent states felt increasingly insecure, worried that they would be subject to attack. They established standing armies, shifted alliances, drafted war plans, and, in the end, went to war.

FOCUS QUESTIONS

What were the main motivations for European imperialism?

In what ways did the worldview of intellectuals living in the belle époque differ from that of a generation earlier?

What factors made parliamentary rule in Great Britain, France, and Italy dysfunctional?

What various crises weakened autocratic rule in Germany, Russia, and the Ottoman Empire?

What responsibility did each of the Great Powers have for the outbreak of war in 1914?

THE NEW IMPERIALISM AND THE SPREAD OF EUROPE'S POPULATION

What were the main motivations for European imperialism?

Part of Europe's self-confidence during the period from the 1880s to 1914 was based on the unchallenged sway it held over the rest of the globe. Europeans brought under political control large swaths of land across the seas and also marked the globe by massive migrations.

The age of empire building that started in Europe in the sixteenth century seemed to have ended by 1750. Then, in the 1880s, the European states launched a new era of expansionism, conquering an unprecedented amount of territory. In only twenty-five years Europeans subjugated 500 million people—one-half of the world's non-European population. European expansion was also manifest in a massive movement of people: between 1870 and 1914, 55 million Europeans moved overseas, mainly to Australia, the United States, Canada, and Argentina.

This era of ambitious conquest is often called the **new imperialism,** to differentiate it from the earlier stage of empire building. Whereas the earlier imperialism focused on the Americas, nineteenth-century imperialism centered on Africa and Asia. And unlike the colonizing of the earlier period, the new imperialism occurred in an age of mass participation in politics and was accompanied by expressions of popular enthusiasm.

ECONOMIC AND SOCIAL MOTIVES

The desire for huge markets and the hope for profit—much of it illusory—stirred an interest in empire. Colonies, it was believed, would provide eager buyers for European goods that would stimulate production at home. Yet colonies did not represent large markets for the metropolitan countries. In 1914 France's colonies represented only 12 percent of its foreign trade. Great Britain's trade with its colonies represented a considerable one-third of its foreign trade, but most of that was with the settlement colonies, such as Canada and Australia, not with those acquired in the era of the new imperialism. As for Germany, colonial trade represented less than 1 percent of its exports. Even protective tariffs imposed on colonies failed to secure trade monopolies. Far more than their colonies, France, Germany, and Great Britain continued to be one another's best customers.

Lack of profitability, however, mattered little to many proponents of empire. Some of them, known as social imperialists, argued that possession of an empire could resolve social as well as economic issues. An empire could be an outlet for a variety of domestic frustrations, especially for those nations concerned about overpopulation. German and Italian imperialists often argued that their nations needed colonies in which to resettle their multiplying poor. Once the overseas territories were acquired, however, few Europeans found them attractive for settlement.

new imperialism   Era of European overseas expansion launched in the 1880s. Europeans subjugated 500 million people in Africa and Asia.

NATIONALISTIC MOTIVES

To a large extent, empire building was triggered by the desire to assert national power. At the end of the nineteenth century, two major powers emerged, Russia and the United States. Compared with these giants, western European nations seemed small and insignificant, and many of their leaders believed that to compete effectively on the world stage, they needed to become large territorial entities. Empires would enable them to achieve that goal.

The British Empire, with India as its crown jewel, constituted the largest, most powerful, and apparently wealthiest of all the European domains. It was the envy of Europe. Although the real source of Britain's wealth and power was the country's industrial economy, many people believed that its success came from its vast empire. And so the British example stimulated other nations to carve out empires. Their activities in turn triggered British anxieties. Britain and France unleashed a scramble for Africa and Asia; in Asia Britain also competed with Russia.

France, defeated by Prussia in 1870, found in its colonies proof that it was still a Great Power. Germany and Italy, which formed their national identities relatively late, cast a jealous eye on the British and French empires and decided that if they were to be counted as Great Powers, they too would need overseas colonies. Belgium's King Leopold II (r. 1876–1909) spun out various plans to acquire colonies to compensate for his nation's small size. And Britain, anxious at the emergence of rival economic and political powers in the late nineteenth century, found in its colonies a guarantee for the future.

In the race for colonies, worldwide strategic concerns stimulated expansion. Because the Suez Canal ensured the route to India, the British established a protectorate over Egypt in 1882. Beginning in the next decade, they feared that a rival power might threaten their position by encroaching on the Nile. They consequently established control over the Nile Valley all the way south to Uganda (see **Map 24.1**). Russia, fearing a British takeover in central Asia, expanded toward Afghanistan, while the British movement northwestward to Afghanistan had a similar motivation—to prevent Russia from encroaching on India. The "great game" played by Russia and Britain in central Asia ended only in 1907, with the signing of the Anglo-Russian Entente.

Much of this expansion was driven by the desire to control the often-turbulent frontiers of newly acquired areas. Once those frontiers had been brought under control, there were, of course, new frontiers that had to be subdued. As a Russian foreign minister said of such an incentive for expansion, "The chief difficulty is to know where to stop." The imperial powers rarely did.

CHRONOLOGY

1873	Three Emperors' League
1882	Britain seizes Egypt
	Triple Alliance of Germany, Italy, and Austria-Hungary
1884	Three Emperors' League renewed
1890	Kaiser Wilhelm II dismisses Bismarck as chancellor
1894	Franco-Russian Alliance
	Beginning of the Dreyfus affair
1900	King of Italy assassinated
1903	Emmeline Pankhurst founds the Women's Social and Political Union
1904	Anglo-French Entente
1905	Einstein proposes theory of relativity
	Revolution in Russia
1907	Anglo-Russian Entente
1908	Young Turk rebellion in Ottoman Empire
1911	Italy colonizes Libya
	Second Moroccan crisis
June 28, 1914	Assassination of Archduke Franz Ferdinand
August 4, 1914	With the entry of Britain, Europe is at war

The bitter rivalry among the Great Powers helps explain the division of the globe, but it also protected some regions from falling under European domination, especially in parts of Asia. Most of China survived because the European powers held one another's ambitions in check. No state alone could conquer all of China; none would allow the others to do so either.

OTHER IDEOLOGICAL MOTIVES

In addition to the search for profit and nationalistic pride, Europeans developed a strong rationalization for imperialism. Because Europeans had gained technological and scientific know-how, many imperialists believed it was Europe's duty to develop Africa and Asia for the benefit of colonizer and colonized. Railroads, telegraphs, hospitals, and schools would transform colonial peoples by opening them to what were seen as the beneficent influences of Europe. If necessary, these changes would be realized by force.

MAP 24.1   Africa in 1914

European powers in the late nineteenth century conquered most of Africa. Only Liberia and Ethiopia were left unoccupied at the start of World War I.

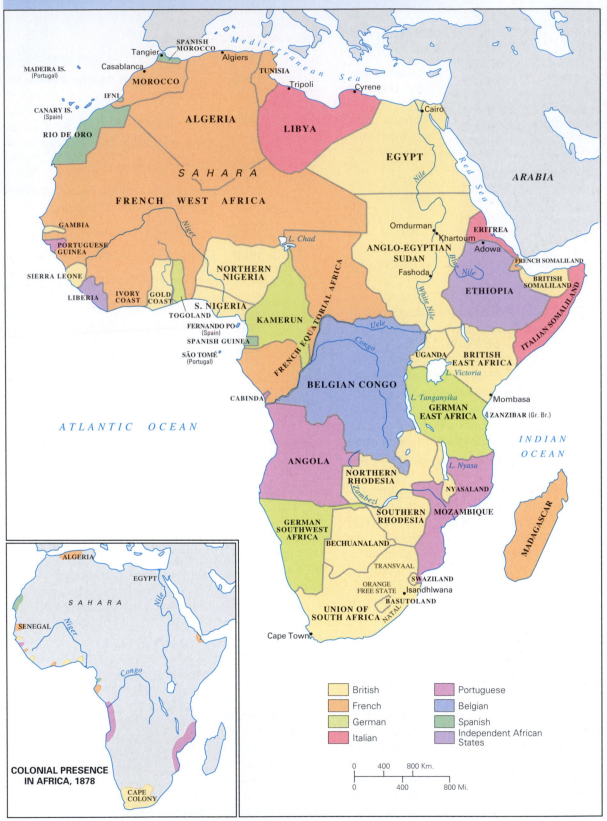

MADEIRA IS.
(Portugal)

SPANISH
MOROCCO

Tangier

Casablanca

Algiers

TUNISIA

Tripoli

Cyrene

Mediterranean Sea

Cairo

CANARY IS.
(Spain)

IFNI

MOROCCO

ALGERIA

LIBYA

EGYPT

Red Sea

ARABIA

RIO DE ORO

S A H A R A

FRENCH   WEST   AFRICA

Nile

GAMBIA

Niger

L. Chad

Omdurman

Khartoum

ERITREA

Adowa

FRENCH SOMALILAND

PORTUGUESE
GUINEA

NORTHERN
NIGERIA

ANGLO-EGYPTIAN
SUDAN

Fashoda

Blue Nile

BRITISH
SOMALILAND

SIERRA LEONE

FRENCH EQUATORIAL AFRICA

White Nile

ETHIOPIA

LIBERIA

IVORY
COAST

GOLD
COAST

S. NIGERIA

TOGOLAND

KAMERUN

Uele

ITALIAN SOMALILAND

FERNANDO PO
(Spain)

SPANISH GUINEA

Congo

UGANDA

BRITISH
EAST AFRICA

SÃO TOMÉ
(Portugal)

L. Victoria

BELGIAN CONGO

L. Tanganyika

GERMAN
EAST AFRICA

Mombasa

CABINDA

ZANZIBAR (Gr. Br.)

ATLANTIC   OCEAN

INDIAN
OCEAN

ANGOLA

NORTHERN
RHODESIA

L. Nyasa

Zambezi

NYASALAND

GERMAN
SOUTHWEST
AFRICA

SOUTHERN
RHODESIA

MOZAMBIQUE

MADAGASCAR

BECHUANALAND

TRANSVAAL

SWAZILAND

Isandhlwana

ORANGE
FREE STATE

BASUTOLAND

UNION OF
SOUTH AFRICA

Natal

Cape Town

COLONIAL PRESENCE
IN AFRICA, 1878

ALGERIA

EGYPT

S A H A R A

Nile

SENEGAL

Niger

Congo

CAPE
COLONY

Legend:

British		Portuguese
French		Belgian
German		Spanish
Italian		Independent African States

0   400   800 Km.

0   400   800 Mi.

At the same time that Europeans were making substantial material progress as a result of industrialization, their wide-scale expansion overseas brought them into contact with Africans and Asians who had traditional economies. They assumed that the dramatic disparity between their own material culture and that of colonial peoples was proof of their own innate superiority. They viewed Africans and Asians as primitive, inferior peoples, still in their evolutionary "infancy."

Influenced by Darwin and his theory of the struggle for survival (see pages 727–729), many argued that just as competition among species existed in nature, so did groups of humans struggle for survival. Dubbed "Social Darwinists," these thinkers envisioned a world of fierce competition. They believed that the most serious struggle was among the races and, further, that the outcome was predetermined: the white race was destined to succeed, the nonwhites to succumb.

Many Europeans paternalistically believed they had a duty to "develop" these "infant" peoples. The British bard of imperialism, Rudyard Kipling (1865–1936), celebrated this view in his poem "White Man's Burden" (1899):

> *Take up the White Man's burden—*
> *Send forth the best ye breed—*
> *Go bind your sons to exile*
> *To serve your captives' need.*

Each nation was certain that providence had chosen it for a colonial mission. France, its leaders announced, had a civilizing mission to fulfill in the world; Prime Minister Ferry (feh-REE) declared it the duty of his country "to civilize the inferior races." Although European states were colonial rivals, they also believed they were engaged in a joint mission overseas. Empire building underscored the belief in a common European destiny, as opposed to the ascribed savagery and backwardness of non-Europeans.

Colonial acquisitions triggered public support for further expansion of the empire—support that was expressed by the founding of various colonial societies. Britain's Primrose League, which lobbied for empire as well as other patriotic goals, had 1 million members.

Dutch Colonial Officials in the Dutch East Indies

In this club in an outpost of empire (in present-day Indonesia), the comforts of European bourgeois life were lovingly re-created. Absent from this photo are the countless Indonesian servants who were part of the colonial officials' lives.

(Royal Tropical Institute, Amsterdam)

Though more limited in size, Germany, France, and Italy had similar organizations. Colonial societies generally drew their membership from the professional middle classes—civil servants, professors, and journalists—who were quite open to nationalist arguments. These societies produced a steady stream of propaganda favoring empire building.

Much of the literature celebrating empire building described it in masculine terms. European men were seen as proving their virility by going overseas, conquering, and running empires. They contrasted their manliness with the supposed effeminacy of the colonial peoples. And in building empires, Europeans asserted their manliness in comparison with their wives, sisters, or mothers. Women were to stay home; if later they came overseas, it was as helpmates to male colonial officials or as missionaries. Believing that they would have a positive influence on the world, women missionaries, either as members of a religious order or joining their husbands, went to the colonies to spread Western religions and European values. A few women heroically explored distant lands; the Englishwoman Mary Kingsley (1862–1900) went on two exploration trips into Africa. Her popular books focused British interest on overseas territories, but they in no way shook the established view that empire was a man's enterprise.

CONQUEST, ADMINISTRATION, AND WESTERNIZATION

Industrialization gave Europeans the means to conquer overseas territories. They manufactured rapid-fire weapons. Their steam-driven gunboats and oceangoing vessels effectively projected power overseas. Telegraphic communications tied the whole world into a single network, allowing Europeans to gather information and coordinate military and political decision making. Such advantages made Europeans virtually invincible in a colonial conflict. One remarkable exception was the 1896 Italian defeat in Adowa at the hands of an Ethiopian force that was not only superior in numbers but better armed.

Conquest was often brutal. In September 1898 British-led forces at the Battle of Omdurman slaughtered 20,000 Sudanese. From 1904 to 1908 an uprising in southwest Africa against German rule led to the killing of an estimated 60,000 of the Herero people. The German general, who had expressly given an order to exterminate the whole population, was awarded a medal by Kaiser Wilhelm II.

Colonial governments could be brutally insensitive to the needs of the indigenous peoples. (See the box "The Global Record: Chief Montshiwa Petitions Queen Victoria.") To save administrative costs in the 1890s, France put large tracts of land in the French Congo under the control of private rubber companies, which systematically and savagely coerced the local people to collect the sap of the rubber trees. When the scandal broke in Paris, the concessionary companies were abolished, and the French state re-established its control. The most notorious example of exploitation, terror, and mass killings was connected with the Belgian Congo. Leopold II of Belgium had acquired it as a personal empire. It was his private domain, and he was not accountable to anyone for his actions there. To his shame, Leopold mercilessly exploited the Congo and its people. An international chorus of condemnation finally forced the king to surrender his empire and put it under the administration of the Belgian government, which abolished some of the worst features of Leopold's rule.

Imperialism also spread Western technologies, institutions, and values. By 1914 Great Britain had built 40,000 miles of rail lines in India—nearly twice as much as in Britain. In India and Egypt, the British erected hydraulic systems that irrigated previously arid lands. Colonials built cities often modeled on the European grid system. In some cases they were graced with large, tree-lined avenues, and some neighborhoods were equipped with running water and modern sanitation. Schools, patterned after those in Europe, taught the imperial language and spread Western ideas and scientific knowledge—though only to a small percentage of the local population.

The European empire builders created political units that had never existed before. In many parts of Africa they ignored tribal and indigenous differences, which had serious repercussions in the postcolonial world. Although there had been many efforts in the past to join the whole Indian subcontinent under a single authority, the British were the first to accomplish this feat (see **MAP 24.2**). Through a common administration, rail network, and trade, Britain gave Indians the sense of a common condition, leading in 1885 to the founding of the India Congress Party. The Congress Party platform included the demand for constitutional government, representative assemblies, and the rule of law—concepts all based on Western theory and practice. Though initially demanding reforms within the British colonial system, the Congress Party eventually became India's major nationalist group.

In contact with the colonizers, intellectuals in colonial societies adopted a European ideology, nationalism. Nationalism was one of the major values Europeans successfully exported to their overseas possessions. Indians, having studied in British schools or visited Britain, were most likely to be nationalists. They founded a movement, known as "Young India," harking back to "Young Italy" and other European nationalist movements founded during the mid-1800s (see page 658).

CHIEF MONTSHIWA PETITIONS QUEEN VICTORIA

In 1885 Bechuanaland, in southern Africa, became a British protectorate. The Bechuana leaders saw British protection as a means to prevent takeover by the Boers, Dutch-speaking white settlers who were aggressively expanding in South Africa. The British were cavalier about their responsibilities, however, and a few years later allowed the British South Africa Company, a particularly exploitive enterprise, to take control of Bechuanaland. In protest, Chief Montshiwa (1815–1896), a major chief of the Baralong people, petitioned Queen Victoria for redress. His petition was supported by missionary lobbying, and most of Bechuanaland was saved from the clutches of the company.

Mafeking, 16 August 1895

To the Queen of England and Her Ministers:

We send greetings and pray that you are all living nicely. You will know us; we are not strangers. We have been your children since 1885.

Your Government has been good, and under it we have received much blessing, prosperity, and peace. . . .

We Baralong are very astonished because we hear that the Queen's Government wants to give away our country in the Protectorate to the Chartered Company; we mean the B[ritish] S[outh] A[frica] Company.

Our land there is a good land, our fathers lived in it and buried in it, and we keep all our cattle in it.

What will we do if you give our land away? My people are increasing very fast and are filling the land.

We keep all the laws of the great Queen; we have fought for her; we have always been the friends of her people; we are not idle; we build houses; we plough many gardens; we sow. . . .

Why are you tired of ruling us? Why do you want to throw us away? We do not fight against your laws. We keep them and are living nicely.

Our words are No: No. The Queen's Government must not give my people's land in the Protectorate to the Chartered Company. . . .

Peace to you all, we greet you;
Please send a good word back.
I am etc,

Montshiwa

QUESTIONS

1. What are Chief Montshiwa's grievances?
2. Why did the missionaries lend their support to the chief?
3. How does Montshiwa view the relationship between his people and the queen?

Source: S. M. Molema, *Montshiwa, 1815–1896* (Cape Town: G. Struik, 1966), pp. 181–182.

Similarly, in French Algeria before World War I, a movement named "Young Algerians" sprang up.

It was to be several decades before nationalism successfully challenged the European empires. In the meantime, Europeans took great satisfaction in their achievements overseas, confirming their sense of themselves as agents of progress, building a new and better world. Europeans arrogantly believed that they knew what was best for other people, and they accepted force as a means of implementing their ideas. Such attitudes may have colored the increasingly caustic relations between European states.

The ties of empire affected metropolitan cultures. The Hindi word for *bandit* became the English word *thug*; the Hindi number five, denoting the five ingredients necessary for a particular drink, became *punch*. Scenes from the colonial world often were the themes of European art, such as Paul Gauguin's paintings of Tahiti and advertising posters for products as different as soap and whiskey. (See the feature "The Visual Record: Empire and Advertising" on pages 750–751.) After the turn of the century, Pablo Picasso's cubism reflected his growing familiarity with African art. In running the largest empire in the world, the British emphasized the need to develop masculine virtues. They cultivated competitive sports and stern schooling, which, they believed, would develop "character" and leadership. To administer their overseas colonies, Europeans developed sophisticated means of gathering and managing information that benefited metropolitan societies. A growing number of people from the colonies also came to live in European cities. By 1900 some former colonial subjects, despite various forms of discrimination, had become full participants in the lives of their host countries; two Indians won election to the British Parliament in the 1890s.

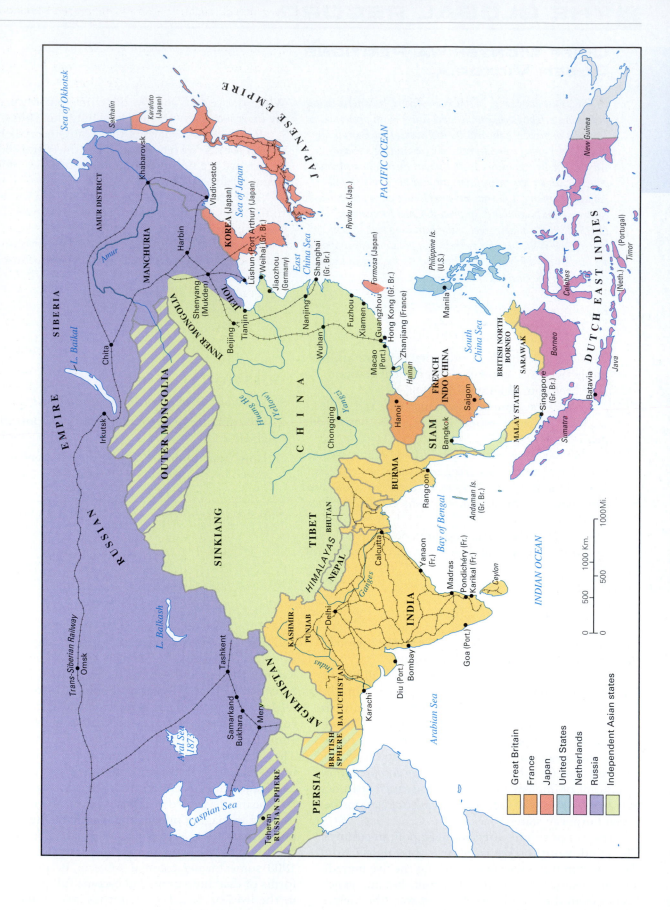

Sea of Okhotsk

Sakhalin

Karafuto (Japan)

JAPANESE EMPIRE

PACIFIC OCEAN

New Guinea

AMUR DISTRICT

Khabarovsk

Vladivostok

KOREA (Japan)

Lüshun (Port Arthur) (Japan)

Weihai (Gr. Br.)

Sea of Japan

East China Sea

Ryuku Is. (Jap.)

Formosa (Japan)

Philippine Is. (U.S.)

Celebes

DUTCH EAST INDIES

Timor (Portugal)

SIBERIA

MANCHURIA

Harbin

Amur

Shenyang (Mukden)

Beijing

Tianjin

Jiaozhou (Germany)

Nanjing

Shanghai (Gr. Br.)

Fuzhou

Xiamen

Guangzhou (Gr. Br.)

Hong Kong (France)

Zhanjiang (France)

Manila

South China Sea

BRITISH NORTH BORNEO

SARAWAK

Borneo

Java

Batavia (Neth.)

Sumatra

EMPIRE

L. Baikal

Chita

INNER MONGOLIA

JEHOL

OUTER MONGOLIA

Wuhan

Huang He (Yellow)

Chongqing

Yangzi

C H I N A

Macao (Port.)

Hainan

FRENCH INDO CHINA

Saigon

Hanoi

SIAM

Bangkok

MALAY STATES

Singapore (Gr. Br.)

RUSSIAN

Irkutsk

SINKIANG

BURMA

Rangoon

Andaman Is. (Gr. Br.)

Bay of Bengal

HIMALAYAS

TIBET

BHUTAN

NEPAL

Calcutta

Yanaon (Fr.)

Madras

Pondichéry (Fr.)

Karikal (Fr.)

Ceylon

INDIAN OCEAN

Trans-Siberian Railway

Omsk

L. Balkash

Tashkent

AFGHANISTAN

KASHMIR

PUNJAB

Delhi

Ganges

Indus

INDIA

BALUCHISTAN

Karachi

Diu (Port.)

Bombay

Goa (Port.)

Arabian Sea

Samarkand

Bukhara

Merv

Aral Sea 1875

BRITISH SPHERE

PERSIA

RUSSIAN SPHERE

Tehran

Caspian Sea

1000 Mi.

1000 Km.

500

500

0

0

Great Britain

France

Japan

United States

Netherlands

Russia

Independent Asian states

MAP 24.2   Asia in 1914
China, Siam (Thailand), and a portion of Persia were the only parts of Asia still independent after the Great Powers, including the United States and Japan, subjugated the continent to alien rule.

Online Study Center   **Improve Your Grade**
Interactive Map: Asia in 1914

OVERSEAS MIGRATIONS AND THE SPREAD OF EUROPEAN VALUES

The nineteenth century saw a phenomenal expansion in European overseas migrations, adding to Europe's impact on other societies (see **MAP 24.3**). Europeans had always migrated. They left villages for towns or, in the case of migrant farm laborers, traveled from village to village as the seasons changed and different crops needed to be harvested. With the expansion of European power abroad beginning in the sixteenth century, Europeans migrated overseas. Between the sixteenth and eighteenth centuries, around 6 million people left Europe. These numbers pale, however, when compared with the nineteenth-century figures. Between 1870 and 1914, 55 million Europeans left the Continent for the Americas, Australia, and New Zealand.

Certain European groups migrated to specific areas. Scandinavians settled in the upper midwestern United States, Italians in Argentina, Germans in Paraguay, Britons in South Africa, and Portuguese in Brazil, with each group leaving its imprint on its adopted land. The upper Midwest was known as "the great desert," but Scandinavians used farming techniques from their homelands to cultivate these dry lands. German Mennonites settled in Kansas and brought with them a strain of wheat that became the basis of the state's prosperity. Immigrants had a similar impact on urban areas. Durban, South Africa, looks like an English city, and some towns in Paraguay resemble Alpine villages of southern Germany. The Germans who came to Milwaukee, Wisconsin, made it a city of beer and strong socialist convictions, reminiscent of home.

Emigration scattered peoples and extended cultures overseas. The settlers consumed many European goods and in turn produced for the European market, increasing the centrality of Europe in the world economy. The migrations around the globe reinforced imperial conquest, further putting Europe's stamp on peoples and societies abroad.

Petersen: Emigrants Preparing to Depart

Edward Petersen's 1890 painting depicts Danish emigrants preparing to leave their homeland. Between 1860 and 1914, 300,000 people emigrated from the small country of Denmark, most of them to the United States.   *(Courtesy of the Aarhus Kunstmuseum. Reproduced with permission of Thomas, Poul, and Ole Hein Pedersen, Aarhus.)*

MAP 24.3 European Migrations, 1820–1910

Throughout the nineteenth century, millions of Europeans left home for overseas, most headed for the United States.   *(Source: The Times Atlas of World History, 3d ed. (Times Books). Reprinted by permission of HarperCollins Publishers, Ltd. © HarperCollins Publishers, Ltd. Some data from Eric Hobsbawm, The Age of Empire, 1875–1914 [New York: Pantheon, 1987].)*

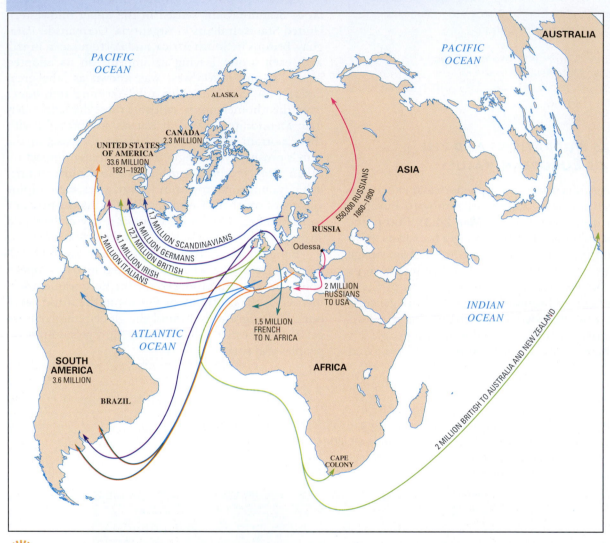

Online Study Center   Improve Your Grade   Interactive Map: European Migrations, 1820–1910

S E C T I O N   S U M M A R Y

- Although the quest for commercial profit helped motivate imperialism, the colonies, for the most part, did not become large markets of the colonizing powers.

- Growing nationalism, rivalry among the Great Powers, and the need to protect the frontiers of already acquired colonies also generated empire building.

- Technological superiority, strong public support, notions of racial and cultural superiority, and a "civilizing mission" justified colonial conquest in the minds of Europeans.

- Industrialization produced powerful weaponry that made colonial conquest possible; European powers brought Western technologies, and methods of administration and education, to the colonized, as well as Western ideologies such as nationalism.

- Colonial cultures influenced metropolitan societies through art, advertising, linguistic practices, and immigration.

- Between 1870 and 1914, 55 million Europeans migrated to the Americas, Australia, and New Zealand, reinforcing Europe's global impact.

FROM OPTIMISM TO ANXIETY: POLITICS AND CULTURE

In what ways did the worldview of intellectuals living in the belle époque differ from that of a generation earlier?

Any of the beliefs and institutions that had seemed so solid in the "age of optimism" found themselves under attack in the next generation. Forces hostile to liberalism became increasingly vocal. In the arts and philosophy, the earlier confidence was replaced by doubt, relativism, and a desire to flee the routines of everyday life.

THE EROSION OF THE LIBERAL CONSENSUS

In 1850 liberals assumed that with the passage of time more and more people would be won over to their worldview. By 1900, however, liberalism faced serious challenges. Various ideas and movements—some new, some rooted in the past—chipped away at the liberal consensus. Prominent among these were socialism, anarchism, a new political right, racism, and anti-Semitism.

The undermining of the liberal consensus began among liberals themselves, who, in the face of changing circumstances, retreated from some of their basic tenets. For example, one of the principal emphases of liberalism had always been free trade. But under the pressure of economic competition, liberals supported tariffs at home and created closed markets in their empires.

Historically, liberals had typically stood for an expansion of civil liberties, yet they saw nothing wrong or inconsistent in continuing to deny women both the vote and free access to education and professional advancement. In the face of labor agitation, many liberals no longer unconditionally supported civil liberties for workers and favored instead the violent crushing of strikes.

Similarly, liberals had always upheld the sanctity of private property, but under the pressure of events, they abandoned this principle as an absolute goal. To ensure workers' safety, they placed limits on employers' liberties by passing legislation requiring them to improve working conditions. In some countries, some liberals supported progressive income taxes, which other liberals perceived as a serious invasion of private property. When it became clear that a free market was unable to meet many human needs, welfare programs were instituted in several countries. These reforms were intended to strengthen the state by winning support from the masses and by fostering the growth of a healthy population through limited aid to mothers and children. In the effort to address real-life problems of the day, however, liberals encountered a paradox at the heart of their ideology: creating rights for one group (such as workers or women) infringed on those of others (such as employers or men). Whatever action liberals took seemed to reveal a willingness to breach fundamental principles.

THE GROWTH OF SOCIALISM AND ANARCHISM

Among the groups challenging the power and liberal ideology of the middle classes were the socialist parties, both Marxist and non-Marxist, whose goal was to win the support of workers by espousing their causes. Socialists varied in their notions of how their goals should be achieved: some favored pursuing objectives gradually and peacefully; others were dedicated to a violent overthrow of capitalist society.

Socialism In Britain, socialists founded the Fabian Society in 1884, named after the Roman general noted for winning by avoiding open, pitched battles. The Fabians criticized the capitalist system as inefficient, wasteful, and unjust. They believed that by gradual, democratic means, Parliament could transfer factories and land from the private sector to the state, which would manage them for the benefit of society as a whole. More efficient and more just, socialism would come into being not through class war but through enlightened ideas. This gradualist approach became the hallmark of British socialism; it shaped the ideology of the Labour Party that would gain electoral success in the 1920s.

In Germany various strands of socialism came together when a single united party was formed in 1875. But within a few years a debate that divided socialism in general broke up the German party: could socialism come about by gradual democratic means, or, as Marx had contended, would it require a violent revolution? The German socialist leader Eduard Bernstein (1850–1932), who had visited England and had soaked up the influence of the Fabians, argued for gradualism in a book with the telling English title *Evolutionary Socialism* (1898). Marx had been wrong, said Bernstein, to suggest that capitalism necessarily led to the increasing wretchedness of the working class. The capitalist economy had in fact expanded and been able to provide for steadily improved conditions. Workers would not need to seize power by some cataclysmic act. Rather, by

THE VISUAL RECORD

Empire and Advertising

In 1822 Joseph Huntley opened a small bakery in Reading, England. It was located near a coaching inn on the busy road between London and Bath. From a handbasket, he sold biscuits to hungry coach travelers passing through. In 1832, Huntley's son, who had an ironmongery across from the bakery, began producing tin boxes for the biscuits, which allowed them to "retain their freshness for years" and to travel worldwide without breaking. The bakery expanded rapidly. George Palmer joined the business in 1841; five years later they purchased a former silk factory of 5,000 square feet that occupied more than half an acre. From this point on, Huntley & Palmers mass-produced their biscuits. By 1898, Huntley & Palmers was the largest biscuit manufacturer in the world; more than 5,000 men and women produced biscuits in a cluster of factory buildings that then occupied 24 acres and had become a "small city" unto itself.*

The image depicted here, a trade card advertising the Huntley & Palmers product, portrays a British hunting party in India around the turn of the nineteenth century. This card and the story behind the company it represents illustrate several themes inherent to nineteenth-century Western civilization: industrial capitalism, the modernization in transportation, global commerce, and most poignantly, the interaction between imperialism and advertising.

The expansion of Huntley & Palmers in the second half of the century could not have occurred without the "second industrial revolution" (see pages 712–713). Improved modes of transportation, improved metal production for packaging, the building of the Suez Canal, and the expansion of empire brought Huntley & Palmers biscuits to ever greater distances. Export to the British colonies began in the 1840s. By 1874 the company could boast that "seldom a ship sails from England that does not bear within [its] ribs a Reading biscuit." By the end of the nineteenth century, Huntley & Palmers had sales representatives in China, Japan, India, South Africa, and North and South America. Ten percent of all its exports went to Britain's most important colony, India. Foreign companies produced biscuits under the Huntley & Palmers license in India, France, New Zealand, and Australia. The company increasingly relied on raw materials imported from overseas—eggs came from Ireland, coconuts came from Barbados and the West Indies, and cocoa came from West Africa.

An important reason for Huntley & Palmers' success lay in advertising. In addition to newspaper advertisements, handbills and posters placarded urban surfaces. Particularly pervasive were trade cards, usually 4 x 6 inches in size, such as the one presented here. Huntley & Palmers produced hundreds of these trade cards, with colorful images on the front and a description of their latest products on the back. They showed not only how the biscuits could be found all over the world, but how they were transported, such as by camel, hot air balloon, elephant, and ship. Retailers distributed the cards, which were so appealing that they became collectors' items.

The card shown here depicts a tiger hunt in India, to which only those who had power and authority—royalty and senior imperial officials—were given the honor of attending. Members of the hunting party sit atop the crates in which 10-pound tins of Huntley & Palmers' biscuits have been shipped, transported by a British-built railroad, and then carried on elephants. Retaining their civilized British custom, the hunters take their tea break after killing tigers, whose carcasses hang from the elephants. The Indians serve not only as their guides, but also as servants to them, performing functions women would perform at home. The relationship the colonizer had to native men was one that effeminized the latter. The scene also suggests the successful and safe insertion of British civilization into an exotic, adventurous, and potentially dangerous context.

In addition to cards, images such as this were placed on the biscuit tins themselves and on calendars, on posters, and in catalogs. Advertisements that included colonial themes conveyed the message that biscuits could bring a "taste of home" to British who found themselves almost anywhere on the globe; they also made imperialism seem safe, adventurous, and appealing.

The colonies themselves were also targets of advertising, especially since they provided such important markets. Advertisements appeared in Indian

*Most of the historical information on Huntley & Palmers comes from "The Huntley & Palmers Collection" on the Reading Museum website, at <http://www.huntleyandpalmers.org.uk>.

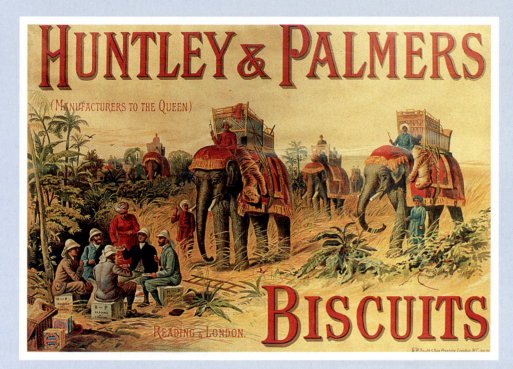

street markets from the mid-nineteenth century. One image from 1902, indeed, depicts an Indian market located in a narrow shadowy street where two upper-class British ladies negotiate with a turbaned figure. Once again, the portrayal suggests potential danger lurking in the shadows; but a tin of Huntley & Palmers biscuits is displayed on the stall, with more stacked in the background, bringing a sense of safety and familiarity to an otherwise strange scene. This 1902 image was used for trade cards as well as for pocket calendars that were placed inside the tins as a promotional gift.

Similar images on the tins made them into collectable objects that are of great value today. One of the most elaborate is an "Arabian Nights" tin from 1888 featuring the adventures of Ali Baba and his encounter with the forty thieves. Folk tales and stories such as these—and the distribution of images depicting such figures in exotic dress—influenced European perceptions of the Muslim world.

Huntley & Palmers iconography turned ordinary objects—trade cards, tins, calendars—into vehicles that carried multiple messages about imperial domination into the homes of ordinary people in Europe and around the globe. The images showed that Huntley & Palmers biscuits could accompany civilized British men (and occasionally women) into

sites of potential danger. The biscuit represented all that was civilized about the British—from its mass production and distribution, to its ability to preserve the habit of tea time—and it offered symbolic proof of British capacity to tame nature and establish order over the "uncivilized." For consumers at home and abroad, Huntley & Palmers represented the success of British imperial dominance.

Huntley & Palmers became so associated with the export business that in 1953 a cartoon depicted their tins of biscuits arriving by spaceship to curious aliens on the planet Mars. So dependent was the company for its success on the British Empire, post–World War II decolonization was one of the factors that caused its closure in 1972.

QUESTIONS

1. What role did the British Empire play in the success of companies such as Huntley & Palmers? What role, in turn, did such a company play in the British experience of empire?

2. How did advertising contribute to the shaping of national, ethnic, and gender identities?

Online Study Center
Improve Your Grade Visual Record Activities

Jean Jaurès

An ideological moderate, the French socialist leader Jean Jaurès (Zhaw-REZ) (1859–1914) was one of France's greatest orators. Much of his socialism was based on ethical notions about social justice, rather than on Marxist doctrine. Here Jaurès addresses a social gathering in 1913. On the eve of World War I, he was assassinated for his efforts to prevent war.

(Roger-Viollet/Getty Images)

piecemeal democratic action, they could win more power and legislate on behalf of their interests. Since he argued for a revision of Marxist theory, Bernstein was labeled a "revisionist." Opposing him in this great debate was the party theoretician, Karl Kautsky (KOUT-skee) (1854–1938). Kautsky insisted that nothing short of a revolution would institute socialism.

Like most other socialists in Europe, the German socialists rejected revisionism and claimed to embrace the doctrine of a violent proletarian revolution. In fact, however, they pursued revisionist policies. Socialists in practice had become another parliamentary party that hoped to reach its goals through legislation.

Despite internal divisions, European socialists also attempted to make their movement international, with some success. In 1864 Marx helped found the Interna-

tional Workers' Association, known as the First International. It was followed by a more robust **Second International,** in 1889. The International met yearly and debated issues of concern to socialists in general, including the worsening relations among European states. As early as 1893 the International urged European states to resolve their conflicts by mandatory arbitration. In 1907, sensing impending war, the International called on workers to strike and refuse military service in case of international conflict.

Anarchism   Another movement that sought to liberate the downtrodden was anarchism, which proclaimed that humans could be free only when the state had been abolished. According to anarchist theory, in a stateless society people would naturally join together in communes and share the fruits of their labor. Some anarchists believed they could achieve their goal by educating people. Others were more impatient and hoped to speed up the process by making direct attacks on existing authority.

The Russian nobleman Michael Bakunin (bah-KOO-neen) (1814–1876), frustrated at the authoritarianism of his homeland, became a lifelong anarchist. He challenged tsarism at home and participated in the 1848 revolutions throughout Europe. He viewed all governments as repressive and declared unilateral war on them: "The passion for destruction is also a creative passion." His ideas were particularly influential in Italy, Spain, and parts of France, especially among the artisan classes.

Many anarchists of this period wanted to bring about the new society by "propaganda of the deed." An attack on the bastions of power, these anarchists believed, could bring about the dissolution of the state. They formed secret terrorist organizations that assassinated heads of state or those close to them. Between 1894 and 1901 anarchists killed a president of France, a prime minister of Spain, an empress of Austria, a king of Italy, and a president of the United States. These murders fixed the popular image of anarchism as a violence-prone ideology. Such "deeds," moreover, produced no particular improvement in the lives of the working-class people on whose behalf they had been undertaken.

Without accepting the anarchists' methods, some in the labor movement shared their hostility toward parliamentary institutions. A working-class program, labor activists argued, could be implemented only by a pure workers' movement, such as unionization. Workers should shun the political arena and concentrate on direct action. According to this line of thought, known

Second International   International socialist organization founded in 1889 that met yearly to debate issues of broad concern. It called for workers to strike and refuse military service.

as "syndicalism" (after the French word for unions), workers would amass their power in unions and at the right moment carry out a general strike, crippling capitalist society and bringing it down. Syndicalism was particularly popular in Mediterranean countries, where its more militant form, anarcho-syndicalism, radicalized labor and made a sizable number of workers hostile to parliamentary government.

THE NEW RIGHT, RACISM, AND ANTI-SEMITISM

The traditional opponents of liberalism on the political right were the conservatives, wedded to preserving the existing order. Beginning in the 1880s, however, a "new right" emerged that was populist and demagogic. Although conservatives had been wary of nationalism, the new right embraced it. Alienated by democracy and social egalitarianism, many in this new right rejected doctrines of human equality and embraced racist ideologies.

Many Europeans believed that human races were not only different physiologically, but also differently endowed in intelligence and other qualities (see page 730). At midcentury the Frenchman Arthur de Gobineau (1816–1882) published his *Essay on the Inequality of Human Races,* declaring that race "dominates all other problems and is the key to it." Biologists and early anthropologists made similar statements, thus giving racism a "scientific" aura. Throughout the second half of the nineteenth century, race was thought to be the principal explanation for the differences that were discovered among human groupings.

These racist ideas helped fuel **anti-Semitism.** For centuries Jews had been the object of suspicion and bigotry. Originally, the basis of the prejudice was religious. As early as the Middle Ages, however, the argument emerged that "Jewish blood" was different. And with the popularization of pseudoscientific racist thinking in the nineteenth century, Jews were commonly viewed as a separate, inferior race, unworthy of the same rights as the majority of the population.

Historically, Christians had relegated the Jews in their midst to marginal positions. In the Middle Ages, when land was the basis of wealth and prestige, Jews were prohibited from owning land, and had thus been confined to urban trades, among which was moneylending. They incurred high risks by lending money: they often were not paid back and faced unsympathetic courts when they tried to collect their debts. To counteract these risks, Jewish moneylenders charged high interest rates that earned them their unpopular reputation as usurers.

The emancipation of the Jews, which began in France with the Revolution and spread to Germany and Austria by the 1860s, provided them with unprecedented opportunities. Some members of society found it hard to adjust to the prominence that some Jews gained. Because their increased social standing and success were concurrent with the wrenching social transformations brought by industrialization and urbanization, anti-Semites pointed to the Jews as the perpetrators of these unsettling changes.

Many people perceived Jews as prototypical of the new capitalist class. Although most of them were of modest means, Jews often became the brunt of resentment toward the rich. Earlier in the century many anti-Semites were socialists, speaking on behalf of the working class. Later they came from among the petite bourgeoisie—small shopkeepers and artisans—who felt threatened by economic change.

Political movements based on anti-Semitism were founded in the 1880s. They depicted Jews as dangerous and wicked and called for their exclusion from the political arena and from certain professions. In some cases proponents suggested that Jews be expelled from the state. Karl Lueger (1844–1928) was elected mayor of Vienna on an anti-Semitic platform. In Berlin the emperor's chaplain, Adolf Stöcker (SHTOE-kur) (1835–1909), founded an anti-Semitic party, hoping to make political inroads among the working-class supporters of socialism. In France Edouard Drumont (1844–1917) published one of the bestsellers of the second half of the nineteenth century, *Jewish France,* in which he blamed all the nation's misfortunes on the Jews.

In Russia organized *pogroms,* or mass attacks, killed two thousand Jews in the 1880s and one thousand in 1905, frightening two million into exile, mostly to the United States. Russian Jews lived under social as well as legal disabilities. Condemned to second-class citizenship, they won full emancipation only with the Bolshevik Revolution of 1917.

In the face of growing hostility, some Jews speculated that they would be safe only in their own nation. The Austrian Jewish journalist Theodore Herzl (HERtsl) (1860–1904), outraged by the Dreyfus affair in France, in which a Jewish officer was imprisoned on trumped-up charges of treason (see pages 758–759), founded the Zionist movement. He advocated establishing a Jewish state in the Jews' ancient homeland of Palestine. In the beginning, the Zionist movement won a following only in eastern Europe, where the Jews were particularly ill-treated, but by 1948 **Zionism** culminated in the creation of the state of Israel.

anti-Semitism Centuries-old prejudice against and demonization of Jews that became virulent in the 1880s with the emergence of the ultranationalist and racist ideologies and political movements.

Zionism Nationalist Jewish movement beginning in the late nineteenth century. In face of anti-Semitism, Zionism advocated establishing a Jewish state in the Jews' ancient homeland of Palestine.

IRRATIONALITY AND UNCERTAINTY

In contrast to the confidence in reason and science that had prevailed at midcentury, the era starting in the 1880s was characterized by a sense of irrationality and uncertainty—in philosophy, in the arts, even in religion. The positivism of the earlier era had emphasized the surface reality of "progress" but had ignored the emotional and intuitive aspects of life. By the 1890s a neo-romantic mood, emphasizing emotion and feeling, stirred major intellectual movements. The spotlight was no longer on reason, but on instinct.

Philosophy   In philosophy the tension between reason and emotion was vividly expressed in the work of the German philosopher Friedrich Nietzsche (FREED-reesh NEET-sheh) (1844–1900), who proclaimed that rationality had led humankind into a meaningless abyss. Reason would not resolve human problems, nor would any preconceived ideas. "God is dead," Nietzsche announced. With no God, humankind was free of all outside constraints, free to overthrow all conventions. Nietzsche admonished his readers to challenge existing institutions and accepted truths and to create new ones.

The French philosopher Henri Bergson (BERK-sohn) (1859–1940) argued that science—and indeed life—must be interpreted not rationally but intuitively. "Science," Bergson declared, "can teach us nothing of the truth; it can only serve as a rule of action." Humans could best understand meaningful truths—such as those of religion, literature, and art—by relying on their feelings.

Social Sciences   Various disciplines of knowledge subscribed to the notion that human beings are often irrational, motivated by deep-seated instinctive forces. The Austro-Hungarian **Sigmund Freud** (1856–1939) founded psychoanalysis, a method of treating psychic disorders by exploring the unconscious. Freud believed that people were motivated not only by observed reality but also by their unconscious feelings and emotions. Whereas earlier physicians had described the frequently diagnosed women's illness of "hysteria" as a physical ailment, Freud saw its roots as psychological, the result of unresolved inner conflicts. He stressed that irrational forces played a significant role in human behavior.

Online Study Center **Improve Your Grade**
Primary Source: The Interpretation of Dreams: Psychoanalysis Is Born

The social theorist Gaetano Mosca (1858–1941) pessimistically argued that the desire to dominate is a basic part of human nature. In his book *Elements of Political Science* (1891), he posited that in all societies—even democratic ones—an elite minority rules over the majority. Beneath slogans touting the public good lies selfish ambition, and the thirst for power is never slaked—a poor prognosis for socialist ideals. Thus, as did Freud, Mosca suggested that surface appearances are deceptive and that irrational forces guide human behavior.

Arts   In the arts, the idea of being ***avant-garde***—French for "forefront"—took hold among creative people. Breaking the taboos of society and the conventions of one's craft seemed to be signs of artistic creativity. Artistic movements proclaimed idiosyncratic manifestoes and constantly called for the rejection of existing forms of expression and the creation of new ones. The symbolists in France and in Italy, the expressionists in Germany, the futurists in Italy, and the secessionists in Austria all reflected the sense that they were living through a fractured period.

In protest against the mass culture of their day, artists focused on images that were unique. Unlike earlier art, which had a clear message, the art of this era did not. Many artists no longer believed their role was to portray or spread ideals. Rather, they tended to be introspective and even self-absorbed. The public at large found it difficult to decipher the meaning of the new art, but a number of patrons supported the avant-garde artists' talent and insight.

Unlike the realists who preceded them, artists in the 1890s surrendered to neo-romanticism, trying to investigate and express inner forces. As the French painter Paul Gauguin (1848–1903) noted, the purpose of painting is to communicate not how things look but the emotions they convey. The Russian Wassily Kandinsky (vass-IH-lee kan-DIN-skee) (1866–1944) asked viewers of his art to "look at the picture as a graphic representation of a mood and not as a representation of objects." Artists appeared to be examining the hidden anxieties of society. The Frenchman Gustave Moreau (mo-RO) (1826–1898) displayed monsters—creations of nightmare and byproducts of the unconscious. The Norwegian painter Edvard Munch (MOONGK) (1863–1944) emphasized scenes of violence, fear, and sheer horror.

Religion and Science   The era of uncertainty undermined both religious belief and confidence in science. Although large numbers of people still held traditional religious beliefs, indifference to organized

---

Sigmund Freud   Austrian founder of psychoanalysis, a method of treating psychic disorders by exploring the unconscious, based on the belief that people are motivated by unconscious feelings and drives.

avant-garde   French for "forefront," the term refers to early-twentieth-century artists who inspired unconventional techniques, considered themselves precursors of new styles, and called for the rejection of existing forms of expression.

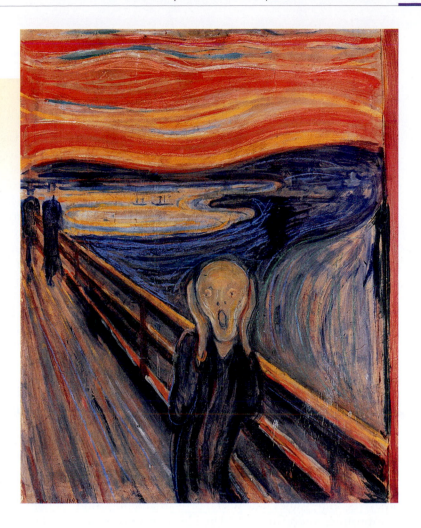

Munch: The Scream
Painted in 1893, this work reflects the fear and horror that some intellectuals experienced at the end of the nineteenth century.
(Nasjonalgalleriet, Oslo/Art Resource, NY. © 2002 Artists Rights Society [ARS], New York/ADAGP, Paris)

religion spread. In urban areas of western Europe, church attendance declined, while various forms and practices of mysticism—such as séances—became more widespread. Some people were attracted to Eastern religions such as Buddhism and Hinduism, perhaps reflecting a loss of faith in Western culture itself.

Scientists of this period questioned long-held commonsense beliefs. During the last week of the century, the German physicist Max Planck (1858–1947) suggested that light and other kinds of electromagnetic radiation, such as radio waves, which had always been considered continuous trains of waves, actually consist of individual packages of well-defined energy, which he called "quanta." In 1905 Albert Einstein (1879–1955) proposed the theory of relativity, which required a drastic change in fundamental ideas about space and time. To the three dimensions of space—length, breadth, and width—was added a complicating fourth dimension, that of time. The new ideas were not easily grasped. The old concept of a fixed cause tied to a fixed effect did not hold, because even though things happen predictably, they also happen randomly.

=== S E C T I O N   S U M M A R Y ===

- The liberal ideology of the early nineteenth century could not address economic and social practicalities by the century's end. Civil and political liberties, some concluded, could not apply to everyone.

- Two strands of socialism emerged by the end of the nineteenth century: one that advocated violent revolution, and another—revisionism—that argued change could come through gradual, democratic means. The latter became more dominant.

- A "new right" of the late nineteenth century embraced nationalism and rejected democracy and the notion of human equality. It also adopted racist and anti-Semitic ideologies.

- By the 1890s a neo-romantic mood emphasized the validity of feeling and emotion, while irrationality and uncertainty permeated philosophy, the social sciences, the arts, religion, and science itself.

VULNERABLE DEMOCRACIES

What factors made parliamentary rule in Great Britain, France, and Italy dysfunctional?

By the end of the nineteenth century, most of Europe's political systems floundered in crisis. The major powers with democratic institutions—Great Britain, France, and Italy—confronted volatile public opinion and had difficulty winning a broad consensus for their policies. They struggled with new challenges emerging from an expanded electorate that was at times frustrated by the failure of the system to respond to its demands. Turning away from the democratic precept of resolving differences through the ballot and legislation, many people—both in government and out—were willing to resort to extraparliamentary means, including violence, to see their interests prevail.

GREAT BRITAIN

In Great Britain the Reform Bill of 1884 extended the vote to two of every three adult men, doubling suffrage to five million. The appeal of this enlarged electorate tempted politicians to make demagogic promises, which were often broken later, to the exasperation of their constituents. Representing a population with more diverse interests and values, members of Parliament found compromise more difficult. Unable to resolve issues peacefully, the British government uncharacteristically resorted to the use of force.

As in earlier periods, the problem of Ireland persisted. The Irish seethed under alien British rule. In 1886, Prime Minister William Gladstone (GLAD-sten) proposed autonomy, or "home rule," for Ireland. But many opposed this plan. If Ireland, a predominantly Catholic country, ruled itself, the local Protestant majority in Ulster (the northeast part of the island) would be overwhelmed by Catholic control. "Home rule is Rome rule," chanted the supporters of Ulster Protestantism. In addition, many opposed changing the existing relationship between England and its neighboring possession. With considerable political maneuvering, the Liberals finally pushed a home-rule bill through the House of Commons in 1911, but it was obstructed in the House of Lords and was not slated to go into effect until September 1914.

Passage of the home-rule bill did not resolve the Irish problem. Many segments of British society showed they were willing to resort to extralegal and even violent means. Fearing Catholic domination, Protestants in northern Ireland armed themselves in their determination to resist home rule. Catholic groups took up arms, too, insisting on the unity of the island. The Conservative Party in Britain, which opposed home rule, called on Ulster Protestants to revolt. British officers threatened to resign their commissions rather than fight Ulster. The behavior of the Conservatives and the army indicated a breakdown of order and authority—a disregard for tradition by two of its major bulwarks. Only the outbreak of world war in 1914 delayed a showdown over Ireland, and then by only a few years.

Irish home rule was not the only issue that eroded civility in the British Parliament. Liberals, who dominated the House of Commons from 1906, committed themselves to an impressive array of social reforms, such as old-age pensions. To finance such measures, the feisty chancellor of the exchequer, David Lloyd George (1863–1945), proposed raising income taxes and death duties, and levying a tax on landed wealth. A bill with these measures easily passed the House of Commons in 1909 but was stymied in the upper chamber, where many members were prominent landowners.

The House of Lords technically had the power to amend or reject a bill passed by Commons, but for nearly 250 years it had been tacitly understood that the Lords did not have the right to reject a money bill. Nonetheless, motivated by economic self-interest and personal spite against the Liberals, a majority in the House of Lords disregarded convention and voted against the bill. Lloyd George expressed his outrage that a handful of magnates in the upper chamber—sitting there not by election but by hereditary right—could thwart the will of the people. A major constitutional crisis ensued.

In 1911 the government sponsored a bill to limit the legislative power in the House of Lords to a suspensive veto—meaning that any bill defeated there would simply be suspended for a predetermined period, such as two years. The House of Lords initially refused to pass the bill, but finally conceded when the king threatened to appoint four hundred new lords.

During the debate over the bill, Conservatives resorted to brawling and refused to let the prime minister speak. It was the first time in British parliamentary history that such a breach of conduct had occurred. The British Parliament, considered the model for supporters of free institutions, had shown itself unable to resolve issues in a civil manner.

Violence also appeared in another unexpected place: the women's suffrage movement. Most liberal males, when speaking of the need to extend human liberty, had

A Suffragist Attempts to Chain Herself to the Gates of Buckingham Palace, London, 1914 In their effort to win the vote, women resorted to civil disobedience, and police often violently intervened. *(Popperfoto/Retrofile.com)*

excluded women because they thought public affairs an inappropriate arena for them. Women were supposed to restrict their concerns to motherhood; they were insufficiently educated and lacking in the capacity for rational and independent thought that voting required. In 1903 Emmeline Pankhurst (1858–1928) and her two daughters founded the Women's Social and Political Union, whose goal was immediate suffrage.

Angered and frustrated by their lack of progress, the **suffragists** (often referred to by contemporaries as "suffragettes"), led by the Pankhursts, began a more militant program of protest in 1906. They disrupted the proceedings in Parliament, broke windows at the prime minister's residence, slashed canvases at the National Gallery, burned down empty houses, dropped acid into mailboxes, and threw bombs. They even threatened the lives of the prime minister and the king. In 1913, Emily Wilding Davidson sacrificed her life to the cause of female suffrage when, before thousands of spectators at the Derby, she threw herself in front of

the king's horse. These acts of violence and tragedy drew condemnation, but they also brought world-wide attention to the cause.

But these acts also incurred severe punishment. Suffragists who were arrested often engaged in hunger strikes, which provoked the authorities to force-feed them—an extremely painful and humiliating procedure that amounts to torture. Female protesters were also physically attacked by male thugs. (See the box "The Written Record: Pankhurst Testifies on Women's Rights.") That women would resort to violence, and that men inside and outside government would retaliate in kind, demonstrated how widespread the cult of force had become.

FRANCE

The Third Republic, founded in 1870 after France's humiliating military defeat at the hands of the Prussians, also struggled with an ongoing series of crises. Challenged by enemies on the political left and right who continually called for the abolition of democracy, the regime found itself buffeted from all sides.

suffragists   Activists who, beginning in the late nineteenth century, organized to win the vote for women and adopted increasingly violent tactics. Also called "suffragettes."

THE WRITTEN RECORD

PANKHURST TESTIFIES ON WOMEN'S RIGHTS

In 1908 the suffragists, led by Emmeline Pankhurst, issued a handbill calling on the people of London to "rush" Parliament and win the vote for women. The legal authorities interpreted their action as a violation of the peace, and several suffragists, including Pankhurst, were put on trial. They put up a spirited defense, in which Pankhurst movingly explained her motives for leading the suffragist cause.

I want you to realise how we women feel; because we are women, because we are not men, we need some legitimate influence to bear upon our law-makers. Now, we have tried every way. We have presented larger petitions than were ever presented for any other reform, we have succeeded in holding greater public meetings than men have ever had for any reform, in spite of the difficulty which women have in throwing off their natural diffidence, that desire to escape publicity which we have inherited from generations of our foremothers; we have broken through that. We have faced hostile mobs at street corners, because we were told that we could not have that representation for our taxes which men have won unless we converted the whole of the country to our side. Because we have done this, we have been misrepresented, we have been ridiculed, we have had contempt poured upon us. The ignorant mob at the street corner has been incited to offer us violence, which we have faced unarmed and unprotected by the safeguards which Cabinet Ministers have. We know that we need the protection of the vote even more than men have needed it. . . .

We believe that if we get the vote it will mean better conditions for our unfortunate sisters. We know what the condition of the woman worker is . . . and we have been driven to the conclusion that only through legislation can any improvement be effected, and that that legislation can never be effected until we have the same power as men have to bring pressure to bear upon our representatives and upon Governments to give us the necessary legislation. . . .

I should never be here if I had the same kind of power that the very meanest and commonest of men have—the same power that the wife-beater has, the same power that the drunkard has. I should never be here if I had that power, and I speak for all the women who have come before you and other magistrates. . . .

If you had power to send us to prison, not for six months, but for six years, for sixteen years, or for the whole of our lives, the Government must not think that they can stop this agitation. It will go on. . . .

We are here not because we are law-breakers; we are here in our efforts to become lawmakers.

QUESTIONS

1. What is the logic behind Pankhurst's comment that women need the "protection of the vote" even more than men? What is her main argument here for why women should get the vote?

2. Do you think women were justified in breaking laws in order to obtain their goal? Why or why not? How did their behavior compare with that of men, both within and outside of the British Parliament?

Source: F. W. Pethick Lawrence, ed., *The Trial of the Suffragette Leaders* (London: The Women's Press, 1909), pp. 21–24.

This situation resulted in part from the French government's lack of strong leadership. The need to build coalitions among the several parties in the parliament rewarded those politicians who had moderate, and often mediocre, programs. Firm ideas and commitments had little purchase, and the prime minister offered conciliation more often than he did leadership. In addition, supporters of the republic actually found lackluster leadership appealing. They continued to fear that a strong leader might—as Louis Napoleon had in 1851—exploit his support to make himself dictator.

The regime lurched from one crisis to another. The most notorious was the Dreyfus affair. In October 1894 Captain Alfred Dreyfus (1859–1935) of the French army was arrested and charged with passing military secrets to the German embassy. Dreyfus (DRY-fooss) seems to have attracted suspicion because he was the only Jewish officer on the general staff. The evidence was flimsy—a handwritten letter that some thought Dreyfus had penned, although other experts testified that the handwriting was not that of the young officer.

This letter, and materials that later turned out to be forged, led the French army to court-martial Dreyfus and sentence him to life imprisonment on Devil's Island off the coast of South America. By March 1896 the general staff had evidence that another officer, Major Esterhazy, was actually the spy. But to reopen the case would be to admit the army had made an error, and the general staff refused to do this.

By late 1897, when the apparent miscarriage of justice became widely known, French society split over "the affair." The political left argued for reopening the case. The army and its supporters—right-wing politicians, royalists, and zealous Catholics—argued that the decision should stand. They believed the army, as a bulwark against internal and foreign threats, should be above the law, and the fate of a single man—guilty or innocent—was immaterial. From the outset, Dreyfus was the target of virulent anti-Semitism.

The affair unleashed a swirl of controversy and rioting, which led the government to order a retrial in 1899. But the court again found Dreyfus guilty—this time with "extenuating circumstances" and the recommendation that he be pardoned. Finally, in 1906, Dreyfus was fully exonerated.

The strong encouragement many Catholics gave to those who supported the original verdict confirmed the republicans' belief that the church was a menace to the regime. The politicians who backed Dreyfus—anticlericals—were voted into the parliament. In 1905 they passed a law separating church and state, thus ending the privileged position the Catholic Church had enjoyed. Violent language and physical confrontations on both sides accompanied this division. Catholics trying to prevent state officials from entering churches to take required inventories sometimes resorted to force, using weapons or, in one case, a bear chained to the church. Armed soldiers broke down church doors and dragged priests away.

Labor problems also triggered repeated confrontations with the government. Increased labor militancy produced long, drawn-out strikes, which in 1904 alone led to the loss of four million workdays. Rural workers agitated as well, particularly in the Midi, the south of France. This region suffered from a crisis in the wine industry caused by a disease that attacked the vines, competition from cheap foreign wines, and fraud. The region witnessed increased rural proletarianization as landholdings became concentrated in fewer hands. Rural militancy led to a revolt in 1907. Troops were sent in; they killed dozens and won for the Radical regime the title "government of assassins."

ITALY

Italy, the third major power in Europe to adopt parliamentary government, also had grave problems. Although unification took place in 1860, genuine national unity proved elusive. As in the past, the south especially challenged the central government. Assertive regionalism, crime, and poverty made this area resistant to most government programs.

The parliamentary system established in 1860 was unrepresentative and far from democratic. Property qualifications limited suffrage to less than 3 percent of the population. And as a result of the persistence of *trasformismo* (see page 689)—the practice by which government corrupted and co-opted the opposition—electoral choice was short-circuited.

Between 1870 and 1890 the Italian government introduced some important reforms, but the relatively low standard of living failed to improve. In the fifty years after unification, the population increased from 25 million to 35 million, and the country had limited resources to deal with such growth. In the south a few wealthy landowners held large private estates, while the majority of the peasants were landless and forced to work the land for minimum wages. In the north industrialization had started, but the region was not rich in coal or iron. To be competitive, industry paid very low wages, and the workers lived in abject misery.

Conditions on the land and in the factories led to widespread protests. In 1893 a Sicilian labor movement

Riots in Italian Parliament
Party strife and conflicts between individuals in the Italian parliament were so severe that often they degenerated into fisticuffs. This illustration catches a particularly violent moment of a parliamentary debate. *(Madeline Grimoldi)*

won the adherence of 300,000 members, who seized land and attacked government offices. The government responded with massive force and declared martial law. As unrest spread throughout the peninsula in 1896, the government placed half of the provinces under military rule. A cycle of violence and repression gripped the nation. In this turbulent atmosphere, an anarchist killed King Umberto I on July 29, 1900.

After the turn of the century, a new prime minister, Giovanni Giolitti (jo-VAH-nee jo-LEE-tee) (1842–1928), tried to end the upheaval. He used government force more sparingly and showed a spirit of cooperation toward the workers. Seeking to divert attention from domestic ills and appeal to nationalist fervor, Giolitti launched an attack on Libya in 1911, wresting it from

the ailing Ottoman Empire. The territory was arid and bereft of economic promise, but its conquest was championed as a test of national virility and the foundation of national greatness. The imperialists proudly proclaimed force the arbiter of the nation's future.

The government also returned to the use of force for its domestic problems when, in June 1914, a national strike led to rioting and workers' seizing power in several municipalities. In northern Italy, workers proclaimed an independent republic. It took 100,000 government troops ten days to restore order. The workers' brazen defiance led some nationalist right-wing extremists to form groups of "volunteers for the defense of order," anticipating the vigilante thugs who were to make up the early bands of Italian fascism.

═══ S E C T I O N   S U M M A R Y ═══

- Democratic governments in western Europe experienced crises that led to forceful repression. The British resorted to violence or uncivil behavior over the issues of Irish home rule, a constitutional crisis over social reform, and women's suffrage.

- Democracy in the French republic was threatened by the nation-splitting Dreyfus affair, the role of the Catholic Church, and labor militancy.

- Regionalism, poverty, social strife, violence, and unrepresentative government challenged Italy's efforts at parliamentary democracy.

AUTOCRACIES IN CRISIS

What various crises weakened autocratic rule in Germany, Russia, and the Ottoman Empire?

Four major autocracies dominated central and eastern Europe: Germany, Austria-Hungary, the Ottoman Empire, and Russia. If the democracies encountered difficulties in these years, the autocracies faced even more vehement opposition. Although many groups in the parliamentary regimes grew impatient at the slowness of change, theoretically at least they could believe that someday their goals would be realized. Not so in the autocracies. In authoritarian states, the demands for more democracy grew louder. Protesters resorted to violence and governments in turn used force to maintain themselves.

The severity of autocratic rule varied from state to state, ranging from the absolutism of the Ottoman Empire to the semiparliamentary regime of Germany; but in all of the states, the ruler had the final political say. Resistance to the autocracies included broad popular challenges to the German imperial system, discontent among ethnic minorities in the nearly ungovernable empire of Austria-Hungary, and revolution and war in the Russian and Ottoman Empires.

GERMANY

Although Germany had a parliament, the government was answerable to the kaiser, not the people's electoral representatives. To rule effectively, Chancellor Otto von Bismarck maneuvered and intrigued to quell opposition. In the face of socialist growth, he used an attempt to assassinate the emperor as the excuse to ban the Socialist Party in 1879. He also turned against the Catholics, who were lukewarm toward Protestant Prussia, persecuting them and their institutions. These measures, however, did not prevent the growth of the Socialist and Catholic Center Parties.

Unfortunately for Bismarck, whose tenure in office depended on the goodwill of the emperor, Wilhelm I died in 1888, to be succeeded first by his son, Friedrich, who ruled only a few months, and then by his grandson, Wilhelm II (r. 1888–1918). The young Kaiser Wilhelm intended to rule as well as reign, but he was ill fit to govern. Convinced of his own infallibility, he bothered to learn very little. Born with a crippled hand,

Wilhelm II
The German emperor liked to be viewed in a heroic and military posture. His crippled left hand is turned away from the viewer. *(Landesarchiv Berlin)*

Wilhelm seemed to want to compensate for this infirmity by appearing forceful, even brutal. He hated any hint of limitation to his power, announcing, "There is only one ruler in the Reich and I am he. I tolerate no other." A restless individual, Wilhelm changed uniforms eight times daily and traveled ceaselessly among his seventy-five castles and palaces. Intimidated by Bismarck and dismayed by his domestic and foreign policies, the kaiser dismissed him.

Wilhelm II was determined to make Germany a world power whose foreign policy would have a global impact. He wanted Germany to have colonies, a navy, and major influence among the Great Powers. This policy, *Weltpolitik,* or "world politics," greatly troubled Germany's neighbors. They were wary of a new, assertive power in central Europe, especially given the kaiser's bombastic threats. Within Germany, however, Weltpolitik won support. Steel manufacturers and shipbuilders received lucrative contracts; workers, in some industries at least, seemed assured of employment.

Weltpolitik Meaning "world politics," the term describes the policy pursued, with nationalistic appeals and bombastic threats, by Kaiser Wilhelm II to make Germany a world power.

Although the nationalist appeals impressed many Germans, the nation could not be easily managed. The emperor's autocratic style was challenged, and his behavior was increasingly viewed as irresponsible. In the elections of 1912 one-third of all Germans voted for Socialist Party candidates. Thus the largest single party in the Reichstag challenged both the capitalist system and autocracy. Labor militancy also reached new heights. In 1912 one million workers—a record number—went on strike. More and more Germans pressed for a government accountable to the people's elected representatives.

The emperor could not tolerate criticism of his behavior. He frequently talked about using the military to crush socialists and the parliament, ideas that were echoed in the officer corps and in government circles. To some observers it seemed likely that the days of German autocracy were numbered—or that the army and the people would come to blows.

AUSTRIA-HUNGARY

A series of crises also wracked the neighboring Austro-Hungarian Empire. In an age of intense nationalism, a multinational empire was an anomaly, as the emperor Franz Joseph (r. 1848–1916) himself acknowledged. Despite the Compromise of 1867 (see page 693) that regulated the relationship between Austria and Hungary, conflict grew, particularly over control of their joint army. Hungary increasingly saw its interests as separate from Austria's and probably would have broken loose from the dual monarchy had world war not occurred.

In the Hungarian half of the empire, the Magyar rule faced growing challenges. Other nationalities opposed Magyarization—the imposition of the Magyar language and institutions—and insisted on the right to use their own languages in their schools and administrations. The Hungarian government censored and imprisoned nationalist leaders. The Austrian half of the empire treated minority nationalities less harshly, but the government was equally strife-ridden.

There were no easy solutions to the many conflicts the empire faced. Hoping to dilute the influence of nationalist middle-class intellectuals, the Habsburg government introduced universal male suffrage in 1907. The result backfired. The extended suffrage produced a parliament that included thirty ethnically based political parties, making a workable majority nearly impossible to achieve. The empire became even more difficult to govern.

The virulence of debate based on nationality and class divisions grew to unprecedented extremes. Within the parliament, deputies threw inkwells at each other, rang sleigh bells, and sounded bugles. Parliament ceased to be relevant. By 1914 the emperor had dissolved it and several regional assemblies. Austria was being ruled by decree. Emperor Franz Joseph feared that the empire would not survive him.

OTTOMAN EMPIRE

In the generation before 1914, no political system in Europe suffered from so advanced a case of dissolution as the Ottoman Empire, undermined by both secessionist movements within its borders and aggression from other European powers. Sultan Abdul Hamid II (r. 1876–1909) ruled the country as a despot and authorized mass carnage against those who contested his rule, earning him the title "the Great Assassin."

Young, Western-educated Turks—the so-called Young Turks—disgusted at one-man rule and the continuing loss of territory and influence, overthrew Abdul Hamid in a coup in July 1908. They set up a government responsible to an elected parliament. The Young Turks hoped to stem the loss of territory by establishing firmer central control, but their efforts had the opposite effect. The various nationalities of the empire resented the imposition of Turkish education and administration. Renewed agitation broke out in Macedonia, in Albania, and among the Armenians. The government carried out severely repressive measures to end the unrest, massacring thousands of Armenians.

To foreign powers, the moment seemed propitious to plunder the weakened empire. In 1911 Italy occupied Libya, an Ottoman province. Greece, Bulgaria, and Serbia—impatient to enlarge their territories—formed an alliance, the Balkan League. In 1912 the League waged a successful war against the empire. Albania became independent, and Macedonia was partitioned among members of the League. This war stripped the empire of most of its European possessions.

RUSSIA

The Great Reforms of the 1860s, intended to resolve Russia's problems, instead unleashed new forces because they coincided with major social changes. Tsarist rule became even more difficult.

The needs of a modernizing country led to an increase in the number of universities and students. The newly educated Russian youths almost instantly began an ardent, sustained critique of autocracy. In the absence of a sizable middle class upholding liberal, advanced ideas, university students and graduates, who came to be known as the *intelligentsia,* saw it as their mission to transform Russia.

In the 1870s university youths by the thousands organized a populist movement, hoping to bring change to the countryside. These young idealists, both men and women, intended to educate the peasants and make them more politically aware. But they met with suspicion from the peasantry and repression by the government. Large numbers of populists were arrested and put on trial. Frustrated at the difficulty of bringing about change from below, disaffected radicals formed the People's Will, which turned to murdering public officials to hasten the day of revolution.

In response, the regime intensified repression. But it also sought to broaden its public support. In 1881 Tsar Alexander II decided to create an advisory committee that some thought would eventually lead to a parliamentary form of government. In March 1881, as he was about to sign the decree establishing this committee, the tsar was assassinated by members of the People's Will.

The new ruler, Tsar Alexander III (r. 1881–1894), who had witnessed the assassination, blamed it on his father's leniency. He thus decided to make the government even more autocratic. He weakened his father's reforms and in the process reduced local self-rule.

When Alexander's son, Nicholas II (r. 1894–1917), succeeded to the throne in 1894, he too was determined to maintain autocratic rule. However, he lacked the methodical, consistent temperament such a pledge required, as well as the forcefulness to establish a coherent policy for his troubled country.

Serious problems had accumulated that threatened the stability of the regime. Conditions worsened in the countryside as explosive population growth increased pressure on the land. Despite the abolition of serfdom, the peasants were not free to come and go as they pleased. Agriculture remained inefficient, far inferior to that of western Europe. Between 1861 and 1914 the peasant population grew by 50 percent, but it acquired only 10 percent more land. In 1891 famine broke out in twenty provinces, killing a quarter of a million people.

Although Russia remained largely agrarian, there were pockets of industrial growth. Some factories and mining concerns were unusually large, with as many as six thousand employees. When workers grew incensed at their condition and insistent on winning the same rights and protection as workers in western Europe, they engaged in massive strikes that crippled industry.

Political dissatisfaction with the autocracy grew among all social classes—the slowly expanding middle classes and aristocrats demanded the right to political participation. Various revolutionary groups committed to socialism flourished. Socialist Revolutionaries, heirs to the People's Will, emerged as a political force in the 1890s. They believed that the peasants would bring socialism to Russia.

In 1898 the Russian Social Democratic Party was founded. A Marxist party, it promoted the industrial

Workers' Demonstration in Moscow, 1905

In 1905 workers as well as peasants protested against the Russian autocracy. To bring the revolution under control, Nicholas II was obliged to grant several concessions. *(Novosti)*

working class as the harbinger of socialism. In 1903 that party split into the Menshevik and Bolshevik factions. The Mensheviks insisted that Russia had to go through the stages of history Marx had outlined—to witness the full development of capitalism and its subsequent collapse before the socialists could come to power. The **Bolsheviks,** a minority group, were led by Vladimir Ilich Lenin (1870–1924), a zealous revolutionary and Marxist. Rather than wait for historical forces to undermine capitalism, he insisted that a revolutionary cadre could seize power on behalf of the working class. Lenin favored a small, disciplined, conspiratorial party, like the People's Will, while the Mensheviks favored a more open, democratic party.

But popular opposition to tsarism soon grew in the face of Russian military ineptitude in the war against Japan, which broke out in February 1904 in a dispute over control of northern Korea. An economic slowdown heightened social tensions, and antagonism to the tsarist regime escalated.

Beginning in January 1905 a series of demonstrations, strikes, and other acts of collective violence erupted. Together they were dubbed "the revolution of 1905." On a Sunday of that month 400,000 workers gathered in front of the tsar's St. Petersburg palace. Rather than hear their demands, officials ordered soldiers to fire on them, resulting in 150 deaths and hundreds more wounded. "Bloody Sunday" inflamed the populace. The tsar, instead of being viewed as an understanding, paternal authority, had become the murderer of his people. Unrest spread to most of the country. The regime's prestige deteriorated further with reports of increasing losses in the war with Japan. By September 1905 Russia had to sue for peace and admit defeat. Challenged in the capital, where independent workers' councils called *soviets* had sprung up, the government also lost control over the countryside, the site of widespread peasant uprisings.

Fearing for his regime, Nicholas hoped to disarm the opposition by meeting some of its demands. He granted major constitutional and civil liberties, including freedom of religion, speech, assembly, and association. At the end of October the tsar established an elective assembly, the Duma, with restricted male suffrage and limited political power. It quickly became the arena for criticism of autocracy. Nicholas responded to the criticism by suspending the Duma and changing its electoral base and rules of operation. Even many conservatives were disillusioned with his breach of the

Bolsheviks Faction of the Russian Socialist Democratic Party led by Marxist Vladimir Ilich Lenin (1870–1924), who insisted that an exclusive revolutionary cadre could seize power on behalf of the working class.

promise he had made in 1905 to establish constitutionalism and parliamentarianism.

Poor social conditions continued to fuel opposition to the tsar. Although the government reduced the peasants' financial obligations, weakened the power of the commune, or *mir* (see pages 696–698), and extended local self-rule to the peasants, these changes did little to alleviate rural poverty. Labor unrest also mounted. In 1912, 725,000 industrial workers went on strike; that number doubled in the first half of 1914. On the eve of the outbreak of the First World War, barricades were rising in the workers' neighborhoods.

S E C T I O N   S U M M A R Y

- In Germany after 1890, Wilhelm II's aggressive foreign policy menaced other European powers; his repressive, irresponsible, and autocratic governing style created widespread opposition to his rule.

- Parliamentary rule in Austria-Hungary failed because of ongoing conflicts between the two monarchies as well as between the multiple nationalities within each.

- The Ottoman Empire continued to suffer from both secessionist movements within its borders and aggression from other European powers; by 1912 the empire had lost most of its European possessions.

- In Russia, the emergence of revolutionary socialist groups, deteriorating conditions of peasants, worker discontent, and defeat in war with Japan fueled opposition to tsarist rule. The revolution of 1905 and subsequent reforms failed to stem the regime's problems.

THE COMING WAR

What responsibility did each of the Great Powers have for the outbreak of war in 1914?

Instability and upheaval characterized international relations in the years between 1880 and 1914. But the outbreak of war was by no means inevitable. Common sense dictated against it, and some intelligent people predicted that in the new modern era, war would become so destructive that it would be unthinkable. Finally, no European state wanted a war, although the Great Powers carried on policies that brought them to its brink.

POWER ALIGNMENTS

Germany enjoyed an unchallenged position in the international order of the 1870s and 1880s. It was united in an alliance with the two other eastern conservative states—Russia and Austria-Hungary—in the Three Emperors' League, formed in 1873 and renewed by treaty in 1884. It also formed part of the **Triple Alliance** with Austria and Italy. France stood alone, without allies. Britain, with little interest in continental affairs, appeared to be enjoying a "splendid isolation."

However, Germany's alliance system was not free from problems. Two of its allies, Austria-Hungary and Russia, were at loggerheads over control of the Balkans. How could Germany be the friend of both? Wary of apparent German preference for Austria, Bismarck signed the Reinsurance Treaty in 1887, assuring Russia that Germany would not honor its alliance with Austria if the latter attacked Russia. After Bismarck's resignation in 1890, Kaiser Wilhelm allowed the Reinsurance Treaty to lapse. Alarmed, the Russians turned to France and, in January 1894, signed the Franco-Russian Alliance, by which each side pledged to help the other should either be attacked by Germany.

The Great Powers on the Continent were now divided into two alliances, the Triple Alliance and the Franco-Russian Alliance. Britain formally belonged to neither, but if it favored any side, it would be the German-led alliance because of colonial rivalries with France over Africa and with Russia over Asia.

In the 1890s Germany lost British goodwill. Launching his Weltpolitik, Wilhelm II built up the German navy. An island nation dependent on international trade for its economic survival, Britain had developed a navy second to none—and it saw the German naval buildup as a threat to its security.

In the face of a mounting German menace, France and Britain decided to reconcile their differences. In 1904 they signed an understanding, or *entente,* resolving their rivalries in Egypt. In 1907 Great Britain and Russia regulated their competition for influence in Persia (present-day Iran) with the Anglo-Russian Entente. Europe was now loosely divided into a new configura-

Triple Alliance   Military alliance established in 1882 among Germany, Austria-Hungary, and Italy to counter the Franco-Russian Alliance (later the Triple Entente).

tion of two groups: the Triple Alliance of Germany, Austria-Hungary, and Italy, and the **Triple Entente** of Great Britain, France, and Russia.

THE MOMENTUM TOWARD WAR

Only through a series of crises did these alignments solidify to the point where their members were willing to go to war to save them. In 1905 and again in 1911, France and Germany nearly went to war over their respective interests in Morocco; both instances left Germany with the appearance of unreasonable aggressiveness. Meanwhile, the unstable situation in the Balkans sharpened tensions between Austria and Russia.

The heightened international tensions forced the European states to increase their arms expenditures, which in turn increased their sense of insecurity. In 1906 Britain introduced a new class of ships with the launching of the *Dreadnought*. Powered by steam turbines, it was the fastest ship afloat; heavily armored, it could not be sunk easily, and its 12-inch guns made it a menace on the seas. The British had thought the Germans incapable of building equivalent ships. But they did, wiping out British supremacy. Older British ships could now easily be sunk by German dreadnoughts. No longer able to depend on its past supremacy, Britain felt less secure than at any time since the Napoleonic Wars, and it continued an expensive and feverish naval race with Germany.

In Germany the growing war-making capacity of Russia created great anxieties. The Japanese defeat of the tsarist empire in 1905 had revealed the Russian military to be inferior—a lumbering giant, slow to mobilize and maneuver. As a result, Germany had not been particularly afraid of its eastern neighbor. But stung by its humiliation in 1905, Russia quickly rebuilt its army and planned an extensive rail network in the west, which would, in the event of war, be used for military purposes. Germany now felt encircled by a hostile Russia to the east and an equally unfriendly France to the west, and by 1912 some military officers and government officials began thinking about a preventive war. If war was inevitable, many Germans argued, it should occur before Russia became even stronger.

Many political leaders viewed the escalating arms race as a form of madness. Between 1904 and 1913 French and Russian arms expenditures increased by 80 percent, those of Germany by 120 percent, those of Austria-Hungary by 50 percent, and those of Italy by 100 percent. British foreign secretary Sir Edward Grey (1862–1933) warned that if the arms race continued, "it will submerge civilization."

But on the whole, warfare was not greatly feared. The Western powers had not experienced a major conflict since the Crimean War (1854–1856). Most policymakers believed that the next war would be short. The wars that had so dramatically changed the borders of European states in the second half of the nineteenth century, notably the Austro-Prussian War of 1866 and the Franco-Prussian War of 1870, had been decided within a few weeks. Because few imagined that the next war would be either long or brutal, Europe's leaders did not make a major effort to prevent it.

The territorial rivalry between Austria and Russia triggered international disaster. For decades enmity had been growing between the two empires over control of the Balkans (see **MAP 24.4**). In 1903, following a

MAP 24.4 The Balkans in 1914
By 1914 the Ottoman Empire was much diminished, containing virtually no European territory. Political boundaries did not follow nationality lines. Serbia was committed to unite all Serbs at the expense of the Austro-Hungarian Empire.

Triple Entente Military alliance between Great Britain, France, and Russia, completed in 1907, countering the Triple Alliance.

bloody military coup that killed the king and queen of Serbia, a pro-Russian party took control of the Serbian government. In 1908 Russia, still not recovered from its defeat in 1905, was surprised when Austria unilaterally declared the annexation of the province of Bosnia (which it had administered since the Congress of Berlin in 1878; see page 696). Austria's action thwarted Serbia's ambition of annexing Bosnia, which had many Serb inhabitants. Fearing war, Russia had to accept diplomatic defeat and abandoned its ally, Serbia. But Russia was determined not to cave in again.

Undeterred, Serbia spread anti-Austrian propaganda and sought to unify under its banner Slavs living in the Balkans—including those under Austrian rule.

As a result, many Austrian officials were convinced that the survival of the Austro-Hungarian Empire required the destruction of Serbia. Talk of an attack on Serbia filled the Austrian court in 1914.

On June 28, 1914, the heir to the Habsburg throne, Archduke Franz Ferdinand, visited Sarajevo in Austrian-ruled Bosnia. A young Bosnian-Serb nationalist hostile to Austrian rule, who had been trained and armed by a Serb terrorist group called the Black Hand, assassinated the archduke and his wife.

The assassination of the heir to the throne provided Austria with an ideal pretext for military action. The German kaiser, fearing that failure to support Vienna would lead to Austrian collapse and a Germany bereft of

The Shot Heard Round the World
The young Serb nationalist Gavril Princip shoots Franz Ferdinand, the heir to the Austro-Hungarian throne, and his consort. The assassination led to the outbreak of World War I. *(Österreichische National-bibliothek, Vienna)*

any allies, urged Austria to attack Serbia. On July 23 Austria issued an ultimatum to Serbia, deliberately worded in such a way as to be unacceptable. When Serbia refused the ultimatum, Austria declared war on July 28.

Perceived self-interest motivated each state's behavior in the ensuing crisis. Russia's status as a Great Power required that it not allow its client state, Serbia, to be humiliated, much less obliterated. In the past the French government had acted as a brake on Russian ambitions in the Balkans. On the eve of the war in 1914, France counseled restraint, but it did not withhold its promise of aid. Since 1911 France had increasingly feared isolation in the face of what it perceived as growing German aggression. Its only ally on the Continent was Russia. To remain a Great Power, France needed to preserve its friendship with Russia and help that country maintain its own Great Power status.

Germany could not allow Austria, its only ally, to be destroyed. Its leaders may also have seen the crisis as a propitious moment to begin a war that was going to occur anyway. The Germans no doubt thought it expedient to strike before the Entente powers, especially Russia, became stronger. After declaring war on Russia, Germany then invaded France through Belgium to prevent it from coming to Russia's aid. The British, concerned for their ally France and outraged by the violation of Belgian neutrality (to which all the Great Powers had been signatories since 1839), on August 4 declared war on Germany. Europe was at war. Eventually so would be much of the world.

SECTION SUMMARY

- By 1907, Europe was loosely divided into the Triple Alliance of Germany, Austria-Hungary, and Italy, and the Triple Entente of Great Britain, France, and Russia.

- Mounting crises solidified the alliances: France and Germany came into conflict over Morocco; all the countries, but especially Britain and Germany, engaged in an arms race; rivalry over the Balkans between Russia and Austria intensified when the latter annexed Bosnia.

- Anti-Austrian sentiments in Serbia led to the assassination of the Austrian archduke Franz Ferdinand, provoking Austria to declare war on Serbia; the system of alliances then brought all of the Great Powers into war.

CHAPTER SUMMARY

Online Study Center **ACE the Test**

What were the main motivations for European imperialism?

In what ways did the worldview of intellectuals living in the belle époque differ from that of a generation earlier?

What factors made parliamentary rule in Great Britain, France, and Italy dysfunctional?

What various crises weakened autocratic rule in Germany, Russia, and the Ottoman Empire?

What responsibility did each of the Great Powers have for the outbreak of war in 1914?

In the decades prior to 1914, Europe appeared to dominate the globe. With the intention of acquiring new sources of wealth, trade, and the trappings of international power and prestige, Europeans forcibly conquered most of Africa and much of Asia. They also conceived of their mission as one that brought civilization to inferior peoples. They introduced both technology and Western education to the colonized subjects.

The scramble to build empires reflected growing competition among the Great Powers, but it also produced anxiety and tensions over them.

Between 1880 and 1914, more Europeans than ever before enjoyed material advantages and improved standards of living. Many intellectuals, however, abandoned the optimism of the generation that preceded them and saw in materialism and democracy the evidence of decline and decadence. Freud and Bergson and artists such as Munch and Moreau suggested that a hidden, irrational dimension of life lurked beneath the tranquil surface. Among the new nationalist right, fear of mass society gave way to racist and anti-Semitic ideologies.

In Western democracies, improved conditions also led to rising expectations. People grew more demanding, insisting in sometimes violent ways on their political and economic rights. Although mass movements such as socialism and women's suffrage generally used peaceful means in their campaigns to change society, some of their members advocated and employed force. Anarchism appeared to stalk Europe. States readily used force in efforts to quell various protest movements, even resorting to martial law.

In central and eastern Europe, similar problems emerged. Added to the mix of extremist ideologies and movements that opposed autocratic rule were the apparently unsolvable conflicts between national and ethnic groups. Everywhere in Europe, domestic ills raised the stakes in competition for overseas empire; at the same time the traditional empires of Austria-Hungary and Turkey were threatened with dissolution.

Every European power had some responsibility for feeding the international tensions that led to the outbreak of war in 1914. France and Germany clashed over Morocco; Austria and Russia competed for influence over the Balkans; Britain and Germany raced each other to build warships. The *Weltpolitik* of Wilhelm II menaced France and Britain. Among European thinkers and leaders, force had become widely accepted as the means to an end; all the powers (except Britain) built up large standing armies with millions of men and lethal modern equipment. As rising tensions tightened the alliance system, Europe divided into two armed camps. Some leaders—notably those of Austria-Hungary and Germany—favored war over negotiation in July 1914.

LOOKING AHEAD

If some leaders still feared war, more dreaded the consequences of not fighting, believing that war would save their regimes from the internal and external challenges they faced. Few could foresee the dire consequences of such a choice. Europe's very success in technological advancement and empire building would make this war a prolonged conflagration that would involve most of the world.

KEY TERMS

new imperialism (p. 740)

Second International (p. 752)

anti-Semitism (p. 753)

Zionism (p. 753)

Sigmund Freud (p. 754)

avant-garde (p. 754)

suffragists (p. 757)

Weltpolitik (p. 761)

Bolsheviks (p. 763)

Triple Alliance (p. 764)

Triple Entente (p. 765)

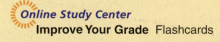
Online Study Center
Improve Your Grade Flashcards

SUGGESTED READING

Burrow, J. W. *The Crisis of Reason: European Thought, 1848–1914*. 2000. A strong emphasis on individual intellectuals and their contributions.

Carrère d'Encaussé, Hélène. *Nicholas II*. 2000. A biography of the tsar, set within the context of an increasingly difficult country to govern.

Hochschild, Adam. *King Leopold's Ghost*. 1998. A dramatic account of Leopold II's brutal rule over the Congo.

Jay, Mike, and Michael Neve, eds. *1900: A Fin-de-Siècle Reader*. 1999. A rich collection of documents on how people imagined the new century.

Johnson, Martin P. *The Dreyfus Affair*. 1999. A brisk review of the major events shaping the affair.

Joll, James. *The Origins of the First World War*. 1984. A clear, concise, readable history tracing how strategic interests and nationalist passions led to the outbreak of war.

Levine, Philippa, ed. *Gender and Empire*. 2004. A collection of essays that examine how gender, and particularly male domination, influenced British imperialism.

Schorske, Carl E. *Fin de Siècle Vienna: Politics and Culture*. 1980. A critically acclaimed work on the arts and social and political thought in the Habsburg capital at the turn of the century.

25

WAR AND REVOLUTION, 1914–1919

Passchendaele, Belgium, 1917
(By courtesy of the Trustees of the Imperial War Museum)

Mud. It was not what soldiers had in mind when they headed off to war in August 1914 amid visions of glory, gallantry—and quick victory. But after heavy rain and constant shelling, mud was a fact of life for those fighting on the western front—Belgium and northern France—during the fall of 1917. The mud was so pervasive, in fact, that soldiers literally drowned in it. These Canadian troops are holding the line on November 14, 1917, at the end of the Battle of Passchendaele (PAH-shun-dale), a British-led assault that began late in July. That assault pushed the Germans back a mere 5 miles—at the cost of 300,000 lives. There was no end to the war in sight.

Some had thought a major war impossible in rational, civilized Europe. Others had devoutly wished for war—precisely to break out of the stifling bourgeois conventions of rational, civilized Europe. When war actually began early in August 1914, the European mood was generally enthusiastic, even festive. No one was prepared for what this war would bring, including the hellish scenes of mud, smoke, artillery craters, blasted trees, decaying bodies, and ruined buildings that came to frame the daily experience of those on the western front. A far wider and more destructive war would follow within a generation, but it was World War I, known to contemporaries as "the Great War," that shattered the old European order, with its comfortable assumptions of superiority, rationality, and progress. After this war, neither Westerners nor non-Westerners could still believe in the privileged place of Western civilization in quite the same way.

The war that began in August was supposed to be over by Christmas. The British government promised "business as usual." But the fighting bogged down in a stalemate during the fall of 1914, then continued for four more years. By the time it ended, in November 1918, the war had strained the whole fabric of life, affecting everything from economic organization to literary vocabulary, from journalistic techniques to the role of women.

Partly because the war grew to become the first "world war," it proved the beginning of the end of European hegemony. The intervention of the United States in 1917 affected the military balance and seemed to give the war more idealistic and democratic purposes. The geographic reach of the

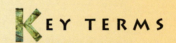CHAPTER OUTLINE

KEY TERMS

Sacred Union

British blockade

total war

Kriegsrohstoffabteilung (KRA)

Petrograd Soviet

provisional government

Vladimir Lenin

Fourteen Points

Treaty of Brest-Litovsk

"stab in the back" myth

Treaty of Versailles

League of Nations

Online Study Center

This icon will direct you to interactive map and primary source activities on the website **college.hmco.com/pic/noble5e**

war was itself unprecedented, especially after the intervention of the Ottoman Empire spread the fighting to the Middle East. Because of European colonial networks, the war also involved many other non-Europeans in combat or support roles. Although the old colonialism continued into the postwar era, the war nourished the forces that would later overthrow it.

Because of all the strains it entailed, the war had many unintended consequences. Revolutions dramatically changed the political landscape first in Russia, then in Germany. The Habsburg and Ottoman Empires collapsed. So when the victors met early in 1919 to shape the peace, they confronted a situation that could not have been foreseen in 1914. Their effort to determine the contours of the postwar world, and thus the immediate meaning of the war, left much unresolved.

FOCUS QUESTIONS

How and why had the course of the war by 1917 defied the expectations that had surrounded the beginning of fighting in August 1914?

Why did this prove a total war, making necessary new forms of socioeconomic coordination and even systematic propaganda?

Why did the first revolution in Russia pave the way for a second, spearheaded by the Bolsheviks?

Why did Germany and its allies end up losing the war even after forcing Russia to make a separate peace by early 1918?

What factors shaped the peace settlement that the victors imposed on Germany and its allies in 1919–1920?

THE UNFORESEEN STALEMATE, 1914–1917

How and why had the course of the war by 1917 defied the expectations that had surrounded the beginning of fighting in August 1914?

When the war began in August 1914, enthusiasm and high morale, based on expectations of quick victory, marked both sides. But fighting on the crucial western front led to a stalemate by the end of 1914, and the brutal encounters of 1916 made it clear that this was not the sort of war most had expected. By early 1917 the difficulties of the war experience brought to the surface underlying questions about what all the fighting was for—and whether it was worth the price.

AUGUST 1914: THE DOMESTIC AND MILITARY SETTING

Although some, including Helmuth von Moltke (MOLT-kuh) (1848–1916), chief of the German general staff, worried that this would prove a long, destructive war testing the very fabric of Western civilization, the outbreak of fighting early in August produced a wave of euphoria and a remarkable degree of domestic unity. To many, war came almost as a relief; at last, the issues that had produced intermittent crisis for the past decade would find a definitive solution. Especially among educated young people, this settling of accounts seemed to offer the prospect of renewal, even a kind of redemption, for themselves and their societies. The war promised an escape from the stifling bourgeois world and, in response to the common danger, an end to the bickering and divisiveness of everyday politics.

An unexpected display of patriotism from the socialist left reinforced the sense of domestic unity and high morale. Forgetting their customary rhetoric about international proletarian solidarity, socialist parties rallied to their respective national war efforts almost everywhere in Europe. To socialists and workers, national defense against a more backward aggressor seemed essential to the eventual creation of socialism. French Socialists had to defend France's democratic republic against autocratic and militaristic Germany; German Socialists had to defend German institutions, and the strong socialist organizations that had proven possible within them, against repressive tsarist Russia. When, on August 4, the German Socialist Party delegation in the Reichstag voted with the other parties to give the government the budgetary authority to wage war, it was clear that the Second International had failed in its long-standing commitment to keep the workers of Europe from slaughtering each other.

In France, the government had planned, as a precaution, to arrest roughly one thousand trade union and socialist leaders in the event of war, but no such arrests were necessary. The order of the day was **Sacred Union,** which meant that French leaders from across the political spectrum agreed to cooperate for the duration of the war. Rather than seek to sabotage the war, Socialist leaders joined the new government of national defense. Germany enjoyed a comparable "Fortress Truce," including an agreement to suspend labor conflict during the war, although no Socialist was invited to join the war cabinet.

In 1914 the forces of the Triple Entente outnumbered those of Germany and Austria-Hungary. Russia had an army of over 1 million men, the largest in Europe, and France had 700,000. Britain, which did not introduce conscription until 1916, had about 250,000. Germany led the Central Powers with 850,000; Austria-Hungary contributed 450,000. Though outnumbered, the Central Powers had potential advantages in equipment, coordination, and speed over their more dispersed adversaries. The outcome was hardly a foregone conclusion in August 1914.

After the fighting began, a second group of nations intervened one by one, expanding the war's scope and complicating the strategic alternatives. In November 1914 the Ottoman Empire, fearful of Russia, joined the Central Powers, thereby extending the war along the Russo-Turkish border and on to Mesopotamia and the approaches to the Suez Canal in the Middle East. For Arabs disaffected with Ottoman Turkish rule, the war presented an opportunity to take up arms—with the active support of Britain and France. Italy, after dickering with both sides, committed itself to the Entente in the Treaty of London of April 1915. This secret agreement specified the territories Italy would receive—primarily the Italian-speaking areas still within Austria-Hungary—in the event of Entente victory. In September 1915 Bulgaria entered the war on the side of the Central Powers, seeking territorial advantages at the expense of Serbia, which had defeated Bulgaria in the Second Balkan War in 1913. Finally, in August 1916, Romania intervened on the side of the Entente, hoping to gain Transylvania, then part of Hungary.

Thus the war was fought on a variety of fronts (see **MAP 25.1**). This fact, combined with uncertainties about the role of sea power, led to ongoing debate among military decision makers about strategic priorities. Some expected that Britain and Germany would quickly be drawn into a decisive naval battle. But

CHRONOLOGY

August 1914	Fighting begins
September 1914	French forces hold off the German assault at the Marne
August–September 1914	German victories repel Russian invasion on eastern front
May 1915	Italy declares war on Austria-Hungary
February–December 1916	Battle of Verdun
July–November 1916	Battle of the Somme
January 1917	Germans resume unrestricted submarine warfare
March 1917	First Russian revolution: fall of the tsar
April 1917	U.S. declaration of war
July 1917	German Reichstag war aims resolution
November 1917	Second Russian revolution: the Bolsheviks take power
March 1918	Treaty of Brest-Litovsk between Germany and Russia
March–July 1918	Germany's last western offensive
June 1918	Initial outbreak of the "Spanish flu"
July 1918	Second Battle of the Marne
November 1918	Armistice: fighting ends
January 1919	Paris Peace Conference convenes
June 1919	Victors impose Treaty of Versailles on Germany

though Britain promptly instituted an effective naval blockade on imports to Germany, the great showdown on the seas never materialized. Even the most significant naval encounter between them, the Battle of Jutland in 1916, was inconclusive. Despite the naval rivalry of the prewar years, World War I proved fundamentally a land war.

Germany faced not only the long-anticipated two-front war against Russia in the east and France and Britain in the west; it also had to look to the southeast, given the precarious situation of its ally Austria-Hungary, which was fighting Serbia and Russia, then also Italy and Romania as well. On the eastern front, Germany was largely successful, forcing first Russia, then Romania, to seek a separate peace by mid-1918. But it was the western front that proved decisive.

Sacred Union An agreement between leaders of different French political groups to cooperate during World War I.

MAP 25.1 Major Fronts of World War I
Although World War I included engagements in East Asia and the Middle East, it was essentially a European conflict, encompassing fighting on a number of fronts.

NORWAY

SWEDEN

FINLAND

Helsinki

Petrograd (St. Petersburg)

Moscow

RUSSIA

Treaty of Brest-Litovsk, March 1918

Don

Dnieper

UKRAINE

Black Sea

Constantinople

OTTOMAN EMPIRE

Gallipoli 1915

Dardanelles

Armistice line, December 1917

Kiev

Riga

ESTONIA

LATVIA

COURLAND

LITHUANIA

Masurian Lakes 1914

Tannenberg 1914

E. PRUSSIA

Warsaw

Brest-Litovsk

POLAND

MAY 1915

Vistula

GALICIA

Farthest Russian Advance, 1914

ROMANIA

Bucharest

TRANSYLVANIA

BULGARIA

SERBIA

Danube

ALBANIA 1917-1918

GREECE

Balkan Front

Mediterranean Sea

Baltic Sea

Berlin

Oder

GERMANY

Elbe

Kiel

Jutland 1916

DENMARK

AUSTRIA-HUNGARY

Vienna

Sarajevo

MONTENEGRO

Caporetto 1917

AUG. 1917

MAR. 1918

Italian Front

ITALY

Rome

Rhine

LUXEMBOURG

SWITZERLAND

NETHERLANDS

Louvain

BELGIUM

Seine

Paris

Western Front

FRANCE

Loire

Bordeaux

Rhone

British blockade line

North Sea

ATLANTIC OCEAN

IRELAND

GREAT BRITAIN

London

SPAIN

Triple Entente and its Allies
Central Powers
Neutral nations
Farthest German-Austrian advance
Major battles
Battle lines

300 Mi.
300 Km.

No Trenches in Sight
Spirits were high early in August 1914, as soldiers like these in Paris marched off to war. None foresaw what fighting this war would be like. None grasped the long-term impact the war would have.
(Giraudon/Art Resource, NY)

INTO THE NIGHTMARE, 1914–1916

With the lessons of the wars of German unification in mind, both sides had planned for a short war based on rapid offensives. According to the Schlieffen (SHLEE-fyn) Plan, drafted in 1905, Germany would concentrate first on France, devoting but one-eighth of its forces to containing the Russians, who would need longer to mobilize. After taking just six weeks to defeat France, Germany would focus on Russia. French strategy, crafted by commander-in-chief Joseph Joffre (JOFF-ruh) (1852–1931), similarly relied on rapid offensives. The boys would be home by Christmas—or so it was thought.

Although German troops encountered more opposition than expected from the formerly neutral Belgians, they moved swiftly through Belgium into northern France during August. By the first week of September they had reached the Marne River, threatening Paris and forcing the French government to retreat south to Bordeaux (bor-DOH). But French and British troops counterattacked from September 6 to 10, forcing the Germans to fall back and begin digging in along the Aisne (ENN) River. By holding off the German offensive at this first Battle of the Marne, the Entente had undercut the Schlieffen Plan—and with it, it turned out, any chance of a speedy victory by either side.

During the rest of the fall of 1914, each side tried—unsuccessfully—to outflank the other. When, by the end of November, active fighting ceased for the winter, a military front of about 300 miles had been established, all the way from Switzerland to the coast of the North Sea in Belgium (see Map 25.2 on page 788). This line failed to shift more than 10 miles in either direction over the next three years. The result of the first six weeks of fighting on the western front was not a gallant victory but a grim and unforeseen stalemate.

Virtually from the start, the war took a fiercely destructive turn. In northern France in September 1914, the Germans fired on the famed Gothic cathedral at Reims (RAANZ), severely damaging its roof and nave, because they believed—apparently correctly—that the French were using one of its towers as an observation post. If such a catastrophe could happen to one of the great monuments in Europe, what else might this war bring?

The two sides were forced to settle into a war of attrition relying on an elaborate network of defensive trenches. Although separated by as much as 5 miles in some places, enemy trenches were sometimes within shouting distance, so there was occasionally banter back and forth, even attempts to entertain the other side. But the trenches quickly became almost unimaginably gruesome—filthy, ridden with rats and lice, noisy and smoky from artillery fire, and foul-smelling, partly from the odor of decaying bodies.

Online Study Center **Improve Your Grade**
Primary Source: The World of the Trenches:
A Deadly Life

As defensive instruments, however, the trenches proved quite effective. Each side quickly learned to take advantage of barbed wire, mines, and especially machine guns to defend its positions. A mass of barbed wire, 3 to 5 feet high and 30 yards wide, guarded a typical trench. The machine gun had been developed before the war as an offensive weapon; few foresaw the decided advantage it would give the defense. But with machine guns, soldiers could defend trenches even against massive assaults—and inflict heavy casualties on the attackers.

In 1916 the British sent the first shipment of tanks to France as an antidote to the machine gun, but, as skeptics had warned, tanks proved too ungainly and unreliable to be widely effective. Although the French used them to advantage in the decisive Allied offensive in 1918, tanks were not crucial to the outcome of the war.

Despite the advantages of defensive trenches, neither side could give up the vision of a decisive offensive. Thus the troops were periodically called on to go "over the top" and then across "no man's land" to assault the dug-in enemy. Again and again, however, such offensives proved futile, producing incredibly heavy casualties: "Whole regiments gambled away eternity for ten yards of wasteland."[1]

For the soldiers on the western front, the war became a nightmarish experience in a hellish landscape. Bombardment by new, heavier forms of artillery scarred the terrain with craters, which became muddy, turning the landscape into a near swamp. Beginning early in 1915, tear gas, chlorine gas, and finally mustard gas found use on both sides. Although the development of gas masks significantly reduced the impact of this menacing new chemical warfare, the threat of poison gas added another nightmarish element to the experience of those who fought the war.

The notions of patriotism, comradeship, duty, and glory that had been prevalent in 1914 gradually dissolved as soldiers experienced the horrors of this war. A French soldier, questioning his own reactions after battle in 1916, responded with sarcasm and irony: "What sublime emotion inspires you at the moment of assault? I thought of nothing other than dragging my feet out of the mud encasing them. What did you feel after surviving the attack? I grumbled because I would have to remain several days more without *pinard* [wine]. Is not one's first act to kneel down and thank God? No. One relieves oneself."[2]

Although the Germans had been denied their quick victory in the west, by the end of 1914 they occupied much of Belgium and almost one-tenth of France, including major industrial areas and mines producing most of France's coal and iron. On the eastern front, as well, the Germans won some substantial advantages in 1914—but not a decisive victory.

Trench Warfare
Grim though they were, the trenches proved effective for defensive purposes. Here a British soldier guards a trench at Ovillers, on the Somme, in July 1916. *(Courtesy of the Trustees of the Imperial War Museum)*

The first season of fighting suggested that the pattern in the east would not be trench warfare but rapid movement across a vast but thinly held front. When hostilities began in August, the Russians mustered more quickly than anticipated, confronting an outnumbered German force in a menacing, if reckless, invasion of East Prussia. But by mid-September German forces under General Paul von Hindenburg (1847–1934) and his chief of staff, General Erich Ludendorff (1865–1937), repelled the Russian advance, taking a huge number of prisoners and seriously demoralizing the Russians.

As a result of this victory, Hindenburg and Ludendorff emerged as heroes, and they would play major roles in German public life thereafter. Hindenburg became chief of staff of the entire German army in August 1916, but the able and energetic Ludendorff proved the key figure as this duo gradually assumed undisputed control of the whole German war effort, both military and domestic.

Seeking a Breakthrough, 1915–1917

After the campaigns of 1915 proved inconclusive, German leaders decided to concentrate in 1916 on a massive offensive against the great French fortress at Verdun, intending to inflict a definitive defeat on France. To assault the fortress, the Germans gathered 1,220 pieces of artillery for attack along an 8-mile front. Included were thirteen "Big Bertha" siege guns, weapons so large that nine tractors were required to position each of them; a crane was necessary to insert the shell, which weighed over a ton. The level of heavy artillery firepower that the Germans applied at Verdun was unprecedented in the history of warfare.

German forces attacked on February 21, taking the outer defenses of the fortress, and appeared poised for victory. The tide turned, however, when General Philippe Pétain (puh-TANH) (1856–1951) assumed control of the French defense. Pétain had the patience and skill necessary to organize supply networks for a long siege. Furthermore, he proved able, through considerate treatment, to inspire affection and confidence among his men. By mid-July the French army had repelled the German offensive, although only in December did the French retake the outer defenses of the fortress. The French had held firm in what would prove the war's longest, most trying battle—one that killed over 700,000 people.

To relieve pressure on Verdun, the British led a major attack at the Somme River on July 1, 1916. On that day alone the British suffered almost 60,000 casualties, including 21,000 killed. Fighting continued into the fall, but the offensive proved futile in the end. One-third of those involved, or over 1 million soldiers, ended up dead, missing, or wounded.

Dominated by the devastating battles at Verdun and the Somme, the campaigns of 1916 finally extinguished the high spirits of the summer of 1914. Both sides suffered huge losses—apparently for nothing. By the end of 1916, the front had shifted only a few miles from its location at the beginning of the year.

In light of the frustrating outcome so far, the French turned to new military leadership, replacing Joffre as commander-in-chief with Robert Nivelle (1856–1924), who promptly sought to prove himself with a new offensive during the spring of 1917. Persisting even as it became clear that this effort had no chance of success, Nivelle provoked increasing resistance among French soldiers, some of whom were refusing to follow orders by the end of April.

With the French war effort in danger of collapse, the French government replaced Nivelle with General Pétain, the hero of the defense of Verdun. Pétain reestablished discipline by adopting a conciliatory approach—improving food and rest, visiting the troops in the field, offering encouragement, even dealing relatively mercifully with the resisters themselves. To be sure, many of the soldiers who had participated in this near mutiny were court-martialed, and over 3,400 were convicted. But of the 554 sentenced to death, only 49 were actually executed.

After the failure of the Nivelle offensive, the initiative fell to the British under General Douglas Haig (1861–1928), who was convinced, despite skepticism in the British cabinet, that Nivelle's offensive had failed simply because of tactical mistakes. Beginning near Ypres (EE-pray) in Belgium on July 31, 1917, and continuing until November, the British attacked. As before, the effort yielded only minimal territorial gains—about 50 square miles—at a horrifying cost, including 300,000 British and Canadian casualties. Known as the Battle of Passchendaele, the British offensive of 1917 ranks with the Battles of Verdun and the Somme as the bloodiest of the war.

1917 as a Turning Point

Meanwhile, the Germans decided to concentrate on the eastern front in 1917 in an effort to knock Russia out of the war. This intensified German military pressure helped spark revolution in Russia, and in December 1917 Russia's new revolutionary regime asked for a separate peace (see page 787). The defeat of Russia freed the Germans at last to concentrate on the west, but by this time France and Britain had a new ally.

On April 6, 1917, the United States entered the war on the side of the Entente, in response to Germany's controversial use of submarines. Germany did not have enough surface ships to respond to Britain's naval blockade, whether by attacking the British fleet directly or by mounting a comparable blockade of the British

Isles. So the Germans decided to use submarines to interfere with shipping to Britain. Submarines, however, were too vulnerable to be able to surface and confiscate goods, so the Germans had to settle for sinking suspect ships with torpedoes. In February 1915 they declared the waters around the British Isles a war zone and served notice that they would torpedo not only enemy ships but also neutral ships carrying goods to Britain.

The German response was harsh, but so was the **British blockade,** which violated earlier international agreements about the rights of neutral shipping and the scope of wartime blockades. The British had agreed that only military goods such as munitions and certain raw materials, not such everyday goods as food and clothing, were to be subject to confiscation. Yet in blockading Germany, the British refused to make this distinction, prompting the sarcastic German quip that Britannia not only rules the waves but waives the rules.[3]

In May 1915 a German sub torpedoed the *Lusitania*, a British passenger liner, killing almost 1,200 people and producing widespread indignation. Partly because 128 of those killed were Americans, U.S. president Woodrow Wilson issued a severe warning, which contributed to the German decision in September 1915 to pull back from unrestricted submarine warfare. But as German suffering under the British blockade increased, pressure mounted on Berlin to put the subs back into action.

The issue provoked bitter debate. Chancellor Theobald von Bethmann-Hollweg (BETT-mahn–HOHL-veg) (1856–1921) and the civilian authorities opposed resumption, fearing it would provoke the United States to enter the war. But Ludendorff and the military finally prevailed, arguing that even if the United States did intervene, U.S. troops could not get to Europe in time to have a major impact. Germany announced it would resume unrestricted submarine warfare on January 31, 1917, and the United States responded with a declaration of war on April 6.

Many on both sides doubted that U.S. intervention would make a pivotal difference; most assumed—correctly—that it would take at least a year for the American presence to materialize in force. Still, the entry of the United States gave the Entente at least the promise of more fighting power. And the United States seemed capable of renewing the sense of purpose on the Entente side, showing that the war had a meaning that could justify the unexpected costs and sacrifice.

SECTION SUMMARY

- Although the war was fought on a variety of fronts and even expanded beyond Europe, it was the fighting on the western front, in a relatively small chunk of Belgium and northern France, that proved decisive.

- At the outset, each side expected a short war of rapid offensives, but the struggle on the western front produced only a stalemate, based on defensive trench warfare, by the end of 1914.

- The defensive trenches proved so difficult to attack, especially because of barbed wire and the machine gun.

- Massive assaults during 1916–1917 failed to produce the intended breakthrough for either side, though they resulted in horrifying numbers of casualties.

- Though the United States declared war in 1917 in response to Germany's resumption of unrestricted submarine warfare, it was not equipped to make an immediate difference on European battlefields.

THE EXPERIENCE OF TOTAL WAR

Why did this prove a total war, making necessary new forms of socioeconomic coordination and even systematic propaganda?

As the war dragged on, the distinction between the military and civilian spheres blurred. Suffering increased on the home front, and unprecedented governmental mobilization of society proved necessary to wage war on the scale that had come to be required. Because it became "total" in this way, the war decisively altered not only the old political and diplomatic order, but also culture, society, and the patterns of everyday life.

HARDSHIP ON THE HOME FRONT

The war meant food shortages, and thus malnutrition, for ordinary people in the belligerent countries, although Britain and France, with their more favorable

British blockade   Britain's naval blockade of Germany during World War I; it seriously impeded the German war effort.

geographic positions, suffered considerably less than others. Germany was especially vulnerable, and the British naval blockade exacerbated an already dire situation. With military needs taking priority, the Germans encountered shortages of the chemical fertilizers, farm machinery, and draft animals necessary for agricultural production. The government began rationing bread, meat, and fats during 1915. The increasing scarcity of food produced sharp increases in diseases such as rickets and tuberculosis and in infant and childhood mortality rates.

The need to pay for the war produced economic dislocations as well. Government borrowing covered some of the cost for the short term, but to underwrite the rest, governments all over Europe found it more palatable to inflate the currency, by printing more money, than to raise taxes. The notion that the enemy would be made to pay once victory had been won seemed to justify this decision. But this way of financing the war meant rising prices and severe erosion of purchasing power for ordinary people all over Europe. In France and Germany, the labor truces of 1914 gave way to increasing strike activity during 1916.

With an especially severe winter in 1916–1917 adding to the misery, there were serious instances of domestic disorder, including strikes and food riots, in many parts of Europe during 1917. In Italy, major strikes developed in Turin and other cities over wages and access to foodstuffs. The revolution that overthrew the tsarist autocracy in Russia that same year began with comparable protests over wartime food shortages.

The strains of war even fanned the flames in Ireland, where an uneasy truce over the home-rule controversy accompanied the British decision for war in 1914. Partly because of German efforts to stir up domestic trouble for Britain, unrest built up again in Ireland, culminating in the Easter Rebellion in Dublin in 1916. The brutality with which British forces crushed the uprising intensified demands for full independence—precisely what Britain would be forced to yield to the Irish republic shortly after the war.

Moreover, new technologies made civilians more vulnerable to wartime violence. Although bombing from aircraft began with an immediate military aim—to destroy industrial targets or to provide tactical support for other military units—it quickly became clear that night bombing, especially, might demoralize civilian populations. In 1915 German airplanes began bombing English cities, provoking British retaliation against cities in western Germany. These raids had little effect on the course of the war, but they showed that new technologies could make warfare more destructive even for civilians.

DOMESTIC MOBILIZATION

Once it became clear that the war would not be over quickly, leaders on both sides realized that the outcome would not be determined on the battlefield alone. Victory required mobilizing all of the nation's resources and energies. So World War I became a **total war,** involving the entire society.

The British naval blockade on Germany, which made no distinction between military and nonmilitary goods, was a stratagem characteristic of total war. The blockade would not affect Germany's immediate strength on the battlefield, but it could damage Germany's long-term war-making capacity. The blockade was effective partly because Germany had not made adequate preparations—including stockpiling—for a protracted war of attrition.

In peacetime, Germany had depended on imports of food, fats, oils, and chemicals, including the nitrates needed for ammunition. With the onset of war, these goods were immediately in short supply, as was labor. Thus Germany seemed to need stringent economic coordination and control. By the end of 1916, the country had coordinated all aspects of economic life for the war effort. Under the supervision of the military, state agencies, big business, and the trade unions were brought into close collaboration. The new system included rationing, price controls, and compulsory labor arbitration, as well as a national service law enabling the military to channel workers into jobs deemed vital to the war effort.

The Germans did not hesitate to exploit the economy of occupied Belgium, requisitioning foodstuffs even to the point of causing starvation among the Belgians themselves. They forced sixty-two thousand Belgians to work in German factories under conditions of virtual slave labor. By the time this practice was stopped in February 1917, nearly a thousand Belgian workers had died in German labor camps.

The body coordinating Germany's war economy was the **Kriegsrohstoffabteilung (KRA)** (kreegs-roh-stoff-AHB-ty-loong), or "War Raw Materials Office." Led initially by the able Jewish industrialist Walther Rathenau (RAT-un-ow) (1867–1922), this agency came to symbolize the unprecedented coordination of the German economy. Recognizing that Germany lacked the raw materials for a long war, Rathenau devised an imaginative program that included the development of synthetic substitute products and the creation of new mixed (private and government) companies to

total war   The concept, first associated with World War I, that war requires the mobilization of all a nation's resources and energies.

Kriegsrohstoffabteilung (KRA)   The "War Raw Materials Office" that coordinated Germany's World War I economy.

allocate raw materials. The KRA's effort was remarkably successful—a model for later economic planning and coordination in Germany and elsewhere.

Although Germany presented the most dramatic example, this sort of domestic coordination was evident everywhere. In Britain, the central figure was David Lloyd George (1863–1945), appointed to the newly created post of minister of munitions in 1915. During his year in office, ninety-five new factories opened, soon overcoming the shortage of guns and ammunition that had impeded the British war effort until then. His performance made Lloyd George seem the one person who could organize Britain for victory. Succeeding Herbert Asquith as prime minister in December 1916, he would direct the British war effort to its victorious conclusion.

ACCELERATING SOCIOECONOMIC CHANGE

Everywhere the war effort quickened the long-term socioeconomic change associated with industrialization. Government orders for war materiel fueled industrial expansion. The needs of war spawned new technologies—advances in food processing and medical treatment, for example—that would carry over into peacetime.

With so many men needed for military service, women were called on to assume new economic roles—such as running farms in France, or working in the new munitions factories in Britain. During the course of the war, the number of women employed in Britain rose from 3.25 million to 5 million. In Italy, 200,000 women had war-related jobs by 1917. Women also played indispensable roles at the front, especially in nursing units.

The expanded opportunities of wartime intensified the debate over the sociopolitical role of women that the movement for women's suffrage had stimulated. The outbreak of war led some antiwar feminists to argue that women would be better able than men to prevent wars, which were essentially masculine undertakings. Women should have full access to public life, not because they could be expected to respond as men did but because they had a distinctive—and valuable—role to play. At the same time, by giving women jobs and the opportunity to do many of the same things men did, the war undermined the stereotypes that had long justified restrictions on women's political roles and life choices.

For many women, doing a difficult job well, serving their country in this emergency situation, afforded a new sense of accomplishment, as well as a new taste of independence. Women were now much more likely to have their own residences and to go out on their own, eating in restaurants, even smoking and drinking. Yet while many seized new opportunities and learned new skills, women frequently had to combine paid employ-

Working Women and the War

All over Europe, governments recruited women to work in munitions factories. This Russian government poster uses an image of working women to rally support for the war. The text reads, "Everything for the war effort! Subscribe to the war loans at 5½ percent." *(Eileen Tweedy/The Art Archive)*

ment with housework and child rearing, and those who left home—to serve in nursing units, for example—often felt guilty about neglecting their traditional family roles.

Online Study Center **Improve Your Grade**
Primary Source: A British Feminist Analyzes the Impact of the War on Women

PROPAGANDA AND THE "MOBILIZATION OF ENTHUSIASM"

Because the domestic front was crucial to sustaining a long war of attrition, it became ever more important to shore up civilian morale as the war dragged on. The result was what the historian Elie Halévy called the "mobilization of enthusiasm"—the manipulation of collective passions by governments on an unprecedented scale.

Every country instituted extensive censorship, even of soldiers' letters from the front. Because of concerns about civilian morale, the French press carried no news of the Battle of Verdun, with its horrifying numbers of casualties. In addition, systematic propaganda included not only patriotic themes but also attempts to discredit the enemy, even through outright falsification of the news. British anti-German propaganda helped draw the United States into the war in 1917.

At the outset of the war, the brutal behavior of the German armies in Belgium made it easy for the French and the British to demonize the Germans. Having expected to pass through neutral Belgium unopposed, the Germans were infuriated by the Belgian resistance they encountered. At Louvain late in August 1914 they responded to alleged Belgian sniping by shooting a number of hostages and setting the town on fire, destroying the famous old university library. This episode led the *London Times* to characterize the Germans as "Huns," a reference to the central Asian tribe that began invading Europe in the fourth century. Stories about German soldiers eating Belgian babies began to circulate.

In October 1914 ninety-three German intellectuals, artists, and scientists signed a manifesto, addressed to "the world of culture," justifying Germany's conduct in Belgium and its larger purposes in the war. As passions heated up, major intellectuals on both sides—from the German theologian Adolf von Harnack (1851–1930) to the French philosopher Henri Bergson (1859–1941)—began denigrating the culture of the enemy and claiming a monopoly of virtue for their own side.

As the war dragged on, some came to believe that real peace with an adversary so evil, so abnormally different, was simply not possible. There must be no compromise but rather total victory, no matter what the cost. At the same time, however, war-weariness produced a countervailing tendency to seek a "white peace," a peace without victory for either side. But in 1917, as Europeans began earnestly debating war aims, the Russian Revolution and the intervention of the United States changed the war's meaning for all the belligerents.

SECTION SUMMARY

- Partly because of the advent of new technologies, the war threatened civilian populations in unforeseen ways.

- The unexpected length of the war forced domestic mobilization, both to maintain civilian morale and to enhance the production necessary to sustain the military effort.

- Britain's naval blockade of Germany forced German leaders to adopt innovative, highly centralized forms of socioeconomic coordination, partly to spearhead the development of substitute products.

- Domestic mobilization accelerated socioeconomic change, especially by enhancing employment opportunities for women.

- Systematic attempts to discredit the enemy, by intellectuals as well as governments, made it harder to envision the scope for a lasting peace.

THE TWO RUSSIAN REVOLUTIONS OF 1917

Why did the first revolution in Russia pave the way for a second, spearheaded by the Bolsheviks?

Strained by war, the old European order cracked first in Russia in 1917. Initially the overthrow of the tsarist autocracy seemed to lay the foundations for parliamentary democracy. But by the end of the year, the Bolsheviks, the smallest and most extreme of Russia's major socialist parties, had taken power, an outcome that was hardly conceivable when the revolution began.

THE WARTIME CRISIS OF THE RUSSIAN AUTOCRACY

The Russian army performed better than many had expected; as late as June 1916, it mounted a successful offensive against Austria-Hungary. Russia had industrialized sufficiently by 1914 to sustain a modern war, at least for a while, and the country's war production increased significantly by 1916. But even early in 1915, perhaps a fourth of Russia's newly conscripted troops were sent to the front without weapons; they were told to pick up rifles and supplies from the dead. Moreover, Russia suffered from problems of leadership and organization that made it less prepared for a long war than the other belligerents.

In August 1915, Tsar Nicholas II (1868–1918) assumed personal command of the army, but his absence from the capital only accelerated the deterioration in government and deepened the divisions within the ruling clique. With the tsar away, the illiterate but charismatic Siberian "holy man" Grigori Rasputin (ca. 1872–1916) emerged as the key political power within the circle of the German-born Empress Alexandra (1872–1918). He won her confidence because of his alleged ability to control the bleeding of her hemophiliac son, Alexis, the heir to the throne. Led by Rasputin, those around the empress made a shambles of the state administration. Many educated Russians, appalled at what was happening, assumed—incorrectly—that pro-German elements at court were responsible for the eclipse of the tsar and the increasing governmental chaos. Asked one Duma deputy of the government's performance, "Is this stupidity, or is it treason?"

Finally, late in December 1916, Rasputin was assassinated by aristocrats seeking to save the autocracy from these apparently pro-German influences. This act indicated how desperate the situation had become, but eliminating Rasputin made little difference.

By the end of 1916, the difficulties of war had combined with the strains of rapid wartime industrialization to produce a revolutionary situation in Russia. The country's urban population had mushroomed, and now, partly because of transport problems, the cities faced severe food shortages. Strikes and demonstrations spread from Petrograd (the former St. Petersburg—

a name abandoned as too German at the start of the war) to other cities during the first two months of 1917. In March renewed demonstrations in Petrograd, spearheaded by women protesting the lack of bread and coal, led to revolution.

THE MARCH REVOLUTION AND THE FATE OF THE PROVISIONAL GOVERNMENT

At first, the agitation that began in Petrograd on March 8, 1917, appeared to be just another bread riot. Even when it turned into a wave of strikes, the revolutionary parties (see page 763) expected it to be crushed by government troops. But when they were called out to help the police break up the demonstrations, the soldiers generally avoided firing at the strikers. Within days, they were sharing weapons and ammunition with the workers; the government's troops were joining what was now becoming a revolution.

Late in the afternoon of March 12, leaders of the strike committees, delegates elected by factory workers, and representatives of the socialist parties formed a *soviet*, or council, following the example of the revolution of 1905, when such soviets had first appeared. Regiments of the Petrograd garrison also began electing representatives, soon to be admitted to the **Petrograd Soviet**, which officially became the Council of Workers' and Soldiers' Deputies. This soviet was now the ruling power in the Russian capital. It had been elected and was genuinely representative—though of a limited constituency of workers and soldiers. Following the lead of Petrograd, Russians elsewhere promptly began forming soviets, so that over 350 local units were represented when the first All-Russian Council of Soviets met in Petrograd in April. The overwhelming majority of their representatives were Mensheviks and Socialist Revolutionaries; about one-sixth were Bolsheviks.

On March 14 a committee of the Duma, recognizing that the tsar's authority had been lost for good, persuaded Nicholas to abdicate, then formed a new **provisional government.** This government was to be strictly temporary, paving the way for an elected constituent assembly, which would write a constitution and establish fully legitimate governmental institutions.

Considering the strains that had produced the revolution of 1905 after the Russo-Japanese War, it was hardly surprising that the autocratic system would shatter now, in light of this far more trying war and the resulting governmental disarray. Russia had apparently

Petrograd Soviet   The *soviet* (council) of leaders of strike committees and army regiments elected in March 1917, when Petrograd's workers protested in response to severe wartime food and coal shortages.

provisional government   The body that ruled Russia from March to November 1917, in the wake of the revolution that overthrew the tsarist regime.

experienced, at last, the bourgeois political revolution necessary to develop a Western-style parliamentary democracy. Even from an orthodox Marxist perspective, the immediate priority was to help consolidate the new democratic order, which would then provide the framework for the longer-term pursuit of socialism.

Although the fall of the tsarist government produced widespread relief, Russia's new leaders faced difficult questions about priorities. Should they focus their efforts on revitalizing the Russian war effort? Or, given the widespread war-weariness in the country, should they focus on domestic political reform? For now, the Petrograd Soviet was prepared to give the provisional government a chance to govern. But the soviet was a potential rival for power if the new government failed to address Russia's immediate problems.

The provisional government took important steps toward democracy, establishing universal suffrage, civil liberties, autonomy for ethnic minorities, and labor legislation, including provision for an eight-hour workday. But the government failed in two key areas, fostering discontents that the Bolsheviks soon exploited. First, it persisted in fighting the war. Second, it dragged its feet on agrarian reform.

The provisional government's determination to renew the war effort stemmed from concern about Russia's obligations to its allies, its national honor and position among the great powers. The long-standing goal of Russian diplomacy—an outlet to the Mediterranean Sea through the Dardanelles—seemed within reach if Russia could continue the war and contribute to an Entente victory. The educated, well-to-do Russians who led the new government expected that ordinary citizens, now free, would fight with renewed enthusiasm, like the armies that had grown from the French Revolution over a century before. These leaders failed to grasp how desperate the situation of ordinary people had become.

Although the March revolution began in the cities, the peasantry soon moved into action as well, seizing land, sometimes burning the houses of their landlords. By midsummer, a full-scale peasant war seemed to be developing in the countryside, and calls for agrarian reform became increasingly urgent. Partly from expediency, partly from genuine concern for social justice, the provisional government promised a major redistribution of land. But it insisted that the reform be carried out legally—not by the present provisional government, but by a duly elected constituent assembly.

Calling elections would thus seem to have been the first priority. The new political leaders kept putting it off, however, waiting for the situation to cool off. But playing for time was a luxury they could ill afford. As unrest grew in the countryside, the authority of the provisional government diminished and the soviets gained in stature. But what role were the soviets to play?

Lenin as Leader
Although he was in exile during much of 1917, Lenin's leadership was crucial to the Bolshevik success in Russia. He is shown here addressing a May Day rally in Red Square, Moscow, on May 1, 1919.
(ITAR-TASS/Sovfoto)

THE BOLSHEVIKS COME TO POWER

In the immediate aftermath of the March revolution, the Bolsheviks had not seemed to differ substantially from their rivals within the socialist movement, at least on matters of immediate concern—the war, land reform, and the character of the revolution itself. But the situation began to change in April when Lenin, assisted by the German military, returned from exile in Switzerland. The Germans assumed—correctly, it turned out—that the Bolsheviks would help undermine the Russian war effort. Largely through the force of Lenin's leadership, the Bolsheviks soon took the initiative within the still-developing revolution in Russia.

Early Years Under Lenin   Born Vladimir Ilich Ulianov, **Vladimir Lenin** (1870–1924) came from a comfortable upper-middle-class family. He was university-educated and trained as a lawyer. But after an older brother was executed in 1887 for participating in a plot against the tsar's life, Lenin followed him into revolutionary activity. Arrested for the first time in 1895, he

Vladimir Lenin   Russian revolutionary and leader of the Bolsheviks since 1903, he masterminded the November 1917 revolution that overthrew the provisional government and led to a communist regime in Russia.

was confined to Siberia until 1900. He then lived in exile abroad for almost the entire period before his return to Russia in 1917.

The Bolshevik Party was identified with Lenin from its beginning in 1903, when it emerged from the schism in Russian Marxist socialism. Because of his emphases, Bolshevism came to mean discipline, organization, and a special leadership role for a revolutionary vanguard. Lenin proved effective because he was a stern and somewhat forbidding figure, disciplined, fiercely intelligent, sometimes ruthless. As a Bolshevik colleague put it, Lenin was "the one indisputable leader . . . a man of iron will, inexhaustible energy, combining a fanatical faith in the movement, in the cause, with an equal faith in himself."[4]

Still, Lenin's reading of the situation when he returned to Petrograd in April astonished even many Bolsheviks. He argued that the revolution was about to pass from the present bourgeois-democratic stage to a socialist phase, involving proletarian dictatorship in the form of government by the soviets. So the Bolsheviks should begin actively opposing the provisional government, especially by denouncing the war as fundamentally imperialist and by demanding the distribution of land from the large estates to the peasants. This latter measure had long been identified with the Socialist Revolutionaries; most Bolsheviks had envisioned collectivization and nationalization instead.

As Lenin saw it, the strains of war had made all of Europe ripe for revolution. A revolution in Russia would provide the spark to ignite a wider proletarian revolution, especially in Germany. He did not envision backward Russia seeking to create socialism on its own. Although some remained skeptical of Lenin's strategy, he promptly won over most of his fellow Bolsheviks. And thus the Bolsheviks began actively seeking wider support by promising peace, land, and bread.

The Bolshevik Revolution   In April 1917 moderate socialists still had majority support in the soviets, so the Bolsheviks sought to build support gradually, postponing any decisive test of strength. But events escaped the control of the Bolshevik leadership in mid-July when impatient workers, largely Bolshevik in sympathy, took to the streets of Petrograd on their own. The Petrograd Soviet refused to support the uprising, and the provisional government had no difficulty getting military units to put it down, killing two hundred in the process. Though the uprising had developed spontaneously, Bolshevik leaders felt compelled to offer public support, and this gave the government an excuse to crack down on the Bolshevik leadership. Lenin managed to escape to Finland, but a number of his colleagues were arrested and jailed.

With the Bolsheviks on the defensive, counterrevolutionary elements in the Russian military decided to seize the initiative with a march on Petrograd in September. To resist this attempted coup, the provisional government, now led by the young Socialist Revolutionary Alexander Kerensky (1881–1970), had to rely on whoever could offer help, including the Bolsheviks. And thanks to Bolshevik propaganda, the soldiers under the command of the counterrevolutionaries refused to fight against the upholders of the revolution in Petrograd. Thus the coup was thwarted. Within days, the Bolsheviks won their first clear-cut majority in the Petrograd Soviet, then shortly gained majorities in most of the other soviets as well.

During the fall of 1917, the situation became increasingly volatile, eluding control by anyone. People looted food from shops; peasants seized land, sometimes murdering their landlords. Desertions and the murder of officers increased within the Russian military.

With the Bolsheviks now the dominant power in the soviets, and with the government's control diminishing, Lenin, from his hideout in Finland, urged the Bolshevik central committee to prepare for armed insurrection. Although some found this step too risky, the majority accepted Lenin's argument that the provisional government would continue dragging its feet,

inadvertently giving right-wing officers time for another coup.

Because Lenin remained in hiding, the task of organizing the seizure of power fell to Leon Trotsky (1870–1940), who skillfully modified Lenin's aggressive strategy. Lenin wanted the Bolsheviks to rise in their own name, in opposition to the provisional government, but Trotsky linked the insurrection to the cause of the soviets and played up its defensive character against the ongoing danger of a counterrevolutionary coup. With the political center at an impasse, the only alternative to such a coup seemed to be a Bolshevik initiative to preserve the Petrograd Soviet, by now the sole viable institutional embodiment of the revolution and its promise. Trotsky's interpretation led people who wanted simply to defend the soviet to support the Bolshevik action.

During the night of November 9, armed Bolsheviks and regular army regiments occupied key points in Petrograd, including railroad stations, post offices, telephone exchanges, power stations, and the national bank. Able to muster only token resistance, the provisional government collapsed. Kerensky escaped and mounted a futile effort to rally troops at the front for a counterattack. In contrast to the March revolution, which had taken about a week, the Bolsheviks took over the capital, overthrowing the Kerensky government, literally overnight and almost without bloodshed.

But though the Bolsheviks enjoyed considerable support in the network of soviets, it was not clear that they could extend their control across the whole Russian Empire. Moreover, from their own perspective, the revolution's immediate prospects, and its potential wider impact, were bound up with the course of the war. Would the Bolshevik Revolution in Russia prove the spark for revolution elsewhere in war-weary Europe, as Lenin anticipated?

THE RUSSIAN REVOLUTION AND THE WAR

Having stood for peace throughout the revolution, the Bolsheviks promptly moved to get Russia out of the war, agreeing to an armistice with Germany in December 1917. They hoped that Russia's withdrawal would speed the collapse of the war effort on all sides and that this, in turn, would intensify the movement toward revolution elsewhere in Europe. The Russian Revolution was but a chapter in this larger story. As Lenin noted to Trotsky, "If it were necessary for us to go under to assure the success of the German revolution, we should have to do it. The German revolution is vastly more important than ours." Indeed, said Lenin to the Bolsheviks' party congress of March 1918, "It is an absolute truth that we will go under without the German revolution."[5]

After assuming control in November, the Bolsheviks published the tsarist government's secret agreements specifying how the spoils were to be divided in the event of a Russian victory. They hoped to inflame revolutionary sentiment elsewhere by demonstrating that the war had been, all along, an imperialist offensive on behalf of capitalist interests. This Bolshevik initiative added fuel to the controversy already developing in all the belligerent countries over the war's purpose and significance.

SECTION SUMMARY

- The strains of war led to a revolution that ended the tsarist order in Russia in March 1917.

- Although the soviet, or workers' and soldiers' council, was a major force in Petrograd, the first Russian revolution of 1917 was not intended to produce a socialist system.

- The provisional government proved ineffective because it dragged its feet on land reform and insisted on maintaining the war effort.

- Due partly to the leadership of Lenin and Trotsky, the Bolsheviks were able to seize the initiative and take power from the provisional government in November 1917.

- The Bolsheviks envisioned their takeover as a spark to revolution elsewhere in war-torn Europe.

THE NEW WAR AND THE ALLIED VICTORY, 1917–1918

Why did Germany and its allies end up losing the war even after forcing Russia to make a separate peace by early 1918?

Because the stakes of the war changed during 1917, the eventual outcome included consequences that Europeans could not have foreseen in 1914. German defeat brought revolution against the monarchy and the beginning of a new democracy. Austro-Hungarian defeat brought the collapse of the Habsburg monarchy and thus the opportunity for its national minorities to form nations of their own. As the old European order fell, grandiose new visions competed to shape the postwar world.

THE DEBATE OVER WAR AIMS

The French and British governments publicly welcomed the March revolution in Russia, partly because they expected Russia's military performance to improve under new leadership, but also because the change of regime seemed to have highly favorable psychological implications. With Russia no longer an autocracy, the war could be portrayed—and experienced—as a crusade for democracy. At the same time, the March revolution could only sow confusion among the many Germans who had understood their own war effort as a matter of self-defense against reactionary Russia. But the November revolution required a deeper reconsideration by all the belligerents.

Allied war aims agreements, such as the Treaty of London that brought Italy into the war in 1915, had remained secret until the Bolsheviks published the tsarist documents. Products of old-style diplomacy, those agreements had been made by a restricted foreign policy elite; even members of the elected parliaments generally did not know their contents. The debate over war aims that developed in 1917 thus became a debate over decision making as well. Many assumed that a more democratic approach to foreign policy would minimize the chances of war, since the people would not agree to wars for dynastic or business interests. In addition, there were exhortations for all the parties in the present war to renounce annexations and settle for a white peace. It was time to call the whole thing off and bring the soldiers home.

Seeking to counter such sentiments, especially the Russian contention that the war was not worth continuing, the idealistic U.S. president, Woodrow Wilson (1856–1924), insisted on the great potential significance of an Allied victory. In his State of the Union speech of January 1918, and in several declarations thereafter, Wilson developed the **Fourteen Points** that he proposed should guide the new international order.

Fourteen Points Proposals by U.S. president Woodrow Wilson to guide the new international order that would follow an Allied victory in World War I.

Notable among them were open diplomacy, free trade, reduced armaments, self-determination for nationalities, a league of nations, and a recasting of the colonial system to ensure equal rights for the indigenous populations.

Online Study Center Improve Your Grade
Primary Source: A New Diplomacy:
    The Fourteen Points

Lenin and Wilson, then, offered radically different interpretations of the war, with radically different implications for present priorities. Yet, compared with the old diplomacy, they had something in common. Together, they seemed to represent a whole new approach to international relations and the possibility of a more peaceful world. Thus they found an eager audience among the war-weary peoples of Europe.

Despite the strains of the war, Sacred Union in France did not weaken substantially until April 1917, with General Nivelle's disastrous offensive. But then, as near mutiny began to develop within the army, rank-and-file pressures forced socialist leaders to demand clarification, and perhaps revision, of French war aims. Suddenly the French government was under pressure to suggest that the war had idealistic and democratic purposes. Doubts about the government's goals were threatening to turn into active opposition to the war.

The same pressures were at work in Germany. Antiwar sentiment grew steadily within the Social Democratic Party (SPD) until the antiwar faction split off and formed the Independent Socialist Party (USPD) in April 1917. A large-scale debate over war aims, linked to considerations of domestic political reform, developed in the Reichstag by the summer of 1917. On July 19, a solid 60 percent majority passed a new war aims resolution, which affirmed that Germany's purposes were solely defensive, that Germany had no territorial ambitions. Germany, too, seemed open to a white peace.

But just as the dramatic events of 1917 interjected new pressures for moderation and peace, pressures in the opposite direction also mounted as the war dragged on. It seemed to some that this war was only the beginning of a new era of cutthroat international competition; the old rules would no longer apply. War aims grew more grandiose as nations tried to gain the leverage for success in the contentious postwar world.

The shape of the current war convinced top German officials that Germany's geography and dependence on imports made it especially vulnerable in a long war. So Germany had to seize the present opportunity to conquer the means to fight the next war on a more favorable footing. Responding in February 1918 to calls for a white peace, General Ludendorff stressed that "if Germany makes peace without profit, it has lost the war." Germany, insisted Ludendorff, must win the mil-

itary and economic basis for future security—to "enable us to contemplate confidently some future defensive war."[6] Many German officials believed that Germany could achieve parity with Britain, and thus the basis for security and peace, only if it maintained control of the Belgian coast. German expansion into Russian Poland and up the Baltic coast of Lithuania and Latvia seemed essential as well.

When, in response to the Russian request for an armistice, Germany was able to dictate the peace terms, as specified in the **Treaty of Brest-Litovsk** of March 1918, it became clear how radically annexationist Germany's war aims had become. European Russia was to be largely dismembered, leaving Germany in direct or indirect control of 27 percent of Russia's European territory, 40 percent of its population, and 75 percent of its iron and coal. All the Reichstag parties except the Socialists accepted the terms of the treaty, which, in fact, produced a renewed determination to push on to victory.

France, less vulnerable geographically than Germany, tended to be more modest. But news of the terms the Germans had imposed at Brest-Litovsk inflamed the French, reinforcing their determination to fight on to an unqualified victory. Only thus could France secure the advantages necessary to ward off an ongoing German menace.

THE RENEWAL OF THE FRENCH WAR EFFORT

The domestic division in France that followed the failure of Nivelle's offensive reached its peak during the fall of 1917. In November, with pressure for a white peace intensifying and France's ability to continue fighting in doubt, President Raymond Poincaré (1860–1934) called on Georges Clemenceau (1841–1929) to lead a new government. The 76-year-old Clemenceau (klem-ahn-SOH) was known as a "hawk"; his appointment portended a stepped-up prosecution of the war. His message was simple as he appeared before the Chamber of Deputies on November 20, 1917: "If you ask me about my war aims, I reply: my aim is to be victorious." For the remainder of the war, France was under the virtual dictatorship of Clemenceau and his cabinet.

Clemenceau moved decisively on both the domestic and military fronts. By cracking down on the antiwar movement—imprisoning antiwar leaders, suppressing defeatist newspapers—he stiffened morale on the home front. Understanding that lack of coordination between French and British military leaders had hampered the Allied effort on the battlefield, Clemenceau persuaded the British to accept the French general Ferdinand Foch

Treaty of Brest-Litovsk   Harsh peace terms that Germany imposed on Russia in March 1918.

(FOHSH) (1851–1929) as the first supreme commander of all Allied forces in the west. In choosing Foch, known for his commitment to aggressive offensives, Clemenceau was pointedly bypassing Pétain, whom he found too passive, even defeatist. After some initial friction, Clemenceau let Foch have his way on the military level, and the two proved an effective leadership combination.

THE GERMAN GAMBLE, 1918

As the military campaigns of 1918 began, Germany seemed in a relatively favorable position: Russia had been knocked out of the war, and American troops were yet to arrive. Moderates in Germany wanted to seize the opportunity to work out a compromise peace while there was still a chance. But military leaders persuaded Kaiser Wilhelm II that Germany could win a definitive victory on the western front if it struck quickly, before U.S. help became significant. Since Germany would be out of reserves by summer, the alternative to decisive victory in the west would be total German defeat.

The German gamble almost succeeded. From March to June 1918, German forces seized the initiative with four months of sustained and effective attacks. By May 30 they had again reached the Marne, where they had been held in 1914. Paris, only 37 miles away, had to be evacuated once more (see **MAP 25.2**). As late as mid-

July, Ludendorff remained confident of victory, but by mid-August it was becoming clear that Germany lacked the manpower to exploit the successes of the offensive.

The German advance had caused mutual suspicion between the French and the British at first, but under Foch's leadership the Western allies eventually managed more effective coordination. By mid-1918 American involvement was also becoming a factor. On June 4, over a year after the U.S. declaration of war, American troops went into action for the first time, bolstering French forces along the Marne. This was a small operation, in which the Americans' performance was amateurish when compared with that of their battle-seasoned allies. But as the Allied counterattack proceeded, 250,000 U.S. troops were arriving per month, considerably boosting Allied morale and battlefield strength.

By June 1918 Europe was experiencing the first outbreak of a virulent new influenza virus, promptly dubbed the "Spanish flu," though it had originated in South Africa. Because of their inferior diets, German soldiers proved far more susceptible to the disease than their adversaries, a fact that significantly affected Germany's combat performance during the crucial summer of 1918.

Germany lost the initiative for good during the second Battle of the Marne, which began on July 15 with yet another German attack. Foch launched a sustained

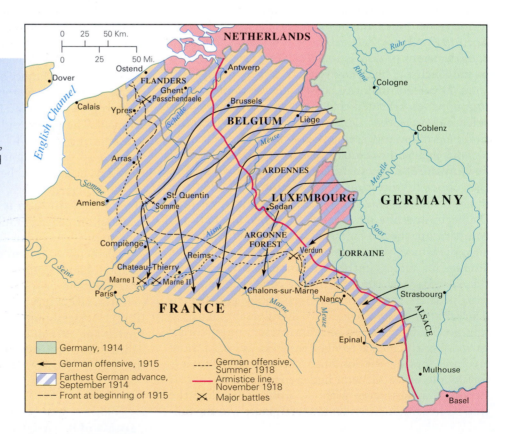

MAP 25.2 Stalemate and Decision on the Western Front
On the western front, in northern France and Belgium, trench warfare developed and the best-known battles of the war were fought. Notable sites include Verdun, Passchendaele, and the Marne and Somme Rivers.

counterattack on July 18, using tanks to good advantage, and maintained the momentum thereafter. By early August the whole western front began to roll back. With astonishing suddenness, the outcome was no longer in doubt, although most expected the war to drag on into 1919. Few realized how desperate Germany's situation had become.

Meanwhile, Germany's allies began falling one by one. In the Balkans an Allied offensive broke through the German-Bulgarian line in September, prompting the Bulgarians to ask for an armistice. The Turkish military effort collapsed in October. With the defeat of Russia in 1917, German troops joined the Austrians on the Italian front, breaking through the Italian line at Caporetto late in 1917 and almost inflicting a decisive defeat. But after retreating, the Italians managed to regroup and hold—and eventually to drive the Austrians back. The Italian victory at Vittorio Veneto forced Austria's unconditional surrender on November 3, 1918. But by this point the armies of the Habsburg empire were disintegrating along nationality lines. And the impending collapse of this centuries-old empire gave its various national minorities the chance to form states of their own.

MILITARY DEFEAT AND POLITICAL CHANGE IN GERMANY

By late September it was clear to Ludendorff that his armies could not stop the Allied advance. On September 29 he informed the government that to avoid invasion, Germany would have to seek an immediate armistice. Hoping to secure favorable peace terms and to foist responsibility for the defeat onto the parliamentary politicians, Hindenburg and Ludendorff asked that a government based on greater popular support be formed. A leading moderate, Prince Max von Baden (BAH-dyn) (1867–1929), became chancellor, and he promptly replaced Ludendorff with General Wilhelm Groener (GREU-nur) (1867–1939), who seemed more democratic in orientation. By now it was clear that ending the war could not be separated from the push for political change in Germany, especially because it was widely assumed that a more democratic Germany could expect more favorable peace terms.

After securing a written request for an armistice from Hindenburg, Prince Max sent a peace note to President Wilson early in October, asking for an armistice based on Wilson's Fourteen Points. During the month that followed, Prince Max engineered a series of measures, passed by the Reichstag and approved by the emperor, that reformed the constitution, abolishing the three-class voting system in Prussia and making the chancellor responsible to the Reichstag. At last Germany had a constitutional monarchy. Not com-

pletely satisfied, President Wilson encouraged speculation that Germany could expect better peace terms if Wilhelm II were to abdicate and Germany became a republic.

But a far more radical outcome seemed possible during late 1918 and early 1919. As negotiations for an armistice proceeded in October, the continuing war effort produced instances of mutiny in the navy and breaches of discipline in the army. By early November workers' and soldiers' councils were being formed all over Germany, just as in Russia the year before. On November 7, antiwar socialists in Munich led an uprising of workers and soldiers that expelled the king of Bavaria and proclaimed a new Bavarian republic. Its provisional government promptly sought its own peace negotiations with the Allies. On November 9, thousands of workers took to the streets of Berlin to demand immediate peace, and the authorities could not muster enough military resources to move against them.

The senior army leadership grew concerned that the collapse of government authority would undermine the ability of officers even to march their troops home. So Hindenburg and Groener persuaded the emperor to abdicate. Having lost the support of the army, Wilhelm II accepted the inevitable and left for exile in the Netherlands.

With the German right, including the military, in disarray, and with the centrist parties discredited by their support for what had become an annexationist war, the initiative passed to the socialists. They, at least, had been in the forefront of the movement for peace. But the socialists had divided in 1917, mostly over the question of response to the war. The mainstream of the SPD, by supporting the war for so long, had irrevocably alienated the party's leftist socialist wing. The most militant of these leftist socialists, led by Karl Liebknecht (1871–1919) and Rosa Luxemburg (1870–1919), envisioned using the workers' and soldiers' councils as the basis for a full-scale revolution, more or less on the Bolshevik model.

The SPD, on the other hand, clung to its reformist heritage and insisted on working within parliamentary institutions. Party leaders argued that a Bolshevik-style revolution was neither appropriate nor necessary under the circumstances. So SPD moderates proclaimed a parliamentary republic on November 9, just hours before the revolutionaries proclaimed a soviet-style republic. The next day the soldiers' and workers' councils in Berlin elected a provisional executive committee, to be led by the moderate socialist Friedrich Ebert (A-bairt) (1871–1925). As the new republic sought to consolidate itself, the radical leftists continued to promote further revolution.

Birth from military defeat was especially disabling for the new republic because the German people were so little prepared for defeat when it came. Vigorous censorship had kept the public in the dark about Germany's real situation, so the request for an armistice early in October came as a shock. At no time during the war had Germany been invaded from the west, and by mid-1918 the German army had seemed on the brink of victory. It appeared inconceivable that Germany had

lost a military decision, plain and simple. Thus the **"stab in the back" myth,** the notion that political intrigue and revolution at home had sabotaged the German military effort, developed to explain what otherwise seemed an inexplicable defeat. This notion would prove a heavy burden for Germany's new democracy to bear.

S E C T I O N   S U M M A R Y

- By 1917, the will to continue the war was flagging on both sides, as some began to question war aims and even to call for a "white peace."

- The idealism of U.S. president Wilson, with his Fourteen Points, suggested to Europeans that the war might indeed be worth fighting to a victorious conclusion.

- The harsh Treaty of Brest-Litovsk that Germany imposed on Russia reflected changes in German war aims.

- The leadership combination of Clemenceau and Foch was crucial to the renewal of the French war effort.

- Germany's gamble on one last massive offensive during the summer of 1918 almost succeeded, but, led by France, the Allies began forcing the Germans back, prompting Germany to ask for an armistice.

- German leaders decided to turn from Wilhelm II's imperial regime toward democracy, partly in an effort to secure more favorable peace terms.

THE OUTCOME AND THE IMPACT

What factors shaped the peace settlement that the victors imposed on Germany and its allies in 1919–1920?

After the armistice officially ended the fighting on November 11, 1918, it was up to the war's four victors—France, Britain, Italy, and the United States—to establish the terms of peace and, it was to be hoped, a new basis for order at the same time. But the peacemakers had to deal with a radically new political and territorial situation. Revolution had undermined, or threatened to undermine, the old political order in much of Europe. And the war had come to involve non-European powers and peoples in unprecedented ways. After all that had happened since August 1914, it was not clear what a restoration of peace and order would require. But it was evident that Europe would no longer dominate world affairs in quite the way it had.

THE COSTS OF WAR

Raw casualty figures do not begin to convey the war's human toll, but they afford some sense of its magnitude. Estimates differ, but it is generally agreed that from 10 million to 13 million military men lost their lives, with another 20 million wounded. In addition, between 7 million and 10 million civilians died as a result of the war and its hardships. In the defeated coun-

tries especially, food shortages and malnutrition continued well after the end of the fighting. Thus the Spanish flu that had affected the balance on the battlefield early in the summer of 1918 returned with particularly devastating results during the fall. The influenza pandemic killed perhaps 40 million people worldwide.

Germany suffered the highest number of military casualties, but France suffered the most in proportional terms. Two million Germans were killed, with another 4 million wounded. Military deaths per capita for France were roughly 15 percent higher than for Germany—and twice as severe as for Britain. Of 8 million Frenchmen mobilized, over 5 million were killed or wounded. Roughly 1.5 million French soldiers, or 10 percent of the active male population, were killed—and this in a country already concerned about demographic decline. The other belligerents suffered less, but still in great numbers. Among the military personnel killed were 2 million Russians, 500,000 Italians, and 114,000 Americans.

Economic costs were heavy as well. In addition to the privations suffered during the years of war, Euro-

> **"stab in the back" myth** The notion, widely held among Germans after their unexpected loss in World War I, that political intrigue and revolution at home had sabotaged the German military effort.

peans found themselves reeling from inflation and saddled with debt, especially to the United States, once the war was over. Although the immediate transition to a peacetime economy did not prove as difficult as many had feared, the war and its aftermath produced an economic disequilibrium that lingered, helping to produce a worldwide depression by the 1930s.

THE SEARCH FOR PEACE IN A REVOLUTIONARY ERA

The war had begun because of an unmanageable nationality problem in Austria-Hungary, and it led not simply to military defeat for Austria-Hungary but to the breakup of the Habsburg system (see **MAP 25.3**). In east-central Europe, the end of the war brought bright hopes for self-determination to peoples like the Czechs, Slovaks, Poles, Serbs, and Croats. Even before the peacemakers opened deliberations in January 1919, some of these ethnic groups had begun creating a new order on their own. For example, a popular movement of Czechs and Slovaks established a Czechoslovak republic on October 29, 1918, and a new Yugoslavia and an independent Hungary similarly emerged from indigenous movements. Czechoslovakia and Yugoslavia were made up of different ethnic groups that found cooperation advantageous now but that might well disagree in the future. Moreover, many of these countries lacked traditions of self-government, and they had reason to feud among themselves. With the Habsburg system no longer imposing one form of stability, a power vacuum seemed likely in this potentially volatile part of Europe.

The Bolshevik Revolution in Russia immeasurably complicated the situation. The unsettled conditions in Germany and the former Habsburg territories seemed to invite the spread of revolution—precisely according to Lenin's script. Shortly after taking power, Lenin and his party had begun calling themselves "communists," partly to jettison the provincial Russian term *bolshevik,* but especially to underline their departure from the old reformist socialism of the Second International. In adopting "communism," they wanted to make it clear that they stood for a revolutionary alternative, and they actively sought to inspire revolution elsewhere.

Outside Russia, the greatest communist success was in Hungary, where a communist regime under Béla Kun (1885–1937) governed Budapest and other parts of the country from March to August 1919, when it was put down by Allied-sponsored forces. At about the same time, communist republics lasted for months in the Slovak part of Czechoslovakia and in the important German state of Bavaria. Even in Italy, which had shared in the victory, socialists infatuated with the Bolshevik example claimed that the substantial labor unrest during 1919 and 1920 was the beginning of full-scale revolution.

Meanwhile, fears that the Russian Revolution might spread had fueled foreign intervention in Russia itself beginning in June 1918, when 24,000 French and British troops landed at Murmansk, in northern Russia. As long as the war with Germany lasted, military concerns helped justify this course, but after the armistice of November 1918, the intervention became overtly anticommunist, intended to help topple the new regime and undercut its efforts to export revolution.

Further complicating the postwar situation were the defeat and dissolution of the Turkish Ottoman Empire, which had controlled much of the Middle East in 1914. The Arab revolt against the Turks that developed in the Arabian peninsula in 1916 did not achieve its major military aims, though it caused some disruption to the Turkish war effort. Its success was due partly to the collaboration of a young British officer, T. E. Lawrence (1888–1935), who proved an effective military leader and an impassioned advocate of the Arab cause. The support that Britain had offered the Arabs suggested that independence, perhaps even a single Arab kingdom, might follow from a defeat of the Ottoman Empire.

But British policy toward the Arabs was uncertain and contradictory. Concerned about the Suez Canal, the British government sought to tighten its control in Egypt by declaring it a protectorate in 1914, triggering increased anti-British sentiment in the region. The secret Sykes-Picot Agreement of May 1916, named for the British and French diplomats who negotiated it, projected a division of the Ottoman territories of the Middle East into colonial spheres of influence. France would control Syria and Lebanon, while Britain would rule Palestine and Mesopotamia, or present-day Iraq.

Potentially complicating the situation in the region was Zionism, the movement to establish a Jewish state in Palestine. Led by Chaim Weizmann (1874–1952), a remarkable Russian-born British chemist, the Zionists reached an important milestone when British foreign secretary Arthur Balfour (1848–1930) cautiously announced, in the Balfour Declaration of November 1917, that the British government "looked with favor" on the prospect of a "Jewish home" in Palestine. At this point Jews were only 10 percent of the population in Palestine. British leaders sympathetic to Zionism saw no conflict in simultaneously embracing the cause of the Arabs against the Ottoman Turks. Indeed, Arabs and Jews, each seeking self-determination, could be expected to collaborate.

In the heat of war, the British established their policy for the former Ottoman territories without careful study. Thus they made promises and agreements that were not entirely compatible. After the war, the victors' efforts to install a new order in the Middle East would create fresh conflicts.

MAP 25.3 The Impact of the War: The Territorial Settlement in Europe and the Middle East

The defeat of Russia, Austria-Hungary, Germany, and Ottoman Turkey opened the way to major changes in the map of east-central Europe and the Middle East. A number of new nations emerged in east-central Europe, while in the Arab world the end of Ottoman rule meant not independence but new roles for European powers.

Legend:
- Boundaries of German, Russian, and Austro-Hungarian empires in 1914
- Areas lost by Austro-Hungarian Empire
- Areas lost by Russian Empire
- Areas lost by German Empire
- Areas lost by Bulgaria
- Areas lost by Ottoman Empire
- Demilitarized Zones
- Boundaries of 1926
- Areas controlled under mandates from the League of Nations, 1920

NORWAY · Oslo · SWEDEN · Stockholm · Helsinki · FINLAND · Murmansk · North Sea · GREAT BRITAIN · DENMARK · Copenhagen · Baltic Sea · Tallinn · ESTONIA · Leningrad (St. Petersburg) · Riga · LATVIA · Memel · Free city of Danzig · LITHUANIA · Vilnius · EAST PRUSSIA · POLISH CORRIDOR · RUSSIAN EMPIRE (Became Union of Soviet Socialist Republics, 1922) · Volga · NETHERLANDS · Amsterdam · GERMANY · Berlin · Brussels · BELGIUM · RUHR · Cologne · Weimar · Frankfurt · POLAND · Warsaw · Paris · LUX. · FRANCE · LORRAINE · ALSACE · Strasbourg · Prague · CZECHOSLOVAKIA · GALICIA · Kiev · Ural · Don · Dnieper · Geneva · Bern · SWITZ. · Locarno · Milan · S. TYROL · AUSTRIA · Vienna · Budapest · HUNGARY · BESSARABIA · Genoa · Venice · Trieste · Zagreb · ROMANIA · Caspian Sea · Rapallo · CROATIA · Belgrade · Bucharest · ITALY · Rome · YUGOSLAVIA · Danube · Black Sea · SERBIA · BULGARIA · Sofia · MONTENEGRO (To Yugoslavia 1921) · Corsica · Naples · ALBANIA · Batum · Baku · Kars · Sardinia · Istanbul (Constantinople) · GREECE · Athens · Izmir (Smyrna) · Ankara · TURKEY · Tabriz · PERSIA (IRAN) · TUNISIA (French) · Mediterranean Sea · Sicily · Crete · Cyprus (Gr. Br.) · Annexed by Turkey 1939 · Aleppo · SYRIA (French Mandate) · Euphrates · Tigris · Baghdad · IRAQ (MESOPOTAMIA) (British Mandate) · Kut el Amara · Beirut · Damascus · Basra · PALESTINE (British Mandate) · Jerusalem · Amman · TRANSJORDAN (British Mandate) · KUWAIT (Gr. Br.) · NEUTRAL ZONES · LIBYA (Italian) · EGYPT (Independent 1922) · Suez Canal · Cairo · Nile · Red Sea · NEJD (SAUDI ARABIA) · Riyadh · Medina

0 200 400 Km.
0 200 400 Mi.

792

An Arab in Paris
Prince Faisal (*foreground*) attended the Paris Peace Conference, where he lobbied for the creation of an independent Arab kingdom from part of the former Ottoman Turkish holdings in the Middle East. Among his supporters was the British officer T. E. Lawrence (*middle row, second from the right*), on his way to legend as "Lawrence of Arabia." (*Courtesy of the Trustees of the Imperial War Museum*)

THE PEACE SETTLEMENT

The peace conference took place in Paris, beginning in January 1919. Its labors led to separate treaties with each of the five defeated states. The first and most significant was the **Treaty of Versailles** with Germany, signed in the Hall of Mirrors of the Versailles Palace on June 28, 1919. Treaties were also worked out, in turn, with Austria, Bulgaria, Hungary, and finally Turkey, in August 1920.

The Participants   This was to be a dictated, not a negotiated, peace. Germany and its allies were excluded, as was revolutionary Russia. The passions unleashed by the long war had dissolved the possibility of a more conciliatory outcome, a genuinely negotiated peace. Having won the war, France, Britain, the United States, and Italy were to call the shots on their own. However, spokesmen for many groups—from Slovaks and Croats to Arabs, Jews, and pan-Africanists—were in Paris as well, seeking a hearing for their respective causes. Both the Arab Prince Faisal (1885–1933), who would later become king of Iraq, and Colonel T. E. Lawrence were on hand to plead for an independent Arab kingdom. (See the box "The Global Record: Prince Faisal at the

Peace Conference.") The African American leader W. E. B. Du Bois (doo BOYS) (1868–1963), who took his Ph.D. at Harvard in 1895, led a major pan-African congress in Paris concurrently with the peace conference.

The fundamental challenge for the peacemakers was to reconcile the conflicting visions of the postwar world that had emerged by the end of the war. U.S. president Wilson represented the promise of a new order that could give this terrible war a lasting meaning. As he toured parts of Europe on his way to the peace conference, Wilson was greeted as a hero. Clemenceau, in contrast, was a hard-liner concerned with French security and dismissive of Wilsonian ideals. Since becoming prime minister in 1917, he had stressed that only permanent French military superiority over Germany, and not some utopian league of nations, could guarantee a lasting peace. The negotiations at Paris centered on this fundamental difference between Wilson and Clemenceau. Although Britain's Lloyd George took a hard line on certain issues, he also sought to mediate, helping engineer the somewhat awkward compromise that resulted. When, after the peace conference, he encountered criticism for the outcome, Lloyd George replied, "I think I did as well as might be expected, seated as I was between Jesus Christ and Napoleon Bonaparte."[7]

Treaty of Versailles   Peace treaty that the victors in World War I imposed on a defeated Germany in 1919.

Shifting Powers In Article 231 of the final treaty, the peacemakers sought to establish a moral basis for their treatment of Germany by assigning responsibility for the war to Germany and its allies. The Germans were required to pay reparations to reimburse the victors for the costs of the war, although the actual amount was not established until 1921. The determination to make the loser pay was one of the factors militating against a compromise peace on both sides by 1917.

Germany was also forced to dismantle much of its military apparatus. The army was to be limited to a hundred thousand men, all volunteers. The treaty severely restricted the size of the German navy as well, and Germany was forbidden to manufacture or possess military aircraft, submarines, tanks, heavy artillery, or poison gas.

France took back Alsace and Lorraine, the provinces it had lost to Germany in 1871 (see Map 25.3). But for France, the crucial security provision of the peace settlement was the treatment of the adjacent Rhineland section of Germany itself. For fifteen years Allied troops were to occupy the west bank of the Rhine River in Germany—the usual military occupation of a defeated adversary. But this would only be temporary. The long-term advantage for France was to be the permanent demilitarization of all German territory west of the Rhine and a strip of 50 kilometers along its east bank. Germany was to maintain no troops on this part

of its own soil; in the event of hostilities French forces would be able to march into Germany unopposed.

French interests also helped shape the settlement in east-central Europe. Wilsonian principles called for self-determination, but in this area of great ethnic complexity, ethnic differences were not readily sorted out geographically. This made it easier for the French to bring their own strategic concerns to bear on the situation. To ensure that Germany would again face potential enemies from both the east and the west, French leaders envisioned building a network of allies in east-central Europe. The first was the new Poland, created from Polish territories formerly in the German, Russian, and Austro-Hungarian Empires. That network might come to include Czechoslovakia, Yugoslavia, and Romania as well. These states would be weak enough to remain under French influence but, taken together, strong enough to replace Russia as a significant force against Germany.

Partly as a result of French priorities, Poland, Czechoslovakia, Yugoslavia, and Romania ended up as large as possible, either by combining ethnic groups or by incorporating minorities that, on ethnic grounds, belonged with neighboring states. The new Czechoslovakia included not only Czechs and Slovaks but also numerous Germans and Magyars. Indeed, Germans, mostly from the old Bohemia, made up 22 percent of the population of Czechoslovakia. By contrast, Austria, Hungary, and Bulgaria, as defeated powers, found themselves diminished (see **MAP 25.4**). What remained of Austria, the German part of the old Habsburg empire, was prohibited from choosing to join Germany, an obvious violation of the Wilsonian principle of self-determination.

Desires to contain revolutionary Russia were also at work in the settlement in east-central Europe. A band of states in east-central Europe, led by France, could serve not only as a check to Germany but also as a shield against the Russian threat. Romania's aggrandizement came partly at the expense of the Russian Empire, as did the creation of the new Poland. Finland, Latvia, Estonia, and Lithuania, all part of the Russian Empire for over a century, became independent states (see Map 25.3).

PRINCE FAISAL AT THE PEACE CONFERENCE

With the war nearing its end in October 1918, British authorities, in line with provisions of the Sykes-Picot Agreement, permitted Faisal ibn-Husayn (1885–1933) to set up a provisional Arab state, with its capital at Damascus. As head of a delegation from this area to the Paris Peace Conference, Faisal claimed to speak for all Arab Asia, but some on the Arabian peninsula challenged his claim. In the memorandum of January 1919 that follows, he outlined the Arab position, mixing pride and assertiveness with a recognition that the Arabs would continue to need the support and help of Western powers. After the peace was concluded, Faisal found himself caught up in British and French rivalries as he was installed as king—first of Syria, then of Iraq (Mesopotamia). But his efforts were central to the eventual achievement of Arab independence in the Middle East.

We believe that our ideal of Arab unity in Asia is justified beyond need of argument. If argument is required, we would point to the general principles accepted by the Allies when the United States joined them, to our splendid past, to the tenacity with which our race has for 600 years resisted Turkish attempts to absorb us, and, in a lesser degree, to what we tried our best to do in this war as one of the Allies. . . .

The various provinces of Arab Asia—Syria, Irak [*sic*], Jezireh, Hedjaz, Nejd, Yemen—are very different economically and socially, and it is impossible to constrain them into one frame of government.

We believe that Syria, an agricultural and industrial area thickly peopled with sedentary classes, is sufficiently advanced politically to manage her own internal affairs. We feel also that foreign technical advice and help will be a most valuable factor in our national growth. We are willing to pay for this help in cash; we cannot sacrifice for it any part of the freedom we have just won for ourselves by force of arms.

. . . The world wishes to exploit Mesopotamia rapidly, and we therefore believe that the system of government there will have to be buttressed by the men and material resources of a great foreign Power. We ask, however, that the Government be Arab, in principle and spirit, the selective rather than the elective principle being necessarily followed in the neglected districts, until time makes the broader basis possible. . . .

In Palestine the enormous majority of the people are Arabs. The Jews are very close to the Arabs in blood, and there is no conflict of character between the two races. In principles we are absolutely at one. Nevertheless, the Arabs cannot risk assuming the responsibility of holding level the scales in the clash of races and religions that have, in this one province, so often involved the world in difficulties. They would wish for the effective super-position of a great trustee, so long as a representative local administration commended itself by actively promoting the material prosperity of the country. . . .

In our opinion, if our independence be conceded and our local competence established, the natural influences of race, language, and interest will soon draw us together into one people; but for this the Great Powers will have to ensure us open internal frontiers, common railways and telegraphs, and uniform systems of education. To achieve this they must lay aside the thought of individual profits, and of their old jealousies. In a word, we ask you not to force your whole civilisation upon us, but to help us to pick out what serves us from your experience. In return we can offer you little but gratitude.

QUESTIONS

1. How does Prince Faisal assess the prospects for unity among the diverse Arab peoples of Asia?
2. What role does Prince Faisal envision for the Western powers in Arab Asia?

Source: J. C. Hurewitz, *Diplomacy in the Near and Middle East: A Documentary Record: 1914–1956*, vol. 2 (Princeton, N.J.: D. Van Nostrand, 1956), pp. 38–39. Reprinted by Archive Editions, UK, 1987.

The territorial settlement cost Germany almost 15 percent of its prewar territory, but German bitterness over the peace terms stemmed above all from a sense of betrayal. In requesting an armistice, German authorities had appealed to Wilson, who had not emphasized war guilt and reparations. He seemed to be saying that the whole prewar international system, not one side or the other, had been responsible for the current conflict. Yet the peacemakers now placed the primary blame on Germany, so for Germans the terms of the peace greatly intensified the sting of defeat.

A New International Order? Wilson had been forced to compromise with French interests in dealing with east-central Europe, but he achieved a potentially significant success in exchange—the establishment of a **League of Nations,** embodying the widespread hope

League of Nations An international organization established at the end of World War I without the membership of the United States. Though its covenant called for the peaceful settlement of disputes and for sanctions against a member that went to war in violation of League provisions, it failed to prevent the escalating violence that culminated in World War II.

MAP 25.4   Ethnicity in East-Central Europe, 1919
Ethnic diversity made it hard to create homogeneous nation-states in east-central Europe. The new states that emerged after World War I mixed ethnic groups, and ethnic tensions would contribute to future problems.

Albanian		Macedonian	
Bosnian		Polish	
Bulgarian		Romanian	
Croatian		Russian, Belorussian, and Ukrainian	
Czech		Serbian	
German		Slovakian	
Hungarian		Slovenian	

0   50   100 Km.
0   50   100 Mi.

Online Study Center **Improve Your Grade**
Interactive Map: Ethnicity in East-Central Europe, 1919

for a new international order. (See the box "The Written Record: The Covenant of the League of Nations.") According to the League covenant worked out by April, disputes among member states were to be settled no longer by war but by mechanisms established by the new assembly. Other members were to participate in sanctions, from economic blockade to military action, against a member that went to war in violation of League provisions.

How could Wilsonian hopes for a new international order be squared with the imperialist system, which seemed utterly at odds with the ideal of self-

determination? Elites among the colonial peoples had tended to support the war efforts of their imperial rulers, but often in the hope of winning greater autonomy or even independence. The Indian leader Mohandas Gandhi (GAHN-dee) (1869–1948), who had been educated in the West and admitted to the English bar in 1889, even helped recruit Indians to fight on the British side. But his aim was to speed Indian independence, and he led demonstrations that embarrassed the British during the war. (See the box "The Global Record: Gandhi Advocates Nonviolence" on page 842 in Chapter 27.)

Colonial peoples participated directly in the war on both sides. In sub-Saharan Africa, for example, German-led Africans fought against Africans under British or French command. France brought colonial subjects from West and North Africa into front-line service during the war. But one result was an expansion of political consciousness that led more of those subject to European imperialism to question the whole system.

The hope that support for the Western powers in wartime would eventually be rewarded led China and Siam (now Thailand) to associate with the Allied side in 1917, in an effort to enhance their international stature. Each was seeking to restore full sovereignty in the face of increasing Western influence. China sent 200,000 people to work in France to help ease France's wartime labor shortage.

At the peace conference, spokesmen for the non-Western world tended to be moderate in their demands. And prodded by Wilson, the peacemakers made some concessions. German colonies and Ottoman territories were not simply taken over by the victors, in the old-fashioned way, but were placed under the authority of the League. The League then assigned them as mandates to one of the victorious powers, which was to report to the League annually on conditions in the area in question. Classes of mandates varied, based on how prepared for sovereignty the area was judged to be. In devising this system, the Western powers formally recognized for the first time that non-Western peoples under Western control had rights of their own and, in principle, were progressing toward independence.

Still, the mandate approach to the colonial question was a halting departure at best. Although Britain granted considerable sovereignty to Iraq in 1932, the victorious powers generally operated as before, assimilating the new territories into their existing systems of colonial possessions. After the hopes for independence raised in the Arab world during the war, this outcome produced a sense of betrayal among Arab leaders.

The Chinese similarly felt betrayed. Despite China's contributions to the Allied war effort, the victors acquiesced in special rights for Japan in China, causing a renewed sense of humiliation among Chinese elites and provoking popular demonstrations and a boycott of

THE COVENANT OF THE LEAGUE OF NATIONS

In its very first part, before treating defeated Germany, the Treaty of Versailles established a new "League of Nations," outlining its aims and procedures as well as the obligations of its members. With this bold experiment, the war's victors sought to organize international relations on a radically new basis. The League's overriding aim was to settle international disputes without resort to war. But the League was also to fulfill an international responsibility, newly recognized here, for the gradual departure from colonialism. Although it instilled great hope at first, the League's inability to prevent aggression and war became clear during the 1930s. Even so, its failure prompted a still more determined effort to order international affairs with the creation of the United Nations in the aftermath of World War II.

The High Contracting Parties,

In order to promote international co-operation and to achieve international peace and security by the acceptance of obligations not to resort to war, by the prescription of open, just and honourable relations between nations, by the firm establishment of the understandings of international law as the actual rule of conduct among Governments, and by the maintenance of justice and a scrupulous respect for all treaty obligations in the dealings of organised peoples with one another,

Agree to this Covenant of the League of Nations. . . .

Article 12.

The Members of the League agree that if there should arise between them any dispute likely to lead to a rupture, they will submit the matter either to arbitration or to inquiry by the Council, and they agree in no case to resort to war until three months after the award by the arbitrators or the report by the Council. . . .

Article 16.

Should any Member of the League resort to war in disregard of its covenants under Articles 12, 13, or 15, it shall *ipso facto* be deemed to have committed an act of war against all other Members of the League, which hereby undertake immediately to subject it to the severance of all trade or financial relations, the prohibition of all intercourse between their nations and the nationals of the covenant-breaking State, and the prevention of all financial, commercial, or personal intercourse between the nationals of the covenant-breaking State and the nationals of any other State, whether a Member of the League or not. . . .

Article 22.

To those colonies and territories which as a consequence of the late war have ceased to be under the sovereignty of the States which formerly governed them and which are inhabited by peoples not yet able to stand by themselves under the strenuous conditions of the modern world, there should be applied the principle that the well-being and development of such peoples form a sacred trust of civilisation and that securities for the performance of this trust should be embodied in this Covenant.

The best method of giving practical effect to this principle is that the tutelage of such peoples should be entrusted to advanced nations who by reason of their resources, their experience or their geographical position can best undertake this responsibility, and who are willing to accept it, and that this tutelage should be exercised by them as Mandatories on behalf of the League.

QUESTIONS

1. How did the League of Nations expect to minimize the resort to war?
2. On what grounds did the League assume responsibility for overseeing the development of the former colonies of the defeated German and Ottoman Empires?

Source: The Treaties of Peace, 1919–1923, vol. 1 (New York: The Carnegie Endowment for International Peace, 1924), pp. 10, 14, 17, 19.

Japanese goods. Although Western leaders were allowing a non-Western power, Japan, access to the imperial club, they were hardly departing from imperialism. For Chinese, Arabs, and others, the West appeared hypocritical. Those whose political consciousness had been raised by the war came to believe not only that colonialism should end, but that the colonial peoples would themselves have to take the lead in ending it.

The incongruities of the postwar settlement prompted Marshal Foch to proclaim, "This is not peace. It is an armistice for twenty years."[8] Would the principal victors have the resolve, and the capacity, to preserve the new order they had established at Paris? Debate over the American role promptly developed in the United States as President Wilson sought Senate ratification of the Versailles treaty, which entailed U.S.

membership in the League of Nations as well as commitments to France and Britain. Wilson's opponents worried that League membership would compromise U.S. sovereignty, but other nations managed to overcome such concerns and join the new organization. American reluctance stemmed especially from the isolationist backlash that was developing against the U.S. intervention in the European war. Late in 1919, at the height of the debate, Wilson suffered a disabling stroke. The Senate then refused to ratify the peace treaty, thereby keeping the United States out of the League of Nations.

American disengagement stemmed partly from doubts about the wisdom of the peace settlement that quickly developed in both Britain and the United States. During the peace conference, a member of the British delegation, the economist John Maynard Keynes (KAINZ) (1883–1946), resigned to write *The Economic Consequences of the Peace* (1920), which helped undermine confidence in the whole settlement. Keynes charged that the shortsighted, vindictive policy of the French, by crippling Germany with a punishing reparations burden, threatened the European economy and thus the long-term peace of Europe. For some, then, the challenge was not to enforce the Versailles treaty but to revise it. This lack of consensus about the legitimacy of the peace made it especially hard to anticipate the longer-term consequences of the war.

THE CULTURAL IMPACT OF THE GREAT WAR

Coming after a century of relative peace and apparent progress, this long and brutal war ended up shaking Europe's social and cultural foundations. The number of casualties, the advent of terrifying new weapons, and the destruction of famous old monuments—all gave the war an apocalyptic aura that heightened its psychological impact.

The war touched virtually everyone, but it marked for life those who had experienced the nightmare of the trenches. At first, traditional notions of glory, heroism, and patriotic duty combined with images of fellowship and regeneration to enable the soldiers to make a certain sense of their wartime experience. But as the war dragged on, such sentiments gradually eroded, giving way, in many cases, to resignation and cynicism. (See the feature "The Visual Record: Max Beckmann's *The Night*.") But others, such as the young German soldier and writer Ernst Jünger (1895–1998), lauded the war as the catalyst for a welcome new era of steel, hardness, discipline, organization, and machine precision.

After the war, many of those who had fought it felt a sense of ironic betrayal. Their prewar upbringing, the values and assumptions they had inherited, had not equipped them to make sense of what they had lived

through. But the effort to find meaning involved not only the survivors but also the families and friends of those killed or maimed. There was much effort to recast traditional, often-religious categories and images for the near-universal experience of bereavement, which transcended national and class divisions.

Beginning in the late 1920s a wave of writings about the war appeared. Many were memoirs, such as *Goodbye to All That* by the English writer Robert Graves (1895–1985) and *Testament of Youth* by Vera Brittain (1893–1970), who had served as a British army nurse at the front. But easily the most famous retrospective was the novel *All Quiet on the Western Front* (1929) by the German Erich Maria Remarque (1898–1970); it sold 2.5 million copies in twenty-five languages in its first eighteen months in print. Remarque provided a gripping portrait of the experience of ordinary soldiers on the western front, but his book also reflected the disillusionment that had come to surround the memory of the war by the late 1920s. Not only were many dead or maimed for life, but all the sacrifices seemed to have been largely in vain, a sentiment that fueled determination to avoid another war in the future.

The novel forms of warfare introduced during World War I intensified fears of renewed war. Thanks to modern technology, which had been central to the West's confident belief in progress, Europeans had now experienced machine-gun fire, poison gas attacks, and the terror-bombing of civilians from airplanes. A generation later, to be sure, the advent of the nuclear age occasioned a measure of terror hardly imaginable earlier, but the experience of World War I was the turning point, the end of an earlier innocence.

What followed from the war, most fundamentally, was a new sense that Western civilization was neither as secure nor as superior as it had seemed. The celebrated French poet Paul Valéry (1871–1945), speaking at Oxford shortly after the war, observed that "we modern civilizations have learned to recognize that we are mortal like the others. We had heard . . . of whole worlds vanished, of empires foundered. . . . Elam, Nineveh, Babylon were vague and splendid names; the total ruin of these worlds, for us, meant as little as did their existence. But France, England, Russia . . . these names, too, are splendid. . . . And now we see that the abyss of history is deep enough to bury all the world. We feel that a civilization is as fragile as a life."[9] Valéry went on to warn that the coming transition to peace would be even more difficult and disorienting than the war itself. So traumatic might be the convulsion that Europe might lose its leadership and be shown up for what it was in fact—a pathetically small corner of the world, a mere cape on the Asiatic landmass. Astounding words for a European, yet even Valéry, for all his foresight, could not anticipate what Europe would experience in the decades to follow.

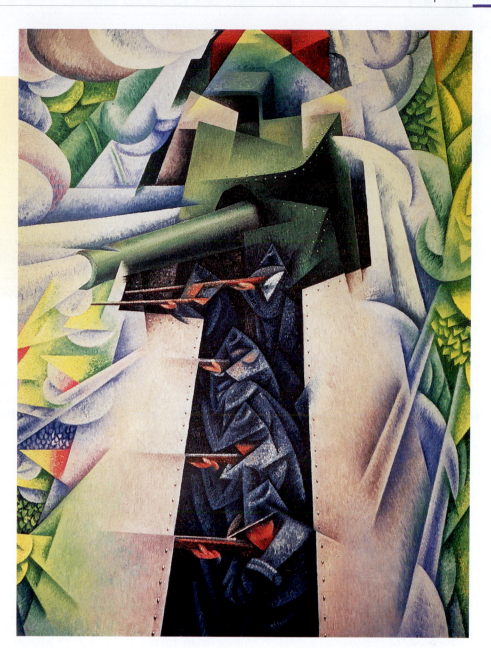

Severini: Armoured Train
In this painting from 1915, the Italian futurist Gino Severini (1883–1966) conveys the hard, steel-like imagery and the sense of disciplined modern efficiency that became associated with war, making it attractive to some young Europeans.
(Richard S. Zeisler Collection, New York/ The Bridgeman Art Library. © 2001 Artists Rights Society [ARS], New York/ADAGP, Paris)

S E C T I O N   S U M M A R Y

- Although Germany suffered the highest number of wartime casualties, France's losses in proportional terms were 15 percent higher—and twice as high as Britain's.

- The breakup of the Habsburg and Ottoman Empires, together with the defeat of Russia and Germany, raised hopes for self-determination among formerly subject peoples but also complicated the challenges of peacemaking.

- The peace settlement represented an awkward compromise between Wilson's idealistic principles and Clemenceau's hardheaded concern for long-term French interests.

- The harsh peace terms imposed on Germany not only inflamed German opinion but also seemed counterproductive to many elsewhere, thereby compromising the moral force of the peace settlement.

- Britain and France divided the Arab parts of the former Ottoman Empire according to the secret Sykes-Picot Agreement of 1916.

THE VISUAL RECORD

Max Beckmann's *The Night*

"One of the most disagreeable images which the art of our century has to show," wrote the noted art historian and critic John Russell in 1981 of the painting we see here.* Max Beckmann (1884–1950) painted *The Night* during 1918–1919, as Germany was suffering military defeat, experiencing political turmoil, and encountering extreme economic hardship. And surely this unprecedented and disturbing image reflects that difficult combination of circumstances. But what are the sources of the imagery we see here, and what does this painting tell us about the war's cultural impact?

The young Beckmann established himself as an innovative painter before the war, working within the idiom of German expressionism. Emerging as a formal movement in 1905, expressionism became the major German contribution to the avant-garde in the visual arts. Expressionists like Ernst Ludwig Kirchner, Ernst Haeckel, and Franz Marc used unnatural colors and deformed natural appearance to convey emotion and to provoke a psychological response in the viewer. In much of their work they sought an appropriately innovative response to the uncanniness, even the menace, of modern life—and especially the modern urban world, at once enticing and threatening.

Like so many of the educated youth of his generation, Beckmann initially welcomed the war as a source of renewal. Indeed he was especially fascinated with its potentially cataclysmic effects, in light of his quasi-Nietzschean faith in the scope for a more intense form of life through struggle and suffering. After volunteering for service in the fall of 1914, he was assigned to the German medical corps. Working in a field hospital on the western front in 1915, Beckmann still found something grandly apocalyptic in the death, the suffering, the wounded bodies. Indeed, he welcomed the chance to observe all that up close; it inspired notes and sketches to be used as material for his art. At the same time, he began to envision conveying his ideas through images recalling the scourging of Christ.

But Beckmann's beliefs were being shaken, and his drawings during 1915 depicted suffering, pain, and death with ever greater intensity. That summer he suffered a nervous breakdown and was sent back to Germany to recuperate. In 1917 he was finally discharged from the army as unfit for further service.

Beckmann turned back to painting in an effort to convey his increasingly disillusioning experience of the war. Like many expressionist artists, he had been influenced by late Gothic German painting, and *The Night* uses certain formal elements from that earlier tradition. Note especially the color—pure but thin, even sour—and the space—shallow and confined, with the figures almost piled atop one another. Beckmann also adapted the religious themes of German Gothic—not, however, as a believer. Rather, he valued their familiarity, as images of suffering, combined with suggestions of cruelty and guilt. Such familiar images seemed to offer the means to create the new, utterly unfamiliar imagery that, Beckmann felt, was necessary to convey what human beings had come to feel as a result of the war and its aftermath.

Here is how Beckmann put it at the end of 1918, precisely as he was working on *The Night:*

> The stronger my determination grows to grasp the unutterable things of this world, the deeper and more powerful the emotion burning inside me about our existence, the tighter I keep my mouth shut and the harder I try to capture the terrible, thrilling monster of life's vitality and to confine it, to beat it down and to strangle it with crystal-clear, razor-sharp lines and planes. . . . We must be a part of all the misery which is coming. We have to surrender our heart and our nerves, we must abandon ourselves to the horrible cries of pain of a poor deluded people.[†]

On the immediate level, *The Night* conveys a scene of violence, torture, and suffering, for three of the figures have apparently broken into a family's home (complete with dog and phonograph) in order to torture, rape, and perhaps kidnap or murder. Yet the complex interplay between the figures suggests that we cannot easily distinguish perpetrators from victims.

---

*John Russell, *The Meanings of Modern Art* (New York: Harper & Row, 1981), p. 95.

[†]Max Beckmann, "Creative Credo," in *Art in Theory, 1900–1990: An Anthology of Changing Ideas,* edited by Charles Harrison and Paul Wood (Oxford: Blackwell, 1993), pp. 267–268.

Beckmann: The Night
(Erich Lessing/Art Resource, NY)

The suffering figure on the left seems to be Beckmann himself, in the pose of the suffering Christ, yet his bandaged torturer may suggest the wounded to whom Beckmann had earlier ministered on the battlefield. In performing his medical duties, he had become haunted with the ambiguity between causing and relieving suffering, especially, perhaps, because he had initially observed the suffering of the wounded with the combination of voyeuristic excitement and clinical detachment we noted earlier. His initial attitude had been symptomatic of the somewhat cavalier attitude with which so many of the educated of his generation had gone off to war.

Another of the torturers is patterned after a blind figure in a fourteenth-century Italian fresco—yet is also made to look like Lenin and/or a contemporary German worker. With bourgeois and proletarian seemingly both implicated in gratuitous violence, there seems no scope for political redemption. Yet neither is the family's home a safe refuge from the violence of politics and war. We all seem to be at once perpetrators and victims, caught in a claustrophobic space, with no place to escape, and little if any scope for action. We are even a hell unto ourselves.

Through this combination of images suggesting suffering and guilt, but seemingly precluding any hope of redemption, "Beckmann achieves," as Reinhard Spieler has put it, "a form which transcends commentary on his own time: the corrup-

tion and cruelty of postwar society is raised to a general and timeless level of human experience, to eternal night, to humanity's hell on earth."[‡]

The Night conveys not simply the disarray of a moment—the German experience of defeat and revolutionary violence—but a changed sensibility; in the wake of World War I the world could never be the same. Although he was determined to avoid sentimentality or collective self-pity, Beckmann still thought that we might hope, through art, to come to terms with all that recent historical experience had revealed. But it had come to seem that we could do so only through "one of the most disagreeable images" in modern art.

QUESTIONS

1. Why does Beckmann place this combination of interconnected figures in such a shallow, confined space?

2. What relationship between the private domestic sphere and the public political sphere does Beckmann seem to be depicting in *The Night*?

[‡]Reinhard Spieler, *Max Beckmann, 1884–1950: The Path to Myth* (Cologne: Taschen, 1995), p. 38.

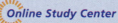
Online Study Center
Improve Your Grade Visual Record Activities

801

CHAPTER SUMMARY

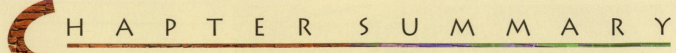

How and why had the course of the war by 1917 defied the expectations that had surrounded the beginning of fighting in August 1914?

Why did this prove a total war, making necessary new forms of socioeconomic coordination and even systematic propaganda?

Why did the first revolution in Russia pave the way for a second, spearheaded by the Bolsheviks?

Why did Germany and its allies end up losing the war even after forcing Russia to make a separate peace by early 1918?

What factors shaped the peace settlement that the victors imposed on Germany and its allies in 1919–1920?

The war that began in August 1914 was supposed to be over in a few months, but after the French held at the first Battle of the Marne in September, it bogged down in a stalemate on the western front, thanks partly to the unforeseen effectiveness of defensive trenches. The massive assaults of 1916–1917 yielded horrifying numbers of casualties—but not the intended breakthrough for either side.

Because it was so much longer and more difficult than expected, this first "world war" proved a total war, calling forth new forms of socioeconomic coordination and even systematic propaganda. Partly as a result, the war accelerated processes, from economic coordination to technological development to women's suffrage, that many deemed progressive.

But the war also caused cracks in the old order, first and most dramatically in Russia, where war-weariness led to a revolution overthrowing the tsarist regime early in 1917. Although this was not a socialist revolution, it paved the way by the end of 1917 to a second revolution, spearheaded by the Bolsheviks, who represented the more extreme wing of Russian Marxism. Although their own tactical prowess was also a factor, they were able to seize the initiative especially because of the mistakes of the provisional government, which kept Russia in the war and balked at systematic land reform. In taking power, the Bolsheviks were seeking not simply to control Russia but to spark the wider revolution they believed essential if a viable new socialist order was to be created.

Although war-weariness on both sides prompted calls for a white peace by 1917, the defection of revolutionary Russia and the intervention of the United States dramatically altered the lineup—and even the potential stakes and meaning of the war. In 1918, Germany mounted a last-ditch offensive in the west that came close to succeeding. But France had toughened under Georges Clemenceau, and a lack of food, provisions, and manpower was fatally weakening the German effort by that point. U.S. intervention gave the anti-German coalition the long-term advantage in any case. Although it entailed far more sacrifice than anyone had expected at the outset, the war reached a definitive outcome with the defeat of Germany and its allies by November 1918.

Conflicting aspirations among the victors led to an awkward peace settlement. Whereas Woodrow Wilson envisioned a new era in world affairs, based on national self-determination and a new League of Nations, Clemenceau was concerned to cement French superiority on the European continent in the face of Germany's greater long-term demographic, economic, and military potential. Such security considerations even compromised the principle of self-determination at the peace conference. But the harshness of the Treaty of Versailles, which produced much resentment even outside Germany, led some observers to doubt the peace could last for long.

LOOKING AHEAD

In destroying the Habsburg empire and the imperial regime in Germany, the war seemed to have overcome the problems that had caused it in the first place. But the future remained uncertain, even after the major provisions of the peace settlement were established in 1919. Did the victors have the unity and will to enforce the peace? Despite a widespread desire to return to normal, many people sensed how radically the world had changed—and that it could never be the same again. Troubling new uncertainties mixed with exciting new possibilities as Europe and the West looked to the future.

KEY TERMS

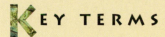

Online Study Center Improve Your Grade Flashcards

Sacred Union (p. 773)

British blockade (p. 778)

total war (p. 779)

Kriegsrohstoffabteilung (KRA) (p. 779)

Petrograd Soviet (p. 783)

provisional government (p. 783)

Vladimir Lenin (p. 784)

Fourteen Points (p. 786)

Treaty of Brest-Litovsk (p. 787)

"stab in the back" myth (p. 790)

Treaty of Versailles (p. 793)

League of Nations (p. 795)

SUGGESTED READING

Beckett, Ian F. W. *The Great War, 1914–1918*. 2001. A thematically organized treatment; especially good on the global dimensions of the conflict.

Boemke, Manfred F., Gerald D. Feldman, and Elisabeth Glaser, eds. *The Treaty of Versailles: A Reassessment After 75 Years*. 1998. Scholars from a number of countries reassess all aspects of the treaty in a major collection of essays.

Chickering, Roger. *Imperial Germany and the Great War, 1914–1918*. 1998. A balanced, comprehensive introduction to the German war effort and experience; especially good on the interpenetration of military and sociopolitical concerns.

Ellis, John. *Eye-Deep in Hell: Trench Warfare in World War I*. 1989. A compelling account of life and death in the trenches, covering topics from trench construction to eating, drinking, and sex; includes striking photographs.

Figes, Orlando. *A People's Tragedy: The Russian Revolution, 1891–1924*. 1997. A lengthy, comprehensive, and gripping account of the revolutionary trajectory, from the famine of 1891 to the death of Lenin in 1924. Seeks to reveal the complexity of the whole process, its many episodes and forms of agency.

Fitzpatrick, Sheila. *The Russian Revolution, 1917–1932*. 2d ed. 1994. An ideal introductory work that places the events of 1917 in the sweep of Russian history.

Holquist, Peter. *Making War, Forging Revolution: Russia's Continuum of Crisis, 1914–1921*. 2002. By focusing on a particular region, this work shows how the Bolsheviks used the tools of mobilization and coercion already called forth by the war in their effort to reshape Russian society.

Keegan, John. *The First World War*. 1999. A comprehensive and accessible study by a widely read military historian.

Morrow, John H., Jr. *The Great War: An Imperial History*. 2004. A clear and balanced chronological account that incorporates the European colonial networks in showing how the war was fought—and in assessing its consequences.

Sharp, Alan. *The Versailles Settlement: Peacemaking in Paris, 1919*. 1991. A brief, clear, and balanced overview that seeks to do justice to the magnitude of the task the peacemakers faced.

Winter, J. M. *The Experience of World War I*. 1989. A beautifully illustrated work that proceeds via concentric circles from politicians to generals to soldiers to civilians, then to the war's longer-term effects.

Winter, Jay. *Sites of Memory, Sites of Mourning*. 1995. Using an effective comparative approach, a leading authority argues that Europeans relied on relatively traditional means of making sense of the bloodletting of World War I.

NOTES

1. Thus wrote the German poet Ivan Goll in 1917; quoted in Modris Eksteins, *Rites of Spring: The Great War and the Birth of the Modern Age* (Boston: Houghton Mifflin, 1989), p. 144.

2. The remarks of Raymond Joubert, as quoted in John Ellis, *Eye-Deep in Hell: Trench Warfare in World War I* (Baltimore: Johns Hopkins University Press, 1989), p. 104.

3. Brian Bond, *War and Society in Europe, 1870–1970* (New York: Oxford University Press, 1986), p. 114.

4. A. N. Potresov, quoted in Richard Pipes, *The Russian Revolution* (New York: Random House, Vintage, 1991), p. 348.

5. Both statements are quoted in Koppel S. Pinson, *Modern Germany: Its History and Civilization*, 2d ed. (New York: Macmillan, 1966), p. 337.

6. Quoted in Arno J. Mayer, *Political Origins of the New Diplomacy, 1917–18* (New York: Random House, Vintage, 1970), p. 135.

7. Quoted in Walter Arnstein, *Britain Yesterday and Today: 1830 to the Present*, 6th ed. (Lexington, Mass.: D. C. Heath, 1992), p. 266.

8. Quoted in P. M. H. Bell, *The Origins of the Second World War* (London and New York: Longman, 1986), p. 14.

9. Paul Valéry, *Variety,* 1st series (New York: Harcourt, Brace, 1938), pp. 3–4.

26

The Illusion of Stability, 1919–1930

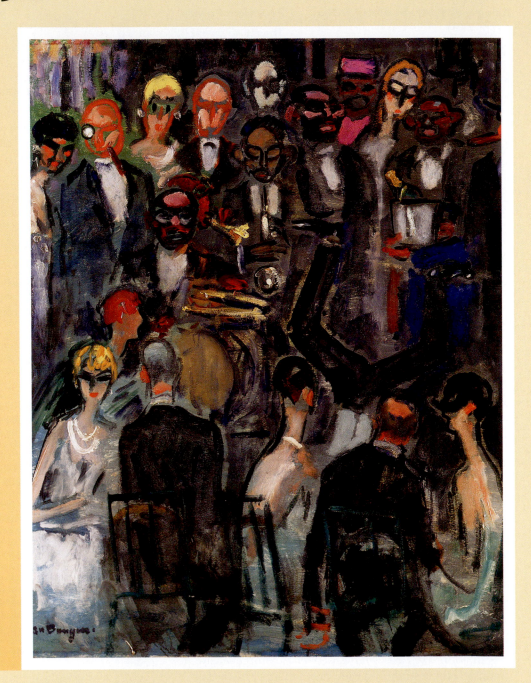

I n 1925 Josephine Baker (1906–1975), a black entertainer from St. Louis, moved from the chorus lines of New York to the bistros of Paris, where she quickly became a singing and dancing sensation. Also a favorite in Germany, she was the most famous of the African American entertainers who took the cultural capitals of Europe by storm during the 1920s. After the disillusioning experience of war, many Europeans found a valuable infusion of vitality in Baker's jazz music, exotic costumes, and "savage," uninhibited dancing (see the poster on page 821).

The European attraction to African Americans as primitive, vital, and sensual reflected a good deal of racial stereotyping, but there really *was* something fresh and uninhibited about American culture, especially its African American variant. And even as they played to those stereotypes, black performers like Baker had great fun ironically subverting them. Many realized they could enjoy opportunities in parts of Europe that were still denied them in the United States. Baker herself was a woman of great sophistication who became a French citizen in 1937, participated in progressive causes, and was decorated for her secret intelligence work in the anti-Nazi resistance during World War II.

The prominence of African Americans in European popular culture was part of a wider infatuation with things American as Europeans embraced the new during the 1920s. Lacking the cultural baggage of Europe, America seemed to offer revitalization and modernity at the same time. With so many old conventions shattered by the war, the ideal of being "modern" became widespread among Europeans, affecting everything from sex education to furniture design. "Modern" meant no-nonsense efficiency, mass production, and a vital popular culture, expressed in jazz, movies, sport, and even advertising. (See the feature "The Visual Record: Advertising" on pages 822–823.)

But Europeans themselves had pioneered modernism in many areas of the arts and sciences, and innovation continued after the war. Paris held its own as an international cultural center, hosting a decorative arts exhibition in 1925 that produced art deco, the sleek, "modernistic" style that helped give the decade its distinctive flavor. And in the unsettled conditions of

KEY TERMS

Maginot Line

fascism

Comintern (Third, or Communist, International)

New Economic Policy (NEP)

Joseph Stalin

Benito Mussolini

Matteotti murder

corporativism, corporative state

Gustav Stresemann

Treaty of Locarno

surrealism

Bauhaus

Online Study Center

This icon will direct you to interactive map and primary source activities on the website **college.hmco.com/pic/noble5e**

postwar Germany, Berlin emerged to rival Paris for cultural leadership during what Germans called "the Golden Twenties." Innovations ranged from avant-garde drama to a sophisticated cabaret scene with a prominent homosexual dimension.

Still, there was something dizzying, even unnerving, about the eager embrace of the new during the 1920s. The war had accelerated the long-term modernization process toward large industries, cities, and bureaucracies, and toward mass politics, society, and culture. That process was positive, even liberating, in certain respects, but it was also disruptive and disturbing. Some Europeans viewed the vogue of black American entertainers as a symptom of decadence that would only undermine further the best of European civilization. In this sense, the postwar sense of release and excitement combined with an anxious longing for stability, for a return to order. Even in embracing the new, many were seeking a new basis for order and security.

Although the immediate disruptions of wartime carried over to 1923, a more hopeful era of relative prosperity and international conciliation followed, continuing until 1929. But there was much that called into question the ideal of a "world safe for democracy" that had surrounded the end of the war. Revolutionary Russia remained an uncertain force, even as it began seeking to build social-

ism on its own. In Italy, the democracy that had emerged in the nineteenth century gave way to the first regime to call itself fascist, and some of the new democracies in east-central Europe did not survive the decade. The postwar efforts at economic restabilization, apparently successful for a while, masked growing strains in the international economy. In one sphere after another, postwar restabilization was fragile—and could quickly unravel.

FOCUS QUESTIONS

How did the differing priorities of Britain and France affect international relations during the 1920s?

Why did Italy turn from parliamentary democracy to fascism even after sharing in the victory in World War I?

Why, and on what basis, did sexuality, gender roles, and the "new woman" provoke so much concern during this period?

What factors made the future of the new German democracy so uncertain during the 1920s?

How did cultural and intellectual leaders differ over the place of "tradition" as they sought to suggest how to come to terms with the new situation of the 1920s?

THE WEST AND THE WORLD AFTER THE GREAT WAR

How did the differing priorities of Britain and France affect international relations during the 1920s?

Although the United States and Japan were becoming important, the major international players before 1914 had been the European powers, who had apportioned much of the non-Western world in imperial networks. But the war and the peace had weakened—and to some extent discredited—the Europeans, who now found themselves saddled with foreign debts and unbalanced economies. Though the United States pulled back from a direct political role in Europe in 1919, it became far more active in world affairs, helping to engineer major conferences on arms limitation and international economic relations during the 1920s. But in crucial respects, the shape of the postwar international order still depended on Europeans. And colonial concerns continued to affect the balance of power in Europe, where it fell to the two major victors in the war, France and Britain, to enforce the controversial peace settlement.

THE EROSION OF EUROPEAN POWER

Emerging from the war as the principal power in East Asia was a non-Western country, Japan, whose claims to the German bases in the region and to special rights in China were formally recognized at the Paris Peace Conference. With the Washington treaty of 1922, Japan won naval parity with Britain and the United States in East Asia. The Western nations were recognizing Japan as a peer, a great power—even a threat. Aspects of the Washington agreements were intended to block Japanese expansion in East Asia. If a new international system was to emerge, it would not be centered in Europe to the extent the old one had been.

As the old Europe lost prestige, President Wilson's ideals of self-determination and democracy were greeted enthusiastically outside the West—in China, for example. At the same time, the Russian revolutionary model appealed to those in the colonial world seeking to understand the mainsprings of Western imperialism—and the means of overcoming it. To some Chinese intellectuals by the early 1920s, Leninism was attractive because it showed the scope for mass mobilization by a revolutionary vanguard.

Non-Western elites were learning to pick and choose from among the elements of the Western tradition. In the 1920s, ever greater numbers of colonial subjects were traveling to western Europe, often for education. Paris was a favored destination, partly because France made an effort to assimilate its colonial peoples. Although those educated in Europe were subject to Westernization, that did not necessarily make them more supportive of Western rule. Many began not only to question colonialism but also to take a fresh look at their own traditions, asking how they might serve the quest for a postcolonial order.

By the 1920s, a generation of anticolonialist, nationalist intellectuals was emerging to lead the non-Western world. Some were more radical than others, but most agreed that the challenge was to learn from the West and to modernize, but without simply copying the West and losing distinctive cultural identities. It was imperative to sift through tradition, determining what needed to be changed and what was worth preserving. The pioneering Chinese nationalist Sun Yixien (Sun Yat-sen, 1866–1925) was typical in recognizing the need to adopt the science and technology of the West. But China, he insisted, could do so in its own way, without sacrificing its unique cultural and political traditions. (See the box "The Global Record: Sun Yixien on Chinese Nationalism.")

As the greatest imperial power, Britain was especially vulnerable to the growing anticolonial sentiment. The struggle to hang on to its empire drew British en-

CHRONOLOGY

March 1919	Founding of the Italian fascist movement
November 1920	Russian civil war ends
March 1921	New Economic Policy announced at Russian Communist Party congress
October 1922	Mussolini becomes Italian prime minister
January 1923	French-led occupation of the Ruhr
November 1923	Peak of inflation in Germany
January 1924	First Labour government in Britain
	Death of Lenin
August 1924	Acceptance of the Dawes Plan on German reparations
October 1925	Treaty of Locarno
May 1926	Pilsudski's coup d'état in Poland
	Beginning of general strike in Britain
May 1927	Lindbergh completes first transatlantic solo flight
January 1929	Stalin forces banishment of Trotsky from Soviet Union
April 1929	Soviets adopt first economic Five-Year Plan
August 1929	Acceptance of the Young Plan on German reparations
October 1929	Death of Stresemann

ergies away from the problems of Europe after the peace settlement.

In light of the strong Indian support for the British war effort, the British government promised in 1917 to extend the scope for Indian involvement in the colonial administration in India. Growing expectations as the war was ending provoked episodes of violence against the British, whose troops retaliated brutally in April 1919, firing indiscriminately into an unarmed crowd. This Amritsar Massacre helped galvanize India's independence movement, even though the British, seeking conciliation in the aftermath, extended self-rule by entrusting certain less essential government services to Indians. Another milestone was reached in 1921, when Mohandas Gandhi, the British-educated leader of the Indian independence movement, shed his European clothes in favor of simple Indian attire. But it was on the basis of Western egalitarianism, not some indigenous value, that Gandhi demanded political rights for the "untouchables," the

Reinforcing Imperialist Rule

In response to episodes of anti-colonialist violence in Amritsar, India, early in 1919, the British brutally cracked down, most notably in the massacre of April 1919. Here British authorities enforce a decree in the wake of the beating of a female British doctor on this road—forcing any Indian using the road to crawl along it. *(National Army Museum, London)*

lowest group in India's long-standing caste system. (See the box "The Global Record: Gandhi Advocates Nonviolence" on page 842 in Chapter 27.)

Online Study Center **Improve Your Grade**
Primary Source: An Indian Nationalist Condemns the British Empire

In Egypt a full-scale anti-British insurrection broke out in 1919. After British troops suppressed the rebellion, British authorities offered to grant moderate concessions, as in India. But Egyptian nationalists demanded independence, which was finally granted in 1922. Egypt gradually evolved into a constitutional monarchy, with representative government and universal suffrage. But Britain retained a predominant influence in Egypt until the nationalist revolution of 1952 (see page 929).

At the same time, nationalism was growing among West Africans who had studied in England. In March 1919 Western-educated Africans in the Gold Coast asked the British governor to establish representative institutions so that Africans could at least be consulted about governmental affairs. The West African National Congress, formed in 1920, made similar demands. The British agreed to new constitutions for Nigeria in 1923 and the Gold Coast in 1925 that took significant steps in that direction. They also agreed to build more schools, though they tended to promote practical education, including African languages and agriculture, whereas the African leaders wanted students to learn the Western classics that "made gentlemen." Such conflicting priorities indicate the complexities of the relationships between colonial rulers and the emerging elites among the colonized peoples.

SUN YIXIEN ON CHINESE NATIONALISM

Sun Yixien (Sun Yat-sen), widely regarded as the father of modern China, founded the Guomindang (Kuomintang), the Chinese nationalist movement, in 1912. Educated by Western missionaries in China, he lived in the United States for extended periods and came to admire the West in important respects. But he insisted that China, to make the best use of what the West offered, had to reconnect with its own unique traditions. Variations on this argument would be heard for decades as the rest of the world sought to come to terms with the seemingly more advanced West. The following passages are from an influential series of lectures that Sun Yixien presented in China in the early 1920s.

What is the standing of our nation in the world? In comparison with other nations we have the greatest population and the oldest culture, of four thousand years' duration. We ought to be advancing in line with the nations of Europe and America. But the Chinese people have only family and clan groups; there is no national spirit. Consequently, in spite of four hundred million people gathered together in one China, we are in fact but a sheet of loose sand. We are the poorest and weakest state in the world, occupying the lowest position in international affairs; the rest of mankind is the carving knife and the serving dish, while we are the fish and the meat. Our position now is extremely perilous; if we do not earnestly promote nationalism and weld together our four hundred millions into a strong nation, we face a tragedy—the loss of our country and the destruction of our race. To ward off this danger, we must espouse nationalism and employ the national spirit to save the country. . . .

But even if we succeed in reviving our ancient morality, learning, and powers, we will still not be able, in this modern world, to advance China to a first place among the nations. . . . [W]e will still need to learn the strong points of Europe and America before we can progress at an equal rate with them. Unless we do study the best from foreign countries, we will go backward. With our own fine foundation of knowledge and our age-long culture, with our own native intelligence besides, we should be able to acquire all the best things from abroad. The strongest point of the West is its science. . . .

As soon as we learn Western machinery we can use it anytime, anywhere; electric lights, for example, can be installed and used in any kind of Chinese house. But Western social customs and sentiments are different from ours in innumerable points; if, without regard to customs and popular feelings in China, we try to apply Western methods of social control as we would Western machinery—in a hard and fast way—we shall be making a serious mistake. . . .

. . . For the governmental machinery of the United States and France still has many defects, and does not satisfy the desires of the people nor give them a complete measure of happiness. So we in our proposed reconstruction must not think that if we imitate the West of today we shall reach the last stage of progress and be perfectly contented. . . .

Only in recent times has Western culture advanced beyond ours, and the passion for this new civilization has stimulated our revolution. Now that the revolution is a reality, we naturally desire to see China excel the West and build up the newest and most progressive state in the world. We certainly possess the qualifications necessary to reach this ideal, but we must not merely imitate the democratic systems of the West.

QUESTIONS

1. Why does Sun Yixien think China, despite its ancient and sophisticated culture, has fallen behind the West?
2. On what grounds does Sun Yixien consider it necessary for China to study Western culture, as opposed to relying on its own traditions?

Source: Sun Yat-sen, *San Min Chu I: The Three Principles of the People* (Taipei, Taiwan: China Cultural Service, 1953), pp. 5, 46, 109–113, 136, 138–139.

ENFORCING THE VERSAILLES SETTLEMENT

It was up to France and Britain to make sure the new international order worked, but it was not clear that either had the will and resources to do so. Cooperation between them was essential, yet sometimes their differences—in geography, in values, and in perceptions—seemed to doom them to work at cross-purposes.

France was the dominant power on the European continent after World War I, and until well into the 1930s it boasted the strongest army in the world. Yet even in the early 1920s a sense of artificiality surrounded France's image of strength—thus the shrillness and the defensiveness that came to mark French thinking and French policy.

In light of Germany's larger population and stronger industrial base, France's long-term security seemed to require certain measures to tip the scales in its favor. By imposing German disarmament and the demilitarization of the Rhineland, the Versailles treaty gave France immediate military advantages. Yet how long could these measures be maintained, once the passions of war had died down and Germany no longer seemed such a threat? France had hoped for British help in enforcing the treaty, but Britain was pulling back from the Continent to concentrate on its empire, just as it had after other major European wars.

In particular, the British wanted to avoid getting dragged into the uncertain situation in east-central Europe, where its own national interests did not seem to be at stake. Yet the French, to replace their earlier link with Russia, promptly developed an alliance system with several of the new or expanded states of the region, including Poland, Czechoslovakia, Romania, and Yugoslavia. France's ties to east-central Europe made the British especially wary of binding agreements with the French.

At first, France felt confident enough to take strong steps even without British support. In response to German foot-dragging in paying reparations, Prime Minister Raymond Poincaré decided to get tough in January 1923. Declaring the Germans in default, he sent French troops at the head of an international force to occupy the Ruhr industrial area and force German compliance. But the move backfired. The Germans adopted a policy of passive resistance in response, and the costs of the occupation more than offset the increase in reparations that France received. The French government ended up having to raise taxes to pay for the venture. Moreover, the move alienated the British, whose lack of support bordered on active hostility.

British leaders now viewed French policy as unnecessarily vindictive and bellicose, and they increasingly saw the Versailles treaty as counterproductive. Instead, they placed great store in the League of Nations and in the international arms reduction effort gaining momentum by the later 1920s. So France found itself with ever less support from its wartime allies as it sought to enforce the peace settlement. The Ruhr occupation of 1923 proved the last time the French dared to go it alone.

From that point on, France gradually lost the advantages it had gained by defeating Germany, and self-confidence gave way to defensiveness and resignation. The defensive mentality found physical embodiment in the **Maginot Line,** a system of fortifications on the country's eastern border. Remembering the defensive warfare of World War I and determined to preclude the sort of invasion France had suffered in 1914, the military convinced France's political leaders to adopt a defensive strategy based on a fortified line. Construction began in 1929, and the Maginot (MAH-zhih-noh) system reached preliminary completion in 1935, when it extended along France's border with Germany from Switzerland to the border with Belgium.

This defensive system was not consistent with the other major strands of French policy, especially its alliances with states in east-central Europe. If France emphasized defense behind an impregnable system of forts, what good were French security guarantees to such new allies as Poland and Czechoslovakia?

Still, the situation remained fluid during the 1920s. In France, as in Britain, national elections in 1924 produced a victory for the moderate left, ending a period of conservative nationalist dominance since the war. In each country, international relations became a major issue in the elections, and the outcome heralded a more conciliatory tack, especially in relations with Germany.

SECTION SUMMARY

- Although the prewar European colonial system remained largely in place after the war, Wilsonian ideals of self-determination spurred anticolonial sentiment in the colonized world.

- On the basis of their study in the West, intellectuals from Europe's colonies sought to combine Western values with indigenous traditions as they began spearheading the anticolonial struggle.

- More vulnerable geographically, France was initially more determined than Britain to keep Germany limited by strictly enforcing the Versailles settlement.

- France's confident, even aggressive, posture gradually gave way to the defensiveness of the "Maginot mentality," evident in the decision to build a series of defensive fortifications.

Maginot Line   A 200-mile system of elaborate permanent fortifications on France's eastern border, named for war minister André Maginot and built primarily during the 1930s. It was a defense against German frontal assault; in 1940 the Germans invaded by flanking the line.

COMMUNISM, FASCISM, AND THE NEW POLITICAL SPECTRUM

Why did Italy turn from parliamentary democracy to fascism even after sharing in the victory in World War I?

In making their revolution in 1917, the Russian Bolsheviks had expected to spark wider revolution. Hopes—and fears—that the revolution would spread were palpable in the immediate postwar period. The Russian Communists initially enjoyed extraordinary prestige on the European left; but as the nature of Leninist communism became clearer, some Marxists grew skeptical or hostile, and the Russian model eventually produced a damaging split in international socialism. By the end of the 1920s revolution elsewhere was nowhere in sight, and it seemed that, for the foreseeable future, the communist regime in Russia would have to go it alone.

By then, a new and unexpected political movement had emerged in Italy, expanding the political spectrum in a different direction. This was the first **fascism,** which brought Benito Mussolini to power in 1922. Emerging directly from the war, Italian fascism was violent and antidemocratic—and thus disturbing to many. Stressing national solidarity and discipline, the fascists were hostile not only to liberal individualism and the parliamentary system, but also to Marxist socialism, with its emphasis on class struggle and the special role of the working class. Claiming to offer a modern alternative to both, Italian fascism quickly attracted the attention of those in other countries who were disillusioned with parliamentary politics and hostile to the Marxist left. The interplay of communism and fascism, as new political experiments, added to the uncertainties of the novel postwar world.

CHANGING PRIORITIES IN COMMUNIST RUSSIA, 1918–1921

Even after leading the revolution that toppled the provisional government in November 1917, the Bolsheviks could not claim majority support in Russia. When the long-delayed elections to select a constituent assembly were held a few weeks after the revolution, the Socialist Revolutionaries won a clear majority, while the Bolsheviks ended up with fewer than one-quarter of the seats. But the Bolsheviks dispersed the assembly by force

when it met in January 1918. And over the next three years the Communists, as the Bolsheviks renamed themselves, gradually consolidated their power, establishing a centralized and nondemocratic regime. Power lay not with the soviets, nor with some coalition of socialist parties, but solely with the Communist Party.

Civil War   During its first years, the new communist regime encountered a genuine emergency that especially seemed to require such a monopoly of power. During 1918 to 1920, in what became a brutal civil war, the communist "Reds" battled counterrevolutionary "Whites," people who had been dispossessed by the revolution or who had grown disillusioned with the Communist Party. Moreover, foreigners eager to topple the communist regime began to intervene militarily. At the same time, several of the non-Russian nationalities of the old Russian Empire sought to take advantage of the unsettled situation to free themselves from Russian and communist control. Appointed "People's Commissar for War" in April 1918, Leon Trotsky forged a loyal and disciplined Red Army in an effort to master the difficult situation.

A series of thrusts, involving troops from fourteen countries at one time or another, struck at Russia from a variety of points along its huge border. The Whites and the foreign troops never managed a coordinated strategy, but the dogged counterrevolutionary assault seriously threatened the young communist regime and the territorial basis of the state it had inherited from the tsarist autocracy. In the final analysis, however, the Whites proved unable to rally much popular support. Peasants feared, plausibly enough, that a White victory would mean a restoration of the old order, including the return of their newly won lands to the former landlords. By the end of active fighting in November 1920, the communist regime had not only survived but regained most of the territory it had lost early in the civil war (see **MAP 26.1**).

The need to launch the new communist regime in this way, fighting counterrevolutionaries supported by foreign troops, inevitably affected Communists' perceptions and priorities. Separatist sentiment might continue to feed counterrevolutionary efforts, so the new regime exerted careful control over the non-Russian nationalities. Thus, when the Union of Soviet Socialist Republics (USSR) was organized in December 1922, it

---

fascism   A violent, antidemocratic movement founded by Benito Mussolini in Italy in 1919. The term is widely used to encompass Hitler's Nazi regime in Germany and other movements stressing disciplined national solidarity and hostile to liberal individualism, the parliamentary system, and Marxist socialism.

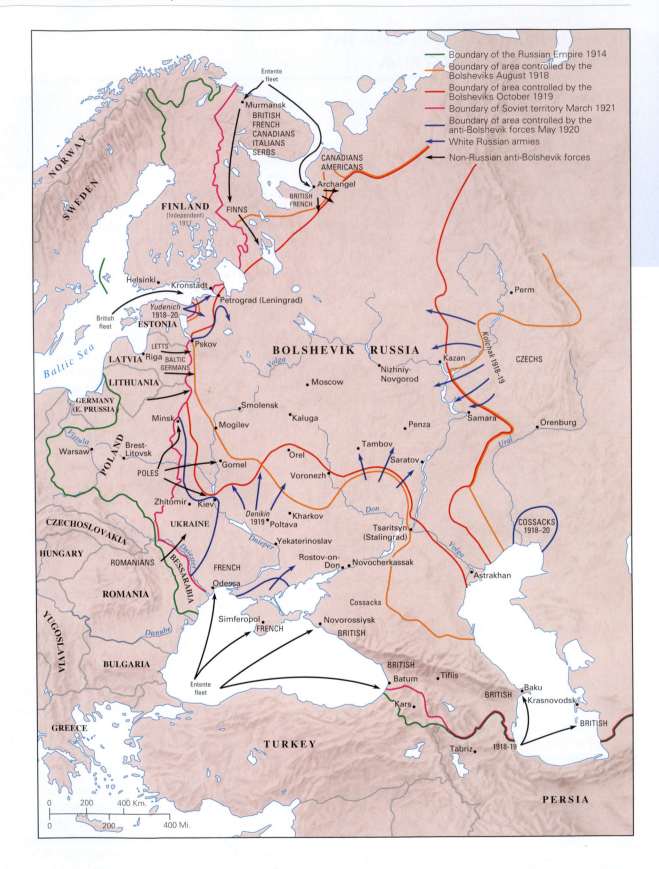

Boundary of the Russian Empire 1914
Boundary of area controlled by the Bolsheviks August 1918
Boundary of area controlled by the Bolsheviks October 1919
Boundary of Soviet territory March 1921
Boundary of area controlled by the anti-Bolshevik forces May 1920
White Russian armies
Non-Russian anti-Bolshevik forces

Entente fleet
Murmansk
BRITISH
FRENCH
CANADIANS
ITALIANS
SERBS
CANADIANS
AMERICANS
Archangel
BRITISH
FRENCH

NORWAY
SWEDEN
FINLAND (Independent) 1917
FINNS

Helsinki
Kronstadt
Petrograd (Leningrad)
Yudenich 1918–20
British fleet
ESTONIA
Pskov
LETTS
LATVIA Riga
BALTIC GERMANS
LITHUANIA
Baltic Sea
GERMANY (E. PRUSSIA)
Minsk
Vistula
Warsaw
Brest-Litovsk
POLAND
POLES
Gomel
Zhitomir
Kiev
Mogilev
Smolensk

Perm
Kolchak 1918–19
CZECHS
Kazan
Nizhniy-Novgorod
Moscow
Kaluga
Penza
Samara
Orenburg
Ural

BOLSHEVIK RUSSIA
Volga

Orel
Voronezh
Tambov
Saratov

Denikin 1919
Kharkov
Poltava
Don
Yekaterinoslav
Dnieper
Tsaritsyn (Stalingrad)
Volga
COSSACKS 1918–20

CZECHOSLOVAKIA
HUNGARY
ROMANIANS
BESSARABIA
Dniester
UKRAINE
FRENCH
Odessa
Rostov-on-Don
Novocherkassak
Cossacks
Astrakhan

ROMANIA
YUGOSLAVIA
Simferopol
FRENCH
Novorossiysk
BRITISH
Danube
BULGARIA
BRITISH
Batum
Tiflis
Baku
BRITISH
Krasnovodsk
GREECE
Kars
BRITISH
Tabriz
1918–19
BRITISH

Entente fleet
TURKEY
PERSIA

0 200 400 Km.
0 200 400 Mi.

MAP 26.1   Foreign Intervention and Civil War in Revolutionary Russia, 1918–1920

By mid-1918 the new communist regime was under attack from many sides, by both foreign troops and anticommunist Russians. Bolshevik-held territory shrank during 1919, but over the next year the Red Army managed to regain much of what had been lost and to secure the new communist state. Anton Denikin, Alexander Kolchak, and Nicholas Yudenich commanded the most significant counterrevolutionary forces. *(Source: Adapted from* The Times Atlas of World History, *3d ed. Reprinted by permission of HarperCollins Publishers Ltd. © HarperCollins Publishers Ltd.)*

was only nominally a federation of autonomous republics; strong centralization from the communist regime's new capital in Moscow was the rule from the start.

The Comintern   In March 1919, while fighting the civil war, the Russian Communists founded the Third, or Communist, International—widely known as the **Comintern**—to make clear their break with the seemingly discredited strategies of the Second International. Through the Comintern, the Russian Communists expected to translate their success in Russia into leadership of the international socialist movement. However, many old-line Marxists elsewhere were not prepared to admit that the leadership of European socialism had passed to the Communist rulers of backward Russia. As early as 1919, the German Karl Kautsky (1854–1938), who had been the leading spokesman for orthodox Marxism after the death of Friedrich Engels in 1895, harshly criticized Leninist communism as a heretical departure that would lead to despotism and severely damage international socialism.

From its founding in March 1919 until the spring of 1920, as a wave of leftist political agitation and labor unrest swept Europe, the Comintern actively promoted the wider revolution that Lenin had envisioned. Seeking to win mass support, the organization accented leftist solidarity and reached out to the rank and file in the labor unions. By the spring of 1920, however, it seemed clear that further revolution was not imminent. Thus Comintern leaders began focusing on a more protracted revolutionary struggle.

The Russians felt that poor organization and planning had undermined the wider revolutionary possibil-

ity in Europe during 1919 and 1920. The Comintern would cut through all the revolutionary romanticism to show what the Leninist strategy, or communism, meant in fact. The Russians themselves would have to call the shots because what communism meant, above all, was tight organization and discipline.

The second Comintern congress, during the summer of 1920, devised twenty-one conditions for Comintern affiliation. Most notably, any socialist party seeking membership had to accept the Comintern's authority, adopt a centralized organization, and purge its reformists. By early 1921, the Comintern's aggressive claim to leadership had split the international socialist movement, for the Comintern attracted some, but not all, of the members of the existing socialist parties. Those who now called themselves "communists" accepted the Leninist model and affiliated with the Comintern. Those who retained the "socialist" label rejected Comintern leadership; they still claimed to be Marxists but declined to embrace the Bolshevik strategy for taking power.

At first, many European socialists had difficulty assessing the Comintern objectively. The Russian Communists enjoyed great prestige because they had made a real revolution, while elsewhere socialists had talked and compromised, even getting swept up in wartime patriotism. When the French Socialist Party debated Comintern membership at its national congress in December 1920, about 70 percent of the delegates voted to join and accept the twenty-one points, while a minority walked out to form a new socialist party. But as the implications of Comintern membership became clearer over the next few years, the balance shifted in favor of the socialists. Membership in the French Communist Party, which stood at 131,000 in 1921, declined to 28,000 by 1932.

Late in 1923 the Comintern finally concluded that revolution elsewhere could not be expected any time soon. The immediate enemy was not capitalism or the bourgeoisie, but the socialists, the Communists' rivals for working-class support. The Communists' incessant criticism of the socialists, whom they eventually dubbed "social fascists," demoralized and weakened the European left, especially in the face of the growing threat of fascism by the early 1930s. The schism on the left remained an essential fact of European political life for half a century.

FROM LENIN TO STALIN, 1921–1929

To win the civil war, the communist regime had adopted a policy of "war communism," a rough-and-ready controlled economy in which food and supplies were commandeered for the Red Army. At the beginning of 1921, the economy was in crisis. Industrial production equaled only about one-fifth the 1913 total,

Comintern (Third, or Communist, International)   An association founded in March 1919 by the Communists (formerly Bolsheviks) to translate their success in Russia into leadership of the international socialist movement.

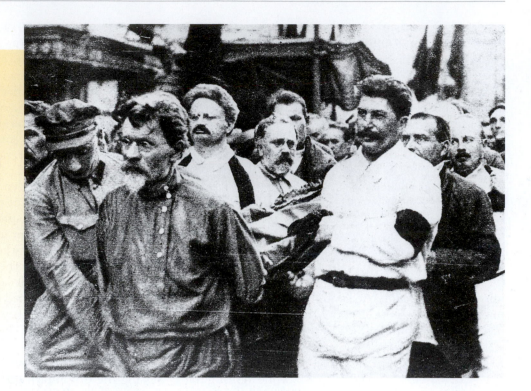

Rivals for the Soviet Leadership
In July 1926 in Moscow, Soviet leaders carry the coffin of Feliks Dzerzhinsky, the first head of the secret police. Among them are Trotsky (*with glasses, center left*), Stalin (*right foreground*), and Bukharin (*with mustache, at far right*), rivals for the Soviet leadership after Lenin's death. The winner, Stalin, would eventually have his two competitors killed.
(*David King Collection*)

workers in key factories went on strike, and peasants were resisting further requisitions of grain. In March 1921 sailors at the Kronstadt naval base near Petrograd mutinied, suffering considerable loss of life as governmental control was reestablished.

With the very survival of the revolution in question, Lenin replaced war communism with the **New Economic Policy (NEP)** in March 1921. Although transport, banking, heavy industry, and wholesale commerce remained under state control, the NEP restored considerable scope for private enterprise, especially in the retail sector and in agriculture. Peasants could again sell some of their harvest. The economy quickly began to revive and by 1927 was producing at prewar levels.

Online Study Center **Improve Your Grade**
Primary Source: A Revolutionary Retreat: The New Economic Policy

But what about the longer term? If revolution elsewhere was not on the immediate horizon, could the Soviet Union—relatively backward economically and scarred by over a decade of upheaval—build a genuinely socialist order on its own? Certain measures were obvious: The new regime engineered rapid improvements in literacy, for example. But the Marxist understanding of

historical progress required industrialization, and so debate focused on how to promote industrial development under Soviet conditions.

This debate about priorities became intertwined with questions about the leadership of the new regime. Lenin suffered the first of a series of strokes in May 1922 and then died in January 1924, setting off a struggle among his possible successors. Leon Trotsky, an effective organizer and powerful thinker, was by most measures Lenin's heir apparent. Although he favored tighter economic controls to speed industrial development, Trotsky insisted that the top priority should be spreading the revolution to other countries.

In contrast, Nikolai Bukharin (1888–1938) wanted to concentrate on the gradual development of the Soviet Union, based on a more open and conciliatory strategy. Rather than tightening controls to squeeze a surplus from agricultural producers, the government should promote purchasing power by allowing producers to profit. By the time of his death Lenin had apparently begun thinking along the same lines. And he had come to have considerable misgivings about the man who would win this struggle to direct the fragile new Soviet regime, **Joseph Stalin** (1879–1953).

Stalin was born Josef Djugashvili into a lower-class family in Georgia, in the Caucasus region. As an ethnic

New Economic Policy (NEP)   A Russian economic liberalization measure aimed at reviving an economy in crisis. The NEP restored considerable scope for private enterprise and allowed peasants to sell some of their harvest.

Joseph Stalin   Soviet dictator who jettisoned the New Economic Policy and instituted a program of crash industrialization and agricultural collectivization. He concluded the Nazi-Soviet Pact in 1939 but joined the Allies after the German invasion of the Soviet Union in 1941.

Georgian, he did not learn to speak Russian until he was 11 years old. From the position of party secretary, which he had assumed in 1922, Stalin established his control within the Soviet system by 1929. Though he lacked Trotsky's charisma and knew little of economics, he was highly intelligent and proved a master of back-stage political maneuvering. Stalin first outmaneuvered Trotsky and his allies, removing them from positions of power and forcing Trotsky himself into exile in 1929. Bitterly critical of Stalin to the end, Trotsky was finally murdered by Stalin's agents in Mexico in 1940. Stalin's victory over those like Bukharin was more gradual, but ultimately just as complete. And his victory proved decisive for the fate of Soviet communism.

By the later 1920s, those who believed in the communist experiment were growing disillusioned with the compromises of the NEP. It was time for the Soviet Union to push ahead to a new order, leaving capitalism behind altogether. Even if revolution was not imminent elsewhere, the Soviet Union could seize the lead and build "socialism in one country." Genuine enthusiasm greeted the regime's turn to centralized economic planning in 1927 and its subsequent adoption of the first Five-Year Plan early in 1929. Central planning led to a program of crash industrialization, favoring heavy industry, by the end of that year. But this new, more radical direction was not fully thought through, and it soon caused incredible suffering.

To buy the necessary plant and equipment, the state seemed to require better control of agricultural output than had been possible under the NEP. The key was to squeeze the agricultural surplus from the peasantry on terms more favorable to the government. By forcing peasants into large, state-controlled collective farms, government leaders could more readily extract the surplus, which would then be sold abroad, earning the money to finance factories, dams, and power plants.

Stalin's effort to mobilize society for the great task of rapid industrialization affected the whole shape of the regime—including cultural and artistic policy. During the 1920s, the possibility of building a new socialist society in the Soviet Union had attracted a number of modernist artists, who assumed that artistic innovation went hand in hand with radical socioeconomic transformation. These artists wanted to make art more socially useful and more central to the lives of ordinary people. With Soviet cultural officials welcoming their experiments, such Soviet artists as Vladimir Tatlin (1885–1956) and Alexander Rodchenko (1891–1956) developed striking new cultural forms.

But in 1929 Soviet officials began mobilizing the cultural realm to serve the grandiose task of building socialism in one country. No longer welcoming experiment and innovation, they demanded "socialist real-

Tatlin: Monument to the Third International Vladimir Tatlin created this model for a monument to the Third International, or Comintern, during 1919 and 1920. He envisioned a revolving structure of glass and iron; it would be twice as tall as the later Empire State Building. Although the monument was never built, Tatlin's bold, dynamic form symbolizes the utopian aspirations of the early years of the communist experiment in Russia. *(David King Collection)*

ism," which portrayed the achievements of the ongoing Soviet revolution in an inspiring, heroic light. Modernism, in contrast, they denounced as decadent and counterrevolutionary.

In retrospect, it is clear that a Stalinist revolution within the Soviet regime had begun by 1930, but where it was to lead was by no means certain—not even to Stalin himself. Still, the Soviet Union was pulling back, going its own way by the end of the 1920s. For the foreseeable future, the presence of a revolutionary regime in the old Russia would apparently be less disruptive for the rest of Europe than it had first appeared.

E CRISIS OF LIBERAL ITALY AND THE CREATION OF FASCISM, 1919–1925

Fascism emerged directly from the Italian experience of World War I, which proved especially controversial because the Italians could have avoided it altogether. No one attacked Italy in 1914, and the country could have received significant territorial benefits just by remaining neutral. Yet it seemed to many, including leading intellectuals and educated young people, that Italy could not stand idly by in a European war, especially one involving Austria-Hungary, which still controlled significant Italian-speaking areas. To participate in this major war would be the test of Italy's maturity as a nation. In May 1915 Italy finally intervened on the side of the Triple Entente. The government's decision stemmed not from vague visions of renewal but from the commitment of tangible territorial gains that France and Britain made to Italy with the secret Treaty of London.

Despite the near collapse of the Italian armies late in 1917, Italy lasted out the war and contributed to the victory over Austria-Hungary. Supporters of the war felt that this success could lead to a thoroughgoing renewal of Italian public life. Yet many Italians had been skeptical of claims for the war from the outset, and the fact that it proved so much more difficult than expected hardly won them over. To socialists, Catholics, and many left-leaning liberals, intervention itself had been a tragic mistake. Thus, despite Italy's participation in the victory, division over the war's significance immensely complicated the postwar Italian political situation.

Their skepticism was only confirmed when Italy did not secure all the gains it sought at the Paris Peace Conference. Italy got most of what it had been promised in the Treaty of London, but appetites increased with the dissolution of the Austro-Hungarian Empire. To some Italians, the disappointing outcome of the peace conference simply confirmed that the war had been a mistake, its benefits not worth the costs. But others were outraged at what seemed a denigration of the Italian contribution by France, Britain, and the United States. The outcome fanned resentment not only of Italy's allies but also of the country's political leaders, who seemed too weak to deliver on what they had pledged.

The leaders of Italy's parliamentary democracy also failed to renew the country's political system in light of the war experience. To be sure, in a spirit of democratic reform, Italy adopted proportional representation to replace the old system of small, single-member constituencies in 1919. The new system meant a greater premium on mass parties and party discipline at the expense of the one-to-one bargaining that character-

ized the earlier *trasformismo*. But the new multiparty system quickly reached an impasse—partly because of the stance of the Italian Socialist Party.

Italian Socialism   In contrast to the French and German parties, the Italian Socialists had never supported the war, and they did not accept the notion that the war experience could yield political renewal in the aftermath. So rather than reaching out to idealistic but discontented war veterans, Socialist leaders talked of imitating the Bolshevik Revolution. And the Italian situation seemed at least potentially revolutionary during 1919 and 1920, when a wave of strikes culminated in a series of factory occupations. But despite their revolutionary rhetoric, Italy's Socialist leaders did not understand the practical aspects of Leninism and did not carry out the planning and organization that might have produced an Italian revolution.

The established parliamentary system was at an impasse, and the Socialist Party seemed at once too inflexible and too romantic to lead some sort of radical transformation. It was in this context that fascism emerged, claiming to offer a third way. It was bound to oppose the Socialists and the socialist working class because of conflict over the meaning of the war and the kind of transformation Italy needed. And this anti-socialist posture made fascism open to exploitation by reactionary interests. By early 1921 landowners in northern and central Italy were footing the bill as bands of young fascists drove around the countryside in trucks, beating up workers and burning down socialist meeting halls. But fascist spokesmen claimed to offer something other than mere reaction—a new politics that all Italians, including the workers, would eventually find superior.

At the same time, important sectors of Italian industry, which had grown rapidly thanks to wartime government orders, looked with apprehension toward the more competitive international economy that loomed after the war. With its relative lack of capital and raw materials, Italy seemed to face an especially difficult situation. Nationalist thinkers and business spokesmen questioned the capacity of the parliamentary system to provide the vigorous leadership that Italy needed. Prone to short-term bickering and partisanship, ordinary politicians lacked the vision to pursue Italy's international economic interests and the will to impose the necessary discipline on the domestic level. Thus the government's response to the labor unrest of 1919 and 1920 was hesitant and weak.

Postwar Italy, then, witnessed widespread discontent with established forms of politics, but those discontented were socially disparate, and their aims were not entirely compatible. Some had been socialists before the war, others nationalists hostile to socialism.

Benito Mussolini

The founder of fascism is shown with other fascist leaders in 1922, as he becomes prime minister of Italy. Standing at Mussolini's right (with beard) is Italo Balbo, later a pioneering aviator and fascist Italy's air force minister.   *(Corbis)*

While some envisioned a more intense kind of mass politics, others thought the masses already had too much power. Still, these discontented groups agreed on the need for an alternative to both parliamentary politics and Marxist socialism. And all found the germs of that alternative in the Italian war experience.

The Rise of Mussolini   The person who seemed able to translate these aspirations into a new political force was **Benito Mussolini** (1883–1945), who had been a prominent socialist journalist before the war. Indeed, he was so talented that he was made editor of the Socialist Party's national newspaper in 1912, when he was only 29 years old. At that point many saw him as the fresh face needed to revitalize Italian socialism.

His concern with renewal made Mussolini an unorthodox socialist even before 1914, and he was prominent among those on the Italian left who began calling for Italian intervention once the war began. The fact that socialists in France, Germany, and elsewhere had immediately rallied to their respective national war efforts raised new questions about conventional socialism, based on international proletarian solidarity. But the Italian Socialist Party refused to follow his call for intervention, remaining neutralist and aloof, so Mussolini found himself cut off from his earlier constituency.

However, through his new newspaper, *Il popolo d'Italia* (*The People of Italy*), Mussolini helped rally the disparate groups that advocated Italian participation in the war. He saw military service once Italy intervened, and after the war he seemed a credible spokesman for those who wanted to translate the war experience into a new form of politics. Amid growing political unrest, he founded the fascist movement in March 1919, taking the term *fascism* from the ancient Roman *fasces,* a bundle of rods surrounding an ax carried on state occasions as a symbol of power and unity.

But fascism found little success at first. And even as it gathered force in violent reaction against the socialist labor organizations by 1921, the movement's direction was uncertain. Although young fascist militants wanted to replace the established parliamentary system with a new political order, Mussolini seemed to be using fascism as his personal instrument to achieve power

Benito Mussolini   Founder of the fascist movement and subsequently dictator within the Italian fascist regime.

within the existing system. When his maneuvering finally won him the prime minister's post in October 1922, it was not at all clear that a change of regime, or a one-party dictatorship, was at hand.

At that point, Mussolini, like most Italians, emphasized normalization and legality. Fascism had apparently been absorbed within the political system, perhaps to provide an infusion of youthful vitality after the war. With Mussolini as prime minister, there would be changes, but not revolutionary changes. Government would become more vigorous and efficient; the swollen Italian bureaucracy would be streamlined; the trains would run on time. But those who had envisioned more sweeping change were frustrated that nothing more had come of fascism than this.

A crisis in 1924 forced Mussolini's hand. In June the moderate socialist Giacomo Matteotti (mah-tay-OH-tee) rose in parliament to denounce the renewed fascist violence that had accompanied recent national elections. His murder by fascist thugs shortly thereafter produced a great public outcry, though the responsibility of Mussolini and his government was unclear. Many establishment figures who had tolerated Mussolini as the man who could keep order now deserted him. A growing chorus called for his resignation. The crisis surrounding the **Matteotti murder** proved pivotal for the fascist regime.

Mussolini sought at first to be conciliatory, but more radical fascists saw the crisis as an opportunity to end the compromise with the old liberal order and to begin creating a whole new political system. The crisis came to a head on December 31, 1924, when thirty-three militants called on Mussolini to demand that he make up his mind. In their view, the way out of the crisis was not to delimit the scope of fascism but to expand it. Mussolini was not an ordinary prime minister but the leader of fascism, *Il Duce* (eel DOO-chay). In that role he would have to accept responsibility even for his movement's violent excesses and finally begin implementing a full-scale fascist revolution.

Mussolini committed himself to this more radical course in a speech to the Chamber of Deputies a few days later, on January 3, 1925. Defiantly claiming the "full political, moral, and historical responsibility for all that has happened," including "all the acts of violence," he promised to accelerate the transformation that he claimed to have initiated with his agitation for intervention in 1914 and 1915.[1] And now began the creation of a new fascist state, although the compromises continued and the direction was never as clear as committed fascists desired.

INNOVATION AND COMPROMISE IN FASCIST ITALY, 1925–1930

Early in 1925, the fascist government began to undermine the existing democratic system by imprisoning or exiling opposition leaders and outlawing nonfascist parties and labor unions. But fascism was not seeking simply a conventional monopoly of political power; the new fascist state was to be totalitarian, all-encompassing, limitless in its reach. Under the old liberal regime, the fascists charged, the state had been too weak to promote the national interest, and Italian society had been too fragmented to achieve its full potential. So Mussolini's regime both expanded the state's sovereignty and mobilized society to create a deeper sense of national identity and shared purpose. To settle labor disputes, a new system of labor judges replaced the right to strike, which, the fascists claimed, had fostered neither productivity nor long-term working-class interests. New organizations—for youth, for women, for leisure-time activities—were to make possible new forms of public participation.

The centerpiece of the new fascist state was **corporativism,** which entailed mobilizing people as producers, through organization of the workplace. Groupings based on occupation, or economic function, were gradually to replace parliament as the basis for political participation and decision making. Beginning in 1926, corporativist institutions were established in stages until a Chamber of Fasces and Corporations at last replaced the old Chamber of Deputies in 1939.

Especially through this **corporative state,** the fascists claimed to be fulfilling their grandiose mission and providing the world with a third way, beyond both outmoded democracy and misguided communism. The practice of corporativism never lived up to such rhetoric, but the effort to devise new forms of political participation and decision making was central to fascism's self-understanding and its quest for legitimacy. And that effort attracted much attention abroad, especially with the Great Depression of the 1930s.

Online Study Center Improve Your Grade
Primary Source: The Fascist "Corporative State"

Despite the commitment to a new regime, however, fascism continued to compromise with pre-existing elites and institutions. The accommodation was especially evident in the arrangements with the Catholic Church that Mussolini worked out in 1929, formally ending the dispute between the church and the Italian state that had festered since national unification in

---

Matteotti murder   The 1924 killing by fascist thugs of Italian moderate socialist Giacomo Matteotti; the public outcry following the murder eventually led Mussolini to commit to a more radical direction, which included the creation of a new, fascist form of state.

corporativism, corporative state   The system established in fascist Italy beginning in 1926 that sought to involve people in public life not as citizens but as producers, through their roles in the economy.

1870. With the Lateran Pact, Mussolini restored a measure of sovereignty to the Vatican; with the Concordat, he gave the church significant roles in public education and marriage law.

This settlement of an old and thorny dispute afforded Mussolini a good deal of prestige among non-fascists at home and abroad. But compromise with the church displeased many committed fascists, who complained that giving this powerful, autonomous institution a role in Italian public life compromised fascism's totalitarian ideal. Such complaints led to a partial crackdown on Catholic youth organizations in 1931, as Mussolini continued trying to juggle traditionalist compromise and revolutionary pretension.

By the end of the 1920s, then, it remained unclear whether Italian fascism was a form of restoration or a form of revolution. It had restored order in Italy, overcoming the labor unrest of the immediate postwar years, but it was order on a new, antidemocratic basis. Yet the fascists claimed to be implementing a revolution of their own at the same time. Fascism could be violent and disruptive, dictatorial and repressive, but Mussolini's regime seemed dynamic and innovative. Though its ultimate direction remained nebulous, fascism attracted those elsewhere who were discontented with liberal democracy and Marxist socialism. It thus fed the volatility and ideological polarization that marked the European political order after World War I.

SECTION SUMMARY

- The question of whether to affiliate with the new Communist International (Comintern), established by the Russian Communists in 1919, split Marxist socialist parties throughout the world.

- The struggle for the Soviet leadership with the death of Lenin became intertwined with questions about communist priorities in the wake of the New Economic Policy adopted in 1921.

- A Stalinist revolution within the Soviet communist experiment had begun by 1930, but where it would lead was not at all clear.

- The fascist reaction against both liberalism and socialism reflected deep divisions in Italy over the significance of the Italian war effort.

- Once Mussolini committed himself to a decisively postliberal direction, the fascists fastened upon corporativism as the basis for a new, specifically fascist form of state.

TOWARD MASS SOCIETY

Why, and on what basis, did sexuality, gender roles, and the "new woman" provoke so much concern during this period?

After a few years of wild economic swings just after the war, Europe enjoyed renewed prosperity by the later 1920s. Common involvement in the war had blurred class lines and accelerated the trend toward what contemporaries began to call "mass society." As the new prosperity spread the fruits of industrialization more widely, ordinary people increasingly set the cultural tone, partly through new mass media such as film and radio. To some, the advent of mass society portended a welcome revitalization of culture and a more authentic kind of democracy, whereas others saw only a debasement of cultural standards and a susceptibility to populist demagoguery. But though the contours of mass society now became evident, social change did not keep up with the promise of—and the requirements for—democratic politics.

ECONOMIC READJUSTMENT AND THE NEW PROSPERITY

In their effort to return to normal, governments were quick to dismantle wartime planning and control mechanisms. But the needs of war had stimulated innovations that helped fuel the renewed economic growth of the 1920s. The civilian air industry, for example, developed rapidly during the decade by taking advantage of wartime work on aviation for military purposes. More generally, newer industries such as chemicals, electricity, and advanced machinery led the way to a new prosperity in the 1920s, which significantly altered patterns of life in the more industrialized parts of the West. The automobile, a luxury plaything for the wealthy before the war, began to be mass-duced in western Europe. In France, automobile production shot up dramatically, from 40,000 in 1920 to 254,000 in 1929.

But the heady pace masked problems that lay beneath the relative prosperity of the 1920s, even in victorious Britain and France. While new industries prospered, old ones declined in the face of new technologies and stronger foreign competition. In Britain, the sectors responsible for Britain's earlier industrial pre-eminence—textiles, coal, shipbuilding, and iron and steel—now had trouble competing. Rather than investing in new technologies, companies in these industries demanded government protection and imposed lower wages and longer hours on their workers. At the same time, British labor unions resisted the mechanization necessary to make these older industries more competitive.

Rather than realistically assessing Britain's prospects in the new international economy, British leaders sought to return to the prewar situation, based on the gold standard, with London the world's financial center. For many Britons, the government's announcement in 1925 that the British pound was again freely convertible to gold at 1914 exchange rates was the long-awaited indication that normality had returned at last. Yet the return to 1914 exchange rates overvalued the pound relative to the U.S. dollar, making British goods more expensive on export markets and making it still more difficult for aging British industries to compete.

The structural decline of older industries was clearest in Britain, but inflation and its psychological impact was most prominent in Germany and France. By the summer of 1923, Germany's response to the French occupation of the Ruhr had transformed an already serious inflationary problem, stemming from wartime deficit spending, into one of the great hyperinflations in history. At its height in November, when it took 4.2 trillion marks to equal a dollar, Germans were forced to cart wheelbarrows of paper money to stores to buy ordinary grocery items. By the end of 1923, the government managed to stabilize prices through currency reform and drastically reduced government spending—a combination that elicited greater cooperation from the victors. But the rampant inflation, and the readjustment necessary to control it, had wiped out the life savings of ordinary people while profiting speculators and those in debt, including some large industrialists. This inequity left scars that remained even as Germany enjoyed a measure of prosperity in the years that followed.

Inflation was less dramatic in France, but there, too, it affected perceptions and priorities in significant ways. For over a century, from the Napoleonic era to the outbreak of war in 1914, the value of the French franc had remained stable. But the war started France on an inflationary cycle that shattered the security of its many small savers—those, such as teachers and shopkeepers, who had been the backbone of the Third Republic. To repay war debts and rebuild war-damaged industries, the French government continued to run budget deficits, and thereby cause inflation, even after 1918. Runaway inflation threatened during 1925 and 1926, but the franc was finally restabilized in 1928, though at only about one-fifth its prewar value.

On the international level, war debts and reparations strained the financial system, creating problems with the financing of trade. But in the course of the 1920s, experts made adjustments that seemed to be returning the international exchange system to equilibrium. Only in retrospect, after the international capitalist system fell into crisis late in 1929, did it become clear how potent those strains were—and how inadequate the efforts at readjustment.

WORK, LEISURE, AND THE NEW POPULAR CULTURE

The wartime spur to industrialization produced a large increase in the industrial labor force all over Europe, and a good deal of labor unrest accompanied the transition to peacetime. Some of that agitation challenged factory discipline and authority relationships. Seeking to re-establish authority on a new basis for the competitive postwar world, business advocates fostered a new cult of efficiency and productivity, partly by adapting Taylorism and Fordism, influential American ideas about mass production. On the basis of his "time-and-motion" studies of factory labor, Frederick W. Taylor (1856–1915) argued that breaking down assembly-line production into small, repetitive tasks was the key to maximizing worker efficiency. In contrast, Henry Ford (1863–1947) linked the gospel of mass production to mass consumption. In exchange for accepting the discipline of the assembly line, the workers should be paid well enough to be able to buy the products they produced—even automobiles. Sharing in the prosperity that mass production made possible, factory workers would be loyal to the companies that employed them. Not all Europeans, however, welcomed the new ideas from America. In the new cult of efficiency and mass production, some saw an unwelcome sameness and a debasement of cultural standards.

Changing Roles for Women   In light of the major role women had played in the wartime labor force, the demand for women's suffrage proved irresistible in Britain, Germany, and much of Europe, though not yet in France or Italy. In Britain, where calls for women's suffrage had earlier met with controversy (see page 757), the right to vote was readily conceded in 1918, though at first only to women over 30. By now women no longer seemed a threat to the political system. And in fact British women, once they could vote, simply flowed into the existing parties, countering earlier hopes—and

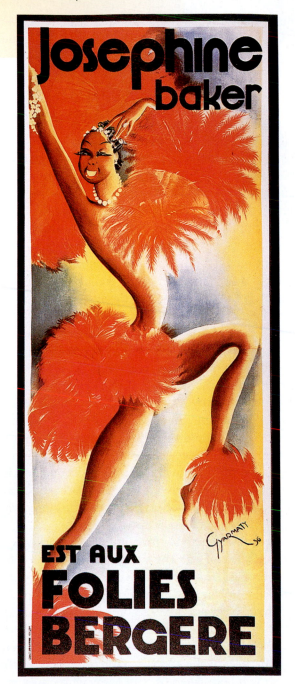

fears—that a specifically feminist political agenda would follow from women's suffrage.

Although there was much discussion of the "new woman," especially in Germany, the wider place of women in society and politics was uncertain during the 1920s, as the new sense of openness clashed with the desire to return to normal. (See the feature "The Visual Record: Advertising.") Female employment remained higher than before the war, but many women—willingly or not—returned home, yielding their jobs to the returning soldiers. The need to replace the men killed in the war lent renewed force to the traditional notion that women served society, and fulfilled themselves, by marrying and rearing families. More generally, some men found the emancipated "new woman" threatening, and after all the disruptions of war, male leaders sometimes assumed that the very stability of the political sphere depended on conventional gender roles. Still, the decade's innovative impulse brought into the public arena subjects—largely taboo before the war—that might portend changes in gender roles later on. The desire to be "modern" produced, for example, a more open, unsentimental, even scientific discussion of sexuality and reproduction.

The new "rationalization of sexuality" fed demands that governments provide access to sex counseling, birth control, and even abortion as they assumed ever greater responsibilities for promoting social health. This trend was especially prominent in Germany, although German innovators learned from experiments in the new Soviet Union and from the birth control movement that Margaret Sanger (1883–1966) was spearheading in the United States.

The more open and tolerant attitude toward sexuality affected popular entertainment—for example, Josephine Baker's dancing and costumes, which would have been unthinkable before the war. Another result was the emergence of a more visible gay subculture, prominent especially in the vibrant cabaret scene in Berlin during the 1920s.

Prosperity and the Culture of Leisure Mass consumption followed from the mass production that created the new prosperity of the 1920s. As it became possible to mass-produce the products of the second industrial transformation, more people could afford automobiles, electrical gadgets such as radios and phonographs, and clothing of synthetic fabrics, developed through innovations in chemistry. First came rayon, produced in small quantities since 1891 but mass-produced beginning in the 1920s. In this new artificial form, silk, long one of the trappings of wealth, was now within the means of ordinary people.

Advertising

A sleek new automobile. A stylish "new woman" who'd adore a Christmas gift of jewelry. These images from the 1920s catch our eye even today, but why? The designs look "modern" somehow, and they convey particular messages about efficiency and the good life. What do such advertisements tell us about the changes at work in Western culture after World War I?

Advertising in one form or another is as old as civilization itself. But the advent of printing expanded possibilities, and the second industrial revolution led to a big boost in advertising by the 1890s, as ads for new products like bicycles and sewing machines appeared in newspapers and magazines. But it was during the 1920s that modern advertising came into its own. As mass consumption grew, advertising budgets expanded dramatically, and professional ad agencies emerged to study tastes and determine how to shape the desires of consumers. Moreover, the advent of commercial radio in 1920 opened a whole new set of possibilities, including the scope for musical jingles.

Mass consumption required advertising to show people what to want. And during the 1920s, ad agencies began offering images of the good life, seeking to define the popular sense of what it meant to be "modern." They often drew from the United States, which stood for efficiency and a fast-paced life of fun, pleasure, and consumerist abundance. So eager were the Germans to follow the U.S. lead in advertising that they adopted the term *sex appeal,* leaving it untranslated.

The new products featured in the print and broadcast media ran the gamut from automobiles to cosmetics, from rayon apparel to chewing gum. When the Wrigley Company of Chicago opened a factory in Germany in 1925, chewing gum quickly became associated with Americanization—and its use increased dramatically. But luxury goods were prominent as well, as in elegant ads such as the two shown here. Even for the many who could not afford expensive jewelry or the six-cylinder Opel, images of the good life stimulated the desire to buy less costly versions. Automobile consumption rose sharply during the 1920s, thanks also to the new techniques of mass production that Henry Ford had pioneered in the United States.

Although advertising served the economic interests of business by stimulating consumption, many began to view it as an art form as well. Far more attention was paid to its design, so the advertising "look" of the 1920s differed dramatically from anything seen before. As in the examples here, the new ads were often self-consciously modern, using simplified typefaces and stylized images suggesting the sleek efficiency and precision of the new machine age. The jewelry ad features an elegant contemporary typeface, and the German automobile ad of 1928 relies on crisp, bold forms and a clean, modern design.

The new prominence of advertising raised issues that were debated all over, but especially in Weimar Germany, where conditions remained unsettled even as a measure of prosperity returned by 1924. From cultural standards to gender roles, much was being called into question, and the wider implications of advertising were central to the "culture wars" of the period.

At an international advertising congress in Berlin in 1929, critics charged that advertising was furthering the debasement of standards already associated with mass culture and Americanization. Defenders countered that advertising was rejuvenating the mainstream culture, which had grown either stale and conventional or overblown and elitist. The fact that advertising served a commercial purpose need not mean cultural debasement. On the contrary, they argued, this new meshing of the best design with popular culture was healthy. In 1928 G. F. Hartlaub, a leading German art dealer, summed up a widespread view when he observed that advertising was a "truly social, collective, mass art, the only one we now have. It shapes the visual habits of that anonymous collectivity, the public. Little by little an artistic attitude is hammered into the mass soul by billboards."[*]

A particular advertising target was the "new woman," with her bobbed hair, short skirts, and freer lifestyle. But the image of women in advertisements was controversial, especially in Weimar Germany. Partly because of the simplification of female attire, images of the new woman in popular magazines provoked much concern about the "masculinization" of women by the mid-1920s. Some men found such images aggressive, even threatening.

---

[*]Quoted in John Willett, *Art and Politics in the Weimar Period: The New Sobriety, 1917–1933* (New York: Pantheon, 1978), p. 137. Translation modified slightly.

Car Ad, 1928: The Six-Cylinder Opel Hits the Jackpot
(From Bärbel Schrader and Jürgen Schebera, The "Golden" Twenties: Art and Literature in the Weimar Republic *[New Haven: Yale University Press, 1990]. Reproduced with permission.)*

Jewelry Ad, 1920s: "Wear jewelry—It makes you a winner. And it's the ideal Christmas gift." *(akg-images)*

Yet at the same time, advertising often assumed women to be master consumers—or perhaps merely mindless shoppers. In the holiday advertisement here, the woman is chic and liberated in one sense, but she is urged to drape herself with jewelry—to indulge in conventional ornamentation. This was also an age that claimed to value efficiency purified of ornament, as with the stripped-down typeface in the automobile ad. So though gender differentiation and women's roles were very much at issue in advertising, the relationship between portrayals of the new woman and genuine liberation remained uncertain.

Despite tensions and contradictions, advertising helped bring new issues to center stage after World War I. Although the ads of the 1920s as-sumed a prosperity that proved fleeting, the cultural change proved enduring. Eye-catching images of the sleek, the chic, the new—all bathed in "sex appeal"—became the staples of twentieth-century advertising, bound up with the new culture of mass consumption.

QUESTIONS

1. What factors led to the upsurge in advertising during the 1920s?

2. What seems specifically modern about the images we see here?

Online Study Center
Improve Your Grade Visual Record Activities

Innovation in Cinema
This poster advertises Fritz Lang's 1926 film *Metropolis*, which explored the dehumanization and exploitation of the modern city. *(Schulz-Neudamm, Metropolis, 1926. Lithograph, 83" × 36½". Gift of Universum-Film-Aktiengesellschaft. Photograph © 1997 The Museum of Modern Art, New York/Art Resource, NY)*

With the eight-hour workday increasingly the norm, growing attention was devoted to leisure as a positive source of human fulfillment—for everyone, not just the wealthy. European beach resorts grew crowded as more people had the time, and the means, to take vacations. An explosion of interest in soccer among Europeans paralleled the growth of professional baseball and college football in the United States. Huge stadiums were built across Europe.

The growth of leisure was linked to the development of mass media and mass culture. During the early 1920s radio became a commercial venture, reaching a mass audience in Europe, as in the United States and Canada. Although movies had begun to emerge as vehicles of popular entertainment even before the war, they came into their own during the 1920s, when the names of film stars became household words for the first time.

Exploiting the new popular fascination with air travel, the American Charles Lindbergh (1902–1974) captured the European imagination in 1927 with the first solo flight across the Atlantic. Lindbergh's feat epitomized the affirmative side of the decade—the sense that there were new worlds to conquer and that there still were heroes to admire, despite the ironies of the war and the ambiguities of the peace.

SOCIETY AND POLITICS IN THE VICTORIOUS DEMOCRACIES

France and Britain seemed the best positioned of the major European countries to take advantage of renewed peace and stability to confront the sociopolitical problems of the postwar era. And during the 1920s, each seemed to return to normal. But was normal good enough, in light of the rupture of the war and the challenges of the emerging mass society?

France Victory in the Great War seemed to belie France's prewar concerns about decadence and decline. In the immediate aftermath of the war, Clemenceau and other French leaders were confident in dealing with radical labor unrest and aggressive in translating the battlefield victory into a dominant position on the European continent. But the tremendous loss of French lives had produced a new fear—that France could not withstand another such challenge. The renewed confidence thus proved hollow.

Although some in prewar France had worried about falling behind rapidly industrializing Germany, victory seemed to have vindicated France's more cautious, balanced economy, with its blend of industry and agriculture. Thus the prewar mistrust of rapid industrial development continued. Rather than foster a program of economic modernization that might have promoted genuine security, the French pulled back even from the measure of state responsibility for the economy that had developed during the war.

To be sure, in France, as elsewhere, the 1920s was a decade of relative prosperity. Led by the oil and electricity industries, the economy grew at an annual rate of 4.6 percent between 1923 and 1929, double the prewar rate. Industrial production by 1929 was 40 percent higher than it had been in 1913. But, with the exception of Britain, other Western economies grew more rapidly during the 1920s, and the opportunity that growth afforded to modernize the French economy was not seized. Although government grants helped reconstruct almost eight thousand factories, most were simply rebuilt as they had been before the war. Moreover, the working class benefited little from the relative prosperity of the 1920s. Housing remained poor, wages failed to keep up with inflation, and France continued to lag behind other countries in social legislation.

Great Britain   Britain, too, made certain adjustments after the war but missed the chance to make others. The government's handling of the Easter Rebellion in Ireland in 1916 (see page 779) intensified anti-British feeling and fed further violence. But the British finally forged at least a provisional resolution. The first step was to partition Ireland, creating a separate Ulster, or Northern Ireland, from those counties with Protestant majorities. Ulster then remained under the British crown when a new independent Republic of Ireland was established in the larger, majority-Catholic part of the island in 1922.

The British political system remained stable between the wars, although the Labour Party supplanted the Liberals to become the dominant alternative to the Conservatives by the early 1920s. The Labour Party even got a brief taste of power when Ramsay MacDonald (1866–1937) formed Britain's first Labour government in January 1924. The coming of Labour to power resulted in a significant expansion of the governmental

elite to incorporate those, like MacDonald himself, with genuinely working-class backgrounds.

However, it was the Conservative leader, Stanley Baldwin (1867–1947), who set the tone for British politics between the wars in three stints as prime minister from 1923 to 1937. Although he was the wealthy son of a steel manufacturer, Baldwin deliberately departed from the old aristocratic style of British Conservative politics. More down-to-earth and pragmatic than his predecessors, he was the first British prime minister to use radio effectively, and he made an effort to foster good relations with workers. Yet Baldwin's era was one of growing social tension.

With exports declining, unemployment remained high in Britain throughout the interwar period, never falling below 10 percent. The coal industry, though still the country's largest employer, had become a particular trouble spot in the British economy. As coal exports declined, British mine owners became ever more aggressive in their dealings with labor, finally, in 1926, insisting on a longer workday and a wage cut of 13 percent to restore competitiveness. The result was a coal miners' strike in May that promptly turned into a general strike, involving almost all of organized labor—about four million workers—in the most notable display of trade-union solidarity Britain had ever seen. For nine days the economy stood at a virtual standstill. But threats of arrest and a growing public backlash forced the union leadership to accept a compromise. The miners continued the strike on their own, but they finally returned to work six months later at considerably lower wages.

Although for somewhat different reasons, Britain and France both failed during the 1920s to take advantage of what would soon seem, in retrospect, to have been a precious opportunity to adjust their economies, heal social wounds, and create more genuinely democratic political systems. The lost opportunity would mean growing social tensions once the relative prosperity of the decade had ended.

═══════ S E C T I O N   S U M M A R Y ═══════

- The inflation that resulted from the war and its aftermath had long-term psychological consequences, most dramatically in Germany, but also in France.

- Adapting influential American ideas about mass production, business leaders throughout much of Europe fostered a new cult of efficiency and productivity as they sought to adjust to the more competitive postwar world economy.

- Although there was much discussion of the "new woman," reflecting a new sense of openness after the war, women were pulled in traditional as well as modernizing directions during the 1920s.

- Mass production yielded mass consumption, the growth of leisure, and the popularity of new media like movies and radio.

- Victory bred a certain complacency in Britain and France, each of which failed to take advantage of what would seem, in retrospect, to have been a precious opportunity to adjust their economies and deepen their democracies.

WEIMAR GERMANY AND THE TRIALS OF THE NEW DEMOCRACIES

What factors made the future of the new German democracy so uncertain during the 1920s?

The war was supposed to have paved the way for democracy, and new democracies emerged in Germany, Poland, and elsewhere in Europe. But almost everywhere they led tortured lives and soon gave way to more authoritarian forms of government. So the postwar decade did not see the extension of the political democracy that optimistic observers associated with the emerging mass society.

The most significant test took place in Germany, where a new democracy emerged from the republic proclaimed in November 1918. Elections in January 1919 produced a constituent assembly that convened in Weimar, a town associated with what seemed the most humane German cultural traditions. The assembly gave this new Weimar Republic, as it came to be called, Germany's first fully democratic constitution. But the Weimar democracy had great difficulty establishing its legitimacy, and it was suffering serious strains by 1930.

DEMOCRACY ABORTED IN EAST-CENTRAL EUROPE

New democracies were established in much of central and eastern Europe after the war, but except in Czechoslovakia and Finland, the practice of parliamentary government did not match the initial promise. Democracy seemed divisive and ineffective, so one country after another adopted a more authoritarian alternative during the 1920s and early 1930s.

Poland offers the most dramatic example. Although its democratic constitution of 1921 established a cabinet responsible to a parliamentary majority, the parliament fragmented into so many parties that instability proved endemic from the start. Poland had fourteen different ministries from November 1918 to May 1926, when Marshal Josef Pilsudski led a coup d'état that replaced parliamentary government with an authoritarian regime stressing national unity. This suppression of democracy came as a relief to many Poles—and was welcomed even by the trade unions. After Pilsudski's death in 1935, a group of colonels ruled Poland until the country was conquered by Nazi Germany in 1939.

Democracy proved hard to manage in east-central Europe partly because of the economic difficulties resulting from the breakup of the Habsburg system. New national borders meant new economic barriers that disrupted long-standing economic relationships. Industrial centers such as Vienna and Budapest found themselves cut off from their traditional markets and sources of raw materials. In what was now Poland, Silesians had long been oriented toward Germany, Galicians toward Vienna, and those in eastern Poland toward Russia. Thus the new Polish nation-state was hardly a cohesive economic unit.

The countries of east-central Europe remained overwhelmingly agrarian, and this, too, proved unconducive to democracy. Land reform that accompanied the transition to democracy made small properties the norm in much of the region. But because these units were often too small to be efficient, agricultural output actually decreased after land was redistributed, most dramatically in Romania and Yugoslavia. When agricultural prices declined in the late 1920s, many peasants had no choice but to sell out to larger landowners. What had seemed a progressive and democratic reform thus failed to provide a stable agrarian smallholder base for democracy.

GERMANY'S CAUTIOUS REVOLUTION, 1919–1920

Meanwhile, in Germany, the Weimar Republic began under particularly difficult circumstances. Born of military defeat, it was promptly forced to take responsibility for the harsh Treaty of Versailles in 1919. During its first years, moreover, the regime encountered severe economic dislocation, culminating in the hyperinflation of 1923, as well as ideological polarization that threatened to tear the country apart.

Although Germany had strong military and authoritarian traditions, the initial threat to the new democracy came not from the right, disoriented and discredited, but from the left, stimulated by the Russian example. Those seeking further revolution, and those who feared it, could easily equate the proclamation of a German republic with the first revolution in Russia; as in Russia, the new, more democratic order could prove a mere prelude to communist revolution. Even after Karl Liebknecht and Rosa Luxemburg were captured and murdered in Berlin in January 1915, a serious chance of further revolution persisted through May 1919, and communist revolutionary agitation continued to flare up until the end of 1923.

As it turned out, there was no further revolution, partly because the parallel between Germany and Russia carried only so far. The new German government had made peace, whereas the leaders of the provisional government in Russia had sought to continue the war. Furthermore, those who ended up controlling the councils that sprang up in Germany during the fall of 1918 favored political democracy, not communist revolution; therefore, they supported the provisional government.

Even so, the revolutionary minority constituted a credible threat. And the new government made repression of the extreme left a priority—even if it meant leaving in place some of the institutions and personnel of the old imperial system. In November 1918, at the birth of the new republic, the moderate socialist leader Friedrich Ebert had agreed with General Wilhelm Groener, the new army head, to preserve the old imperial officer corps to help prevent further revolution. But when the regular army, weakened by war and defeat, proved unable to control radical agitation in Berlin in December, it seemed the republic would have to take extraordinary measures to defend itself from the revolutionary left. With the support of Ebert and Groener, Gustav Noske (1868–1946), the minister of national defense, began to organize "Free Corps," volunteer paramilitary groups to be used against the revolutionaries. Noske, who was a socialist, but one long supportive of the military, noted that "somebody will have to be the bloodhound—I won't shirk the responsibility."[2]

During the first five months of 1919, the government unleashed the Free Corps to crush leftist movements all over Germany, often with wanton brutality. In relying on right-wing paramilitary groups, the republic's leaders were playing with fire, but the immediate threat at this point came from the left. In 1920, however, the government faced a right-wing coup attempt, the Kapp Putsch. The army declined to defend the republic, but the government managed to survive thanks largely to a general strike by leftist workers. The republic's early leaders had to juggle both extremes because, as one of them put it, the Weimar Republic was "a candle burning at both ends."

Though sporadic street fighting by paramilitary groups continued, the republic survived its traumatic birth and achieved an uneasy stability by 1924. But Germany's postwar revolution had remained confined to the political level. There was no program to break up the cartels, with their concentrations of economic power. Even on the level of government personnel, continuity was more striking than change. There was no effort to build a loyal republican army, and no attempt to purge the bureaucracy and the judiciary of antidemocratic elements from the old imperial order. When right-wing extremists assassinated prominent leaders, such as the Jewish industrialist Walther Rathenau in 1922, the courts often proved unwilling to prosecute those responsible.

In light of the republic's eventual failure, the willingness of its early leaders to leave intact so much from the old order has made them easy targets of criticism. It can be argued, however, that the course they followed—heading off the extreme left, reassuring the established elites, and playing for time—was the republic's best chance for success. The new regime might establish its legitimacy by inertia, much like the Third Republic in France, which had similarly been born of defeat. Even lacking the sentimental fervor that had earlier surrounded democratic ideals, Germans might gradually become "republicans of reason," recognizing that this regime could be a framework for prosperity and renewed German prominence in international affairs. In the event of an early crisis, however, a republic consolidating itself in this cautious way might well find fewer defenders than opponents.

The constituent assembly elections of January 1919 took place before the peace conference had produced the widely detested Treaty of Versailles. When the first regular parliamentary elections finally were held in June 1920, the three moderate parties that had led the new government, and that had been forced to accept the treaty, suffered a major defeat, together dropping from 76 to 47 percent of the seats. These were the parties most committed to democratic institutions, but they were never again to achieve a parliamentary majority.

The 1920 elections revealed the problems of polarization and lack of consensus that would bedevil, and eventually ruin, the Weimar Republic. Because the electorate found it difficult to agree, or even to compromise, Germany settled into a multiparty system that led to unstable coalition government. And the strength, or potential strength, of the extremes immeasurably complicated political life for those trying to make the new democracy work. On the left, the Communist Party constantly criticized the more moderate Socialist Party for supporting the republic. On the right, the Nationalist Party (DNVP) played on nationalist resentments and fears of the extreme left—but the result was similarly to dilute support for the new republic. To the right even of the Nationalists were Adolf Hitler's National Socialists, or Nazis, who were noisy and often violent, but they attracted little electoral support before 1930.

GUSTAV STRESEMANN AND THE SCOPE FOR GRADUAL CONSOLIDATION

All was not necessarily lost for the republic when the three moderate, pro-Weimar parties were defeated in 1920. Germans who were unsupportive or hostile at first might be gradually won over. After the death of President Ebert in 1925, Paul von Hindenburg, the emperor's field marshal, was elected president. Depending on the circumstances, having a conservative military leader from the old order in this role could prove

advantageous, or damaging, for the future of democracy. As long as there was scope for consolidation, Hindenburg's presidency might help persuade skeptics that the new regime was legitimate and a worthy object of German patriotism. But when crisis came by 1930, Hindenburg was quick to give up on parliamentary government—with devastating results.

The individual who best exemplified the possibility of winning converts to the Weimar Republic was **Gustav Stresemann** (STRAY-zuh-mahn) (1878–1929), the leader of the German People's Party (DVP), a conservative party that did not support the republic at the outset. But it was relatively flexible and offered at least the possibility of broadening the republic's base of support. As chancellor, and especially as foreign minister, Stresemann proved the republic's leading statesman.

Stresemann's background and instincts were not democratic, but by the end of 1920 Germany's postwar political volatility had convinced him that if the new republic should go under, the outcome would not be

the conservative monarchy he preferred but the triumph of the extreme left. Moreover, it had become clear that the new democratic republic was not likely to be revolutionary on the socioeconomic level. It made sense, then, to work actively to make the new regime succeed. From within this framework Germany could pursue its international aims, negotiating modifications of the Versailles treaty and returning to great power status.

Stresemann became chancellor in August 1923, when inflation was raging out of control. Within months his government managed to get the German economy functioning effectively again, partly because the French agreed that an international commission should review the reparations question, specifying realistic amounts based on Germany's ability to pay. During the summer of 1924, a commission led by the American financier Charles G. Dawes produced the Dawes Plan, which remained in force until 1929. The plan worked well by pinpointing revenue sources, lowering payments, providing loans, and securing the stability of the German currency. With the expiration of the Dawes Plan in 1929, the Young Plan, conceived by American businessman Owen D. Young, removed Allied controls over the German economy and specified that Germany pay reparations until 1988. The annual amount was less than Germany had been paying, so it was expected that this plan constituted a permanent, and reasonable, settlement.

Quite apart from the immediate economic issue, Stresemann understood that better relations with France had to be a priority if Germany was to return to great power status. French foreign minister Aristide Briand (bree-AHN) (1862–1932) shared Stresemann's desire for improved relations, and together they engineered a new, more conciliatory spirit in international affairs. Its most substantial fruit was the **Treaty of Locarno** of 1925. France and Germany accepted the postwar border between the two countries, which meant that Germany gave up any claim to Alsace-Lorraine. France, for its part, renounced the sort of direct military intervention in Germany that it had attempted with the Ruhr invasion of 1923 and agreed to begin withdrawing troops from the Rhineland ahead of schedule. Germany freely accepted France's key advantage, the demilitarization of the Rhineland, and Britain and Italy now explicitly guaranteed the measure.

By accepting the status quo in the west, Stresemann was freeing Germany to concentrate on eastern Europe, where he envisioned gradual but substantial revision in the territorial settlement that had resulted from the war. Especially with the creation of Poland, that settlement had come partly at Germany's expense. Stresemann, then, was pursuing German interests, not subordinating them to some larger European vision. But he was willing to compromise and, for the most part, to play by the rules as he did so.

With the Locarno treaty, the victors accepted Germany as a diplomatic equal for the first time since the war. Germany's return to good graces culminated in its entry into the League of Nations in 1926. The new spirit of reconciliation was widely welcomed. Indeed, Stresemann and Briand were joint winners of the Nobel Peace Prize for 1926.

Still, those to the right in Germany continually exploited German resentments by criticizing Stresemann's compromises with Germany's former enemies—in accepting the Dawes and Young Plans, for example. Even when successful from Stresemann's own perspective, these negotiations cost his party electoral support. The controversy that surrounded Stresemann, a German conservative pursuing conventional national interests, indicates how volatile the German political situation remained, even with the improved economic and diplomatic climate of the later 1920s. Still, Strese-

mann's diplomatic successes were considerable, and his death in October 1929, at the age of 51, was a severe blow to the republic.

An Uncertain Balance Sheet

Although Weimar Germany was better off in 1929 than it had been in 1923, the political consensus remained weak, the political party system remained fragmented, and unstable coalition government remained the rule. Although the immediate threat from the extreme left had been overcome, many German conservatives continued to fear that the unstable Weimar democracy would eventually open the way to a socialist or communist regime.

The Weimar Republic epitomized the overall European situation during the 1920s. As long as prosperity and international cooperation continued, the new democracy in Germany might endure, even come to thrive. But the new institutions in Germany, like the wider framework of prosperity and stability, were fragile indeed. At the first opportunity, antidemocratic elites, taking advantage of their access to President Hindenburg, would begin plotting to replace the Weimar Republic with a more authoritarian alternative.

─── S E C T I O N   S U M M A R Y ───

- Although new democracies were established in central and eastern Europe after the war, parliamentary government proved divisive and ineffective in much of the region, so one country after another adopted a more authoritarian alternative.

- Germany's democratic political revolution was not accompanied by major changes in socioeconomic relations—or even in the administrative structures inherited from Wilhelm II's government.

- Because of polarization and lack of consensus in the electorate, the Weimar Republic quickly fell into a

multiparty system that led to unstable coalition government.

- A conservative monarchist by instinct, Gustav Stresemann rallied to the Weimar Republic because he found it the best framework for restoring Germany to prosperity and international influence—and for heading off leftist revolution.

- Although many Germans continued to resent the peace settlement, the Treaty of Locarno of 1925 seemed to suggest a hopeful new spirit of reconciliation between France and Germany.

The Search for Meaning in a Disordered World

How did cultural and intellectual leaders differ over the place of "tradition" as they sought to suggest how to come to terms with the new situation of the 1920s?

For all its vitality, the new culture of the 1920s had something brittle about it. The forces that produced a sense of openness, liberation, and innovation were disruptive and disturbing at the same time.

Perhaps the frenetic pace only masked a deeper sense that things had started to come apart and might well get worse. The era called forth some notable diagnoses and prescriptions, but, not surprisingly, they differed dramatically.

ANXIETY, ALIENATION, AND DISILLUSIONMENT

Concern about the dangers of the emerging mass civilization was especially clear in the *Revolt of the Masses* (1930), by the influential Spanish thinker José Ortega y Gasset (1883–1955). In his view, contemporary experience had shown that ordinary people, incapable of creating standards, remained content with the least common denominator. Communism and fascism indicated the violent, intolerant, and ultimately barbaric quality of the new mass age. But Ortega found the same tendencies in American-style democracy. The fact that much of Europe seemed to be moving toward the mass politics and culture of the United States was a symptom of the deeper problem, not a solution.

Concern with cultural decline was part of a wider pessimism about the condition of the West, which stood in stark contrast to the belief in progress, and the attendant confidence in Western superiority, that had been essential to Western self-understanding before 1914. The German thinker Oswald Spengler (1880–1936) made concern with decline almost fashionable with his bestseller of the immediate postwar years, *The Decline of the West* (1918), which offered a cyclical theory purporting to explain how spirituality and creativity were giving way to a materialistic mass-based culture in the West.

To Sigmund Freud (1856–1939), the eruption of violence and hatred during the war and afterward indicated a deep, instinctual problem in the human makeup (see page 754). In his gloomy essay *Civilization and Its Discontents* (1930), Freud suggested that the progress of civilization requires individuals to bottle up their aggressive instincts, which are directed inward as guilt, but which may erupt in violent outbursts. This notion raised questions not only about the scope for continued progress but also about the plausibility of the Wilsonian ideals that had surrounded the end of the war. Perhaps, with civilization growing more complex, the Great War had been only the beginning of a new era of hatred and violence.

The sense that something incomprehensible, even nightmarish, haunted modern civilization, with its ever more complex bureaucracies, technologies, and cities, found vivid expression in the work of the Czech Jewish writer Franz Kafka (1883–1924), most notably in the novels *The Trial* and *The Castle,* published posthumously in the mid-1920s. In a world that claimed to be increasingly rational, Kafka's individual is the lonely, fragile plaything of forces utterly beyond reason, comprehension, and control. In such a world, the quest for law, or meaning, or God, is futile, ridiculous.

Especially in the unsettled conditions of Weimar Germany, the anxiety of the 1920s tended to take extreme forms, from irrational activism to a preoccupation with death. Suicides among students increased dramatically. Youthful alienation prompted the novelist Jakob Wassermann (1873–1934) to caution German young people in 1932 that not all action is good simply because it is action, that feeling is not always better than reason and discipline, and that youth is not in itself a badge of superiority.

RECASTING THE TRADITION

Expressions of disillusionment revealed something about human experience in the unsettled new world, but they were sometimes morbid and self-indulgent. Other cultural leaders sought to be more positive; the challenge was not to give vent to new anxieties but to find antidotes to them. One direction was to recast traditional categories—in the arts, in religion, in politics—to make them relevant to contemporary experience. Although not all were optimistic about human prospects, many found such a renewal of tradition to be the best hope for responding to the disarray of the postwar world.

Among artists, even those who had been prominent in the modernist avant-garde before the war now pulled back from headlong experimentation and sought to pull things back together, though on a new basis. In music, composers as different as Igor Stravinsky (1882–1971) and Paul Hindemith (1895–1963) adapted earlier styles, although often in a somewhat ironic spirit, as they sought to weave new means of expression into familiar forms. The overall tendency toward neoclassicism during the period was an effort to give musical composition a renewed basis of order.

One of the most striking responses to the anxieties of this increasingly secular age was a wave of neoorthodox religious thinking, most prominent in Protestants like the German-Swiss theologian Karl Barth (1886–1968). In his *Epistle to the Romans* (1919), Barth reacted against the liberal theology, the attempt to marry religious categories to secular progress, that had become prominent by the later nineteenth century. The war, especially, had seemed to shatter the liberal notion that the hand of God was at work in history, and Barth emphasized the radical cleft between God and our human, historical world, sunken in sin. Recalling the arguments of Augustine and Luther, he portrayed humanity as utterly lost, capable only of a difficult relationship with God, through faith, grace, and revelation.

With democracy faring poorly in parts of Europe, and with fascism and communism claiming to offer superior alternatives, some sought to make new sense of the liberal democratic tradition. In Italy, Benedetto Croce (CROH-chay) (1866–1952) agreed with critics that the old justifications, based on natural law or util-

THE WRITTEN RECORD

TRADITION AND WOMEN: THE CONDITIONS OF INDEPENDENCE

Speaking in 1928 about the situation of women writers, the British novelist Virginia Woolf raised questions that were relevant to all women seeking the opportunity to realize their potential. Indeed, her reflections about the value of difference and the need for particular traditions inspired those seeking equal opportunity for decades to come. And her question about why we know so little about women's lives in the past helped stimulate later historians to investigate the experiences of ordinary people.

Woman . . . pervades poetry from cover to cover; she is all but absent from history. . . . Occasionally an individual woman is mentioned, an Elizabeth, or a Mary; a queen or a great lady. But by no possible means could middle-class women with nothing but brains and character at their command have taken part in any one of the great movements which, brought together, constitute the historian's view of the past. . . . What one wants . . . is a mass of information; at what age did she marry; how many children had she as a rule; what was her house like; had she a room to herself; did she do the cooking; would she be likely to have a servant? All these facts lie somewhere, presumably, in parish registers and account books; the life of the average Elizabethan woman must be scattered about somewhere, could one collect it and make a book of it. It would be ambitious beyond my daring, I thought, looking about the shelves for books that were not there, to suggest to the students of those famous colleges that they should rewrite history, though I own that it often seems a little queer as it is, unreal, lop-sided. . . .

But whatever effect discouragement and criticism had upon their writing—and I believe they had a very great effect—that was unimportant compared with the other difficulty which faced them (I was still considering those early nineteenth-century novelists) when they came to set their thoughts on paper—that is that they had no tradition behind them, or one so short and partial that it was of little help. For we think back through our mothers if we are women. It is useless to go to the great men writers for help, however much one may go to them for pleasure. . . .

. . . Women have sat indoors all these millions of years, so that by this time the very walls are permeated by their creative force, which has, indeed, so overcharged the capacity of bricks and mortar that it must needs harness itself to pens and brushes and business and politics. But this creative power differs greatly from the creative power of men. And one must conclude that it would be a thousand pities if it were hindered or wasted, for it was won by centuries of the most drastic discipline, and there is nothing to take its place. It would be a thousand pities if women wrote like men, or lived like men, or looked like men. . . . Ought not education to bring out and fortify the differences rather than the similarities?

QUESTIONS

1. Why does Woolf find something "lop-sided" about the body of historical writing available in her own time, and how does she believe the problem might be overcome?
2. Why does Woolf suggest that education ought to nurture a distinctive female voice?

Source: Virginia Woolf, *A Room of One's Own* (San Diego: Harcourt Brace Jovanovich, Harvest/HBJ, 1989), pp. 43–45, 76, 87–88.

---

itarianism, were deeply inadequate, but he also became one of Europe's most influential antifascists. The most significant innovations in modern thought, he argued, show us why democratic values, institutions, and practices are precisely what we need. We human beings are free, creative agents of a history that we make as best we can, without quite understanding what will result from what we do. Humility, tolerance, and equal access to political participation are essential to the process whereby the world is endlessly remade.

The new political challenges also stimulated fresh thinking within the Marxist tradition. By showing that Marxism could encompass consciousness as well as economic relationships, the Hungarian Georg Lukács (LOO-kash) (1885–1971) invited a far more sophisticated Marxist analysis of capitalist culture than had been possible before. Lukács accented the progressive role of realistic fiction and attacked the disordered fictional world of Kafka, which seemed to abandon all hope for human understanding of the forces of history. Though more eclectic, the Institute for Social Research, founded in Frankfurt, Germany, in 1923, gave rise to an influential tradition of criticism of capitalist civilization in what came to be known as the Frankfurt

School. These innovations helped give the Marxist tradition a new lease on life in the West, even as it was developing in unforeseen ways in the Soviet Union.

THE SEARCH FOR A NEW TRADITION

While some intellectuals sought renewal from within the European tradition, others insisted that a more radical break was needed—but also that the elements for a viable new cultural tradition were available.

Reflecting on the situation of women writers in 1928, the British novelist Virginia Woolf (1882–1941) showed how women in the past had suffered from the absence of a tradition of writing by women. By the 1920s, women had made important strides, but Woolf suggested that further advance required a more self-conscious effort by women to develop their own tradition. Most basically, women needed greater financial independence so that they could have the time for scholarship, the leisure for cultivated conversation and travel, and the privacy of "a room of one's own." Woolf also envisioned a new sort of historical inquiry, focusing on how ordinary women lived their lives, that could show contemporary women where they came from—and thus deepen their sense of identity. (See the box "The Written Record: Tradition and Women: The Conditions of Independence.")

A very different effort to establish a new tradition developed in Paris, where the poet André Breton (1896–1966) spearheaded the surrealist movement in literature and the visual arts. **Surrealism** grew directly from Dada, an artistic movement that had emerged in neutral Zurich, Switzerland, and elsewhere during the war. Radically hostile to the war, Dada artists developed shocking, sometimes nihilistic forms to deal with a reality that now seemed senseless and out of control. Some made collages from gutter trash; others indulged in nonsense or relied on chance to guide their art. By the early 1920s, however, the surrealists felt it was time to create a new and deeper basis of order after the willful disordering of Dada. Having learned from Freud about the subconscious, they sought to adapt Dada's novel techniques—especially the use of chance—to gain access to the subconscious mind, which they believed contains a deeper truth, without the overlay of logic, reason, and conscious control.

But other artists, seeking to embrace the modern industrial world in a more positive spirit, found surrealism merely escapist. Among them was Walter Gropius (1883–1969), a pioneering modernist architect and leader of an influential German art school, the **Bauhaus,** during the 1920s. Gropius held that it was possible to establish new forms of culture, even a new tradition, that could be affirmative and reassuring in the face of the postwar cultural disarray. Rather than putting up familiar neoclassical or neo-Gothic buildings, "feigning a culture that has long since disappeared," society had to face up to the kind of civilization it had become—industrial, technological, efficient, urban, mass-based. If people chose carefully from among the elements of this new machine-based civilization, they could again have a culture that worked, an "integrated pattern for living."[3]

This "constructive," pro-modern impulse was particularly prominent in Germany, but it could be found all over—in the modernists of the Russian Revolution, in the French painter Fernand Léger (leh-ZHAY) (1881–1955), in the Swiss architect Le Corbusier (luh cor-BOO-zee-ay) (1887–1965). Whereas many of their contemporaries were at best ambivalent about the masses, these artists sought to bring high art and mass society together in the interests of both. And they welcomed the new patterns of life that seemed to be emerging in the modern world of mass production and fast-paced cities.

═══════════ S E C T I O N   S U M M A R Y ═══════════

- The shock of the war produced a sense of disillusionment and even decline that took many forms in the culture of the 1920s.

- Some accented the scope for recasting traditions during the 1920s, but others insisted on the need to form new traditions if the era's challenges were to be met.

- The contrast between surrealism and the German Bauhaus suggested a wider disagreement over whether Western culture was excessively rational or not rational enough.

- Whereas some, like Ortega y Gasset, were at best ambivalent about the advent of modern mass society, others welcomed it and sought to devise cultural forms that seemed more appropriate to a mass machine age.

surrealism   A literary and artistic movement that emerged in Paris in the early 1920s, it sought to explore the subconscious, which it believed to hold something liberating for human beings.

Bauhaus   An influential German art school, founded in 1919, that sought to adopt contemporary materials to develop new forms of architecture, design, and urban planning in response to the cultural uncertainty that followed World War I.

The Bauhaus Building, Dessau

The Bauhaus, an influential but controversial German art school, was established in Weimar in 1919 and then moved to Dessau in 1925. Walter Gropius, its founding director, spearheaded the design of its headquarters building. Constructed in 1925–1926, it immediately became a symbol of the Weimar modernism that some admired and others detested.   *(Vanni/Art Resource, NY)*

 # CHAPTER SUMMARY

Online Study Center ACE the Test

How did the differing priorities of Britain and France affect international relations during the 1920s?

Why did Italy turn from parliamentary democracy to fascism even after sharing in the victory in World War I?

Why, and on what basis, did sexuality, gender roles, and the "new woman" provoke so much concern during this period?

What factors made the future of the new German democracy so uncertain during the 1920s?

How did cultural and intellectual leaders differ over the place of "tradition" as they sought to suggest how to come to terms with the new situation of the 1920s?

n the wake of the most destructive war in history, questions about the new international framework, established at the peace conference of 1919–1920, were bound to be central. Although they bore the major responsibility for enforcing the peace, France and Britain seemed to drift apart as the British, preoccupied with colonial concerns, distanced themselves from politics on the Continent. Whereas France was willing to intervene actively to enforce the Versailles treaty, Britain placed greater faith in reconciliation and the new League of Nations.

The threat of leftist revolution was a major factor in the emergence of fascism in Italy, although the fascists claimed to offer a "third way," a modern alternative to *both* Marxist socialism and liberal democracy. Once Mussolini committed himself to a decisively postliberal direction, the fascists fastened upon corporativism as the basis for a new, specifically fascist form of state. Corporativism, they claimed, offered a way of transcending the class divisions accented by Marxism while also involving people in public life in more constant and direct ways than democratic institutions had made possible.

The war had seemingly enhanced opportunities for women, and a new sense of openness and possibility carried into the postwar period. During the 1920s sexuality, reproductive choices, gender roles, and family life were open to discussion as never before in the West. But in light of demographic losses and the seemingly brutalizing effects of the war, women encountered considerable pressure to conform to traditional roles of mothering and nurturing. Although the image of the liberated "new woman" was central to the era, women themselves were sometimes torn between conflicting roles and expectations.

Germany's Weimar Republic provided the central test of the bright hopes for democracy that marked the beginning of the postwar era. Yet the new German democracy was launched under the difficult circumstances of defeat, harsh peace terms, and ongoing revolutionary unrest. Moreover, the limits of political consensus in Germany meant a fragmented electorate, a complicated multiparty system, and a reliance on unstable coalition governments. Although the improved economic and diplomatic situation by 1925 enhanced the prospects for democracy, the Weimar Republic remained fragile and vulnerable.

In light of the cultural disruptions of the war and its aftermath, many intellectuals insisted that certain traditions could be recast to provide the sense of direction that people needed. But there was wide disagreement over which traditions were relevant. Whereas some pointed to religion, others fastened upon Marxism. Still others found it essential to return to more accessible forms in the arts, turning from the avant-garde experiment that had marked the immediate prewar period. At the same time, however, figures as disparate as Virginia Woolf, André Breton, and Walter Gropius insisted that the means were available to develop *new* traditions, more appropriate to the needs and possibilities of the postwar world.

LOOKING AHEAD

Despite the ferment that marked the years since World War I, Europe seemed on its way to restabilization by early 1929. Of the three most volatile of the major countries, Italy and Germany seemed to be settling down, and the Soviet Union, though embarking on an unprecedented experiment in socioeconomic engineering, was by this point looking inward, not actively seeking to export revolution. But the Great Depression, growing from the strains in the postwar economic restabilization, was just around the corner. When the decade of the 1920s is taken on its own terms, it is clear that the vitality, the renewed prosperity, and the diplomatic goodwill were all real. But so were the unresolved problems that made the 1920s a prelude to the more difficult 1930s, when the notion that postwar Europe had returned to normal came to seem but a fairy tale.

KEY TERMS

Maginot Line (p. 810)

fascism (p. 811)

Comintern (Third, or Communist, International) (p. 813)

New Economic Policy (NEP) (p. 814)

Joseph Stalin (p. 814)

Benito Mussolini (p. 817)

Matteotti murder (p. 818)

corporativism, corporative state (p. 818)

Gustav Stresemann (p. 828)

Treaty of Locarno (p. 828)

surrealism (p. 832)

Bauhaus (p. 832)

Online Study Center
Improve Your Grade Flashcards

SUGGESTED READING

Bush, Barbara. *Imperialism, Race, and Resistance: Africa and Britain, 1919–1945*. 1999. Focuses on western and southern Africa; probes the changing nature of British colonial rule in light of growing resistance during the pivotal interwar period.

De Grazia, Victoria. *Irresistible Empire: America's Advance Through Twentieth-Century Europe*. 2005. An illuminating account of the impact of the American business ethos—from Rotary Clubs to chain stores to advertising—on twentieth-century Europe, including key steps during the 1920s.

Gay, Peter. *Weimar Culture: The Outsider as Insider*. 1970. An influential study providing a good sense of the conflicting impulses—the embrace of modernity, the nostalgia for wholeness, the sense of foreboding—that made German culture so intense and vital during the 1920s.

Gentile, Emilio. *The Sacralization of Politics in Fascist Italy*. 1996. An engaging account of the rituals, symbols, and myths that, beginning in Italy during the 1920s, fed the first overtly totalitarian experiment.

Kolb, Eberhard. *The Weimar Republic*. 1988. Provides a good overall survey, then pinpoints the recent trends in research and the questions at issue among historians of the period.

Pedersen, Susan. *Family, Dependence, and the Origins of the Welfare State: Britain and France, 1914–1945*. 1993. An effective comparative study showing how concerns about gender roles and family relations helped shape discussion and policy as government assumed greater responsibility for social welfare. Detailed but readable; a landmark in the new gender history.

Peukert, Detlev. *The Weimar Republic: The Crisis of Classical Modernity*. 1992. An influential interpretive study, accenting the strains stemming from the rapid modernization of the 1920s. Stresses the loss of political legitimacy even before the onset of the Depression.

Stites, Richard. *Revolutionary Dreams: Utopian Visions and Experimental Life in the Russian Revolution*. 1989. A vivid account of the utopian aspirations that gave the new communist regime emotional force from 1917 to 1930.

Tucker, Robert C. *Stalin as Revolutionary, 1879–1929: A Study in History and Personality*. 1973. A pioneering account of Stalin's early years and rise to power, probing the sources of the elements of character and personality that helped shape his subsequent rule.

Wright, Jonathan. *Gustav Stresemann: Weimar's Greatest Statesman*. 2002. A balanced study showing that Stresemann's willingness to play by the democratic rules was important in giving Weimar democracy a chance.

NOTES

1. Benito Mussolini, speech to the Italian Chamber of Deputies, January 3, 1925, from Charles F. Delzell, ed., *Mediterranean Fascism, 1919–1945* (New York: Harper & Row, 1970), pp. 59–60.

2. Quoted in Robert G. L. Waite, *Vanguard of Nazism: The Free Corps Movement in Postwar Germany, 1918–1923* (New York: W. W. Norton, 1969), pp. 14–15.

3. Walter Gropius, *Scope of Total Architecture* (New York: Collier Books, 1962), pp. 15, 67.

27

The Tortured Decade, 1930–1939

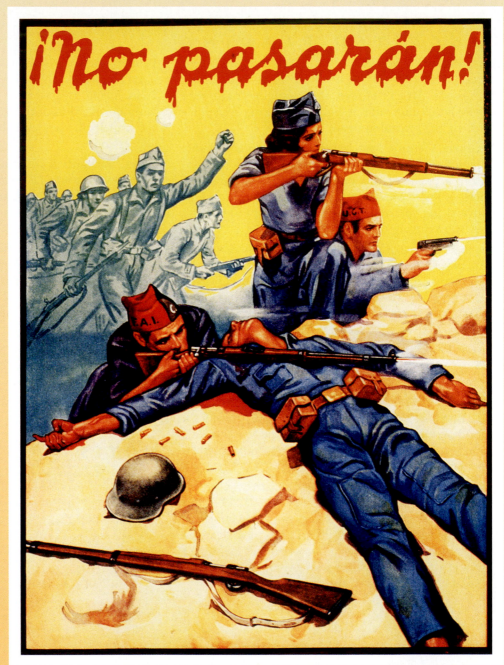

¡No pasarán! ("They shall not pass")
Defending the democratic republic during the Spanish civil war. *(Biblioteca Nacional, Madrid)*

"They shall not pass," proclaimed the charismatic Spanish communist Dolores Ibarruri (ee-bah-RUHR-ee) (1895–1989), whose impassioned speeches and radio broadcasts helped inspire the heroic defense of Madrid during the civil war that gripped Spain, and captured the attention of the world, during the later 1930s. Known as *La Pasionaria*—the passion flower—Ibarruri became a living legend for her role in defending the Spanish republic against the antidemocratic Nationalists seeking to overthrow it. But the Republican side lost, and she spent thirty-eight years in exile before returning to Spain in 1977, after the end of the military dictatorship that had resulted from the Spanish civil war.

In her effort to rally the Republican side, Ibarruri stressed the political power of women, and indeed women were prominent in the citizen militias defending Madrid and other Spanish cities. Women fought for the republic partly because it seemed to open new opportunities for them, especially as it became more radical by 1936. But just as some women welcomed the new direction, others became politically active on the opposing Nationalist side—to support the church, to combat divorce, to defend a separate sphere for women as the guardians of private life and family values.

The ideological polarization that characterized the Spanish civil war reflected the expanding reach of politics in the 1930s, when economic depression and the challenge from new, antidemocratic governments immeasurably complicated the European situation. The mechanisms used to realign the international economy after World War I had seemed effective for most of the 1920s, but by 1929 they were beginning to backfire, helping to trigger the Great Depression. During the early 1930s the economic crisis intensified sociopolitical strains all over the Western world—and beyond, heightening anti-Western feeling. In Germany the Depression helped undermine the Weimar Republic and opened the way for the new Nazi regime under Adolf Hitler, whose policies led through a series of diplomatic crises to a new European war.

German Nazism paralleled Italian fascism in its reliance on a single charismatic leader, its willingness to use violence, and its hostility to both parliamentary democracy and Marxist socialism. But Nazism emphasized racism

CHAPTER OUTLINE

THE GREAT DEPRESSION

THE STALINIST REVOLUTION IN THE SOVIET UNION

HITLER AND NAZISM IN GERMANY

FASCIST CHALLENGE AND ANTIFASCIST RESPONSE, 1934–1939

THE COMING OF WORLD WAR II, 1935–1939

KEY TERMS

collectivization
show trials
gulag
Adolf Hitler
National Socialist (Nazi) Party
Schutzstaffel (SS)
Kristallnacht (Crystal Night)

"euthanasia" program
popular front
Rome-Berlin Axis
remilitarization of the Rhineland
appeasement
Nazi-Soviet Pact

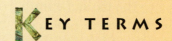

Online Study Center

This icon will direct you to interactive map and primary source activities on the website **college.hmco.com/ pic/noble5e**

and anti-Semitism in a way that Italian fascism did not, and it more radically transformed its society.

At the same time, Stalin's communist regime in the Soviet Union seemed to converge, in some ways, with these new fascist regimes—especially with German Nazism. So though they expressed widely different aims, Stalinism and Nazism are sometimes lumped together as instances of "totalitarianism." Both apparently sought control over all aspects of society, partly through the use of secret police agencies. But on closer inspection, the forms of coercion and violence in the Soviet and German regimes by the later 1930s were quite different, and the extent to which each can be understood as an instance of totalitarianism remains controversial.

Fascism, Nazism, and communism seemed able to sidestep—or surmount—the ills of the Depression, yet they stood opposed to the parliamentary democracy that had long seemed the direction of progressive political change. So the democratic movement appeared to lose its momentum in the face of the political and economic challenges of the 1930s. The defeat, by early 1939, of the democratic republic in Spain by the authoritarian Nationalists seemed to exemplify the political direction of the decade.

FOCUS QUESTIONS

With what array of measures did governments respond to the Great Depression?

Why did the Stalinist attempt to build "socialism in one country" lead to the "terror-famine" of 1932–1933 and the "great terror" of 1937–1938?

Through what measures did the Nazi regime claim to be improving the quality of the German population?

Why did the "popular front" strategy prove counterproductive in both France and Spain?

Why did the other countries not stop Hitler's Germany before it was strong enough to start a new European war in 1939?

THE GREAT DEPRESSION

With what array of measures did governments respond to the Great Depression?

If any single event can be said to have triggered the world economic crisis of the early 1930s, it was the stock market crash of October 1929 in the United States. But that crash had such an impact only because the new international economic order after World War I was extremely fragile. By October 1929, in fact, production was already declining in all the major Western countries except France.

The economies of Germany and the states of east-central Europe remained particularly vulnerable after the war, and in the increasingly interdependent economic world, their weaknesses magnified problems that started elsewhere. The crash of the U.S. stock market led to a restriction of credit in central Europe, which triggered a more general contraction in production and trade. Facing cruel dilemmas, policymakers proved unable to master the situation for the first few years of the crisis.

CAUSES OF THE DEPRESSION

Certain economic sectors, especially coal mining and agriculture, were already suffering severe problems by the mid-1920s, well before the stock market crash. British coal exports fell partly because oil and hydroelectricity were rapidly developing as alternatives. Unemployment in Britain was never less than 10 percent even in the best of times between the wars. In agriculture high prices worldwide during the war produced oversupply, which, in turn, led to a sharp drop in prices once the war was over. During the later 1920s, bumper harvests of grain and rice in many parts of the world renewed the downward pressure on prices. The result of low agricultural prices was a diminished demand for industrial goods, which impeded growth in the world economy.

Throughout the 1920s, finance ministers and central bankers had difficulty juggling the economic imbalances created by the war, centering on war debts to the United States and German reparations obligations to France, Britain, and Belgium. The strains in the system finally caught up with policymakers by 1929, when an international restriction of credit forced an end to the international economic cooperation that had been attempted throughout the decade.

The shaky postwar economic system depended on U.S. bank loans to Germany, funneled partly by international agreements but also drawn by high interest rates. By 1928, however, U.S. investors were rapidly withdrawing their capital from Germany in search of the higher returns that could be made in the booming U.S. stock market. This shift tightened credit in Germany. Then the crash of the overpriced U.S. market in October 1929 deepened the problem by forcing suddenly strapped American investors to pull still more of their funds out of Germany. This process continued over the next two years, weakening the major banks in Germany and the other countries of central Europe, which were closely tied to the German economy. In May 1931 the bankruptcy of Vienna's most powerful bank, the Credit-Anstalt, made it clear that a crisis of potentially catastrophic proportions was in progress.

Despite attempts at adjustment on the international level, fears of bank failure or currency devaluation led to runs on the banks and currencies of Germany and central Europe. To maintain the value of the domestic currency in world markets, and thereby to resist the withdrawal of capital, government policymakers raised interest rates. This measure was not sufficient to stem the capital hemorrhage, but by restricting credit still more, it further dampened domestic economic activity.

Finally, the Germans seemed to have no choice but to freeze foreign assets—that is, to cease allowing conversion of assets held in German marks to other currencies. In this atmosphere, investors seeking the safest place for their capital tried to cash in currency for gold—or for British pounds, which could then be converted to gold. Europe's flight to gold, however, soon put such pressure on the British currency that Britain was forced to devalue the pound and sever it from the gold standard in September 1931. This proved the definitive end of the worldwide system of economic exchange based on the gold standard that had gradually crystallized during the nineteenth century.

The absence of a single standard of exchange, combined with various currency restrictions, made foreign trade more difficult, thereby diminishing it further. So did the scramble for tariff protection that proved a widespread response to the developing crisis. Crucial was the U.S. Smoot-Hawley Tariff Act of June 1930, which raised taxes on imports by 50 to 100 percent,

CHRONOLOGY

October 1929	U.S. stock market crash helps trigger Great Depression
December 1929	Forced collectivization in Soviet agriculture begins
June 1930	Smoot-Hawley Tariff Act (U.S.)
May 1931	Bankruptcy of Vienna's Credit-Anstalt
January 1933	Hitler becomes German chancellor
December 1934	Assassination of Kirov
March 1935	Hitler announces rearmament
October 1935	Italy invades Ethiopia
March 1936	Germany remilitarizes the Rhineland
May 1936	Blum becomes French popular front prime minister
July 1936	Spanish civil war begins
March 1938	Third Moscow show trial; Bukharin and others convicted and executed
	Anschluss: Germany absorbs Austria
September 1938	"Appeasement": Munich conference ends Sudetenland crisis
November 1938	Crystal Night pogrom
March 1939	Dismemberment of Czechoslovakia
May 1939	Pact of Steel binds fascist Italy and Nazi Germany
August 23, 1939	Nazi-Soviet Pact
September 1, 1939	Germany invades Poland
September 3, 1939	Britain and France declare war on Germany

forcing other nations to take comparable steps. Even Britain, long a bastion of free trade, adopted a peacetime tariff for the first time in nearly a century with the Import Duties Act of 1932, which imposed a 10 percent tax on most imports.

The decline of trade spread depression throughout the world economic system. By 1933 most major European countries were able to export no more than two-thirds, and in some cases as little as one-third, of the amount they had sold in 1929. At the same time, losses from international bank failures contracted credit and purchasing power and furthered the downward spiral, until by 1932 the European economies had shrunk to a little over half their 1929 size. This was the astonishing outcome of the short-lived prosperity of the 1920s.

Unemployment in Britain
The Depression hit Britain hard—and its effects continued to be felt throughout the 1930s. These unemployed shipyard workers from Jarrow, in northeastern England, are marching to London in 1936 to present a protest petition. *(Hulton Archive/Getty Images)*

CONSEQUENCES AND RESPONSES

The Depression was essentially a radical contraction in economic activity; with less being produced and sold, demand for labor declined sharply. In Germany industrial production by early 1933 was only half what it had been in 1929, and roughly six million Germans, or one-third of the labor force, were unemployed.

Although its timing and severity varied, the Depression profoundly affected the lives of ordinary people throughout the Western world and beyond. Unemployment produced widespread malnutrition, which led, in turn, to sharp increases in such diseases as tuberculosis, scarlet fever, and rickets. The decline in employment opportunities helped produce a backlash against the ideal of the "new woman," working outside the home, which had been a prominent aspect of the new freedom of the 1920s in Germany and elsewhere. Even those men and women who hung on to jobs suffered from growing insecurity. In his aptly titled *Little Man, What Now?* (1932), the German novelist Hans Fallada (1893–1947) explored the effects of the Depression on members of the lower middle class—store clerks, shop owners, civil servants. Such people were first resentful, then resigned, as their dreams of security, of "order and cleanliness," fell apart.

During the first years of the Depression, central bankers everywhere sought to balance budgets in order to reassure investors and stabilize currencies. With economies contracting and tax revenues declining, the only way to balance the budget was to sharply reduce government spending. In addition, governments responded to the decline in exports by forcing wages down, seeking to enhance competitiveness abroad. But by cutting purchasing power at home, both these measures reinforced the slowdown in economic activity.

Economic policymakers based their responses on the "classical" economic model that had developed from the ideas of Adam Smith in the eighteenth century (see page 658). According to this model, a benign "invisible hand" ensured that a free-market price for labor, for capital, and for goods and services would produce an ongoing tendency toward economic equilibrium. A downturn in the business cycle was a normal and necessary adjustment; government interference would only upset this self-adjusting mechanism.

By 1932, however, it was clear that the conventional response was not working, and governments began seeking more actively to stimulate the economy. Although the British economist John Maynard Keynes would outline the rationale for governmental intervention in technical economic terms in 1936, governments could only experiment, and strategies varied widely. (See the box "The Written Record: The Government's Role in Managing a Free-Market Economy.") In the United States, Franklin D. Roosevelt (1882–1945) defeated the incumbent president, Herbert Hoover, in 1932 with the promise of a New Deal—a commitment to increase government spending to restore purchasing power. In fascist Italy, a state agency created to infuse capital into failing companies proved a reasonably effective basis for collaboration between government and business. In Germany, economics minister Hjalmar Schacht (1877–1970) mounted an energetic assault on the economic problem after Hitler came to power in 1933. Government measures sealed off the German mark from international

THE WRITTEN RECORD

THE GOVERNMENT'S ROLE IN MANAGING A FREE-MARKET ECONOMY

In 1936, at the height of the Depression, the British economist John Maynard Keynes published The General Theory of Employment, Interest and Money, *which proved the most influential work in economics of the twentieth century. While recognizing the advantages of a free-market economy, Keynes noted that capitalism seemed to entail a built-in tendency toward unemployment, dramatically evident in the Depression. Thus some people were attracted to socialist or statist alternatives, which might include, for example, the wholesale nationalization of industry. But Keynes insisted that a more active role for government in managing the capitalist economy could overcome the tendency toward unemployment while preserving a democratic framework and the advantages of a market economy. Government could manage the economy especially through the "socialization of investment"—absorbing money through taxation and spending it to stimulate the economy toward full employment.*

The outstanding faults of the economic society in which we live are its failure to provide for full employment and its arbitrary and inequitable distribution of wealth and incomes. . . .

. . . I conceive, therefore, that a somewhat comprehensive socialisation of investment will prove the only means of securing an approximation to full employment; though this need not exclude all manner of compromises and of devices by which public authority will co-operate with private initiative. But beyond this no obvious case is made out for a system of State Socialism which would embrace most of the economic life of the community. It is not the ownership of the instruments of production which it is important for the State to assume. If the State is able to determine the aggregate amount of resources devoted to augmenting the instruments and the basic rate of reward to those who own them, it will have accomplished all that is necessary. Moreover, the necessary measures of socialisation can be introduced gradually and without a break in the general traditions of society. . . .

. . . The central controls necessary to ensure full employment will, of course, involve a large extension of the traditional functions of government. Furthermore, the modern classical theory has itself called attention to various conditions in which the free play of economic forces may need to be curbed or guided. But there will still remain a wide field for the exercise of private initiative and responsibility. Within this field the traditional advantages of individualism will still hold good.

Let us stop for a moment to remind ourselves what these advantages are. They are partly advantages of efficiency—the advantages of decentralisation and of the play of self-interest. . . .

Whilst, therefore, the enlargement of the functions of government, involved in the task of adjusting to one another the propensity to consume and inducement to invest, would seem to a nineteenth-century publicist or to a contemporary American financier to be a terrific encroachment on individualism, I defend it, on the contrary, both as the only practicable means of avoiding the destruction of existing economic forms in their entirety and as the condition of the successful functioning of individual initiative. . . .

The authoritarian state systems of to-day seem to solve the problem of unemployment at the expense of efficiency and of freedom. It is certain that the world will not much longer tolerate the unemployment which, apart from brief intervals of excitement, is associated—and, in my opinion, inevitably associated—with present-day capitalistic individualism. But it may be possible by a right analysis of the problem to cure the disease whilst preserving efficiency and freedom.

QUESTIONS

1. Why does Keynes argue for a considerably expanded role for government in coordinating the capitalist economy?

2. In what sense is Keynes trying to save free-market capitalism in light of the Depression and the appeal of the alternatives emerging in Italy, Germany, and the Soviet Union?

Source: John Maynard Keynes, *The General Theory of Employment, Interest and Money* (New York: Harcourt, Brace & World, n.d.), pp. 372, 378–381. Reprinted by permission of J. S. Dring.

---

fluctuations, stimulated public spending—partly on rearmament—and kept wages low. By 1935 Germany was back to full employment. This success added tremendously to Hitler's popularity.

High unemployment in Norway, Sweden, and Denmark helped Social Democrats win power in all three of these Scandinavian countries by the mid-1930s. The new left-leaning governments responded to the economic

GANDHI ADVOCATES NONVIOLENCE

Mohandas Gandhi, a successful English-educated lawyer, emerged as a major force in the movement for Indian independence just after World War I. Calling first for a strategy of noncooperation with the British colonial overlords, Gandhi gradually developed a philosophy of nonviolent civil disobedience, which won widespread sympathy for the cause of Indian independence. The following excerpts from articles published in 1935 and 1939—years notable for outbreaks of violence elsewhere—explain the significance of nonviolence to Gandhi's overall strategy.

Non-violence to be a creed has to be all-pervasive. I cannot be non-violent about one activity of mine and violent about others. That would be a policy, not a life-force. That being so, I cannot be indifferent about the war that Italy is now waging against Abyssinia. . . . India has an unbroken tradition of non-violence from times immemorial. But at no time in her ancient history, as far as I know it, has it had complete non-violence in action pervading the whole land. Nevertheless, it is my unshakeable belief that her destiny is to deliver the message of non-violence to mankind. . . .

. . . India as a nation is not non-violent in the full sense of the term. . . . Her non-violence is that of the weak. . . . She lacks the ability to offer physical resistance. She has no consciousness of strength. She is conscious only of her weakness. If she were otherwise, there would be no communal problems, nor political. If she were non-violent in the consciousness of her strength, Englishmen would lose their role of distrustful conquerors. We may talk politically as we like and often legitimately blame the English rulers. But if we, as Indians, could but for a moment visualize ourselves as a strong people disdaining to strike, we should cease to fear Englishmen whether as soldiers, traders or administrators, and they to distrust us. Therefore if we became truly non-violent we should carry Englishmen with us in all we might do. In other words, we being millions would be the greatest moral force in the world, and Italy would listen to our friendly word. . . .

. . . [W]hen society is deliberately constructed in accordance with the law of non-violence, its structure will be different in material particulars from what it is today. But I cannot say in advance what the government based wholly on non-violence will be like.

What is happening today is disregard of the law of non-violence and enthronement of violence as if it were an eternal law. The democracies, therefore, that we see at work in England, America and France are only so called, because they are no less based on violence than Nazi Germany, Fascist Italy or even Soviet Russia. The only difference is that the violence of the last three is much better organized than that of the three democratic powers. Nevertheless we see today a mad race for outdoing one another in the matter of armaments. And if and when the clash comes, as it is bound to come one day, the democracies win, they will do so only because they will have the backing of their peoples who imagine that they have a voice in their own government whereas in the other three cases the peoples might rebel against their own dictatorships.

Holding the view that without the recognition of non-violence on a national scale there is no such thing as a constitutional or democratic government, I devote my energy to the propagation of non-violence as the law of our life—individual, social, political, national and international. I fancy that I have seen the light, though dimly. I write cautiously, for I do not profess to know the whole of the Law. If I know the successes of my experiments, I know also my failures. But the successes are enough to fill me with undying hope. I have often said that if one takes care of the means, the end will take care of itself. Non-violence is the means, the end for every nation is complete independence.

QUESTIONS

1. What is the difference between "strong" and "weak" nonviolence in Gandhi's thinking?
2. Why does Gandhi play down the difference between the democracies and the dictatorships of the West?

Source: Raghavan Iyer, ed., *The Essential Writings of Mahatma Gandhi* (Delhi: Oxford University Press, 1991), pp. 245–247, 262–263. Copyright © 1991 by Navajivan Trust. Reprinted by permission of Navajivan Trust.

crisis not by a frontal assault on capitalism but by pioneering the "welfare state," providing such benefits as health care, unemployment insurance, and family allowances. To pay for the new welfare safety net, the Scandinavian countries adopted a high level of progressive taxation and pared military expenditures to a minimum. The turn to a welfare state eased the imme-diate human costs of the Depression and helped restore production by stimulating demand. At the same time, the Scandinavian model attracted much admiration as a "third way" between free-market capitalism and the various dictatorial extremes.

In the other European democracies the Depression proved more intractable. Although Britain saw some recovery by the mid-1930s, it was especially the rearmament of the later 1930s, financed by borrowing, or deficit spending, that got the British economy growing again. France, less dependent on international trade, experienced the consequences of the world crisis only gradually. But by the early 1930s, France, too, was suffering its effects, which lingered to the end of the decade, helping to poison the political atmosphere.

THE IMPACT BEYOND THE WEST

The radical restriction of international trade meant a sharp decline in demand for the basic commodities that colonial and other regions exported to the industrialized West. Economic strains fed nationalist, anti-Western sentiments in colonial nations. The increase in misery among rural villagers in India, for example, spread the movement for national independence from urban elites to the rural masses. In this context Mohandas Gandhi, who had become known by 1920 for advocating noncooperation with the British, became the first leader to win a mass following throughout the Indian subcontinent (see pages 897 and 901). Encouraging villagers to boycott British goods, Gandhi accented simplicity, self-reliance, and an overall strategy of nonviolent civil disobedience based on Indian traditions. (See the box "The Global Record: Gandhi Advocates Nonviolence.")

In Japan, the strains of the Great Depression helped produce precisely the turn to imperialist violence that Gandhi sought to counter. Densely populated yet lacking raw materials, Japan was particularly dependent on international trade and reacted strongly as increasing tariffs elsewhere cut sharply into Japanese exports. Led by young army officers who were already eager for a less subservient form of Westernization, Japan turned to aggressive imperialism. As justification, the Japanese began arguing that they were spearheading a wider struggle to free East Asia from Western imperialism. (See the box "The Global Record: Japan's 'Pan-Asian' Mission" on page 887 in Chapter 28.) Attacking in 1931, Japanese forces quickly reduced Manchuria to a puppet state, but the Japanese met stubborn resistance when they began seeking to extend this conquest to the rest of China in 1937.

Japanese pressure indirectly advanced the rise of the Chinese communist movement, led by Mao Zedong (Mao Tse-tung, 1893–1976). Securing a base in the Yanan district in 1936, Mao began seeking to apply Marxism-Leninism to China through land reform and other measures to link the Communist Party elite to the Chinese peasantry. Mao was notable among those adapting Western ideas to build an indigenous movement that would at once overcome Western imperialism and create an alternative to Western liberal capitalism.

═══════ S E C T I O N   S U M M A R Y ═══════

- The new international economic interdependence after World War I entailed strains that were difficult to understand at the time—and that eventually helped produce the Great Depression.

- The effort to respond to the economic downturn through the principles of classical economics only deepened the crisis.

- The new regimes of the extreme left and right won greater prestige in some circles because they seemed

- to be surviving the global economic crisis more successfully than the capitalist democracies.

- Gradually the democratic governments began trying out more innovative, interventionist responses to the Depression.

- By restricting imports into the industrialized West, the Depression hurt the non-Western world and helped fuel anticolonialist sentiment.

THE STALINIST REVOLUTION IN THE SOVIET UNION

Why did the Stalinist attempt to build "socialism in one country" lead to the "terror-famine" of 1932–1933 and the "great terror" of 1937–1938?

Seeking to build "socialism in one country," Joseph Stalin led the Soviet Union during the 1930s through an astounding transformation that mixed achievement with brutality and terror in often tragic ways. The resulting governmental system, which gave Stalin unprecedented power, proved crucial to the outcome of the great experiment that had begun with the Russian Revolution of 1917. But whether the fateful turn of the 1930s had been implicit in the Leninist revolutionary model all along or stemmed mostly from unforeseen circumstances and Stalin's idiosyncratic personality remains uncertain.

Collectivization in Soviet Agriculture

At the "New Life" collective farm, not far from Moscow, women stand for the morning roll call. The Soviet collectivization effort of the 1930s rested in important measure on the forced mobilization of peasant women.

(Endeavor Group UK)

CRASH INDUSTRIALIZATION AND FORCED COLLECTIVIZATION

Stalin's program of rapid industrialization based on forced **collectivization** in agriculture began in earnest at the beginning of 1930. It entailed an assault on the better-off peasants, or *kulaks,* who were often sent to labor camps in Siberia while their lands were taken over by the government. The remaining peasants were herded into new government-controlled collective farms. So unpopular was this measure that many peasants simply killed their livestock or smashed their farm implements rather than have them collectivized. During the first two months of 1930, as many as fourteen million head of cattle were slaughtered, resulting in an orgy of meat eating and a shortage of draft animals. By 1934 the number of cattle in the Soviet Union was barely half what it had been in 1928.

Online Study Center **Improve Your Grade**
Primary Source: Collectivization in the Soviet Union: A Peasant's Report

Collectivization served, as intended, to squeeze from the peasantry the resources needed to finance industrialization, but it was carried out with extreme brutality. What was being squeezed was not merely a surplus—the state's extractions cut into subsistence. So while Soviet agricultural exports increased after 1930,

collectivization Soviet program under Stalin that reshaped agriculture by forcing peasants into government-controlled collective farms in order to better finance rapid industrialization.

large numbers of peasants starved to death. The great famine that developed during 1932–1933 resulted in between five million and six million deaths, over half of them in Ukraine. This "terror-famine" went unrecorded in the Soviet press, and the Soviets refused help from international relief agencies.

By 1937 almost all Soviet agriculture took place on collective farms—or on state farms set up in areas not previously under agriculture. However, restrictions on private plots and livestock ownership were eased slightly after 1933, and partly as a result, agriculture rebounded and living standards began to rise. By the late 1930s, moreover, significant increases in industrial output had established solid foundations in heavy industry, including the bases for military production.

In pursuing this program, Stalin played up the great historical drama surrounding the Soviet experiment, with its incredible targets and goals. Suggestions by some that the pace could not be maintained only proved grist for Stalin's mill: "No, comrades," he told a workers' conference early in 1931, "the tempo must not be reduced. On the contrary, we must increase it as much as is within our powers and capabilities. . . . To slow the tempo would mean falling behind. And those who fall behind get beaten. . . . Do you want our socialist fatherland to be beaten and to lose its independence? . . . We are fifty or a hundred years behind the advanced countries. We must make good this distance in ten years. Either we do this or they will crush us."[1]

Soviet propaganda, including art in the official socialist realist style, glorified the achievements of the new Soviet industrial and agricultural workers. "Stakhanovism (stah-KAH-nov-izm)," named for a coal miner who had heroically exceeded his production quota in 1935, became the term for the prodigious economic achievements that the regime valued as it proclaimed the superiority of the communist system.

But whatever its successes, this forced development program created many inefficiencies and entailed tremendous human costs. The Soviet Union could probably have done at least as well, with much less suffering, through other strategies of industrial development. Moreover, Stalin's program departed from certain socialist principles—egalitarianism in wages, for example—that the regime had taken very seriously during the late 1920s. By 1931, bureaucratic managers, concerned simply with maximizing output, were openly favoring workers in certain industries. Collective bargaining and the right to strike had vanished from the workers' arsenal.

FROM OPPOSITION TO TERROR, 1932–1938

Stalin's radical course, with its brutality and uncertain economic justification, quickly provoked opposition. During the summer of 1932, a group centered on M. N. Ryutin (ree-YOU-tin) (1890–1937) circulated among party leaders a two-hundred-page tract calling for a retreat from Stalin's economic program and a return to democracy within the party. It advocated readmitting those who had been expelled—including Stalin's archenemy, Leon Trotsky. Moreover, the document strongly condemned Stalin personally, describing him as "the evil genius of the Russian Revolution, who, motivated by a personal desire for power and revenge, brought the Revolution to the verge of ruin."[2]

Stalin promptly had Ryutin and his associates ousted from the party, then arrested and imprisoned. But especially as the international situation grew menacing during the 1930s, Stalin became ever more preoccupied with the scope for further opposition. Both Germany and Japan exhibited expansionist aims that might threaten Soviet territories. Trotsky from exile might work with foreign agents and Soviet dissidents to sabotage the Soviet development effort.

In December 1934 the assassination of Sergei Kirov (KIH-roff) (1888–1934), party leader of Leningrad (the former Petrograd), indicated the potential for violence. But whether Stalin was actually responsible for the assassination, or simply felt vulnerable because of it, remains uncertain. In any case, the determination to root out "wreckers," those assumed to be sabotaging the great Soviet experiment, led gradually to purges, **show trials,** and even a kind of terror, with several categories

of citizens vulnerable to arbitrary arrest by the secret police. By the time it wound down, early in 1939, this "great terror" had significantly changed the communist regime—and Soviet society. But though the bare facts are clear, what to make of them is not.

In the three Moscow show trials, which took place during a twenty-month period from 1936 to 1938, noted Bolsheviks, including Nikolai Bukharin and major functionaries such as Genrikh Yagoda, recently removed as chief of the secret police, confessed to a series of sensational trumped-up charges: that they had been behind the assassination of Kirov, that they would like to have killed Stalin, that they constituted an "anti-Soviet, Trotskyite center," spying for Germany and Japan and preparing to sabotage Soviet industry in the event of war. Almost all the accused, including Bukharin and others who had been central to the 1917 revolution, were convicted and executed. Soviet authorities did not dare risk public trial for the few who refused, even in the face of torture, to play their assigned roles and confess. Among them was Ryutin, who was shot in secret early in 1937.

During 1937 a purge wiped out much of the top ranks of the army, with half the entire officer corps shot or imprisoned in response to unfounded charges of spying and treason. The Communist Party underwent several purges, culminating in the great purge of 1937 and 1938. Of the roughly two thousand delegates to the 1934 congress of the Communist Party, over half were shot during the next few years. The most prominent were especially vulnerable. Indeed, 114 of the 139 central committee members elected at the 1934 party congress had been shot or sent to a forced labor camp by 1939.

The first such camps were established under Lenin in 1918, during the civil war, but the camp system expanded exponentially under Stalin during the 1930s, coming to play a major economic role. This network of forced labor camps—there were eventually at least 476 of them—became known as the **gulag,** originally an acronym for "main camp administration."

Although considerable controversy remains over the number of victims of the Stalinist revolution, the totals are staggering. According to one influential high-end estimate, 8.5 million of the approximately 160 million people in the Soviet Union were arrested during 1937 and 1938, and of these perhaps 1 million were executed by shooting. Half of those belonging to the Communist Party—1.2 million people—were arrested; of these, 600,000 were executed, and most of the rest died in gulag camps. Altogether, the terror surrounding the several purges resulted in as many as 8 million deaths. Estimates of the death toll from all of Stalin's

show trials Trials staged for ideological and propaganda reasons in the USSR.

gulag An acronym for "main camp administration," it was a network of forced labor camps for political prisoners in the Soviet Union.

policies of the 1930s, including the forced collectiviza-
tions, range as high as 20 million.

COMMUNISM AND STALINISM

What was going on in this bizarre and lethal combination of episodes? Obviously Stalinism was one possible outcome of Leninist communism, but was it the
logical, even the inevitable, outcome? Leninism had
accented centralized authority and the scope for human will to force events, so it may have created a
framework in which Stalinism was likely to emerge.
Yet Stalin's personal idiosyncrasies and growing para-
noia seem to have been crucial for the Soviet system to
develop as it did. But though he ended up the
regime's undisputed leader, Stalin was part of a wider
dynamic.

It was long assumed that Stalin was pursuing a coordinated policy of terror to create a system of total
control. Yet recent research has shown that he was often merely improvising, responding to a situation that
had become chaotic, out of control, as the Communists tried to carry through a revolution in a backward
country. No one had ever attempted this sort of forced
industrialization based on a centrally planned economy. At once idealistic, inexperienced, and suspicious,
the regime's leaders really believed that failures must be
due to sabotage—that "wreckers" were seeking to undermine the heroic Soviet experiment. Moreover, though
Stalin tended to blow them out of proportion, there
were genuine threats to the Soviet regime and his own
leadership by the mid-1930s.

Whereas the terror was long viewed as almost random, it is now clearer that those in the upper and middle
reaches of the Soviet system were the most vulnerable.
Top officials encouraged ordinary workers to provide information about plant managers and local party officials
who seemed incompetent or corrupt. And whether to
serve the revolution or to vent personal resentments,
such workers often took the initiative in denouncing
their superiors, thereby playing important roles in the
dynamic that developed.

But what explains the "confessions" that invariably
resulted from the bizarre show trials? The accused
sometimes succumbed to torture, and to threats to
their families. But some, at least, offered false confessions because they believed that in doing so they were
still serving the communist cause. All along, the revolution had required a willingness to compromise personal scruples, including "bourgeois" concerns about
personal honor and dignity. Even though false, these
confessions could help the communist regime ward off
the genuine dangers it faced. So in confessing, the accused would be serving the long-term cause, which
they believed to be bigger than Stalin and the issues of
the moment. What some could not see—or admit—was
that the triumph of Stalinism was fatally compromising the original revolutionary vision.

Although much was unplanned and even out of
control, Stalin's ultimate responsibility for the lethal
dynamic of the later 1930s is undeniable. At the height
of the terror, he personally approved lists for execution,
and he took advantage of the chain of events to crush
all actual or imagined opposition. By 1939 Stalin loyalists constituted the entire party leadership.

Even as some turned away in disillusionment or despair, others found the regime's ruthlessness in rooting
out its apparent enemies evidence of its ongoing revolutionary purpose. And whereas Stalin was not a charismatic leader like Hitler or Mussolini, he was coming for
many to embody the ongoing promise of the communist experiment.

═══ S E C T I O N　 S U M M A R Y ═══

- Forced collectivization was a way—ultimately a brutal way—of extracting the agricultural surplus from
the peasantry to finance rapid industrialization in
the Soviet Union.

- The *gulag,* the network of forced labor camps, expanded dramatically with the Stalinist revolution of
the 1930s—and especially with the "great terror" of
1937–1938.

- Soviet leaders really believed that failures must be
due to sabotage—that "wreckers" were seeking to
undermine the heroic communist experiment.

- Although Stalin's ultimate responsibility is clear, the
great terror of 1937–1938 grew not from some conscious design but from a momentum that spun out
of control.

- Stemming from an effort to root out "wreckers," the
terror especially affected those in the upper and
middle reaches of the Soviet system.

HITLER AND NAZISM IN GERMANY

Through what measures did the Nazi regime claim to be improving the quality of the German population?

Beset with problems from the start, the Weimar Republic lay gravely wounded by 1932. Various antidemocratic groups competed to replace it. The winner was the Nazi movement, led by **Adolf Hitler,** who became chancellor in January 1933. It was especially Hitler's new regime in Germany that made the 1930s so tortured, for Hitler not only radically transformed German society but fundamentally altered the power balance in Europe.

Nazism took inspiration from Italian fascism, but Hitler's regime proved more dynamic—and more troubling—than Mussolini's. Nazism was not conventionally revolutionary, in the sense of mounting a frontal challenge to the existing socioeconomic order. Some of its themes were traditionalist and even antimodernizing. But in the final analysis Nazism was anything but conservative. Indeed, it constituted a direct assault on what had long been held as the best of Western civilization.

THE EMERGENCE OF NAZISM AND THE CRISIS OF THE WEIMAR REPUBLIC

The **National Socialist German Workers' (Nazi) Party** (NSDAP) emerged from the turbulent situation in Munich just after the war. A center of leftist agitation, the city also became a hotbed of the radical right, nurturing a number of new nationalist, militantly anticommunist political groups. One of them, a workers' party founded under the aegis of the right-wing Thule Society early in 1919, attracted the attention of Adolf Hitler, who soon gave it his personal stamp.

Adolf Hitler (1889–1945) had been born not German but Austrian, the son of a middling government official. As a young man he had gone to Vienna, hoping to become an artist, but he failed to gain admission to the Viennese Academy of Fine Arts. By 1913 he had become a German nationalist hostile to the multinational Habsburg empire, and he emigrated to Germany to escape service in the Austrian army. He was not opposed to military service per se, however, and

when war broke out in 1914, he immediately volunteered for service in the German army.

Corporal Hitler experienced firsthand the fighting at the front and, as a courier, performed bravely and effectively. Indeed, he was in a field hospital being treated for gas poisoning when the war ended. Although his fellow soldiers considered him quirky and introverted, Hitler found the war experience crucial; it was during the war, he said later, that he "found himself."

Following his release from the hospital, Hitler worked for the army in routine surveillance of extremist groups in Munich. In this role he joined the infant German Workers' Party late in 1919. When his first political speech at a rally in February 1920 proved a resounding success, Hitler began to believe he could play a special political role. From this point, he gradually developed the confidence to lead a new nationalist, anticommunist, and anti-Weimar movement.

But Hitler jumped the gun in November 1923 when, with Erich Ludendorff at his side, he led the Beer Hall Putsch in Munich, an abortive attempt to launch a march on Berlin to overthrow the republic. On trial after this effort failed, Hitler gained greater national visibility as he denounced the Versailles treaty and the Weimar government. Still, *Mein Kampf* (*My Battle*), the political tract that he wrote while in prison during 1924, sold poorly. To most, Hitler was simply a right-wing rabble-rouser whose views were not worth taking seriously.

His failure in 1923 convinced Hitler that he should exploit the existing political system, but not challenge it directly, in his quest for power on the national level. Yet Hitler did not view the NSDAP as just another political party, playing by the same rules as the others within the Weimar system. Thus, most notably, the Nazi Party maintained a paramilitary arm, the *Sturmabteilung* (SA), which provoked a good deal of antileftist street violence. Still, the Nazis remained confined to the margins of national politics even as late as 1928, when they attracted only 2.6 percent of the vote in elections to the Reichstag.

The onset of the economic depression by the end of 1929 produced problems that the Weimar democracy could not handle—and that radically changed the German political framework. The pivotal issue was unemployment insurance, which became a tremendous financial burden for the government as unemployment grew. The governing coalition fell apart over the issue in March 1930, and this proved to be the end of normal parliamentary government in Weimar Germany.

Adolf Hitler   German dictator whose aggressive foreign policy led to World War II and whose policies of anti-Semitism and racial purity led to the murder of millions.

National Socialist (Nazi) Party   The political party that grew from the movement that German dictator Adolf Hitler made his vehicle to power.

President Paul von Hindenburg called on Heinrich Brüning (1885–1970), an expert on economics from the Catholic Center Party, to become chancellor. Brüning was to spearhead a hard-nosed, deflationary economic program intended to stimulate exports by lowering prices. Like most of the German middle classes, Brüning feared inflation, disliked unemployment insurance, and believed that Germany could not afford public works projects to pump up demand—the obvious alternative to his deflationary policy. But when he presented his program to the Reichstag, he encountered opposition not only from those on the left but also from conservatives, eager to undermine the republic altogether. As a result, Brüning could get no parliamentary majority. Rather than resigning or seeking a compromise, he invoked Article 48, the emergency provision of the Weimar constitution, which enabled him to govern under presidential decree.

When this expedient provoked strenuous protests, Brüning dissolved the Reichstag and scheduled new elections for September 1930. At this point there was still some chance that a more conciliatory tack would have enabled the chancellor to build a new parliamentary majority—and save parliamentary government. The Socialists were seeking to be more cooperative in the face of the deepening economic crisis and the prospect of new parliamentary elections, which, under these difficult circumstances, seemed to invite trouble. However, Brüning persisted, believing the electorate would vindicate him.

In fact, the outcome of the elections of September 1930 was disastrous—for Brüning, and ultimately for Germany as well. While two of the democratic, pro-Weimar parties lost heavily, the two extremes, the Communists and the Nazis, improved their totals considerably. Indeed, this was a major breakthrough for the Nazis, whose share of the vote jumped from 2.6 percent to 18.3 percent of the total.

Brüning continued to govern, still relying on President Hindenburg and Article 48 rather than majority support in the Reichstag. But his program of raising taxes and decreasing government spending failed to revive the economy. Meanwhile, the growth of the political extremes helped fuel an intensification of the political violence and street fighting that had bedeviled the Weimar Republic from the beginning. As scuffles between Nazis and Communists sometimes approached pitched battles, the inability of the government to keep order further damaged the prestige of the republic. And as the crisis deepened in 1932, conservative fears of a Marxist outcome played into Hitler's hands.

By this point, conservatives close to Hindenburg sensed the chance to replace the fragmented parliamentary system with some form of authoritarian government. A new, tougher regime would not only attack the economic crisis but also stiffen governmental resistance against the apparent threat from the extreme left. In May 1932 those advisers finally persuaded Hindenburg to dump Brüning, and two of them, Franz von Papen (PAH-pin) (1878–1969) and General Kurt von Schleicher (SHLY-shur) (1882–1934), each got a chance to govern in the months that followed. But neither succeeded, partly because of the daring strategy Hitler adopted.

When, following the ouster of Brüning, new elections were held in July 1932, the Nazis won 37.3 percent of the vote and the Communists 14.3 percent. Together, the two extremes controlled a majority of the seats in the Reichstag. Hitler, as the leader of what was now the Reichstag's largest party, refused to join any coalition—unless he could lead it as chancellor. Meanwhile, the authoritarian conservatives around President Hindenburg wanted to take advantage of the Nazis' mass support for antidemocratic purposes. Finally, in January 1933, with government at an impasse, Papen lined up a new coalition that he proposed to Hindenburg to replace Schleicher's government. Hitler would be chancellor, Papen himself vice chancellor, and Alfred Hugenberg (1865–1951), the leader of the Nationalist Party, finance minister. For months, Hindenburg had resisted giving Hitler a chance to govern, but he felt this combination might work to establish a parliamentary majority, to box out the left and to contain Nazism. So Hindenburg named Hitler Germany's chancellor on January 30, 1933.

It became clear virtually at once that the outcome of the crisis was a dramatic change of regime, the triumph of Hitler and Nazism. But though the Nazis had always wanted to destroy the Weimar Republic, they were not directly responsible for overthrowing it. The rise of Nazism was more a symptom than a cause of the crisis of Weimar democracy.

In one sense, the Weimar Republic collapsed from within, largely because the German people disagreed fundamentally about priorities after the war—and then again with the onset of the Depression. Thus the new democracy produced unstable government based on multiparty coalitions, and it fell into virtual paralysis when faced with the economic crisis by 1930. At the same time, however, those around Hindenburg were particularly quick to begin undercutting democratic government in 1930, as the economic crisis seemed to intensify the threat from the extreme left.

With unemployment growing during the first years of the 1930s, both the Nazis and the Communists gained electoral support, but the Germans voting for the Nazis were not simply those most threatened economically. Nor did the Nazi Party appeal primarily to the uneducated or socially marginal. Rather, the party served as a focus of opposition for those alienated from the Weimar Republic itself. Although the Nazis did relatively poorly among Catholics and industrial workers, they put together a broad, fairly diverse base of electoral support, ranging from artisans and small shopkeepers to university students and civil servants. But though Hitler was clearly anti-Weimar, anticommunist, and anti-Versailles, his positive program remained vague; those who voted for the Nazis were not clear what they might be getting. In light of economic depression and political impasse, however, it seemed time to try something new.

THE CONSOLIDATION OF HITLER'S POWER, 1933–1934

When Hitler became chancellor, it was not obvious that a change of regime was beginning. Like his predecessors, he could govern only with the president's approval, and governmental institutions like the army, the judiciary, and the diplomatic corps, though hardly bastions of democracy, were not in the hands of committed Nazis. But even though an element of caution and cultivated ambiguity remained, a revolution quickly began, creating a new regime, the Third Reich.

On February 23, just weeks after Hitler became chancellor, a fire engulfed the Reichstag building in Berlin. It was set by a young Dutch communist acting on his own, but it seemed to suggest that a communist uprising was imminent. This sense of emergency gave Hitler an excuse to restrict civil liberties and imprison leftist leaders, including the entire Communist parliamentary delegation. Even in this atmosphere of crisis, the Nazis could not win a majority in the Reichstag elections of March 5. But support from the Nationalists and the Catholic Center Party enabled the Nazis to win Reichstag approval for an enabling act granting Hitler the power to make laws on his own for the next four years, bypassing both the Reichstag and the president.

Although the Weimar Republic was never formally abolished, the laws that followed fundamentally altered government, politics, and public life in Germany. The other parties were either outlawed or persuaded to dissolve, so that in July 1933 the Nazi Party was declared the only legal party. When President Hindenburg died in August 1934, the offices of chancellor and president were merged, and Germany had just one leader, Adolf Hitler, holding unprecedented power. Members of the German armed forces now swore loyalty to him personally.

Hitler and Children
Adolf Hitler was often portrayed as the friend of children. This photograph accompanied a story for an elementary school reader that described how Hitler, told it was this young girl's birthday, picked her from a crowd of well-wishers to treat her "to cake and strawberries with thick, sweet cream." *(Bayerisches Staatsbibliotek, Munich)*

During this period of power consolidation, Hitler acted decisively but carefully, generally accenting normalization. To be sure, his methods occasionally gave conservatives pause, most notably when he had several hundred people murdered in the "blood purge" of June 30, 1934. But this purge was directed especially against the SA, led by Ernst Röhm (1887–1934), who had had pretensions of controlling the army. His removal seemed evidence that Hitler was taming the radical elements in his own movement. In fact, however, this purge led to the ascendancy of the **Schutzstaffel (SS),** the select Nazi elite, led by Heinrich Himmler (1900–1945). Linked to the Gestapo, the secret political police, the SS became the institutional basis for the most troubling aspects of Nazism.

HITLER'S WORLDVIEW AND THE DYNAMICS OF NAZI PRACTICE

In achieving the chancellorship and in expanding his power thereafter, Hitler showed himself an adept politician, but he was hardly a mere opportunist, seeking to amass power for its own sake. Power was only the instrument for the grandiose transformation he believed necessary. And the most troubling aspects of Nazism, from personal dictatorship to the eventual effort to exterminate the Jews of Europe, stemmed from an overall vision of the world that radiated from Hitler himself. It had coalesced in Hitler's mind by about 1924.

This is not to say that Hitler was an original thinker or that his ideas were true—or even plausible. But he sought to make systematic sense of things, and the most disturbing features of his political activity stemmed directly from the resulting worldview. His most committed followers shared certain of his ideas, although fanatical loyalty to Hitler himself was more important for some of them. The central components of Hitler's thinking—geopolitics, biological racism, anti-Semitism, and Social Darwinism—were by no means specifically German. They could be found all over the Western world by the early twentieth century.

Geopolitics claimed to offer a scientific understanding of world power relationships based on geographical determinism. In his writings of the 1920s, Hitler warned that Germany faced imminent decline unless it confronted its geopolitical limitations. To remain fully sovereign in the emerging new era of global superpowers like the United States, Germany would have to act quickly to expand its territory. Otherwise it would end up like Switzerland or the Netherlands.

For decades German imperialists had argued about whether Germany was better advised to seek overseas colonies or to expand its reach in Europe. As Hitler saw it, Germany's failure to make a clear choice had led to its defeat in World War I. Now choice was imperative, and current geopolitical thinking suggested the direction for expansion. Far-flung empires relying on naval support were said to be in decline. The future lay with land-based states—unified, geographically contiguous, with the space necessary for self-sufficiency. By expanding eastward into Poland and the Soviet Union, Germany could conquer the living space, or *Lebensraum,* necessary for agricultural-industrial balance—and ultimately for self-sufficiency.

Though limited and mechanistic, this geopolitical way of thinking is at least comprehensible, in light of the German vulnerabilities that had become evident during World War I. The other three strands of Hitler's worldview were much less plausible, though each had become prominent during the second half of the nineteenth century. Biological racism insisted that built-in racial characteristics determine what is most important about any individual. Anti-Semitism went beyond racism in claiming that Jews had played, and continued to play, a special and negative role in history. The fact that the Jews were dispersed and often landless indicated that they were different—and parasitical. Finally, Social Darwinism, especially in its German incarnation, accented the positive role of struggle—not among individuals, as in a prominent American strand, but among racial groups.

The dominant current of racist thinking labeled the "Aryans" as healthy, creative, superior. Originally the Sanskrit term for "noble," *Aryan* gradually came to indicate the ancient language assumed to have been the common source of the modern Indo-European languages. An Aryan was simply a speaker of one of those languages. By the late nineteenth century, however, the term had become supremely ill defined. In much racist thinking, Germanic peoples were somehow especially Aryan, but race mixing had produced impurity—and thus degeneration. Success in struggle with the other races was the ultimate measure of vitality, the only proof of racial superiority for the future.

Hitler brought these themes together by emphasizing that humanity is not special, but simply part of nature, subject to the same laws of struggle and selection as the other animal species. Humanitarian ideals are thus dangerous illusions. As he put it to a group of officer cadets in 1944:

> Nature is always teaching us . . . that she is governed by the principle of selection: that victory is to the strong and that the weak must go to the wall. She teaches us that what may seem cruel to us, because it affects us personally or because we have been brought up in ignorance of her laws, is nevertheless often essential if a higher way of life

Schutzstaffel (SS) Specially selected Nazi elite, entrusted with the most sensitive ideological tasks of the Nazi regime—and responsible for many of its worst atrocities.

is to be attained. Nature . . . knows nothing of the notion of humanitarianism, which signifies that the weak must at all costs be protected and preserved even at the expense of the strong.

Nature does not see in weakness any extenuating reasons . . . on the contrary, weakness calls for condemnation.[3]

To Hitler, the Jews were not simply another of the races involved in this endless struggle. Rather, as landless parasites, they embodied the principles—from humanitarianism to class struggle—that were antithetical to the healthy natural struggle among racial groups. "Jewishness" was bound up with the negative, critical intellect that dared suggest things ought to be not natural but just, even that it was up to human beings to change the world, to make it just. The Jews were the virus keeping the community from a healthy natural footing. Marxist communism, embodying divisive class struggle as well as utopian humanitarian ideals, was fundamentally Jewish.

The central features of Nazism in practice, from personal dictatorship to the extermination of the Jews, followed from Hitler's view of the world. First, the racial community must organize itself politically for this ceaseless struggle. Individuals are but instruments for the success of the racial community. Parliamentary democracy, reflecting short-term individual interests, fosters selfish materialism and division, thereby weakening that community. The political order must rest instead on a charismatic leader, united with the whole people through bonds of common blood.

NAZI AIMS AND GERMAN SOCIETY

Although Hitler's worldview provided the underlying momentum for the Nazi regime, it did not specify a consistent program that could be implemented all at once. Moreover, the regime sometimes found it necessary to adopt short-term expedients that conflicted with its long-term aims. Thus it was possible for Germans living under Nazi rule in the 1930s to embrace aspects of Nazism in practice without seeing where it was all leading.

To create a genuine racial community, or *Volksgemeinschaft*, it was necessary to unify society and instill Nazi values, thereby making the individual feel part of the whole—and ultimately an instrument to serve the whole. This entailed more or less forced participation in an array of Nazi groupings, from the Women's Organization to the Hitler Youth, from the Labor Front to the Strength Through Joy leisure-time organization. Common participation meant shared experiences such as weekend hikes and a weekly one-dish meal. Even the most ordinary, once-private activities took on a public or political dimension. Moreover, the Nazis devised un-precedented ways to stage-manage public life, using rituals like the Hitler salute, symbols like the swastika, new media like radio and film, and carefully orchestrated party rallies—all in an effort to foster this sense of belonging. (See the feature "The Visual Record: Film as Propaganda.")

Online Study Center **Improve Your Grade**
Primary Source: Nazi Recreation: Summer Camps for Girls

The Response of the German People   The Nazi regime enjoyed considerable popular support, but even after Hitler was well entrenched in power, most Germans did not grasp the regime's deeper dynamic. Some welcomed the sense of unity, the feeling of belonging and participation, especially after what had seemed the alienation and divisiveness of the Weimar years. Moreover, Hitler himself was immensely popular, partly because of his personal charisma, partly because his apparently decisive leadership was a welcome departure from the near paralysis of the Weimar parliamentary system. But most important, before the coming of war in 1939, he seemed to go from success to success, surmounting the Depression and repudiating the major terms of the hated Versailles treaty.

Hitler's propaganda minister, Joseph Goebbels (1897–1945), played on these successes to create a "Hitler myth," which made Hitler seem at once a hero and a man of the people, even the embodiment of healthy German ideals against the excesses and corruption that could be attributed to the Nazi Party. This myth became central to the Nazi regime, but it merely provided a façade behind which the real Hitler could pursue partially hidden, longer-term aims. These aims were not publicized directly because the German people did not seem ready for them. In this sense, then, support for Hitler and his regime was broad but shallow during the 1930s.

Moreover, resistance increased as the regime became more intrusive. Youth gangs actively opposed the official Hitler Youth organization as it became more overbearing and militaristic by the late 1930s. But people resisted especially by minimizing their involvement with the regime, retreating into the private realm, in response to the Nazi attempt to make everything public.

Did such people feel constantly under threat of the Gestapo, the secret police? In principle, the Gestapo could interpret the will of the *Führer*, or leader, and decide whether any individual citizen was "guilty" or not. And the Gestapo was not concerned about due process; on occasion it simply bypassed the regular court system. But the Gestapo did not terrorize Germans at random. Its victims were generally members of specific groups, people suspected of active opposition, or people who protected those the Gestapo had targeted.

Film as Propaganda

One of the extraordinary pieces of evidence from the Nazi period is *Triumph of the Will*, a documentary film on the sixth Nazi Party rally, which took place from September 4 to 10, 1934, in the historic city of Nuremberg, by this time the official site for such party rallies. Directed by a talented young woman named Leni Riefenstahl (1902–2003), *Triumph of the Will* has long been recognized as one of the most compelling propaganda films ever made. What can we learn from this film about how the Nazis understood and used propaganda? What was the Nazi regime trying to convey in sponsoring the film, with the particular images it contained?

A sense of the scope for political propaganda was one of the defining features of the Nazi movement virtually from its inception. In his quest for power Hitler allotted an especially significant role to his future propaganda minister, Joseph Goebbels. Both Hitler and Goebbels saw that new media and carefully orchestrated events might be used to shape the political views of masses of people.

The Nazi Party held the first of what would become annual conventions in Nuremberg in 1927. From the start, these meetings were rallies of the faithful, intended to give the Nazi movement a sense of cohesion and common purpose; but they increasingly became carefully staged propaganda spectacles, with banners and searchlights, parades and speeches. When, by 1934, the regime had completed the task of immediate power consolidation, it seemed time to seize the potential of the film medium to carry the spectacle beyond those present in Nuremberg. The intention to make a film thus influenced the staging of the 1934 rally. Film would transform the six-day event into a single potent work of art.

When Hitler came to power, Goebbels, as propaganda minister, assumed control of the German film industry, and he was particularly jealous of his prerogatives in this sphere. If there was to be a film of one of the Nuremberg rallies, he assumed that he would be in charge. So he objected strenuously when Hitler decided that Riefenstahl, who was not even a party member, should film the 1934 rally.

Already popular as an actress, Riefenstahl had established her own filmmaking company in 1931, before she turned 30. Her first film won the admiration of Hitler, who sought her out and eventually proposed that she direct the film of the party rally.

Although she was an artist with no special interest in politics, Riefenstahl, like many Germans, believed at this point that Hitler might be able to revive Germany's fortunes. So despite considerable reluctance, she bowed to Hitler's persistence and agreed to do the film—though only after she was guaranteed final control over editing. Her relations with Goebbels remained strained, but Hitler continued to support her as she made *Triumph of the Will*.

Riefenstahl developed the 107-minute film by editing 61 hours of footage that covered everything from Hitler's arrival and motorcade to the closing parades and speeches. As depicted on film, the party rally does not convey an overt ideological message. We hear Hitler simply trumpeting German renewal, not attacking Jews or glorifying conquest. Most striking in Riefenstahl's portrayal are the unity and epic monumentality that Nazism had apparently brought to Germany thanks to Hitler's leadership.

The film opens as Hitler emerges from dramatic cloud formations to arrive by airplane, descending from the sky like a god. He appears throughout the film as an almost superhuman figure, even, as in the shot shown here, as inspired, possessed, uncanny. Above all, he is a creator who shapes reality by blending will and art, forging masses of anonymous individuals into one people, one racial community, ready for anything. Those individuals seem, from one perspective, to lose their individuality in a monolithic mass, as in the shot of the parade grounds. But their sense of involvement in grandiose purposes charges them emotionally, even gives them a kind of ecstasy. The symbols, the massed banners, the ritualistic show of conformity, all strengthened this sense of participation in the new people's community. But unity and community were not ends in themselves; the film exalted military values and depicted a disciplined society organized for war.

Triumph of the Will extended participation in the spectacle to those who were not actually present in Nuremberg. Because the film chiseled the sprawling event into a work of art, seeing the film was in some ways more effective than being there. The Nazis looked for every means possible to involve the whole society in ritualistic spectacles that could promote a sense of belonging and unity. In addition to film, they made effective use of radio, even subsidizing the purchase of radio sets, or "people's

. . . and the Disciplined, Tightly Knit Community of Followers *(Both photos from the Museum of Modern Art/Film Stills Archive)*

As seen in *Triumph of the Will,* the Leader . . .

receivers." Such new media were to help ordinary Germans feel a more meaningful kind of belonging than Weimar democracy made possible. But this was only an emotional involvement, not the active participation of free citizens invited to make rational choices.

Triumph of the Will had its premiere in March 1935, with Hitler in the audience. It won several prizes in Germany and abroad but enjoyed only mixed success with the German public, especially outside the large cities. For some, it was altogether too artistic, and the Nazi regime did not use it widely for overt propaganda purposes. Still, the Nazis commissioned no other film about Hitler, for

Triumph of the Will captured the way he wanted to be seen. Indeed, Hitler praised the film as an "incomparable glorification of the power and beauty of our Movement."

QUESTIONS

1. Why did Hitler feel it so important to film a Nazi party rally—and even to plan the rally with the filming in mind?

2. What relationship between Hitler and the Nazi movement does *Triumph of the Will* convey?

Online Study Center
Improve Your Grade Visual Record Activities

Women, Family, and Reproduction   More-over, changes and contradictions in Nazi goals allowed considerable space for personal choice. During the struggle for power, the Nazis had emphasized the woman's role as wife and mother and deplored the on-going emancipation of women. Once Hitler came to power, concerns about unemployment reinforced these views. Almost immediately Hitler's government began offering interest-free loans to help couples set up house-keeping if the woman agreed to leave the labor force. Such efforts to increase the German birthrate reinforced the emphasis on child rearing in Nazi women's organi-zations. Nonetheless, the size of the family continued to decrease in Germany as elsewhere in the industrial-ized world during the 1930s.

Beginning in 1936, when rapid rearmament began to produce labor shortages, the regime did an about-face and began seeking to attract women back to the workplace, especially into jobs central to military prep-aration. These efforts were not notably successful, and by 1940 the military was calling for the conscription of women into war industries.

Further, the Nazis valued the family only insofar as it was congruent with the "health" of the racial com-munity. They were determined to promote that health by actually implementing radical eugenics measures that had been discussed, but not seriously imple-mented, during the Weimar years. The Nazi regime en-couraged childbearing and large families on the part of those considered fit, while simultaneously discourag-ing those considered unfit from having children. In pursuit of these goals, the regime regulated marriage, essentially politicized the family, and compromised tra-ditional family values again and again.

Just months after coming to power in 1933, Hitler brushed aside the objections of Vice Chancellor Franz von Papen, a Catholic, and engineered a law mandating the compulsory sterilization of persons suffering from certain allegedly hereditary diseases. Medical personnel sterilized some 400,000 people, the vast majority of them "Aryan" Germans, during the Nazi years.

Nazi Policy Toward the Jews   Eugenics was es-sentially one of two prongs of the Nazis' radical popu-lation policy. The other sought ethnic homogeneity, especially through measures directed against Germany's small Jewish minority. Although the regime began imme-diately to single out the Jews, Nazi Jewish policy remained an improvised hodgepodge prior to World War II. Within weeks after Hitler became chancellor in 1933, new re-strictions limited Jewish participation in the civil service, in the professions, and in German cultural life—and quickly drew censure from the League of Nations. The Nuremberg Laws, announced at a party rally in 1935, in-cluded prohibition of sexual relations and marriage be-tween Jews and non-Jewish Germans. Beginning in 1938,

the Jews had to carry special identification cards and to add "Sarah" or "Israel" to their given names.

Online Study Center   **Improve Your Grade**
Primary Source: The Centerpiece of Nazi Racial Legislation: The Nuremberg Laws

But though Hitler and other Nazi leaders claimed periodically to be seeking a definitive solution to Ger-many's "Jewish problem," the dominant objective dur-ing the 1930s was to force German Jews to emigrate. About 60,000 of Germany's 550,000 Jews left the coun-try during 1933 and 1934, and perhaps 25 percent had gotten out by 1938. The fact that the regime stripped emigrating Jews of their assets made emigration more difficult. Potential host countries, concerned about un-employment during the Depression, were especially un-willing to take in substantial numbers of Jews if they were penniless.

On November 9, 1938, using the assassination of a German diplomat in Paris as a pretext, the Nazis staged the ***Kristallnacht* (Crystal Night)** pogrom, during which almost all the synagogues in Germany and about seven thousand Jewish-owned stores were destroyed. Between 30,000 and 50,000 relatively prosperous Jews were arrested and forced to emigrate after their prop-erty was confiscated. Although the German public had generally acquiesced in the earlier restrictions on Jews, this pogrom, with its wanton violation of private prop-erty, shocked many Germans.

Concentration camps—supplementary detention centers—had become a feature of the Nazi regime virtu-ally at once, but prior to 1938 they were used primarily to hold political prisoners. As part of the Crystal Night pogrom, about 35,000 Jews were rounded up and sent to the camps, but most were soon released as long as they could document their intention to emigrate. When World War II began in 1939, the total camp population was about 25,000. The systematic physical extermination of the Jews began only during World War II.

Euthanasia and Nazi Preparation for War
However, the killing of others deemed superfluous or threatening to the racial community began earlier, with the so-called **euthanasia program** initiated under volunteer medical teams in 1939. Its aim was to elimi-nate chronic mental patients, the incurably ill, and people with severe physical handicaps. Those subject to

---

***Kristallnacht* (Crystal Night)**   Organized Nazi assault on Jewish businesses and synagogues during the night of November 9–10, 1938, following the assassina-tion of a German diplomat in Paris.

"euthanasia" program   The Nazi program of sys-tematically killing people deemed superfluous or threatening to Germany's racial health because of their physical or mental disabilities.

such treatment were overwhelmingly ethnic Germans, not Jews or foreigners. Although the regime did all it could to make it appear the victims had died naturally, a public outcry developed, especially among relatives and church leaders by 1941, when the program was largely discontinued. But by then it had claimed 100,000 lives and seems essentially to have achieved its initial objectives.

This "euthanasia" program was based on the sense, fundamental to radical Nazism, that war was the norm and readiness for war the essential societal imperative. In war, societies send individuals to their deaths and, on the battlefield, make difficult distinctions among the wounded, letting some die in order to save those most likely to survive and return to battle. Struggle necessitates selection, which requires overcoming humanitarian scruples—especially the notion that "weakness" calls for special protection. Thus it was desirable to kill even ethnic Germans who were deemed unfit, as "life unworthy of life."

Preparation for war was the core of Nazism in practice. The conquest of living space in the east would make possible a more advantageous agricultural-industrial balance. The result would be not only the self-sufficiency necessary for sovereignty but also the land-rootedness necessary for racial health. Such a war of conquest would strike not only the allegedly inferior Slavic peoples of the region but also detested communism, centered in the Soviet Union.

The point of domestic reorganization was to marshal the community's energies and resources for war. Because German business interests generally seemed congruent with Nazi purposes, Nazi aims did not appear to require some revolutionary assault on business elites or the capitalist economy. But the Nazis had their own road to travel, and beginning in 1936 they proved quite prepared to bend the economy, and to coordinate big business, to serve their longer-term aims of war-making.

The Nazi drive toward war during the 1930s transformed international relations in Europe. The responses of the other European powers, as they sought to deal with Hitler, reflected the increasingly polarized political context of the period. Before considering the fortunes of Hitler's foreign policy, we must consider fascism as a wider phenomenon—and the efforts of the democracies, on the one hand, and the Soviet Union, on the other, to come to terms with it.

S E C T I O N   S U M M A R Y

- The Nazis did not directly overthrow the Weimar Republic but ended up the beneficiaries when it reached an impasse during 1930–1933.

- The central components of Hitler's thinking—geopolitics, biological racism, anti-Semitism, and Social Darwinism—were neither original with Hitler nor specifically German.

- Among ordinary Germans, support for Hitler and his regime was broad but shallow during the 1930s.

- A radical eugenics program, entailing forced sterilization and eventually the actual killing of those deemed unfit, was central to Nazi action on the domestic level during the 1930s.

- During the 1930s the Nazis began stripping German Jews of citizenship rights as part of a haphazard effort to encourage—or force—Jews to emigrate.

FASCIST CHALLENGE AND ANTIFASCIST RESPONSE, 1934–1939

Why did the "popular front" strategy prove counterproductive in both France and Spain?

Communism, fascism, and Nazism all repudiated the parliamentary democracy that had been the West's political norm. Each seemed subject to violence and excess, yet each had features that some found attractive, especially in light of the difficult socioeconomic circumstances of the 1930s. But communists and adherents of the various forms of fascism were bitterly hostile to each other, and the very presence of these new political systems caused polarization all over Europe.

Beginning in 1934 communists sought to join with anyone who would work with them to defend the democratic framework against further fascist assaults. Without democracy, the very survival of communist parties was in doubt. This effort led to new antifascist coalition governments in Spain and France. In each case, however, the Depression restricted maneuvering room, and these governments ended up furthering the polarization they were seeking to avoid. By mid-1940, democracy had fallen in Spain, after a brutal civil war, and even in France, in the wake of military defeat.

EUROPEAN FASCISM AND THE POPULAR FRONT RESPONSE

Although some across Europe who were disaffected with democracy and hostile to communism found genuine fascism attractive, the line between fascism and conservative authoritarianism blurred in the volatile political climate of the 1930s. To many, any retreat from democracy appeared a step toward fascism.

In east-central Europe, political distinctions became especially problematic. Movements like the Arrow Cross in Hungary and the Legion of the Archangel Michael in Romania modeled themselves on the Italian and German prototypes, but they never achieved political power. Those who controlled the antidemocratic governments in Hungary and Romania, as in Poland, Bulgaria, and Yugoslavia, were authoritarian traditionalists, not fascists. Still, many government leaders in the region welcomed the closer economic ties with Germany that Hitler's economics minister, Hjalmar Schacht, engineered. The difference between authoritarianism and fascism remained clearest in Austria, where Catholic conservatives undermined democracy during 1933 and 1934. They were actively hostile to the growing pro-Nazi agitation in Austria, partly because they wanted to keep Austria independent.

In France various nationalist, anticommunist, and anti-Semitic leagues gathered momentum during the early 1930s. They covered a spectrum from monarchism to outspoken pro-fascism, but together they constituted at least a potential threat to French democracy. In February 1934, right-wing demonstrations against the Chamber of Deputies provoked a bloody clash with police and forced a change of ministry. As it began to seem that even France might be vulnerable, those from the center and left of the political spectrum began to consider collaborating to resist fascism. The communists, especially, took the initiative by promoting **popular fronts** of all those seeking to preserve democracy.

This was a dramatic change in strategy for international communism. Even as Hitler was closing in on the German chancellorship in the early 1930s, German Communists, following Comintern policy, continued to attack their socialist rivals rather than seek a unified response to Nazism. From the communist perspective, fascism represented the crisis phase of monopoly capi-

popular front   A term for antifascist electoral alliances and governing coalitions that communists promoted from 1934 until 1939 to resist the further spread of fascism.

Ideological Confrontation

At a major international exhibition in Paris in 1937, the new antidemocratic political regimes made bold propaganda statements. With a sculpture from fascist Italy's pavilion in the foreground, we look across the Seine River to a classic representation of the ideological warfare of the 1930s: the Soviet Pavilion, on the left, facing the German Pavilion, on the right. Crowning the Soviet building is the noted sculpture by Vera Muchina, *Worker and Collective Farmer*. *(AP/Wide World Photos)*

talism, so a Nazi government would actually be useful to strip away the democratic façade hiding class oppression in Germany. But by 1934 the threat of fascism seemed so pressing that Communists began actively promoting electoral alliances and governing coalitions with socialists and even liberal democrats to resist its further spread. From 1934 until 1939, Communists everywhere consistently pursued this "popular front" strategy.

By the 1930s, however, it was becoming ever harder to know what was fascist, what was dangerous, what might lead where. As fears intensified, perceptions became as important as realities. Popular front governments, intended to preserve democracy against what appeared to be fascism, could seem to conservatives to be leaning too far to the left. Ideological polarization made democracy extraordinarily difficult. The archetypal example proved to be Spain, where a tragedy of classical proportions was played out.

FROM DEMOCRACY TO CIVIL WAR IN SPAIN, 1931–1939

Spain became a center of attention in the 1930s, when its promising new parliamentary democracy, launched in 1931, led to civil war in 1936 and the triumph of a repressive authoritarian regime in 1939. An earlier effort at constitutional monarchy had fizzled by 1923, when King Alfonso XIII (1886–1941) supported a new military dictatorship. But growing opposition led first to the resignation of the dictator in 1930 and then, in April 1931, to the end of the monarchy and the proclamation of a republic. The elections for a constituent assembly that followed in June produced a solid victory for a coalition of liberal democrats and Socialists, as well as much hope for substantial reform.

A significant agrarian reform law was passed in 1932, but partly because of the difficult economic context, the new government was slow to implement it. Feeling betrayed, Socialists and agricultural workers became increasingly radical, producing growing upheaval in the countryside. Radicalism on the left made it harder for the moderates to govern and, at the same time, stimulated conservatives to become more politically active.

A right-wing coalition known as the CEDA, led by José Maria Gil Robles (heel ROH-blayce) (1898–1980), grew in strength, becoming the largest party in parliament with the elections of November 1933. In light of its parliamentary strength, the CEDA had a plausible claim to a government role, but it was kept from participation in government until October 1934. It seemed to the left, in the ideologically charged atmosphere of the time, that the growing role of the CEDA was a prelude to fascism. To let the CEDA into the government would be to hand the republic over to its enemies.

A strong Catholic from the traditional Spanish right, Gil Robles refused to endorse the democratic republic as a form of government, but he and the CEDA were willing to work within it. So the Spanish left may have been too quick to see the CEDA as fascist—and to react when the CEDA finally got its government role. However, Mussolini and Hitler had each come to power more or less legally, from within parliamentary institutions. The German left had been criticized for its passive response to the advent of Hitler; the Spanish left wanted to avoid the same mistake.

Thus, when the CEDA finally got a role in the government, the left responded during the fall of 1934 with quasi-revolutionary uprisings in Catalonia and Asturias, where a miners' commune was put down only after two weeks of heavy fighting. In the aftermath,

the right-leaning government of 1935 began undoing some of the reforms of the left-leaning government of 1931–1933, though still legally, within the framework of the parliamentary republic.

In February 1936 a popular front coalition to ward off fascism won a narrow electoral victory, sufficient for an absolute majority in parliament. As would be true in France a few months later, electoral victory produced popular expectations that went well beyond the essentially defensive purposes of the popular front. Hoping to win back the leftist rank and file and head off what seemed a dangerous attempt at revolution, the new popular front government began to implement a progressive program, now including the land reform that had been promised but not implemented earlier. It was too late, however, to undercut the growing radicalization of the masses.

A wave of land seizures began in March 1936, followed by the most extensive strike movement in Spanish history, which by June was becoming clearly revolutionary in character. To many, the government's inability to keep order had become the immediate issue. By the early summer of 1936, leaders of the democratic republic had become isolated between the extremes of left and right, each preparing an extralegal solution.

Finally, in mid-July, several army officers initiated a military uprising against the government. Soon led by General Francisco Franco (1892–1975), these Nationalist insurgents took control of substantial parts of Spain. But elsewhere they failed to overcome the resistance of the Republicans, or Loyalists, those determined to defend the republic. So the result was not the intended military takeover but a brutal civil war (see **MAP 27.1**). The substantial Italian fascist and Nazi German intervention on the Nationalist side by the end of 1936 intensified the war's ideological ramifications. At the same time, the remarkable, often heroic resistance of the Loyalists captured the imagination of the world. Indeed, forty thousand volunteers came from abroad to fight to preserve the Spanish republic.

It proved a war of stunning brutality on both sides. Loyalist anticlericalism led to the murder of twelve bishops and perhaps one-eighth of the parish clergy in Spain. On the other side, the German bombing of the Basque town of Guernica (gair-NEE-kah, in Spanish; GWAIR-nee-kah, as customarily rendered in English) on a crowded market day in April 1937, represented unforgettably in Pablo Picasso's painting, came to symbolize the violence and suffering of the whole era (see the painting on page 859).

Republican Loyalists assumed that Franco and the Nationalists represented another instance of fascism. In fact, however, Franco was no fascist, but rather a traditional military man whose leadership role did not rest on personal charisma. He was an authoritarian emphasizing discipline, order, and Spain's Catholic traditions.

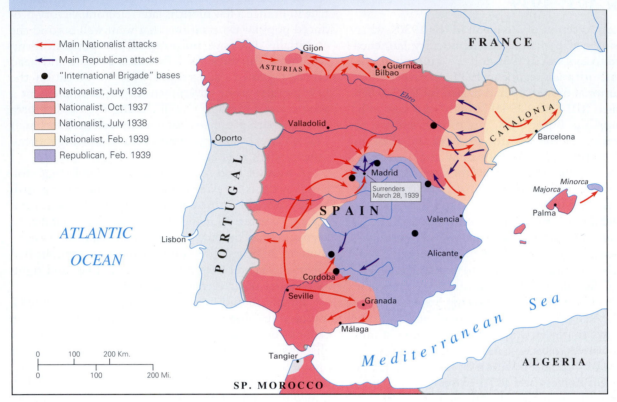

MAP 27.1   The Spanish Civil War, 1936–1939
The Nationalist insurgents quickly took over most of northern and eastern Spain in 1936 and then gradually expanded their territory. The fall of Madrid early in 1939 marked the end of the fighting. The revolutionary effort of 1936 and 1937 within the Republican zone was centered in Barcelona.   *(Source: Adapted from The Times Atlas of World History, 3d ed. Reprinted by permission of HarperCollins Publishers Ltd. © HarperCollins Publishers Ltd.)*

Still, in their effort to rally support during the civil war, Franco's forces found it expedient to take advantage of the appeal of the Falange (fah-LAHN-hay), a genuinely fascist movement that had emerged under the leadership of the charismatic young José Antonio Primo de Rivera (1903–1936). Although extremely weak at the time of the elections in February 1936, the Falange grew rapidly in opposition to the leftist radicalism that followed the popular front victory. As street fighting between left and right intensified that spring, the republic arrested José Antonio, as he was called, and he was in prison when the civil war began.

José Antonio decided that his best hope was alliance with the military. Although he was contemptuous of their shortsighted conservatism, he felt that their very absence of ideas afforded an opening for the Falange to provide direction, a genuine alternative. But it worked out the other way. In November 1936, the republican government tried and executed José Antonio for conspiring to overthrow the republic. The Nationalists promptly began invoking his memory, and using other trappings of the Falange, to increase their popular appeal.

Meanwhile, the republic's leaders had to fight a civil war while dealing with continuing revolution in their own ranks. Developing especially in Catalonia from the uprisings of 1936, that revolution was not communist but anarcho-syndicalist in orientation. The Communists, true to popular front principles, insisted that this was no time for such "infantile leftist" revolutionary experiments. What mattered, throughout the Republican zone, was the factory discipline necessary to produce essential war materiel. As a consequence, the Communists, under Stalin's orders, were instrumental in putting down the anarchist revolution in Catalonia in June 1937.

Under these extraordinary circumstances, the Communists, at first a distinct minority on the Spanish left, gradually gained ascendancy on the Republican side, partly because they were disciplined and effective, partly because Soviet assistance enhanced their prestige. However, this single-minded prosecution of the civil war did not prove enough to defeat the military insurgency, despite the considerable heroism on the Loyalist side. The war ended with the fall of Madrid to the Nationalists in March 1939. General Franco's authoritarian regime governed Spain until his death in 1975.

Picasso: Guernica

Created for the Spanish Pavilion at the famed 1937 Paris Exhibition, Picasso's painting conveys horror and outrage—his response to the German bombing of Guernica on a crowded market day in 1937, during the Spanish civil war. Picasso's stark, elemental imagery helped define this era of violence and suffering for the generations that followed.   *(Pablo Picasso, Guernica [1937, May–early June]. Oil on canvas. Art Resource, NY. © 2002 Artists Rights Society [ARS], New York/ADAGP, Paris)*

In Spain, as in Weimar Germany, the lack of consensus in a new republic made parliamentary democracy difficult, and the wider ideological framework magnified the difficulties. With the political boiling point so low, the left and the right each saw the other in extreme terms and assumed that extraordinary response to the other was necessary. Thus the left tended to view even conservatives operating within a parliamentary framework as "fascist," and both sides were relatively quick to give up on a democratic republic that seemed to be tilting too far in the wrong direction.

FRANCE IN THE ERA OF THE POPULAR FRONT

In France, as in Spain, concern to arrest the spread of fascism led to a popular front coalition, here including Socialists, Communists, and Radicals, that governed the country from 1936 to 1938. Although it did not lead to civil war, the popular front was central to the French experience of the 1930s, producing polarization and resignation and undermining confidence in the Third Republic.

Beginning in 1934, the French Communists took the initiative in approaching first the Socialists, then the Radicals, to develop a popular front coalition against fascism. In reaching out to the Radicals, the Commu-

nists stressed French patriotism and made no demand for significant economic reforms. Stalin gave this effort a major push in 1935 when, in a stunning change in the communist line, he stressed the legitimacy of national defense and explicitly endorsed French rearmament.

In the elections of April and May 1936, the popular front won a sizable majority in the Chamber of Deputies, putting the Socialists' leader, Léon Blum (1872–1950), in line to become France's first Socialist prime minister. The Communists pledged full support of the new Blum government, but to avoid fanning fears, they did not participate directly. However, despite the popular front's moderate and essentially defensive aims, the situation quickly began to polarize after the elections.

Fearing that the new Blum government would be forced to devalue the French currency, and thereby diminish the value of assets denominated in francs, French investors immediately began moving their capital abroad. At the same time, the popular front victory produced a wave of enthusiasm among workers that escaped the control of popular front leaders and culminated in a spontaneous strike movement, the largest France had ever seen. By early June it had spread to all major industries nationwide. Although the workers' demands—for collective bargaining, a forty-hour workweek, and paid vacations—were not extraordinary, the movement involved sit-down strikes as well as the normal walkouts and thus seemed quasi-revolutionary in character. The major trade union confederation, the Communists, and most Socialists, including Blum himself, saw the strikes as a danger to the popular front, with its more modest aims of defending the republic, and eagerly pursued a settlement.

That settlement, the Matignon (mah-tin-YON) Agreement of June 8, 1936, was a major victory for the French working class. Having been genuinely frightened by the strikes and now reassured that the popular front government would at least uphold the law, French industrialists were willing to make significant concessions. So the workers got collective bargaining, elected shop stewards, and wage increases as a direct result of Matignon, then a forty-hour week and paid vacations in a reform package promptly passed by the parliament.

In the enthusiasm of the summer of 1936, other reforms were enacted as well, but after that the popular front was forced onto the defensive. Two problems undermined its energy and cohesion: the noncooperation of French business and the Spanish civil war. The cautious response of Blum, the Socialist prime minister, is striking in each case, but he faced a situation with little maneuvering room.

From the outset Blum stressed that he had no mandate for revolution, and as France's first Socialist prime minister, he felt it essential to prove that a Socialist could govern responsibly. Thus Blum did not respond energetically to the capital flight, even though it produced serious currency and budgetary difficulties. Perhaps, as critics suggest, he should have acted more aggressively to overhaul the French banking and credit system. But Blum shied away from any such drastic measures, both to prove he could be moderate and to avoid antagonizing business.

Blum was also uncertain as he faced the dilemmas surrounding the Spanish civil war. The key question was whether the French government should help the beleaguered Spanish republic, at least by sending sup-plies. Although he initially favored such help, Blum changed his mind under pressure from three sides. The Conservative government of Stanley Baldwin in Britain was against it. So was the French right; some even suggested that French intervention would provoke a comparable civil war in France. Moreover, the Radicals in his own coalition were generally opposed to helping the Spanish republic, so intervention would jeopardize the cohesion of the popular front itself.

Thus, rather than help supply the Spanish republic, Blum promoted a nonintervention agreement among the major powers, including Italy and Germany. Many Socialists and Communists disliked Blum's cautious policy, especially as it became clear that Mussolini and Hitler were violating their hands-off pledges. As Blum stuck to nonintervention, the moral force of the popular front dissolved.

In 1938 a new government under the Radical Edouard Daladier (dah-lah-dee-YAY) (1884–1970), still nominally a creature of the popular front, began dismantling some of the key gains of 1936, even attacking the forty-hour week. Citing productivity and national security concerns, Daladier adopted pro-business policies and succeeded in attracting capital back to France. But workers, watching the gains they had won in 1936 slip away, felt betrayed. At the same time, businessmen and conservatives began blaming the workers' gains—such as the five-day week—for slowing French rearmament. Although such charges were not entirely fair, they indicated how poisoned the atmosphere in France had become in the wake of the popular front.

As France began to face the possibility of a new war, the popular front was widely blamed for French weakness. When war came at last, resignation and division were prevalent, in contrast with the patriotic unity and high spirits of 1914. It was partly for that reason that France was so easily defeated by Germany in 1940. And when France fell, the democratic Third Republic fell with it.

S E C T I O N   S U M M A R Y

- In light of the ideological polarization of the 1930s, many people found it difficult to distinguish between conservative authoritarianism and fascism.

- In a dramatic change in their international strategy, the Communists in 1934 began promoting "popular fronts," which were to bring together all those seeking to preserve democracy against the threat of fascism.

- The wider ideological framework magnified the difficulties of parliamentary democracy in Spain, contributing to the polarization that soon led to civil war.

- Although he sometimes exploited the trappings of fascism, General Franco was not a fascist but an authoritarian Catholic traditionalist.

- Although it was intended to preserve the Third Republic, the popular front experiment in France produced a backlash and was widely blamed for French weakness as war again loomed by the end of the 1930s.

THE COMING OF WORLD WAR II, 1935–1939

Why did the other countries not stop Hitler's Germany before it was strong enough to start a new European war in 1939?

Even as the Great Depression added to their burdens, Western leaders faced the challenge of maintaining the peace during the 1930s. But despite the promising adjustments of the 1920s, many of the problems that accompanied the World War I peace settlement were still in place when Hitler came to power. And Hitler had consistently trumpeted his intention to overturn that settlement. What scope was there for peaceful revision? Could the threat of war stop Hitler? By the last years of the 1930s, these questions tortured the Western world as Hitler went from one success to another, raising the possibility of a new and more destructive war. And the power balance rested on the responses not only of the Western democracies, but of fascist Italy and the communist Soviet Union as well.

THE REORIENTATION OF FASCIST ITALY

During its first decade in power, Benito Mussolini's fascist regime in Italy concentrated on domestic reconstruction, especially the effort to mobilize people through their roles as producers within a new corporative state (see page 861). But though corporativist institutions were gradually constructed, with great rhetorical fanfare, they bogged down in bureaucratic meddling. Corporativism proved more the vehicle for regimentation than for a more direct kind of participation. Mussolini offered assurances that, despite the necessary compromises, fascism's corporativist revolution was continuing, but many committed fascists were sharply critical of the new system. Fascism seemed to have stalled, partly as the result of compromise with prefascist elites and institutions, and partly as the result of its own internal contradictions.

Mussolini was never merely the instrument of the established elites, but neither was he a consistent ideologue like Hitler. By the early 1930s, he sometimes seemed satisfied with ritual, spectacle, and the growing cult of his own infallibility as he juggled the contending forces in fascist Italy. But the limitations he had encountered on the domestic level increasingly frustrated him. On the international level, in contrast, the new context after Hitler came to power offered some welcome space for maneuver.

Though Italy, like Germany, remained dissatisfied with the territorial status quo, it was not obvious that fascist Italy and Nazi Germany had to end up in the same camp. For one thing, Italy was anxious to preserve an independent Austria as a buffer with Germany, whereas many Germans and Austrians favored the unification of the two countries. Such a greater Germany might then threaten the gains Italy had won at the peace conference at Austria's expense. When, in 1934, Germany seemed poised to absorb Austria, Mussolini helped force Hitler to back down. He even warned that Nazism, with its racist orientation, posed a significant threat to the best of European civilization.

As it began to appear that France and Britain might have to work with the Soviet Union to check Hitler's Germany, French and British conservatives pushed for good relations with Mussolini's Italy to provide ideological balance. So Italy was well positioned to play off both sides as Hitler began shaking things up on the international level. In 1935, just after Hitler announced significant rearmament measures, unilaterally repudiating provisions of the Versailles treaty for the first time, Mussolini hosted a meeting with the French and British prime ministers at Stresa, in northern Italy. In an overt warning to Hitler's Germany, the three powers agreed to resist "any unilateral repudiation of treaties which may endanger the peace of Europe."

However, Mussolini was already preparing to extend Italy's possessions in East Africa to encompass Ethiopia (formerly called Abyssinia). He assumed that the French and British, who needed his support against Hitler, would not offer significant opposition. Ethiopia had become a League of Nations member in 1923—sponsored by Italy, but opposed by Britain and France because it still practiced slavery. After a border incident, Italian troops invaded in October 1935, prompting the League to announce sanctions against Italy.

These sanctions were applied haphazardly, largely because France and Britain wanted to avoid damaging their longer-term relations with Italy. In any case, the sanctions did not deter Mussolini, whose forces prevailed through the use of aircraft and poison gas by May 1936. But they did make Italy receptive to German overtures in the aftermath of its victory. And the victory made Mussolini more restless. Rather than seeking to play again the role of European balancer, he sent Italian troops and materiel to aid the Nationalists in the Spanish civil war, thereby further alienating democratic opinion elsewhere.

Conservatives in Britain and France continued to push for accommodation with Italy, hoping to revive the "Stresa front" against Hitler. Some even defended Italian imperialism in East Africa. But Italy continued its drift toward Germany. Late in 1936 Mussolini spoke of a new **Rome-Berlin Axis** for the first time. During 1937 and 1938 he and Hitler exchanged visits. Finally, in May 1939, Italy joined Germany in an open-ended military alliance, the Pact of Steel, but Mussolini made it clear that Italy could not be ready for a major European war before 1943.

Partly to strengthen this developing relationship, fascist Italy adopted anti-Semitic racial laws, even though Italian fascism had not originally been anti-Semitic. Indeed, the party had attracted Jewish Italians to its membership in about the same proportion as non-Jews. Although the imperial venture in Ethiopia had been popular among the Italian people, the seeming subservience to Nazi Germany displeased even many fascists. Such opposition helped keep Mussolini from intervention when war broke out in September 1939.

RESTORING GERMAN SOVEREIGNTY, 1935–1936

During his first years in power, through 1936, Hitler could be understood as merely restoring German sovereignty, revising a postwar settlement that had been misconceived in the first place. However uncouth and abrasive he might seem, it was hard to find a basis for opposing him. Yet with the beginning of rearmament in 1935, and especially with the **remilitarization of the Rhineland** in March 1936, Hitler fundamentally reversed the power balance established in France's favor at the peace conference.

France's special advantage had been the demilitarization of the entire German territory west of the Rhine River and a 50-kilometer strip on the east bank. The measure had been reaffirmed at Locarno in 1925, now with Germany's free agreement, and it was guaranteed by Britain and Italy. Yet on a Saturday morning in March 1936, that advantage disappeared as German troops moved into the forbidden area. The French and British acquiesced, uncertain of what else to do. After all, Hitler was only restoring Germany to full sovereignty.

But Hitler was not likely to stop there. As a result of the war and the peace, three new countries—Austria, Czechoslovakia, and Poland—bordered Germany (see **MAP 27.2**). In each, the peace settlement had left trouble spots involving the status of ethnic Germans; in each, the status quo was open to question.

AUSTRIA, CZECHOSLOVAKIA, AND APPEASEMENT

As early as 1934, Hitler had moved to encompass his homeland, Austria, but strenuous opposition from Italy led him to back down. The developing understanding with Mussolini by 1936 enabled Hitler to focus again on Austria—initiating the second, more radical phase of his prewar foreign policy. On a pretext in March 1938, German troops moved into Austria, which was promptly incorporated into Germany. This time Mussolini was willing to acquiesce, and Hitler was genuinely grateful.

The Treaty of Versailles had explicitly prohibited this *Anschluss*, or unity of Austria with Germany, though that prohibition violated the principle of self-determination. It was widely believed in the West, no doubt correctly, that most Austrians favored unity with Germany now that the Habsburg empire had broken up. The *Anschluss* could thus be justified as revising a misconceived aspect of the peace settlement.

Czechoslovakia presented quite a different situation. Although it had preserved democratic institutions, the country included restive minorities of Magyars, Ruthenians, Poles, and—concentrated especially in the Sudetenland, along the German and Austrian borders—about 3.25 million Germans. After having been part of the dominant nationality in the old Habsburg empire, those Germans were frustrated with their minority status in the new Czechoslovakia. Worse, they seemed to suffer disproportionately from the Depression. Hitler's agents actively stirred up their resentments.

Leading the West's response, when Hitler began making an issue of Czechoslovakia, was Neville Chamberlain (1869–1940), who followed Stanley Baldwin as Britain's prime minister in May 1937. An intelligent, vigorous, and public-spirited man from the progressive wing of the Conservative Party, Chamberlain has long been derided as the architect of the **"appeasement"** of Hitler at the Munich conference of 1938, which settled the crisis over Czechoslovakia. Trumpeted as the key to peace, the Munich agreement proved but a step to the war that broke out less than a year later. Yet though it failed, Chamberlain's policy of appeasement stemmed not from cowardice or mere drift, and certainly not from some unspoken pro-Nazi sentiment.

Rather than let events spin out of control, as seemed to have happened in 1914, Chamberlain sought to

---

Rome-Berlin Axis   Alliance between Hitler's Nazi Germany and Mussolini's fascist Italy, which began informally in 1936, then was cemented by an open-ended military alliance, the Pact of Steel, in 1939.

remilitarization of the Rhineland   The reoccupation of Germany's Rhineland territory by German troops in March 1936, in clear violation of the Treaty of Versailles.

appeasement   The policy employed by Britain's prime minister, Neville Chamberlain, to defuse the 1938 crisis with Germany's Adolf Hitler. Chamberlain acquiesced to Hitler's demands to annex the Sudetenland portion of Czechoslovakia, but this proved merely a step toward the war that broke out less than a year later.

MAP 27.2   The Expansion of Nazi Germany, 1936–1939

Especially with the remilitarization of the Rhineland in 1936, Hitler's Germany began moving, step by step, to alter the European power balance. In September 1939 the Soviet Union also began annexing territory, capitalizing on its agreement with Germany the month before.

Online Study Center **Improve Your Grade** Interactive Map: The Growth of Nazi Germany, 1933–1939

master the difficult international situation through creative bargaining. Surely, he felt, the excesses of Hitler's policy resulted from the mistakes of Versailles; redo the settlement on a more realistic basis, and Germany would behave responsibly. The key was to pinpoint the sources of Germany's frustrations and, as Chamberlain put it, "to remove the danger spots one by one."

Moreover, in Britain as elsewhere, there were some who saw Hitler's resurgent Germany as a bulwark against communism, which might spread into east-central Europe—especially in the event of another war. Indeed, the victor in another war might well be the revolutionary left. To prevent such an outcome was worth a few concessions to Hitler.

The Czechs, led by Eduard Beneš (BAY-naish) (1884–1948), made some attempt to liberalize their nationality policy. But by April 1938 they were becoming ever less sympathetic to Sudeten German demands for

autonomy, especially as German bullying came to accompany them. Tensions between Czechoslovakia and Germany mounted, and by late September 1938 war appeared imminent, despite Chamberlain's efforts to mediate. Both the French and the British began mobilizing, with French troops manning the Maginot Line for the first time.

A 1924 treaty bound France to come to the aid of Czechoslovakia in the event of aggression. Moreover, the Soviet Union, according to a treaty of 1935, was bound to assist Czechoslovakia if the French did so. And throughout the crisis, the Soviets pushed for a strong stand in defense of Czechoslovakia against German aggression. For both ideological and military reasons, however, the British and French were reluctant to line up for war on the side of the Soviet Union. The value of the Soviet military was uncertain, at best, at a time when the Soviet officer corps had just been purged.

By September, Hitler seemed eager to smash the Czechs by force, but when Mussolini proposed a four-power conference, he was persuaded to talk again. At Munich late in September, Britain, France, Italy, and Germany settled the matter, with Czechoslovakia—and the Soviet Union—excluded. Determined not to risk war over what seemed Czech intransigence, the Brit-

ish ended up agreeing to what Hitler had wanted all along—not merely autonomy for the Sudeten Germans but German annexation of the Sudetenland.

The Munich agreement specified that all Sudeten areas with German majorities be transferred to Germany. Plebiscites were to be held in areas with large German minorities, and Hitler pledged to respect the sovereignty of the now diminished Czechoslovak state. Chamberlain and his French counterpart, Edouard Daladier, each returned home to a hero's welcome, having transformed what had seemed certain war to, in Chamberlain's soon-to-be-notorious phrase, "peace in our time."

Rather than settle the nationality questions bedeviling Czechoslovakia, the Munich agreement only provoked further unrest. Poland and Hungary, eager to exploit the new weakness of Czechoslovakia, agitated successfully to annex disputed areas with large numbers of their respective nationalities. Then unrest stemming from Slovak separatism afforded a pretext for Germany to send troops into Prague in March 1939. The Slovak areas were spun off as a separate nation, while the Czech areas became the Protectorate of Bohemia and Moravia. Less than six months after the Munich conference, most of what had been Czechoslovakia had landed firmly within the Nazi orbit (see Map 27.2). It was no longer possible to justify Hitler's actions as an effort to unite all Germans in one state.

POLAND, THE NAZI-SOVIET PACT, AND THE COMING OF WAR

With Poland, the German grievance was still more serious, for the new Polish state had been created partly at German expense. Especially galling to Germans was the Polish corridor, which cut off East Prussia from the bulk of Germany in order to give Poland access to the sea. The city of Danzig (now Gdansk, in Poland), historically Polish but part of Germany before World War I, was left a "free city," supervised by the League of Nations.

Disillusioned by Hitler's dismemberment of Czechoslovakia and angered by the Germans' menacing rhetoric regarding Poland, Chamberlain announced on March 31, 1939, that Britain and France would intervene militarily should Poland's independence be threatened. Chamberlain was not only abandoning the policy of appeasement; he was making a clear commitment to the Continent, of the sort that British governments had resisted since 1919. He could do so partly because Britain was rapidly rearming. By early 1940, in fact, Britain was spending nearly as large a share of its national income on the military as Germany was.

Chamberlain's assertive statement was not enough to deter Hitler, who seems to have been determined to settle the Polish question by force. In an effort to localize the conflict, however, Hitler continued to insist that German aims were limited and reasonable. Germany simply wanted Danzig and German transit across the corridor; it was the Polish stance that was rigid and unreasonable. Hitler apparently believed that Polish stubbornness would alienate the British and French, undercutting their support. And as the crisis developed by mid-1939, doubts were increasingly expressed, on all sides, that the British and French were really prepared to aid Poland militarily—that they had the will "to die for Danzig."

Although they had been lukewarm to Soviet proposals for a military alliance, Britain and France began to negotiate with the Soviet Union more seriously during the spring and summer of 1939. But reservations about the value of a Soviet alliance continued to gnaw at Western leaders. For one thing, Soviet troops could gain access to Germany only by moving through Poland or Romania. But each had territory gained at the expense of Russia in the postwar settlement, so the British and French, suspicious of Soviet designs, were reluctant to insist that Soviet troops be allowed to pass through either country.

Even as negotiations between the Soviet Union and the democracies continued, the Soviets came to their own agreement with Nazi Germany on August 23, 1939, in a pact that astonished the world. Each side had been denouncing the other, and although Hitler had explored the possibility of Soviet neutrality in May, serious negotiations began only that August, when the Soviets got the clear signal that a German invasion of Poland was inevitable. It now appeared that no Soviet alliance with Britain and France could prevent war. Under these circumstances, a nonaggression pact with Germany seemed better to serve Soviet interests than a problematic war on the side of Britain and France. So the Soviets agreed with the Germans that each would remain neutral in the event that either became involved in a war with some other nation.

The Soviet flip-flop stemmed partly from disillusionment with the British and French response to the accelerating threat of Nazism. The democracies seemed no more trustworthy, and potentially no less hostile, than Nazi Germany. But the Soviets were playing their own double game. A secret protocol to the **Nazi-Soviet Pact** apportioned major areas of east-central Europe between the Soviet Union and Germany. As a result, the Soviets soon regained much of what they had lost after World War I, when Poland, Finland, and other states had been created or aggrandized with territories that had been part of the tsarist empire.

The Nazi-Soviet Pact seemed to give Hitler the free hand he wanted in Poland. With the dramatic change in alignment, the democracies were surely much less likely to intervene. But Chamberlain, again determined to avoid the hesitations of 1914, publicly reaffirmed the British guarantee to Poland on August 25. Britain would indeed intervene if Germany attacked. And after Hitler ordered the German invasion of Poland on September 1, the British and French responded with declarations of war on September 3.

With each step on the path to war, Hitler had vacillated between apparent reasonableness and wanton aggressiveness. Sometimes he accented the plausibility of his demands in light of problems with the postwar settlement; sometimes he seemed to be actively seeking war. Even in invading Poland, he apparently still hoped to localize hostilities. But he was certainly willing to risk a more general European war, and the deepest thrust of his policy was toward an all-out war of conquest—first against Poland, but ultimately against the Soviet Union. War was essential to the Nazi vision, and only when the assault on Poland became a full-scale war did the underlying purposes of Nazism become clear.

SECTION SUMMARY

- In light of the ideological polarization of the period, even the efforts to check Hitler by Britain and France, the major European democracies, depended partly on their relations with fascist Italy and the Soviet Union.

- Germany's remilitarization of the Rhineland in March 1936 prompted no military response by France and Britain, even though Germany's move removed the trump card that France had won with the Versailles treaty.

- In "appeasing" Hitler, Neville Chamberlain was not simply caving in but was seeking, through creative diplomacy, to remove the present sources of international hostility.

- Disillusioned by Hitler's course after the Munich agreement of September 1938, Chamberlain announced in March 1939 that Britain and France would intervene militarily should Germany threaten Poland's independence.

- Although they came to terms with Hitler's Germany in 1939 partly from mistrust of Britain and France, the Soviets quickly pursued their own aggressive aims in north-central Europe.

Nazi-Soviet Pact   Surprise agreement between the Soviet Union and Nazi Germany in August 1939 that each would remain neutral if the other went to war against some other nation.

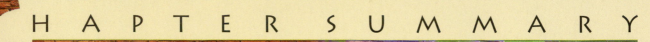

With what array of measures did governments respond to the Great Depression?

Why did the Stalinist attempt to build "socialism in one country" lead to the "terror-famine" of 1932–1933 and the "great terror" of 1937–1938?

Through what measures did the Nazi regime claim to be improving the quality of the German population?

Why did the "popular front" strategy prove counterproductive in both France and Spain?

Why did the other countries not stop Hitler's Germany before it was strong enough to start a new European war in 1939?

The Great Depression caught decision makers in the democracies unprepared. Reflecting conventional economic thinking, their initial response was to keep government budgets balanced. But this required cutting government spending on such measures as unemployment benefits, which not only added to the human misery but also intensified the economic contraction. The further effort to protect domestic economies through higher tariffs also worsened the downturn by restricting global trade. Only after several years, and for quite disparate reasons, did governments begin increasing spending and thereby stimulating renewed economic growth.

Stalin sought to rekindle the Russian revolutionary experiment by attempting to build "socialism in one country." The essential prerequisite was rapid industrialization, to be financed by squeezing the peasantry through forced collectivization in agriculture. Both the collectivization itself and the ensuing extractions of agricultural produce were extremely brutal, culminating in the "terror-famine" of 1932–1933. Partly because of its brutality, and partly because its economic results were mixed at best, the Stalinist departure produced opposition even from within the Communist Party. Seeking to root out those who might be sabotaging the great Soviet experiment, Communist leaders embarked on a series of purges and show trials, but their effort gradually spun out of control, producing the "great terror" of 1937–1938.

Population engineering, based on eugenics—on the one hand, racism and anti-Semitism, on the other—was central to the Nazis' domestic program. Determined to implement radical eugenics measures that had been discussed but not implemented under the Weimar Republic, the regime launched a program of forced sterilization in 1933. By the eve of World War II, German

medical personnel were actually killing mental patients, the terminally ill, and others deemed unfit. Even as they sought to "improve" the "Aryan" population through such eugenics measures, the Nazis also sought ethnic homogeneity, especially by stripping German Jews of citizenship rights in an effort to force emigration.

Hitler's consolidation of power in Germany and the apparent threat of fascism in France in 1934 prompted leaders of the Comintern to make resistance to the further spread of fascism their top priority. To that end, communists spearheaded the formation of "popular fronts" with socialists and others concerned to preserve democratic institutions. But though it produced electoral successes in 1936 in Spain and France, the strategy proved polarizing. Popular front electoral victories produced radical pressures that the new popular front governments had trouble containing. Those pressures eventually produced a backlash from the right. Partly as a result, democracy was defeated in both Spain and France by 1940.

Hitler's aggressive foreign policy provided an unprecedented challenge to the European order, but the leading democracies, Britain and France, were slow to respond. Eagerness to avoid another war affected their reactions, as did the ideological polarization of the decade. But up to a point, Hitler's steps could seem legitimate, in terms of principles of national sovereignty and ethnic self-determination that had been compromised to Germany's disadvantage at the Paris Peace Conference. In 1939, when Hitler's further steps could no longer be justified in such terms, the democracies, led by Britain, at last began to stiffen. But Hitler was determined to crush Poland. The Nazi-Soviet Pact seemed to make the intervention of Britain and France unlikely, but the Nazi leader was more than willing to risk another European war.

LOOKING AHEAD

During the 1930s the democracies had to respond to three novel regimes—Italian fascism, German Nazism, and Stalinist communism—that did not play by the expected rules. Although they involved ordinary people in new ways, each of the three regimes concentrated power in the hands of dictators. Thus they were at once dynamic and unpredictable—and thus, in part, the hesitancy and uncertainty of the democracies in dealing with them. The hesitations of the democracies during the 1930s tended to confirm the view of the three dictators that democracy was weak, decadent, passé. Such contempt inclined Mussolini and Hitler to ever greater recklessness and persuaded Stalin finally to make his own deal with the Nazis in August 1939. When Germany invaded Poland on September 1, Hitler believed the democracies would let him have his way. It was hardly clear that this would end up another European war, let alone the most destructive, cataclysmic war the world had ever seen.

KEY TERMS

Online Study Center **Improve Your Grade** Flashcards

collectivization (p. 844)

show trials (p. 845)

gulag (p. 845)

Adolf Hitler (p. 847)

National Socialist (Nazi) Party (p. 847)

Schutzstaffel (SS) (p. 850)

Kristallnacht (Crystal Night) (p. 854)

"euthanasia" program (p. 854)

popular front (p. 856)

Rome-Berlin Axis (p. 862)

remilitarization of the Rhineland (p. 862)

appeasement (p. 862)

Nazi-Soviet Pact (p. 865)

SUGGESTED READING

Applebaum, Anne. *Gulag: A History*. 2003. A major survey of the Soviet camp network, based on extensive new research. Comprehensive, but sensitive and accessible.

Bell, P. M. H. *The Origins of the Second World War in Europe*. 2d ed. 1997. A well-organized and fair-minded survey.

Burleigh, Michael. *The Third Reich: A New History*. 2000. A lengthy reinterpretation by a major authority who uses the notions of totalitarianism and political religion to place the Nazi experience within the wider context of the era.

Fitzpatrick, Sheila. *Everyday Stalinism, Ordinary Life in Extraordinary Times: Soviet Russia in the 1930s*. 1999. An engaging, balanced account of urban life in the Soviet Union in the context of the upheavals of the 1930s.

Kershaw, Ian. *Hitler*, vol. 1, *1889–1936, Hubris,* and vol. 2, *1936–1945, Nemesis*. 1999, 2000. Thorough and readable, the most important biography of Hitler.

Northrop, Douglas. *Veiled Empire: Gender and Power in Stalinist Central Asia*. 2004. Examines the anomalies that resulted as the Communists sought to bring their revolution to Uzbekistan, in Soviet central Asia, by reforming Muslim gender relations.

Paxton, Robert O. *The Anatomy of Fascism*. 2004. Comes to an effective conclusion based on a careful account of the actual trajectories of the major fascist movements and regimes.

Roberts, David D. *The Totalitarian Experiment in Twentieth-Century Europe*. 2006. Seeks to reassess the historically specific common elements in the Soviet communist, Italian fascist, and Nazi German experiments of the interwar period.

Watt, Donald Cameron. *How War Came: The Immediate Origins of the Second World War, 1938–1939*. 1989. A detailed but readable narrative account, based on thorough research.

Weber, Eugen. *The Hollow Years: France in the 1930s*. 1994. A lively account of French life and manners during a decade that led to humiliation and defeat.

NOTES

1. Quoted in Martin McCauley, *The Soviet Union Since 1917* (London and New York: Longman, 1981), pp. 72–73.

2. Quoted in Robert Conquest, *The Great Terror: A Reassessment* (New York: Oxford University Press, 1990), p. 24.

3. Quoted in Helmut Krausnick et al., *Anatomy of the SS State* (New York: Walker, 1968), p. 13.

28

THE ERA OF THE SECOND WORLD WAR, 1939–1949

Atomic Bombing of Nagasaki, August 9, 1945

When this photo was taken, from an observation plane 6 miles up, thirty-five thousand people on the ground had already died.

(By courtesy of the Trustees of the Imperial War Museum)

"The effects could well be called unprecedented, magnificent, beautiful, stupendous and terrifying. No man-made phenomenon of such tremendous power had ever occurred before.... Thirty seconds after the explosion came first, the air blast pressing hard against the people and things, to be followed almost immediately by the strong, sustained, awesome roar which warned of doomsday and made us feel that we puny things were blasphemous to dare tamper with the forces heretofore reserved to The Almighty."[1]

So wrote Brigadier General Thomas F. Farrell, who had just witnessed the birth of the atomic age. On July 16, 1945, watching from a shelter 10,000 yards away, Farrell had seen the first explosion of an atomic bomb at a remote, top-secret U.S. government testing ground near Alamogordo, New Mexico. Such a weapon had been little more than a theoretical possibility when World War II began, and it required a remarkable concentration of effort, centered first in Britain, then in the United States, to make possible the awesome spectacle that confronted General Farrell. Exceeding most expectations, the test revealed a weapon of unprecedented power and destructiveness.

Within weeks, the United States dropped two other atomic bombs—first on Hiroshima, then on Nagasaki—to force the surrender of Japan in August 1945. Thus ended the Second World War, the conflict that had begun six long years earlier with the German invasion of Poland. At first Germany enjoyed remarkable success, prompting Italy to intervene and encouraging Japanese aggressiveness as well. But Britain held on even after its ally, France, fell to Germany in 1940. Then the war changed character in 1941 when Germany attacked the Soviet Union and Japan attacked the United States.

Britain, the United States, and the Soviet Union quickly came together in a "Grand Alliance," which spearheaded the victorious struggle against the Axis powers—Germany, Italy, and Japan. In Europe, the Soviet victory in a brutal land war with Germany proved decisive. In East Asia and the Pacific, the Americans gradually prevailed against Japan. The American use of the atomic bomb to end the war was the final stage in an escalation of violence that made World War II the most destructive war in history. What the

CHAPTER OUTLINE

THE VICTORY OF NAZI GERMANY, 1939–1941

THE ASSAULT ON THE SOVIET UNION AND THE NAZI NEW ORDER

A GLOBAL WAR, 1941–1944

THE SHAPE OF THE ALLIED VICTORY, 1944–1945

INTO THE POSTWAR WORLD

KEY TERMS

Vichy France

Charles de Gaulle

Winston Churchill

Auschwitz-Birkenau

Stalingrad

"the Great Patriotic War"

Franklin Delano Roosevelt

Lend-Lease Act

D-Day

Yalta conference

United Nations

Potsdam conference

Nuremberg trials

"iron curtain"

cold war

Truman Doctrine

Online Study Center

This icon will direct you to interactive map and primary source activities on the website **college.hmco.com/pic/noble5e**

advent of this terrifying new weapon would mean for the future remained unclear in the war's immediate aftermath.

The ironic outcome of the Second World War was a new cold war between two of the victors, the United States and the Soviet Union. Emerging from the war with far greater power and prestige, each assumed a world role that would have been hard to imagine just a few years earlier. By the end of the 1940s, these two new superpowers had divided Europe into competing spheres of influence. Indeed, the competition between the United States and the Soviet Union almost immediately became global in scope, creating a bipolar world. And the cold war between them was especially terrifying because, seeking military advantage, they raced to stockpile ever more destructive nuclear weapons. Thus the threat of nuclear annihilation helped define the cold war era.

World War II led to the defeat of Italy, Germany, and Japan and in this sense resolved the conflicts that had caused it. But the experience of this particular war changed the world forever. Before finally meeting defeat, the Nazis were sufficiently successful to begin implementing their "new order" in Europe, especially in the territories they conquered to the east. As part of this effort, in what has become known as the Holocaust, they began systematically murdering Jews in extermi-

nation camps, eventually killing as many as six million. The most destructive of the camps was at Auschwitz (OWSH-vits), in what had been Poland. Often paired after the war, Auschwitz and Hiroshima came to stand for the incredible new forms of death and destruction that the war had spawned—and that continued to haunt the world long after it had ended, posing new questions about the meaning of Western civilization.

FOCUS QUESTIONS

What were the outcomes of the war as of late spring 1941, before the German invasion of the Soviet Union and before the intervention of the United States?

What was the place of the Holocaust in the Nazi effort to begin constructing a "new order" in eastern Europe?

How did the Grand Alliance of Britain, the United States, and the Soviet Union come together against the Axis powers?

How did the Allies manage to defeat Nazi Germany in World War II, after Germany's remarkable initial successes?

What was the relationship between the Allied victory in World War II and the coming of the cold war?

THE VICTORY OF NAZI GERMANY, 1939–1941

What were the outcomes of the war as of late spring 1941, before the German invasion of the Soviet Union and before the intervention of the United States?

Instead of the enthusiasm evident in 1914, the German invasion of Poland on September 1, 1939, produced a grim sense of foreboding, even in Germany. Well-publicized incidents such as the German bombing of civilians during the Spanish civil war and the Italian use of poison gas in Ethiopia suggested that the frightening new technologies introduced in World War I would now be used on a far greater scale. The new conflict would be a much uglier war, more directly involving civilians.

Still, as in 1914, there were hopes that this war could be localized and brief—that it would not become a "world war." Hitler and the Germans envisioned a *Blitzkrieg*, or "lightning war," and the initial outcome seemed to confirm these expectations. Poland fell quickly, and Hitler publicly offered peace to Britain and France, seriously thinking that might be the end of it. The British and French refused to call off the war, but from 1939 through 1941 the Nazis won victory after victory, establishing the foundation for their new order in Europe.

INITIAL CONQUESTS AND "PHONY WAR"

The Polish army was large enough to have given the Germans a serious battle. But in adapting the technological innovations of World War I, Germany had developed a new military strategy based on rapid mobility. This Blitzkrieg strategy employed swift, highly concentrated offensives based on mobile tanks covered with concentrated air support, including dive-bombers that struck just ahead of the tanks. In Poland this strategy proved decisive. The French could offer only token help, and the last Polish unit surrendered on October 2, barely a month after the fighting had begun. The speed of the German victory stunned the world.

Meanwhile, the Soviets began cashing in on the pact they had made with Nazi Germany a few weeks before. It offered a precious opportunity to undo provisions of the World War I settlement that had significantly diminished the western territories of the former Russian Empire. On September 17, with the German victory in Poland assured, Stalin sent Soviet forces westward to share in the spoils. Soon Poland was again divided between Germany and Russia, just as most of it had been before 1914. The Baltic states of Estonia, Latvia, and Lithuania soon fell as well.

When Finland proved less pliable, the Soviets invaded in November 1939. In the ensuing "Winter War," the Finns held out bravely, and the Soviets managed to prevail by March 1940 only by taking heavy casualties. The difficult course of the war in Finland seemed to confirm suspicions that Stalin's purge during the mid-1930s had substantially weakened the Soviet army. Still, by midsummer 1940, the Soviet Union had regained much of the territory it had lost during the upheavals that followed the revolution of 1917.

In the west, little happened during the strained winter of 1939–1940, known as the "Phony War." Then, on April 9, 1940, the Germans attacked Norway and Denmark in a surprise move to preempt a British and French scheme to cut off the major route for the shipment of Swedish iron ore to Germany. Denmark fell almost at once, while the staunch resistance in Norway was effectively broken by the end of April. The stage was set for the German assault on France.

THE FALL OF FRANCE, 1940

The war in the west began in earnest on May 10, 1940, when Germany attacked France and the Low Countries. The Germans launched their assault on France through the Ardennes Forest, above the northern end of the Maginot Line—terrain so difficult the French had discounted the possibility of an enemy strike there (see page 810). As in 1914, northern France quickly became the focus of a major war pitting French forces and

their British allies against invading Germans. But this time, in startling contrast to World War I, the Battle of France was over in less than six weeks, a humiliating defeat for the French.

The problem for France was not lack of men and materiel, but strategy. Germany had only a slight numerical

CHRONOLOGY

September 1, 1939	Germany invades Poland
1939–1940	Soviets wage "Winter War" against Finland
1940	Germany attacks Denmark and Norway (April)
	Germany attacks the Netherlands, Belgium, and France (May 10)
1941	Germany attacks the Soviet Union (June 22)
	Churchill and Roosevelt agree to the Atlantic Charter (August)
December 7, 1941	Japan attacks Pearl Harbor
August 1942–February 1943	Battle of Stalingrad
November 1942	Allied landings in North Africa
1943	Warsaw ghetto revolt (April–May)
	Soviet victory in Battle of Kursk-Orel (July)
	Allied landings in Sicily; fall of Mussolini; Italy asks for an armistice (July)
	Teheran conference (November)
June 6, 1944	D-Day: Allied landings in Normandy
February 1945	Yalta conference
May 7–8, 1945	Germany surrenders
June 1945	Founding of the United Nations
July–August 1945	Potsdam conference
August 6, 1945	U.S. atomic bombing of Hiroshima
August 15, 1945	Japan announces surrender
March 1947	Truman Doctrine
June 1948–May 1949	Berlin blockade and airlift
August 1949	First Soviet atomic bomb
September 1949	Founding of the Federal Republic in West Germany

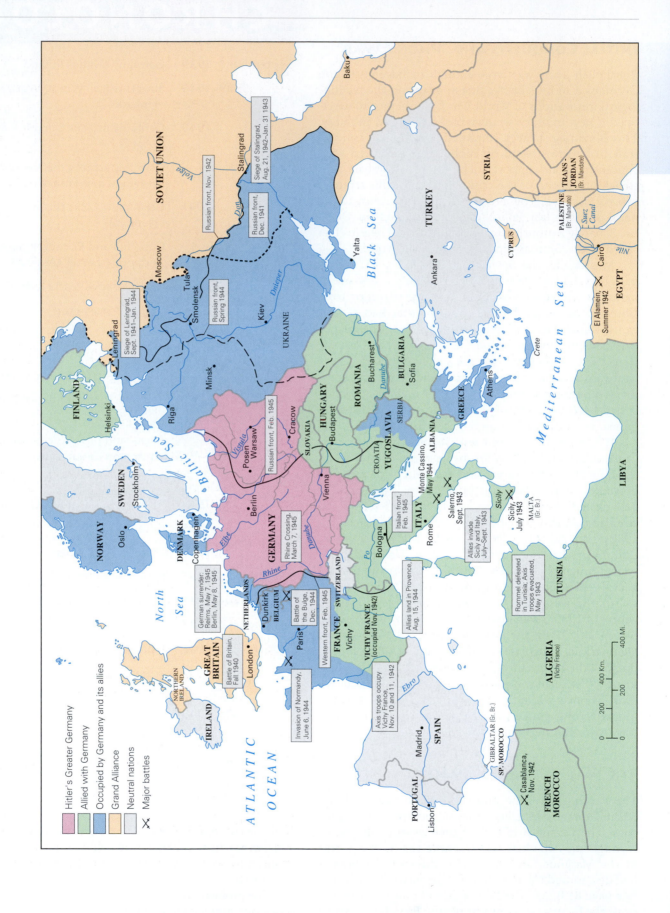

SOVIET UNION

Baku

Volga

Russian front, Nov. 1942

Stalingrad

Siege of Stalingrad, Aug. 21, 1942–Jan. 31 1943

Russian front, Dec. 1941

Don

SYRIA

Moscow

TURKEY

PALESTINE (Br. Mandate)

TRANS-JORDAN (Br. Mandate)

Tula

Black Sea

Smolensk

Russian front, Spring 1944

Dnieper

Yalta

Ankara

CYPRUS

Suez Canal

Nile

Leningrad

Siege of Leningrad, Sept. 1941–Jan. 1944

Kiev

UKRAINE

El Alamein, Summer 1942

Cairo

EGYPT

FINLAND

Minsk

Bucharest

Danube

BULGARIA

Sofia

Mediterranean Sea

Helsinki

Riga

ROMANIA

Crete

NORWAY

SWEDEN

Stockholm

Baltic Sea

Vistula

Posen

Warsaw

Cracow

Russian front, Feb. 1945

SLOVAKIA

HUNGARY

Budapest

CROATIA

YUGOSLAVIA

SERBIA

ALBANIA

GREECE

Athens

Oslo

DENMARK

Copenhagen

Elbe

Berlin

GERMANY

Rhine Crossing, March 7, 1945

Vienna

Danube

Po

Bologna

Italian front, Feb. 1945

ITALY

Rome

Monte Cassino, May 1944

Salerno, Sept. 1943

Sicily, July 1943

Sicily

MALTA (Gr. Br.)

LIBYA

German surrender: Reims, May 7, 1945 Berlin, May 8, 1945

North Sea

NETHERLANDS

Dunkirk

BELGIUM

Battle of the Bulge, Dec. 1944

Rhine

Paris

Western front, Feb. 1945

FRANCE

SWITZERLAND

VICHY FRANCE (occupied Nov 1942)

Vichy

Allies land in Provence, Aug. 15, 1944

Allies invade Sicily and Italy, July–Sept. 1943

Rommel defeated in Tunisia, Axis troops evacuated, May 1943

TUNISIA

GREAT BRITAIN

Battle of Britain, Fall 1940

London

Invasion of Normandy, June 6, 1944

NORTHERN IRELAND

IRELAND

ATLANTIC OCEAN

Axis troops occupy Vichy France, Nov. 10 and 11, 1942

Ebro

Madrid

SPAIN

GIBRALTAR (Gr. Br.)

SP. MOROCCO

ALGERIA (Vichy France)

PORTUGAL

Lisbon

Casablanca, Nov. 1942

FRENCH MOROCCO

400 Mi.

400 Km.

200

200

0

0

Hitler's Greater Germany

Allied with Germany

Occupied by Germany and its allies

Grand Alliance

Neutral nations

Major battles

MAP 28.1   World War II: European Theaters
Much of Europe saw fighting during World War II, although different fronts were important at different times. What proved decisive was the fighting that ensued in the vast expanse of the Soviet Union after the Germans invaded in June 1941.

advantage in tanks but used mobile tanks and dive-bombers to mount rapid, highly concentrated offensives. Anticipating another long, defensive war, France had dispersed its tanks among infantry units along a broad front. Once the German tank column broke through the French lines, it quickly cut through northern France and moved toward the North Sea. France's poor showing convinced the British that rather than commit troops and planes to a hopeless battle in France, they should get out and regroup for a longer global war. Finally, in early June, 200,000 British troops—as well as 130,000 French—escaped German encirclement and capture through a difficult evacuation at Dunkirk (see **MAP 28.1**).

By mid-June, Germany had won a decisive victory. As the French military collapsed, the French cabinet resigned, to be replaced by a new government under Marshal Philippe Pétain, who had led the successful French effort in the Battle of Verdun during World War I. Pétain's government first asked for an armistice and then engineered a change of regime. The French parliament voted by an overwhelming majority to give Pétain exceptional powers, including the power to draw up a new constitution. So ended the parliamentary democracy of the Third Republic, which seemed responsible for France's weakness. The republic gave way to the more authoritarian **Vichy** (VEE-shee) regime, named after the resort city to which the government retreated as the Germans moved into Paris. The end of the fighting in France resulted in a kind of antidemocratic revolution, but one in which the French people, stunned by military defeat, at first acquiesced.

According to the armistice agreement, the French government was not only to cease hostilities but also to collaborate with the victorious Germans. French resistance began immediately, however. In a radio broadcast from London on June 18, **Charles de Gaulle** (1890–1970), the youngest general in the French army, called

Vichy France   Authoritarian French government, headquartered in the town of Vichy, that followed the Third Republic after France's defeat by Nazi Germany in 1940. The government collaborated with the victorious Germans, who occupied Paris.

Charles de Gaulle   The youngest general in the French army, he called on French forces to follow his lead and continue the fight against Nazi Germany after the fall of France in June 1940.

on French forces to rally to him to continue the fight against Nazi Germany. The military forces stationed in the French colonies, as well as the French troops that had been evacuated at Dunkirk, could form the nucleus of a new French army. Under the present circumstances of military defeat and political change, de Gaulle's appeal seemed quixotic at best. Most French colonies went along with what seemed the legitimate French government at Vichy—to which de Gaulle was a traitor. Yet a new Free French force grew from de Gaulle's remarkable appeal, and its subsequent role in the war compensated, in some measure, for France's humiliating defeat in 1940.

WINSTON CHURCHILL AND THE BATTLE OF BRITAIN

With the defeat of France, Hitler seems to have expected that Britain, now apparently vulnerable to German invasion, would come to terms. And certainly some prominent Britons questioned the wisdom of remaining at war. But the British war effort found a new and effective champion in **Winston Churchill** (1874–1965), who replaced Neville Chamberlain as prime minister on May 10, when the German invasion of western Europe began. Although Churchill had been prominent in British public life for years, his career to this point had not been noteworthy for either judgment or success. He was obstinate, difficult, something of a curmudgeon. Yet he rose to the wartime challenge, becoming one of the notable leaders of the modern era. In speeches to the House of Commons during the remainder of 1940, he inspired his nation with perhaps the most memorable words of the war. Though some found a negotiated settlement with Germany even more sensible in light of the outcome in France, Churchill's dogged promise of "blood, toil, tears, and sweat" helped rally the British people, so that later he could say, without exaggeration, that "this was their finest hour."

Online Study Center   Improve Your Grade
Primary Source: "This Was Their Finest Hour"

After the fall of France, Churchill's Britain promptly moved to full mobilization for a protracted war. Indeed, Britain developed the most thoroughly coordinated war economy of all the belligerents, producing more tanks, aircraft, and machine guns than Germany did between 1940 and 1942. The National Service Act of 1941 subjected men ages 18 to 50 and women ages 20 to 30 to military or civilian war service. The upper age limits were subsequently raised to meet the demand for labor. Almost 70 percent of the three million

Winston Churchill   British prime minister during World War II, his courage and decisiveness made him widely seen as one of modern Britain's greatest leaders.

people added to the British work force during the war were women.

Britain, then, intended to continue the fight even after France fell. Hitler weighed his options and decided to attack. In light of British naval superiority, he hoped to rely on aerial bombardment to knock the British out of the war without an actual invasion. The ensuing Battle of Britain culminated in the nightly bombing of London from September 7 through November 2, 1940, killing fifteen thousand people and destroying thousands of buildings. But the British held. Ordinary people holed up in cellars and subway stations, while the fighter planes of the Royal Air Force fought back effectively, inflicting heavy losses against German aircraft over Britain.

Although the bombing continued into 1941, the British had withstood the worst the Germans could deliver, and Hitler began looking to the east, his ultimate objective all along. In December 1940 he ordered preparations for Operation Barbarossa, the assault on the Soviet Union. Rather than continuing the attack on Britain directly, Germany would use submarines to cut off shipping—and thus the supplies the British needed for a long war. Once Germany had defeated the Soviet Union, it would enjoy the geopolitical basis for world power, while Britain, as an island nation relying on a dispersed empire, would sooner or later be forced to come to terms.

ITALIAN INTERVENTION AND THE SPREAD OF THE WAR

Lacking sufficient domestic support, and unready for a major war, Mussolini could only look on as the war began in 1939. But as the Battle of France neared its end, it seemed safe for Italy to intervene, sharing in the spoils of what appeared certain victory. Thus in June 1940 Italy entered the war, expecting to secure territorial advantages in the Mediterranean, starting with Corsica, Nice, and Tunisia, at the expense of France. Italy also hoped eventually to supplant Britain in the region—and even to take the Suez Canal.

Although Hitler and Mussolini got along reasonably well, their relationship was sensitive. When Hitler seemed to be proceeding without Italy during the first year of the war, Mussolini grew determined to show his independence. Finally, in October 1940, he ordered Italian forces to attack Greece. But the Greeks mounted a strong resistance, thanks partly to the help of British forces from North Africa.

Meanwhile, Germany had established its hegemony in much of east-central Europe without military force, often by exploiting grievances over the outcome of the Paris Peace Conference in 1919. In November 1940 Romania and Hungary joined the Axis camp, and Bulgaria followed a few months later. But in March 1941, just after Yugoslavia had similarly committed to

British Resistance
At the height of the German bombing of Britain in 1940, Winston Churchill and his wife, Clementine, survey the damage in London.
(*Hulton Archive/Getty Images*)

the Axis, a coup overthrew the pro-Axis government in Yugoslavia, and the new Yugoslav government prepared to aid the Allies.

By this point Hitler had decided it was expedient to push into the Balkans with German troops, both to reinforce the Italians and to consolidate Axis control of the area. As the war's geographic extent expanded, its stakes increased, yet the Germans continued to meet every challenge. By the end of May 1941 they had taken Yugoslavia and Greece (see Map 28.1).

At the same time, the war was spreading to North Africa and the Middle East because of European colonial ties. The native peoples of the area sought to take advantage of the conflict among the Europeans to pursue their own independence. Iraq and Syria became involved as the Germans, operating from Syria, which was administered by Vichy France, aided anti-British

Arab nationalists in Iraq. But most important proved to be North Africa, where Libya, an Italian colony since 1912, lay adjacent to Egypt, where the British presence remained strong.

In September 1940 the Italian army drove 65 miles into Egypt, initiating almost three years of fighting across the North African desert. A British counteroffensive from December 1940 to February 1941 drove the Italians back 340 miles into Libya, prompting Germany to send some of its forces from the Balkans into North Africa. Under General Erwin Rommel (1891–1944), the famous "Desert Fox," Axis forces won remarkable victories in North Africa from February to May 1941. But successful though they had been, the German forays into North Africa and the Balkans had delayed the crucial attack on the Soviet Union.

===== S E C T I O N   S U M M A R Y =====

- In implementing its innovative *Blitzkrieg* strategy, Germany employed rapid, highly concentrated offensives that combined tanks and airpower to great effect.

- After Poland fell quickly, Hitler offered peace to Britain and France, seriously thinking that this particular war might be over.

- Once German victory in Poland was assured, the Soviet Union began sharing the spoils and, by midsummer 1940, had regained much of the territory lost during the upheavals that followed the Russian Revolution.

- In dramatic contrast with World War I, France in 1940 fell to German invasion in less than six weeks.

- The defeat of France led to the end of the Third Republic and the advent of the authoritarian Vichy regime, which, according to the armistice agreement, was obliged to collaborate with Nazi Germany.

- Inspired by Churchill's determined leadership, the British withstood the sustained German air assault during the second half of 1940 and finally forced Hitler to alter his overall strategy.

THE ASSAULT ON THE SOVIET UNION AND THE NAZI NEW ORDER

What was the place of the Holocaust in the Nazi effort to begin constructing a "new order" in eastern Europe?

German troops invaded the Soviet Union on June 22, 1941, initiating what proved to be the decisive confrontation of World War II. Although the Nazis enjoyed the expected successes for a while, the Soviets eventually prevailed, spearheading the Allied victory in Europe. Supplies from their new Allies—Britain and eventually the United States—aided the Soviet cause, but the surprising strength of the Soviet military effort was the most important factor in the eventual outcome. In the process, the Soviets suffered incredible casualties, and after they gained the

initiative, they proceeded with particular brutality as they forced the invading Germans back into Germany.

In doing so, the Soviets were responding to the unprecedented form of warfare that the Nazis had unleashed. While preparing for the attack on the Soviet Union, Hitler had made it clear to the Nazi leadership that this was to be no ordinary military engagement but a war of racial-ideological extermination. The Germans penetrated well into the Soviet Union, reaching the apex of their power late in 1942. German conquests by that point enabled Hitler to begin constructing the

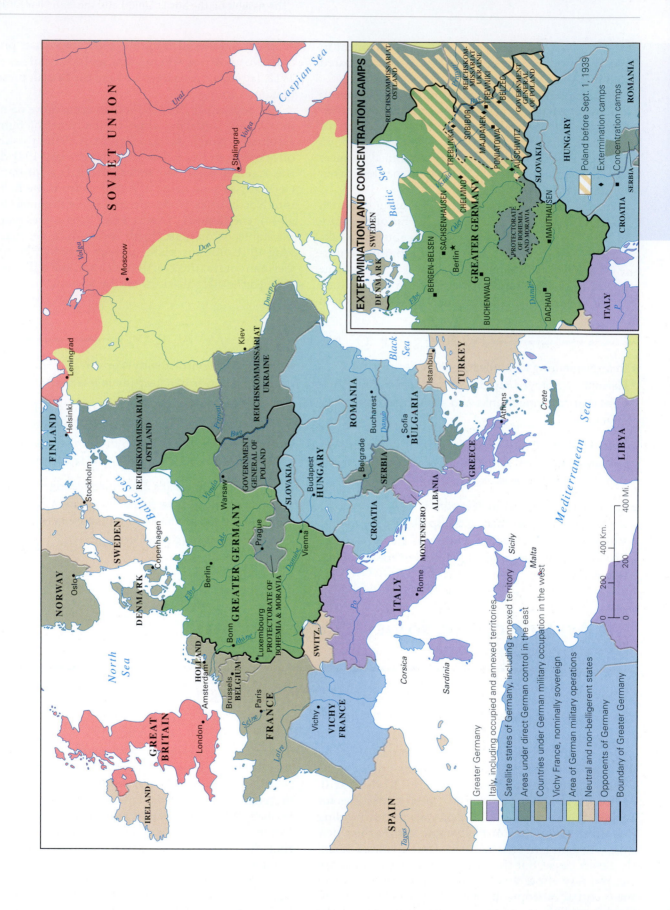

SOVIET UNION

Caspian Sea

Ural

Volga

• Stalingrad

Volga

Don

• Moscow

Dnieper

• Kiev

REICHSKOMMISSARIAT UKRAINE

Leningrad •

FINLAND

Helsinki •

Pripyat

Bug

GOVERNMENT GENERAL OF POLAND

Black Sea

TURKEY

ROMANIA

Bucharest •

Danube

Istanbul •

Crete

REICHSKOMMISSARIAT OSTLAND

Baltic Sea

Vistula

Warsaw •

Oder

SLOVAKIA

Budapest •

HUNGARY

Belgrade •

SERBIA

BULGARIA

Sofia •

Mediterranean Sea

Stockholm •

SWEDEN

Copenhagen •

Prague •

GREATER GERMANY

Berlin •

Elbe

Bonn •

Vienna •

Danube

Rhine

PROTECTORATE OF BOHEMIA & MORAVIA

Luxembourg •

CROATIA

ALBANIA

GREECE

Athens •

LIBYA

NORWAY

Oslo •

DENMARK

North Sea

HOLLAND

Amsterdam •

BELGIUM

Brussels •

SWITZ.

Po

ITALY

Rome •

Sicily

Malta

GREAT BRITAIN

London •

Paris •

Seine

FRANCE

Loire

Vichy •

VICHY FRANCE

Corsica

Sardinia

IRELAND

SPAIN

Tagus

EXTERMINATION AND CONCENTRATION CAMPS

ROMANIA

REICHSKOMMISSARIAT OSTLAND

REICHSKOMMISSARIAT UKRAINE

GOVERNMENT GENERAL OF POLAND

SOBIBOR

TREBLINKA

MAJDANEK

BELZEC

PONIATOWA

AUSCHWITZ

HUNGARY

SLOVAKIA

CROATIA

SERBIA

Baltic Sea

SWEDEN

DENMARK

CHELMNO

SACHSENHAUSEN

Berlin ★

Oder

BERGEN-BELSEN

GREATER GERMANY

BUCHENWALD

PROTECTORATE OF BOHEMIA AND MORAVIA

MAUTHAUSEN

DACHAU

Danube

ITALY

Vistula

Elbe

Poland before Sept. 1, 1939

Extermination camps

Concentration camps

Greater Germany

Italy, including occupied and annexed territories.

Satellite states of Germany, including annexed territory

Areas under direct German control in the east

Countries under German military occupation in the west

Vichy France, nominally sovereign

Area of German military operations

Neutral and non-belligerent states

Opponents of Germany

Boundary of Greater Germany

400 Km.

400 Mi.

0   200

0   200

MAP 28.2   The Nazi New Order in Europe, 1942

At the zenith of its power in 1942, Nazi Germany controlled much of Europe. Concerned most immediately with winning the war, the Nazis sought to coordinate the economies of their satellite states and conquered territories. But they also began establishing what was supposed to be an enduring new order in eastern Europe. The inset shows the locations of the major Nazi concentration camps and the six extermination camps the Nazis constructed in what had been Poland.

Forgive me, comrade . . .

On June 23, 1941, the day after Nazi Germany attacked the Soviet Union, the *London Daily Mail* published this cartoon depicting Hitler's betrayal of his 1939 pact with Stalin.   (*Daily Mail*, London, 23 June 1941. *Reprinted with permission of Solo Syndication Limited*)

—by Illingworth.

new, race-based European order he had dreamed of. Although in western Europe the Nazis generally sought the collaboration of local leaders, in the Soviet Union, as in Poland, the new order meant brutal subjugation of local populations. As part of this process, the Nazis began systematically killing Jews, first by shooting, then by mass-gassing them in specially constructed death camps.

AN AMBIGUOUS OUTCOME, 1941–1942

In ordering preparations for Operation Barbarossa in December 1940, Hitler decided to risk attacking the Soviet Union before knocking Britain out of the war. Then he invaded the Balkans and North Africa in what may have been an unnecessary diversion. In retrospect, it is easy to pinpoint that combination as his fatal mistake. But in light of the Soviet purges of the 1930s and what seemed the poor performance of the Soviet army against Finland, Hitler had reason to believe the Soviet Union would crack relatively easily. Western military experts had come to similar conclusions, estimating that German forces would need but six weeks to take Moscow. And if Germany were to defeat the Soviet Union with another Blitzkrieg, it could gain control of the oil and other resources required for a longer war against Britain and, if necessary, the United States.

Attacking the Soviet Union on June 22, 1941, German forces achieved notable successes during the first month of fighting, partly because Stalin was so unprepared for this German betrayal. Ignoring warnings of an impending German assault, he had continued to live up to his end of the 1939 bargain with Hitler, even supplying the Germans with oil and grain. After the attack, Russia's defenses were at first totally disorganized, and by late November German forces were within 20 miles of Moscow.

But the Germans were ill-equipped for Russian weather, and as an early and severe winter descended, the German offensive bogged down. In December the Soviets mounted a formidable surprise counterattack

near Moscow. The German Blitzkrieg, which had seemed a sure thing in July, had failed. Germany might still prevail, but a different strategy would be required.

Although their initial assault had stalled, the Germans still had the advantage. German forces failed to take the key city of Leningrad in 1941, but they cut it off by blockade and, until early 1944, kept it under siege with relentless bombing and shelling. During the summer of 1942, they mounted another offensive, moving more deeply into the Soviet Union than before, reaching Stalingrad in November. But this proved the deepest penetration of German forces—and the zenith of Nazi power in Europe.

HITLER'S NEW ORDER

By the summer of 1942, Nazi Germany dominated the European continent as no power had before (see **MAP 28.2**). German military successes allowed the Nazi regime to begin building a new order in the territories under German domination. Satellite states in Slovakia and Croatia, and client governments in Romania and Hungary, owed their existence to Nazi Germany and readily adapted themselves to the Nazi system. Elsewhere in the Nazi orbit, some countries proved eager collaborators; others did their best to resist; still others were given no opportunity to collaborate but were ruthlessly subjugated instead.

The Nazis' immediate aim was simply to exploit the conquered territories to serve the continuing war effort. Precisely as envisioned, access to the resources of so much of Europe made Germany considerably less vulnerable to naval blockade than during World War I. France proved a particularly valuable source of raw materials; by 1943, for example, 75 percent of French iron ore went to German factories.

But the deeper purposes of the war were also clear in the way the Nazis treated the territories under their control, especially in the difference between east and west. Western Europe experienced plenty of atrocities, but Nazi victory there still led to something like conventional military occupation. The Germans tried to enlist the cooperation of local authorities in countries like Denmark, the Netherlands, and France, though with mixed results. And whereas the Nazis exploited the economy of France, for example, it never became clear what role France might play in Europe after a Nazi victory. However, in Poland and later in the conquered parts of the Soviet Union, there was no pretense of cooperation, and it was immediately clear what the Nazi order would entail.

After the conquest of Poland, the Germans annexed the western part of the country outright and promptly executed, jailed, or expelled members of the Polish elite—professionals, journalists, business leaders, and priests. The Nazis prohibited the Poles from entering the professions and restricted even their right to marry. All the Polish schools and most of the churches were simply closed.

In the rest of Poland, known as the General Government, Nazi policy was slightly less brutal at first. Most churches remained open, and Poles were allowed to practice the professions, but the Nazis closed most schools above the fourth grade, as well as libraries, theaters, and museums, as they sought to root out every expression of Polish culture. Some Poles in this area were forced into slave labor, but a final decision as to whether the Polish population was to be exterminated, enslaved, or shipped off to Siberia was postponed—to be made after the wider war had been won.

With the conquest of Poland, Nazi leaders proclaimed that a new era of monumental resettlement in eastern Europe had begun for Germany. Germans selected for their racial characteristics were now resettled in the part of Poland annexed to Germany. Most were ethnic Germans who had been living outside Germany.

During the fall of 1942, Heinrich Himmler's *Schutzstaffel* (SS), the select Nazi elite, began to arrest and expel peasants from the rest of Poland to make way for further German resettlement. By 1943 perhaps one million Germans had been moved into what had been Poland.

After the assault on the Soviet Union, Hitler made it clear that eastern Europe as far as the Ural Mountains was to be opened for German settlement. War veterans were to be given priority, partly because the German settlers would have to be tough to resist the Slavs, who would be concentrated east of the Urals. To prepare for German colonization, Himmler told SS leaders that Germany would have to exterminate thirty million Slavs in the Soviet Union. After the German invasion, the SS promptly began executing prisoners of war, as well as any Soviet leaders they could find. However, the Nazis expected that several generations would be required for the resettlement of European Russia.

THE HOLOCAUST

Conquest of the east also opened the way to a more radical solution to the "Jewish problem" than the Nazis had contemplated before. Under the cover of war, they began actually killing the Jews within their orbit. Thus began the process, and the experience, that has come to be known as the Holocaust.

When and why this radical policy was chosen remains controversial. Although prewar Nazi rhetoric occasionally suggested the possibility of actual physical extermination, talk of a "final solution to the Jewish problem" seemed to mean forced emigration. Although the precise chain of events that led to a more radical approach will no doubt remain uncertain, it was surely bound up with the fortunes of the war.

The Ghettos   The conquest of Poland, with a Jewish population of 3.3 million, gave the Nazis control over a far greater number of Jews than ever before. In 1940, as part of their effort to create a new order, the Nazis began confining Polish Jews to ghettos set up in Warsaw and five other cities. Although much brutality and many deaths accompanied this process, the Nazis had not yet adopted a policy of systematic killing. Indeed, at first no one knew what was to become of these Jews. At this point Nazi authorities were concentrating on removing, or even killing, non-Jewish Poles to make way for German resettlement into former Polish lands. The fate of the Jews would be decided later.

Online Study Center **Improve Your Grade**
Primary Source: The Ghettoization of the Jews: Prelude to the Final Solution

After the defeat of France, Himmler and the SS made tentative plans to develop a kind of superghetto for perhaps four million Jews on the island of Madagascar, at that point still a French colony, once the war had been won. However, as the Polish ghettos grew more crowded and difficult to manage, Nazi officials in Poland began pressing for a more immediate solution.

The SS Plan for Annihilation

At the same time, Hitler made it clear that the invasion of the Soviet Union would launch something new, a racial-ideological war of annihilation. Accompanying the military forces were specially trained SS units, essentially mobile killing squads, assigned to get rid of Communist Party officials and adult male Jews. But soon some began murdering Jewish women and children as well. By late November 1941, the Nazis had killed 136,000 Jews, most by shooting, in the invaded Soviet territories. But this mode of killing proved both inefficient and psychologically burdensome—even for these specially trained killers. Their experience in the Soviet Union combined with the problems in the Polish ghettos to lead Nazi leaders to begin seeking a more systematic and impersonal method of mass extermination by late summer 1941.

The most likely scenario is that Hitler settled on physical extermination of the Jews in the thrill of what seemed impending victory over the Soviet Union. At the end of July 1941, Reinhard Heydrich of the SS began developing a detailed plan, and by the fall the Nazis were sending German and Austrian Jews to the ghettos in Poland and actively impeding further Jewish emigration from Europe.

Heydrich explained his plan for the extermination of the Jews in January 1942 at a conference of high-ranking officials at Wannsee, a suburb of Berlin. The conference had been postponed from early December, and by January the operation had already begun. The Nazis took advantage of the personnel and the methods—especially the use of poison gas—that had proven effective during the "euthanasia" campaign of 1939 through 1941 in Germany (see pages 854–855). By March 1942 they had constructed several extermination camps with gas chambers and crematoria, intended to kill large numbers of Jews and dispose of their bodies as efficiently as possible. Now they began full-scale mass killing, targeting first the Polish Jews who had already been confined to ghettos. The Nazis brutally suppressed attempts at resistance, like the Warsaw ghetto uprising of April and May 1943.

The End of the Warsaw Ghetto

In April 1943 the sixty thousand Jews remaining in the Warsaw ghetto revolted rather than face shipment to the extermination camps. Many died in the ensuing fighting; others perished as the Germans set fire to the ghetto. Almost all the rest were captured and sent to their deaths at Treblinka. Before it was put down in May, the uprising killed at least three hundred Germans. *(AP/Wide World Photos)*

Nazi Death Camps   During the war the Nazis constructed six full-scale death camps, although not all were operating at peak capacity at the same time. All six were located in what had been Poland (see inset, Map 28.2). Horrifying though they were, the concentration camps in Germany, such as Dachau, Buchenwald, and Bergen-Belsen, were not extermination camps, although many Jews died in them late in the war.

The largest of the six death camps was the **Auschwitz-Birkenau** complex, which became the principal extermination center in 1943. The Nazis shipped Jews from all over Europe to Auschwitz, which was killing about twelve thousand people a day at the height of its operation in 1944. Auschwitz was one of two extermination camps that included affiliated slave-labor factories, in which Jews considered most able to work were often literally worked to death. Among the companies profiting from the arrangement were two of Germany's best known, Krupp and IG Farben.

The Jews typically arrived at one of the camps crammed into cattle cars on special trains. SS medical doctors subjected new arrivals to "selection," picking some for labor assignments and sending the others, including most women and children, to the gas chambers. Camp personnel made every effort to deceive the Jews who were about to be killed, to lead them to believe they were to be showered and deloused. Even in camps without forced-labor factories, Jews were compelled to do much of the dirty work of the extermination operation. But under the brutal conditions of the camps, those initially assigned to work inevitably weakened; most were then deemed unfit and put to death.

Secrecy Surrounding the Camps   The Nazis took every precaution to hide what was going on in the death camps. The SS personnel involved were sworn to silence. Himmler insisted that if secrecy was to be maintained, the operation would have to be quick—and total, to include women and children, "so that no Jews will remain to take revenge on our sons and grandsons." Himmler constantly sought to accelerate the process, even though it required labor and transport facilities desperately needed for the war effort. Indeed, as the fortunes of war turned against Germany, the extermination of the Jews became a kind of end in itself.

Himmler and the other major SS officials, such as Rudolf Höss (HOESS), the commandant at Auschwitz, or Adolf Eichmann (IKE-mahn), who organized the transport of the Jews to the camps, were not simply sadists who enjoyed humiliating their victims. Rather, they took satisfaction in doing what they believed was their duty without flinching, without signs of weakness. Addressing a group of SS members in 1943, Himmler portrayed the extermination of the Jews as a difficult "historical task" that they, the Nazi elite, must do for their racial community: "Most of you know what it means to see a hundred corpses piled up, or five hundred, or a thousand. To have gone through this and—except for cases of human weakness—to have remained decent, that has made us tough. This is an unwritten, never to be written, page of glory in our history."[2]

However, as Himmler's casual reference to "cases of human weakness" suggests, a minority of camp guards and others failed to live up to this image and indulged in wanton cruelty toward their helpless victims. For some, the extermination process became the occasion to act out sadistic fantasies. But though this dimension is surely horrifying, the bureaucratic, factory-like nature of the extermination process has seemed still more troubling in some respects, for it raises questions about the nature of modern rationality itself. The mass killing of Jews required the expertise of scientists, doctors, and lawyers; it required the bureaucratic organization of the modern state—all to provide the most efficient means to a monstrous end.

Despite the overriding emphasis on secrecy, reports of the genocide reached the West almost immediately in 1942. At first, however, most tended to discount them as wartime propaganda of the sort that had circulated during World War I, when stories about Germans eating Belgian babies whipped up war fever. Skepticism about extermination reports was easier because there were a few concentration camps, like Theresienstadt (teh-REZ-ay-en-shtat) in the former Czechoslovakia, that housed Jews who had been selected for special treatment. These camps were not used for extermination and were not secret; the Red Cross was even allowed to inspect Theresienstadt several times. Those outside, and the German people as well, were led to believe that all the Jews were being interned, for the duration of the war, in camps like these, much as Japanese Americans were being interned in camps in the western United States at the same time. But even as the evidence grew, Allied governments, citing military priorities, refused pleas from Jewish leaders in 1944 to bomb the rail line into Auschwitz.

An Array of Victims   The Nazis' policy of actually murdering persons deemed undesirable or superfluous did not start with, and was not limited to, the Jews. First came the "euthanasia" program in Germany, and the war afforded the Nazis the chance to do away with an array of other "undesirables," including Poles, Sinti and Roma ("Gypsies"), communists, homosexuals, and vagrants. The Nazis also systematically killed perhaps 2 million Soviet prisoners of war. So the most radical

Auschwitz-Birkenau   The largest of Nazi Germany's six extermination camps, all of which were located in what had been Poland.

and appalling aspect of Nazism did not stem from anti-Semitism alone. This must not be forgotten, but neither must the fact that the Jews constituted by far the largest group of victims—perhaps 5.7 to 6 million, almost two-thirds of the Jews in Europe. (See the feature "The Visual Record: Holocaust Snapshots.")

COLLABORATION IN NAZI EUROPE

In rounding up Jews for extermination, and in establishing their new order in Europe, the Nazis found willing collaborators among some of the countries within their orbit. Several of them found collaboration with the victorious Nazi regime the best way to pursue their own nationalist agendas. Croatia, earlier part of the new state of Yugoslavia, was eager to round up Jews and Gypsies, as well as to attack Serbs, as part of its effort to establish itself as a nation-state. But national circumstances varied across Europe, and so did degrees of collaboration. In Denmark, Norway, and the Netherlands, the Nazis thought racial kinship would matter, but they never found sufficient support to make possible genuinely independent collaborationist governments. Denmark did especially well at resisting the German effort to round up Jews, as did Italy and Bulgaria.

Vichy France was somewhere in the middle, and thus it has remained particularly controversial. When the Vichy regime was launched during the summer of 1940, Marshal Pétain, its 84-year-old chief of state, enjoyed widespread support. Pétain promised to maximize French sovereignty and shield his people from the worst aspects of Nazi occupation. At the same time, the Vichy government claimed to be implementing its own "national revolution," returning France to authority, discipline, and tradition after the shambles of the Third Republic. Vichy's revolution was anti-Semitic and hostile to the left, so it seemed compatible, up to a point, with Nazism. And at first Germany seemed likely to win the war. Thus, Pétain's second-in-command, Pierre Laval (1883–1945), was willing to collaborate actively with the Nazis. The Vichy regime ended up doing much of the Nazis' dirty work for them—rounding up workers for forced shipment to German factories, hunting down members of the anti-German resistance, and picking up Jews to be sent to the Nazi extermination camps.

After the war, Pétain, Laval, and others were found guilty of treason by the new French government. Because of his advanced age, Pétain was merely imprisoned, while Laval and others were executed. Despite the contributions of de Gaulle's Free French and the French resistance, the shame of Vichy collaboration continued to haunt France, deepening the humiliation of the defeat in 1940.

TOWARD THE SOVIET TRIUMPH

The import of what happened elsewhere in Europe depended on the outcome of the main event, the German invasion of the Soviet Union. Although the German Sixth Army, numbering almost 300,000 men, reached Stalingrad by late 1942, the Germans could not achieve a knockout. The Soviets managed to defend the city in what was arguably the pivotal military engagement of World War II. While some Soviet troops fought street by street, house by house, others counterattacked, encircling the attacking German force. Hitler refused a strategic retreat, but his doggedness backfired. By the end of January 1943, the Soviets had captured what remained of the German force, about 100,000 men, very few of whom survived to return to Germany. Perhaps 240,000 German soldiers died in the Battle of **Stalingrad** or as prisoners afterward. But the price to the Soviets for their victory was far greater: a million Soviet soldiers and civilians died at Stalingrad.

Although the Germans resumed the offensive on several fronts during the summer of 1943, the Soviets won the tank battle of Kursk-Orel in July, and from then on Stalin's Red Army moved relentlessly westward, forcing the Germans to retreat. By February 1944 Soviet troops had pushed the Germans back to the Polish border, and the outcome of the war was no longer in doubt.

The Soviet victory on what proved the decisive front of World War II was incredible, in light of the upheavals of the 1930s and the low esteem in which most held the Soviet military in 1941. Portraying the struggle as **"the Great Patriotic War"** for national defense, Stalin managed to rally the Soviet people as the Germans attacked. Rather than emphasize communist themes, he recalled the heroic defenses mounted against invaders in tsarist times, including the resistance to Napoleon in 1812. But though the Soviets ultimately prevailed, the cost in death, destruction, and suffering was almost unimaginable. For example, by the time Soviet forces finally broke the siege of Leningrad in January 1944, a million people in the city had died, most from starvation, freezing, or disease. And the Soviets won on the battlefield partly by taking incredible numbers of casualties.

The invading Germans gained access to major areas of Soviet industry and oil supply, and by the end of 1941 the country's industrial output had been cut in half. Yet the Soviet Union was able to weather this blow and go

Stalingrad   Decisive World War II battle in which Soviet forces launched repeated counterattacks on Germany's Sixth Army, stopping it from advancing farther and finally forcing it to surrender.

"the Great Patriotic War"   Term for World War II devised by Joseph Stalin to rally Soviet citizens against the German invasion.

THE VISUAL RECORD

Holocaust Snapshots

What are we to make of these pictures? In one sense, they appear to be ordinary snapshots of the sort that became popular between the wars, as inexpensive cameras became common consumer items for the first time. But these photographs are hardly ordinary; they depict disturbing aspects of the Nazi effort to exterminate the Jews between 1941 and 1945. So we wonder who took these pictures—and why. Why did these particular images seem worth preserving? What do such photographs tell us about the mentality that made possible the monstrous process that we have come to know as the Holocaust?

More than 50 percent of the victims of the Holocaust died in the six extermination camps, the camps with systematic gassing facilities. Almost a quarter died from such factors as malnutrition, disease, or exhaustion while in transit, in the ghettos, or in the labor or concentration camps. The rest—more than one quarter of the victims—were killed individually, mostly by shooting, up close.

These photos, and many others like them, were taken by members of Hamburg-based Reserve Battalion 101 of the "order police," made famous through the somewhat conflicting accounts of Christopher R. Browning and Daniel Jonah Goldhagen.[3] This local branch of the complex German police system was sent to assist in the removal of Jews from a remote section of Poland in July 1942. Only upon arriving in the village of Józefów did these ordinary policemen find that their first task was to shoot large numbers of defenseless Jews one by one. When given their collective charge, these men were offered a chance to pull back from the actual murder of Jews. But the vast majority did what they were told—why?

We know that the men of Battalion 101 had not been specially selected and trained for such a task. Indeed, they were unprepared and surprised when, upon arriving in Józefów, they learned what they were there to do. Browning suggests that many of the men felt that they had to be tough, following orders based on government policy, whatever it entailed. Moreover, they did not want to appear weak or leave the dirty work to their comrades. Others tried not to think about what they were doing or masked it through heavy drinking.

But photographs like these suggest a further step. Ordinary Germans took them not so that they could forget, obviously, but precisely to remember and commemorate their participation. Indeed, the very act of taking the photographs was essential to their dehumanization and humiliation of the Jews. Notice the photo on the left, taken during the liquidation of the ghetto at Lukow, Poland, probably in the fall of 1942. Three of the four police officers are looking directly at the camera. Some of the officers have stern facial expressions, as if they are trying to convey their toughness and power. Others, such as the officer at far left, smile broadly for the camera. The Jews, meanwhile, are humiliated by being forced to kneel and raise their hands above their heads.

In the other photograph, Jews are shown digging their own graves. Unlike the one taken at Lukow, no officers appear in this photo and no one is posing for the camera. Yet somehow even this image seemed worth preserving in a snapshot.

What did these Germans find so memorable about what they were doing? We may first assume that sheer anti-Semitism was the key, a notion that Goldhagen wholeheartedly supports. He argues that these photographs manifest a virulent anti-Semitism endemic in German society even before the rise of Nazism. But most experts deny that German anti-Semitism had been especially pronounced before Hitler came to power, so something more complex was surely at work in the minds of these policemen. Especially as the Nazi revolution yielded an apocalyptic war of race, ideology, and annihilation, the Nazi regime's ongoing campaign to demonize the Jews affected the responses to the Jews by ordinary Germans. The Jews came to seem not merely superfluous, but alien and threatening.

Thus the key variable was not anti-Semitism per se but the momentum of the Nazi revolution itself. By 1942 a sense of the extraordinariness of the overall Nazi enterprise had produced an altered frame of mind in many reaches of German society. For example, a doctor involved in the earlier "euthanasia" program, Friedrich Mennecke, sought, in his letters to his wife, to chronicle for posterity this, "the greatest of times" in which he was privileged to participate.[4] In the same vein, historians Michael Burleigh and Wolfgang Wippermann found, as central to the Holocaust, "the group intoxication with violence and the prospect of going outside the limits of received moral norms."[5]

The ongoing Nazi revolution caught up even the members of Reserve Battalion 101 in essential

Lukow, Poland, July 1942   *(Yad Vashem Film and Photo Archive)*

roles. So those who took, and kept, and perhaps showed off these photographs were not merely ordinary human beings, or even ordinary Germans, but ordinary *Nazified* Germans. To some extent they, too, believed themselves to be involved in an enterprise that was grandiose, unprecedented, and of world-historical import. They did not merely follow orders but came to experience the "extraordinary exhilaration" that Saul Friedländer found central to the overall extermination process.[6] Partly as a result, they sometimes fell into the gratuitous cruelty evident in many of the photographs they took. Most of these men would not have been capable of such cruelty under ordinary circumstances.

When the veterans of police Battalion 101 were put on trial in the 1960s, one of them, Erwin Graffman, noted that only after the fact had it occurred to him that the killing had been wrong.[7] When acting, he had believed in the essential rightness of the wider Nazi revolution. The participation of such people is not to be explained simply through universal, ahistorical mechanisms, as if "we all could have done it." Those operating from within the framework of the Nazi revolution were especially likely to have treated the Jews as they did, not just killing them, but often humiliating them—and finding something memorable in the process.

Thus, for these perpetrators, the import of capturing the extraordinary enterprise through snapshots. But twenty years later, those who took them found it almost impossible to explain what had been their mindset at the time. As Browning noted, "it was a different time and place, as if they

Lomazy, Poland, August 1942   *(Courtesy, ZstL, Ludwigsburg, Germany)*

had been on another political planet, and the political values and vocabulary of the 1960s were useless in explaining the situation in which they had found themselves in 1942."[8] Yet these haunting images remain.

QUESTIONS

1. What, beyond sheer anti-Semitism, seems to have stimulated the policemen of Battalion 101 to preserve these scenes for posterity?

2. Does Erwin Graffman seem credible, or merely self-serving, when he says that, at the time these photographs were taken, he genuinely believed what he was doing was right?

Online Study Center
Improve Your Grade Visual Record Activities

Stalingrad, November 1942
From September 1942 until the German surrender early in February 1943, this city on the Volga River saw some of the heaviest fighting of World War II. The Soviet victory, in the face of incredible casualties, was arguably the turning point of the war in Europe. *(Sovfoto/Eastfoto)*

on to triumph. Outside help contributed, but only 5 to 15 percent of Soviet supplies came from the West. Between 1939 and 1941, Soviet leaders had begun building a new industrial base east of the Urals. And when the Germans invaded in 1941, the plant and equipment of 1,500 enterprises were dismantled and shipped by rail for reassembly farther east, out of reach of German attack. Then, beginning in 1942, thousands of brand-new factories were constructed in eastern regions as well.

Moreover, the earlier purges of the armed forces proved to have done less long-term damage than outside observers had expected. If anything, the removal of so many in the top ranks of the military hierarchy made it easier for talented young officers like Georgi Zhukov (1896–1974), who would become the country's top military commander, to rise quickly into major leadership positions.

When the United States entered the war in December 1941, the Soviets were fighting for survival. They immediately began pressuring the United States and Britain to open another front in Europe, preferably by landing in northern France, where an Allied assault could be expected to have the greatest impact. But the Allies did not invade northern France and open a major second front until June 1944. By then the Soviets had turned the tide in Europe on their own.

SECTION SUMMARY

- Although the German invasion of the Soviet Union in 1941 failed to bring the expected quick victory, the Germans drove still further into the country in 1942—but then met defeat at the Battle of Stalingrad.

- Brutal though it was, Nazi policy in northern and western Europe approached something like conventional military occupation, whereas in the conquered territories of the east, first and most dramatically in the former Poland, the Nazis engaged in radical population engineering as they began constructing a race-based "new order."

- By the end of 1941, the Holocaust became a systematic program as the Nazis decided to kill Jews and others by adapting the methods developed through the "euthanasia" program.

- Although the Jews constituted by far the largest group of victims, the Nazis also killed an array of others, from homosexuals to Soviet prisoners of war.

- After defeating the Germans at Kursk-Orel in July 1943, the Soviets began steadily advancing toward Germany, thereby turning the tide in Europe well before the U.S.-British landing in northern France opened a major second front in June 1944.

A GLOBAL WAR, 1941–1944

How did the Grand Alliance of Britain, the United States, and the Soviet Union come together against the Axis powers?

World War II proved unprecedented in its level of violence partly because it eclipsed even World War I in its geographical reach. The European colonial presence quickly drew the war to North Africa and the Middle East. But the war's early results in Europe also altered the power balance in East Asia and the Pacific, where the Russians and the Japanese had long been antagonists. During the 1930s, the United States had also become involved in friction with Japan. By 1941 President **Franklin Delano Roosevelt** was openly favoring the anti-Axis cause, though it took a surprise attack by the Japanese in December 1941 to bring the United States into the war.

JAPAN AND THE ORIGINS OF THE PACIFIC WAR

As a densely populated island nation lacking the raw materials essential for industry, Japan had been especially concerned about foreign trade and spheres of economic influence as it modernized after 1868. By the interwar period, the Japanese had become unusually reliant on exports of textiles and other products. During the Depression of the 1930s, when countries all over the world adopted protectionist policies, Japan suffered from increasing tariffs against its exports. This situation tilted the balance in Japanese ruling circles from free-trade proponents to those who favored a military-imperialist solution.

To gain economic hegemony by force, Japan could choose either of two directions. The northern strategy, concentrating on China, would risk Soviet opposition as well as strong local resistance. The southern strategy, focusing on southeast Asia and the East Indies, would encounter the imperial presence of Britain, France, the Netherlands, and the United States.

Japan opted for the northern strategy in 1931, when it took control of Manchuria, in northeastern China. But the Japanese attempt to conquer the rest of China, beginning in 1937, led only to an impasse by 1940. Japanese aggression in China drew the increasing hostility of the United States, a strong supporter of the Chinese nationalist leader Jiang Jieshi (Chiang Kai-shek) (1887–1975), as well as the active opposition of the Soviet Union. Clashes with Soviet troops along the border between Mongolia and Manchuria led to significant defeats for the Japanese in 1938 and 1939. The combination of China and the Soviet Union seemed more than Japan could handle.

By 1941, Germany's victories in Europe had seriously weakened Britain, France, and the Netherlands, the major European colonial powers in southeast Asia and the East Indies. The time seemed right for Japan to shift to a southern strategy. To keep the Soviets at bay, Japan agreed to a neutrality pact with the Soviet Union in April 1941. Rather than worry about China and the areas of dispute with the Soviet Union, the Japanese would seek control of southeast Asia, a region rich in such raw materials as oil, rubber, and tin—precisely what Japan lacked.

Japan had already joined with Nazi Germany and fascist Italy in an anticommunist agreement in 1936. In September 1940, the three agreed to a formal military alliance. For the Germans, alliance with Japan was useful to help discourage U.S. intervention in the European war. Japan, for its part, could expect the major share of the spoils of the European empires in Asia. However, diplomatic and military coordination between Germany and Japan remained minimal.

The United States began imposing embargoes on certain exports to Japan in 1938, in response to the Japanese aggression in China. After Japan had assumed control of Indochina, nominally held by Vichy France, by the summer of 1941, the United States imposed total sanctions, and the British and Dutch followed, forcing Japan to begin rapidly drawing down its oil reserves. Conquest of the oil fields of the Dutch East Indies now seemed a matter of life and death to the Japanese.

These economic sanctions heightened the determination of Japanese leaders to press forward aggressively now, when the country's likely enemies were weakened or distracted. But the Japanese did not expect to achieve a definitive victory over the United States in a long, drawn-out war. Rather, they anticipated, first, that their initial successes would enable them to grab the resources to sustain a longer war if necessary, and, second, that Germany would defeat Britain, leading the United States to accept a compromise peace allowing the Japanese what they wanted—a secure sphere of economic hegemony in southeast Asia.

Some Japanese leaders—diplomats, businessmen, naval officers, and even the emperor and some of his circle—were dismayed by the prospect of war with the United States. But as the influence of the military grew

Franklin Delano Roosevelt   U.S. president who served from 1933 to 1945, through the Great Depression of the 1930s and most of World War II.

MAP 28.3 The War in East Asia and the Pacific

After a series of conquests in 1941 and 1942, the Japanese were forced gradually to fall back before advancing U.S. forces. When the war abruptly ended in August 1945, however, the Japanese still controlled much of the territory they had conquered.

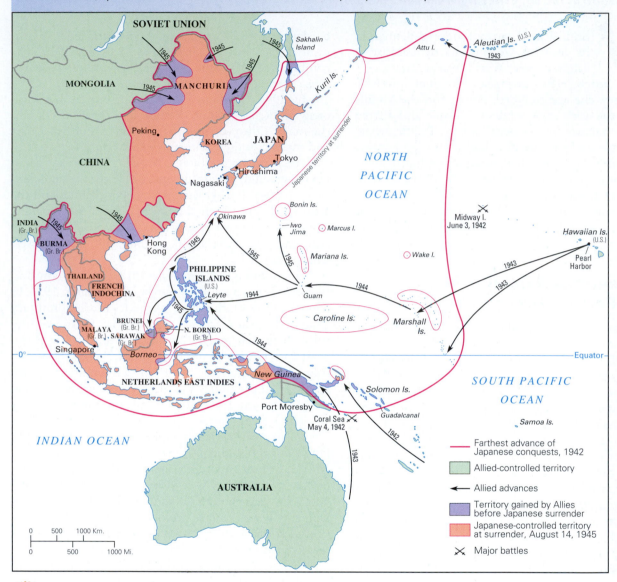

Online Study Center **Improve Your Grade** Interactive Map: World War II in the Pacific

during the 1930s, it became ever more difficult for those opposing Japan's new imperialist direction to make themselves heard. By 1941, a conformist confidence in victory was demanded, and dissenters dared not speak out for fear of being labeled traitors.

The Japanese finally provoked a showdown on December 7, 1941, with a surprise attack on Pearl Harbor, a U.S. naval base in Hawaii. The next day, Japanese forces seized Hong Kong and Malaya, both British colonies, and Wake Island and the Philippines, both under U.S. control. The United States promptly declared war; in response, Hitler kept an earlier promise

to Japan and declared war on the United States. World War II was now unprecedented in its geographic scope (see **MAP 28.3**).

Much like their German counterparts, Japanese forces got off to a remarkably good start. By the summer of 1942, Japan had taken Thailand, the Dutch East Indies, the Philippines, and the Malay Peninsula. Having won much of what they had been seeking, the Japanese began devising the Greater East Asia Co-Prosperity Sphere, their own "new order" in the conquered territories. (See the box "The Global Record: Japan's 'Pan-Asian' Mission.")

JAPAN'S "PAN-ASIAN" MISSION

With the coming of war against the Western powers in 1941, the Japanese could claim to be freeing Asians from Western imperialism and establishing a new economic order in East Asia and the Pacific. This selection from an essay titled "Our Present War and Its Cultural Significance," written just after the bombing of Pearl Harbor by the well-known author Nagayo Yoshio (1888–1961), accents Japan's anti-Western mission in the region. Yoshio understood, especially from his country's recent experience in China, that Asians might find Japanese hegemony just as oppressive as Western domination. Although it served Japan's own economic interests and was often applied brutally, Japanese "pan-Asianism" helped fuel the reaction against Western imperialism in Asia and the Pacific, with lasting results after the war.

Whenever Japan has faced a powerful enemy it has been the *yamato damashii* [Japanese national spirit] which provided the basis of our courage. Now that we can talk in retrospect of the Sino-Japanese War, I am afraid our national spirit has not been given a proper chance to be aroused, due to the deplorable fact that we had to fight with China, our sister nation, with no foreseeable conclusion to look forward to.... While desperately fighting with a country which we made our enemy only reluctantly we were trying to find out a principle, an ethic based upon a new view of the world, which would justify our course of action.... The China incident was not only insufficient to fulfill this goal but also met with insurmountable obstacles. Consequently, time and opportunity ripened to declare war against the United States and England....

... We would have nothing to say for ourselves if we were merely to follow the examples of the imperialistic and capitalistic exploitation of Greater East-Asia by Europe and the United States....

... It is true that the science of war is one manifestation of a nation's culture. But from this time on we have to realize the increasing responsibility on our part if we are to deserve the respect of the people of East-Asian countries as their leaders, in the sphere of culture in general (not only the mere fusion and continuance of Western and Oriental cultures but something surpassing and elevating them while making the most out of them) such as the formation of national character, refinement, intellect, training to become a world citizen, etc. ...

The sense of awe and respect with which the Orientals have held the white race, especially the Anglo-Saxons, for three hundred years is deep-rooted almost beyond our imagination. It is our task to realize this fact and deal with this servility at its root, find out why the white people became the objects of such reverence. It goes without saying that we cannot conclude simplemindedly that their shrewdness is the cause. Also we have to be very careful not to impose the *hakko ichiu* [the gathering of the whole world under one roof] spirit arbitrarily upon the Asians. If we make this kind of mistake we might antagonize those who could have become our compatriots and thus might also blaspheme our Imperial rule....

To sum up, we have finally witnessed the dawn of a new principle which we had been searching for over ten years.... The phrase "Greater East-Asian Co-prosperity Sphere" is no longer a mere abstract idea.

QUESTIONS

1. Why, according to the author, did the Japanese effort in China sow confusion about Japan's wider aims?

2. What role was Japan to play in southeast Asia if it was *not* merely to replace Western imperialistic exploitation with another form?

Source: "Our Present War and Its Cultural Significance" by Nagayo Yashio, translated by Mitsuko Iriye, in *Modern Asia and Africa,* edited by William H. McNeill and Mitsuko Iriye (New York: Oxford University Press, 1971), pp. 232–236.

THE UNITED STATES IN EUROPE AND THE PACIFIC

During the first years of the war in Europe, the United States did not have armed forces commensurate with its economic strength; in 1940, in fact, its army was smaller than Belgium's. But the United States could be a supplier in the short term and, if it chose to intervene, a major player over the longer term. With the **Lend-Lease Act** of March 1941, intended to provide war materiel without the economic dislocations of World War I, the United States lined up on the side of Britain against the Axis powers. In August 1941 a meeting between Churchill and Roosevelt aboard a cruiser off the coast of Newfoundland produced the Atlantic Charter, the first tentative agreement about the aims

Lend-Lease Act Act by the U.S. Congress authorizing President Franklin Roosevelt to lend or lease weapons or other aid to countries the president designated.

and ideals that were to guide the anti-Axis war effort. The Americans extended lend-lease to the Soviet Union the next month.

But though Roosevelt was deeply committed to the anti-Axis cause, isolationist sentiment remained strong in the United States. The Japanese attack on Pearl Harbor in December inflamed American opinion and enabled Roosevelt at last to bring his country into the war as an active belligerent. By May 1942 the United States had joined with Britain and the Soviet Union in a formal military alliance against the Axis powers.

The two democracies had joined with Stalin's Soviet Union in a marriage of expediency, and mutual suspicions marked the relationship from the start. Initially, Britain and the United States feared that the Soviet Union might even seek a separate peace, as Russia had in World War I. The Soviets, for their part, worried that these newfound allies, with their long-standing anticommunism, might hold back from full commitment or even seek to undermine the Soviet Union.

In response to pressure from Stalin, Britain and the United States agreed to open a second front in Europe as soon as possible. But the Nazis dominated the Continent, so opening such a front required landing troops from the outside. It proved far more difficult to mount an effective assault on Europe than either Churchill or Roosevelt anticipated in 1942. The resulting delays furthered Stalin's suspicions that his allies were only too eager to have the Soviets do the bulk of the fighting against Nazi Germany—and weaken themselves in the process.

The United States agreed with its new allies to give priority to the war in Europe. But because it had to respond to the direct Japanese assault in the Pacific, the United States was not prepared to act militarily in Europe right away. What it could do, however, was supply the British with the ships needed to overcome German submarines, which seriously threatened shipping to Britain by 1942.

In the Pacific theater, in contrast, it was immediately clear that the United States would bear the brunt of the fighting against Japan. Although the Japanese went from one success to another during the first months of the war, they lacked the long-term resources to exploit their initial victories. In May 1942 the Battle of Coral Sea—off New Guinea, north of Australia—ended in a stalemate, stopping the string of Japanese successes. Then in June, the United States defeated the Japanese navy for the first time in the Battle of Midway, northwest of Hawaii. After the United States stopped attempted Japanese advances in the Solomon Islands and New Guinea early in 1943, U.S. forces began steadily advancing across the islands of the Pacific toward Japan (see Map 28.3).

THE SEARCH FOR A SECOND FRONT IN EUROPE

As the Soviet army fought the Germans in the Soviet Union, the United States and Britain tried to determine how they could help tip the scales in Europe, now an almost impregnable German fortress. Stalin kept urging a direct assault across the English Channel, which, if successful, would have the greatest immediate impact. Churchill, however, advocated attacking the underbelly of the Axis empire by way of the Mediterranean, which would first require winning control of North Africa. And it was that strategy the Allies tried first, starting in 1942.

By May 1943, step one of Churchill's plan had succeeded, but North Africa was valuable only as a staging ground for an Allied attempt to penetrate Europe from the south (see Map 28.1). Meeting at the Moroccan city of Casablanca in January 1943, Churchill and Roosevelt agreed that British and American forces would proceed from North Africa to Sicily and on up through Italy. The Soviets, still pushing for an invasion across the English Channel into France, objected that the Germans could easily block an Allied advance through the long, mountainous Italian peninsula.

Crossing from North Africa, Allied troops landed in Sicily in July 1943, prompting the arrest of Mussolini and the collapse of the fascist regime. Supported by King Victor Emmanuel III, the Italian military commander, Pietro Badoglio (bah-DOHL-yo), formed a new government to seek an armistice. Meanwhile, Allied forces moved on to the Italian mainland, but the Germans quickly occupied much of Italy in response. They even managed a daring rescue of Mussolini and promptly re-established him as puppet leader of a new rump republic in northern Italy, now under German control. Just as the Soviets had warned, the Germans sought to block the Italian peninsula, and it was not until nine months later, in June 1944, that the Allies reached Rome. So Churchill's strategy of assaulting Europe from the south proved less than decisive.

Only when Churchill, Roosevelt, and Stalin met for the first time, at Teheran, Iran, in November 1943, did they agree that the next step would be to invade western Europe from Britain. Preparations had been underway since early 1942, but the operation was complex and hazardous in the extreme. Finally, Allied troops crossed the English Channel to make an amphibious landing on the beaches of Normandy, in northern France, on June 6, 1944, known to history as **D-Day.** Partly by deceiving the Germans seeking to defend the area, they were quickly able to consolidate their positions.

D-Day   The complex Allied amphibious landings in Normandy, France, on June 6, 1944, that opened a second major European front in World War II.

The success of the D-Day invasion opened a major second front in Europe at last. Now American-led forces from the west and Soviet forces from the east worked systematically toward Germany. The one substantial German counterattack in the west, the Battle of the Bulge in December 1944, slowed the Allies' advance, but on March 7, 1945, Allied troops crossed the Rhine River (see Map 28.1).

By June 1944, when Allied forces landed at Normandy, Soviet forces had already crossed the 1939 border with Poland as they moved steadily westward. But in August the Soviets stopped before reaching Warsaw, allowing the Nazis to crush a notable uprising by the Polish resistance from August to October. The Polish Home Army, as it was called, was seeking to liberate Warsaw on its own, without waiting for the Soviets, who seemed likely to impose communism on Poland. In putting down the uprising, the German occupying forces suffered ten thousand casualties, then destroyed much of the city in retaliation. Meanwhile, the major Soviet thrust began cutting south, through Romania, which surrendered in August, and on into the Danube Valley in Hungary and Yugoslavia during the fall. The Soviets resumed their advance, taking Warsaw and moving westward toward Germany, only in January 1945.

Now, with the defeat of Germany simply a matter of time, Allied concern shifted to the postwar order. Churchill, especially, worried about the implications of the Soviet advances in east-central Europe and the Balkans. As a supplement to the D-Day landings, he wanted to strike from Italy through Yugoslavia into east-central Europe. But the Americans resisted; Churchill's priorities, they felt, reflected old-fashioned concerns over spheres of influence that were no longer appropriate. So the Allies concentrated instead on a secondary landing in southern France in August 1944. This assault, in which Free French forces were prominent, led quickly to the liberation of Paris. But because the Allies made both their landings in France, and not in southeastern Europe, the Western democracies were involved only in the liberation of western Europe. It was the Soviets who drove the Germans from east-central Europe and the Balkans. This fact, and the resulting geographic distribution of military strength, fundamentally affected the postwar order in Europe.

D-Day, 1944
Allied forces land at Normandy, early in the morning of June 6, 1944, at last opening a major second front in Europe.   *(National Archives, Washington)*

S E C T I O N   S U M M A R Y

- Japan turned to a more aggressive, expansionist foreign policy during the 1930s largely because its economy, heavily dependent on exports, proved especially vulnerable during the Great Depression.

- Although Japan and Nazi Germany each had reasons for a military alliance with the other, diplomatic and military coordination between them was minimal during World War II.

- Delays in opening a major second front in Europe furthered Stalin's suspicions that Britain and the United States were happy to let the Soviets bear

the brunt of the burden in the fight against Nazi Germany.

- After the Allied invasion of Italy failed to make a conclusive difference on the continental level, Churchill, Roosevelt, and Stalin agreed in November 1943 that, as the next step, the democracies would invade western Europe from Britain.

- In making their continental landings in Italy and France, the Western democracies left it to the Soviets to drive the German forces from east-central Europe and the Balkans.

THE SHAPE OF THE ALLIED VICTORY, 1944–1945

How did the Allies manage to defeat Nazi Germany in World War II, after Germany's remarkable initial successes?

The leaders of the Soviet Union, Britain, and the United States sought to mold that postwar order at two notable conferences in 1945. Even as they brought different aspirations for the postwar world, they had to deal together with the legacy of a war of unprecedented violence and destruction. At the same time, they also had to face the hard military realities that had resulted from the fighting so far: each country had armies in certain places but not in others. The result was an informal division of Europe into spheres of influence among the victors.

The most serious question the Allies faced concerned Germany, which was widely held responsible for the two world wars, as well as for Nazism with all its atrocities—including the concentration and extermination camps, discovered with shock and horror by the advancing Allied armies in 1945. Germany was to be forced to surrender unconditionally; there would be no negotiation or armistice. But what should be done with the country over the longer term?

In the Pacific theater, as in Europe, the way the war ended had major implications for the postwar world. The United States decided to use the atomic bomb, a weapon so destructive that it forced a quick Japanese surrender. The suddenness of the ending helped determine the fate of the European empires in Asia.

THE YALTA CONFERENCE: SHAPING THE POSTWAR WORLD

When Stalin, Roosevelt, and Churchill met at Yalta, a Soviet Black Sea resort, in February 1945, Allied victory was assured, and the three leaders accomplished a great

deal. Yet controversy has long surrounded the **Yalta conference.** Western critics have charged that the concessions made there to Stalin consigned east-central Europe to communist domination and opened the way to the dangerous cold war of the next forty years. At the time, however, the anticipation of victory produced a relatively cooperative spirit among the Allies. Thus they firmed up plans for military occupation of Germany in separate zones, for joint occupation of Berlin, and for an Allied Control Council, composed of the military commanders-in-chief, which would make policy for all of Germany by unanimous agreement.

Each of the Allies had special concerns, but each got much of what it was seeking at Yalta. Roosevelt was eager for Soviet help against Japan as soon as possible, and he won Soviet commitment to an agreement tentatively worked out earlier. In exchange for territorial concessions in Asia and the Pacific, Stalin agreed to declare war on Japan within three months of the German surrender.

Churchill, meanwhile, worried about the future of Europe in light of the American intention, which Roosevelt announced at Yalta, to maintain occupation troops in Europe for only two years after the war. To help balance Soviet power on the Continent, Churchill felt it essential to restore France as a great power. To this end, he urged that France be granted a share in the occupation of Germany and a permanent seat on the Security Council of the proposed new international organization,

Yalta conference 1945 meeting between Stalin, Roosevelt, and Churchill in which they began outlining plans for the postwar order, including the military occupation of Germany.

The Big Three at Yalta
With victory over Nazi Germany assured, Churchill, Roosevelt, and Stalin were in reasonably good spirits when they met at Yalta, a Black Sea resort in the Soviet Union, in February 1945. Important sources of friction among them were evident at the meeting, but the differences that led to the cold war did not seem paramount at this point. The Yalta conference proved to be the last meeting of the three leaders. *(F.D.R. Library)*

the **United Nations** (see page 898). Roosevelt agreed, even though he had little use for Charles de Gaulle or what he viewed as the pretensions of the French.

It seemed to the Americans that both Britain and the Soviet Union remained too wedded to traditional conceptions of national interest as they sought to shape the postwar world. Hence one of Roosevelt's major priorities was to secure British and Soviet commitment to the United Nations before the three allies began to disagree over particular issues. He won that commitment at Yalta, but only by giving in to Churchill on the sensitive matter of British colonies.

Because anti-imperial sentiment worked to Japan's advantage in Asia, the United States had pestered Britain on the colonial issue since early in the war. Roosevelt even asked Churchill in 1941 about British intentions in India. So prickly was Churchill that he proclaimed in 1942, "I have not become the King's First Minister in order to preside over the liquidation of the British Empire." The parties agreed at Yalta that the British Empire would be exempt from an anticipated measure to bring former colonies under United Nations trusteeship after the war.

Although it was not the only question on the table, the future of the former Axis territories was central to the seaside deliberations. By the time of the conference, those territories were already being divided into spheres of influence among the Allies, and in light of the location of Allied troops, the eventual alignment was probably inevitable. In Italy, where U.S. and British troops held sway, the two democracies had successfully resisted Stalin's claim for a share in the administration. In east-central Europe, however, the Soviet army was in control. Still, the United States, with its vision of a new world order, objected to spheres of influence and insisted that democratic principles be applied everywhere. At Yalta this American priority led to an awkward compromise over east-central Europe: the new governments in the area were to be both democratic and friendly to the Soviet Union.

Most important to the Soviets was Poland, with its crucial location between the Soviet Union and Germany. Although they insisted that communists lead the new Polish government at the outset, the Soviets compromised by allowing a role for the noncommunist Polish government-in-exile in London and by promising free elections down the road. The Allies agreed that Poland would gain substantial German territory to its west to make up for the eastern territory it had already lost to the USSR (see **Map 28.4**).

In addition, the United States and Britain were to have a role in committees set up to engineer the transition to democracy in the rest of east-central Europe. However, only the Soviets had troops in the area, and those committees proved essentially powerless. The sources of future tension were already at work at Yalta, but they generally remained hidden by the high spirits of approaching victory.

United Nations   International organization of nations founded in 1945 to encourage peace, cooperation, and recognition of human rights.

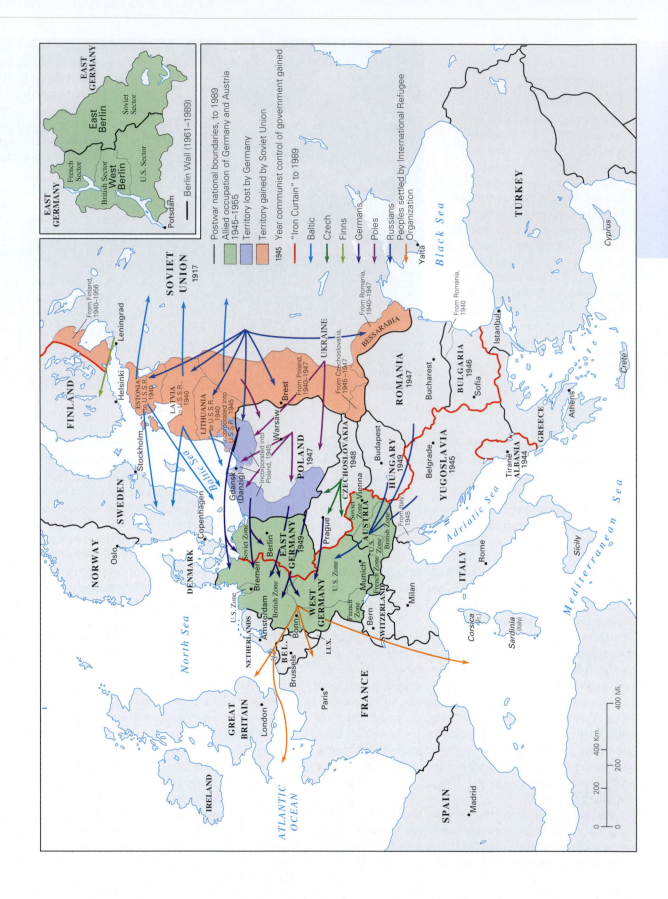

MAP 28.4   The Impact of World War II in Europe

As a result of World War II the Soviet Union expanded its western borders and Poland shifted westward at the expense of Germany. Territorial changes added to the wartime disruption and produced a flood of refugees. The cold war division of Europe did not depend on immediate territorial changes, but soon Germany itself came to be divided on east-west lines.

Online Study Center **Improve Your Grade**
Interactive Map: The Impact of World War II in Europe

VICTORY IN EUROPE

Although the tide had turned in 1943, Germany managed to continue the war by exploiting its conquered territories and by more effectively allocating its domestic resources for war production. Thanks partly to the efforts of armaments minister Albert Speer, war production grew sharply between 1941 and 1944, so Germany had plenty of weapons even as the war was ending. The Germans even proved able to withstand the systematic bombing of cities that the British, especially, had thought might prove decisive.

Beginning in 1942, British-led bombing attacks destroyed an average of half the built-up area of seventy German cities, sometimes producing huge firestorms. The bombing of the historic city of Dresden in February 1945 killed at least sixty thousand civilians in the most destructive air assault of the war in Europe. But despite this widespread destruction, such bombing did not undermine morale or disrupt production to the extent expected. Even in the face of steady Allied bombing, Germany increased its war production during 1943 and 1944.

But Germany encountered two crucial bottlenecks that finally crippled its military effort: it was running out of both oil and military personnel. Despite making effective use of synthetics, the Nazi war machine depended heavily on oil from Romania. And although the terror bombing of cities did not have the anticipated impact, the more precisely targeted bombing favored by U.S. strategists significantly affected the outcome. In May 1944 the United States began bombing oil fields in Romania and refineries and synthetic oil plants in Germany. Then, late in August 1944, Soviet troops crossed into Romania, taking control of the oil fields. Soon Germany lacked enough fuel even to train pilots. So serious were the bottlenecks by 1945 that the German air force could not use all the aircraft that German industry was producing.

Soviet troops moving westward finally met U.S. troops moving eastward at the Elbe River in Germany on April 26, 1945. With his regime now thoroughly defeated and much of his country in ruins, Hitler committed suicide in his underground military head-

The Soviet Victory in Europe

After forcing the Germans back for almost two years, Soviet troops reached Berlin in April 1945. After a day of heavy fighting and bombardment, the Soviets took the Reichstag building, in the heart of the devastated German capital, on April 30. Here two Soviet sergeants, Yegorov and Kantariya, plant the Soviet flag atop the Reichstag, symbolizing the Soviet victory in the decisive encounter of World War II in Europe. *(ITAR-TASS/Sovfoto)*

quarters in Berlin on April 30, 1945. The war in Europe finally ended with the German surrender to General Dwight D. Eisenhower (1890–1969) at Reims, France, on May 7 and to Marshal Zhukov at Berlin on May 8. The world celebrated the end of the fighting in Europe, but an element of uncertainty surrounded the Allied victory. East-West differences were increasingly coming to the fore within the anti-German alliance.

THE POTSDAM CONFERENCE AND THE QUESTION OF GERMANY

The immediate question for the victorious Allies was the fate of Germany, which they confronted at the last of their notable wartime conferences, at **Potsdam,** just outside Berlin, from July 17 to August 2, 1945. The circumstances were dramatically different from those at Yalta just months before. With Hitler dead and Germany defeated, no common military aim provided unity. And of the three Allied leaders who had been at Yalta, only Stalin remained. President Roosevelt had died in April, so his successor, Harry Truman (1884–1972), represented the United States. In Britain, Churchill's Conservatives lost the general election during the first days of the conference, so Clement Attlee (1883–1967), the new Labour prime minister, assumed the leadership of the British delegation.

At Potsdam the Allies had to determine how to implement their earlier agreements about Germany, which, devastated by bombing and devoid of a government, depended on the Allied occupying forces even for its day-to-day survival. For a time, U.S. policymakers had even considered destroying Germany's industrial capacity in perpetuity. However, cooler heads understood that the deindustrialization, or "pastoralization," of Germany would not be in anyone's economic interests. Moreover, as the democracies grew increasingly suspicious about Soviet intentions, an economically healthy Germany seemed necessary to help in the balance against the Soviet Union.

For their part, the Soviets had reason to take a much harder line against Germany. Having been ravaged by invading German forces twice within living memory, the Soviet Union wanted to weaken Germany both territorially and economically. And of the three victors, the Soviets had suffered a greatly disproportionate share of the wartime destruction and economic loss, so they also sought to exploit the remaining resources of Germany by exacting heavy reparations. Moreover, the British and the Americans accepted the

Soviet proposal that Germany's eastern border with Poland be shifted substantially westward, to the line formed by the Oder and Neisse (NYE-suh) Rivers. But just as Poland gained at the expense of Germany, the Soviet Union kept a substantial slice of what had been eastern Poland (see Map 28.4).

Each of the three Allies had responsibility for administering a particular zone of occupation, but they were supposed to coordinate their activities in a common policy toward Germany. This effort was to include de-Nazification, demilitarization, and an assault on concentrations of economic power—to root out what seemed to have been the sources of Germany's anti-democratic and aggressive tendencies. But East-West disagreements over economic policy soon undermined the pretense of joint government.

THE ATOMIC BOMB AND THE CAPITULATION OF JAPAN

In the Pacific, Japan had been forced onto the defensive by September 1943, and though it mounted two major counterattacks during 1944, the Japanese navy was crippled by shortages of ships and fuel by the end of the year. However, as the situation grew more desperate for Japan, Japanese ground soldiers battled ever more fiercely, often fighting to the death or taking their own lives rather than surrendering. Beginning late in 1944, aircraft pilots practiced *kamikaze* (kah-mih-KAH-zee), suicidally crashing planes filled with explosives into U.S. targets. The Japanese used this tactic especially as the Americans sought to take Okinawa in the spring of 1945. The U.S. forces finally prevailed in June, but only after the most bitter combat of the Pacific war (see Map 28.3).

In conquering Okinawa, American forces got close enough for air raids on the Japanese home islands. But though the United States was now clearly in control, it seemed likely that an actual invasion of Japan would be necessary to force a Japanese surrender. Some estimated that, because the Japanese could be expected to fight even more desperately to defend their own soil, invasion might well cost the United States one million additional casualties. It was especially for this reason that the Americans decided to try to end the war in an altogether different way—by using an atomic bomb.

In 1939 scientists in several countries, including Germany, had started to advise their governments that new, immensely destructive weapons based on thermonuclear fission were theoretically possible. The German economics ministry began seeking uranium as early as 1939, but Hitler promoted jet- and rocket-propelled terror weaponry instead, especially the V-2 rocket bombs that the Germans began showering on England in the fall of 1944. Still, fear that the Nazis were developing

Potsdam conference   A July–August 1945 meeting held at Potsdam, Germany, between the USSR, the United States, and Great Britain to implement their earlier agreements concerning the treatment of defeated Germany.

atomic weapons lurked behind the Allied effort to produce the ultra-lethal bomb as quickly as possible.

Although the British were the first to initiate an atomic weapons program, by late 1941 the Americans were building on what they knew of British findings to develop their own crash program, known as the Manhattan Project. Constructing an atomic bomb proved far more difficult and costly than most had expected in 1941, and it took a concerted effort by the United States to have atomic weapons ready for use by mid-1945.

Online Study Center **Improve Your Grade**
Primary Source: Witness to the Birth of the Atomic Age

The U.S. decision to use the atomic bomb on Japanese civilians has been one of the most controversial of modern history. The decision fell to the new president, Harry Truman, who had known nothing of the bomb project when Roosevelt died in April 1945. During the next few months, Truman listened to spirited disagreement among American policymakers. Was it necessary actually to drop the bomb to force the Japanese to surrender? Since the ultimate victory of the United States was not in doubt, some argued that it would be enough simply to demonstrate the new weapon to the Japanese in a test firing.

By July, when the Allies met at Potsdam, the United States was prepared to use the bomb. But President Truman first warned Japan that if it did not surrender at once, it would be subjected to destruction immeasurably greater than Germany had just suffered. The Japanese ignored the warning, although the United States had begun area-bombing Japanese cities a few months before. The bombing of Tokyo in March produced a firestorm that gutted one-fourth of the city and killed over 80,000 people. In light of the Japanese refusal to surrender, the use of the atomic bomb seemed to Truman to be the logical next step.

At 8:15 on the morning of August 6, 1945, from a height of 32,000 feet above the Japanese city of Hiroshima, an American pilot released the first atomic bomb to be used against an enemy target. The bomb exploded after 45 seconds, 2,000 feet above the ground, killing 80,000 people outright and leaving tens of thousands more to die in the aftermath. Three days later, on August 9, the Americans exploded a second atomic bomb over Nagasaki, killing perhaps 50,000 people. Although sectors of the Japanese military held out for continued resistance, Emperor Hirohito (hee-roh-HEE-toh) (1901–1989) finally announced Japan's surrender on August 15. The bombing of civilians had discredited the Japanese military, which not only had proved unable to defend the country but had systematically misled the Japanese people about their country's prospects.

The war in the Pacific ended more suddenly than had seemed possible just a few months earlier (see Map 28.3). This worked in favor of the various national liberation or decolonization movements that had developed in Asia during the war, for the Europeans had little opportunity to re-establish their dominance in the colonial territories they had earlier lost to the Japanese. In the Dutch East Indies, the Japanese had encouraged anticolonial sentiment, even helping local nationalists create patriotic militias. After the war, the Dutch were never able to reassert their control against this Indonesian nationalist movement. But though the war had severely weakened the old Western imperialism in Asia and the Pacific, what would replace it remained unclear.

DEATH, DISRUPTION, AND THE QUESTION OF GUILT

World War II left as many as 60 million people dead—three times as many as World War I. About that same number were left homeless for some length of time, or found themselves forced onto the mercies of others as refugees. The Soviet Union, Poland and Germany suffered by far the highest casualty figures; for each, the figure was considerably higher than in World War I. An appalling 23 million Soviet citizens died, of whom 12 million to 13 million were civilians. Poland lost over 6 million, the vast majority civilians, including perhaps 3 million Jews. Germany lost 5 million to 6 million, including perhaps 2 million civilians.

In contrast, casualty rates for Italy, Britain, and France were lower than in World War I. Italy suffered 200,000 military and 200,000 civilian deaths. Total British losses, including civilians, numbered 450,000, to which must be added 120,000 from the British Empire. Despite its quick defeat, France lost more lives than Britain because of the ravages of German occupation: the 350,000 deaths among French civilians considerably exceeded the British figure, closer to 100,000.

The United States lost 300,000 servicemen and 5,000 civilians. Figures for Japan are problematic, partly because the Japanese claim that 300,000 of those who surrendered to the Soviets in 1945 have remained unaccounted for. Apart from this number, 1.74 million Japanese servicemen died from 1941 to 1945, more from hunger and disease than from combat, and 300,000 civilians died in Japan, most from U.S. bombing.

During the war, Jews, Poles, and others deemed undesirable by the Nazis had been rounded up and shipped to ghettos or camps, where the great majority had died. Of those Jews who were still alive when the Nazi camps were liberated, almost half died within a few weeks. Even those who managed to return home sometimes faced pogroms during the difficult months that followed; forty Jews were killed in the worst of them, at Kielce (KYEL-tsuh), Poland, in 1946.

Late in the war, as German forces in the east retreated, ethnic Germans living in Poland, Czechoslovakia, Hungary, and elsewhere in east-central Europe began seeking refuge in Germany. They were fleeing the Soviet advance but also seeking to escape the growing wave of anti-German resentment in those countries. Once the war was over, the Poles began expelling ethnic Germans from the historically German areas that were now to become Polish. These Germans were sometimes sent to detention camps, and when they were shipped out, it was often in cattle cars. According to some estimates, as many as two million died in the process. At the same time, the uprooting of Poles that had begun during the war continued as Poles were systematically forced from the Polish territories incorporated into the Soviet Union.

In Czechoslovakia the government expelled 3.5 million Germans from the Sudetenland area by 1947. All told, at least 7 million German refugees moved west into the shrunken territory of the new Germany by 1947. They were among the 16 million Europeans who were permanently uprooted and transplanted during the war and its immediate wake. And the process continued at a diminished rate thereafter. By 1958 perhaps 10 million Germans had either left or been forced out of the new Poland, leaving only about 1 million Germans still living there.

As the end of the war approached, Europeans began attempting to assess guilt and to punish those responsible for the disasters of the era. In the climate of violence, resistance forces in France, Italy, and elsewhere often subjected fascists and collaborators to summary justice, sometimes through quick trials in ad hoc courts. In Italy this process led to 15,000 executions, in France 10,000. French women accused of sleeping with German soldiers were shamed by having their heads shaved.

The most sensitive confrontation with the recent past took place in Germany, where the occupying powers imposed a systematic program of de-Nazification. In the western zones, German citizens were required to attend lectures on the virtues of democracy and to view the corpses of the victims of Nazism. In this context, the Allies determined to identify and bring to justice those responsible for the crimes of Hitler's regime. This effort led to the **Nuremberg trials** of 1945 and 1946, the most famous of a number of war crimes trials held in Germany and the occupied countries after the war.

Although Hitler, Himmler, and Goebbels had committed suicide, the occupying authorities apprehended for trial twenty-four individuals who had played important but very different roles in Hitler's Third Reich. All but three were convicted of war crimes and "crimes against humanity." Twelve were sentenced to death; of those, two committed suicide, and the other ten were executed.

Questions about their legitimacy dogged the Nuremberg trials from the start. To a considerable extent the accused were being judged according to law made after the fact. The notion of "crimes against humanity" remained vague. Moreover, even insofar as a measure of international law was in force, it was arguably binding only on states, not individuals. But in light of the unprecedented atrocities of the Nazi regime, there was widespread agreement among the victors that the Nazi leaders could not be treated simply as defeated adversaries.

S E C T I O N   S U M M A R Y

- The future of east-central Europe was but one of the items on the agenda at Yalta, where each of the Big Three achieved some of its major aims concerning the shape of the postwar world.

- As a result of the agreements at Yalta and Potsdam, the reconstituted Poland was shifted substantially westward at the expense of Germany.

- Although the terror bombing of cities did not undermine the German war effort, the more precisely targeted bombing of industrial and military targets hastened Germany's defeat, especially by cutting off oil supplies.

- Because the war in the Pacific ended so suddenly, as the result of the atomic bombing of Japan by the United States, the Europeans had little opportunity to re-establish their dominance in the colonial territories they had earlier lost to the Japanese.

- Of the twenty-four Germans charged with war crimes and "crimes against humanity" in the Nuremberg trials of 1945 and 1946, twenty-one were convicted, of whom twelve were sentenced to death.

Nuremberg trials The war crimes trials conducted in Nuremberg, Germany. Most of the twenty-four defendants were convicted of war crimes and "crimes against humanity."

INTO THE POSTWAR WORLD

What was the relationship between the Allied victory in World War II and the coming of the cold war?

Even after the fighting stopped in 1945, remarkable changes continued as the forces unleashed by the war played themselves out. In a number of war-torn countries, the legacies of wartime resistance movements helped shape the political order and priorities for beginning anew. At the same time, differences between the Soviets and the Western democracies began to undermine the wartime alliance, soon producing the division of Germany and a bipolar Europe. Thus the conclusion of World War II led directly to the danger of a third world war, which might involve nuclear weapons and thus prove immeasurably more destructive than the last.

In addition to the dramatic changes in Europe, the wider effects of the war brought to the forefront a whole new set of issues, from anticolonialism to the Arab-Israeli conflict to the spread of communism in the non-Western world. These issues would remain central for decades. By 1949, however, it was already possible to discern the contours of the new postwar world, a world with new sources of hope but also with conflicts and dangers hardly imaginable ten years earlier.

RESISTANCE AND RENEWAL

Though the Nazis had found some willing collaborators, the great majority of those living under German occupation came to despise the Nazis as their brutality became ever clearer. Nazi rule meant pillage, forced labor in Germany, and the random killing of hostages in reprisal for resistance activity. In one extreme case, the Germans destroyed the Czech village of Lidice (LIH-dyit-seh), killing all its inhabitants, in retaliation for the assassination of SS security chief Reinhard Heydrich in 1942.

Clandestine movements of resistance to the occupying Nazi forces gradually developed all over Europe. In western Europe, resistance was especially prominent in France and, beginning in 1943, northern Italy, which was subjected to German occupation after the Allies defeated Mussolini's regime. But the anti-German resistance was strongest in Yugoslavia, Poland, and the occupied portions of the Soviet Union, where full-scale guerrilla war against the Germans and their collaborators produced the highest civilian casualties of World War II. The Polish resistance achieved some notable successes in sabotaging roads and railroads, although it met disastrous defeat when it sought to tackle the Germans head-on in Warsaw in 1944.

The role of the resistance proved most significant in Yugoslavia, where the Croatian Marxist Josip Broz, taking the pseudonym Tito (1892–1980), forged the opponents of the Axis powers into a broadly based guerrilla army. Its initial foe was the inflated Croatian state that the Germans, early in 1941, carved from Yugoslavia and entrusted to the pro-Axis Croatian separatist movement, the Ustashe (oo-STAH-zhiy). But Tito's forces soon came up against a rival resistance movement, led by Serb officers, that tended to be pro-Serb, monarchist, and anticommunist. By 1943 Tito led 250,000 men and women in what had become a vicious civil war, one that deepened ethnic divisions and left a legacy of bitterness. Tito's forces prevailed, enabling him to create a communist-led government in Yugoslavia late in the war.

In France and Italy as well, communists played leading roles in the wartime resistance movements. As a result, the Communist Party in each country overcame the disarray that followed from the Nazi-Soviet Pact of 1939, and after the war each enjoyed a level of prestige that would have been unthinkable earlier.

In the French case, the indigenous resistance, with its significant communist component, generally worked well with de Gaulle and the Free French, operating outside France until August 1944. Still, de Gaulle took pains to cement his own leadership in the overall struggle. Among the measures to this end, he decreed women's suffrage for France, partly because women were playing a major role in the resistance. After the liberation of France in 1944, he sought to control a potentially volatile situation by disarming the resistance as quickly as possible.

The western European resistance movements are easily romanticized, their extent and importance overstated. Compared with regular troops, resistance forces were poorly trained, equipped, and disciplined. In France fewer than 30 percent of the nearly 400,000 active resisters had firearms in 1944. But though the Allies never tried to use them in a systematic way, the resistance movements made at least some military contribution, especially through sabotage. And they boosted national self-esteem for the longer term, helping countries humiliated by defeat and occupation make a fresh start after the war.

But had governments and institutions outside Germany done all they could—especially as the dimensions of the Nazi exterminations began to come into focus? For example, President Roosevelt, in the face of appeals from Jewish groups, declined to try to disrupt the Nazi killing machine by bombing the rail lines to Auschwitz. As he saw it, the way to save as many Jews as possible was to win the war as quickly as possible.

Especially controversial has been the response of Pope Pius XII (r. 1939–1958), who declined to take the moral high ground and denounce Nazi atrocities explicitly. He felt that he could not censure the Nazis without also censuring the Soviets, at that point allies in the anti-Nazi cause. He also feared for the fortunes of the Catholic Church as an institution in areas under German control, including Rome itself during the pivotal nine months from September 1943 to June 1944. The mission of the church was not merely to save lives but above all to save souls—and for that the institution was essential. Many felt, however, that stronger moral leadership by the Catholic Church would have stiffened resistance to the Nazis, stimulated aid to individual Jews, and enhanced the overall self-confidence of the West as it faced the post-Holocaust future.

CONFLICTING VISIONS AND THE COMING OF THE COLD WAR

Starting with the Atlantic Charter conference of 1941, Roosevelt had sought to ensure that the common effort against the Axis powers would lead to a firmer basis for peace, to be framed through a new international organization after the war. At a conference at Dumbarton Oaks in Washington, D.C., in September 1944, the United States proposed the structure for a new "United Nations." Meeting in San Francisco from April to June 1945, delegates from almost fifty anti-Axis countries translated that proposal into a charter for the new organization. As Roosevelt had envisioned, the major powers were given a privileged position in the organization as permanent members of the Security Council, each with veto power. To dramatize its departure from the Geneva-based League of Nations, which the United States had refused to join, the United Nations was headquartered in New York. In July 1945 the U.S. Senate approved U.S. membership in the international body almost unanimously.

By the end of the war, several international meetings had used the United Nations title. In July 1944 the United Nations Monetary and Financial Conference at Bretton Woods, New Hampshire, brought together delegates from forty-four nations to deal with problems of currency and exchange rates. Although it produced only recommendations subject to ratification by the individual countries, the conference indicated a new determination to cooperate on the international level after the failures of the interwar period. The outcome of the conference, the Bretton Woods Agreement, laid the foundation for international economic exchange in the noncommunist world for the crucial quarter century of economic recovery after the war. In addition, the conference gave birth to the International Monetary Fund and the International Bank for Reconstruction and Development, which played major roles in the decades that followed.

Whereas the United States envisioned a world order based on the ongoing cooperation of the three victors, the Soviet Union had a different agenda. Its top priority was to create a buffer zone of friendly states in east-central Europe, especially as a bulwark against Germany. While seeking this sphere of influence in east-central Europe, Stalin gave the British a free hand to settle the civil war between communists and anti-communists in Greece, and he did not push for revolution in western Europe. The strong communist parties that had emerged from the resistance movements in Italy and France were directed by Moscow to work within broad-based democratic fronts rather than try to take power. Although no formal deal was made, Stalin saw this moderate position in western and southern Europe as a tacit exchange with the West for a free hand in east-central Europe.

THE DIVISION OF GERMANY

The site of greatest potential stress between the Soviets and the democracies was Germany. At first, the Western Allies were concerned especially to root out the sources of Germany's antidemocratic, aggressive behavior, but that concern faded as communism, not Nazism, came to seem the immediate menace. And it was especially conflict over Germany that cemented the developing division of Europe. Neither the democracies nor the Soviets lived up to all their agreements concerning Germany, but in light of the fundamental differences in priorities, cooperation between the two sides was bound to be difficult at best.

Disagreements over economic policy proved the major source of the eventual split. At Potsdam, the West had accepted Soviet demands for German reparations, but rather than wait for payment, the Soviets began removing German factories and equipment for reassembly in the Soviet Union. To ensure that they got their due, the Soviets wanted access to the economic resources not simply of the Russian occupation zone but of the whole of Germany. The United States and Britain, in contrast, gave priority to economic reconstruction and quickly began integrating the economies of the Western zones for that purpose.

Friction developed from 1945 to 1948 as the West insisted on reduced reparations and a higher level of industrial production than the Soviets wanted. Finally, as part of their effort to spur economic recovery, the United States and Britain violated Allied agreements by introducing a new currency without Soviet consent. Stalin answered in June 1948 by blockading the city of Berlin, cutting its western sectors off from the main

Western occupation zones, almost 200 miles west (see Map 28.4). The Western Allies responded with a massive airlift that kept their sectors of Berlin supplied for almost a year, until May 1949, when the Soviets finally backed down.

By 1948 two separate German states began emerging from the Allied occupation zones. The Western occupying powers had begun restoring local government immediately after the war, to create the administrative framework necessary to provide public utilities and food distribution. Gradually a governing structure was built from the ground up in the Western zones, which were increasingly coordinated.

With Allied support, a "parliamentary council" of West German leaders met during 1948 and 1949 and produced a document that, when ratified in September 1949, became the "Basic Law" of a new Federal Republic of Germany, with its capital at Bonn. This founding document was termed simply the Basic Law, as opposed to the constitution, to emphasize the provisional character of the new West German state. To create a state limited to the west was not to foreclose the future reunification of Germany. But as it became clear that a new state was being created in the Western zones, the Soviets settled for a new state in their zone, in eastern Germany. Thus the Communist-led German Democratic Republic, with its capital in East Berlin, was born in October 1949.

The "Iron Curtain" and the Emergence of a Bipolar World

In east-central Europe, only Yugoslavia and Albania had achieved liberation on their own, and the communist leaders of their resistance movements had a plausible claim to political power. Elsewhere, the Soviet army had provided liberation, and the Soviet military presence remained the decisive political fact as the war ended. In much of the region, authoritarianism and collaboration had been the rule for a decade or more, so there was no possibility of returning to a clearly legitimate prewar political order. To be sure, each country had local political groups, some representing former governments in exile, that now claimed a governing role, but their standing in relation to the Soviet army was uncertain.

Under these circumstances, the Soviets were able to work with local communists to install new regimes, led by communists and friendly to the Soviet Union, in most of east-central Europe. But though Churchill warned as early as 1946 that an **"iron curtain"** was de-

scending from the Baltic to the Adriatic, the process of Soviet power consolidation was not easy, and it took place gradually, in discrete steps over several years. The Communist-led government of Poland held elections in January 1947—but rigged them to guarantee a favorable outcome. In Czechoslovakia the Communist Party anticipated serious losses in upcoming elections and so finally took power outright in 1948. By 1949 communist governments, relying on Soviet support, controlled Poland, Czechoslovakia, East Germany, Hungary, Romania, and Bulgaria, with Yugoslavia and Albania also communist but capable of a more independent line.

Communism might have spread still farther in Europe, and perhaps beyond, but the West drew the line at Greece. There, as in Yugoslavia, an indigenous, communist-led resistance movement had become strong enough to contend for political power by late 1944. But when it sought to oust the monarchical government that had just returned to Greece from exile, the British intervened, helping the monarchy put down the leftist uprising. Although Stalin gave the Greek communists little help, communist guerrilla activity continued, thanks partly to support from Tito's Yugoslavia. In 1946 a renewed communist insurgency escalated into civil war.

As U.S.-Soviet friction turned into a **cold war,** both countries began taking a more active interest in the Greek conflict, though Soviet intentions remained uncertain. After the financially strapped Labour government in Britain reduced its involvement early in 1947, the United States stepped in to support the Greek monarchy against the communists. American policymakers feared that communism would progress from the Balkans through Greece to the Middle East. Thus, in March 1947, President Truman announced the **Truman Doctrine,** which committed the United States to the "containment" of communism throughout the world. (See the box "The Written Record: 'Containment' as a Cold War Strategy.") American advisers now began re-equipping the anticommunist forces in Greece. Faced with this determined opposition from the West, Stalin again pulled back, but the Greek communists, with their strong indigenous support, were not defeated until 1949.

Thus the wartime marriage of expediency between the Soviet Union and the Western democracies gradually fell apart in the war's aftermath. Only in Austria,

"iron curtain"   Term used by Winston Churchill in a speech on March 5, 1946, to warn that, thanks to Soviet policy, a formidable de facto barrier was emerging in Europe, cutting the Soviet sphere off from the West and threatening the long-term division of the Continent.

cold war   The hostile standoff between the Soviet Union and the United States that began after World War II as Europe was divided into spheres of influence between the two superpowers and the United States vowed to resist the further spread of communism.

Truman Doctrine   The U.S. policy of containment, or limiting communist expansion, as outlined by President Harry Truman in 1947.

"CONTAINMENT" AS A COLD WAR STRATEGY

As a foreign service officer, George F. Kennan (1904–2005) emerged as the U.S. government's leading authority on the dynamics of Soviet foreign policy by the later 1940s. After analyzing Soviet postwar objectives in his now-famous "long telegram" from Moscow to the U.S. State Department in 1946, Kennan returned to the United States to become director of the State Department's Policy Planning Staff from 1947 to 1949. With hawks pondering a preemptive strike on the Soviet Union and doves stressing mutual accommodation, Kennan forcefully advocated a middle position, a strategy of "containment," in an article published anonymously in the journal Foreign Affairs *in 1947. And his views prevailed. An uncertain experiment when it began in 1947, containment proved successful—arguably for the reasons Kennan anticipated.*

[The Soviet Union] is under no ideological compulsion to accomplish its purposes in a hurry. . . . Thus the Kremlin has no compunction about retreating in the face of superior force. And being under the compulsion of no timetable, it does not get panicky under the necessity for such retreat. Its political action is a fluid stream which moves constantly, wherever it is permitted to move, toward a given goal. . . .

. . . The patient persistence by which it is animated means that it can be effectively countered not by sporadic acts which represent the momentary whims of democratic opinion but only by intelligent long-range policies on the part of Russia's adversaries—policies no less steady in their purpose, and no less variegated and resourceful in their application, than those of the Soviet Union itself.

In these circumstances it is clear that the main element of any United States policy toward the Soviet Union must be that of a long-term, patient but firm and vigilant containment of Russian expansive tendencies. It is important to note, however, that such a policy has nothing to do with outward histrionics: with threats or blustering or superfluous gestures of outward "toughness." While the Kremlin is basically flexible in its reaction to political realities, it is by no means unamenable to considerations of prestige. . . . It is a *sine qua non* of successful dealing with Russia that the foreign government in question should remain at all times cool and collected and that its demands on Russian policy should be put forward in such a manner as to leave the way open for a compliance not too detrimental to Russian prestige.

In the light of the above, it will be clearly seen that the Soviet pressure against the free institutions of the western world is something that can be contained by the adroit and vigilant application of counter-force at a series of constantly shifting geographical and political points, corresponding to the shifts and manœuvres of Soviet policy, but which cannot be charmed or talked out of existence. . . .

. . . Soviet power is only a crust concealing an amorphous mass of human beings among whom no independent organizational structure is tolerated. . . . If, consequently, anything were ever to occur to disrupt the unity and efficacy of the Party as a political instrument, Soviet Russia might be changed overnight from one of the strongest to one of the weakest and most pitiable of national societies. . . .

. . . It is . . . a question of the degree to which the United States can create among the peoples of the world generally the impression of a country which knows what it wants, which is coping successfully with the problems of its internal life and with the responsibilities of a World Power, and which has a spiritual vitality capable of holding its own among the major ideological currents of the time. To the extent that such an impression can be created and maintained, the aims of Russian Communism must appear sterile and quixotic, the hopes and enthusiasm of Moscow's supporters must wane, and added strain must be imposed on the Kremlin's foreign policies. For the palsied decrepitude of the capitalist world is the keystone of Communist philosophy. . . .

. . . The United States has it in its power to increase enormously the strains under which Soviet policy must operate, to force upon the Kremlin a far greater degree of moderation and circumspection than it has had to observe in recent years, and in this way to promote tendencies which must eventually find their outlet in either the break-up or the gradual mellowing of Soviet power.

QUESTIONS

1. What conception of the Soviet Union and its aims led Kennan to propose a policy of containment?

2. What would containment actually entail on a practical level as a response to Soviet moves?

3. Why did Kennan believe that the United States had to be unified, consistent, and principled in everything it did if it was eventually to prevail in the cold war?

Source: "X" [George F. Kennan], "The Sources of Soviet Conduct," *Foreign Affairs* 25, no. 4 (July 1947). Reprinted by permission of *Foreign Affairs.* Copyright 1947 by the Council on Foreign Relations, Inc.

jointly occupied by the Soviets and the Western democracies, were the former Allies able to arrange the postwar transition in a reasonably amicable way. The Soviets accepted the neutralization of a democratic Austria as the occupying powers left in 1955. Elsewhere, Europe was divided into two antagonistic power blocs.

The antagonism between the two superpowers became more menacing when the Soviets exploded their first atomic bomb in August 1949, intensifying the postwar arms race. By then, in fact, the United States was on its way to the more destructive hydrogen bomb. The split between these two nations, unmistakable by 1949, established the framework for world affairs for the next forty years.

THE WEST AND THE NEW WORLD AGENDA

At the same time, other dramatic changes around the world suggested that, with or without the cold war, the postwar political scene would be hard to manage. Events in India in 1947, in Israel in 1948, and in China in 1949 epitomized the wider new hopes and uncertainties spawned by World War II.

Independence in India   Although the British, under U.S. pressure, had reluctantly promised independence for India in order to elicit Indian support during the war, British authorities and Indian leaders had continued to skirmish. Mohandas Gandhi (see pages 807 and 843) was twice jailed for resisting British demands and threatening a massive program of nonviolent resistance to British rule. But by 1946 the British lacked the will and the financial resources to maintain their control on the subcontinent. Thus Britain acquiesced as the new independent states of India and Pakistan emerged on August 15, 1947. Allowing independence to India, long the jewel of the British Empire, raised questions about Britain's role in the postwar world and portended a wider disintegration of the European colonial system. There would be new countries, many of them poor—and resentful of Western imperialism. What would that mean for the new world order, centering on the United Nations, that Roosevelt had envisioned?

The Creation of Israel   Questions about the fate of the Jews, who had suffered so grievously during World War II, were inevitable as well. Almost two-thirds of the Jews of Europe had been killed, and many of the survivors either had no place to go or had decided that they could never again live as a minority in Europe. Many concluded that the Jews must have a homeland of their own. For decades such Zionist sentiment (see page 791) had centered on the biblical area of Israel, in what had become, after World War I, the British mandate of Palestine. Jewish immigration to the area accelerated during the interwar period, but it caused increasing friction between the Jews and the Palestinian Arabs.

Concerned about access to Middle Eastern oil, the British sought to cultivate good relations with the Arab world after the war. Thus they opposed further immigration of Jews to Palestine, as well as proposals to carve an independent Jewish state from the area. The United States, however, was considerably more sympathetic to the Zionist cause. As tensions built, Jewish terrorists blew up the British headquarters in Jerusalem,

Gandhi and Anticolonialism

An apostle of nonviolence, Mohandas Gandhi became one of the most admired individuals of the century as he spearheaded the movement for Indian independence. He is pictured (*center*) in December 1942 with the British statesman Sir Stafford Cripps (*left*), who had come to India to offer a plan for Indian self-government. Despite the good spirit evident here, Cripps's mission failed; Gandhi and his movement held out for full independence.   (*Corbis*)

MAP 28.5 The Proposed Partition of Palestine and the Birth of the State of Israel
In November 1947 the United Nations offered a plan to partition the British mandate of Palestine, but complications immediately arose. The Jews of the area won their own state, Israel, but the Palestinian Arabs were left stateless. Thus tensions continued in the area.

Online Study Center **Improve Your Grade**
Interactive Map: The Proposed Partition of Palestine and the Birth of the State of Israel

and the British decided to abandon what seemed a no-win situation. In September 1947 they announced their intention to withdraw from Palestine, leaving its future to the United Nations. In November the UN voted to partition Palestine, creating both a Jewish and a new Arab Palestinian state (see **MAP 28.5**).

Skirmishing between Jews and Arabs became full-scale war in December 1947, and in that context the Jews declared their independence as the new state of Israel on May 14, 1948. When the fighting ended in 1949, the Israelis had conquered more territory than had been envisioned in the original partition plan, and the remaining Arab territories fell to Egypt and Jordan, rather than forming an independent Palestinian state. Thus was born the new state of Israel, partly a product of the assault on the Jews during World War II. Yet it was born amid Arab hostility and Western concerns about oil, and so its long-term prospects remained uncertain.

Communism in China In 1949 the communist insurgency in China under Mao Zedong (Mao Tse-tung) (see page 843) finally triumphed over the Chinese Nationalists under Jiang Jieshi (Chiang Kai-shek), who fled to the island of Taiwan. During the war, the Communists had done better than the Nationalists at identifying themselves with the Chinese cause against both Japanese and Western imperialism. And after their victory, the Chinese Communists enjoyed great prestige among other "national liberation" movements struggling against Western colonialists. To many in the West, however, the outcome in China by 1949 simply intensified fears that communism was poised to infect the unsettled postwar world.

--- SECTION SUMMARY ---

- Although it had spurned the League of Nations after World War I, the U.S. Senate approved U.S. membership in the United Nations almost unanimously in July 1945.

- Concerned primarily to win a secure sphere of influence in east-central Europe, especially as a bulwark against Germany, Stalin took a moderate position with regard to western Europe and did not seek to foment communist revolution.

- Disagreements over economic policy, especially, fed the split that led to the creation of two separate

- German states, one oriented toward the West, the other oriented toward the Soviet Union, in 1949.

- The communist challenge in Greece by 1947 prompted the Truman Doctrine, which committed the United States to the "containment" of communism throughout the world.

- The granting of independence to India in 1947, the creation of the state of Israel in 1948, and the communist takeover in China in 1949 indicated the new world agenda emerging after World War II.

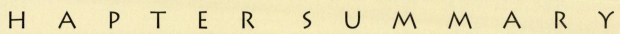

CHAPTER SUMMARY

Online Study Center **ACE the Test**

What were the outcomes of the war as of late spring 1941, before the German invasion of the Soviet Union and before the intervention of the United States?

What was the place of the Holocaust in the Nazi effort to begin constructing a "new order" in eastern Europe?

How did the Grand Alliance of Britain, the United States, and the Soviet Union come together against the Axis powers?

How did the Allies manage to defeat Nazi Germany in World War II, after Germany's remarkable initial successes?

What was the relationship between the Allied victory in World War II and the coming of the cold war?

Using an effective new offensive strategy, Germany quickly defeated Poland in 1939, but Britain and France refused Hitler's peace overtures in the aftermath. After France fell to German invasion eight months later, the Third Republic gave way to the authoritarian Vichy regime, which was obliged to collaborate with Nazi Germany. When the British again refused to come to terms, Hitler launched a sustained air assault on Britain. The British withstood it, but Hitler remained confident of containing Britain over the longer term. Even when the reckless intervention of Italy forced Hitler's attention to North Africa and the Balkans, the Germans won further successes, which suggested that the Soviet Union would fall in a matter of weeks in the wake of Germany's invasion of June 1941.

In dealing with their conquered territories first in Poland, then in the Soviet Union, the Nazis were concerned with population engineering and ideology; Jewish policy was distinctly secondary. Even when Jews were confined to ghettos in Poland, there was no plan to kill them. But ghettoization produced problems of its own, so Nazi forces were instructed to shoot Soviet Jews once the invasion of the Soviet Union began. Such shooting also proved to be problematic, so gradually the Nazi leadership decided on a more systematic method—mass extermination by gassing, to start with the Jews in the ghettos in Poland. Such a program could be envisioned, and implemented, especially because of the precedent of the "euthanasia" program in Germany. Once it began, the process of mass killing developed a momentum of its own, especially as it became clear that Germany was likely to lose the war.

After a disastrous start in the face of German invasion, Soviet forces stiffened in the fall of 1941,

then, in December, mounted a formidable counterattack. That same month the United States declared war on Germany in the aftermath of the bombing of Pearl Harbor by the Japanese. Meanwhile, the British, having withstood the German air assault, were regrouping for a protracted war. Common hostility to the Axis powers brought Britain, the Soviet Union, and the United States together in a "Grand Alliance" early in 1942, but mutual suspicions between the democracies, on the one hand, and the Soviet Union, on the other, marked the relationship. Above all, Stalin worried that Britain and the United States were dragging their feet in opening a major second front on the European continent. By the time of the D-Day landings in France in June 1944, the Soviets were steadily forcing the Germans back on the eastern front.

Even after all the upheavals of the 1930s, the Soviets proved able to spearhead the Allied victory in Europe, though they suffered incredibly heavy casualties in the process. Stalin managed to rally the Soviet people, and the Soviet military and industrial effort proved more effective than outside observers had thought possible. But the efforts of the democracies in North Africa, Italy, and France contributed to the final victory as well. And American-led bombing of military and industrial targets, especially oil refining facilities, seriously compromised Germany's capacity to wage war by the end.

The Grand Alliance began unraveling soon after the war was over, especially because the priorities of the Soviets differed considerably from those of the two democracies. Having been invaded, and devastated, by German forces twice in a generation, the Soviets were determined to have friendly states on their

903

borders, especially in Poland. And having suffered from direct German military invasion as the other two victors had not, the Soviets were also determined to extract reparations from Germany, even including plant and equipment to be dismantled and carried back to the Soviet Union. By 1949 two competing German states had emerged, and Europe was clearly divided between East and West.

 OOKING AHEAD

Whereas there had been, for a while, some illusion of a "return to normal" after World War I, it was obvious after World War II that the old Europe was gone forever. As a result of the war, the two major fascist powers collapsed, and fascist forms of politics, with their hostility to democracy and their tendencies toward violence and war, stood discredited. But it was not clear whether Europe would be able to develop effective democratic political systems amid defeat and destruction. Indeed, much of Europe's proud culture, on the basis of which it had claimed to lead the world, lay in the ruins of war, apparently exhausted. What role could Europe play in Western civilization, and in the wider world, after all that had happened? What lessons had been learned, and what foundations for the future could be found, now in the shadow of the cold war?

KEY TERMS

Vichy France (p. 873)

Charles de Gaulle (p. 873)

Winston Churchill (p. 873)

Auschwitz-Birkenau (p. 880)

Stalingrad (p. 881)

"the Great Patriotic War" (p. 881)

Franklin Delano Roosevelt (p. 885)

Lend-Lease Act (p. 887)

D-Day (p. 888)

Yalta conference (p. 890)

United Nations (p. 891)

Potsdam conference (p. 894)

Nuremberg trials (p. 896)

"iron curtain" (p. 899)

cold war (p. 899)

Truman Doctrine (p. 899)

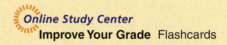
Online Study Center **Improve Your Grade** Flashcards

SUGGESTED READING

Browning, Christopher R. *The Origins of the Final Solution: The Evolutions of Nazi Jewish Policy, September 1939–March 1942.* 2004. A leading expert's detailed but gripping account of the often haphazard steps that led to the Nazi program to exterminate the Jews.

Campbell, John, ed. *The Experience of World War II.* 1989. Focusing on the experience of those touched by the war, this collaborative volume covers everything from prisoners of war to the uses of the arts for propaganda purposes; large format, with superb illustrations and maps.

Gaddis, John Lewis. *The Cold War: A New History.* 2005. A comprehensive but accessible synthesis that finds the cold war to have been necessary to settle the contest between American democracy and Soviet communism in a definitive and desirable way.

Hilberg, Raul. *Perpetrators, Victims, Bystanders: The Jewish Catastrophe, 1933–1945.* 1992. The dean of Holocaust historians offers an accessible, compelling account by weaving capsule portraits delineating the many layers of involvement and responsibility at issue in the Holocaust.

Jackson, Julian. *The Fall of France: The Nazi Invasion of 1940.* 2003. After assessing causes and consequences from a variety of angles, this major study of a long-standing problem concludes that, in light of the anomalous Nazi determination to wage war, the fall of France was not a "strange defeat."

_____. *France: The Dark Years, 1940–1944.* 2001. A major reassessment of the Vichy period, set within the broader sweep of modern French history.

Keegan, John. *The Second World War.* 1989. A detailed but readable study featuring military operations; well illustrated.

Overy, Richard J. *Why the Allies Won.* 1995. Denying that the sheer weight of numbers made the outcome inevitable, this account focuses on the differences in political, economic, and even moral mobilization to explain why the Allies defeated the Axis powers.

Parker, R. A. C. *Struggle for Survival: The History of the Second World War.* 1990. An accessible, comprehensive, and well-balanced survey, especially good on debates over strategy and the wider implications of the strategies chosen.

Trachtenberg, Marc. *A Constructed Peace: The Making of the European Settlement, 1945–1963.* 1999. An original work that pushes beyond the long-standing cold war framework to argue that concerns about Germany and nuclear weapons were central to the postwar settlement.

Weinberg, Gerhard L. *A World at Arms: A Global History of World War II.* 1994. An enlightening global approach by a leading historian of the period that stresses the interrelationship among simultaneous events and decisions in the various theaters of the war around the world.

NOTES

1. From Farrell's full account as related by General Leslie Groves in his "Memorandum to the Secretary of War," dated July 18, 1945, in *The American Atom: A Documentary History of Nuclear Policies from the Discovery of Fission to the Present,* ed. Philip L. Cantelon, Richard G. Hewlett, and Robert C. Williams, 2d ed. (Philadelphia: University of Pennsylvania Press, 1991), pp. 56–57.

2. Quoted in Karl Dietrich Bracher, *The German Dictatorship: The Origins, Structure, and Effects of National Socialism,* trans. Jean Steinberg (New York: Praeger, 1970), p. 423.

3. Christopher R. Browning, *Ordinary Men: Reserve Police Battalion 101 and the Final Solution in Poland,* with a new afterward (New York: HarperCollins, 1998); Daniel Jonah Goldhagen, *Hitler's Willing Executioners: Ordinary Germans and the Holocaust* (New York: Random House [Vintage], 1997).

4. Michael Burleigh, *Death and Deliverance: "Euthanasia" in Germany, c. 1900–1945* (Cambridge: Cambridge University Press, 1994), p. 221.

5. Michael Burleigh and Wolfgang Wippermann, *The Racial State: Germany, 1933–1945* (Cambridge: Cambridge University Press, 1991), p. 98.

6. Martin Broszat and Saul Friedländer, "A Controversy About the Historicization of National Socialism," in Peter Baldwin, ed., *Reworking the Past: Hitler, the Holocaust, and the Historians' Debate* (Boston: Beacon Press, 1990), pp. 120–121.

7. Goldhagen, *Hitler's Willing Executioners,* pp. 279–280.

8. Browning, *Ordinary Men,* p. 72.

29

AN ANXIOUS STABILITY: THE AGE OF THE COLD WAR, 1949–1989

Berlin Wall, November 1989
East Germans stream through the dismantled Berlin Wall into West Berlin. *(Lionel Cironneau/AP/ Wide World Photos)*

The atmosphere was festive, euphoric. Those who came to celebrate could hardly believe it was happening, for it had been unthinkable just a few months before. Yet happening it was, one of the defining events of the twentieth century, live on television. This was November 1989, and the Berlin Wall was coming down.

Erected to stop emigration from communist East Germany to the West in 1961, the wall had become an all-too-tangible symbol of the division of Europe, and much of the world, for more than four decades after World War II. The two superpowers that had emerged from the war, the Soviet Union and the United States, had settled into a cold war marked by ideological competition, an arms race, and nuclear stalemate.

As a physical barrier of concrete and barbed wire, the Berlin Wall had divided families and caused much human suffering. Indeed, 191 people died and 5,000 were arrested trying to cross it. But the East German government, desperate by 1989 to preserve its legitimacy, opened the wall on November 9 and began dismantling it within days. However, it proved too late. The communist regime in East Germany collapsed as part of a wider anticommunist revolution that finally enveloped even the Soviet Union in 1991. The anxious cold war era was suddenly over; virtually no one had foreseen its abrupt ending.

Although Berlin had been a particular hot spot, the cold war was global in scope. It seemed that confrontation between the Soviet Union and the United States might take place almost anywhere, sparking the cold war into a hot war threatening nuclear annihilation. And indeed confrontation came closest not over Berlin but over Soviet missiles in Cuba in 1962. That crisis was surmounted, and East-West relations alternately warmed and cooled during the quarter century that followed.

Both halves of Europe had to operate within the bipolar framework, but the Western and Soviet blocs confronted different challenges and evolved in different ways. The countries of western Europe adjusted to a diminished international role as they recognized their dependence on U.S. leadership and gradually lost their overseas colonies. The change in scale led many

CHAPTER OUTLINE

THE SEARCH FOR CULTURAL BEARINGS

PROSPERITY AND DEMOCRACY IN WESTERN EUROPE

THE COMMUNIST BLOC: FROM CONSOLIDATION TO STAGNATION

EUROPE, THE WEST, AND THE WORLD

THE COLLAPSE OF THE SOVIET SYSTEM, 1975–1991

KEY TERMS

existentialism

North Atlantic Treaty Organization (NATO)

welfare state

Konrad Adenauer

Willy Brandt

Margaret Thatcher

Warsaw Pact

Prague Spring

Suez crisis

European Economic Community (EEC)

Helsinki Accords

Solidarity

Mikhail Gorbachev

Online Study Center

This icon will direct you to interactive map and primary source activities on the website **college.hmco.com/ pic/noble5e**

politicians and intellectuals to advocate some form of European union, which might eventually enable the western Europeans to deal with the superpowers on a more equal basis. On the domestic level, the immediate postwar situation was so unsettled that few western European countries could simply return to the prewar norm. Postwar reconstruction rested on a new consensus that government must play a more active role in promoting economic growth and social welfare. By the 1960s the promise of shared prosperity was realized to a remarkable extent. But changing circumstances by the early 1970s threatened the consensus that postwar prosperity had made possible.

Although the Soviet Union had suffered immensely in winning World War II, the communist regime emerged from the war with renewed legitimacy. During the 1950s and 1960s, the Soviet system achieved some significant successes, but its efforts to outgrow its Stalinist framework were halting. By 1980 the system was becoming rigid and stagnant. And thus the dramatic changes in the Soviet bloc that came to a head in 1989, leading to

the opening of the Berlin Wall and, by 1991, to the end of communism in Europe. Only as it was ending, more than four decades after World War II, did observers realize that the anxious cold war era had been one of relative stability and peace.

FOCUS QUESTIONS

What seemed the most likely overall directions as western Europeans pondered priorities in light of all the disasters surrounding the era of the two world wars?

What factors led to the surprisingly rapid restoration of democracy in much of continental western Europe after World War II?

How did Soviet policy evolve after the death of Stalin in 1953?

How did the place of western Europe in world affairs change during the cold war era?

What led to the collapse of the communist system in the Soviet Union and its satellite states?

THE SEARCH FOR CULTURAL BEARINGS

What seemed the most likely overall directions as western Europeans pondered priorities in light of all the disasters surrounding the era of the two world wars?

The events from World War I to the cold war added up to an unprecedented period of disaster for Europe. Europeans were bound to ask what had gone wrong and what could be salvaged from the ruins of a culture that had made possible the most destructive wars in history, as well as fascism, totalitarianism, and the Holocaust. With so much discredited or called into question, Europeans faced an unprecedented period of experiment.

The cold war framework crucially shaped responses all over the Western world. Some embraced the Soviet Union or sought a renewed Marxism. Opposition to communism helped stimulate others to return to religious or classical traditions or to embrace new ideas associated with America's recent successes. In western Europe, at least, this effort to take stock led promptly to the renewed determination that helped

produce the dramatically successful reconstruction of the postwar years. But the anxieties stemming from superpower rivalry, and especially the nuclear arms race, were bound to temper any renewed optimism.

ABSURDITY AND COMMITMENT IN EXISTENTIALISM

The postwar mood of exhaustion and despair found classic expression in the work of the Irish-born writer Samuel Beckett (1906–1989), especially in his plays *Waiting for Godot* (1952) and *Endgame* (1957). Through Beckett's characters, we see ourselves going through the motions, with nothing worth saying or doing, ludicrously manipulating the husks of a worn-out culture. The only redeeming element is the comic pathos we feel as we watch ourselves.

The same sense of anxiety and despair led to the vogue of **existentialism,** a movement that marked philosophy, the arts, and popular culture from the later 1940s until well into the 1950s. Existentialism developed from the ideas of the German thinker Martin Heidegger (1889–1976), especially *Being and Time* (1927), one of the most influential philosophical works of the century. Though it was a philosophy of sorts, existentialism was most significant as a broader cultural tendency, finding expression in novels and films. The existentialists explored what it means to be human in a world cast adrift from its cultural moorings, with no mutually accepted guideposts, standards, or values.

The most influential postwar existentialists were the Frenchmen Jean-Paul Sartre (SAH-truh) (1905–1980) and Albert Camus (kah-MOO) (1913–1960), each of whom had been involved in the French resistance, Camus in a particularly central role as editor of an underground newspaper. For both, an authentic human response to a world spinning out of control entails engagement, commitment, and responsibility—even though every action is fraught with risk.

Rather than accept the bleak, ludicrously comic vision of Beckett's plays, Camus sought to show how we might go on living in a positive, affirmative spirit, even in a world that seemed simply absurd in one sense, especially after the recent disasters in Europe. Conventional values like friendship and tolerance could be made usable again, based on the simple fact that we human beings are all caught up in this unmasterable situation together. People suffer and die, but as we come together to help as best we can, we might at least learn to stop killing one another.

Camus split from Sartre in a disagreement over the ongoing value of Marxism and the communist experiment in the Soviet Union. Though never an orthodox communist, Sartre found potential for human liberation in the working class, in communist political parties, even in the Soviet Union itself, which he saw as the strongest alternative to U.S. imperialism. By the 1950s he was portraying existentialism as fundamentally a way to revitalize Marxism.

Online Study Center **Improve Your Grade**
Primary Source: Existentialism Defined

By contrast, Camus, who had started as a communist in the 1930s, had grown disillusioned with communism even before the war, and his major political tract, *The Rebel* (1951), was partly an attack on Marxism and communism. Establishing new bases for human happiness and solidarity meant recognizing limits to

existentialism A philosophical and cultural movement, often associated with Jean-Paul Sartre and Albert Camus, for whom an authentic human response to an apparently meaningless universe entailed commitment and responsibility.

CHRONOLOGY

1947	India and Pakistan achieve independence
	Marshall Plan announced
1949	Formation of NATO
1951	Formation of the European Coal and Steel Community
1953	Death of Stalin
	Workers' revolt in East Germany
1955	West Germany joins NATO
	Warsaw Pact
1956	Khrushchev de-Stalinization speech
	Suez crisis
	Hungarian reform movement crushed
1957	*Sputnik I* launched
	Common Market established
1958	Beginning of Fifth Republic in France
1959	Bad Godesberg congress: reorientation of German socialism
1961	Berlin Wall erected
1962	Algerian independence from France
	Cuban missile crisis
1964	Ouster of Khrushchev
1968	Days of May uprising in France
	Prague Spring reform movement crushed
1969	Brandt becomes West German chancellor
1973	First OPEC oil crisis
1975	Communist victory in Vietnam
1978	Election of Pope John Paul II
1979	Thatcher becomes prime minister of Britain
1980	Formation of Solidarity in Poland
	Formation of independent Zimbabwe from Southern Rhodesia
1981	Mitterrand elected president of France
1982	Death of Brezhnev
1985	Gorbachev comes to power in the Soviet Union
1986	Chernobyl disaster
1989	Collapse of communism in east-central Europe
1991	Collapse of communism in the Soviet Union
	Dissolution of the Soviet Union

what human beings could accomplish, limits even to our demands for freedom and justice. These were precisely the limits that the new political movements of the century had so disastrously overstepped. Communism, like fascism, was part of the problem, not the solution.

Marxists and Traditionalists

Sartre was among the many European intellectuals who believed that Marxism had won a new lease on life from the wartime resistance. As they saw it, Marxism could be revamped for the West, without the Stalinist excesses of the Soviet Union. Marxism remained a significant strand in Western political culture throughout the cold war era, but it also attracted periodic waves of denunciation.

In Italy, as in France, the communists' major role in the resistance enhanced their prestige, preparing the way for the extraordinary posthumous influence of Antonio Gramsci (GRAHM-she) (1891–1937), a founder of the Italian Communist Party who had spent most of the fascist period in prison. His *Prison Notebooks,* published during the late 1940s, became influential throughout the world and helped make Marxism a powerful force in postwar Italian culture. Seeking to learn the lessons of the fascist triumph in Italy, Gramsci pointed Marxists toward a flexible political strategy, attuned to the special historical circumstances of each country. Thanks partly to Gramsci's legacy, Italy had the most innovative and important communist party outside the communist world for several decades after the war.

Loosely Marxist ideas were central to the renewal of political activism in the West by the late 1960s, although Marxism proved more effective as a critique of capitalism than as a blueprint for change. The best-known spokesman for a renewed radicalism on both sides of the Atlantic during the late 1960s and early 1970s was the German-born social thinker Herbert Marcuse (mar-KOO-zuh) (1898–1979), who explored the cultural mechanisms through which capitalism perpetuates itself in *One-Dimensional Man* (1964).

Even during the late 1940s, however, others, like Camus, denied that any recasting could overcome the inherent flaws in Marxism. Damaging revelations about the excesses of Stalinism during the 1930s seemed to confirm this view. Such writers as the Hungarian-born Arthur Koestler (KEST-lur) (1905–1983) who had believed in communism during the 1930s now denounced it as "the God that failed." Whatever its initial promise, Marxism anywhere would inevitably lead to the kind of tyranny that had developed in the Soviet Union. In his futuristic novel *Nineteen Eighty-Four,* published in 1949, the British intellectual George Orwell (1903–1950), long a partisan of leftist causes, chillingly portrayed the dehumanization that totalitarianism—and, by association, communism—seemed bound to entail.

By the mid-1970s, the disturbing portrait of the Soviet gulag, or forced-labor-camp system, by the exiled Soviet writer Alexander Solzhenitsyn (soul-zhen-EET-sin) (b. 1918) stimulated another wave of anticommunist thinking. And whether or not Marxism was necessarily Stalinist and repressive in implication, its relevance to the increasingly prosperous industrial democracies of western Europe was open to question. By the early 1980s, many had come to believe that the Marxist understanding of capitalism and class relations was simply passé.

Those hostile to Marxism often insisted that the West had to reconnect with older traditions if it were to avoid further horrors like those it had just been through. Especially in the first years after the war, many, like the French Catholic thinker Jacques Maritain (mar-eh-TAN) (1882–1973), held that only a return to religious traditions would suffice. For the American-born British writer T. S. Eliot (1888–1965), the essential return to tradition had to embrace family and locality, as well as religion. Without a return to tradition, Eliot warned, the West could expect more excesses such as fascism and totalitarianism in the future.

The Intellectual Migration and Americanism

The extraordinary migration of European artists and intellectuals to the United States to escape persecution during the 1930s and 1940s profoundly affected the cultural life of the postwar period. An array of luminaries arrived on American shores, from the composer Igor

Stravinsky to the theoretical physicist Albert Einstein, from the architect Walter Gropius to the radical social theorist Herbert Marcuse.

Before this cross-fertilization, American culture had remained somewhat provincial, sometimes proudly and self-consciously so. All the direct contact with these Europeans by the 1940s helped propel the United States into the Western cultural mainstream. No longer could "Western" culture be identified primarily with Europe. In some spheres—painting, for example—Americans were now confident enough to claim the leadership for the first time.

But the American abstract expressionism emerging by the later 1940s owed something to European existentialism, and it became possible only because so many of the most innovative European painters had come to New York, where the Americans had been able to learn their lessons firsthand. At the same time, European painters such as Jean Dubuffet (doo-boo-FAY) (1901–1985) in France and Francis Bacon (1910–1992) in Britain created new forms of their own—sometimes playful, sometimes brutal—as they sought the startling new visual imagery that seemed appropriate to Western culture after the era of fascism and war. Even in the United States, artists began reacting against the deep seriousness of abstract expressionism during the mid-1950s. One new direction led by the early 1960s to "pop art," which was "American" in a different sense, featuring the ordinary objects and mass-produced images of modern consumerist culture. (See the feature "The Visual Record: Pop Art.")

Some Europeans were eager to embrace what seemed distinctively American because America had remained relatively free of the political ideologies that seemed to have led Europe to totalitarianism and ruin. By the 1950s, there was much talk of "the end of ideology," with America indicating a healthier alternative combining technology, value-free social science, and scientific management. Whereas the old European way led either to mere theorizing, to political extremism, or to polarization and impasse, the American approach got results by tackling problems one at a time, so that they could be solved by managerial or technical experts.

Such Americanism fed the notion that Europe needed a clean break based on technological values. If such a break was necessary, however, what was to become of the European tradition, for centuries the center of gravity of the West and until recently dominant in the world? Did anything distinctively European remain, or was Europe doomed to lick its wounds in the shadow of America? These questions lurked in the background as Europeans faced the difficult task of economic and political restoration.

Dubuffet: Spinning Round

Seeking to depart from the European tradition of sophisticated, well-made art, Jean Dubuffet developed imagery that was at once crude and primitive, playful and whimsical. *(Tate Gallery, London/Art Resource, NY. © 2003 Artists Rights Society [ARS], New York/ADAGP, Paris)*

Pop Art

Hamburgers, comic strips, soup-can labels, familiar images of entertainment icons—such was the stuff of "pop art," which burst onto the New York art scene in the early 1960s and came to exert a widespread cultural influence. Indeed, with their imaginative renderings of familiar images and whimsical sculptures of everyday objects, artists like Andy Warhol (1928–1987), Roy Lichtenstein (1923–1997), and Claes Oldenburg (b. 1929) helped shape the experience of the later twentieth century. But was this serious art or simply a joke, a parody, a put-on? Were the pop artists poking fun at the triviality of modern society, or were they deepening our encounter with defining aspects of contemporary culture? Whatever their intent, what does this striking new art form tell us about the direction of Western culture in the decades after World War II?

The term *pop art* was coined in England in the 1950s, when a group of artists and critics became interested in bridging the cultural gap between "fine art" and the emerging popular culture of mass media and machine-produced images, of advertising and automobiles. Like everyone else, they associated that consumerist mass culture with America—the America of Hollywood, Detroit, and Madison Avenue. And they found it more vital than the conventional fine art of the period. The American pop artists were similarly fascinated by the impersonal, mass-produced, often expendable quality of the objects and images that have come to surround us.

Oldenburg: Floor Burger, 1962 *(Claes Oldenburg [American, b. 1929], Floor Burger, 1962. Canvas filled with foam rubber and cardboard boxes, painted with acrylic paint, 132.1 x 213.4 cm. Art Gallery of Ontario, Toronto. Reproduced with permission of Claes Oldenburg.)*

Pop art was part of a wider reaction against the deeply serious abstract expressionist painting that emerged in New York just after the Second World War. By the early 1950s, abstract expressionists like Jackson Pollock (1912–1956) and Mark Rothko (1903–1970) had created images of unprecedented power, whether seeking to forge an artistic identity in the face of nothingness or to transcend selfhood in a cosmic wholeness. In the mid-1950s, however, younger artists, "tired of the stink of artists' egos," began reacting against the self-importance of abstract expressionism. For these younger artists, art did not have to be a vehicle for the psychological expression of the artist or a quest for "the tragic and timeless." Although the reaction took several forms, pop art proved the most influential. The pop movement emerged especially in the United States, and it interested Europeans as typically American—fresh and fascinating or garish and vulgar, depending on one's point of view.

Whereas the abstract expressionists had sought to rise above the everyday world, Claes Oldenburg's sculptures played with the scale and context of the most ordinary objects—a mixer, a three-pronged plug, a lipstick, a hamburger—to deepen our involvement with the everyday things that surround us. In this sense, the aim of pop art was not simply to parody or satirize, but to affirm our relationship with the trappings of ordinary life. Hollywood, Detroit, and Madison Avenue were all right after all; indeed, they had become the centers of Western culture by the later twentieth century.

Though anonymous and impersonal, the modern world of mass production, mass consumption, and mass media is "popular" because its images and objects are accessible to us all. In fact, they bombard us from all directions, giving shared shape and definition to our everyday lives. This is our world, the pop artists were saying, and they were creating the art appropriate to our time. They invite us to relax and enjoy that world, but they also enhance our experience by making art from it, thereby awakening us to its novelty and vitality.

But some viewers have found an element of melancholy, nostalgia, even tragedy just beneath pop art's eye-catching surface. In a world of mass media and reproduced images, more of our experience becomes secondhand and literally superficial. Likewise, pop subjects, from fast food to billboards,

Warhol: Marilyn Diptych, 1962 *(Tate Gallery, London/Art Resource, NY. © Artists Rights Society [ARS], New York/ADAGP, Paris)*

have no deeper meaning, no expressive personal agenda. With his multiplied image of Marilyn Monroe, Andy Warhol dealt not with the actress herself but with the obsessive familiarity of her image. He cultivated a deadpan, detached style that reflected the machine-made quality of his subject matter—the quality that made the images he started with so familiar in the first place. But even as, on one level, he embraced aspects of the new mass culture, Warhol was exploring precisely the emotional detachment—and the accompanying trivialization of emotion—at work in the culture that had produced the images he adapted. Especially in his paintings treating impersonal newspaper images of disaster and death, Warhol bore witness to our indifference—and perhaps to a cosmic meaninglessness as well. One expert has noted that "in Warhol's pictures of the material objects and other false idols that most of us worship, the pain lies just below the bright surfaces of the images and waits passively to engage us."*

_____
* Eric Shanes, *Warhol* (New York: Portland House, 1991), p. 41.

The advent of pop art provoked a series of questions that remain unanswered: Is the embrace of the mass-produced and commercial, at the expense of traditional "fine art" values, a symptom of exhaustion or a healthy affirmation of contemporary popular culture, so bound up with the commercial world? Or is pop art perhaps a valuable comment on the emptiness of that culture, with its impersonal conformity, garish commercialism, and mechanical repetition? In the final analysis, were the pop artists abandoning the artist's lofty mission and giving in to the ordinary? Or were they the first to show us what "Western civilization" had come to mean by the late twentieth century?

QUESTIONS

1. Does pop art seem to be embracing, or poking fun at, the modern world of consumerism and advertising?

2. What is "popular" about pop art?

Online Study Center
Improve Your Grade Visual Record Activities

━━━━ S E C T I O N   S U M M A R Y ━━━━

- Existentialism and the plays of Samuel Beckett expressed the sense of exhaustion and lack of bearings in Western culture after World War II.

- Cold war concerns helped fuel an often bitter debate between Marxists and anti-Marxists that continued, off and on, from the later 1940s well into the 1970s.

- Some held that a return to religious and other traditions offered the only antidote in light of the disasters surrounding the era of the two world wars.

- The migration of European artists and intellectuals to America profoundly affected cultural relations between America and western Europe, especially during the early years of the cold war era.

- As they sought a fresh start for Europe, many western Europeans sought to adapt what they took to be American practicality.

PROSPERITY AND DEMOCRACY IN WESTERN EUROPE

What factors led to the surprisingly rapid restoration of democracy in much of continental western Europe after World War II?

By 1941 democracy seemed to be dying on the European continent, yet it quickly revived in western Europe after World War II, taking root more easily than most had thought possible. The bipolar international framework helped. The United States actively encouraged democracy, and Europeans fearing the spread of communism were happy to follow the American lead. Success at economic reconstruction was important as well. Not only was there greater prosperity, but governments could afford to deliver on promises of enhanced security, social welfare, and equal opportunity. It also mattered that western Europeans learned from past mistakes.

ECONOMIC RECONSTRUCTION AND THE ATLANTIC ORIENTATION

It is hard to imagine how desperate the situation in much of western Europe had become by 1945. Major cities like Rotterdam, Hamburg, and Le Havre lay largely in ruins, and normal routines suffered radical disruption. Production had declined to perhaps 25 percent of the prewar level in Italy, to 20 percent in France, and to a mere 5 percent in southern Germany. Cigarettes, often gained through barter from American soldiers, served widely as a medium of exchange.

Although the U.S. commitment to assist European economic reconstruction was not originally a cold war measure, the developing cold war context added urgency to the American effort. The key was the Marshall Plan, which U.S. secretary of state General Marshall outlined in 1947 and which channeled $13.5 billion in aid to western Europe by 1951.

Online Study Center **Improve Your Grade**
Primary Source: An American Plan to Rebuild a Shattered Europe

Cold war concerns deepened the partnership in April 1949, when the United States spearheaded a military alliance, the **North Atlantic Treaty Organization (NATO),** that included much of western Europe. The Soviets were tightening their grip on their satellite states in east-central Europe, and the NATO alliance was intended to check any Soviet expansion westward. The Soviets had considerable superiority in conventional forces, which had ready access to western Europe, but U.S. nuclear superiority provided a balance. Indeed, the American nuclear guarantee to western Europe was the cornerstone of the NATO alliance.

On the economic level, the western Europeans quickly proved worthy partners. So impressive was the recovery in continental western Europe by the 1950s that some dubbed it an "economic miracle." Western Europeans took advantage of the need to rebuild by adopting up-to-date methods and technologies, though economic strategies differed from one country to the next. The new German government intervened in the economy only to ensure free competition. In France, by contrast, many were determined to use government to modernize the country, thereby overcoming the weakness that had led to defeat. So France adopted a flexible, pragmatic form of government-led economic

North Atlantic Treaty Organization (NATO)
An alliance for regional defense, created in 1949 by the United States, Canada, and western European nations, whose members agree to defend one another from attack by nonmember countries.

Ban the Bomb

As nuclear tension escalated during the 1950s, some people built air-raid shelters; others took to the streets in antinuclear protests. The protest movement was especially prominent in Britain, where the noted philosopher Bertrand Russell (1872–1970) played a central role. Here, at the right of those seated, he awaits arrest during a sit-in demonstration outside the British Defense Ministry.

planning, spearheaded by the technocrat Jean Monnet (moh-NAY) (1888–1979). By 1951 French industrial production had returned to its prewar peak, and by 1957 it had risen to twice the level of 1938. Indeed, strong and sustained rates of economic growth were achieved throughout much of western Europe until the late 1960s, although Britain lagged considerably.

As part of the new postwar consensus, labor was supposed to be brought more fully into economic decision making. Thus, for example, the trade unions participated in the planning process in France. In Germany the codetermination law of 1951 provided for labor participation in management decisions in heavy industry, and labor representatives were given access to company books and full voting memberships on boards of directors. This measure ultimately made little difference in the functioning of the affected firms, but it helped head off any return to trade-union radicalism.

During the first years of rapid economic growth, the labor movement remained fairly passive in western Europe, even though wages stayed relatively low. By the 1960s, however, labor began demanding—generally with success—to share more fully in the new prosperity. Now, rather abruptly, much of western Europe took on the look of a consumer society, with widespread ownership of automobiles, televisions, and other household appliances.

SOCIAL WELFARE AND THE ISSUE OF GENDER

Western governments began to adopt social welfare measures late in the nineteenth century (see page 726), and by the 1940s some degree of governmental responsibility for unemployment insurance, workplace safety, and old-age pensions was widely accepted. Some Europeans, seeking renewal after the war, found attractive models in Sweden and Denmark, where the outlines of a **welfare state** had emerged by the 1930s. Sweden, especially, drew attention as a "middle way" that avoided the extremes of either Soviet Marxism, with its coercive statism, or American-style capitalism, with its brash commercialism and selfish individualism.

Sweden   Sweden's economy remained fundamentally capitalist, based on private ownership; even after World War II, its nationalized, or government-run, sector was not large by European standards. But the system of social insurance in Sweden was the most extensive in Europe, and the government worked actively with business to promote full employment and to steer the economy in directions deemed socially desirable. Moreover, the

welfare state   The concept, especially prevalent in Western countries after World War II, that government should adopt large-scale social welfare measures, while maintaining a primarily capitalistic economy.

Social Welfare in Sweden

With the state playing a major role, Sweden proved a pioneer in responding to the family and children's issues that became increasingly prominent after World War II. Here children play at a day-care center in Stockholm in 1953.   *(Roland Janson/Pressens Bild, Stockholm)*

welfare state came to mean a major role for the Swedish trade unions, which won relatively high wages for workers and even enjoyed a quasi-veto power over legislation.

At the same time, the Swedish government began playing a more active role in spheres of life that had formerly been private, from sexuality to child rearing. Thus, for example, drugstores were required to carry contraceptives beginning in 1946. Sweden was the first country to provide sex education in the public schools; optional beginning in 1942, it became compulsory in 1955. By 1979 the Swedes were limiting corporal punishment—the right to spank—and prohibiting the sale of war toys. This deprivatization of the family stemmed from a sense, especially pronounced in Sweden, that society is collectively responsible for the well-being of its children.

Britain   Although the Swedish model was extreme in certain respects, most of western Europe moved in the same direction in an effort to restore consensus and establish the foundations for democratic renewal after the war. Even Britain, one of the war's major victors, quickly began constructing a welfare state, dumping Winston Churchill in the process.

Early in the war most Britons began to take it for granted that major socioeconomic changes would follow from victory. Greater collective responsibility for the well-being of all British citizens seemed appropriate in light of the shared hardships the war had imposed. Moreover, the successes of government planning and control during the wartime emergency sug-

gested that once the war was over, government could assume responsibility for the basic needs of the British people, guaranteeing full employment and providing a national health service. But the Labour Party, led by Clement Attlee (1883–1967), seemed better equipped to deliver on that promise than the Conservatives, whose leader, Churchill, was in fact quite hostile to welfare state notions. So when Britain held its first postwar elections, in July 1945, Churchill's Conservatives suffered a crushing loss to Labour, which promptly began creating the British welfare state.

Although some expected, and others feared, that the result would be a form of socialism, the new direction did not undermine the capitalist economic system. The Labour government nationalized some key industries, but 80 percent of the British work force remained employed in private firms in 1948. Moreover, even under Labour, the British government did not seek the kind of economic planning role that government was playing in France.

The core of the British departure was a set of government-sponsored social welfare measures that significantly affected the lives of ordinary people. These included old-age pensions; insurance against unemployment, sickness, and disability; and allowances for pregnancy, child rearing, widowhood, and burial. The heart of the system was free medical care, to be provided by the National Health Service, created in November 1946 and operating by 1948.

In Britain, as elsewhere, gender roles were inevitably at issue as government welfare measures were debated and adopted. Were married women to have access to the welfare system as individual citizens or as members of a family unit, responsible for child rearing and dependent on their husbands as breadwinners? Should government seek to enable women to be both mothers and workers, or should government help make it possible for mothers not to have to work outside the home?

As during the First World War, the percentage of women in the work force had increased significantly during World War II, but both women and men proved eager to embrace the security of traditional domestic patterns once the war was over. So the war did not change gender patterns of work even to the extent that World War I had done. In Britain women made up about 30 percent of the labor force in 1931, 31 percent in 1951. Thus the embrace of welfare measures took place at a time of renewed conservatism in conceptions of gender roles.

British feminists initially welcomed provisions of the British welfare state that recognized the special role of women as mothers. The government was to ease burdens by providing family allowances, to be paid directly to mothers of more than one child to enable them to stay home with their children. This seemed a more progressive step than the perpetual British trade-union demand for a "family wage," sufficient to enable the male breadwinner to support a family. But though women were now to be compensated directly for their role as mothers, the assumptions about gender roles remained essentially the same.

France   In France, which had refused even to grant women the vote after World War I, the very different situation after 1945 stimulated an especially innovative response to gender and family issues. After the experience of defeat, collaboration, and resistance, the French were determined to pursue both economic dynamism and individual justice. But they also remained concerned with population growth, so they combined incentives to encourage large families with measures to promote equal opportunity and economic independence for women.

As they expanded the role of government after the war, the French tended more than the British to assume that paid employment for women was healthy and desirable. New laws gave French women equal access to civil service jobs and guaranteed equal pay for equal work. At the same time, the French recognized that women had special needs as mothers, but also that husbands shared the responsibility for parenting. So the French system provided benefits for women during and after pregnancy and then family allowances that treated the two parents as equally essential. At the same time, the system viewed women as individual citizens, regardless of marital or economic status. Thus all were

equally entitled to pensions, health services, and job-related benefits.

Although female participation in the paid labor force declined just after the war, it began rising throughout the West during the 1950s, then accelerated during the 1960s, reaching new highs in the 1970s and 1980s. Thanks partly to the expansion of government, the greatest job growth was in the service sector—in social work, health care, and education, for example—and many of these new jobs went to women. From about 1960 to 1988, the percentage of women aged 25 to 34 in the labor force rose from 38 to 67 in Britain, from 42 to 75 in France, and from 49 to 87 in Germany.

These statistics reflect significant changes in women's lives, but even as their choices expanded in some respects, women became more deeply aware of enduring limits to their opportunities. Thus a new feminist movement emerged by the early 1970s, drawing intellectual inspiration from *The Second Sex*, a pioneering work published in 1949 by the French existentialist Simone de Beauvoir (1908–1986).

THE RESTORATION OF DEMOCRACY

Much of continental western Europe faced the challenge of rebuilding democracy after defeat and humiliation. With the developing cold war complicating the situation, the prospects for democracy were by no means certain in the late 1940s. Although the division of Germany weakened communism in the new Federal Republic, in France and Italy strong communist parties had emerged from the wartime resistance and claimed to point the way beyond conventional democracy altogether.

Germany   The new Federal Republic of Germany held its first election under the Basic Law in August 1949, launching what proved to be a stable and successful democracy. Partly to counter the Soviet Union, but also to avoid what seemed the disastrous mistake of the harsh peace settlement after World War I, the victors sought to help get West Germany back on its feet as quickly as possible. At the same time, West German political leaders, determined to avoid the mistakes of the Weimar years, now better understood the need to compromise, to take responsibility for governing the whole nation.

To prevent the instability that had plagued the Weimar Republic, the creators of the new government strengthened the chancellor in relation to the Bundestag, the lower house of parliament. In the same way, the Basic Law helped establish a stable party system by discouraging splinter parties and by empowering the courts to outlaw extremist parties. And the courts found reason to outlaw both the Communist Party and a Neo-Nazi Party during the formative years of the new German democracy.

The West German republic proved more stable than the earlier Weimar Republic partly because the political party system was now considerably simpler. Two mass parties, the Christian Democratic Union (CDU) and the Social Democratic Party (SPD), were immediately predominant, although a third, the much smaller Free Democratic Party (FDP), proved important for coalition purposes.

Konrad Adenauer (1876–1967), head of the CDU, the largest party in 1949, immediately emerged as West Germany's leading statesman. A Catholic who had been mayor of Cologne under Weimar, he had withdrawn from active politics during the Nazi period, but he reemerged after the war to lead the council that drafted the Basic Law. As chancellor from 1949 to 1963, he oriented the new German democracy toward western Europe and the Atlantic bloc, led by the United States.

The new bipolar world confronted West Germany with a cruel choice. By accepting the bipolar framework, the country could become a full partner within the Atlantic bloc. But by straddling the fence instead, it could keep open the possibility that Germany could be reunified as a neutral and disarmed state. When the outbreak of war in Korea in 1950 intensified the cold war, the United States pressured West Germany to rearm and join the Western bloc. Although some West Germans resisted, Adenauer prevailed, committing the Federal Republic to NATO in 1955. Adenauer was eager to anchor the new Federal Republic to the West, partly to buttress the new democracy in West Germany, but also to cement U.S. support in the face of what seemed an ongoing Soviet threat to German security.

By the late 1950s the West German economy was recovering nicely, and the country was a valued member of the Western alliance. Adenauer's CDU seemed so potent that the other major party, the SPD, appeared to be consigned to permanent—and sterile—opposition. Frustrated with its outsider status, the SPD began to shed its Marxist trappings in an effort to widen its appeal. Prominent among those pushing in this direction was **Willy Brandt** (1913–1992), who became mayor of West Berlin in 1957, and who would become the party's leader in 1963. At its watershed national congress at Bad Godesberg in 1959, the party officially gave up talk of the class struggle and adopted a more moderate program.

Adenauer stepped down in 1963 at the age of 87, after fourteen years as chancellor. The contrast with Weimar, which had known twenty-one different cabinets in a comparable fourteen-year period, could not be more striking. The Adenauer years proved to Germans that democracy could mean effective government, economic prosperity, and foreign policy success. Still, Adenauer had become somewhat authoritarian by his later years, and it was arguable that West Germany had become overly reliant on him and his party.

During the years from 1963 to 1969, the CDU proved it could govern without Adenauer, and the SPD came to seem ever more respectable, even joining as the junior partner in a government coalition with the CDU in 1966. Finally, in October 1969, new parliamentary elections brought Brandt to the chancellorship, and the SPD became responsible for governing West Germany for the first time since the war.

Brandt sought to provide a genuine alternative to the CDU without undermining the consensus that had developed around the new regime since 1949. He wanted

Konrad Adenauer Leading statesman of post–World War II Germany who oriented the country toward western Europe and the United States and proved to Germans that democracy could mean effective government, economic prosperity, and foreign policy success.

Willy Brandt Social Democratic West German chancellor whose policy of opening to the East, or *Ostpolitik,* made possible closer economic ties between West and East Germany and helped ordinary citizens interact across the east-west border.

especially to improve relations between West Germany and the Soviet bloc, but this required a more independent foreign policy than Adenauer and his successors had followed. Under Adenauer, the Federal Republic had refused to deal with East Germany at all. So Brandt's opening to the East, or *Ostpolitik* (OST-po-luh-teek), was risky for a socialist chancellor seeking to prove his respectability. But he pursued it with skill and success.

In treaties with the Soviet Union, Czechoslovakia, and Poland during the early 1970s, West Germany accepted the main lines of the postwar settlement. This was to abandon any claim to the former German territory east of the Oder-Neisse line, now in Poland. Brandt also managed to improve relations with East Germany. After the two countries finally agreed to mutual diplomatic recognition, each was admitted to the United Nations in 1973. Brandt's overtures made possible closer economic ties between them, and even broader opportunities for ordinary citizens to interact across the east-west border. His *Ostpolitik* was widely popular and helped deepen the postwar consensus in West Germany.

France, Italy, and Southern Europe

In France and Italy, unlike West Germany, the communists constituted a potent force in light of their major roles in wartime resistance movements. The presence of Western troops in France and Italy gave the leverage to noncommunists, however, and Moscow directed the communists in both countries to settle for the moderate course of participation in broad political coalitions. But in each nation the United States intervened persistently to minimize the communists' role. Though support for the communists in France continued to grow until 1949, the French Communist Party settled into a particularly doctrinaire position, maintaining strict subservience to the Soviet Union, and found itself increasingly marginalized thereafter.

As the leader of the French resistance effort, Charles de Gaulle immediately assumed the dominant political role after the liberation of France in August 1944. But he withdrew, disillusioned, from active politics early in 1946, as the new Fourth Republic returned to the unstable multiparty coalitions that had marked the later years of the Third Republic. Still, governmental decision making changed significantly as the nonpolitical, technocratic side of the French state gained power in areas such as economic planning. And government technocrats survived the fall of the Fourth Republic in 1958, when de Gaulle returned to politics in a situation of crisis stemming from France's war to maintain control of Algeria (see page 930).

It was clear that de Gaulle's return signified a change of regime. After the French legislature gave him full powers for six months, his government drafted a new constitution, which was then approved by referendum in the fall of 1958. The result was the new Fifth Republic, which featured a stronger executive—and soon a president elected directly by the people and not dependent on the Chamber of Deputies. It was only in 1958, with the return of de Gaulle and the advent of the Fifth Republic, that government in postwar France began to assume definitive contours.

Italy's political challenge, after more than twenty years of fascism, was even more dramatic than France's. Shortly after the war, the Italians adopted a new democratic constitution and voted to end the monarchy, thereby making modern Italy a republic for the first time. But much depended on the balance of political forces, which quickly crystallized around the Christian Democratic Party (DC), oriented toward the Catholic Church, and the strong Communist Party. Many Italian moderates with little attachment to the church supported the Christian Democrats as the chief bulwark against communism. And though they consistently had to work with smaller parties to attain a parliamentary majority, the Christian Democrats promptly assumed the dominant role, which they maintained until the early 1990s.

The Communists continued to offer the major opposition, typically winning 25 to 35 percent of the vote in national elections. Taking their cue from Gramsci's writings, they adopted a proactive strategy to make their presence felt in Italian life and to demonstrate the superiority of their diagnoses and prescriptions. And they found considerable success as they organized profit-making cooperatives for sharecroppers, ran local and regional governments, and garnered the support of intellectuals, journalists, and publishers. But though they had proven capable of operating constructively within a democratic framework, their longer-term role remained unclear into the 1970s. What were the Communists trying to accomplish on the national level, and how long was it supposed to take? Could they function as part of a majority governing coalition within a democratic political system?

By the 1960s the new democracies in Germany, France, and Italy seemed firmly rooted, and during the 1970s Greece, Spain, and Portugal also established workable democracies after periods of dictatorial rule. Following the death of Francisco Franco in 1975, almost forty years after his triumph in the Spanish civil war, democracy returned to Spain more smoothly than most had dared hope. Franco ordained that a restoration of the monarchy would follow his death, and King Juan Carlos (b. 1938; r. 1975–) served as an effective catalyst in the transition to democracy. The new constitution of 1978 dismantled what was left of the Franco system so that, for example, Catholicism was no longer recognized as the official religion of the Spanish state.

NEW DISCONTENTS AND NEW DIRECTIONS

Even as democracy seemed to be thriving in western Europe, political disaffection began to threaten the consensus by the late 1960s. At that point western Europe was at the height of the new prosperity, so the discontent did not stem from immediate economic circumstances. A new radicalism similarly emerged in the United States during the 1960s. Although this American radicalism developed especially from the civil rights movement and from opposition to the U.S. war in Vietnam, a sense that ordinary people were not truly empowered by contemporary democratic institutions fed the new radicalism on both sides of the Atlantic.

Long in gestation, the American civil rights movement sought to overcome racial segregation and other limitations on the rights of African Americans in the United States. It gathered momentum during the 1950s, inspired partly by decolonization struggles elsewhere. A Baptist minister, Martin Luther King, Jr. (1929–1968), emerged as the movement's best-known leader after he spearheaded a successful bus boycott in Montgomery, Alabama, during 1955 and 1956. Professing the technique of nonviolence that Mohandas Gandhi had practiced in India (see the box "The Global Record: Gandhi Advocates Nonviolence" on page 842 in Chapter 27), King won widespread sympathy for the movement among American whites. In 1963 he led a mixed-race throng of 200,000 in a march on Washington, D.C., that helped produce the landmark Civil Rights Act of 1964 and other legislation ending segregation and overt forms of racial discrimination. Although discrimination and de facto segregation could still be found thereafter, the civil rights movement transformed American society and helped stimulate movements for change around the world for decades thereafter.

The most dramatic instance of radical protest in western Europe was the "Days of May" uprising of students and workers that shook France during May and June of 1968. The movement's aims were amorphous or utopian, and cooperation between students and workers proved sporadic. But the episode gave vent to growing discontent with the aloofness of the technocratic leaders and the unevenness of the modernization effort in de Gaulle's France. Despite the impressive economic growth, many ordinary people were coming to feel left out as public services were neglected and problems worsened in such areas as housing and education. French universities were a particular target, drawing protests and even full-scale takeovers by radical students.

Enrollment in French universities more than doubled between 1939 and 1960, then more than doubled again between 1960 and 1967. Apart from a few highly selective *grandes écoles*, the institutions of the state-run university system were open to anyone who passed a standard examination. To limit enrollments by restricting access did not seem politically feasible. Instead, the government tried to build to keep up with demand—thereby creating vast, impersonal institutions with professors increasingly inaccessible to students. But overcrowding persisted, and the value of a university degree diminished, leaving graduates with uncertain job prospects.

In Italy frustration with the stagnation of the political system bred radical labor unrest by 1969 and then a major wave of terrorism during the 1970s. By this time many radical young people found the Communists too caught up in the system to be genuinely innovative, yet still too weak to break the Christian Democrats' lock on power. Because the Italian Communists, unlike the German Social Democrats, never established their credibility as a national governing party, the Christian Democrats grew ever more entrenched, becoming increasingly arrogant and corrupt.

In Germany the Green movement formed by peace and environmental activists during the late 1970s took pains to avoid acting like a conventional party. Concerned that Germany, with its central location, would end up the devastated battleground in any superpower confrontation, the Greens opposed deployment of additional U.S. missiles on German soil and called for an alternative to the endless arms race. The SPD, as the governing party in an important NATO state, seemed unable to confront this issue and lost members as a result.

Prominent among the new political currents emerging by the early 1970s was the renewed feminist movement, which recalled the earlier movement for women's suffrage. This drive for "women's liberation" sought equal opportunities for women in education and employment. It was striking, for example, that despite major steps toward equal educational opportunity in postwar France, the country's prestigious engineering schools were still not admitting women in the late 1960s and would begin doing so only during the 1980s. But feminists also forced new issues onto the political stage as they worked, for example, to liberalize divorce and abortion laws.

As the established Marxist left seemed unable to deal persuasively with contemporary concerns, new coalitions developed around newly politicized issues such as abortion and the environment. The successes of this new left fed renewed hopes for a more systematic change in socioeconomic relations by the early 1980s, when revitalized socialist parties in France, Spain, and Italy marginalized the communists and, for a time, seemed poised to reorient government, even to spearhead that systematic change.

The pivotal case was France, where François Mitterrand (MEE-tuh-rahn) (1916–1996) was elected president in 1981, promising to create the first genuinely democratic socialism. Despite a vigorous start, how-

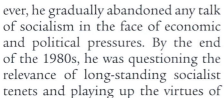

Thatcher's Conservative Revolution

As British prime minister from 1979 to 1990, Margaret Thatcher led an assault on the welfare state and a renewed embrace of free-market economics in Britain. Together with U.S. president Ronald Reagan, who greatly admired her, she came to symbolize the retreat from government that marked the 1980s. Thatcher is shown at a political rally in London in 1987.

(D. Hudson/Corbis Sygma)

ever, he gradually abandoned any talk of socialism in the face of economic and political pressures. By the end of the 1980s, he was questioning the relevance of long-standing socialist tenets and playing up the virtues of entrepreneurship, the profit mechanism, and free-market competition. Mitterrand realized that France, like the other industrial democracies, had to operate in an increasingly competitive international economy, which seemed to impose the same rules on all.

RETHINKING THE WELFARE STATE

In much of western Europe the reach of government continued to expand into the 1970s, when reforms in Italy, for example, made available a wider range of state services—from kindergarten and medical care to sports and recreational facilities—than ever before. But during the 1970s some began to question both the monetary costs of such measures and their implications for European competitiveness in the global economy.

Although much publicity surrounded the postwar British welfare state, by the early 1970s the percentage of the British economy devoted to public expenditure for welfare, housing, and education—18.2 percent—was about average for the industrialized nations of the West. Sweden had the highest figure at 23.7 percent, and by that point 40 percent of Sweden's national income was devoted to taxes to finance the system—the highest rate of taxation in the world. But pressures on the welfare state were especially striking in Sweden at the same time. Swedish opinion-makers grew increasingly doubtful that a welfare state could nurture the initiative and productivity needed for success in international economic competition. Sweden found itself less competitive, both because its wages were high and because it was not keeping abreast of technological developments.

In Britain a dramatic assault on the welfare state began developing at the same time, especially because the postwar British economy, having lagged behind the others of the industrialized West, suffered especially with the more difficult economic circumstances of the 1970s. Between 1968 and 1976, the country lost one million manufacturing jobs. By the mid-1970s this economic decline threatened to shatter Britain's postwar consensus around the welfare state, as the British people could not agree on how to apportion the pain of the necessary austerity measures.

During the 1970s each of Britain's two major political parties made a serious effort to come to grips with the situation, but neither succeeded, especially because neither could deal effectively with Britain's strong trade unions. But when the militantly conservative **Margaret Thatcher** (b. 1925) became prime minister in 1979, it was clear that Britain was embarking on a radically different course.

Thatcher insisted that Britain could reverse its economic decline only by fostering a new "enterprise culture," restoring the individual initiative that had been sapped, as she saw it, by decades of dependence on government. So her government made substantial cuts in taxes and corresponding cuts in spending for education, national health, and public housing. It also fostered privatization, selling off an array of state-owned firms from Rolls-Royce to British Airways. The government even sold public housing to tenants, at as much

Margaret Thatcher   Conservative prime minister of Britain from 1979 to 1990, she promoted privatization and free enterprise at the expense of the welfare state and the British labor unions.

as 50 percent below market value, a measure that helped win considerable working-class support.

At the same time, several new laws curtailed trade-union power, and Thatcher refused to consult with union leaders as her predecessors had done since the war. A showdown was reached with the yearlong coal miners' strike of 1984–1985, one of the most bitter and violent European strikes of the century. Its failure in the face of government intransigence further discred-ited the labor movement and enhanced Thatcher's prestige.

Even critics admitted that Thatcher's policies had produced a significant change in British attitudes in favor of enterprise and competition. And Britain's economic performance certainly improved in the wake of the Thatcher revolution. But the gap between rich and poor widened, and the old industrial regions of the north were left ever farther behind.

S E C T I O N   S U M M A R Y

- The continuing American commitment to western Europe, on both the economic and military-diplomatic levels, helped provide a framework for democratic restoration.

- Government promises of enhanced social welfare and equality of opportunity were essential to a new social compact in the years of democratic recon-struction in western Europe.

- Konrad Adenauer led West Germany into the American-led Atlantic bloc as part of his effort to cement democratic institutions in the new West Germany.

- Discontent with the quality of democracy surfaced on both sides of the Atlantic by the 1960s, even before the economic downturn of the 1970s.

- The traditional socialist left and even the welfare state were on the defensive in many parts of western Europe by the 1980s.

THE COMMUNIST BLOC: FROM CONSOLIDATION TO STAGNATION

How did Soviet policy evolve after the death of Stalin in 1953?

By the late 1950s, policymakers in the West were increasingly concerned that the Soviet Union, though rigid and inhumane in important re-spects, might have significant advantages in the race with the capitalist democracies. Westerners worried es-pecially about producing enough scientists and engi-neers to match the Soviets. With the Great Depression still in memory, some economists held that central planning might prove more efficient, and more likely to serve social justice, than capitalism. The sense that the communist system offered formidable competition added to the anxieties in the U.S.-led Atlantic bloc.

Nonetheless, the flawed political and economic or-der that had emerged under Stalin continued in the So-viet Union. And when it was imposed on the countries within the Soviet orbit after the war, it produced wide-spread resentment—and new dilemmas for Soviet lead-ers. Efforts to make communism more flexible after Stalin's death in 1953 proved sporadic at best. The So-viet suppression of the reform movement in Czechoslo-vakia during the "Prague Spring" of 1968 seemed to prove the inherent rigidity of the Soviet system.

DILEMMAS OF THE SOVIET SYSTEM IN POSTWAR EUROPE, 1949–1955

Even in victory, the Soviet Union had suffered enor-mously in the war with Nazi Germany. Especially in the more developed western part of the country, thousands of factories and even whole towns lay destroyed, and there were severe shortages of everything from labor to housing. Yet the developing cold war seemed to require that military spending remain high.

At the same time, the Soviet Union faced the chal-lenge of solidifying the new system of satellite states it had put together in east-central Europe. Most of the re-gion had no desirable interwar past to reclaim, and thus there was widespread sentiment for significant change. Even in Czechoslovakia, which had been the most prosperous and democratic state in the region, considerable nationalization of industry was completed even before the communist takeover in 1948. And what-ever integration into the new Soviet bloc might mean politically, it was not clear in the late 1940s that it had to be economically disadvantageous over the long term.

The Soviet system seemed to have proved itself in standing up to the Nazis, and many believed that a socialist economic system could be made to work.

Partly in response to U.S. initiatives in western Europe, the Soviets sought to mold the new communist states into a secure, coordinated bloc of allies. In the economic sphere, the Soviets founded a new organization, COMECON, as part of their effort to lead the economies of the satellite states away from their earlier ties to the West and toward the Soviet Union (see **Map 29.1**). In the military-diplomatic sphere, the Soviets countered NATO in 1955 by bringing the Soviet bloc countries together in a formal alliance, the **Warsaw Pact,** which provided for a joint military command and mutual military assistance.

From the start, Yugoslavia had been a point of vulnerability for the Soviet system. Communist-led partisans under Josip Tito had liberated Yugoslavia from the Axis on their own, and they had not needed the Red Army to begin constructing a new communist regime (see page 897). Tito was willing to work with the Soviets, but because he had his own legitimacy, he could be considerably more independent than those elsewhere whose power rested on Soviet support. Thus the Soviets deemed it essential to bring Tito to heel, lest his example encourage too much independence in the other communist states. When Soviet demands became intolerably meddlesome from the Yugoslav point of view, Tito broke with the Soviet Union altogether in 1948. Yugoslavia then began developing a more flexible socialist economic system, with greater scope for local initiatives.

Stalin's response to Tito's defection was a crackdown on potential opponents throughout the Soviet bloc. Though the terror did not approach the massive scale of 1937–1938 (see pages 845–846), again the secret police executed those suspected of deviation, inspiring fear even among the top leadership. As such repression proceeded in the satellite states, opposition strikes and demonstrations developed as well, finally reaching a crisis point in East Germany in 1953.

In East Berlin a workers' protest against a provision to increase output or face wage cuts promptly led to political demands, including free elections and the withdrawal of Soviet troops. Disturbances soon spread to the other East German cities. Though this spontaneous uprising was not well coordinated, Soviet military forces had to intervene to save the East German communist regime. But the East German protest helped stimulate strikes and antigovernment demonstrations elsewhere in the Soviet bloc as well, convincing Soviet leaders that something had to be done. However, at this point the leadership of the Soviet Union was again being sorted out, for Stalin had died

early in 1953, a few months before the crisis in East Germany came to a head.

De-Stalinization Under Khrushchev, 1955–1964

Although a struggle for succession followed Stalin's death, the political infighting involved a reasonable degree of give-and-take, as opposed to terror and violence. To be sure, the contestants quickly ganged up on the hated secret police chief, who was tried and executed within months, but this stemmed from their prior agreement to limit the role of the secret police. Moreover, although one of the eventual losers was sent to Siberia to run a power station and the other was made ambassador to Outer Mongolia, it was a major departure that the winner, Nikita Khrushchev (KROOSH-choff) (1894–1971), ordered neither of them exiled or executed.

Slightly crude, even something of a buffoon, Khrushchev outmaneuvered his rivals by 1955 partly because they repeatedly underestimated him. Although his period of leadership was brief, it was eventful indeed—and in some ways the Soviet system's best chance for renewal.

At a closed session of the Soviet Communist Party's twentieth national congress in February 1956, Khrushchev made a dramatic late-night speech denouncing the criminal excesses of the Stalinist system and the "cult of personality" that had developed around Stalin himself. Khrushchev's immediate aim was to undercut his hard-line rivals, but he also insisted that key features of Stalinism had amounted to an unnecessary deviation from Marxism-Leninism. So the advent of Khrushchev suggested that there might be liberalization and reform.

In the face of the East German uprising of 1953, the Soviets backed off from hard-line Stalinism in the satellite states, making room for more moderate communists they had previously shunned, such as the Hungarian Imre Nagy (NAHZH) (1896–1958). Khrushchev even sought to patch things up with Tito, exchanging visits with him in 1955 and 1956. In his speech to the party congress in 1956, Khrushchev suggested that different countries might take different routes to communism.

But could liberalization be contained within the larger framework of Soviet leadership, or were openness and innovation bound to threaten the system itself? The test case proved to be Hungary, where reformers led by the moderate communist Nagy had taken advantage of the liberalizing atmosphere by mid-1956 to begin dismantling collective farms and moving toward a multiparty political system. They even called for Soviet troops to withdraw, to enable Hungary to leave the Warsaw Pact and become neutral. These were not changes within the system, but challenges to the

Warsaw Pact   Military-diplomatic alliance of Soviet bloc countries, created to counter NATO.

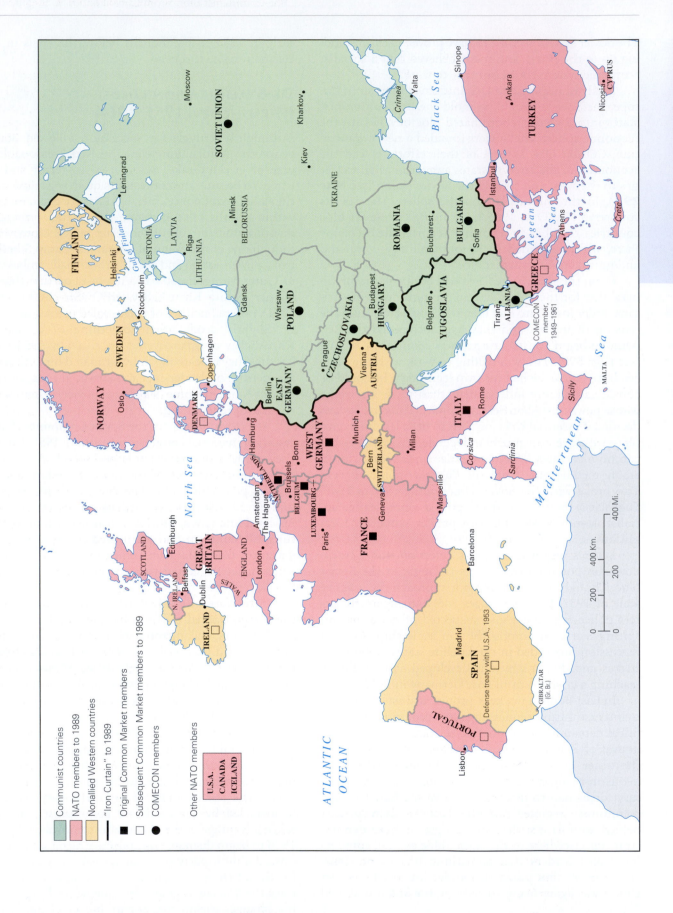

FINLAND
Helsinki
Gulf of Finland
Leningrad
Moscow
SOVIET UNION
Minsk
BELORUSSIA
Kharkov
Kiev
Crimea
Yalta
Black Sea
Sinope
Ankara
TURKEY
Nicosia
CYPRUS
ESTONIA
LATVIA
Riga
LITHUANIA
UKRAINE
ROMANIA
Bucharest
BULGARIA
Sofia
Istanbul
Aegean Sea
Athens
Crete
SWEDEN
Stockholm
NORWAY
Oslo
Copenhagen
DENMARK
Gdansk
Warsaw
POLAND
Prague
CZECHOSLOVAKIA
Budapest
HUNGARY
Belgrade
YUGOSLAVIA
Tiranë
ALBANIA
GREECE
COMECON member, 1949–1961
MALTA
Sea
Berlin
EAST GERMANY
Vienna
AUSTRIA
ITALY
Rome
Sicily
Corsica
Sardinia
Mediterranean Sea
North Sea
Hamburg
NETHERLANDS
Bonn
WEST GERMANY
Munich
Bern
SWITZERLAND
Milan
Brussels
BELGIUM
LUXEMBOURG
Amsterdam
The Hague
Paris
FRANCE
Geneva
Marseille
SCOTLAND
Edinburgh
GREAT BRITAIN
ENGLAND
London
WALES
N. IRELAND
Belfast
Dublin
IRELAND
Barcelona
Madrid
SPAIN
Defense treaty with U.S.A., 1953
GIBRALTAR (Gr. Br.)
PORTUGAL
Lisbon
ATLANTIC OCEAN

400 Mi.
400 Km.
200
200
0
0

Communist countries
NATO members to 1989
Nonallied Western countries
"Iron Curtain" to 1989
Original Common Market members
Subsequent Common Market members to 1989
COMECON members

U.S.A.
CANADA
ICELAND

Other NATO members

MAP 29.1 Military Alliances and Multinational Economic Groupings, 1949–1989

The cold war split was reflected especially in the two military alliances: NATO, formed in 1949, and the Warsaw Pact, formed in 1955. Each side also had its own multinational economic organization, but the membership of the EEC, or Common Market, was not identical to that of NATO. Although communist, Yugoslavia remained outside Soviet-led organizations, as did Albania for part of the period.

Online Study Center **Improve Your Grade**
Interactive Map: Military Alliances and Multinational Economic Groupings, 1949–1989

system itself. When a democratic coalition government was set up by November, the Soviets used tanks to crush the Hungarian reform movement. Thousands were killed during the fighting or subsequently executed, and 200,000 Hungarians fled to the West.

Yet even the crackdown in Hungary did not mean a return to the old days of Stalinist rigidity in the Soviet bloc. The Soviets understood that the system had to become more palatable, but liberalization was to be contained within certain limits. Above all, it could not challenge communist monopoly rule and the Warsaw Pact. After 1956 the satellites were granted greater leeway, and showed greater diversity, than had previously seemed possible. Hungary's new leader, János Kádár (1912–1989), collectivized agriculture more fully than before, but he also engineered a measure of economic decentralization, allowing scope for local initiatives and market mechanisms.

In East Germany, in contrast, Walter Ulbricht (1893–1973) concentrated on central planning and heavy industry in orthodox fashion. The East German economy became the most successful in the Soviet bloc, primarily because here the new communist regime fell heir to a skilled industrial labor force. Still, that economic growth was built on low wages, so East German workers were tempted to emigrate to West Germany as the West German economic miracle gleamed ever brighter during the 1950s. The special position of Berlin, in the heart of East Germany yet still divided among the occupying powers, made such emigration relatively easy, and 2.6 million East Germans left for the West between 1950 and 1962. With a population of only 17.1 million, East Germany could not afford to let this hemorrhaging continue. Thus, in August 1961 the Ulbricht regime erected the Berlin Wall, an ugly symbol of the cold war division of Europe.

FROM LIBERALIZATION TO STAGNATION

As a domestic leader, Khrushchev proved erratic, but he was an energetic innovator, willing to experiment. He jettisoned the worst features of the police state apparatus, including some of the infamous forced-labor camps, and offered several amnesties for prisoners. He also liberalized cultural life and gave workers greater freedom to move from one job to another. The economic planning apparatus was decentralized somewhat, affording more scope for local initiatives and placing greater emphasis on consumer goods. The government expanded medical and educational facilities and, between 1955 and 1964, doubled the nation's housing stock, substantially alleviating a severe housing shortage.

Even Khrushchev's claim in 1961 that the Soviet Union would surpass the Western standard of living within twenty years did not seem to be an idle boast. The Soviets had launched *Sputnik I* in 1957, assuming the lead in the ensuing space race, and they sent the first human into space in 1961. Such achievements suggested that even ordinary Soviet citizens had reason for optimism. More generally, the communist regimes throughout the Soviet bloc entered the 1960s with confidence after achieving excellent rates of economic growth during the 1950s.

Yet Khrushchev had made enemies with his erratic reform effort, and this led to his forced retirement in October 1964. After the unending experiment in the economy, his opponents wanted to consolidate, to return to stability and predictability. But not until 1968 did it become clear that the liberalization and innovation of the Khrushchev era were over.

By early 1968 a significant reform movement had developed within the Communist Party in Prague, the capital of Czechoslovakia. Determined to avoid the fate of the Hungarian effort in 1956, the reformers emphasized that Czechoslovakia was to remain a communist state and a full member of the Warsaw Pact. But within that framework, they felt, it should be possible to invite freer cultural expression, to democratize the Communist Party's procedures, and to broaden participation in public life.

However, efforts to reassure the Soviets alienated some of the movement's supporters, who stepped up their demands. As earlier in Hungary, the desire for change seemed to outstrip the intentions of the movement's organizers. Finally, in August 1968, Soviet leaders decided to crack down, sending Soviet tanks into Prague to crush the reform movement. This end of the **Prague Spring** closed the era of relative flexibility and

Prague Spring The attempt by Czechoslovakian reformers in 1968 to gain freer cultural expression, democratization of Communist Party procedures, and broader participation in public life within the framework of a communist state.

The End of the Prague Spring

Moving tanks into Prague in August 1968, Soviet leaders ended the widely admired reform movement in Czechoslovakia. Though there were protests, as shown here on August 20, the outcome was a foregone conclusion once the Soviets decided to intervene. The ending of the Prague Spring proved a watershed for the fate of communism in Europe. *(Josef Kondelka/Magnum Photos)*

cautious innovation in the Soviet bloc that had begun in 1953.

A period of relative stagnation followed under Leonid Brezhnev (BREZH-nef) (1906–1982), a careful, consensus-seeking bureaucrat. In dealing with the United States, Brezhnev helped engineer significant moves toward arms control and an easing of tensions.

But despite this *détente*, the "Brezhnev Doctrine" made it clear that the Soviet Union would intervene as necessary to help established communist regimes remain in power. For the Soviet satellite states, there seemed to be no further hope of reform from within. But even as resignation marked the first years after 1968, forces soon emerged that undermined the whole communist system.

═══ S E C T I O N   S U M M A R Y ═══

- The imposition of Stalinist forms of governing in the new Soviet satellite states produced tensions that led the whole satellite system to a breaking point by 1953.

- Nikita Khrushchev's speech of February 1956 denouncing the excesses of Stalinism opened the way to a measure of liberalization and reform in the Soviet Union.

- The Soviet suppression of the Hungarian revolution in the fall of 1956 indicated a strict set of limits, but the Soviet satellite states had some freedom to set their own course thereafter.

- The East German government erected the Berlin Wall in August 1961 to stop people from moving to West Berlin—and from there to other parts of West Germany.

- In light of the Soviet suppression of the Prague Spring reform movement in 1968, there seemed little scope for reforming the communist systems from within.

EUROPE, THE WEST, AND THE WORLD

How did the place of western Europe in world affairs change during the cold war era?

By the early 1950s, the old Europe seemed dwarfed by the two superpowers and, for the foreseeable future, divided by the conflict between them. The colonial networks that had manifested European predominance unraveled rapidly at the same time. One obvious response was some form of European integration. A unified Europe might eventually become a global superpower in its own right. Although the first steps toward European unity did not go as far as visionaries had hoped, a new group of leaders established lasting foundations by the late 1950s. Still, the cold war framework limited the new union's geographical extent and the scope of its activity for decades.

THE COLD WAR FRAMEWORK

That cold war tensions could produce dangerous military conflict quickly became clear as superpower divisions over Korea, which had been jointly liberated from the Japanese by the Americans and the Soviets, helped produce the complex Korean War (1950–1953). Although the United States had previously declared Korea outside the U.S. defense perimeter, it intervened in support of noncommunist South Korea in the face of an attempt by communist North Korea, encouraged by Stalin, to unify Korea as a communist state. The war was inconclusive, leaving the Korean peninsula divided more or less as before, but it prompted the United States to extend containment to the global level and to step up military production.

In retrospect, however, it is clear that the most intense phase of the cold war ended with Stalin's death in 1953. In his speech to the twentieth party congress in 1956, Khrushchev repudiated the previous Soviet tenet that the very existence of Western capitalist imperialism made a military showdown with the communist world inevitable. During a visit to the United States in 1959, he stressed that the ongoing competition between the two sides could be peaceful. However, despite summit conferences and sporadic efforts at better relations, friction between the Soviet Union and the United States continued to define the era.

Indeed, a new peak of tension was reached in October 1962, when the Soviets began placing missiles in Cuba, just 90 miles from the United States. Cuba had developed close ties with the Soviet Union after a 1959 revolution led by Fidel Castro (b. 1926). With Castro beginning to develop a communist system, a U.S.-supported force of Cuban exiles sought to invade Cuba and foment insurrection against the new regime in April 1961. This effort proved a fiasco, but it demonstrated to the Soviets that the new Cuban regime was vulnerable to overthrow from the United States.

Although the United States had placed offensive missiles in NATO member Turkey, adjacent to the Soviet Union, the Soviet attempt to base missiles in Cuba seemed an intolerable challenge to the U.S. administration. President John F. Kennedy (1917–1963) responded with a naval blockade of Cuba, and for several days the superpowers seemed on the verge of military confrontation. Finally, the Soviets agreed to withdraw their missiles in exchange for a U.S. promise not to seek to overthrow the communist government of Cuba. The Americans also agreed informally to remove their offensive missiles from Turkey. Khrushchev's willingness to retreat antagonized hard-liners in the Soviet military and contributed to his ouster from power two years later. Yet Khrushchev himself viewed the outcome in Cuba as a victory. By challenging the United States with missiles, the Soviets had helped secure the survival of the Cuban communist regime, which was now less vulnerable to overthrow by the United States. The Cuban missile crisis was the closest the superpowers came to direct, armed confrontation during the cold war period.

At the same time, it became increasingly clear that international communism was not the monolithic force it had once seemed. The most dramatic indication was the Sino-Soviet split, which developed during the 1950s as the Chinese Communist Party under Mao Zedong solidified its power. In the long struggle that led to their victory in 1949, the Chinese Communists had often had no choice but to go their own way, and during the 1940s especially, Stalin had been willing to subordinate any concern for their cause to Soviet national interests. After taking power in 1949, the Chinese Communists pursued their own path to development without worrying about the Soviet model. Not without reason, the Soviets feared that the independent, innovative Chinese might be prepared to challenge Soviet leadership in international communism. By the early 1960s, the Chinese Communists' path had become appealing to many in the non-Western world, though it attracted dissident communists in the West as well.

MAP 29.2 Decolonization, 1945–1980
During a thirty-five-year period after World War II, the European empires in Africa, Asia, and the Pacific gradually came apart as the former colonies became independent nations.

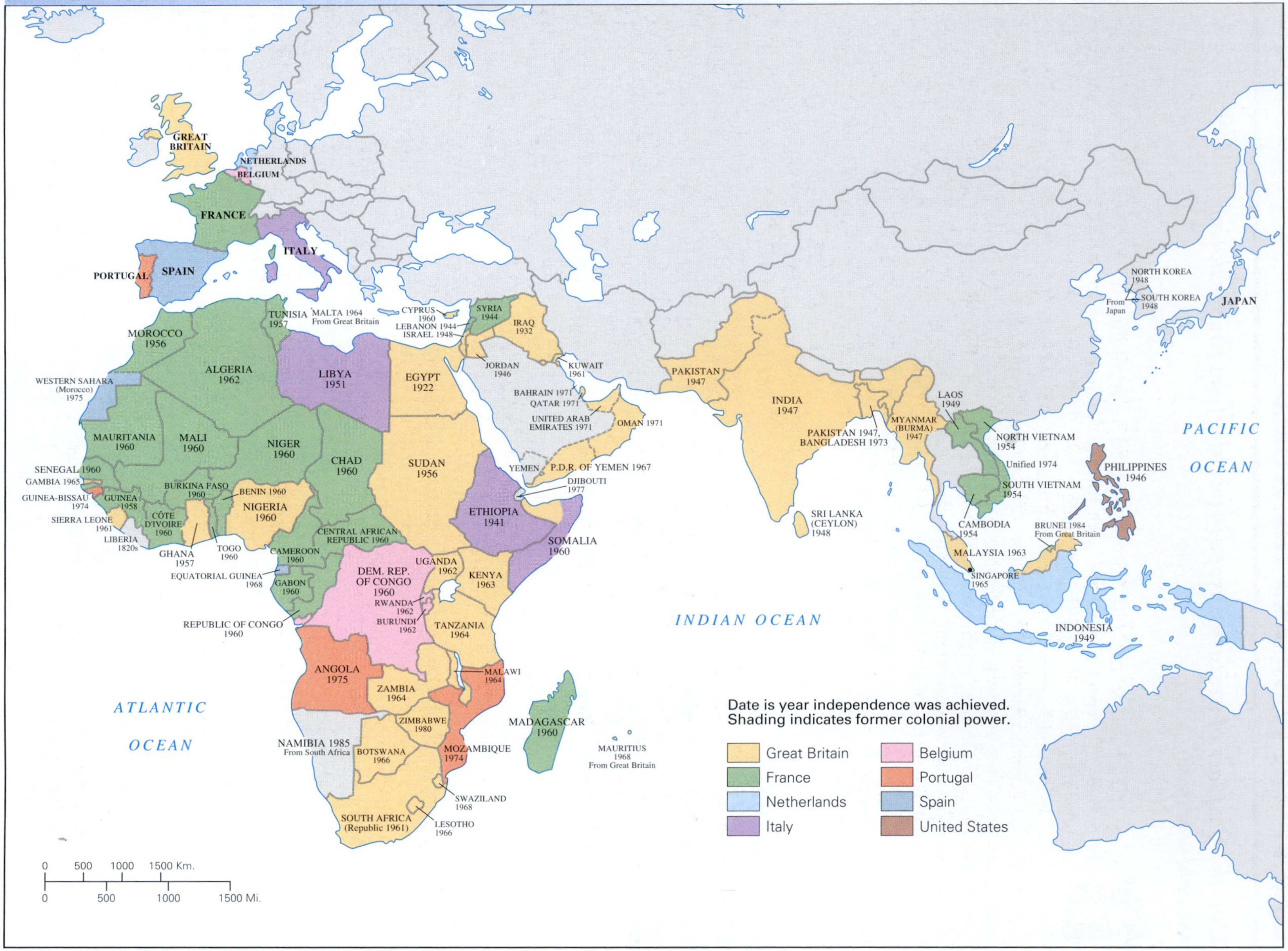

Date is year independence was achieved.
Shading indicates former colonial power.

Great Britain
France
Netherlands
Italy
Belgium
Portugal
Spain
United States

PACIFIC OCEAN
INDIAN OCEAN
ATLANTIC OCEAN

JAPAN
NORTH KOREA 1948 (From Japan)
SOUTH KOREA 1948
PHILIPPINES 1946
BRUNEI 1984 From Great Britain
INDONESIA 1949
NORTH VIETNAM 1954
Unified 1974
SOUTH VIETNAM 1954
CAMBODIA 1954
MALAYSIA 1963
SINGAPORE 1965
LAOS 1949
MYANMAR (BURMA) 1947
PAKISTAN 1947
BANGLADESH 1973
INDIA 1947
PAKISTAN 1947
SRI LANKA (CEYLON) 1948
OMAN 1971
P.D.R. OF YEMEN 1967
DJIBOUTI 1977
YEMEN
KUWAIT 1961
BAHRAIN 1971
QATAR 1971
UNITED ARAB EMIRATES 1971
IRAQ 1932
JORDAN 1946
SYRIA 1944
CYPRUS 1960
LEBANON 1944
ISRAEL 1948
MALTA 1964 From Great Britain
TUNISIA 1957
ITALY
NETHERLANDS
BELGIUM
FRANCE
GREAT BRITAIN
PORTUGAL
SPAIN
MOROCCO 1956
WESTERN SAHARA (Morocco) 1975
MAURITANIA 1960
ALGERIA 1962
MALI 1960
NIGER 1960
LIBYA 1951
CHAD 1960
EGYPT 1922
SUDAN 1956
ETHIOPIA 1941
SOMALIA 1960
KENYA 1963
UGANDA 1962
DEM. REP. OF CONGO 1960
RWANDA 1962
BURUNDI 1962
TANZANIA 1964
CENTRAL AFRICAN REPUBLIC 1960
CAMEROON 1960
GABON 1960
REPUBLIC OF CONGO 1960
EQUATORIAL GUINEA 1968
NIGERIA 1960
BENIN 1960
TOGO 1960
GHANA 1957
COTE D'IVOIRE 1960
BURKINA FASO 1960
GUINEA 1958
GUINEA-BISSAU 1974
SENEGAL 1960
GAMBIA 1965
SIERRA LEONE 1961
LIBERIA 1820s
ANGOLA 1975
ZAMBIA 1964
ZIMBABWE 1980
MALAWI 1964
MOZAMBIQUE 1974
BOTSWANA 1966
NAMIBIA 1985 From South Africa
SOUTH AFRICA (Republic 1961)
SWAZILAND 1968
LESOTHO 1966
MADAGASCAR 1960
MAURITIUS 1968 From Great Britain

0   500   1000   1500 Mi.
0   500   1000   1500 Km.

THE VARIETIES OF DECOLONIZATION

The advent of a new world configuration, with a circumscribed place for Europe, found dramatic expression in the rapid disintegration of the European colonial empires after World War II (see **MAP 29.2**). The war itself had been a major catalyst for independence movements throughout the world. In southeast Asia and the Pacific, quick Japanese conquests revealed the tenuous hold of France, the Netherlands, and Britain on their domains. And it was not colonial reconquest that marked the end of the war, but the atomic bomb and the victory of the United States, which took a dim view of conventional European colonialism.

New Nations in Asia

The effort of the Netherlands to regain control of the Dutch East Indies led to four years of military struggle against the Indonesian nationalist insurgency. Although most independent observers felt that the Dutch could not win, the Dutch were reluctant to relinquish control of the East Indies, which had been in their hands since the seventeenth century. Especially after the humiliations of defeat and occupation during World War II, many of the Dutch took pride in their imperial role. The struggle lasted from 1945 to 1949, when the Dutch finally had to yield as their former colony became independent Indonesia.

Unlike the Netherlands, Britain was still a great power in the twentieth century, and its empire had long seemed essential to its stature. But the structure of the British Empire had been evolving for decades before World War II. With the Statute of Westminster, passed by the British Parliament in 1931, such dominions as Canada, Australia, New Zealand, and South Africa became truly independent, controlling their own foreign policies and joining the League of Nations. This statute was essentially the founding document of the British Commonwealth of Nations. Though it initially encompassed only former British possessions dominated by people of European origin, the commonwealth provided the basis for relatively orderly decolonization after World War II.

In granting independence to India and Pakistan in 1947, the British understood that traditional colonial arrangements were ending, but they envisioned playing an ongoing leadership role by incorporating their former colonies into the British Commonwealth. However, the commonwealth idea proved to have little appeal for those winning independence, and the British Commonwealth proved to be little more than a voluntary cooperative association. Still, Britain was the most realistic of the European colonial powers, grasping the need to compromise and work with emerging national leaders in light of decolonization pressures.

The Suez Crisis

Nevertheless, even Britain decided to resist in 1956, when it provoked an international crisis over the status of the Suez Canal in Egypt (see Map 28.1 on page 872). Once a British protectorate, Egypt had remained under heavy British influence even after nominally becoming sovereign in 1922. But a revolution in 1952 produced a new government of Arab nationalists, led by the charismatic Colonel Gamal Abdel Nasser (1918–1970). In 1954 Britain agreed with Egypt to leave the Suez Canal zone within twenty months, though the zone was to be international, not Egyptian, and Britain was to retain special rights there in the event of war. In 1956, however, Nasser announced the nationalization of the canal, partly so that Egypt could use its revenues to finance public works projects.

Led by the Conservative Anthony Eden (1897–1977), Britain decided on a showdown. Eden won the support of Israel and France, each of which had reason to fear the pan-Arab nationalism that Nasser's Egypt was now spearheading. Israel had remained at odds with its Arab neighbors since its founding in 1948, and Nasser was helping the Arabs who were beginning to take up arms against French rule in Algeria.

Late in 1956 Britain, Israel, and France orchestrated a surprise attack on Egypt. After the Israelis invaded, the British and French bombed military targets, then landed troops to take the canal. But the troops met stubborn Egyptian resistance, and the British and French encountered decisive defeat in the diplomatic maneuvering that accompanied the outbreak of fighting. Both the United States and the Soviet Union opposed the Anglo-French-Israeli move, as did world opinion. The old European powers had sought to act on their own, by the old rules, but the outcome of this **Suez crisis** demonstrated how limited their reach had become.

The French in Vietnam

Still, the 1956 debacle did not convince France to abandon its struggle to retain Algeria. And that struggle proved the most wrenching experience that any European country was to have with decolonization. For the French the process started not in North Africa but in Indochina, in southeast Asia, during World War II.

Led by the communist Ho Chi Minh (1890–1969), the Indochinese anticolonialist movement gained strength resisting the Japanese during the war. Then, before the French could return, Ho established a political base in northern Vietnam in 1945. Although the French reestablished control in the South, negotiations between the French and the Vietnamese nationalists

Suez crisis Crisis prompted by Egypt's nationalization of the British-owned Suez Canal. The effort of Britain, France, and Israel to seize the canal prompted a strong negative reaction in world opinion, forcing them to withdraw.

seemed at first to be moving toward some form of self-government for Vietnam. But in 1946 French authorities in Indochina deliberately provoked an incident to undercut negotiations and start hostilities. Eight years of difficult guerrilla war followed, creating a major drain on the French economy.

With its strongly anticolonialist posture, the United States was unsympathetic to the French cause at first. But the communist takeover in China in 1949 and the outbreak of war in Korea in 1950 made the French struggle in Indochina seem to be a battle in a larger war against communism in Asia. By 1954 the United States was covering 75 percent of the cost of the French effort in Indochina. Nonetheless, when the fall of the fortified area at Dien Bien Phu in May 1954 signaled a decisive French defeat, the United States decided to pull back and accept a negotiated settlement. Partly at the urging of its European allies, the United States had concluded that the Soviet threat in Europe must remain its principal concern.

France worked out the terms of independence for Vietnam in 1955. The solution, however, entailed a North-South partition to separate the communist and anticommunist forces, pending elections to unify the country. The anticommunist regime the United States sponsored in the South resisted holding the elections, so the country remained divided (see Map 29.2). With the Americans providing first advisers, then, beginning in 1964, active military support, South Vietnam sought unsuccessfully to defeat a guerrilla insurgency supported by the communist North. After finally defeating the United States and South Vietnam in 1975, the communist heirs of those who had fought the French assumed the leadership of a reunified Vietnam.

In France the defeat in Indochina in 1954 left a legacy of bitterness, especially among army officers, many of whom felt that French forces could have won had they not been undercut by politicians at home. When the outcome in Indochina emboldened Arab nationalists in North Africa to take up arms against the French colonial power, the French army was anxious for a second chance—and the French government was willing to give it to them. Algeria had been under French control since 1830, and it had a substantial minority of ethnic Europeans, totaling over a million, or 10 percent of the population.

The War in Algeria   Although France gradually committed 500,000 troops to Algeria, the war bogged down into what threatened to become a lengthy stalemate, with increasing brutality on both sides. As it drained French lives and resources, the war became a highly contentious political issue in France. The situation came to a head during the spring of 1958, when the advent of a new ministry, rumored to favor a compromise settlement, led to violent demonstrations, en-

gineered by the sectors of the French army in Algeria. Military intervention in France itself seemed likely to follow—and with it the danger of civil war.

It was at this moment of genuine emergency that Charles de Gaulle returned to lead the change to the Fifth Republic. Those determined to hold Algeria welcomed him as their savior. But de Gaulle fooled them, working out a compromise with the nationalist rebels that ended the war and made Algeria independent in 1962. Only de Gaulle could have engineered this outcome without provoking still deeper political division in France.

Independence in sub-Saharan Africa   By the end of the 1950s, the colonialist impulse, which had still been significant immediately after World War II, was waning noticeably all over Europe. But resistance remained, though its forms varied considerably, as the colonies of sub-Saharan Africa continued to move toward independence. Outcomes depended on several factors: the number and intransigence of European settlers, the extent to which local elites had emerged, and the confidence of the Europeans that they could retain their influence if they agreed to independence. Of the major imperial powers in the region, Britain had done best at preparing local leaders for self-government and proved the most willing to work with indigenous elites. The two smallest countries, Belgium and Portugal, were less certain they could maintain their influence, and they proved the most reluctant to give up their imperial status.

The transition was smoothest in British West Africa, where the Gold Coast achieved independence as Ghana, first as a commonwealth dominion in 1957, then as a fully independent republic in 1960. Few British settlers lived in that part of Africa, and the small, relatively cohesive African elite favored a moderate transition, not revolution. Where British settlers were relatively numerous, however, the transition to independence was much more difficult. The very presence of Europeans had impeded the development of cohesive local elites, so movements for independence in those areas tended to become more radical, threatening the expropriation of European-held property. In Southern Rhodesia, unyielding European settlers resisted the British government's efforts to promote a compromise. A white supremacist government declared its independence from Britain in 1965, fueling a guerrilla war. The Africans won independence as Zimbabwe only in 1980.

The reaction against Eurocentrism that accompanied the turn from colonialism was not confined to those who had been subjected to European imperialism. There was also much interest among Westerners in the work of Frantz Fanon (1925–1961), a black intellectual from Martinique who became identified especially with the cause of the Algerian rebels. In *The Wretched of the Earth* (1961), Fanon found the West spir-

THE GLOBAL RECORD

THE LEGACY OF EUROPEAN COLONIALISM

In the following passages from The Wretched of the Earth *(1961), Frantz Fanon probes the negative consequences of colonialism—for both colonizers and colonized—and tries to show why a radical, even violent break from colonialism was necessary. In his conclusion, he offers a stirring call to the colonized world to repudiate the West, whose claims to offer universal values he finds hypocritical in the extreme.*

The violence which has ruled over the ordering of the colonial world, which has ceaselessly drummed the rhythm for the destruction of native social forms and broken up without reserve the systems of reference of the economy, the customs of dress and external life, that same violence will be claimed and taken over by the native at the moment when, deciding to embody history in his own person, he surges into the forbidden quarters. . . .

. . . In the colonial context the settler only ends his work of breaking in the native when the latter admits loudly and intelligibly the supremacy of the white man's values. In the period of decolonization, the colonized masses mock at these very values, insult them, and vomit them up.

. . . All that the native has seen in his country is that they can freely arrest him, beat him, starve him: and no professor of ethics, no priest has ever come to be beaten in his place, nor to share their bread with him. As far as the native is concerned, morality is very concrete; it is to silence the settler's defiance, to break his flaunting violence—in a word, to put him out of the picture. . . .

. . . The colonialist bourgeoisie, in its narcissistic dialogue, expounded by the members of its universities, had in fact deeply implanted in the minds of the colonized intellectual that the essential qualities remain eternal in spite of all the blunders men may make: the essential qualities of the West, of course. . . . Now it so happens that during the struggle for liberation, at the moment that the native intellectual comes into touch again with his people, . . . [a]ll the Mediterranean values—the triumph of the human individual, of clarity, and of beauty . . . are revealed as worthless, simply because they have nothing to do with the concrete conflict in which the people is engaged.

Individualism is the first to disappear. . . . The colonialist bourgeoisie had hammered into the native's mind the idea of a society of individuals where each person shuts himself up in his own subjectivity, and whose only wealth is individual thought. Now the native who has the opportunity to return to the people during the struggle for freedom will discover the falseness of this theory. The very forms of organization of the struggle will suggest to him a different vocabulary. Brother, sister, friend—these are words outlawed by the colonialist bourgeoisie, because for them my brother is my purse, my friend is part of my scheme for getting on. The native intellectual . . . will . . . discover the substance of village assemblies, the cohesion of people's committees, and the extraordinary fruitfulness of local meetings and groupments. Henceforward, the interests of one will be the interests of all, for in concrete fact *everyone* will be discovered by the troops, *everyone* will be massacred— or *everyone* will be saved. . . .

Leave this Europe where they are never done talking of Man yet murder men everywhere they find them. . . . For centuries they have stifled almost the whole of humanity in the name of a so-called spiritual experience. Look at them today swaying between atomic and spiritual disintegration. . . .

Come then, comrades, the European game has finally ended; we must find something different. We today can do everything, so long as we do not imitate Europe, so long as we are not obsessed by the desire to catch up with Europe.

QUESTIONS

1. On what basis does Fanon believe that even native intellectuals who have embraced Western values can be won back for the anticolonialist cause?

2. What Western value does Fanon claim is the first to be repudiated—and why?

Source: Frantz Fanon, The Wretched of the Earth *(New York: Grove, 1968), pp. 40–47, 311–312.*

itually exhausted and called on the peoples of the non-Western world to go their own way, based on their own values and traditions. (See the box "The Global Record: The Legacy of European Colonialism.")

The process of decolonization led to a remarkable transformation in the thirty-five years after World War II. Forms of colonial rule that had been taken for granted before World War I stood discredited, virtually without defenders, by the late twentieth century. Europeans were now accepting the principle of national self-determination for non-Europeans. But decolonization hardly offered a neat and definitive solution. In formerly colonial territories, new political boundaries often stemmed from the ways Europeans had carved things up, rather than from indigenous ethnic or national patterns. Moreover, questions remained about the longer-term economic relationships between the Europeans and their former colonies.

ECONOMIC INTEGRATION AND THE ORIGINS OF THE EUROPEAN UNION

As the old colonialism increasingly fell into disrepute, many found in European unity the best prospect for the future. Although hopes for full-scale political unification were soon frustrated, the movement for European integration achieved significant successes in the economic sphere, especially through the European Economic Community, or Common Market, established in 1957.

The impetus for economic integration came especially from a new breed of "Eurocrats"—technocrats with a supranational, or pan-European, outlook. A notable example was Robert Schuman (1886–1963), a native of Lorraine, which had passed between France and Germany four times between 1870 and 1945. After serving as a German officer in World War I, he was elected to the French Chamber of Deputies in 1919 just after Lorraine was returned to France. As French foreign minister after World War II, Schuman was responsible for a 1950 plan to coordinate French and German production of coal and steel. The Schuman Plan quickly encompassed Italy, Belgium, the Netherlands, and Luxembourg to become the European Coal and Steel Community (ECSC) in 1951. Working closely with Schuman was Jean Monnet, who served as the ECSC's first president. From this position, he pushed for more thoroughgoing economic integration. The successes of the ECSC led the same six countries to agree to a wider "Common Market," officially known as the **European Economic Community (EEC),** in 1957.

After the merger of the governing institutions of the several European supranational organizations in 1967, the term *European Community* (EC) and later *European Union* (EU) came to indicate the institutional web that had emerged since the launching of the European Coal and Steel Community in 1951. Meanwhile, its membership gradually expanded, encompassing, during the cold war era, Denmark, Ireland, and Britain in 1973, Greece in 1981, and Spain and Portugal in 1986 (see Map 29.1). For newly democratic countries like Spain, Portugal, and Greece, Common Market membership became a pillar of the solidifying democratic consensus.

The immediate aim of the original EEC was to facilitate trade by eliminating customs duties between its member countries and by establishing common tariffs on imports from the rest of the world. For each member of the EEC, tariff reduction meant access to wider markets abroad, but also the risks of new competition in its own domestic market. However, the EEC proved advantageous to so many that tariff reduction proceeded well ahead of schedule. By 1968 the last internal tariffs had been eliminated.

With tariffs dropping, trade among the member countries nearly doubled between 1958 and 1962. For example, French exports of automobiles and chemicals to Germany increased more than eightfold. Partly because the increasing competition stimulated initiative and productivity, industrial production within the EEC increased at a robust annual rate of 7.6 percent during those years.

Despite these successes, vigorous debate accompanied the development of the EEC during the 1960s. To enable goods, capital, and labor to move freely among the member countries, some coordination of social and economic policy was required. But were the member states prepared to give up some of their own sovereignty to the Common Market to make that coordination possible?

In the mid-1960s French president de Gaulle forced some of the underlying uncertainties to the fore. Though he had willingly turned from the old colonialism, de Gaulle was not prepared to compromise French sovereignty, and he was not persuaded that supranational integration offered the best course for postwar Europe. With the end of the Algerian war in 1962, France began playing an assertively independent role in international affairs. Thus, for example, de Gaulle developed an independent French nuclear force, curtailed the French role in NATO, and recognized the communist People's Republic of China.

This determination to assert France's sovereignty led to friction between de Gaulle and the supranational Eurocrats of the Common Market. Matters came to a head in 1965, when a confrontation developed over agricultural policy. The immediate result was a compromise, but de Gaulle's tough stance served to check the increasing supranationalism evident in the EEC until then. As the economic context became more difficult during the 1970s, it became still harder to maintain the EEC's cohesion. So though the Common Market was an important departure, it did not overcome traditional national sovereignty or give western Europe a more muscular world role during the first decades after World War II.

THE ENERGY CRISIS AND THE CHANGING ECONOMIC FRAMEWORK

As the political situation in western Europe became more volatile by the early 1970s, events outside Europe made it clear how interdependent the world had become—and that the West did not hold all the trump cards. In the fall of 1973, Egypt and Syria attacked Is-

European Economic Community (EEC)
Common market formed by Belgium, France, West Germany, Italy, Luxembourg, and the Netherlands to promote free trade.

rael, seeking to recover the losses they had suffered in a brief war in 1967. Although the assault failed, the Arab nations of the oil-rich Middle East came together in the aftermath to retaliate against the Western bloc for supporting Israel. By restricting the output and distribution of the oil its members controlled, the Arab-led Organization of Petroleum Exporting Countries (OPEC) produced a sharp increase in oil prices and a severe economic disruption all over the industrialized world.

The 1970s proved to be an unprecedented period of "stagflation"—sharply reduced rates of growth combined with inflation and rising unemployment. The economic miracle was over, partly because the process soon to be known as globalization was now taking off. The European economies were subject to growing competition from non-Western countries, most notably Japan. In light of increasing global competition and rising unemployment, the labor movement was suddenly on the defensive throughout the industrialized West. And the changing circumstances inevitably strained the social compact that had enabled western Europe to make a fresh start after the war.

SECTION SUMMARY

- Dependent on the United States for their security, the western European countries had limited freedom of action in world affairs during the cold war era.

- Though the decolonization process varied considerably from case to case, the long-standing European colonial networks gradually dissolved after World War II.

- Desires to remove the sources of war and to enhance Europe's economic competitiveness fueled the movement toward European integration, including the formation of the European Economic Community (Common Market) in 1957.

- French president Charles de Gaulle envisioned a more independent role for Europe from within the cold war framework, but that role was to be based on French leadership, not European integration.

- The difficult economic circumstances of the 1970s raised questions about the long-term sustainability of welfare state measures.

THE COLLAPSE OF THE SOVIET SYSTEM, 1975–1991

What led to the collapse of the communist system in the Soviet Union and its satellite states?

Though the reasons were different, the Soviet Union also encountered economic stagnation during the 1970s. The deteriorating situation finally produced a major Soviet reform effort by the mid-1980s. At the same time, new forms of opposition developed in the satellite states after the crushing of the Prague reform movement in 1968. The intersection of these forces led to the unraveling of the satellite system in 1989, then to the collapse of the Soviet communist regime in 1991. This outcome stunned Western observers, who had come to take the anxious stability of the cold war framework for granted.

ECONOMIC STAGNATION IN THE SOVIET BLOC

The impressive rates of economic growth achieved in the Soviet Union and several of the satellite states continued into the 1960s. However, much of that success came from adding labor—women and underemployed peasants—to the industrial work force. By the end of the 1960s that process was reaching its limits, so increasingly the challenge for the Soviet bloc was to boost productivity through technological innovation.

By the late 1970s, however, the Soviets were falling seriously behind the West as a new technological revolution gathered force. The state-directed Soviet economy had proven quite capable of technological leadership when marshaling resources for a particular task was required. Thus, for example, the Soviets led the way in space travel. But continuing development in high technology demanded the freedom to experiment and exchange ideas and the flexibility to anticipate innovation and shift resources. In these areas, the Soviet system, with its direction from the top, proved too rigid. Moreover, as the Soviet system bogged down, the expense of the arms race with the United States dragged ever more seriously on the Soviet economy. Ordinary Soviet citizens grew increasingly frustrated as the communist economy proved erratic in providing the most basic consumer goods. Yet major functionaries now enjoyed access to special shops and other privileges.

Women's Work in the Soviet Union
This cartoon adapts the caryatid form from ancient sculpture to depict the special burdens that were coming to wear more heavily on women as the Soviet economy bogged down. Intended to commemorate International Women's Day, the image appeared in the Soviet magazine *Krokodil* in 1984.
(Krokodil Magazine, March 1984)

In satellite countries such as Poland and Hungary, the communist governments managed for a while to win mass support by borrowing from foreign banks to provide meat and other consumer goods at artificially low prices—"sausage-stuffing," some called it. But as the lending banks came to realize, by the end of the 1970s, that such loans were not being used to enhance productivity, these governments found it much harder to borrow. Thus they began having to impose greater austerity.

Throughout the Soviet bloc, frustration grew especially among women, who seemed to bear a disproportionate share of the burdens. Women were more likely to be employed outside the home in the communist countries than in the West. About 90 percent of adult women in the Soviet Union and East Germany had paid jobs outside the home by 1980. Yet not only were these women concentrated in jobs with low pay and prestige, but they also still bore the major responsibility for child-care, housework, and shopping. They had few of the labor-saving devices available in the West, and they often had to spend hours in line to buy ordinary consumer items. Dissatisfaction among women fed an underground protest movement that began developing in the Soviet bloc in the mid-1970s—an indication of the growing strains in the overall system.

THE CRISIS OF COMMUNISM IN THE SATELLITE STATES

For many intellectuals in the Soviet bloc, the Soviet suppression of the Prague Spring in 1968 ended any hope that communism could be made to work. The immediate outcome was a sense of hopelessness, but by the mid-1970s a new opposition movement had begun to take shape, especially in Hungary, Poland, and Czechoslovakia. It centered initially on underground (or *samizdat*) publications, privately circulated writings that enabled dissidents to share ideas critical of the regime.

In one sense, these dissidents realized, intellectuals and ordinary people alike were powerless in the face of heavy-handed communist government. But they came to believe they could make a difference simply by "living the truth," ceasing to participate in the empty rituals of communist rule. And mere individual honesty could have political potential especially because of the Helsinki Accords on human rights that the Soviet bloc countries had accepted in 1975.

The meeting of thirty-five countries in Helsinki, Finland, in 1975 was one of the most important fruits of the *Ostpolitik,* or opening to the East, that Willy Brandt began pursuing after becoming West Germany's chancellor in 1969 (see page 919). Eager to grasp Brandt's offer to regularize the status of East Germany and to confirm the western border of Poland, the Soviet bloc found it expedient to accept the detailed agreement on human rights included in the resulting **Helsinki Accords.**

Though merely symbolic in one sense, the human rights agreement proved a touchstone for initiatives that would help bring the whole Soviet system crashing down. Through various "Helsinki Watch" groups monitoring civil liberties, anticommunists in the satellite states managed to assume moral leadership. By demanding that the communist governments live up to their agreements, and by noting the gap between idealistic pretense and grim reality, opposition intellectuals began to cast doubts on the very legitimacy of the communist regimes.

The most significant such group was Charter 77, which emerged in Czechoslovakia in response to the arrest of a rock group called "The Plastic People of the Universe." Longhaired and anti-establishment like their counterparts in the West, the Plastic People were deemed filthy, obscene, and disrespectful of society by the repressive Czechoslovak regime. In 1977, protesting the crackdown on the group, 243 individuals signed "Charter 77"—using their own names and addresses, living the truth, acting as if they were free to register such an opinion.

A leader in Charter 77 was the writer Václav Havel (HA-vul) (b. 1936), who noted that, after 1968, the hope for change depended on people organizing themselves, outside the structures of the party-state, in diverse, independent social groupings. (See the box "The Written Record: Power from Below: Living the Truth.") Havel and a number of his associates were in and out of jail as the government sought to stave off this protest movement. Despite the efforts of Havel and his colleagues, government remained particularly repressive and ordinary people relatively passive in Czechoslovakia until the late 1980s. For quite different reasons, Hungary and Poland offered greater scope for change.

Even after the failed reform effort of 1956, Hungary proved the most innovative of the European communist countries. Partly because its government allowed small-scale initiatives outside the central planning apparatus, Hungary was able to respond more flexibly to the growing economic stagnation. By the mid-1980s various alternative forms of ownership were responsible for one-third of Hungary's economic output.

This openness to economic experimentation enabled reformers within the Hungarian Communist Party to gain the upper hand. Amid growing talk of "socialist pluralism," the Hungarian elections of 1985 intro-

duced an element of genuine democracy. Increasingly open to a variety of viewpoints, the Hungarian Communists gradually pulled back from their long-standing claim to a monopoly of power.

The reform effort that built gradually in Hungary stemmed especially from aspirations within the governing elite. More dramatic was the course of change in Poland, where workers and intellectuals, at odds even as recently as 1968, managed to come together during the 1970s. When Polish workers struck in 1976, in response to a cut in food subsidies, intellectuals formed a committee to defend them. This alliance had become possible because dissident intellectuals were coming to emphasize the importance of grass-roots efforts that challenged the logic of the communist system without attacking it directly.

An extra ingredient from an unexpected quarter also affected the situation in Poland, perhaps in a decisive way. In 1978 the College of Cardinals of the Roman Catholic Church departed from long tradition and, for the first time since 1522, elected a non-Italian pope. Even more startling was the fact that the new pope was from Poland, behind the iron curtain. He was Karol Cardinal Wojtyla (voy-TILL-ah) (1920–2005), the archbishop of Cracow, who took the name John Paul II.

After World War II, the Polish Catholic Church had been unique among the major churches of east-central Europe in maintaining and even enhancing its position. It worked just enough with the ruling Communists to be allowed to carve out a measure of autonomy. For many Poles, the church thus remained a tangible institutional alternative to communism and the focus of national self-consciousness in the face of Soviet domination. Thus the new pope's visit to Poland in 1979 had an electrifying effect on ordinary Poles, who took to the streets by the millions to greet him—and found they were not alone. This boost in self-confidence provided the catalyst for the founding of a new trade union, **Solidarity,** in August 1980.

Led by the remarkable shipyard electrician Lech Walesa (va-WEN-sah) (b. 1944), Solidarity emerged from labor discontent in the vast Lenin shipyard in Gdansk, on the Baltic Sea (see Map 29.1). Demanding the right to form their own independent unions, seventy thousand workers took over the shipyard, winning support both from their intellectual allies and from the Catholic Church. Support for Solidarity grew partly because the government, facing the crisis of its "sausage-stuffing" strategy, was cutting subsidies and raising food prices. But the new union developed such force because it placed moral demands first—independent

Helsinki Accords   Agreements signed by thirty-five countries in Helsinki, Finland, that committed the signatories to recognize existing borders, to increase economic and environmental cooperation, and to promote freedom of expression, religion, and travel.

Solidarity   A trade union formed in communist Poland, it became the nucleus of widespread demands for change—including independent labor organizations, the right to strike, and freedom of expression.

POWER FROM BELOW: LIVING THE TRUTH

Considering the scope for change in the communist world by the late 1970s, Václav Havel imagines a conformist grocer who routinely puts a sign in his window with the slogan "Workers of the world, unite!" simply because it is expected. That same grocer, says Havel, has the power to break the system, which rests on innumerable acts of everyday compliance. Havel finds this system "post-totalitarian" because it rests on neither the coercion nor the fanatical belief that, in some combination, had sustained the earlier totalitarian systems. At the same time, he senses that aspects of the "post-totalitarian" order reveal, in stark and garish terms, more general modern tendencies that are merely masked in the Western democracies. So the West did not offer an easy model; in fact, it might actually have something to learn from the forms of opposition that Havel saw emerging in the communist bloc.

The real meaning of the greengrocer's slogan has nothing to do with what the text of the slogan actually says. Even so, this real meaning is quite clear and generally comprehensible because the code is so familiar: the greengrocer declares his loyalty . . . in the only way the regime is capable of hearing; that is, by accepting the prescribed *ritual,* by accepting appearances as reality, by accepting the given rules of the game. In doing so, however, he has himself become a player in the game, thus making it possible for the game to go on, for it to exist in the first place. . . .

In the end, is not the greyness and emptiness of life in the post-totalitarian system only an inflated caricature of modern life in general? And do we not stand (although in the external measures of civilization, we are far behind) as a kind of warning to the West, revealing its own latent tendencies?

Let us now imagine that one day something in our greengrocer snaps and he stops putting up the slogans merely to ingratiate himself. He stops voting in elections he knows are a farce. He begins to say what he really thinks at political meetings. . . . He rejects the ritual and breaks the rules of the game. He discovers once more his suppressed identity and dignity. . . .

. . . By breaking the rules of the game, he has disrupted the game as such. He has exposed it as a mere game. He has shattered the world of appearance, the fundamental pillar of the system. . . . He has shown everyone that it *is* possible to live within the truth. Living within the lie can constitute the system only if it is universal. The principle must embrace and permeate everything. There are no terms whatsoever on which it can coexist with living within the truth, and therefore everyone who steps out of line *denies it in principle* and threatens it in its entirety. . . .

And since all genuine problems and matters of critical importance are hidden beneath a thick crust of lies, it is never quite clear when the proverbial last straw will fall, or what that straw will be. This . . . is why the regime prosecutes, almost as a reflex action preventively, even the most modest attempts to live within the truth.

. . . The crust presented by the life of lies is made of strange stuff. As long as it seals off hermetically the entire society, it appears to be made of stone. But the moment someone breaks through in one place, when one person cries out, "The emperor is naked!"— when a single person breaks the rules of the game, thus exposing it as a game—everything suddenly appears in another light and the whole crust seems then to be made of a tissue on the point of tearing and disintegrating uncontrollably. . . .

The post-totalitarian system is only one aspect . . . of this general inability of modern humanity to be the master of its own situation. The automatism of the post-totalitarian system is merely an extreme version of the global automatism of technological civilization. The human failure that it mirrors is only one variant of the general failure of modern humanity.

. . . It would appear that the traditional parliamentary democracies can offer no fundamental opposition to the automatism of technological civilization and the industrial-consumer society, for they, too, are being dragged helplessly along by it. People are manipulated in ways that are infinitely more subtle and refined than the brutal methods used in the post-totalitarian societies.

QUESTIONS

1. Why does Havel believe that small, everyday acts of conformity actually constitute the post-totalitarian system?

2. What relationship between the communist bloc and the Western democracies is Havel positing?

Source: Václav Havel et al., *The Power of the Powerless: Citizens Against the State in Central-Eastern Europe* (Armonk, N.Y.: M. E. Sharpe, 1985), pp. 31, 37–40, 42–43, 90–91. Reprinted by permission from M. E. Sharpe, Inc., Armonk, NY 10504.

labor organizations, the right to strike, and freedom of expression. Reflecting the wider opposition thinking in east-central Europe, Solidarity was not to be bought off with lower meat prices, even had the government been able to deliver them.

After over a year of negotiation, compromise, and broken promises, the tense situation came to a head in December 1981, when the government under General Wojciech Jaruzelski (yah-roo-ZELL-skee) (b. 1923) declared martial law and outlawed Solidarity, imprisoning its leaders. Strikes in protest were crushed by military force. So much for that, it seemed: another lost cause, another reform effort colliding with inflexible communist power, as in 1953, 1956, and 1968. But this time it was different, thanks especially to developments in the Soviet Union.

THE QUEST FOR REFORM IN THE SOVIET UNION

The death of Leonid Brezhnev in 1982 paved the way for a concerted reform effort that began in earnest when **Mikhail Gorbachev** (GOR-ba-choff) (b. 1931) became Soviet Communist Party secretary in 1985. Gorbachev's effort encompassed four intersecting initiatives: arms reduction; liberalization in the satellite states; *glasnost* (GLAHZ-nost), or "openness" to discussion and criticism; and *perestroika* (pair-es-TROY-kah), or economic "restructuring." This was to be a reform within the Soviet system. There was no thought of giving up the Communist Party's monopoly on power or embracing a free-market economy. The reformers still took it for granted that communism could point the way beyond Western capitalism, with its shallow consumerism. But they had to make communism work.

Gorbachev understood that "openness" was a prerequisite for "restructuring." The freedom to criticize was essential to check abuses of power, which, in turn, was necessary to overcome the cynicism of the workers and improve productivity. Openness was also imperative to gain the full participation of the country's most creative people, whose contributions were critical if the Soviet Union was to become competitive in advanced technology.

The main thrust of perestroika was to depart from the rigid economic planning mechanism by giving local managers more autonomy. But any restructuring was bound to encounter resistance, especially from those with careers tied to the central planning apparatus. And Gorbachev's program made only partial headway in this crucial sector.

Online Study Center **Improve Your Grade**
Primary Source: The Last Heir of Lenin Explains His Reform Plans: Perestroika and Glasnost

THE ANTICOMMUNIST REVOLUTION IN EAST-CENTRAL EUROPE

Meanwhile, in Poland, repression continued, as dramatized especially by the murder of the charismatic priest and Solidarity supporter Jerzy Popieluszko (pope-yeh-LUSH-koh) by the secret police in 1984. But Walesa

Mikhail Gorbachev Soviet Communist Party secretary who attempted to reform the Soviet communist system through arms reduction; liberalization in the satellite states; *glasnost;* and *perestroika.*

remained a powerfully effective leader even from prison. He was able to keep his heterogeneous movement together as the ideas of Solidarity continued to spread underground. Then the advent of Gorbachev in 1985 changed the overall framework, for Gorbachev was convinced that restructuring the Soviet system required reform in the satellites as well. As the Polish economy, already in difficulty by 1980, reached a crisis in 1987, Solidarity began stepping up its efforts.

When proposed price increases were rejected in a referendum, the Polish government imposed them by fiat. Strikes demanding the relegalization of Solidarity followed during the spring of 1988. The government again responded with military force, but Solidarity-led strikes in August forced government leaders to send signals that they might be prepared to negotiate. With the economy nearing collapse, the government recognized that it could no longer govern on its own.

The negotiations that followed early in 1989 proved pivotal. When they began, Walesa and his advisers wanted primarily to regain legal status for Solidarity within the Communist-dominated system, still under Jaruzelski. In exchange, they assumed they would have to help legitimate a rigged election to approve painful but necessary economic measures. But as these "Round Table" negotiations proceeded, the government gave ever more in exchange for Solidarity's cooperation. Not only did it consent to legalize Solidarity, but it agreed to make the forthcoming elections free enough for the opposition genuinely to participate.

The elections of June 1989 produced an overwhelming repudiation of Poland's communist government. Even government leaders running unopposed failed to win election as voters crossed out their names. In the aftermath of the elections, President Jaruzelski was forced to give Solidarity a chance to lead. Not all members of the opposition felt it wise to accept government responsibility under such difficult economic circumstances, but finally Tadeusz Mazowiecki (mah-zo-VYETS-kee) (b. 1927), Walesa's choice and one of the movement's most distinguished intellectuals, agreed to form a government.

The chain of events in Poland culminated in one of the extraordinary events of modern history—the negotiated end of communist rule. That a communist government might give up power voluntarily had been utterly unforeseen. It happened partly because the Soviet Union under Gorbachev was seeking reform and thus had become much less likely to intervene militarily. It also helped that the Polish Catholic Church was available to act as mediator, hosting meetings, reminding both sides of their shared responsibilities in the difficult situation facing their country. By some accounts, General Jaruzelski, who seemed for most of the 1980s to be just another mili-

tary strongman and Soviet lackey, had proved to be a national hero for his grace, perhaps even ingenuity, in yielding power to the opposition. But most important was the courage, the persistence, and the vision of Solidarity itself.

Although the Hungarians were already breaking out of the communist mold, it was especially the Polish example that suggested to others in the Soviet bloc that the whole system was open to challenge. During 1989 demands for reform and, increasingly, for an end to communist rule spread through east-central Europe by means of the domino effect that had preoccupied the Soviets from the start. By the end of that year, the Soviet satellite system was in ruins (see Map 30.1 on page 948).

By 1989 a number of grass-roots movements, involving especially young people, had emerged across the Soviet bloc to challenge governmental authority in indirect ways. Although they were indebted to older leaders like Havel, who had stressed the power of simply "living the truth," these movements fastened upon such new issues as disarmament, the treatment of the elderly, and environmental threats like nuclear power. And their modes of action often had an absurd, carnival-like dimension, such as traveling about in an open sightseeing bus. Precisely because it was not obviously subversive, such activity backed the regimes into uncomfortable corners—even made the authorities appear weak and flatfooted. The remaining legitimacy of the communist systems was dissipating.

A marked increase in illegal emigration from East Germany to the West had been one manifestation that the system was starting to unravel. During 1989 the reform-minded Hungarian Communists decided to stop impeding East Germans, many of whom vacationed in Hungary, from emigrating to the West at the Hungarian border with Austria. If the communist reformers in East Germany were to have any chance of turning the situation around, they had to relax restrictions on travel and even grant the right to emigrate. They began preparing to do both as part of a host of reforms intended to save the system. On November 9, 1989, the East German communist regime did the unthinkable and opened the Berlin Wall, which was promptly dismantled altogether. Germans now traveled freely back and forth between East and West. Although the fate of the Soviet Union itself remained uncertain, the opening of the wall signaled the end of the cold war. It was no longer a bipolar world.

By this point, discontented East Germans envisioned not simply reforming the communist system but ending it altogether. Within weeks it was clear that the rhythm of events was beyond the control of East

Germany's reform communists, who opened the way for German reunification in 1990. Despite some nervousness, the four postwar occupying powers—the United States, Britain, France, and the Soviet Union—gave their blessing as the Federal Republic incorporated the five East German states. The communist system in East Germany simply dissolved.

Although some in West Germany were hesitant about immediate reunification, especially because of the economic costs that seemed likely, West German chancellor Helmut Kohl (KOLE) (b. 1930) sought to complete the process as quickly as possible. By early 1990 the emigration of East Germans to the West had become a flood. West German law treated these Germans as citizens, entitled to social benefits, so their arrival in such numbers presented a considerable financial burden. It seemed imperative for West Germany to regularize the situation as quickly as possible, assuming responsibility for the East and restoring its economy.

The division of Germany, symbolized by the Berlin Wall, had been the central fact of the bipolar cold war world. Now Germany was a unified country for the first time since Nazism and the Second World War. What would it mean?

THE END OF THE SOVIET UNION

Meanwhile, in the Soviet Union, what began as a restructuring of the communist system became a struggle for survival of the system itself. The much-trumpeted glasnost produced greater freedom in Soviet culture and politics, but Gorbachev sought to avoid alienating hard-line Communists, so he compromised, watering down the economic reforms essential to perestroika. The result proved a set of half measures that only made things worse. Because so little was done to force the entrenched Soviet bureaucracy to go along, the pace of economic reform was lethargic. The essential structures of the command economy weakened, but free-market forms of exchange among producers, distributors, and consumers did not emerge to replace them.

In 1986 an accidental explosion at the Soviet nuclear power plant at Chernobyl, in Ukraine (see **MAP 29.3**), released two hundred times as much radiation as the atomic bombs dropped on Hiroshima and Nagasaki combined. The accident contaminated food supplies and forced the abandonment of villages and thousands of square miles of formerly productive land. The radioactivity released would eventually hasten the deaths of at least 100,000 Soviet citizens. Despite his commitment to openness, Gorbachev reverted to old-fashioned Soviet secrecy for several weeks after the accident, in an effort to minimize what had happened. As a result, the eventual toll was far greater than it need have been. The accident and its aftermath seemed stark manifestation

of all that was wrong with the Soviet system—its arrogance and secrecy, its premium on cutting corners to achieve targets imposed from above.

By the end of the 1980s, Soviet citizens felt betrayed by their earlier faith that Soviet communism was leading to a better future. A popular slogan spoke sarcastically of "seventy years on the road to nowhere." The economic situation was deteriorating, yet people were free to discuss alternatives as never before. As the discussion came to include once-unthinkable possibilities such as privatization and a market economy, it became clear that the whole communist system was in jeopardy.

By mid-1990, moreover, the union of Soviet republics itself tottered on the verge of collapse. Lithuania led the way in calling for outright independence. But the stakes were raised enormously when the Russian republic, the largest and most important in the USSR, followed Lithuania's lead. In June 1990 the newly elected chairman of Russia's parliament, Boris Yeltsin (b. 1931), persuaded the Russian republic to declare its sovereignty. Yeltsin had grown impatient with the slow pace of economic and political change, and by threatening that Russia might go its own way, he hoped to force Gorbachev's reform effort beyond the present impasse. As a further challenge to Gorbachev, Yeltsin dramatically resigned from the Communist Party during its televised national congress in July 1990. When, in June 1991, free elections in the Russian republic offered the first clear contest between communists determined to preserve the system and those seeking to replace it, the anticommunist Yeltsin was elected the republic's president by a surprising margin.

After tilting toward the hard-liners late in 1990, Gorbachev sought a return to reform after Yeltsin's dramatic election as Russia's president in June 1991. He even engineered a new party charter that jettisoned much of the Marxist-Leninist doctrine that had guided communist practice since the revolution. In August the hard-liners struck back with a coup that forced Gorbachev from power—but only for a few days. Yeltsin, supported by ordinary people in Moscow, stood up to the conspirators, while the secret police refused to follow orders to arrest Yeltsin and other opposition leaders. The coup quickly fizzled, but the episode galvanized the anticommunist movement and radically accelerated the pace of change.

Although Gorbachev was restored as head of the Soviet Union, the winner was Yeltsin, who quickly mounted an effort to dismantle the party apparatus before it could regroup. Anticommunist demonstrations across much of the Soviet Union toppled statues of Lenin and dissolved local party networks. In a referendum in December 1991, Ukraine, the second most populous Soviet republic, overwhelmingly voted for

MAP 29.3   The Dissolution of the Soviet Union

As crisis gripped the Soviet system by the late 1980s, the republics of the Soviet Union began declaring first their sovereignty, then their independence. Most of the fifteen republics that had made up the Soviet Union became part of a much looser confederation, the Commonwealth of Independent States, in 1991 and 1992.

Online Study Center Improve Your Grade
Interactive Map: The Dissolution of the Soviet Union

independence. Not only the communist system but the Soviet Union itself was simply disintegrating. Late in December, Gorbachev finally resigned, paving the way for the official dissolution of the Soviet Union on January 1, 1992 (see Map 29.3). The European map again included Russia, as well as, in a matter of months, fourteen other sovereign states from what had been the Soviet Union.

One of the notable experiments in the history of the West, nourished by the hopes and ideals of generations, the communist regime in the Soviet Union had proved a resounding failure.

S E C T I O N   S U M M A R Y

- The economies of the Soviet bloc were encountering stagnation by the 1970s, especially because they proved less adept than the capitalist economies at technological innovation.

- Disparate factors converged in Poland to yield the trade union Solidarity, which proved decisive in un-

dermining the communist system not only in Poland but throughout the Soviet bloc.

- Seeking to overcome Soviet stagnation, Mikhail Gorbachev spearheaded a reform effort around *glasnost*, or "openness," and *perestroika*, or economic "restructuring," beginning in 1985.

- Changes in government policy in Poland and Hungary during 1989 produced a domino effect that led to the opening of the Berlin Wall and the fall of the communist regimes in east-central Europe.

- As Gorbachev's reform effort proved insufficient, the republics of the Soviet Union began pulling away, leading, by 1991, to the disintegration of the communist system and the breakup of the Soviet Union itself.

CHAPTER SUMMARY

Online Study Center **ACE the Test**

What seemed the most likely overall directions as western Europeans pondered priorities in light of all the disasters surrounding the era of the two world wars?

What factors led to the surprisingly rapid restoration of democracy in much of continental western Europe after World War II?

How did Soviet policy evolve after the death of Stalin in 1953?

How did the place of western Europe in world affairs change during the cold war era?

What led to the collapse of the communist system in the Soviet Union and its satellite states?

estern Europeans faced a situation of unprecedented cultural uncertainty as they pondered priorities in the wake of all that had befallen Europe from 1914 to 1949. Whereas some explored the loss of bearings, others called for a return to tradition, and still others found renewed possibilities in the Marxist tradition. At the same time, deeper interaction with the United States during and immediately after World War II led many to look to America for a more successful model, free of the ideological extremes that, it seemed, had helped lead Europe to disaster.

The United States sought to assist the rebuilding of western Europe, and partly because of American help, the western Europeans were able to restore their economies—and even surpass prewar production levels—with remarkable speed. And economic success greatly facilitated the restoration of democracy. At the same time, the shared experience of wartime led to a new social compact based on greater government responsibility for economic well-being and social welfare. By 1968, however, the Western democracies were beginning to experience unforeseen strains, some of which then deep-ened with the slowdown in economic growth during the 1970s.

In the Soviet bloc, Stalin's death in 1953 brought an end to the most repressive features of the communist system. Under his successor, Nikita Khrushchev, the Soviet Union seemed able to compete with the United States in areas from education to space travel. But the experiment with various forms of central planning in the Soviet bloc proved ever less successful. At the same time, the crushing of a series of opposition and reform efforts, from East Berlin in 1953 to Prague in 1968, suggested that the Soviets were prepared to intervene as necessary to keep their satellites on a communist path.

The bipolar cold war framework meant a diminished influence in world affairs for the states of western Europe. Even their own security, in the face of the potential Soviet threat, seemed to depend on the United States. At the same time, the western Europeans gradually gave up control of their remaining colonial possessions, though not without instances of fighting and bitterness, evident most notably in the French effort to retain Algeria. However, France joined with Germany in the first key steps toward European integration, and such leaders as Charles de Gaulle and Willy Brandt showed the scope for European initiatives from within the limiting cold war framework.

Even as they faced new economic and political strains by the 1970s, the nations of western Europe could take for granted a substantial measure of prosperity and political legitimacy. In the communist part of Europe, in contrast, growing economic stagnation fueled a much deeper form of political disaffection during the 1970s and 1980s. New modes of opposition arose in Poland and Czechoslovakia, while in Hungary and eventually in the Soviet Union itself, communist leaders sought to renew the system from within. But the crisis of Soviet-style communism proved too deep, and by the end of 1991 discontent had produced forces for change that led to the breakup of the Soviet Union and the unraveling of the communist system in Europe.

LOOKING AHEAD

Thus ended the cold war era. The immediate response in the West was euphoria, for the anxieties that had resulted from superpower rivalry seemed to vanish almost overnight. But what would follow remained unclear. Reformers in the former communist countries claimed to want individual freedom, political democracy, and free-market capitalism, but it would be necessary to build these on the ruins of the now-discredited communist system, a task never confronted before. And what sort of international order might replace the dangerous but stable bipolar framework that had stood since World War II?

KEY TERMS

existentialism (p. 909)

North Atlantic Treaty
   Organization (NATO) (p. 914)

welfare state (p. 915)

Konrad Adenauer (p. 918)

Willy Brandt (p. 918)

Margaret Thatcher (p. 921)

Warsaw Pact (p. 923)

Prague Spring (p. 925)

Suez crisis (p. 929)

European Economic Community
   (EEC) (p. 932)

Helsinki Accords (p. 935)

Solidarity (p. 935)

Mikhail Gorbachev (p. 937)

Online Study Center
Improve Your Grade Flashcards

SUGGESTED READING

Bark, Dennis L., and David R. Gress. *A History of West Germany,* vol. 1, *From Shadow to Substance, 1945–1963,* and vol. 2, *Democracy and Its Discontents, 1963–1991.* 2d ed. 1993. A favorable account of West Germany's democracy and its Atlantic and European roles in the face of ongoing suspicion and criticism.

Caute, David. *The Dancer Defects: The Struggle for Cultural Supremacy During the Cold War.* 2003. An engaging, comprehensive treatment of the efforts of both sides during the cold war to use culture for political advantage.

Crockatt, Richard. *The Fifty Years' War: The United States and the Soviet Union in World Politics, 1941–1991.* 1995. A balanced history of U.S.-Soviet relations, showing the global impact of their cold war rivalry.

Dedman, Martin J. *The Origins and Development of the European Union, 1945–95: A History of European Integration.* 1996. A concise and accessible introductory work.

Hitchcock, William I. *The Struggle for Europe: The Turbulent History of a Divided Continent, 1945–2002.* 2003. A highly regarded survey—comprehensive, balanced, and engaging.

Kenney, Padraic. *A Carnival of Revolution: Central Europe 1989.* 2002. A ground-level account of the diverse popular initiatives that helped undermine the legitimacy of communist systems in varied parts of the Soviet bloc.

Marwick, Arthur. *The Sixties: Cultural Revolution in Britain, France, Italy, and the United States, c. 1958–c. 1974.* 1998. A lengthy but gripping portrait of a pivotal decade.

Saxonberg, Steven. *The Fall: A Comparative Study of the End of Communism in Czechoslovakia, East Germany, Hungary, and Poland.* 2001. Contrasts the governmental initiatives in Poland and Hungary with the initiatives from below that undermined the communist regimes in Czechoslovakia and East Germany.

Schulze, Max-Stephan, ed. *Western Europe: Economic and Social Change Since 1945.* 1999. A superior collection of essays accenting economic change; some treat individual countries, others overarching topics.

Springhall, John. *Decolonization Since 1945: The Collapse of European Overseas Empires.* 2001. An accessible and comprehensive survey.

30

A CONTINUING EXPERIMENT: THE WEST AND THE WORLD SINCE 1989

Cartoon Protest
On February 18, 2006, Muslims march through central London in an angry but peaceful protest against the publication in the Western press of cartoons seeming to caricature the prophet Muhammad. *(AP/Wide World Photos)*

The relationship between the West and the wider world was sorely tested early in 2006 as it gradually became known that the previous September a Danish newspaper, *Jyllands-Posten,* had published twelve cartoons depicting the Islamic prophet Muhammad, one wearing a turban in the shape of a bomb. The stated aim was to confront the fear, the sense of intimidation, that some claimed had resulted from the cultural interface with Muslims in European countries. Especially unsettling had been the brutal assassination, by a Dutch national of Moroccan descent, of Theo Van Gogh in the Netherlands in 2004. Van Gogh had been targeted for having made a film denouncing the treatment of women in Islamic societies.

The editor who invited the cartoons claimed that fears of violence against anyone perceived to be denigrating Islam were leading to self-censorship. The episode unfolded against a backdrop of increasing tensions in several European countries over the assimilation of immigrants, or the children or grandchildren of immigrants—and especially, it seemed, of those who professed Islam.

A number of predominantly Islamic nations promptly protested the Danish cartoons, but Denmark's prime minister refused to meet with their ambassadors, saying that he did not, and should not, have any control over what Danish newspapers published. But as news of the cartoons gradually became known, there was outrage across the Muslim world, including violence first against Danish interests, then against Europeans and Westerners more generally. Scores of people were killed. The cartoonists themselves received death threats and had to go into hiding.

Any depiction of the prophet Muhammad would have offended Muslims, who traditionally have been particularly concerned to ward off idolatry, the worship of images. Muslims had periodically protested a frieze dating from the 1930s in the U.S. Supreme Court, which included Muhammad, portrayed between Charlemagne and the Roman emperor Justinian, as one of eighteen "great lawgivers of history." But Muslims found the Danish cartoons gratuitously offensive.

Defenders of the cartoons stressed the Western values of free speech and a free press, and, as the controversy grew, a number of news outlets published one or more of the cartoons in solidarity with the now-beleaguered Danish publication. But others, especially in Britain and the United States, refused to

CHAPTER OUTLINE

THE UNCERTAIN INTERNATIONAL FRAMEWORK AFTER THE COLD WAR

THE CONTINUING EXPERIMENT WITH DEMOCRATIC CAPITALISM

LIFESTYLES AND IDENTITIES

THE WEST IN A GLOBAL AGE

QUESTIONING THE MEANING OF THE WEST

KEY TERMS

G-8 (Group of 8)
European Union (EU)
Maastricht agreements
euro
Common Agricultural Policy (CAP)
ethnic cleansing
unilateralism
Vladimir Putin

social market economy
World Health Organization (WHO)
information technology
World Trade Organization (WTO)
digital divide
nongovernmental organizations (NGOs)

Online Study Center

This icon will direct you to interactive map and primary source activities on the website **college.hmco.com/pic/noble5e**

republish them, stressing the wisdom of voluntary restraint. Whatever the formal freedom of the press, matters of taste, decorum, and responsibility were also at issue. Yet some charged that such refusal to republish, despite the undeniable news value of the cartoons, reflected not responsibility but plain fear.

Compounding the problem were charges of hypocrisy from both the Western and the Islamic worlds. Islamic spokespersons doubted that Western publications would have been equally open to cartoons about, for example, the Holocaust, or slavery in the American South. Conversely, it was widely noted that Christians and especially Jews had long been caricatured in the most grotesque terms in a number of Islamic countries.

Both defenders and critics of the cartoons noted limitations on freedom of speech in the West. Hitler's *Mein Kampf* could not be sold in Germany. It was illegal to deny the Holocaust in Germany and indeed in fourteen Western countries. Charges of hypocrisy produced pressure to get rid of such laws and embrace freedom of speech more consistently in the West.

Whatever was to be made of tensions between the West and the Islamic world, they played in complex ways against the process known as globalization, through which ever more of the world was drawn into the competitive market economy that had gradually spread from Europe over the previous millennium. It seemed to make the world more unified and homogeneous, yet it also produced a backlash, including the embrace of traditional cultural expressions like the headscarf worn by many Muslim women in Europe. But that backlash also included violence and terrorism.

Within the West itself, the end of the cold war led not to a new era of peace and stability but to unforeseen tensions, including ethnic and sectarian conflict in parts of Europe and splintering within the Western alliance. The former communist countries scrambled to institute Western-style democratic capitalism, and during the first decade of the twenty-first century many of them were accepted into the European Union (EU). But even in the established Western democracies, unprecedented economic and technological change raised new questions, some of which threatened to challenge the political consensus that had crystallized since World War II. Nervousness among Europeans about the pace of change even seemed, by 2005, to arrest the notable progress the EU had made since the mid-1980s.

FOCUS QUESTIONS

Why and how did the relationship between western Europe and the United States change after the end of the cold war?

What forces raised new questions about the effectiveness of Western-style democracy by the early years of the twenty-first century?

How did the changes bound up with globalization affect identities in the West?

What questions emerged as the West faced new crises all over the globe after the end of the cold war?

On what basis was the wider contemporary relevance of "Western civilization" being debated by the first decade of the twenty-first century?

THE UNCERTAIN INTERNATIONAL FRAMEWORK AFTER THE COLD WAR

Why and how did the relationship between western Europe and the United States change after the end of the cold war?

The disintegration of the Soviet system from 1989 to 1991 meant the swift, unexpected end of the bipolar cold war framework that had defined the era since World War II (see **MAP 30.1**). An immediate and troubling outcome was renewed ethnic conflict in parts of Europe. Although Czechoslovakia divided peacefully into two nations, the Czech and Slovak Republics, on January 1, 1993, ethnic concerns elsewhere produced violence and massive human rights violations. Violence also found expression in increased international terrorism by the early twenty-first century.

Although the need to respond to such problems unified the West up to a point, differences soon surfaced, differences that threatened to fragment the West as never before since World War II. At the same time, efforts to address the unforeseen problems of the post–cold war world raised questions about the respective roles of multinational entities such as the UN, NATO, and the EU.

NEW POWER RELATIONSHIPS IN THE WEST

That the end of the cold war had left the United States "the world's only superpower" quickly became a cliché, and the Americans continued to offer leadership through the framework they had established after World War II. Although NATO's role was less clear with the end of the Soviet threat, NATO expanded first in 1999, then in 2004, to encompass most of the former Soviet satellite states of eastern Europe, from Poland to Bulgaria. To the former communist countries, NATO membership meant the definitive repudiation of the cold war division of Europe.

Whereas the collapse of communism meant renewed pride and independence for the former satellite states, Russia felt humiliated as a onetime superpower that was now diminished in size, struggling economically, and far less influential in world affairs. But the West was anxious not to alienate the new Russia. Germany and France each developed strong bilateral relations with the former communist power. Moreover, Russia was invited to join the informal grouping of the world's seven largest economic powers (the United States, Japan, Germany, France, Britain, Italy, and Canada), which had begun meeting during the 1970s in an effort to coordinate economic policies. Although the size of the Russian economy did not warrant inclusion in this "Group of Seven," or G-7, it seemed worthwhile to give the new Russia a voice in what thus became the **G-8 (Group of 8)**.

Germany, which promptly reunified as communism collapsed, seemed a major beneficiary of the end of the cold war. Whereas some worried that the new Germany might return to bullying and aggressiveness, others—Germans and non-Germans alike—were eager to have Germany assume a stronger diplomatic role, and thus the responsibilities commensurate with its population and economic strength.

G-8 (Group of 8) Originally a Group of Seven, or G-7, this informal association of the world's seven largest economic powers (the United States, Japan, Germany, France, Britain, Italy, and Canada) began meeting during the 1970s in an effort to coordinate economic policies. After the fall of communism, the group added Russia.

CHRONOLOGY

1990	Reunification of Germany
1991	Beginning of fighting in Yugoslavia
	Maastricht agreements expand scope of European Union
1996	Peace in Bosnia
1997	Blair becomes prime minister of Britain
1998	UN establishes international criminal court in The Hague
1999	Euro launched as currency of European Union
	NATO bombing of Serbia in response to Serb policies in Kosovo
	Renewal of Russia's war with Chechnya
2000	Putin elected president of Russia
2001	Milosevic put on trial for war crimes at The Hague
	Terrorist attacks on United States
2003	U.S.- and British-led forces overthrow Saddam Hussein's regime in Iraq
	WTO meeting in Cancún, Mexico, breaks up amid protests
2004	EU adds ten new member countries, for a total of twenty-five
	Terrorist bombings on commuter trains in Madrid
2005	EU draft constitution rejected in referenda in France and the Netherlands
	Terrorist attack on the London public transportation system
	Angela Merkel becomes German chancellor
	Riots by Muslim youth in Paris and other French cities
2006	Demonstrations in France protesting new labor legislation

The Federal Republic officially moved its capital from provincial Bonn to Berlin in 1999, when a costly makeover of the old parliament (Reichstag) building had been completed. As it happened, precisely as the refurbished building was opened, German forces were involved in their first combat roles since World War II, participating in NATO air strikes responding to what seemed genocidal aggression in Yugoslavia. German chancellor Gerhard Schroeder, a socialist, insisted that Germany, in light of its recent history, could not turn away but indeed had a particular responsibility to respond. Still, though Germany contributed significantly

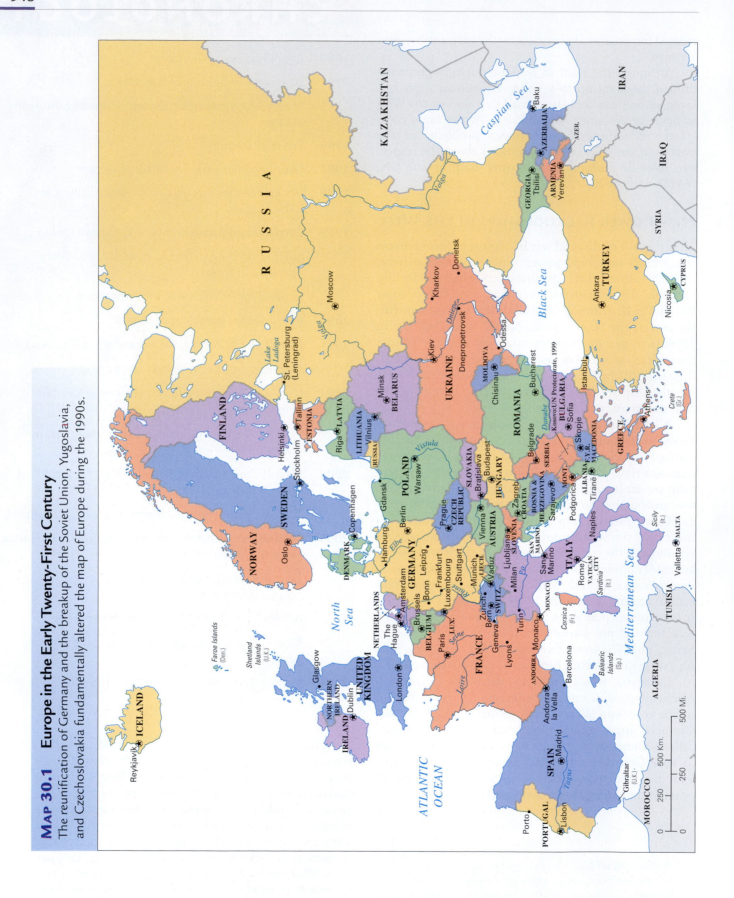

MAP 30.1   Europe in the Early Twenty-First Century

The reunification of Germany and the breakup of the Soviet Union, Yugoslavia, and Czechoslovakia fundamentally altered the map of Europe during the 1990s.

The Democratic Reichstag, Berlin The centerpiece of the renovation of the German parliament building, completed in 1999, was the addition of a glass dome, intended to manifest the openness of Germany's democracy as its capital moved from Bonn to Berlin. *(Reimer Wulf/ akg-images)*

to international peacekeeping efforts, many Germans remained reluctant to support an expanded international military role. German military spending remained low compared with that of the United States, Britain, and France. Germany had to lease planes from Ukraine to transport its troops to Afghanistan for peacekeeping in 2002.

THE EUROPEAN UNION

As the **European Union (EU)** continued to expand and deepen by the early twenty-first century, it became clear that it constituted one of the notable experiments in Western history. Though still very much in progress, that experiment had produced a complex web of institutional arrangements that was bizarre and complex in one sense, bold and innovative in another.

Origins of the Union   After the oil crises of the 1970s, and amid concern over lack of innovation and competitiveness, the twelve members of the European Community committed themselves in 1985 to creating a true single market with genuinely free competition by the end of 1992. Goods, services, and money would circulate freely among the member countries; manufacturing would conform to uniform product standards; and equal competition for government contracts would apply.

Meeting at Maastricht, in the Netherlands, in 1991, leaders of the member countries agreed to a new "Treaty on European Union," which, among other things, pro-

vided for a common policy on workers' rights and a common currency and central banking structure by 1999. Although the EU's members eventually ratified most of the **Maastricht agreements,** member countries could opt out of certain provisions. Even as the new common currency, the **euro,** was introduced in two major steps, in 1999 and 2002, four of the now-fifteen EU members, including Britain, remained outside the common currency mechanism. Still, the common currency facilitated a notable increase in supranational mergers and takeovers—a trend that threatened some but promised greater international competitiveness for European firms.

So successful was the EU that others clamored to join. In 2004 the EU added ten new member countries, eight of them recently communist, thereby increasing the membership to twenty-five. The lure of membership significantly strengthened democracy in the candidate states, for the EU insisted on democratic institutions and alignment with EU procedures as a condition of membership.

Structure and Organization   Although the EU made democracy a condition for membership, it had its own "democratic deficit": major decisions were made

Maastricht agreements   1991 agreements among member states of the European Union. They agreed to expand cooperation on social, foreign, judicial, and security matters and adopted a timetable for common economic policies.

euro   The common currency launched by the European Union in 1999 and 2002 to eliminate the cost of currency exchange and boost trade and economic interaction.

European Union (EU)   New name for the European Community after the Maastricht agreements of 1991. It consists of twenty-five member countries.

by an unelected elite of technical experts. By the early twenty-first century, the EU included a network of five interlocking core institutions, variously seated in Brussels, Strasbourg, Luxembourg, and Frankfurt. The executive branch was the Commission in Brussels, consisting of twenty appointed members, but with a professional staff of sixteen thousand. Charged to pursue the wider interests of the community, not to represent national interests, the Commission had considerable power to initiate and enforce EU legislation.

The legislative branch of the EU was the Council of Ministers, composed of ministers from the governments of the member countries. On routine matters, the Council voted by majority, weighted by the size of each country's population. More sensitive issues required unanimity; thus each member country had veto power. Especially as the EU prepared to expand, reformers sought to extend the role of majority rule and minimize the scope for veto.

EU membership entailed some loss of national sovereignty, thanks especially to the increasingly powerful role of the judicial branch, the European Court of Justice, headquartered in Luxembourg. In contrast, the power of the European Parliament, which had developed from the assembly of the European Coal and Steel Community, and which divided its time between Strasbourg and Brussels, was more potential than actual. Although it had some oversight over budget and expanding powers to block or amend legislation, the parliament remained the weakest of the core EU institutions.

The fifth core institution, the European Central Bank, headquartered in Frankfurt, was born with the commitment to a common monetary policy and currency in 1991. Like central banks everywhere, it sought to regulate the money supply and thereby to help the EU's economies function in a smooth and coordinated way.

By the early twenty-first century, "Europe" had become a kind of hybrid, at once a collection of sovereign states and a genuinely supranational entity, thanks to the gradual, incremental emergence of the EU over more than fifty years. In spheres such as trade, agriculture, and the environment, the EU was dominant; national governments had little freedom of action. But other spheres, such as defense, taxation, and criminal justice, remained mostly national prerogatives. The question was whether the EU would continue to expand its sphere of competence—and in what directions. For example, by 2006 there was not yet a true single market for services, though services accounted for 70 percent of economic activity in the EU. Thus reformers advocated that the EU specify uniform standards for professional qualifications.

The creation of an internal customs union, benign though it seemed, had never committed the EU to freer trade with nonmember countries—the United States, for example, or the developing nations of the non-Western world. Indeed, half the EU budget at the end of the 1990s went to the widely criticized **Common Agricultural Policy (CAP),** entailing subsidies to protect farmers from outside competition. Efforts by the EU Commission to lower price supports led to several massive demonstrations by French farmers during the 1990s. Political opposition to change remained strong, especially in France, so the scope for reform was uncertain at best.

The Constitution and New Member States

Especially with expansion coming in 2004, it seemed essential that the EU clarify and streamline its procedures through a formal constitution. But as questions about further expansion loomed, the EU's momentum was halted dramatically and unexpectedly when, in May 2005, French voters rejected the EU's new draft constitution in a referendum. It was the biggest check to European integration since the 1970s. Voters in the Netherlands followed suit shortly thereafter. Most of the EU's member states required approval of the constitution only by their elected parliaments, and such approval had, for the most part, been readily forthcoming. So the surprising setbacks in France and the Netherlands constituted a wake-up call; they indicated strains, doubts, and frustrations that could be found throughout Europe.

The rejection reflected a sense that the recent expansion had itself been too radical a step. But especially troubling was the prospect of further expansion to include not just Romania and Bulgaria, for example, but Turkey, Serbia, Albania, Ukraine, and others.

The case of Turkey, a key NATO member, was particularly controversial. Although it had a tradition of secular government, Turkey was a predominantly Islamic country at a time of growing tensions between Europe and the Islamic world and growing concerns about militant Islamic fundamentalism. Even as skeptical Europeans pointed to aspects of the Turkish constitution that were not congruent with EU norms, the Turks worked to make the adjustments necessary to meet those norms. Still, the Turkish candidacy raised questions about how far the EU was prepared to expand, even about the meaning of "Europe."

Matters of European and national identities were very much at issue in the 1995 referenda. "We want to stay Dutch" was one of the slogans used to mobilize voters against the constitution in the Netherlands.[1] The increasingly volatile issues surrounding immigration and assimilation heightened concerns. In its specific measures, the proposed EU constitution would have given more power to the European parliament and

Common Agricultural Policy (CAP) A major pillar of the European Union, it entailed subsidies to protect farmers from outside competition. The CAP was widely criticized by advocates of freer world trade.

Such measures reflected the notion that key firms in areas like utilities, transportation, and banking should be immune from foreign takeover, even if government-sanctioned near-monopoly on the national level was required. But such nationality was not supposed to matter in the EU economy; mergers were to be based on business decisions, not political criteria. Although some began to proclaim that "Europe is dead," it remained to be seen whether this wave of defensive measures by governments would seriously compromise the cohesion of the EU.

Although it was surely a setback, the rejection of the proposed constitution did not undermine the existing union, which continued as before. EU membership had played a major role in transforming the economies of once-poor countries like Greece, Ireland, Spain, and Portugal; comparable successes could apparently be expected for the new members from east-central Europe. And expansion to include Romania and Bulgaria remained likely, even if, in light of the new restiveness, still further expansion appeared unlikely for the foreseeable future.

ETHNIC CONFLICT AND PEACEKEEPING ROLES

As the members of the European Union struggled to create a supranational entity, forces in the opposite direction—subnational, religious, ethnic, tribal—grew more powerful in parts of the West, sometimes producing violent conflict. Beginning in 1969, the British had to use troops in Northern Ireland to keep order in the face of ongoing threats from Irish Catholics seeking the end of British rule and unification with the Republic of Ireland. The result was more than three decades of conflict between Protestants and Catholics that eluded definitive solution into the twenty-first century. A movement to separate French-speaking Quebec from the rest of Canada periodically achieved prominence, almost succeeding in 1995.

The War in Bosnia   The most dramatic situation, however, was in postcommunist Yugoslavia, where ethnic and religious conflict led to the disintegration of the country in a series of brutal wars among Serbs, Croats, Bosnian Muslims, and ethnically Albanian Kosovars (see **MAP 30.2**). Defining events of the 1990s, these wars proved a major challenge for the new international order after the cold war.

Although much was made of ancient ethnic and religious differences once Yugoslavia began falling apart, the area had long traditions of pluralism and tolerance. Ethnic relations had been poisoned, however, by recent events, especially the civil war during World War II (see page 897). The situation had remained reasonably stable under Josip Tito's independent communist regime,

significantly restricted national veto power. So it proved controversial because it seemed to entail a further sacrifice of sovereignty to an ever larger and more diffuse entity.

Concerns about economic well-being were also at work; meshing with more general concerns about globalization was a sense that the recent eastward expansion of the EU had intensified competition from lower-wage countries. It was clear especially in France that those most vulnerable to economic change were the most likely to shift from approval of the EU to rejection of the new constitution.

Evidence of increasing economic nationalism among EU members also worried proponents of European integration. In 2006 the French government acted to facilitate a merger of two major firms in the French energy-utilities industry to head off a hostile takeover of one of the companies by an Italian firm. Further measures followed to make French firms harder for foreigners to acquire. But the Italian government had taken comparable measures to prevent the takeover of two Italian banks, as had the Spanish government in the wake of an acquisition attempt by a German firm.

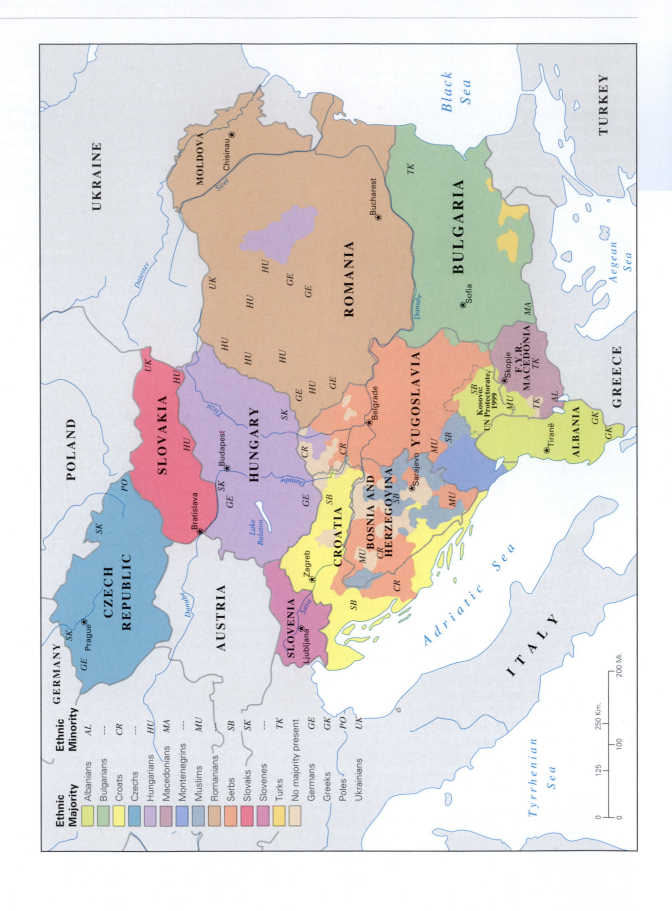

Ethnic Majority

	Ethnic Minority
Albanians	AL
Bulgarians	---
Croats	CR
Czechs	---
Hungarians	HU
Macedonians	MA
Montenegrins	---
Muslims	MU
Romanians	---
Serbs	SB
Slovaks	SK
Slovenes	---
Turks	TK
No majority present	
Germans	GE
Greeks	GK
Poles	PO
Ukrainians	UK

POLAND

UKRAINE

TURKEY

GERMANY

CZECH REPUBLIC

Prague

SLOVAKIA

Bratislava

AUSTRIA

HUNGARY

Budapest

MOLDOVA

Chisinau

ROMANIA

Bucharest

Black Sea

BULGARIA

Sofia

Aegean Sea

SLOVENIA

Ljubljana

CROATIA

Zagreb

YUGOSLAVIA

Belgrade

BOSNIA AND HERZEGOVINA

Sarajevo

Kosovo: UN Protectorate, 1999

Skopje

F.Y.R. MACEDONIA

GREECE

ALBANIA

Tiranë

ITALY

Adriatic Sea

Tyrrhenian Sea

Lake Balaton

Danube

Sava

Tisza

Siret

Dniester

Danube

200 Mi.

250 Km.

125   100

0   0

MAP 30.2   Ethnic Conflict in the Balkans and East-Central Europe

Much of east-central Europe, and particularly the Balkans, has long been an area of complex ethnic mixture. The end of communist rule opened the way to ethnic conflict, most tragically in what had been Yugoslavia. This map shows ethnic distribution in the region in the mid-1990s.

which insisted on Yugoslav unity while affording some measure of regional autonomy. But within a few years of Tito's death in 1980, intellectuals concerned about cultural distinctiveness began undermining the wider Yugoslav identity that Tito had sought to foster.

After the fall of communism, Slovenia and Croatia declared themselves independent of Yugoslavia in May 1991. At the same time, the Serb leader of the remaining Yugoslavia, Slobodan Milosevic (mih-LOH-suh-vitch) (1941–2006), a former communist, embraced Serb nationalism at least partly to maintain his own power. His aim was to unite all the Serbs, two million of whom lived outside Serbia, mostly in Croatia and Bosnia-Herzegovina. He would start by taking over the substantial parts of Croatia with Serb majorities, then divide Bosnia-Herzegovina with Croatia.

Starting in 1991, Milosevic proceeded with extreme brutality, fostering **ethnic cleansing**—forced relocation or mass killing to rid the territory in question of non-Serb inhabitants. In the Bosnian capital, Sarajevo, a culturally diverse city long known for its tolerant, cosmopolitan atmosphere, more than 10,000 civilians, including 1,500 children, were killed by shelling and sniper fire during a Serb siege from 1992 to early 1996.

When a Serb mortar killed thirty-seven civilians in a marketplace in Sarajevo in August 1995, NATO forces responded with air strikes that led to peace accords and the end of fighting by early 1996. Although the peace agreement envisioned a unified Bosnian state, the contending Serbs, Croats, and Bosnian Muslims quickly began carving out separate spheres, violating agreements about repatriation and the rights of minorities. A decade later Bosnia remained an ethnically divided international protectorate, still dependent on the international peacekeeping force stationed there.

The War in Kosovo   The next phase of the Yugoslav tragedy centered on the province of Kosovo (KOH-soh-voh), which Serbs viewed as the cradle of their nationhood (see Map 30.2). For complex historical reasons, however, Serbs had long constituted only a minority of its population. The majority were ethnically Albanian, and by the late 1980s they were talking independence—and sometimes mistreating the minority Serbs. As part of his effort to foster Serb nationalism, Milosevic countered by suspending autonomy for Kosovo within the Yugoslav confederation in 1991. The fissuring of Yugoslavia over the next few years emboldened the Kosovars, who had come to envision full independence, as opposed to mere autonomy within the Serbian part of what remained of Yugoslavia. By provoking Serb intransigence, they could expect to win international support as they demanded independence.

When Milosevic struck against the Kosovars in the spring of 1999, ruthlessly pursuing ethnic cleansing, the Western powers again intervened, first convening a meeting with Serb and Kosovar leaders on Kosovo's future. When the Serb-led remnant of Yugoslavia refused to sign, NATO made good on its threats to bomb Serbia in retaliation. The bombing, concentrated on such economic targets as bridges and power stations, continued for eleven weeks in late 1999.

Critics argued that it set a dubious precedent to attack Serbia for refusing a settlement that would have ceded territory and opened the rest of Serbia to quasi-occupation by NATO. No one denied that Kosovo was part of Serbia, so the NATO action was an overt interference in the internal affairs of a sovereign state. Even the notion that the operation was a humanitarian response to genocide seemed hypocritical to some, who asked why the international community had done nothing in response to the far more systematic genocide in Rwanda in 1994, when 800,000 people had been killed in a hundred days. Defenders countered that it was partly because of the soul-searching in the aftermath of Rwanda that the Western countries were now changing the rules and taking responsibility for concerted action.

Once the NATO bombing began, the Serbs intensified their ethnic cleansing of Kosovo, burning homes, forcing 800,000 refugees to flee into neighboring Macedonia and Albania. But the bombing finally led both the Serbs and the Kosovars to pull back from their more extreme demands, and Russia agreed to join in the multinational peacekeeping force in Kosovo in the aftermath. Still, the outcome bore little relationship to the multi-ethnic pluralism NATO had been seeking. As Kosovars came to dominate the now-ravaged territory, still nominally part of Serbia, the rule was ethnic separation, portending some sort of division. Moreover, the new Kosovo was dominated first by lawless gangs, then increasingly by criminal organizations that the peacekeepers proved powerless to control.

ethnic cleansing   An effort, through forced relocation or even mass killing, to remove an unwanted ethnic group from a particular geographical area. This tactic was implemented by Yugoslavian ruler Slobodan Milosevic to unite all Serbs.

War Crimes Tribunals Authority over Kosovo was transferred to the UN, and talks to settle the province's future began early in 2006. With ethnic Albanians constituting 90 percent of Kosovo's 2 million people by this point, it was widely expected that the province would be made independent. The potential for renewed ethnic violence remained, so Serbia could only try to get the best deal possible for the remaining Serbs.

Although Milosevic was the first sitting head of state to be indicted for war crimes, he proved resilient, initially surviving his defeat in Kosovo in 1999. He lost the presidential election in September 2000, however, and the following year, under pressure from the international community, the Serbian government within the rump Yugoslav confederation turned him over to a UN war crimes tribunal in The Hague. There, as his trial dragged on, he died in prison in 2006. Meanwhile, those who led Serbia after Milosevic's defeat fought a difficult battle against systematic corruption and organized crime as they sought to make their country worthy of membership in the EU.

It was increasingly clear that if Serbia was to have any hope of such membership, it would have to be more helpful in the ongoing effort to apprehend the Bosnian Serb general Ratko Mladic (MLAH-ditch) for his own war crimes trial at The Hague. Charged with the slaughter of as many as 8,000 Bosnian Muslim men and boys when his forces took the town of Srebrenica

(shreb-reh-NEET-sah) in 1995, Mladic had been indicted but had managed to evade capture, most basically because he was still deemed a hero by many Serbs.

RESPONDING TO GLOBAL TERRORISM

Further complicating international relations after the cold war was an increase in the scale and extent of terrorism, sometimes pitting non-Westerners against the West. European venues ranged from Northern Ireland to the Basque region of northern Spain to the rebellious Russian republic of Chechnya to the subways of London. In the United States right-wing extremists bombed a federal government building in Oklahoma City in 1995, and U.S. embassies in Kenya and Tanzania were subjected to terrorist attacks in 1998.

With this new terror already erupting, a terrorist attack of unprecedented proportions shook the United States on September 11, 2001. Suicide hijackers seized four large airliners, crashing one into each of the towers of the World Trade Center in New York City and another into the Pentagon, just outside Washington, D.C. The fourth plane, apparently also headed for Washington, crashed in Pennsylvania. The World Trade Center crashes collapsed both towers, which had been among the world's most visible landmarks. The coordinated attacks claimed the lives of over three thousand people from eighty-two countries.

The United States proclaimed this assault an act of war, and the NATO alliance invoked Article 5 for the first time: the attack on one of its members was to be treated as an attack against all. U.S. leaders promptly assigned responsibility to al Qaeda, an international terrorist network led by the wealthy Saudi Arabian Osama bin Laden, who was living in exile in Afghanistan. There he and others of his network were protected by the Taliban regime, whose extreme, radically fundamentalist version of Islam they shared in certain respects.

Led by President George W. Bush, the United States initiated military action against the Taliban regime later in 2001. Several weeks of U.S. bombing enabled Afghan opposition forces to oust the Taliban and force al Qaeda onto the defensive. But bin Laden survived, and al Qaeda regrouped sufficiently to launch terrorist

attacks against Western interests in Morocco and Saudi Arabia in 2002 and 2003. Then, in March 2004, the network struck in Europe for the first time with a series of terrorist bombings on commuter trains in Madrid that killed over 200 people.

But terror could be bred in Western countries as well. The suicide bombers who led a coordinated attack on the London public transportation system, killing 56, in July 2005 seemed to have been British citizens, Muslims of Pakistani descent, acting on their own. Whatever its sources, such terrorism posed an ongoing threat to Western security and complicated the West's relations with the non-Western world.

DIVISIONS OVER THE INVASION OF IRAQ

The United States won widespread support for its effort to root out international terrorist networks. But the Americans encountered formidable opposition in 2002 when the Bush administration began to call for the overthrow of Saddam Hussein's regime in Iraq. Saddam was charged with stockpiling chemical and bi-

ological weapons of mass destruction in violation of the UN peace agreement that followed the Persian Gulf War of 1991. In that war a broad, U.S.-led coalition defeated an Iraqi effort to conquer Kuwait. Iraq was also accused of developing a nuclear weapons program and supporting terrorist networks like al Qaeda. Moreover, Saddam had long tyrannized the Iraqi people.

As it began to appear that the United States might be prepared to act unilaterally, the Iraq issue became one of the most divisive in recent history, seriously straining Western relations. No one denied that the Iraqi regime was a brutal dictatorship that had developed, and even used, weapons of mass destruction in the past. But an array of countries, with France, Germany, Russia, and China in the forefront, insisted that UN weapons inspectors be given more time to assess Iraq's compliance with the peace terms. Moreover, they held that any punitive action in the event of noncompliance be directed by the UN Security Council, not the United States acting unilaterally.

Yet the Americans won a good deal of international support. Most notably, British prime minister Tony Blair, despite considerable opposition from within his own Labour government, made Britain a full partner of the United States. The governments of Italy, Spain, Denmark, Poland, Hungary, and the Czech Republic supported Bush's get-tough policy. Romania and Bulgaria cooperated, even letting their military bases be used as staging points for the ensuing U.S. assault on Iraq. Each hoped to gain not only NATO membership but also permanent American bases as the United States contemplated redeploying some of its forces in Europe in light of the changing international configuration. But even in countries whose governments supported U.S. policy, the public tended to be strongly opposed to a military showdown in Iraq.

When it became clear they could not win UN Security Council endorsement, the United States and Britain sent military forces into Iraq in March 2003 and toppled Saddam Hussein's regime within six weeks. The military success proved easier than most people had expected, but the tasks of reconstruction proved far more difficult than U.S. officials had envisioned. Although there were steps toward what might eventually prove genuine democracy, an anti-occupation insurgency developed after the United States declared active hostilities ended on May 1, 2003. Sectarian and ethnic violence further complicated the effort of Iraqi leaders to develop a workable new government.

In the aftermath of the invasion it had gradually become clear that Saddam Hussein's Iraq had not been actively developing weapons of mass destruction. In addition, evidence suggested that both the U.S. and British governments had relied to some extent on faulty intelligence or had used intelligence selectively to justify the invasion. And whereas no links between Saddam's regime and al Qaeda had been shown, the newly chaotic Iraq seemed a far more dangerous breeding ground for international terrorists than Saddam's Iraq had been.

In the Spanish elections that followed the terrorist bombings in Madrid of March 2004, voters elected the Socialist leader José Luis Rodríguez Zapatero, who charged that the U.S.-led occupation of Iraq was becoming a fiasco. He promptly followed through on an earlier pledge to withdraw the 1,300 Spanish troops from Iraq. But though some of America's European partners gradually pulled back, the coalition remained reasonably stable, despite the difficulties encountered.

U.S. UNILATERALISM

A major source of friction between the United States and Europe was growing U.S. **unilateralism**—the country's willingness, even determination, to go its own way in the world on the basis of what it took to be its own interests. As the world's military-diplomatic superpower, the United States was increasingly prone to such unilateralism during the 1990s, then moved more decisively in that direction in the aftermath of the terrorist attacks of September 2001. In pursuing its own course, the United States was departing from the multilateral international system that it had fostered since World War II. Foreshadowed in the Atlantic Charter of 1941 (see pages 887–888), multilateralism found expression in NATO, in the economic organizations growing from the Bretton Woods Agreement, and in a whole array of multilateral understandings and institutions governing matters such as arms control and war crimes.

While an overwhelming majority of nations—120, to be exact—supported the establishment of the UN's International Criminal Court in The Hague in 1998, the United States was among only 7 that opposed it. Then, as the court was being established, the United States sought an exemption for itself because it worried that American peacekeepers might be especially tempt-

ing targets of false accusations of war crimes. Such concerns were not groundless, and they indicated the unique problems the United States faced as the world's undisputed, and often resented, superpower. But many found it disturbing that the United States did not want to play by the same rules as the vast majority.

Some Europeans continued to look to the UN to check American hegemony, but others, including many non-Europeans, found a stronger European military and diplomatic presence the only potential balance to the United States. EU forces were prominent in peacekeeping missions in Macedonia, Bosnia, Kosovo, Afghanistan, and Congo. Yet the Europeans were much less willing than Americans to use force in the first place. As of early 2006, the United States was spending 3.4 percent of its gross domestic product (GDP) on defense, Europe 1.9 percent. Moreover, the Europeans were devoting only half as much of their defense spending to modernizing equipment and twice as much to pay and pensions. The Iraq War dramatized how far the U.S. military had outpaced even the British in technological capacities. Many experts found this gap between the Europeans and the Americans a threat to NATO, which might become simply useless as a battle-ready alliance.

Some suggested that Europeans had grown soft in their reliance on the United States since World War II. While they agreed that, in principle, the West must be prepared to fight on occasion, they were unwilling to pay if it meant cutting the welfare benefits they had come to expect. Moreover, Europeans could muster no unified military and diplomatic policy. It was attractive for a variety of reasons to let the United States shoulder the military burden in a dangerous world.

Still, some observers noted the scope for the United States and Europe to play complementary roles in world affairs. Americans were better at fighting wars, but Europeans might be better at preventing them. Precisely because they were not prone to threaten force, Europeans could play a constructive role of moral suasion, even if it was up to the Americans to provide the muscle.

SECTION SUMMARY

- The end of the cold war opened the way to a series of new issues that the West had to confront, even as it also changed power relationships within the West itself.

- The European Union expanded and gathered strength but also encountered unforeseen setbacks.

unilateralism Term describing the increasing willingness of the United States to go its own way in world affairs after the end of the cold war, and especially after the terrorist attacks on the United States in September 2001.

- Ethnic conflict contributed to the breakup of Yugoslavia in a series of wars that included major human rights violations and significant dilemmas for peacekeepers.

- International terrorism, often reflecting tensions between the West and the Islamic world, became a major concern throughout the Western world.

- Increasing U.S. unilateralism, evident most dramatically in the U.S.-led invasion of Iraq, alienated others in the West.

THE CONTINUING EXPERIMENT WITH DEMOCRATIC CAPITALISM

What forces raised new questions about the effectiveness of Western-style democracy by the early years of the twenty-first century?

 emocracy had become the unchallenged norm in western Europe by the 1980s, and after the fall of communism the former Soviet bloc countries seemed eager to adopt the western European model. But though patterns in several of the former communist countries increasingly approximated those of the mature democracies of western Europe, disaffection and even some unforeseen new political and economic forms emerged as well. The problems of adjustment were especially dramatic, and even tragic, in Russia.

The mainstream tendency was toward democratic procedures, the rule of law, and an orderly alternation of competing political parties within a framework of stability, consensus, and tolerance. But even in the established democracies, technological change and globalization were altering the socioeconomic framework, producing new challenges for governments and even threatening the socioeconomic compact that had emerged after World War II.

THE POSTCOMMUNIST EXPERIMENT

The former communist countries had little experience with the give-and-take of democratic politics, and their fragile new political systems had to engineer the difficult transition to a free-market economy. With the economies close to chaos as the transition began, the effort led to unemployment, inflation, and widespread corruption. No longer could ordinary people count on the subsidized consumer goods or the welfare safety net the communist regimes had provided. While many suffered great hardship, some former communist functionaries quickly got rich by taking over state-owned companies.

The pattern of change and the degree of success varied considerably from country to country, though in per capita income the whole region continued to lag behind western Europe considerably. Still, by the mid-1990s, the transition to a market economy seemed to be working (see **MAP 30.3**). Thanks partly to the lure of EU membership, most of the postcommunist countries made considerable progress toward mainstream democracy. Even the election of former Communists in Poland and Hungary during the mid-1990s did not compromise democracy or the market economy.

Still, the case of Poland manifested certain enduring strains and risks. On the one hand, the country by 2006 had experienced changes scarcely imaginable in 1989. A full member of both NATO and the EU, it was now numbered among Europe's new "big six," together with Germany, France, Britain, Italy, and Spain. GDP grew by 50 percent from 1990 to 2005, as Poland attracted considerable foreign investment.

But, on the other hand, the costs were high for those left out. In 2006 unemployment stood at 18 percent, ever more people were falling into poverty, and the gap between rich and poor was widening. The state was widely seen as weak, bloated, inefficient, and highly corrupt. Services were poor, and the tax system was full of loopholes. Low electoral turnouts manifested the widespread disillusionment with the new political class—and even doubts about democracy itself.

In Russia, where communism had far deeper roots than elsewhere in the former Soviet bloc, the transition from communism proved especially difficult. Although privatization proceeded rapidly, it mostly benefited former Communist Party functionaries, some of whom became instant multimillionaires. By the mid-1990s Russia had evolved a kind of "crony capitalism," with a small group of economic oligarchs manipulating much of the economy through dubious banking practices and outright extortion—and paying no taxes. After ten years the postcommunist Russian economy had shrunk to perhaps half its former size. Especially sobering were the demographic effects: Russians were dying young and having few children. By 2001 the population had dropped to 143 million—a decline of 6 million people in ten years.

The combination of economic stringency and governmental weakness produced a chilling increase in street crime, from muggings to auto theft. By the end of the 1990s, moreover, dozens of journalists, politicians, and business leaders had been murdered gangland style, with the killers never apprehended. Particularly appalling was the death of Galina Starovoitova (stah-ro-VOY-to-vah), a widely admired liberal legislator and potential presidential candidate who was gunned down outside her St. Petersburg apartment in 1998.

As Russia's president during the first postcommunist years, Boris Yeltsin seemed a committed reformer—surely the best hope for an orderly transition to democracy and a market economy. He enjoyed widespread support from the Western democracies, but among Russians the difficult circumstances produced disenchantment with reform, nostalgia for the stability of communism, and much resentment of the West.

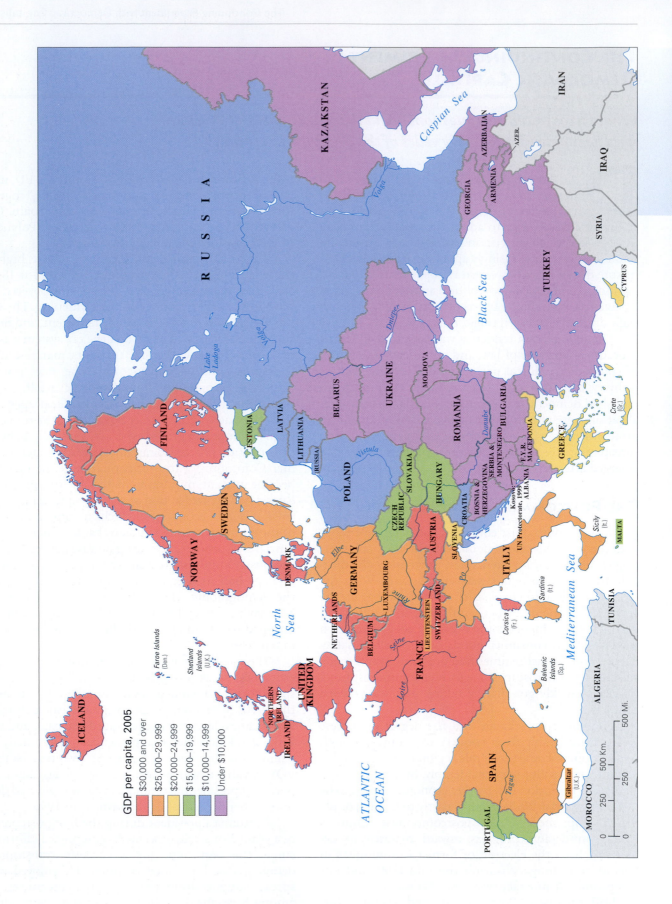

GDP per capita, 2005

$30,000 and over
$25,000–29,999
$20,000–24,999
$15,000–19,999
$10,000–14,999
Under $10,000

ICELAND

FINLAND

NORWAY

SWEDEN

ESTONIA

LATVIA

LITHUANIA

DENMARK

IRELAND

NORTHERN IRELAND

UNITED KINGDOM

NETHERLANDS

BELGIUM

LUXEMBOURG

GERMANY

POLAND

BELARUS

UKRAINE

MOLDOVA

ROMANIA

CZECH REPUBLIC

SLOVAKIA

HUNGARY

AUSTRIA

SLOVENIA

CROATIA

LIECHTENSTEIN

SWITZERLAND

FRANCE

ITALY

BOSNIA & HERZEGOVINA

SERBIA & MONTENEGRO

ALBANIA

F.Y.R. MACEDONIA

BULGARIA

GREECE

Kosovo, 1999 UN Protectorate

TURKEY

CYPRUS

Crete (Gr.)

RUSSIA

KAZAKSTAN

GEORGIA

ARMENIA

AZERBAIJAN

AZER.

IRAN

IRAQ

SYRIA

PORTUGAL

SPAIN

Gibraltar (U.K.)

MOROCCO

ALGERIA

TUNISIA

Corsica (Fr.)

Sardinia (It.)

Sicily (It.)

MALTA

Balearic Islands (Sp.)

Faroe Islands (Den.)

Shetland Islands (U.K.)

KALININGRAD (RUSSIA)

Caspian Sea

Black Sea

Volga

Dnieper

Danube

Lake Ladoga

Volga

Vistula

Elbe

Rhine

Seine

Loire

Po

Tagus

North Sea

ATLANTIC OCEAN

Mediterranean Sea

500 Mi.

500 Km.

250

250

0

0

Map 30.3   GDP per Capita in Europe, 2005

Gross domestic product (GDP) per capita is a widely recognized measure of national economic success. By 2005, this measure varied dramatically among the European countries, revealing the wide disparity in economic well-being across the Continent. The former communist countries continued to lag, even as some were growing at impressive rates. The U.S. figure was $42,000, and Canada's was $32,900.

As it sought to engineer the transition to democratic capitalism, the Yeltsin government had to deal with the attempted defection of Chechnya (CHECH-nyah), a small, largely Muslim republic located in the Caucasus (see Map 29.3 on page 940). Long restive under Russian control, the Chechens began demanding independence after the collapse of the Soviet Union in 1991, finally provoking war with Russia in 1994. In the aftermath of a compromise in 1996, Chechen hardliners oppressed the Russian minority, kidnapping and enslaving some, and even killed journalists and international aid workers. When Islamic militants began spreading the anti-Russian message from Chechnya to adjacent Dagestan, Russia renewed full-scale war with Chechnya in 1999.

This renewed confrontation made possible the rise of **Vladimir Putin** (POO-tin), who had been director of Russia's secret police, though he was virtually unknown in political circles. Calling for a tough stance on Chechnya, Putin was Yeltsin's choice for prime minister in 1999, and he immediately delivered on his promise to clear Dagestan of Chechen terrorists. Whereas most Russians had disliked the earlier confrontation with Chechnya, by now they had had enough—not only of Chechen defiance but also of Russian weakness. Putin's popularity soared as he talked tough and acted tougher. A brutal Russian assault late in 1999 left much of Chechnya, especially the capital, Grozny, in ruins.

In poor health and increasingly erratic, Yeltsin resigned at the end of 1999, essentially to make way for Putin, who was elected president early in 2000. Reelected in 2004, Putin remained quite popular among Russians. Still, outside observers tended to give his performance decidedly mixed marks. In the economic sphere, there was considerable evidence that, thanks partly to Putin's leadership, the post-Soviet decline had at last been reversed by 2006. Tax collection had improved, some well-run companies had emerged, and

Vladimir Putin   President of Russia since 2000, he strengthened the Russian state against the forces of disintegration that emerged after communism, but critics accused him of authoritarianism and excessive governmental secrecy.

the Russian middle class was clearly expanding. Especially as a result of high oil prices, life was much better for average Russians—perhaps better than ever before. But the political order suffered from secrecy and governmental inaccessibility. The media were increasingly concentrated and subject to restrictions and controls.

Especially contested was the relationship between state power and business power. A showdown between Putin and the economic barons led in 2003 to the arrest of Russia's richest person, Yukos Oil chief Mikhail Khodorkovsky (koh-dor-KOV-skee), who was given an eight-year sentence in Siberia for corruption and tax evasion. The company itself was essentially renationalized, thereby reversing the earlier, largely fraudulent privatization from which Khodorkovsky had benefited. Whereas some read the move as a welcome notice to such tycoons to start paying taxes, others charged that Putin was merely jealous of Khodorkovsky, who had been willing to act independently and who had been admired in the West as the embodiment of Russia's new capitalist spirit.

As itself an unprecedented experiment, the effort to move from communism to democratic capitalism made clearer what was required to make democratic capitalism work. The Russian case demonstrated that even a turn to free elections and a market economy could yield an exploitative and brutal "gangster capitalism." If democracy and a market economy were to be socially beneficial, a deeper consensus around civic responsibility and the rule of law was required. People had to be willing to pay taxes, and the state had to be strong enough to collect taxes, to limit corruption, and to sustain genuinely open markets and an orderly banking system. Merely getting government out of the way was not sufficient.

Consensus in the Established Democracies

During the half century since World War II, renewed prosperity came together with the new compact concerning economic and social welfare to sustain the Western democracies. At the same time, something like an orderly alternation of moderately conservative and moderately progressive parties or coalitions became the norm, or at least the direction, helping to sustain the democratic consensus. Even Italy, long notorious for the surface instability of its government, moved toward a system of alternating left-leaning and right-leaning coalitions after major scandals during the early 1990s undermined the long-standing political establishment.

Although the European left had won reforms that were now central to the consensus around democratic capitalism, by the 1990s it had abandoned much of what it had stood for in its earlier socialist forms—from class struggle and revolution to state ownership and a centrally planned economy. Though still nominally socialist, the German SPD, for example, could serve only as the mildly left-leaning alternative within the framework of capitalist democracy. When the Labour Party returned to power in Britain in 1997, the popular new prime minister, Tony Blair, did not offer a bold new program or reverse Margaret Thatcher's privatization measures of the 1980s. To be sure, he was more concerned to care for those worst-off and to enhance equality of opportunity. But he expressed admiration for her concerted effort to modernize the British economy, and he was no more sympathetic than she to trade-union efforts to protect jobs at the expense of productivity.

TWO MODELS OF DEMOCRATIC CAPITALISM

By the 1980s much of western Europe had caught up with the United States in standard of living, and it was increasingly clear that two models of democratic capitalism were at work—and to some extent in competition. The U.S. model, largely shared by Britain since the Thatcher years, placed greater emphasis on free enterprise and the market, whereas continental western Europe had evolved a **social market economy,** with greater commitment to security, consensus, and communitarian values. The European model provided a more substantial safety net—in health care, for example—as well as a stronger commitment to subsidized transportation and day care. Generous pensions, especially for government workers, had been one aspect of the postwar compact. By 2003 Italy and Austria were devoting 15 percent of their economies to public-sector pensions, the highest figures in Europe. Few Austrians worked past age 60.

In France by the mid-1990s, five-week paid vacations were mandatory, with the government sometimes subsidizing the cost of transportation to seaside or mountain resorts. Indeed, the French welfare system had emerged as a model. In 2000 the UN's **World Health Organization (WHO)** rated the French health-care system the world's best. Moreover, social services in France were delivered with less paperwork and intrusiveness than elsewhere.

In some respects, it was almost as if the Americans

and Europeans had passed in the night in the decades since World War II. In the United States, which had long prided itself on its egalitarianism vis-à-vis class-bound Europe, disparities between rich and poor had become greater than anywhere in the developed world by the early twenty-first century. In business firms, the ratio of executive compensation to worker salaries was dramatically higher in the United States than in Europe.

Perhaps still more significant was the difference in attitudes toward such disparities. Wary of extreme inequalities of income, Europeans tended to view unrestricted competition more as a threat than an opportunity. Whereas most Europeans found the inequalities and insecurities of American life unacceptable, Americans accented the scope for upward mobility that their system offered. As long as anyone could get rich, it did not matter that some were much richer than others. Americans were far more likely than Europeans to see themselves as moving up.

At the same time, Americans had grown more skeptical about government and its capacity to provide social services. Whereas 62 percent of those surveyed in Britain in 2002 said they would accept higher taxes for better services, less than 1 percent of those in the United States held this view. Friction over particular policies from pollution control to product testing reflected similar differences in priorities and values. The United States was more likely than Europe to rely on unfettered freedom, competition, and the market. Europe was more cautious—more willing to err on the side of health and the environment. Accustomed to a strong government role in society, Europeans had difficulty understanding how measures such as government-sponsored health care could cause such controversy among Americans.

By the 1990s the changing socioeconomic framework was producing new challenges for governments on both sides of the Atlantic. But continental western Europe seemed especially vulnerable because of the difficulties it encountered in squaring its social market model with increasing global competition.

NEW ECONOMIC COMPETITORS

During most of the 1990s the United States experienced remarkable prosperity as it asserted its leadership in the "new economy" revolving around **information technology.** The technological revolution encompassed everything from robotics to fiber optics but was based especially on the computer. Some new firms were able to exploit technology and start from scratch, while

social market economy The socially oriented model of capitalism practiced in continental western Europe, providing a substantial safety net in health care and a commitment to public services such as transportation and day care.

World Health Organization (WHO) Established as a specialized agency of the United Nations in 1948, it serves as the coordinating authority on international public health. It is headquartered in Geneva, Switzerland.

information technology Term for the revolution in information availability and communications resulting from the late-twentieth-century development of personal computers and the Internet.

older competitors often faced problems of redundant workers or outmoded plants and equipment. In all cases, manufacturing jobs were lost, as competition forced the industrial sector to become more efficient through computers and automation. In the German steel industry, which had spearheaded a remarkable industrial transformation a century before, more than half the jobs disappeared during the 1970s and 1980s.

Just as the West became concerned with economic challenges from the Soviet Union in the 1950s, Japan by the later 1970s, and a wider array of East Asian "tigers" by the 1980s, it came to view China and to a lesser extent India as potential economic superpowers by the early twenty-first century. Although still nominally communist, China was increasingly willing to compete in the global economic marketplace and did well at manufacturing, thanks especially to a cheap, disciplined labor force. With its favorable trade balance, China came to hold such a large share of the U.S. national debt that it seemed capable, at least potentially, of compromising the independence of American foreign policy.

By the 1980s Italy had become Europe's leading producer of clothing and shoes, thanks primarily to the initiatives of small and medium-sized family firms. Having established a global presence in the 1980s, the well-known clothing retailer Benetton had exemplified Italy's success. Even in 1990, almost 90 percent of its output was being produced in Italy. By early 2006, however, that figure had fallen to 30 percent—and was expected to fall still further, to 10 percent, by 2010. Responding to global competition, Benetton was relying increasingly on Chinese suppliers, who offered low labor costs and rapidly improving production skills.

In 2003 France's Peugeot Citroën chose Trnava, a town in western Slovakia, for a site of a major automobile assembly plant, to start turning out cars in 2006. At the same time, the British firm MG Rover was making a major investment in Poland, and France's Renault was launching a new budget model at its factory in Romania. The former communist countries of east-central Europe were proving tremendously appealing to automakers elsewhere. Although the communist system had not proved competitive over the long term, it had left a reasonably good infrastructure, as well as a skilled and disciplined labor force costing only about 20 percent as much as the EU labor force.

By 2006, major carmakers in France, Germany, and Italy were being forced to cut costs—and thus jobs and benefits—at home in order to remain competitive in light of the much lower labor costs in east-central Europe. There was much sensitivity in western Europe that competition from new EU members in east-central Europe was causing downward pressure on living standards. But it was not only the new EU members that

were attracting such investment. Volkswagen was building new plants in Russia and China. Some were predicting that auto manufacture in western Europe would have ceased altogether in ten to fifteen years.

UNEMPLOYMENT AND ECONOMIC CHALLENGES IN WESTERN EUROPE

As global economic competition intensified, governments throughout western Europe found it more difficult to pay for all the benefits they had gradually come to promise. By the early 1990s some found the social compact all too generous—and unsustainable. Pension reform, labor legislation, and the costs of education became flash points across much of western Europe.

Falling birthrates and aging populations meant that relatively fewer workers would have to foot the pension and health-care bills for increasing numbers of older people. Although most agreed that reform was necessary, massive union-led demonstrations against government proposals to scale back pensions brought France almost to a halt in May 2003. Comparable protests greeted reform proposals in Germany, Italy, and Austria. As a result, little was done anywhere to address the problem.

Even with the renewed prosperity of the 1980s, unemployment in western Europe reached levels not seen since the Great Depression. During the 1990s high unemployment persisted in much of Europe, even as it declined to postwar lows in the United States. Most people attributed the difference in unemployment rates to the different structure of labor markets and, more generally, to the greater flexibility of the U.S. economy. As a result of laws, labor agreements, and the postwar consensus now in place, European workers who had jobs were more secure than their American counterparts. But European employers were less able to adapt to changing conditions by laying off workers or hiring new ones with different skills. Government reform efforts provoked strenuous protests.

Widespread demonstrations in France in the spring of 2006 forced the government to abandon legislation that would have adjusted labor laws to enable employers to fire, without cause, workers under 26 years of age within two years after hiring. It was thought that such flexibility would encourage employers to hire more younger workers, thereby reducing France's 22 percent employment rate among youth. Yet it was French youth, supported by France's trade unions, that led the protests. One poll indicated that 75 percent of French young people aspired to a civil service job, primarily because of the security such a job seemed to entail.

In Germany, the ongoing costs of assimilating the former communist East complicated reform efforts. By early 2006, Germany was still transferring 80 billion euros a year to the former East. As of that point, the subsidy to the East since reunification totaled 1.3 trillion euros overall. Yet young people continued to migrate from East to West, and the birthrate in the former East was even lower than in the West.

Upon becoming Germany's first female chancellor in November 2005, the conservative Angela Merkel sought the measures necessary to streamline the German economy. But Merkel led an unstable "grand coalition" of the two largest parties, her own conservatives and the socialists, in light of the near dead heat in the national elections that September. It remained to be seen whether her awkward coalition could muster the unified will and the political muscle to tackle Germany's problems in a concerted way.

The difficulties that Merkel faced seemed to suggest a certain political paralysis, not only in Germany but in Europe more widely. It was symptomatic that with the German electorate split and the postwar social compact eroding, an increasing number of private schools emerged in Germany—for those who could afford them. At the same time, a growing black market economy had come to constitute an estimated 15 percent of Germany's GDP by early 2006.

Although the extent of the problem varied from country to country, the increasingly obvious role of money in politics—needed to finance campaigns and win elections—raised doubts throughout the Western world about the capacity of elected governments to pursue some common public interest. This tendency toward corruption yielded political cynicism—and declining voter turnouts—all over the Western world.

Whatever the patterns of divergence and convergence within the West, what was ultimately at issue, after its roughly two-hundred-year experiment with liberal capitalism, was the scope for creating and maintaining a genuine public sphere. It rested on the capacity for citizenship, as opposed to the mere pursuit of individual or group interests. It required a capacity for compromise and shared sacrifice. Conversely, a government worthy of public trust would be not a mere dispenser of favors but a shared responsibility of the entire citizenry. In terms of its sustaining commitments, the democracy that the West held up as a model for the non-Western world remained very much an experiment in progress.

IMMIGRATION, ASSIMILATION, AND THE NEW RIGHT

With the decline of socialism as a political alternative, and with the welfare state increasingly open to question, a new right gained prominence in much of Europe by the mid-1990s. Though differing considerably in priorities, respectability, and success, leaders such as José María Aznar in Spain, Jean-Marie Le Pen in France, Jörg Haider (HY-dur) in Austria, Gianfranco Fini (FEE-nee) in Italy, and Pim Fortyn (for-TOON) in the Netherlands tapped into political frustration and economic uncertainty. Some were absorbed into the mainstream, while others provoked renewed political division.

In addressing economic anxieties, the new conservatives sometimes articulated problems that mainstream politicians ignored, but they often disagreed among themselves—over the relative merits of free trade and protectionism, for example. On one issue, however, they were in clear agreement. This was the issue of assimilation, citizenship, and national identity as globalization proceeded and immigration increased. The arrival of refugees from the former Yugoslavia and other trouble spots during the 1990s added another dimension. Even figures like Le Pen and Haider, who typically won only 15 to 20 percent of the vote, articulated a wider sense among the public that immigrant communities were responsible not only for increasing crime but also for a weakening of the common values necessary to sustain society.

By the first years of the new millennium, concerns about national community, cultural diversity, and the meaning of citizenship were taking center stage all over Europe. It was striking that the Netherlands and Denmark, two small countries widely known for openness and tolerance, became flash points. But especially cen-

On Her Way to the Chancellorship

As leader of the German conservative party (Christian Democratic Union), Angela Merkel launches her campaign to become German chancellor in 2005. Her party won a narrow victory in the September elections, and she became chancellor as head of a broad coalition in November.   *(David Bathgate/Corbis)*

tral was France, proud of what had seemed its traditions of inclusiveness, and by 2006 home of the largest concentration of Muslims in western Europe, roughly 6 million, or 10 percent of the French population.

Most were recent immigrants or members of immigrant families established since World War II. Indeed, many French Muslims were French citizens, the second- or third-generation descendants of immigrants who had begun coming to France from Algeria and other former French African colonies in the 1950s when, as the postwar economic miracle gathered force, France needed workers. But beginning in the early 1970s, jobs had become increasingly scarce.

With open citizenship central to the French self-understanding, French law accorded citizenship automatically to second-generation immigrants, on the assumption that these offspring would be readily assimilated. However, the Muslim community in France had not been well assimilated, and by the end of the 1980s finger-pointing on all sides had begun. Whereas the French left defended cultural diversity and its compatibility with citizenship, the right complained that citizenship was being devalued as a mere convenience, requiring no real commitment to the national community. Critics such as Le Pen charged that many from recent immigrant families did not want to assimilate.

An especially symptomatic episode in 1989—the "affair of the scarves"—made it clear that the place of Muslims in France had become a central and volatile issue. Three teenaged Muslim girls were suspended from school on the grounds that, in wearing the traditional Muslim headscarf, they were violating a long-standing law banning religious displays in public schools. The girls insisted they were not seeking to flaunt their religion or to convert others; the point was simply that Islamic teaching required women to cover their heads in public as a sign of modesty. Yet in the eyes of some Westerners, that practice reflected the second-class status of women in Islamic civilization. To defend the right to wear the scarves was thus to condone the oppression of women.

An uncertain compromise resulted from this episode, but the issue continued to smolder, becoming more intense as the Muslim presence in France increased and tensions between Muslims and non-Muslims grew. Early in 2004 the French National Assembly passed, by an overwhelming margin, a new law to ban conspicuous religious displays in French public schools, hospitals, and other governmental buildings. Although large Christian crosses and Jewish yarmulkes, or skullcaps, were also at issue, the law seemed especially to target the headscarves traditionally worn by Muslim women. The law was passed despite massive protest marches, especially featuring Muslim women, in cities throughout France and in a number of major cities elsewhere.

Polls indicated that whereas 69 percent of the French backed the new law, these issues divided the French Muslim community. Muslim support for the ban on the headscarf reflected a fear of backlash against indications of Islamic separatism, but a genuine desire for assimilation was also at work. However, many Muslims were reluctant to accept full assimilation if it was to mean the gradual loss of their religious identity in France's secular society. At the same time, many non-Muslims supported the right of women to wear the scarf precisely on the grounds of pluralism, tolerance, and freedom of expression. Yet some of those opposing the new law sought not to preserve diversity but to keep Muslim girls in the public schools to expose them to secular influence and to promote long-term assimilation. In the short term, they argued, any law restricting religious expression would spawn separate Islamic schools, thereby deepening the divisions already evident in France.

By the first decade of the new century French Muslims were clustered in deteriorating high-rise ghetto suburbs ringing Paris and other cities. Whereas young Muslims were widely blamed for criminality, they complained of police harassment and job discrimination. Certainly they experienced very high rates of unemployment, well over 40 percent in many areas. And thus, it was feared, they were increasingly prone to militancy or Islamic fundamentalism.

As the police sought to crack down on crime, an incident late in October 2005 provoked a riot among Muslim youth in the ghetto suburb of Clichy-sous-Bois. During the next few days waves of looting and car-burning spread to cities throughout France. The rioting continued well into November, until the government declared a state of emergency and deployed sharply increased security forces. It was France's worst civil unrest since the Days of May demonstrations of 1968 (see page 920). President Jacques Chirac admitted that the riots had dramatized problems that had to be addressed vigorously and promptly. Some observers called for a form of affirmative action to bring French Muslims, or French citizens of North African descent, into positions of greater prominence in business, politics, and the media, spheres in which they were virtually absent.

But the problem was by no means confined to France. Germany started from a very different set of assumptions than France about assimilation and citizenship, yet ended up with many of the same problems. Germany had actively recruited foreign workers during the decades of economic boom and labor shortage that followed the war. At first these "guest workers" had been viewed not as immigrants but as temporary, almost migrant, laborers. But many of the 14 million guest workers let in from 1955 to 1973, especially the Turks, remained in Germany. Although their family patterns came to approximate those of the rest of the population, their birthrates were considerably higher. By the 1980s Germany had a large and increasingly settled population of non-Germans, many of them born and educated there.

In addition, the German Federal Republic had adopted a generous asylum law as one bit of atonement for the crimes of the Nazi period. With the turmoil surrounding the end of communism in the Soviet bloc, the newly reunified Germany found 60,000 new arrivals seeking asylum every month by 1993. At that point Germany had a large foreign population of 6.4 million, or roughly 8 percent of the population.

Germany's law governing citizenship for immigrants and their descendants reflected a long-standing German assumption that citizenship presupposed German ethnicity—or at least full assimilation. Thus ethnic Germans—more than a million of whom moved to Germany from the former Soviet bloc between 1988 and 1991—were immediately accorded German citizenship. But the many Turks, for example, who had been born in Germany were denied citizenship. Precisely because citizenship seemed to entail full assimilation, some Germans opposed it for "foreigners" out of respect for cultural diversity.

In 1999, however, the law was reworked to make naturalization much easier. In principle, citizenship was now available to almost everyone born in Germany or whose parents had resided and worked in Germany for at least eight years. But as of 2006, this formal change had not made the expected difference in practice. The Turks in Germany remained largely separate, as many Turks seemed to prefer to remain in Turkish ghettos, having minimal contact with ethnic Germans. At the same time, many ethnic Germans remained wedded to the notion that belonging is based on descent, or ethnic origin. Even as access to citizenship on the national level became easier, some German states erected new barriers to naturalization during the first decade of the twenty-first century. And although citizenship was more accessible in light of the 1999 law, the national government concentrated not on liberaliz-

ing immigration rules but on tightening security and fostering the assimilation of those of non-German descent already in Germany. Thus, for example, a 2004 law required new immigrants to take German lessons.

Indeed, by the early twenty-first century, the tendency all over Europe was to push assimilation—the formation of national citizens. Whereas some conflated the impulse with racism, others insisted that, on the contrary, anyone could belong, regardless of race or ethnicity, but that belonging required a positive commitment, adopting the mainstream values of the national community, not holding to cultural differences.

In the wake of the assassination of Theo Van Gogh in 2004 and the controversy over the Danish cartoons of 2005, the Netherlands in 2006 adopted a law, the first of its kind anywhere, requiring that prospective immigrants take a "civic integration examination" testing their willingness to accept the tolerant openness of Dutch culture. The chairman of a leading Dutch Muslim organization defended the measure, suggesting that all immigrants needed to be prepared to embrace modernity.

The Dutch were in the forefront of a wider retreat from the multiculturalism that had been prevalent especially on the European left, and that had made the persistence of immigrant subcultures in European countries seem a virtue. A veteran, highly respected observer of the contemporary European scene, Jane Kramer, summed up the dilemma that seemed to face well-meaning Europeans as they came to grasp the implications of the cultural differences separating them from many in the immigrant communities in their midst. Noting that the Internet in the Netherlands was awash in hate-mail by Muslims, who often equated the pluralistic tolerance of the Netherlands with mere decadence, Kramer suggested that the Dutch were coming to recognize that democracy without assimilation might be a dangerous contradiction in terms. "But," she concluded, "like everybody else in Europe, they have no answer to the question What now?"[2]

SECTION SUMMARY

- Although the transition from communism to some variety of democratic capitalism proved difficult throughout the former Soviet bloc, it proved especially problematic in Russia.

- With the decline of the traditional left, accenting class division and anticapitalism, the established democracies tended toward a new level of consensus around some variety of a two-party framework.

- From within the wider democratic census, there was a split between much of continental western Europe,

with its "social market economy," and the United States, which had greater confidence in free-market capitalism and less confidence in government.

- Especially in continental western Europe, the challenges of globalization suggested the need for reforms—reforms that proved difficult to engineer through the democratic process.

- Concerns about the assimilation of immigrant communities in much of Europe strengthened the political right and raised newly volatile political issues.

LIFESTYLES AND IDENTITIES

How did the changes bound up with globalization affect identities in the West?

Even as matters of diversity and citizenship were becoming mainstream political concerns, they were very much bound up with wider issues of personal identity. And in that respect they intersected in complex ways with other potential influences on identity, from consumerism to religion to gender.

By the mid-1960s, the remarkable postwar economic growth had created a secular, consumerist society throughout much of the West, establishing patterns of life that continued into the twenty-first century, when cell phones and personal computers were commonplace. But changing lifestyles dictated new choices, and the new affluence challenged traditional sources of personal identity in unexpected ways, producing new concerns—and sometimes conflict. Important groups of non-Westerners rejected Western secular consumerism altogether. At the very least, it indicated a kind of decadence. For the various forms of Islamic fundamentalism, it was nothing less than an abomination.

SUPRANATIONAL, NATIONAL, AND SUBNATIONAL IDENTITIES

By the late 1980s consumerism and the widening impact of American popular culture—from blue jeans and American TV to shopping malls and theme parks—suggested a growing homogenization in the capitalist democracies. A Euro-Disneyland opened in France in 1992 and, after a slow start, proved increasingly popular. American fast-food chains such as McDonald's, adopting some European ways and even serving beer and wine, satisfied hungry locals in cities all over Europe.

But Americanization threatened long-standing European identities, and Europeans sometimes adopted special measures to preserve distinctiveness. The EU specified that EU television programming had to be at least 40 percent EU-made, while the French mandated that at least every third popular song played on the radio had to be French.

Prominent among European critics of Americanization was José Bové, the outspoken leader of France's small farmers. When he stood trial in 2000 for vandalizing a McDonald's restaurant in France, thirty thousand people turned out to demonstrate their support. Typically equating globalization with Americanization, Bové articulated a widespread concern for French distinctiveness and identity in the face of U.S. "cultural imperialism," as France seemed increasingly overrun by American films, television, music, even novels in French translation.

But were quotas and mandates really necessary to preserve distinctiveness? The American chain Starbucks, which had revolutionized the serving of coffee in the United States, found it hard to penetrate continental Europe, which had its own long traditions of coffee-making. Even as many were coming to assume that American pop culture was irresistible, it became clear that European viewers were increasingly picking local TV programming on their own, quite apart from quotas. Between 1996 and 2002, the number of hours of American TV programming fell 26 percent in Spain, 17 percent in Germany, and 9 percent in Italy. By 2003 every EU country was well above the 40 percent minimum for local programming, with the average at 62 percent.

Meanwhile, the growing prominence of the supranational EU, and doubts about the significance of national politics, nourished a renewed premium on subnational identities in such distinctive European regions as Flanders, Corsica, Scotland, and Catalonia. Flemings and Corsicans, Scots and Catalans, actively sought to preserve some measure of their distinct cultures and languages in the face of all the contemporary pressures toward standardization. In Britain Tony Blair fostered the "devolution" of powers from the central government in London to Scottish and Welsh assemblies in 1999.

National sentiment grew especially uncertain in Italy, which had had a relatively brief and problematic history as a unified nation. Although its movement for national unification had drawn widespread enthusiasm throughout the Western world in the nineteenth century (see pages 685–689), by the 1990s disillusionment with national politics made many Italians particularly eager to embrace the EU, while others turned in the opposite direction, renewing their identification with region or locality. Resentful of the national government's ties to the less prosperous south, a new political movement, the Northern League, emerged during the 1990s to push for the north to become an independent state. Whatever the seriousness of such literal separatism, the Northern League's persistent strength suggested that "Italian" was becoming less important as a basis of individual identity in Italy's prosperous north.

CLASS IDENTITIES AND TRADE UNIONS

The advent of a media-driven consumerist society produced greater homogeneity of experience and taste and a corresponding de-emphasis on class as a basis of identity. One symptom was the decline of the trade-union movement, long central to working-class identity and advancement.

Changing labor patterns reinforced the decline of organized labor, which was decidedly on the defensive throughout western Europe and the United States by the 1980s. The increasing danger of unemployment undercut the leverage of the unions. And as the economy grew more complex, workers were less likely to think of themselves as members of a single, unified working class.

Still, union membership varied considerably from country to country, and some unions found new ways of exerting influence. In a survey of union membership as a percentage of the work force in twelve industrialized countries in 2001, Denmark and Sweden had the highest figures—around 80 percent. The figures for Italy, Germany, and Britain were all around 30 percent. The lowest figures were in France (10 percent) and the United States (14 percent). Despite some much-publicized militancy in resisting government efforts at pension reform, the unions generally had moved beyond their earlier confrontational posture to an increasing pragmatism.

In Germany local union councils were more willing to make informal agreements with big companies that, while technically violating Germany's restrictive labor regulations, helped keep jobs in Germany. At the same time, some German-based multinational companies such as Volkswagen actively sought to head off trouble with German unions by agreeing to guidelines specifying how they would operate worldwide. By committing itself to offering its workers elsewhere proper pay and working conditions, as well as the right to unionize, Volkswagen was saying that it would not merely seek the lowest bidder, as globalization sometimes seemed to demand. In this respect, too, the unions were still making a difference.

ECONOMIC GROWTH AND ENVIRONMENTAL CONCERNS

The impact of rapid economic growth on the European landscape and cityscape provoked ever greater concern by the last third of the twentieth century. The number of automobiles in western Europe increased from 6 million in 1939 to 16 million by 1959 to 42 million by 1969. Almost overnight, traffic and air pollution fundamentally changed the face of Europe's old cities. In 1976 five statues that had supported the Eastern Portico of the Erectheum Temple on the Acropolis in Athens since the fifth century B.C. were replaced by replicas and put in a museum to save them from the rapid decay that air pollution was causing.

With the end of communist rule, it became obvious that the years of communism had produced environmental degradation on an appalling scale in the Soviet bloc. In the Soviet Union itself, the overproduction of cotton in central Asia, stemming from efforts to foster regional specialization, led to the desiccation of the Aral Sea, an ecological catastrophe. Even with the fall of communism, it was hard to break from the old, often polluting patterns because jobs and energy sources often depended on them. For years Ukraine could not afford to replace the remaining nuclear reactors at Chernobyl, despite safety and environmental risks that the 1986 accident had only worsened (see page 939). International aid finally enabled Ukraine to close the plant in 2000.

The greater affluence in western Europe made possible, and sometimes dictated, more creative responses to pollution and other environmental side effects of economic growth. Many cities adopted pedestrian-only zones to restrict automobile traffic, and some experimented with road-pricing measures in an effort to reduce traffic in central cities.

It was not only the urban environment that proved vulnerable to the byproducts of the new affluence. By the early 1980s acid rain had damaged one-third of the forests of West Germany, including the famous Black Forest of the southwest. Water pollution was a major problem from the Rhine to the Mediterranean to the Black Sea.

Differences in response to environmental concerns sometimes produced friction among Western countries or complicated the West's relations with the non-Western world. Especially symptomatic was the controversy over genetically altered foods, widely consumed in the United States since 1996. European concerns over safety led the EU to impose a moratorium on genetically modified products, including imports from the United States, in 1998. The United States considered the moratorium illegal under existing trade agreements and filed suit with the **World Trade Organization (WTO)** in 2003 to compel the EU to lift the moratorium.

In May 2003, on the eve of the annual G-8 meeting, U.S. president George W. Bush charged that European restrictions on genetically altered foods were undercutting efforts to provide food aid to Africa. The European example had led Africans to avoid investments in such crops. Moreover, some famine-ridden African countries

World Trade Organization (WTO)   Growing from a multilateral trade agreement in 1947, it sought, with mixed success, to promote freer trade throughout the world. By the early twenty-first century WTO meetings tended to draw demonstrations by anti-globalization activists.

had refused U.S. food aid because of European-induced concerns about safety. Partly at issue was the fear that genetically modified crops might infiltrate native crops and thereby jeopardize African exports to Europe. Americans countered that Europeans were using a bogus issue to help limit U.S. food exports to Europe—and hurting African development in the process.

The United States had joined the other industrialized nations in signing the Kyoto agreement of 1997, designed to limit emissions of the "greenhouse gases" widely held by scientists to be causing global warming, with potentially catastrophic consequences. But questioning the scientific evidence and citing concerns about economic growth, the United States pulled out of the agreement in 2001, causing much resentment in Europe and elsewhere. With 5 percent of the world's population, the United States was responsible for 25 percent of the world's greenhouse gas emissions per year.

Still, global warming was increasingly recognized, in the United States as elsewhere, as a serious issue that had to be addressed promptly. The question was what needed to be done, and how to muster the political will to do it. New technologies might make it possible to reduce the emissions in question without compromising living standards in the developed world—or the chance for growth in the less-developed world.

RELIGIOUS IDENTITIES

Whereas religious affiliation and church or synagogue attendance remained relatively stable in the United States, Europeans abandoned churches in droves after the mid-1950s. As church attendance dropped, popular culture revolved less around religious festivals and holy days. Moreover, in assuming responsibility for social welfare, European governments had gradually taken over much of the charitable role that the churches had long played.

Seeking to change with the times, the Catholic Church undertook a notable modernization effort under the popular Pope John XXIII (r. 1958–1963). But under his more conservative successors, the church became caught up in controversy, especially over issues such as abortion that women had forced to the fore. By the 1990s its conservative social policy had put the Catholic Church on the defensive. Still, the active, highly visible role of Pope John Paul II (r. 1978–2005) in a variety of spheres attracted widespread admiration. His death in 2005 led to an enormous outpouring of affection.

In such traditionally Catholic countries as France, Italy, and Spain, many people considered themselves "cultural Catholics" and ignored church rulings they found inappropriate, especially those concerning sexuality, marriage, and gender roles. In referenda in 1974 and 1981, two-thirds of Italians defied the Vatican by voting to legalize divorce and approve abortion rights.

Even in heavily Catholic Ireland, the electorate approved, though narrowly, the legalization of divorce in 1995, after having defeated it overwhelmingly in a referendum just nine years before.

When surveys showed that 80 percent of Spaniards considered themselves Catholic by the twenty-first century, even the cardinal-bishop of Madrid admitted that for many, "Catholic" was not a way of life but merely a label, perhaps linked to national identity. Other surveys showed that whereas in 1975, the year of the dictator Francisco Franco's death, 61 percent of Spaniards reported regular church attendance, that figure had dropped to 19 percent by the early twenty-first century. Even 46 percent of those calling themselves Catholic admitted that they almost never went to church.

A survey of church attendance in eleven western European countries in 1999–2000 found Spain somewhere in the middle, with 25 percent of the population saying they had been to church at least once a month. Ireland had the highest rate of attendance (58 percent), followed by Italy (about 40 percent). The lowest rates were in Denmark (3 percent) and Sweden (4 percent). Other surveys suggested that such self-responses probably doubled the actual rate of church attendance. While religious affiliations weakened in western Europe, the Russian Orthodox Church experienced a notable revival after the collapse of communism and the breakup of the Soviet Union.

In parts of the West, religious and ethnic identities blurred, sometimes enhancing the potential for conflict. Even after the breakup of the wider Soviet Union gave independence to the predominantly Muslim central Asian republics, the remaining Russian Federation included more than twenty million Muslims, or about 15 percent of the overall population. In both absolute numbers and percentage terms, this was the largest Muslim population in Europe. Included were those who identified themselves as Muslims in cultural terms even if they did not practice the Islamic religion.

A significant Islamic revival among Russian Muslims followed the collapse of communism, producing increasing friction with the central authorities. In 2002 the interior ministry banned women from wearing headscarves in photos for official documents. The Russian supreme court upheld the ban in response to an appeal by Islamic women that it violated Russia's constitutionally guaranteed freedom of religion. At the same time, the Russian army refused to allow Muslim services on military bases.

FAMILY LIFE AND GENDER ROLES

The new affluence significantly affected demographic patterns, partly because contraception became more readily available. Indeed, the advent of the birth control pill, widely obtainable by the late 1960s, fostered a

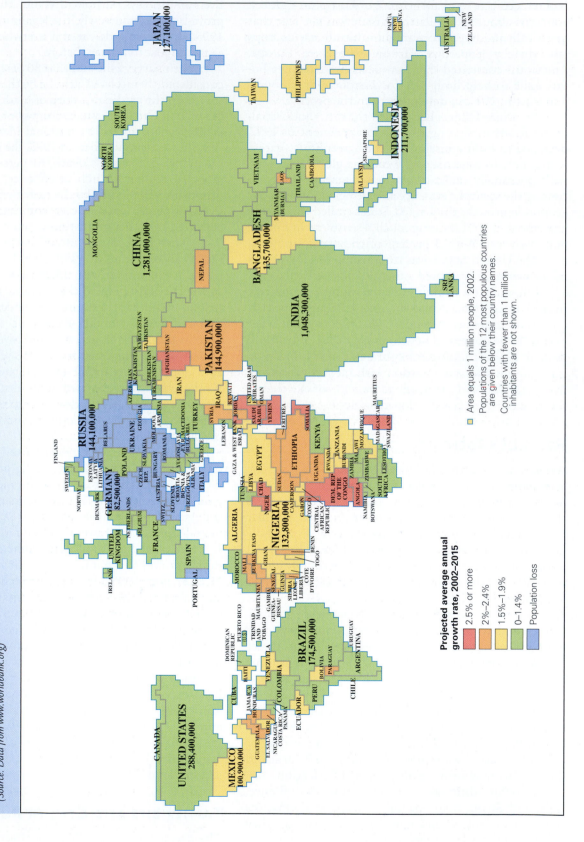

MAP 30.4 World Population Trends, 2002–2015

This map shows populations in 2002, as well as projected average annual growth rates from 2002 to 2015, in countries throughout the world. In the developed countries of the West, populations are relatively high but growing slowly, if at all. Most of the world's population growth is occurring in the less developed countries outside the West.

(*Source: Data from www.worldbank.org*)

Projected average annual growth rate, 2002–2015

2.5% or more
2%–2.4%
1.5%–1.9%
0–1.4%
Population loss

Area equals 1 million people, 2002.

Populations of the 12 most populous countries are given below their country names.

Countries with fewer than 1 million inhabitants are not shown.

sexual revolution that was central to the emerging secular lifestyle. At the same time, falling birthrates meant an aging population, and thus all the concerns about paying for the pensions and other welfare measures central to the postwar social compact.

In western Europe, as in the United States, a remarkable baby boom had followed the end of World War II and carried into the early 1960s. But the birthrate declined rapidly thereafter, so family size had diminished markedly by 1990. In Italy the number of births in 1987 was barely half the number in 1964, when the postwar baby boom reached its peak. Between 1993 and 2003, Italy's population increased by but 0.01 percent, to 57.5 million, and it was expected to shrink to 56 million by 2010. By 1995 the population was not sustaining itself in a number of European countries (see **Map 30.4**).

The feminist movement that had re-emerged in the late 1960s gradually expanded its focus beyond the quest for formal equality of opportunity. Examining subtle cultural obstacles to equality led feminists to the more general issue of gender—the way societies make sense of sexual difference and allocate social roles on that basis. By the late twentieth century, gender was central not only to public policy but also to private relationships and life choices in much of the Western world.

By the 1970s women sought measures such as government-subsidized day care that would enable them to combine paid employment with raising a family. At the same time, governments increasingly understood the value of policies to encourage both productive working parents and effective childhood development. Setting the pace was France, where the government began making quality day care available to all during the 1980s. Government subsidies kept costs within reach for ordinary working families. In addition, 95 percent of French children ages 3 to 6 were enrolled in the free public nursery schools available by the early 1990s. The figures for Italy (85 percent) and Germany (65 to 70 percent) were also relatively high, but Britain lagged behind (35 to 40 percent).

As some people saw it, the increasing reliance on child-care at once reflected and reinforced a decline in the socializing role of the traditional family. But the social changes at work were complex, and their longer-term implications for the well-being of parents, children, and society itself remained unclear. Some studies showed that an early day-care experience enhanced the socialization of children. Others cautioned against romanticizing the traditional nuclear family, which had been less prevalent than widely believed and not always successful in any case. Moreover, the responsibilities of parenting did not have to fall primarily on mothers. The biological difference in childbearing and nursing remained, however, and even committed feminists disagreed about whether parenting entailed a special role for women and, if so, about the policy implications that followed from it.

Although much remained contested or uncertain, the scope for greater sharing of parental responsibilities and the need for equal career opportunities across gender lines were widely recognized by the 1990s. The French model seemed to work well in combining child support with equal opportunity for paid employment. In simultaneously offering day care and allowances to concentrate on parenting, French government programs seemed to give French mothers a genuine choice as to whether to work outside the home. French family policy was widely popular; the key question by 2006 was whether France could afford it.

Also much at issue by the early twenty-first century were the rights of homosexual couples—to adopt children, for example, or to have their partnerships legally recognized as marriage. Whether married or not, were homosexual partners entitled to job benefits such as health care, which often were available to heterosexual couples?

The interrelationship of family, gender, sexuality, and personal self-realization, never static, was evolving in new ways—a crucial aspect of the ongoing experiment in the West.

= S E C T I O N   S U M M A R Y =

- The advent of a consumer society, increasingly on a global level, affected national, supranational, and subnational identities in complex, often unforeseen ways.

- The de-emphasis on class and class distinction as a basis of identity contributed to the decline of the trade-union movement.

- Economic growth seemed to have adverse effects on the environment, though there was disagreement over how best to respond.

- In the face of pressures toward secularization, the strength of religious identities varied considerably from country to country throughout the West.

- Affluence led to new ways of conceiving gender roles and family life.

NELSON MANDELA AND THE UNIVERSALITY OF HUMAN VALUES

For all the admiration that continued to surround those who had helped undermine Soviet-style communism, the most revered person in the West and the world at the beginning of the twenty-first century was surely the black South African Nelson Mandela (b. 1918). As a militant in the African National Congress, which was seeking to overcome the brutally segregationist apartheid system in South Africa, he spent twenty-seven years in prison. He was released in 1990 as part of a wider amnesty granted by South Africa's new president, F. W. De Klerk (b. 1936). Responding to international pressures, including effective trade sanctions, De Klerk wanted Mandela's help in restructuring the South African system. The two were central to the ensuing negotiations that repealed apartheid and began the transition to a nonracial democracy in South Africa. When the first elections were held under the new system in 1994, Mandela was elected president of South Africa. In this passage from the conclusion to his autobiography, he articulates the idealism that inspired his remarkable achievement and made him a symbol of shared human values to Westerners and non-Westerners alike.

On the day of the inauguration, I was overwhelmed with a sense of history. In the first decade of the twentieth century, a few years after the bitter Anglo-Boer War and before my own birth, the white-skinned peoples of South Africa patched up their differences and erected a system of racial domination against the dark-skinned peoples of their own land. The structure they created formed the basis of one of the harshest, most inhumane societies the world has ever known. Now, in the last decade of the twentieth century, and my own eighth decade as a man, that system had been overturned forever and replaced by one that recognized the rights and freedoms of all peoples regardless of the color of their skin.

That day had come about through the unimaginable sacrifices of thousands of my people, people whose suffering and courage can never be counted or repaid. I felt that day, as I have on so many other days, that I was simply the sum of all those African patriots who had gone before me. That long and noble line ended and now began again with me. I was pained that I was not able to thank them and that they were not able to see what their sacrifices had wrought. . . .

I never lost hope that this great transformation would occur. Not only because of the great heroes I have already cited, but because of the courage of the ordinary men and women of my country. I always knew that deep down in every human heart, there is mercy and generosity. No one is born hating another person because of the color of his skin, or his background, or his religion. People must learn to hate, and if they can learn to hate, they can be taught to love, for love comes more naturally to the human heart than its opposite. Even in the grimmest times in prison, when my comrades and I were pushed to our limits, I would see a glimmer of humanity in one of the guards, perhaps just for a second, but it was enough to reassure me and keep me going. . . .

I was not born with a hunger to be free. I was born free—free in every way that I could know. . . .

But then I slowly saw that not only was I not free, but my brothers and sisters were not free. I saw that it

THE WEST IN A GLOBAL AGE

What questions emerged as the West faced new crises all over the globe after the end of the cold war?

By the early twenty-first century, the West was part of a world that was, in one sense, dramatically less Eurocentric than it had been a century before, when European imperialism was at its peak. Events in the West competed for attention with OPEC oil prices, Chinese trade practices, and Iran's nuclear program. Decisions vitally affecting, or demanding the response of, the industrialized countries of the West might be made anywhere. Just as capital and information flowed more quickly than ever across national borders, so could epidemic diseases emerging in some distant forest or jungle. This was the reverse side of the new interconnectedness of a global world. A planetary culture, a threatened environment, an interdependent economy, and an increasing sense of international responsibility required people to think in global terms as never before. (See the box "The Global Record: Nelson Mandela and the Universality of Human Values.")

was not just my freedom that was curtailed, but the freedom of everyone who looked like I did. That is when I joined the African National Congress, and that is when the hunger for my own freedom became the greater hunger for the freedom of my people. It was this desire for the freedom of my people to live their lives with dignity and self-respect that animated my life, that transformed a frightened young man into a bold one, that drove a law-abiding attorney to become a criminal, that turned a family-loving husband into a man without a home, that forced a life-loving man to live like a monk. I am no more virtuous or self-sacrificing than the next man, but I found that I could not even enjoy the poor and limited freedoms I was allowed when I knew my people were not free. Freedom is indivisible; the chains on any one of my people were the chains on all of them, the chains on all of my people were the chains on me.

It was during those long and lonely years that my hunger for the freedom of my own people became a hunger for the freedom of all people, white and black. I knew as well as I knew anything that the oppressor must be liberated just as surely as the oppressed. A man who takes away another man's freedom is a prisoner of hatred, he is locked behind the bars of prejudice and narrow-mindedness. I am not truly free if I am taking away someone else's freedom, just as surely as I am not free when my freedom is taken from me. The oppressed and the oppressor alike are robbed of their humanity.

When I walked out of prison, that was my mission, to liberate the oppressed and the oppressor both. Some say that has now been achieved. But I know that that is not the case. The truth is that we are not yet free; we have merely achieved the freedom to be free, the right not to be oppressed. We have not taken the final step of our journey, but the first step on a longer and even more difficult road. For to be free is not merely to cast off one's chains, but to live in a way that respects and enhances the freedom of others. The true test of our devotion to freedom is just beginning.

. . . After climbing a great hill, one only finds that there are many more hills to climb. I have taken a moment here to rest, to steal a view of the glorious vista that surrounds me, to look back on the distance I have come. But I can rest only for a moment, for with freedom comes responsibilities, and I dare not linger, for my long walk is not yet ended.

QUESTIONS

1. In what sense is Mandela appealing to human values, as opposed to the values or special circumstances of a particular group?

2. Why does Mandela suggest that the struggle for freedom is essentially endless?

Source: Long Walk to Freedom by Nelson Mandela, pp. 541–544. Copyright © 1994 by Nelson Rolihlahla Mandela. Reprinted by permission of Little, Brown and Company (Inc.).

UNIFORMITY AND DIVERSITY IN THE "GLOBAL VILLAGE"

By the last decades of the twentieth century, a kind of global culture began to emerge for the first time. Indeed, talk of a single "global village" became commonplace. But just as "Americanization" produced concerns about preserving distinctiveness elsewhere in the West, "globalization" produced comparable concerns on a global level. Although the process promised a better life for many people in less developed countries, valuable diversity was seemingly being lost in an ever more uniform world. For instance, half of the world's 6,500 languages were expected to disappear during the twenty-first century.

Skyscrapers in booming Asian cities looked much like skyscrapers in the West. Indeed, they were often designed by the same architects. Businessmen in conservative Western dress made postwar Japan the world's second-largest economy. American firms transferred billing and even customer service operations to lower-cost India, even as India was becoming a major player in computer technology. "Americanization" made products such as Coca-Cola and McDonald's burgers familiar not just in Europe but worldwide. Especially among urban youth, a common style emerged that owed much to American popular culture. Meanwhile, for everyone from scientists to business leaders to airline pilots, English became the common language.

At work, however, was not simply Western or American cultural imperialism. What resulted in many spheres, from food to popular music, was not homogenization but a more complex kind of fusion, as elements from diverse cultures interpenetrated and enriched one another while retaining distinctive features. The British tourist board declared Indian curry to be the official British dish, testimony to the number of Indian restaurants in Britain—itself testimony to the enduring cultural impact of the Indian heritage on Britain.

Even multinational media conglomerates increasingly accented local content. When Viacom launched MTV in the 1980s, the producers assumed that since the pop music culture was universal, a single channel would succeed everywhere. But it quickly became evident that success required local variation. Between 2001 and 2003, MTV launched fourteen new channels, for a total of thirty-eight around the world. Each was tailored to local tastes, with no emphasis on an American link. One MTV executive observed, "we don't even call it an adaptation of American content: it's local content creation. . . . The American thing is irrelevant."[3] So whereas the advent of MTV had initially seemed to entail overt cultural imperialism, the program's evolution manifested—and contributed to—the more complex global cross-fertilization in process.

THE "NORTH-SOUTH" DIVIDE AND MUTUAL INTERDEPENDENCE

Beginning especially in the 1970s, western Europe and North America encountered formidable economic competition first from Japan and then from other countries of the East Asian Pacific rim. What increasingly mattered, as globalization proceeded, was the difference between the industrialized, relatively affluent "North" and the less developed "South," including much of Africa and Latin America, southern Asia, and the Middle East. Indeed, "North-South" tensions, resulting from demographic and economic patterns, quickly moved to center stage to replace the East-West tensions that had ended with the cold war. World population reached six billion in 1999, having doubled since 1960. This was the fastest rate of world population growth ever, and by the 1990s virtually all of that growth was in Africa, Asia, and Latin America (see Map 30.4).

As the population exploded in the less developed world, the gap between rich and poor nations widened. One aspect of this process, producing much concern by the early twenty-first century, was the growing **digital divide**—the disparity in access to the computing and Internet technologies that seemed essential to compete in the global economy. New technologies were not bridging, but rather widening, the gap between the richer and poorer nations of the world.

The West recognized some responsibility to assist economic development in the developing world, but individual countries differed considerably in the ways they claimed to be doing so. Whereas most Americans assumed that they led the world in foreign aid, the United States, among the twenty-one richest countries, actually devoted the smallest percentage of its overall economy to direct foreign aid as of 2002. The most generous countries—Denmark, Norway, and the Netherlands—gave almost seven times as much. But such direct aid was only one measure of the ways the developed world might assist development elsewhere. Also important were direct investment, trade policy, and a willingness to accept immigrants, who often sent money back to their countries of origin, thereby providing essential foreign exchange. As the least protectionist of the wealthy nations, the United States was most helpful on trade because its markets were more open to products from developing countries.

Growing concern about the environment intensified the sense of global interdependence and pointed to the need for international cooperation. Problems such as global warming, the loss of biodiversity, and the deterioration of the ozone layer were inherently supranational in scope. Yet environmental concerns also complicated relations between the industrialized nations and the rest of the world. Countries seeking to industrialize encountered environmental constraints that had not been at issue when the West industrialized. The challenge for the West was to foster protection of the environment in poorer regions of the globe without imposing unfair limitations on economic growth.

Also bringing home mutual interdependence was the rapid spread of disease with the intensification of contacts around the world. Moreover, there was evidence that new diseases were emerging more frequently as the world grew more crowded. The human population intruded into previously untouched jungles and forests, intensifying interaction among species that had formerly remained largely separated. The crowding of animals for food production also fed the genesis and spread of new diseases.

AIDS (acquired immune deficiency syndrome), a sexually transmitted disease caused by the HIV virus, had apparently spread from chimpanzees to humans in Africa earlier in the twentieth century, although it began to be recognized only in the late 1970s. It then spread throughout the world beginning in the 1980s. Particularly devastating in Africa, AIDS remained a major concern in the early twenty-first century.

In the late 1990s, West Nile virus and monkey pox appeared at almost the same time. SARS (severe acute

digital divide A term for the disparity in access to the computing and Internet technologies that seemed essential to compete in the twenty-first-century global economy.

respiratory syndrome), a highly contagious and often fatal disease, was first reported in southern China in 2003, apparently contracted by a human being from a civet cat. The disease reached epidemic proportions in some areas of China and was carried elsewhere by travelers. The fact that Toronto, one of the most successful North American cities, was especially hard hit made clear the wider vulnerability of the West in this age of rapid transport and communication.

By 2006, there was much concern with "bird flu," a new strain of influenza virus first identified in Hong Kong in 1997. Cases involving humans were rare; as of early 2006, 170 people had been infected, of whom 92 had died. But this was an especially dangerous strain that might mutate further to facilitate the jump from birds to human populations. It might then produce a pandemic to rival the so-called Spanish flu, which killed perhaps forty million people in 1918 and 1919 (see page 790).

Seemingly under control at first, bird flu was eventually spread by migratory birds to southeast Asia and from there westward, reaching Turkey, then Africa and western Europe. When, in France in 2006, it infected a European poultry farm for the first time, 43 countries promptly banned the import of French poultry and foie gras, to the dismay of French producers. Officials of the UN's World Health Organization (WHO) stressed that they lacked the global infrastructure to head off the sort of pandemic that could develop.

THE CONTROVERSY OVER ECONOMIC GLOBALIZATION

Although many forces fed globalization, arguably the most potent, and increasingly controversial, was international capitalism itself. The capitalist ideal of free and open markets sounded appealing, and economic models, based on comparative advantage, could explain how everybody wins through expanded international economic exchange. The world economy was not a zero-sum game. But whatever the virtues of free global markets in principle, experience showed globalization to be a multi-edged sword, producing complex, often-contradictory results.

Indeed, globalization bred increasingly vocal opposition, fueled by concerns over fairness, exploitation, and the "Americanization" of the world. Critics charged that globalization was not helping the poorer nations to catch up, as theory would have it, but leaving them ever further behind. Meetings of the G-8 proved prominent targets of opposition, but at least as important was the network of supranational agencies, starting with the World Bank and the International Monetary Fund (IMF), that had developed from the Bretton Woods Agreement near the end of World War II (see page 898). Also central, especially in promoting free trade, was the World Trade Organization (WTO), which grew from a multilateral trade agreement in 1947.

These organizations had long drawn praise for helping to keep the world economy stable and growing. By the late 1990s, however, they had come to constitute a focal point for the growing concerns about accelerating economic globalization.

Meetings of the WTO in Seattle in 1999 and of the World Bank and IMF in Washington, D.C., in 2000 drew large demonstrations. Riots accompanied G-8 meetings in 2001 and 2003. Those protesting were often naive about economics and the benefits of free trade. But their protests raised significant questions about wages, working conditions, environmental impact, and international financial arrangements that were not always adequately addressed in the prevailing economic models. Most fundamentally at issue was whether it made sense to foster free trade and globalization without greater consistency in social and environmental policy. In the absence of common standards, free trade was not likely to be fair trade. The challenge was to find some balance between free trade and regulation within an increasingly global economy.

Heading Off Disease

As "bird flu" was becoming a major international concern, the disease struck a turkey farm in the Ain region in southeastern France, prompting many foreign countries to suspend French poultry imports. The French responded quickly. Here a veterinarian vaccinates a duck at a poultry farm in Horsarrieu, in southwestern France, on March 6, 2006. *(AP/Wide World Photos)*

In September 2003 the WTO meeting in Cancún, Mexico, broke up amid much bitterness. A group of twenty-one poorer nations, led by Brazil, India, and China, walked out, accusing the United States and the EU of hypocrisy in calling for freer trade while still subsidizing their own farmers. By helping the richer countries export agricultural products at lower prices, such subsidies made it harder for poorer countries to develop their own crops and to sell them to the richer countries. West African cotton farmers suffered as the United States spent more than $3 billion a year on subsidies to 25,000 U.S. cotton growers, helping to make the United States the world's largest cotton exporter and depressing cotton prices worldwide. The United States claimed to be eager to cut farm subsidies, but only as part of a more systematic reduction that would also involve Japan and the EU, which was devoting 40 percent of its budget to such subsidies.

THE QUESTION OF GLOBAL RESPONSIBILITY

If people were forced to think in global terms as never before, how far did global responsibility extend in a world that remained divided into sovereign nation-states? The series of brutal, sometimes genocidal conflicts from Yugoslavia to Rwanda to Liberia that marked the post–cold war period fostered a growing sense of collective responsibility on the part of what was increasingly called "the international community." Amorphous though it was, that entity seemed to take on real existence by the end of the 1990s. But who or what constituted "the international community" and the conditions under which it should act remained uncertain.

Of course, a prominent international organization was already in place—the United Nations, the fruit of the hopes for a better world in light of World War II. By the 1990s no one denied that it had achieved significant successes in areas such as nutrition, health, and education. Kofi Annan (b. 1938) of Ghana, who became its secretary-general in 1997, was highly regarded worldwide. Indeed, he, together with the UN itself, was awarded the Nobel Peace Prize in 2001. But scandals surrounding the implementation of the UN's "oil-for-food" program in Iraq partly discredited the UN, especially among those skeptical about it in the first place. This program was initiated in 1996 to diminish the suffering of ordinary Iraqis in the wake of sanctions imposed on Iraq after its invasion of Kuwait in 1990. An exhaustive independent report made it clear that whereas the program had achieved considerable success, even saving lives, it had suffered from mismanagement and corruption. As an organization of 191 member states with diffuse lines of authority, the UN was simply not equipped to run so complicated a program without mishap.

More generally, UN forces were often overburdened as they took on the often-incompatible objectives of peacekeeping and humanitarian relief—sometimes in areas where there was no real peace to keep. And the organization's members, especially its leaders on the Security Council, were frequently divided about what should be done. The need to seem impartial sometimes paralyzed UN peacekeepers. In July 1995 four hundred Dutch troops failed to prevent the massacre of more than 7,000 Muslim men and boys in a UN "safe area" around Srebrenica, in Bosnia. But the UN Security Council had not allocated enough troops or weapons to protect the victims in any case, despite the secretary-general's pleas for additional resources.

Still, the UN was a visible presence even as concerns for national sovereignty compromised its ability to act. UN inspectors assumed the burden of policing Iraqi compliance with the peace that followed the Persian Gulf War of 1991. After ad hoc UN war crimes tribunals began dealing with the atrocities that had taken place in the Balkans and Rwanda, the UN established its permanent International Criminal Court (ICC) in The Hague in 1998. Its charge was to bring to justice those responsible for war crimes or crimes against humanity. And the UN was sufficiently credible that, for many people throughout the world, the lack of UN sanction undermined the legitimacy of the U.S.-led invasion and occupation of Iraq.

Whatever its center of gravity, the international community rested on the commitment and initiative of the rich Western countries, because only they had the means to act globally in response to natural or human-made disasters. Supplementing the efforts of governments was a network of **nongovernmental organizations (NGOs),** such as the Red Cross, Amnesty International, and Doctors Without Borders, that had emerged over the years to deal with humanitarian relief or human rights issues. Collectively they were a major presence on the international scene by the early twenty-first century and central to the international community.

But those seeking to provide aid or maintain peace were often forced to deal with semicriminal elements who diverted humanitarian aid to buy weapons or who took peacekeepers and aid workers hostage—or even killed them. In 1994, for the first time, more UN civilian aid workers (twenty-four) than peacekeeping soldiers were killed in the line of duty. And the death toll for aid workers rose rapidly during the decade.

The conflicts that developed in hot spots around the world after the cold war spawned an increasing sense that it was up to the Western-led international community to "do something." But do what—and at

nongovernmental organizations (NGOs)
Private, independent organizations designed to deal with humanitarian relief and human rights issues. Though unaffiliated with governments or the United Nations, they became central to the international community.

THE WRITTEN RECORD

THE QUESTION OF WESTERN RESPONSIBILITY

The end of the cold war helped open the way to ethnic conflict, terrorism, and, in some areas, the breakdown of government as violent warlords fought for control. With the world more interconnected than ever before, it was increasingly assumed that "the international community," spearheaded by the rich countries of the West, ought to respond to tragedy anywhere. But quite apart from the difficult questions of leadership and coordination, it was not clear what level of risk, and expense, the West was prepared to assume. In the following excerpt, Brian Urquhart, born in Britain in 1919 and long a senior official of the United Nations, offers a pointed analysis of the issues that came to the fore as the West experimented with a more active response to tragedies around the world.

What is to be done when hundreds of thousands of people in a hitherto little-known region of the world are hounded from their homes, massacred, or starved to death in a brutal civil war, or even in a deliberate act of genocide? To our credit, we no longer turn away from the face of evil, but we still don't know how to control it. As the new century dawns, one of the biggest problems for international organizations and their member governments is to learn how to react to the great human emergencies that still seem to occur regularly in many parts of the world. . . .

The so-called "international community" is anything but a constitutional system. As far as it is organized at all, it is an institutional arrangement, unpredictable and slow to act. It usually responds only when disaster has already struck and when its members, usually in the UN Security Council, can agree to take action. Even then, since the UN has no standing forces or substantial resources of its own, its action, if it can be agreed upon, is likely to be too little and too late.

In his opening address to the General Assembly on September 20, 1999, Secretary-General Kofi Annan made an impassioned plea for UN intervention in cases of gross violations of human rights. The reactions of governments to Annan's remarks showed very clearly how far the world still has to go before evil can be systematically dealt with internationally. Most comments on Annan's speech were critical and stressed the paramount importance of national sovereignty; some even saw humanitarian intervention as a cloak for American or Western hegemony or neo-colonialism. Only a small minority of Western countries supported Sweden's position that the collective conscience of mankind demands action.

A new idea of "human security" has now taken its place alongside the much older concept of "international peace and security." It has emerged as the result of a vaguely defined and fitful international conscience on the part of the liberal democracies, and it has been encouraged both by the prodigious growth of nongovernmental organizations and by the communications revolution. However, the rules and the means for protecting human security are still tentative and controversial, not least because virtually any situation threatening human security is likely to raise questions of national sovereignty. No government wants to set up a system which may, at some point in the future, be invoked against itself.

. . . Humanitarian action as it emerged in the aftermath of World War II was principally concerned with refugee resettlement and the reconstruction of war-shattered countries. In those innocent days, humanitarian relief was seen as a nonpolitical activity, dictated by the needs of the afflicted and by the resources and expertise available to meet them. . . . That relatively nonpolitical concept of humanitarianism has come to a brutal end with the rising importance of warlords and the conflicts within states of the post–cold war world. The international sponsors of humanitarian aid are no longer dealing with more or less responsible governments. . . .

. . . "The whole aid community has been overtaken by a new reality," the IRC [International Rescue Committee] stated. "Humanitarianism has become a resource . . . and people are manipulating it as never before. Sometimes we just shouldn't show up for a disaster." . . .

QUESTIONS

1. Why did the West find it so difficult to respond to the sorts of disasters that came to the fore after the cold war?
2. Why did even humanitarian aid come to seem increasingly ineffective under certain circumstances?

Source: "In the Name of Humanity" by Brian Urquhart, *The New York Review of Books,* April 27, 2000, pp. 19–21. Reprinted with permission from *The New York Review of Books.* Copyright © 2000 NYREV, Inc.

what cost? What aims were realistic? During the first decade of the new century the international community was widely called upon to end the apparent ongoing genocide in the Darfur region of Sudan. But there was no consensus on what degree of response was appropriate or on how it should be coordinated. (See the box "The Written Record: The Question of Western Responsibility.")

- Although globalization meant cultural homogeneity in one sense, it also produced unforeseen forms of cultural fusion and a deeper appreciation of cultural diversity.

- New diseases dramatized global interdependence even as the gap between the rich countries of the "North" and many of the poorer countries of the "South" seemed to widen.

- Economic globalization produced a backlash, often targeting multinational entities like the World Trade Organization, on the grounds that free trade was too often exploitative and unfair.

- Even as it increasingly felt responsible for dealing with disasters around the world, the West, leading "the international community," was often unsure how best to respond.

QUESTIONING THE MEANING OF THE WEST

On what basis was the wider contemporary relevance of "Western civilization" being debated by the first decade of the twenty-first century?

Although in one sense "globalization" meant "Westernization" to advocates and critics alike, its accelerating pace bred deeper uncertainty about what was specifically Western—about the meaning and value of the Western tradition. During the cold war, the West had offered two competing visions to the world. But with the fall of communism, one of them stood discredited, and democratic capitalism emerged the clear winner. As the end of the cold war also ended the division of Europe and removed the common adversary, the ties that had helped bind western Europe to the United States loosened. Indeed, the need to respond both to the challenges of the competitive global economy and to the increasingly volatile international environment occasioned friction and fragmentation within the West.

CULTURAL DIFFERENCES WITHIN THE WEST

Even on the cultural level, differences between Europeans and Americans seemed to be deepening by the early twenty-first century. As a corollary of religious differences between the two, the United States experienced periodic controversy over the teaching of Darwinian evolution in the public schools—controversy that would have been unthinkable in Europe. In the same way, homosexuality and abortion continued to stir greater controversy in America than they did in most of Europe.

In light of the disruptions and disasters of the twentieth century, the place of history became especially problematic in Europe. At the same time, the radical transformation in the half century since World War II in some ways cut Europeans off from their own traditions. The uneasy contemporary relationship with the past, especially the traumatic past of the earlier twentieth century, took especially pointed form in the neo-expressionist painting prominent in Germany and Italy by the late twentieth century.

For a generation after World War II European artists, unsure of their direction, had tended to follow the lead of New York. But by the late 1960s, the new generation that included such artists as the German Anselm Kiefer (b. 1945) and the Italian Sandro Chia (KEE-ah) (b. 1946) sought to confront the recent past—and thus the meaning of a tradition that now included fascism, total war, and the Holocaust. What did it mean to be German, Italian, or even European in light of this difficult past and the globalizing present and future? Wrestling with the interface of recent history and national identity, Kiefer and Chia conveyed the paradox and ambiguity that many felt as the rapidly changing West encountered the layers of its own cultural tradition.

The ongoing effort to come to terms with the recent past produced controversy and sometimes seemed to open old wounds, as earlier fascist or communist sympathies came under scrutiny. In Italy and France questions about collaboration and resistance during World War II produced periodic waves of bitterness. Even how to remember and commemorate the Holocaust produced much dispute, although Berlin's Holocaust memorial, opened in 2005, was one prominent indication of the widespread agreement that some such remembrance and commemoration was essential.

Kiefer: Osiris and Isis

The German artist Anselm Kiefer combined unusual materials to create haunting images that often suggested the horrors of recent history. In this work, dated 1985–1987, the interpenetrating layers of human culture include images of ruin and death, hope and resurrection.   *(Anselm Kiefer,* Osiris und Isis, *1985–1987. Mixed media on canvas, 150" × 220½" × 6½". San Francisco Museum of Modern Art. Purchased through a gift of Jean Stein by exchange, the Mrs. Paul L. Wattis Fund, and the Doris and Don Fisher Fund. Photo: Ben Blackwell)*

COMMON VALUES AND THE PARADOX OF PLURALISM

The West was surely more willing than some of the non-Western world to embrace the messy, inconclusive openness, the ongoing give-and-take, associated with freedom of speech and freedom of religion. But did Western approaches enjoy some universal sanction, or was Western pluralism—including the right to religious freedom, even the right to ridicule someone else's religion—itself merely one value in a wider global pluralism?

Some observers noted that democracy rested on such rights, with the scope for diversity and the implication of tolerance that they implied. But arguably that notion was relevant only to the rules *within* democratic, pluralistic societies. It was surely symptomatic that the Netherlands and Denmark, as prominent examples of such societies, took extraordinary steps to establish that membership in their democratic societies required acceptance of precisely the messy, inconclusive openness that some outside the West found objectionable. But what expectations and even rules were required for a genuinely democratic society was only "half" the question. Was the West to take a further step and say to non-Western countries that Western-style pluralism was the ultimate value? Was Western democracy, revolving around "human rights," the one-size-fits-all model for the world, even to be imposed by force under certain circumstances?

To be sure, the UN convention on human rights was at least nominally accepted around the world. And non-Western figures from Mohandas Gandhi to Nelson

THE VISUAL RECORD

Postmodern Architecture

Three building complexes, one by an Italian working in Japan, another by an American working in Germany, and a third by a Spaniard working in Spain: they look dramatically different, yet they were built at roughly the same time. Do they have anything in common? In fact, each was rejecting earlier "modern" architecture, and each expressed what came to be known as "postmodernism" by the last two decades of the twentieth century.

Modernism in architecture, design, and urban planning had emerged especially during the 1920s from sources like the German Bauhaus, which turned resolutely from tradition to embrace the modern industrial age (see page 832). During the first two decades after World War II, this modernist approach triumphed at last, transforming cities throughout the world. Now known as "the international style," it reflected the wider self-understanding of the modern world, centered in the West. "Modern" meant rationality and efficiency, clarity and regularity, machine precision and mass culture. Ornament, decoration, symbolism, and historical reference had little or no place.

At issue, in fact, was not just a particular style of building but a new relationship with history. As modern, we seemed to be living on the cutting edge of history, in the eternal present, endlessly being cut off from our past. Henry Ford, widely taken as the personification of modernity in his time, put the matter directly: "History is bunk."

But by the 1960s, a reaction began to develop in architecture and urban planning, reflecting deeper thinking about history, about what it meant to be modern, and about the contemporary relationship with cultural traditions, including older buildings. In 1977 the architectural critic Charles Jencks, in his book *The Language of Post-Modern Architecture,* used the term "post-modernism" to characterize what now seemed to be a new movement or direction.

The earlier notion of modernity was coming to seem dubious in an emerging world of global interchange and plural perspectives. Memory, history, and the presence of the past were more, not less, important as accelerating technological change made possible instant communication and constant access to information across the globe. Yet there was sometimes irony, uncertainty, or paradox in the coexistence of old and new.

Postmodernist architects did not merely reject the earlier modernism, and certainly their aim was

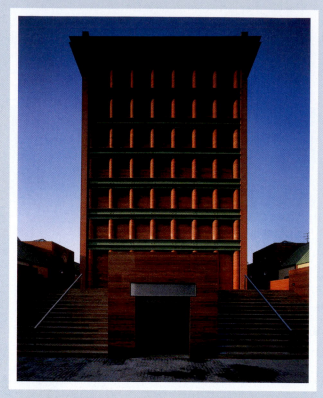

Aldo Rossi: Il Palazzo Hotel, Fukuoka, Japan
(Courtesy, Nacasa & Partners, Inc.)

not simply to revive previous styles such as classical or Gothic, though elements of them, as embodiments of our living history, might be incorporated in postmodern buildings. For example, look at the photo above of the Palazzo Hotel, designed by the Italian Aldo Rossi (1931–1997). Set in a Japanese city, the hotel clearly recalls Italian buildings, even those of the fascist period, themselves ambiguously modern, with references to the classical tradition and especially ancient Rome. For the façade, constructed of red marble and brick crossed with green steel moldings, Rossi combined contrasting materials, uncertain scale, and historical reference in a striking, even uncanny way.

Moreover, postmodernist architects were just as committed to modern techniques and materials as the modernists. They reacted, however, against the modernist pretense of a single right way, the rejection of ornament and history, and the reduction of architecture to function and the logic of machines. Postmodernists did not simply accept but actively celebrated messiness, variety, mixture, and complexity. The American Frank Gehry (b. 1929) suggested impermanence as well as postmodern pluralism in

Frank Gehry: Der Neue Zollhof
(The New Customs House),
Düsseldorf, Germany
(*Thomas Mayer, photographer*)

Santiago Calatrava: City of Arts
and Sciences, Valencia, Spain
(*Barbara Burg and Oliver Schuh, Palladium
Photodesign, Cologne, Germany*)

his complex of three office buildings in Düsseldorf, Germany (above left). Notice how the project incorporates modernist elements—flat roofs, identical prefabricated windows—but provides remarkable variety and contrast by cladding one of the units in red brick, one in mirror-polished stainless steel, and the third in white plaster. At the same time, the uniform, angled windows contrast with the curved surfaces. None of the three is the right way; rather, they play evocatively against one another.

Santiago Calatrava (b. 1951) drew on an even wider frame of reference to create shapes that were never before part of our built environment. Calatrava used highly sculptured forms for the building shown here (above right)—the centerpiece of a science museum complex built in the bed of a diverted river in his native Valencia, Spain. Taking advantage of his engineering background, he created unexpected spaces and sculptural surfaces that went beyond tradition altogether. With structures suggesting bones and tendons, he conveyed the dynamics of movement, of folding, opening, and closing—even the opening and closing of an eye.

Dramatically different though they appear, these three architectural statements share the wider postmodern framework. Rossi invokes the past to resist change; Gehry plays with the past, even the recent modernist past, while suggesting impermanence; Calatrava transcends the present outcome of the past, but without the limitations, the particular discipline, that modernism imposed. Rather than submit to the logic of the machine, he felt free to experiment more boldly, devising radically new forms. Each of the three architects represents a strand in the wider, complex, and contradictory postmodernist approach to history and tradition, including the tradition of modernism itself.

QUESTIONS

1. In what sense are the buildings we see here recognizably *post*-modern, in the sense of consciously rejecting earlier modernist tenets?

2. How do Rossi, Gehry, and Calatrava differ in their approach to change and history?

Online Study Center
Improve Your Grade Visual Record Activities

Mandela were widely admired in the West, precisely as spokesmen for what seemed universal human values. But the UN human rights convention was engineered by the dominant powers under the very particular circumstances surrounding the end of World War II. Were freedom of speech, freedom of religion, and equality for women to be understood as genuinely universal "human rights," even if parts of the world had difficulty grasping them? Or was there a place for genuine cultural diversity on the global level, including, for example, the differential handling of gender relations and religious freedom?

Although they were contested even then, these issues seemed less troubling to the Western world a century before. The West set the standard, and spearheading "Westernization" even seemed a moral duty. But the events of the tumultuous century that followed shook the West's self-confidence. Reflecting on what seemed the special European or Western path "from Athens to Auschwitz," the noted German classicist Christian Meier insisted that the Holocaust marked the end of the notion that European civilization had a special role to play, even that Europe could understand itself in terms of a continuous and unified history.[4]

Yet even if the West had long since abandoned "the white man's burden" in its late nineteenth century forms, it was hardly prepared to embrace the mode of multiculturalism that meant a thoroughgoing cultural relativism, the notion that you have your practices and I have mine, that we live and let live and learn to appreciate and even celebrate the differences. On the contrary, the West held to the notion that ideals and institutions most fully developed in the West—democracy, human rights, notions of equality—are not only relevant for the West but somehow of universal value. The West still claimed to have a privileged template that enabled it to assess the practices—and the progress—of everybody else.

The question was where lines were to be drawn. Westerners of goodwill differed, for example, over the Muslim headscarf issue in France. Most defenders of the right to wear the headscarf in public schools were not claiming to discern some hidden wisdom in the traditional Islamic handling of gender; rather, they were insisting on the right to individual self-expression. The choice of women to wear the headscarf deserved respect—as, say, the disproportionate abortion of female fetuses in India did not. Pluralism and the embrace of diversity had their limits, even if there was disagreement over where lines should be drawn.

Arguably what distinguished the West at that point was precisely the growing recognition that some measure of such disagreement was inevitable, legitimate, and even healthy. During the first decade of the twenty-first century, the West was wrestling with matters of humanity and diversity, human rights and national

sovereignty, as never before. Whereas "the West" had always been a continuing experiment, that experiment would now continue in a more self-conscious way.

WESTERN CIVILIZATION IN A POSTMODERN WORLD

By the end of the twentieth century, bitter debate had raged in the West for two decades and more over the legitimacy of "Western civilization" as a concept. Some critics highlighted the geographical imprecision of "the West" and claimed that the words *Western* and *civilization* had been juxtaposed simply to justify conquest and domination. Even among those who recognized a distinctive Western cultural tradition, some found it elitist and limiting. In their view, Western culture had defined itself around a group of artifacts—writings, paintings, monuments—that reflected the experience of a very restricted circle.

Others countered that imperialism and assumptions of superiority had not been confined to the West. Moreover, they continued, the West had been the source of ideas—the "rights of man," the scope for eliminating exploitation—that were now being eagerly embraced in the non-Western world. Even the charges of cultural elitism directed against the Western tradition stemmed from a democratic impulse that had itself grown from within that Western tradition. And by the last decades of the twentieth century, that impulse had prompted historians to focus on ordinary people and a far wider circle of cultural interpreters, thereby dramatically expanding the "canon"—the body of works considered worthy of our attention.

Questions about the Western tradition and its contemporary relevance were bound up with the advent of *postmodernism,* a term widely used by the early 1990s for a cultural orientation that had been gathering force for decades. (See the feature "The Visual Record: Postmodern Architecture.") Postmodernism reflected a certain conception of what *modernism* had meant, even a sense that modernism had defined an era that was ending. But what was ending—and how it was bound up with the debate over Western civilization—was not so clear.

Postmodernism emerged partly as confidence in the scope for a neutral, objective social science began to decline during the 1960s. That confidence had reflected the belief in reason that had emerged from the Scientific Revolution and the Enlightenment. Reason had seemed universal, not limited to any particular culture, and it was assumed to be applicable to the human as well as the natural world.

To apply reason seemed "modern," and the West, apparently having progressed by applying reason, had long understood itself to be in the forefront of modernity. Everyone else was scrambling to catch up through the universal process of modernization. Such was the

Old and New in Contemporary Europe
Especially with the transformation of Europe since World War II, new styles intersect with living artifacts from the past to form sometimes ironic combinations. Here, in a neighborhood in Milan, Italy, teenagers wearing blue jeans and backpacks seem oblivious to the legacies of Roman antiquity and Christianity that are prominent around them.   *(© 1999, George Steinmetz)*

"master narrative" through which the West had understood its place in the world during the modern era.

But even as globalization proceeded during the late twentieth century, Western thinkers retreated from this long-standing master narrative. There was no question that capitalism had spread from Europe, but the West was not necessarily the model, the standard of development. Thus the growing interest in the non-Western world, the increasing respect for its diverse traditions, that came to mark Western culture by the last decades of the twentieth century.

Postmodernists questioned claims of certainty, objective truth, and intrinsic meaning in language, in works of art, and ultimately in all cultural expressions. Some held that such claims were assertions of privilege in what was essentially a political struggle for power—the power to set the wider social agenda. Especially in the United States, the postmodernist reaction led by the 1980s to the vogue of the French philosopher and historian Michel Foucault (foo-KOH) (1926–1984), who had sought to show that the power to specify what counts as knowledge was the key to social or political power. Since, from this perspective, all knowledge was suspect, Foucault's accents invited mistrust and disruption.

At the same time, however, an array of equally innovative thinkers, from the German Jürgen Habermas (b. 1929) to the American Richard Rorty (b. 1931), sought a more constructive orientation based on a renewed, no longer arrogant understanding of Western traditions, including the place of reason and democracy.

For those embracing this more constructive approach, the point was not to celebrate Western civilization but simply to understand it—as the framework that continued to shape the West and, less directly, the world. That tradition included much that might be criticized, and its present outcome entailed much that might be changed. Habermas, in particular, was a persistent and often radical critic of what he saw as the disparity between Western democratic ideals and contemporary social and political practices. But effective criticism had to rest on free inquiry and rational understanding, as opposed to prejudice or wishful thinking. The invitation to think freely about the Western tradition, to criticize and change it, rested on precisely that tradition; indeed, the scope for such criticism and change had been central to the Western belief in reason. That openness remained perhaps the West's most fundamental legacy.

S E C T I O N   S U M M A R Y

- Cultural differences between Europeans and Americans, as reflected, for example, in attitudes toward religion or the role of government, seemed to be deepening by the early twenty-first century.

- Even as encounters with the Muslim world, especially, brought home the distinctiveness of Western traditions, there was disagreement over the degree of multicultural pluralism that was healthy in a democratic society.

- Although the existence of universal human values was widely accepted in principle, it was not always clear how such values meshed with cultural pluralism and diversity on the global level.

- The advent of postmodernism suggested the end of the "modern" period, partly defined by the assumption that the West was in the forefront, playing a privileged role in world development.

- Even as the very legitimacy of "Western civilization" was debated in the West, intellectual leaders sought to show how Western notions of reason and democracy could be given renewed relevance.

C H A P T E R   S U M M A R Y

Online Study Center **ACE the Test**

Why and how did the relationship between western Europe and the United States change after the end of the cold war?

What forces raised new questions about the effectiveness of Western-style democracy by the early years of the twenty-first century?

How did the changes bound up with globalization affect identities in the West?

What questions emerged as the West faced new crises all over the globe after the end of the cold war?

On what basis was the wider contemporary relevance of "Western civilization" being debated by the first decade of the twenty-first century?

With the end of the cold war, the United States and the nations of western Europe no longer faced a common communist adversary, so close collaboration seemed less pressing to both sides. Greater freedom for Europe to set its own course provided a further impetus to the expansion and deepening of the European Union. And whereas the West was mostly united in response to increasing terrorism, Western nations split over the wisdom of the U.S.-led invasion of Iraq, which, to many Europeans, seemed to indicate an unwelcome unilateralism on the part of the United States.

Although democracy was the unquestioned norm, especially with the decline of the traditional left, a variety of changes posed new challenges for governments and the political order more generally. In light of aging populations and increasing global competition, western European countries found it ever harder to pay for the benefits promised as part of the postwar social compact.

Yet effort at reform provoked protests that led governments to back down. Adding to political volatility was growing concern over the assimilation of immigrants.

Increasing economic globalization expanded horizons but also affected the self-understanding of individuals in complex ways. Skeptical Europeans often equated globalization with Americanization and promoted various measures to preserve distinctiveness. However, people disagreed over whether what was to be preserved was "European," national, or local. Ways of understanding class, gender, and the place of religion also changed, though in some countries more than others.

An array of challenges, from new diseases to genocidal aggression, called for coordinated multinational responses. Although the UN played more visible roles after the cold war, it was an unwieldy organization whose effectiveness was sometimes limited. Even its specialized entities, such as the World Health Organization, sometimes lacked the resources and the clout to coordinate multinational responses to new problems. In dealing with politically inspired humanitarian crises in the non-Western world, the West found it difficult to develop a consistent and workable policy of intervention.

Changing relationships between the West and the non-Western world prompted new questions about the meaning and ongoing relevance of "Western civilization" as a concept. Some suggested that the whole "modern" conception of history, which had assumed a privileged leadership role for the West, had fallen away. But wider cultural encounters helped bring home the centrality of Western notions of openness and pluralism.

KEY TERMS

Online Study Center **Improve Your Grade** Flashcards

G-8 (Group of 8) (p. 947)
European Union (EU) (p. 949)
Maastricht agreements (p. 949)
euro (p. 949)
Common Agricultural Policy (CAP) (p. 950)
ethnic cleansing (p. 953)
unilateralism (p. 956)
Vladimir Putin (p. 959)

social market economy (p. 960)
World Health Organization (WHO) (p. 960)
information technology (p. 960)
World Trade Organization (WTO) (p. 966)
digital divide (p. 972)
nongovernmental organizations (NGOs) (p. 974)

SUGGESTED READING

Brubaker, Rogers. *Citizenship and Nationhood in France and Germany*. 1992. A lucid comparative study showing how very different conceptions of citizenship emerged in these two countries as a result of their contrasting historical experiences over the past two centuries.

Calleo, David P. *Rethinking Europe's Future*. 2001. Against a carefully drawn historical backdrop, this important work pinpoints the key issues in the evolving partnership between Europe and the United States and stresses the potential for a greater European contribution to world affairs.

Cohen, Daniel. *Globalization and Its Enemies*. 2006. A French writer's brief but probing and original analysis of the West's complex relations with the non-Western world in an age of globalization.

Fehrenbach, Heide, and Uta G. Poigner, eds. *Transactions, Transgressions, Transformations: American Culture in Western Europe and Japan*. 2000. A superior collection of essays reassessing the United States's cultural impact on Europe and Japan. Several of the essays treat film or popular music, while others are more comparative or synthetic in approach.

Garton Ash, Timothy. *Free World: America, Europe, and the Surprising Future of the West*. 2004. In the face of Western self-doubt, features the scope for the West to offer renewed global leadership, with Britain positioned to point the way by mediating between continental Europe and the United States.

Jack, Andrew. *Inside Putin's Russia*. 2004. While offering a balanced assessment of Putin's priorities and style of governance, questions whether Russia can have economic reform without more genuine democracy.

Judt, Tony. *Postwar: A History of Europe Since 1945*. 2005. A masterly and comprehensive survey by a leading expert on the period.

Lebovics, Herman. *Bringing the Empire Back Home: France in the Global Age*. Features the interplay of France's capital city, its provinces, and its former colonies in the ongoing consideration of what it means to be French in a changing European and global context.

McCormick, John. *Understanding the European Union: A Concise Introduction*. 1999. A clear introduction to the history, structure, and functioning of the central institutions of the EU.

Shawcross, William. *Deliver Us from Evil: Peacekeepers, Warlords, and a World of Endless Conflict*. 2000. Accents the limits and contradictions of the Western response to crises in areas lacking an indigenous political class.

NOTES

1. William Pfaff, "What's Left of the Union?" *New York Review of Books*, July 14, 2005, p. 27.

2. Jane Kramer, "The Dutch Model: Multiculturalism and Muslim Immigrants," *The New Yorker*, April 3, 2006, p. 67.

3. Quoted in *The Economist*, April 5, 2003, p. 59.

4. Christian Meier, *From Athens to Auschwitz: The Uses of History* (Cambridge, Mass.: Harvard University Press, 2005), pp. 170, 173.

GLOSSARY

This Glossary covers the complete text, Chapters 1 through 30.

absolutism Extraordinary concentration of power in royal hands, achieved particularly by the kings of France, most notably **Louis XIV,** in the seventeenth century. Proponents argued that hereditary monarchy was the divinely ordained form of government. *(Ch. 16)*

Act of Supremacy (1534) Act of the English Parliament during the Protestant Reformation that finalized the break with the Catholic Church by declaring the king to be head of the Church of England. Henry VIII required a public oath supporting the act, which Sir **Thomas More** refused to take; More was then executed for treason. *(Ch. 14)*

Adenauer, Konrad (1876–1967) Leading statesman of post–World War II Germany. As chancellor (1949–1963), he oriented the country toward western Europe and the United States and proved to Germans that democracy could mean effective government, economic prosperity, and foreign policy success. *(Ch. 29)*

agricultural revolution Dramatic increase in food production from the sixteenth to eighteenth centuries, brought about by changes in agricultural practices, cultivation of new crops, greater availability of animal manure, and introduction of the nutrient-rich potato from the Americas. *(Ch. 18)*

Alexander the Great (356–323 B.C.) King of **Macedon** (r. 336–323) and conqueror of the **Persian Empire**. Son of **Philip II** of Macedon, Alexander was an ingenious warrior who, in the course of his conquests, spread Greek civilization to western Asia, Egypt, and India. His despotism and ruler-worship set a precedent for later monarchs, including many Roman emperors. *(Ch. 4)*

Alexandria Mediterranean seaport in northern Egypt founded by **Alexander the Great** in 332 B.C. It was a thriving Hellenistic city with great harbors, marketplaces, banks, inns, courts, shipbuilding facilities, and a renowned library. *(Ch. 4)*

Amarna reform Term for the ancient Egyptian king Amenhotep IV's seizure of power from temple priests by replacing the god Amun-Re with Aten and renaming himself Akhenaten. After Akhenaten's death, the Amun-Re cult regained power. *(Ch. 1)*

Anabaptists Radical religious reformers in Germany and Switzerland during the Reformation. They rejected the practice of infant baptism, believing that baptism should occur only after confession of sin. They also believed that Christians should live apart in communities of the truly redeemed. Mennonites and Hutterites are their modern descendants. *(Ch. 14)*

Antigonids Dynasty of Macedonian rulers founded in 276 B.C. by Antigonus Gonatas, grandson of Antigonus the One-Eyed, a general of **Alexander the Great.** The Antigonid dynasty lasted about 140 years, until the Roman conquest. *(Ch. 4)*

Antioch Greatest of the cities founded by Seleucus, a general of **Alexander the Great.** Located near the present-day Turkish-Syrian border, it became one of the wealthiest and most luxurious of all eastern Mediterranean cities. *(Ch. 4)*

anti-Semitism Centuries-old prejudice against and demonization of Jews. Anti-Semitism became virulent in Europe in the 1880s with the emergence of the ultranationalist and racist "new right" ideologies and political movements. An essential part of the Nazi worldview, it led to the Holocaust. *(Ch. 24)*

appeasement The term for the policy employed by Britain's prime minister, Neville Chamberlain, to defuse the 1938 crisis with Germany's **Adolf Hitler.** Chamberlain acquiesced to Hitler's demands to annex the Sudetenland portion of Czechoslovakia, which proved a giant step toward the war that broke out less than a year later. *(Ch. 27)*

Aquinas, Thomas (1225–1274) Dominican friar and theologian. In his two most famous works, *Summa Contra Gentiles* and *Summa Theologiae,* he distinguished between natural truth, or what a person could know by reasoning, and revealed truths, which can be known only through faith in God's revelation. No one before him had so rigorously followed the dialectical method of reasoning through a whole field of knowledge. *(Ch. 10)*

Archaic Greece Period of ancient Greek history from around 700 to 500 B.C. Archaic Greece was characterized by artistic achievement, increased individualism amid communal solidarity, and a moving away from divine and toward abstract, mechanistic explanations. The Western philosophical tradition began during this period. *(Ch. 3)*

Arianism Popular heresy advocated by the priest Arius (ca. 250–336), emphasizing that Jesus was the "first born of all creation." It sought to preserve and purify Christianity's monotheism by making Jesus slightly subordinate to the Father. It was condemned by the **Council of Nicaea.** *(Ch. 7)*

Aristotle (384–322 B.C.) Ancient Greek philosopher, student of **Plato** and tutor of **Alexander the Great.** Aristotle emphasized the goal (*telos* in Greek) of change; in his view the entire cosmos is teleological, and every one of its parts has an essential purpose. Aristotle's scientific writings were the most influential philosophical classics of Greek and Roman civilization and remained so during the Middle Ages. *(Ch. 3)*

Armada (1588) Massive fleet of Spanish warships sent against England by **Philip II** but defeated by the English navy and bad weather. The tactics used by the English helped set the future course of naval warfare. *(Ch. 15)*

Assyrians Warlike people who ruled the ancient Near East during the first millennium B.C. Their innovations included using cavalry as their main striking force and having weapons and armor made of iron. *(Ch. 2)*

Augsburg Confession (1532) Document written by Philipp Melanchthon (1497–1560), with the approval of **Martin Luther,** that became the most widely accepted statement of the Lutheran faith. It constitutes part of the creedal basis for today's Lutheran churches. *(Ch. 14)*

Augustine (354–430) North African bishop and one of the most influential Christian thinkers. Augustine wrote that all people were sinners in need of God's redemption, that history is the struggle between those who call on divine grace and those who sin, and that learning was useful only to the extent that it equipped individuals to read and understand the Bible's message of salvation. *(Ch. 7)*

Augustus (63 B.C.–A.D. 14) Honorific title of Gaius Julius Caesar Octavianus, grandnephew of **Julius Caesar** and first Roman emperor. After defeating Mark Antony and Cleopatra at the Battle of Actium (31 B.C.), Augustus ruled the empire for forty-five years. His rule laid the foundations of two hundred years of prosperous Roman peace. See also **Principate.** *(Ch. 6)*

Auschwitz-Birkenau The largest and principal extermination center of Nazi Germany's six death camps, all of which were located in what had been Poland. The Nazis shipped Jews from all over Europe to Auschwitz, which killed about twelve thousand people a day at the height of its operation in 1944. *(Ch. 28)*

avant-garde French for "forefront," the term refers to early-twentieth-century artists who, inspired by novel or unconventional techniques, considered themselves precursors of new styles. Avant-garde movements proclaimed idiosyncratic manifestos and constantly called for the rejection of existing forms of expression and the creation of new ones. *(Ch. 24)*

Aztecs Amerindian people that dominated central Mexico from the fourteenth through the sixteenth centuries from their capital Tenochtitlán (present-day Mexico City). Weakened by exposure to virulent Old World diseases, they were conquered in 1521–1523 by Spanish forces led by **Hernán Cortés.** *(Ch. 13)*

Babylonian Captivity of the Papacy Term used to describe the period from 1309 to 1378 when popes resided north of the Alps rather than in central Italy or Rome, where the pope was the bishop. The term refers to the period when the tribes of Israel lived in exile. *(Ch. 11)*

Bacon, Francis (1561–1626) England's lord chancellor during the reign of James I and author of a utopian essay extolling science's benefits for a peaceful society and human happiness. His influential works encouraged the empirical method and inductive reasoning. See also **empirical method.** *(Ch. 17)*

baroque Style of European art and architecture popular from the late sixteenth to early eighteenth century. Baroque artists, such as Peter Paul Rubens, modified Renaissance techniques, adding dynamism and emotional energy. Baroque painting used light to portray dramatic illusion, and baroque churches were both impressively grand and emotionally engaging. *(Ch. 15)*

Bauhaus An influential German art school, founded in 1919, that sought to adopt contemporary materials to develop new forms of architecture, design, and urban planning in response to the cultural uncertainty that followed World War I. Though it arguably failed in its immediate German context, the Bauhaus helped shape the whole idea of "the modern" in the West and throughout the world for decades to come. *(Ch. 26)*

Bernard of Clairvaux (1090–1153) Monk, church reformer, and influential adviser to kings and popes. Bernard believed that faith and divine inspiration were more important than dialectical reasoning. He was instrumental in the success of the Cistercian religious order. *(Ch. 10)*

Bismarck, Otto von (1815–1898) Nineteenth-century German statesman. A Prussian aristocrat, Bismarck was the autocratic architect who, through a series of aggressive wars, united Germany and served as the nation's first chancellor. He administered an emperor-controlled country that became the dominant power in Europe. See also *Realpolitik. (Ch. 22)*

Black Death (1348–1351) First of a series of epidemics, possibly bubonic plague, that raged in Europe and western Asia for three centuries. The Black Death killed about 60 percent of those infected. The huge population decline fueled the economic and social transformations of the late Middle Ages. *(Ch. 11)*

Bolsheviks Members of a faction of the Russian Socialist Democratic Party led by **Vladimir Ilyich Lenin** (1870–1924), a zealous Marxist who insisted that a revolutionary cadre could seize power on behalf of the working class. The Bolsheviks gained control of Russia in November 1917. *(Ch. 24)*

Bonaparte, Napoleon. See **Napoleon Bonaparte.**

bourgeois century Characterization of the nineteenth century, especially the latter half. In western Europe, the bourgeois elites (middle classes), which had expanded dramatically in the wake of industrialization, helped fashion much of society. *(Ch. 23)*

Brandenburg-Prussia Group of German territories, ruled by the Hohenzollern family, that became one of Europe's most powerful states in the seventeenth century. Its military strength was supported by its hereditary landowners, who were granted autonomy in their territories. *(Ch. 16)*

Brandt, Willy (1913–1992) Socialist West German chancellor (r. 1969–1974). Brandt's widely popular policy of opening to the East, or *Ostpolitik,* made possible closer economic ties between West and East Germany and broader opportunities for ordinary citizens to interact across the east-west border. *(Ch. 29)*

Brest-Litovsk, Treaty of (1918) Treaty in which Russia accepted its defeat by Germany and its allies in World War I. The treaty forced the Russians to cede much of European Russia to Germany. After Germany's defeat by the Allies later in the year, the **Bolsheviks** recaptured Ukraine and the Caucasus region. *(Ch. 25)*

British blockade   Britain's naval blockade of Germany during World War I. By means of this tactic, which cut off supplies to Germany but which also violated several provisions of international law, the British seriously impeded the German war effort. *(Ch. 25)*

Caesar, Gaius Julius (63 B.C.– A.D. 14)   Roman general gifted at war and politics. Named dictator in 49 B.C., he was assassinated by the members of the **senate** in 44 B.C. He introduced to Europe the calendar of 365¼ days. He was succeeded as ruler by his grandnephew Octavian (**Augustus**). Later Roman emperors were also called *caesar. (Ch. 5)*

caliphate   Arab empire established by the successors of **Muhammad**; *caliph* means "successor to the prophet." The Umayyad caliphate, with its capital in Damascus, ruled from 661 to 750; the Abbasid caliphate, based in Baghdad, from 750 to 1258. *(Ch. 8)*

Calvin, John (1509–1564)   Franco-Swiss theologian and founder of the Reformed Church in Geneva. Calvin's theological writings, most notably *Institutes of the Christian Religion* (1536), were widely disseminated and hugely influential. Calvin stressed the absolute power of God and the need for moral reform of the Christian community. *(Ch. 14)*

canon law   Collection of orderly rules for the government of the Catholic Church, based on papal decrees and decisions of church councils. In 1140 the monk Gratian published the *Decretum,* the first systematic collection of canon law. *(Ch. 10)*

Carlowitz, Treaty of (1699)   Treaty imposed by the European allies on a weakening Ottoman Empire. The Habsburgs, Venetians, Russians, and Poles gained territory and power at the Turks' expense. *(Ch. 16)*

Carolingian Renaissance   Major revival of learning, combined with reform of religious and political institutions, that occurred under **Charlemagne** and his successors. The revival encompassed the founding of schools in religious institutions, production of textbooks, dissemination of early church teachings and of **canon law,** as well as secular reforms such as regularization of royal estates. *(Ch. 8)*

Catherine the Great (r. 1762–1796)   Empress of Russia. Through an astute policy of wars and alliances, Catherine expanded her country's borders south to the Black Sea and west into Europe. An "enlightened despot," she advanced the Westernizing reforms begun by **Peter the Great.** *(Ch. 18)*

Cato the Censor (234–149 B.C.)   Marcus Porcius Cato, Roman general and statesman. Known as Cato the Censor because he denounced luxury goods, he was the first Roman historian to write in Latin. *(Ch. 5)*

Charlemagne (r. 768–814)   Frankish king, crowned emperor in 800. He carried out a program of legal and ecclesiastical reform, patronized learning, and revitalized the western Roman Empire. See also **Carolingian Renaissance.** *(Ch. 8)*

Charles V (r. 1519–1558)   Holy Roman emperor and, as Charles I, king of Spain. His empire included Spain, Italy, the Low Countries, and Germany. Though he vigorously opposed the spread of Protestantism during the Reformation, he was forced to sign the Religious Peace of Augsburg in 1555, which acknowledged the right of German princes to choose the religion to be practiced in their territories, Lutheran or Catholic. Charles abdicated his imperial and royal titles the next year, ceding the empire to his brother Ferdinand and his Spanish possessions to his son **Philip II.** *(Ch. 14)*

Chartism   Nineteenth-century British political movement whose goal was to transform Britain from an oligarchy to a democracy. The Chartists' demands were contained in the 1838 "people's charter," which called for universal male suffrage, electoral districts with equal population, salaries and the abolition of property qualifications for Members of Parliament, the secret ballot, and annual general elections. The movement failed, but most of its measures eventually became law. See also **Second Reform Bill.** *(Ch. 21)*

chivalry   Initially, a medieval code of conduct for mounted warriors, focusing on military prowess, open-handed generosity, and earning a glorious reputation. Later it evolved into an elaborate set of rules governing relations between men and women. *(Ch. 10)*

Christianity   Sect originally rooted in Judaism that emerged as a fully separate religion by around A.D. 200. Emphasizing belief in one God and the mission of his son, **Jesus of Nazareth,** as savior, Christianity offered salvation in the next world and a caring community in the present one. A messianic religion, Christianity emphasized Christ's return, leading to the beginning of a heavenly kingdom on earth. *(Ch. 6)*

Churchill, Winston (1874–1965)   British prime minister (1940-1945; 1951-1955). As the leader of his country during World War II, Churchill's courage, decisiveness, memorable words, and boundless energy made him widely seen as one of Britain's greatest leaders of the twentieth century. See also **Yalta conference.** *(Ch. 28)*

Cicero, Marcus Tullius (106–43 B.C.)   Philosopher, writer, and statesman who was Rome's greatest orator. He was crucial in making the Latin language a vessel for the heritage of Greek thought. *(Ch. 5)*

city-state   State consisting of an independent city and the surrounding territory under its control. Early examples were the Sumerian city-states in the third millennium B.C. *(Ch. 1)*

civic humanism   An ideology, championed by Florentine writers and public officials during the Renaissance, that emphasized their city's classical republican virtues and history. They argued that a moral and ethical value was intrinsic to public life. *(Ch. 12)*

Civil Code   Law code established under Napoleon in 1804 that included limited acceptance of revolutionary gains, such as a guarantee of equality before the law and taxation of all social classes. Also known as the Napoleonic Code, it enshrined modern forms of property ownership and civil contracts, enhanced paternal control of families, outlawed divorce in most circumstances, and placed women under the legal domination of fathers and husbands. *(Ch. 19)*

Classical Greece   Period of ancient Greek history from about 480 to 323 B.C. Classical Greek culture emphasized public life as the central theme of art and literature, and its sculpture was the most anatomically precise yet. Classical Greece set many standards for modern Western culture. See also **demokratia.** *(Ch. 3)*

Cluny (Cluniacs)   A spiritual reform begun in 910 in central France. The movement emphasized strict adherence to the Benedictine Rule, as well as the ideas that the church should pray for the world without being deeply involved in it and must be free from lay control. *(Ch. 10)*

cold war   The hostile standoff between the Soviet Union and the United States that began after World War II, when communist governments, relying on Soviet support, took control of most of east-central Europe. The Soviets' first atomic bomb explosion in 1949 intensified the conflict, which shaped world affairs for the next forty years. *(Ch. 28)*

collectivization   The program that reshaped agriculture in the Soviet Union under **Joseph Stalin** during the early 1930s. By forcing peasants into government-controlled collective farms, the Soviet regime sought to take control of agricultural production in order better to finance rapid industrialization. *(Ch. 27)*

Columbian Exchange   Historians' term for the blending of cultures between the Old World and the New after Christopher Columbus's arrival in the New World in 1492. The Spanish and other Europeans brought their plants, domesticated animals, and diseases to the Americas. The Americas contributed New World crops, most notably maize (corn) and potatoes, transforming the Old World diet. *(Ch. 13)*

Comintern (Third, or Communist, International)   An association founded in March 1919 by the Communists (formerly **Bolsheviks**) to translate their success in Russia into leadership of the international socialist movement. Its program of tight organization and discipline under Russian leadership produced a schism between communists and socialists in Europe and throughout the world. *(Ch. 26)*

Common Agricultural Policy (CAP)   A major pillar of the **European Union,** accounting for half of its budget by 2000, the Common Agricultural Policy entailed subsidies to protect farmers from outside competition. The CAP was widely criticized by advocates of freer world trade. *(Ch. 30)*

communes   Form of government in Italian towns that rose in the eleventh century. Despite numerous local variations, communes involved common decision making by local notables, including both landed aristocrats and wealthy merchants or industrialists. *(Ch. 9)*

Compromise of 1867   Agreement that divided the Habsburg empire into Austria in the west and Hungary in the east, a dual monarchy under Emperor Franz Joseph called Austria-Hungary. The compromise confirmed Magyar dominance in Hungary. *(Ch. 22)*

conciliarists   These people argued that the pope was not a universal monarch, but rather the first among equals in the church. Thus, church councils had the right and duty to reform and correct even the pope. *(Ch. 11)*

congress system   System of European international relations in the first half of the nineteenth century in which the major European states cooperated to preserve the balance of power. This system disappeared as political leaders increasingly used force to pursue their narrow interests. *(Ch. 22)*

Congress of Vienna (1814–1815)   Conference called by the victorious powers—Austria, Great Britain, Prussia, and Russia—who defeated Napoleon. Guided by the Austrian foreign minister, Prince Metternich, the Great Powers drew new territorial boundaries advantageous to themselves. They also attempted to provide long-term stability on the European continent and restored some of the rulers who had been overthrown. See also **congress system.** *(Ch. 21)*

conservatism   Ideology underlying the order established in Europe in 1815. Conservatives emphasized resistance to change and preservation of the existing order of monarchy, aristocracy, and an established church. *(Ch. 21)*

Copernicus, Nicholas (1473–1543)   Polish astronomer who initiated the Scientific Revolution by proposing that the earth and other planets orbit the sun, a theory called the heliocentric, or sun-centered, system. See also **heliocentric theory.** *(Ch. 17)*

corporativism, corporative state   The system established in fascist Italy beginning in 1926 that sought to involve people in public life not as citizens but as producers, through their roles in the economy. A system based on such occupational groupings eventually replaced parliament as the basis of political representation in fascist Italy. *(Ch. 26)*

Cortés, Hernán (1485–1546)   Spanish commander who conquered the **Aztecs** and claimed the Valley of Mexico for Spain. Cortés had only five hundred men but was aided by an outbreak of smallpox and the help of Amerindian peoples eager to end Aztec control. *(Ch. 13)*

Cossacks   Originally the term (from a Russian word meaning "free man" or "adventurer") for peoples of Tatar origin who inhabited the hinterland of the Black and Caspian Seas. Their numbers swelled, after 1500, by peasants who fled serfdom in Poland-Lithuania and the growing Russian state. The Cossacks helped to provide a military buffer between the Polish-Lithuanian and Russian states and the Ottomans to the south, and they resisted Polish domination in the seventeenth century, but slowly lost their autonomy to the expanding Russian state in the eighteenth century. *(Ch. 16)*

Council of Constance (1414–1418)   Assembly convened by Holy Roman Emperor Sigismund to heal deep religious and civil divisions. The council declared that its rulings were binding even on the pope. Its selection of Pope Martin V ended the **Great Schism.** *(Ch. 11)*

Council of the Indies   Body established by the king of Spain in 1524 to oversee Spain's colonial possessions. Located at court, eventually in Madrid, it supervised all legal, administrative, and commercial activity in the colonies until the early eighteenth century. *(Ch. 13)*

Council of Nicaea (325)   History's first ecumenical, or "all-church," council, convened by the emperor Constantine. The council condemned **Arianism** and proclaimed key elements of the Nicene Creed, especially the doctrine that Christ was "one in being with the Father," co-equal and co-eternal. *(Ch. 7)*

Council of Trent (1545–1563)   Ecumenical council of the Roman Catholic Church during the Reformation. Though rejecting many Protestant positions, the council reformed and reorganized the church partly in response to Protestant criticisms. Its decrees reaffirmed and defined the basic tenets of Roman Catholicism for the next four hundred years. *(Ch. 14)*

covenant   As told in the Hebrew Bible, the pact God made with Abraham, the first patriarch of Israel. In return for the land of Canaan and the promise of becoming a great nation, the Israelites agreed to worship no other gods. *(Ch. 2)*

Cromwell, Oliver (1599–1658)   English Puritan general and statesman. A military genius and leader in the English civil war, Cromwell governed as Lord Protector during the Interregnum from 1653 to 1658. *(Ch. 16)*

Crusades   A series of largely unsuccessful wars waged by western European Christians to recapture the Holy Land from the Muslims and ensure the safety of Christian pilgrims to Jerusalem. Later, the term came to designate any military effort by Europeans against non-Christians. *(Ch. 9)*

Crystal Night (*Kristallnacht*)   Organized Nazi assault on Jewish businesses and synagogues during the night of November 9–10, 1938, following the assassination of a German diplomat in Paris. Almost all the synagogues in Germany and about seven thousand Jewish-owned stores were destroyed. The broken shop windows gave the episode its name. Although the German public generally deplored this wanton destruction of property, the Crystal Night pogrom initiated a more radical phase of Nazi anti-Jewish policy. *(Ch. 27)*

cuneiform   First writing system in Mesopotamia, consisting of wedge-shaped impressions in soft clay. Named from the Latin word for "wedge-shaped," it was developed about 3500–3100 B.C. *(Ch. 1)*

Darwinism   Profoundly influential theory of biological evolution, first put forth by Charles Darwin (1809–1882). He proposed that all forms of life continuously develop through natural selection, whereby those that are better adapted to the environment have the advantage and are more likely to survive and pass on their beneficial traits to their offspring. *(Ch. 23)*

D-Day   The complex Allied amphibious landings in Normandy, France, on June 6, 1944, that opened a second major European front in World War II. In the aftermath of this invasion, American-led forces in the west began moving toward Germany, complementing the Soviet effort, which was already forcing the Germans back on the eastern front. *(Ch. 28)*

Decembrists   Group of Russian military officers who led the December 1825 rebellion after the death of Tsar Alexander I, seeking to install a constitutional monarchy

with Alexander's eldest brother, Constantine, as tsar. They were defeated and executed by Constantine's younger brother, Nicholas. The Decembrists were seen as martyrs by later Russian revolutionaries. *(Ch. 21)*

Declaration of the Rights of Man and the Citizen (1789)   Document issued by the **National Assembly** of France in August 1789. Modeled on the U.S. Constitution, the declaration set forth the basis for the new French government and asserted "the natural, inalienable and sacred rights of man." *(Ch. 19)*

De Gaulle, Charles (1890–1970)   The youngest general in the French army, he called on French forces to follow his lead and continue the fight against Nazi Germany after the fall of France in June 1940. As the leader of the new Free French force that emerged thereafter, he won renewed respect for France as a major power and sought to exercise political leadership after France's liberation in 1944. Though he retired from public life in 1946, disillusioned with politics, he returned in 1958 to spearhead the creation of the new Fifth Republic. He served as its president from 1958 to 1969. *(Ch. 28)*

demokratia   Term coined in Athens in the fifth century B.C. to describe the city's system of direct government. It means "the power *(kratos)* of the people *(demos)*." Athenian society pioneered today's key democratic principles, including freedom, equality, universal citizenship, and the rule of law. *(Ch. 3)*

Descartes, René (1596–1650)   French philosopher, scientist, and mathematician. Descartes emphasized skepticism and deductive reasoning in his most influential treatise, *Discourse on Method.* He offered the first alternative physical explanation of matter after the Copernican revolution. *(Ch. 17)*

digital divide   A term for the disparity in access to the computing and Internet technologies that seemed essential to compete in the twenty-first-century global economy. It was one way that new technologies were widening the gap between the world's haves and have-nots. *(Ch. 30)*

Directory   French revolutionary government from 1795 to 1799, consisting of an executive council of five men chosen by the upper house of the legislature. It was overthrown in a coup led by **Napoleon Bonaparte.** *(Ch. 19)*

Dominic de Guzman (1170–1221)   Spanish priest and founder of the spiritually influential Dominican mendicant order. The order was known for the irreproachable life of its members, its learning, and its desire to emulate the apostolic life of the early church by poverty and preaching. *(Ch. 10)*

Dutch East India Company   Commercially innovative Dutch company formed in 1602 that combined government management of trade with both public and private investment. The formation of the company created a permanent pool of capital to sustain trade and resulted in a dramatic expansion of commerce with Asia. *(Ch. 16)*

Edict of Milan (313)   Proclamation issued primarily by Emperor Constantine that made Christianity a legal religion in the Roman Empire. Constantine promoted the

Christian church, granting it tax immunities and relieving the clergy of military service. *(Ch. 7)*

Edict of Nantes (1598)   Edict of Henry IV granting France's Protestants **(Huguenots)** the right to practice their faith and maintain defensive garrisons. They were also guaranteed access to schools, hospitals, royal appointments, and separate judicial institutions. The edict was revoked by **Louis XIV** in 1685. *(Ch. 15)*

Elizabeth I (r. 1558–1603)   First woman to occupy the English throne successfully. Elizabeth's adroit rule brought stability to England after the turmoil of previous reigns. She firmly established Protestantism in England, encouraged English commerce, defended the nation against the Spanish **Armada,** and fostered the English Renaissance in poetry and drama. *(Ch. 15)*

empirical method   Philosophical view developed by the seventeenth-century English philosophers **Francis Bacon** and **John Locke,** asserting that all knowledge is based on observation and experimentation and that general principles should be derived from particular facts. *(Ch. 17)*

encomienda   A Spanish royal grant of protectorship over a group of Amerindians. The receivers of the grants (encomenderos) were obliged to Christianize the people under their charge, but instead most forced the natives to work as virtual slaves in mines and on Spanish lands. See also **Bartolomé de Las Casas.** *(Ch. 13)*

enlightened despotism   Term for the reform-oriented rule of eighteenth-century monarchs such as **Frederick the Great,** Joseph II of Austria, and **Catherine the Great.** Enlightened despots applied Enlightenment remedies to economic problems, encouraged education and legal reform, and improved agricultural productivity by enabling some peasants to own the land they worked. *(Ch. 18)*

entrepreneurs   People who assume the risks of organizing and investing in a new business venture. Entrepreneurship is closely connected with the inventions and innovations made during the industrial age. *(Ch. 20)*

Epicureans   Adherents of the Athenian philosopher Epicurus (341–270 B.C.), who taught that the soul is made up of atoms that do not exist after death. Epicureans emphasized the avoidance of pain and the pursuit of intellectual pleasure. *(Ch. 4)*

Erasmus, Desiderius (1466–1536)   Prominent Dutch humanist during the Renaissance, best known for his satire *Praise of Folly.* Erasmus's works reinterpreted Greek and Roman wisdom and emphasized tolerance, reason, and faith in the goodness and educability of the individual. *(Ch. 12)*

ethnic cleansing   A term describing attempts to remove an unwanted ethnic group from an area, which can include forced relocation and mass killing. Beginning in 1991, this tactic was implemented by Yugoslavian ruler Slobodan Milosevic (b. 1941) to unite all Serbs, many of whom lived in neighboring Croatia, Bosnia-Herzegovina, and Kosovo. *(Ch. 30)*

Etruscans   Inhabitants of twelve loosely confederated city-states north of Rome in Etruria that flourished in the seventh to sixth centuries B.C. They were conquered by the Romans by the early third century B.C. *(Ch. 5)*

euro   The common currency launched by the **European Union** in 1999 to eliminate the cost of currency exchange and boost trade and economic interaction. As of January 1, 2002, it replaced the national currencies of the participating countries (the "Eurozone"). *(Ch. 30)*

European Economic Community (EEC) (1957–1967)   Common market formed by Belgium, France, West Germany, Italy, Luxembourg, and the Netherlands to promote free trade. The EEC was replaced by the European Community (EC) in 1967. *(Ch. 29)*

European Union (EU)   New name for the European Community after the **Maastricht agreements** of 1991. It consists of twenty-five member countries. See also **euro.** *(Ch. 30)*

"euthanasia" program   The Nazi program of systematically killing people, overwhelmingly ethnic Germans, whom the Nazis deemed superfluous or threatening to the German racial health. Victims included chronic mental patients, the incurably ill, and people with severe physical handicaps. Initiated in 1939, the program had claimed 100,000 lives by the time it was discontinued in 1941. *(Ch. 27)*

existentialism   A philosophical and cultural movement, influential from the late 1940s into the 1950s, that explored life in a world cast adrift from its cultural moorings. Highly influential were the Frenchmen Jean-Paul Sartre (1905–1980) and Albert Camus (1913–1960), for whom an authentic human response to an apparently meaningless universe entailed commitment and responsibility. *(Ch. 29)*

factories   Centralized workplaces where a number of people cooperate to mass-produce goods. The first factories of industrializing Europe were made possible by the development of the **steam engine** as a central power source. The mechanized production of factories led to huge productivity increases in the nineteenth century. See also **industrialization; mass production.** *(Ch. 20)*

fascism   A violent, antidemocratic movement founded by **Benito Mussolini** in Italy in 1919. The term is widely used to encompass Hitler's Nazi regime in Germany and other movements stressing disciplined national solidarity and hostile to liberal individualism, the parliamentary system, and Marxist socialism. *(Ch. 26)*

February Patent (1861)   Enactment issued in February 1861 by the Austrian emperor Franz Joseph (r. 1848–1916) that established a constitutional monarchy in the old Austrian Empire. The patent guaranteed civil liberties and provided for local self-government and an elected parliament. *(Ch. 22)*

feudal revolution   The societal change in tenth-century France from prince-dominated territories with loyal, reliable, but few vassals to the advent of many locally powerful magnates with numerous vassals whose fidelity was uncertain and who primarily provided military service. *(Ch. 9)*

Five Pillars The basic teachings of Islam: (1) the profession of faith, "There is no God but Allah and **Muhammad** is His Prophet"; (2) individual prayer five times daily, plus group prayers at noon on Friday; (3) the sunup-to-sundown fast during the month of Ramadan; (4) giving generous alms to the poor; and (5) pilgrimage to Mecca at least once in a person's lifetime. *(Ch. 8)*

Flavians Dynasty of the Roman emperors Vespasian (r. 69–79), Titus (r. 79–81), and Domitian (r. 81–96), whose rule was a time of relative peace and good government. Unlike the Julio-Claudians, the Flavians descended from Italian landowners, not old Roman nobility. Domitian persecuted the nobility and was assassinated. *(Ch. 6)*

Fourteen Points Proposals by U.S. president Woodrow Wilson (1856–1924) to guide the new international order that would follow an Allied victory in World War I. Specifics included open diplomacy, free trade, reduced armaments, self-determination for nationalities, and a league of nations. *(Ch. 25)*

Francis of Assisi (1181–1226) Italian monk and founder of a new order of friars ("brothers," from the Latin *fratres*). Francis was born wealthy but adopted a life based on the scriptural ideals of poverty, preaching, and service. His apostolate to the urban poor was highly popular. *(Ch. 10)*

Frankfurt Assembly (1848–1849) Popularly elected national assembly that attempted to create a unified German state. The assembly drew up a constitution and offered the German throne to Friedrich Wilhelm IV, king of Prussia, who declined, fearing a war with Austria and not wanting an office offered by representatives of the people. *(Ch. 21)*

Frederick the Great (r. 1740–1786) Autocratic king of Prussia who transformed the country into a major military power, acquired Polish Prussia, and waged three wars against Austria. He participated in and encouraged the study of philosophy, history, poetry, and French literature. *(Ch. 18)*

Freud, Sigmund (1856–1939) Austrian founder of psychoanalysis, a method of treating psychic disorders by exploring the unconscious. Freud believed that people were motivated in part by their unconscious feelings and drives. He helped call attention to the concept that irrational forces play a significant role in human behavior. *(Ch. 24)*

friendly societies Nineteenth-century organizations formed by workers; members pooled their resources to provide mutual aid. Combining business activity with feasts, drinking bouts, and other social functions, friendly societies promoted group solidarity and a sense of working-class identity. *(Ch. 20)*

G-8 (Group of 8) Originally a Group of Seven, or G-7, this informal association of the world's seven largest economic powers (the United States, Japan, Germany, France, Britain, Italy, and Canada) began meeting during the 1970s in an effort to coordinate economic policies. After the fall of communism, the group added Russia, thereby becoming the G-8. *(Ch. 30)*

Galilei, Galileo (1564–1642) Italian physicist and astronomer who provided evidence supporting the **heliocentric theory** of **Nicholas Copernicus** and helped develop the physics of mechanics. His publication of his astronomical observations and his subsequent condemnation by the Catholic Church spurred popular debate and greatly influenced the future of science. *(Ch. 17)*

gentry Class of wealthy, educated, and socially ambitious families in western Europe, especially England, whose political and economic power was greatly enhanced during the sixteenth century. They shared with traditional old-family warrior-aristocrats certain legal privileges, security of landownership, and a cooperative relationship with the monarchy. See also **price revolution.** *(Ch. 15)*

Glorious Revolution (1688) Bloodless English revolution in which Parliament replaced the Catholic King James II with William (of Orange) and his wife, Mary (James's Protestant daughter). Parliament imposed on the new sovereigns a Bill of Rights that confirmed Parliament's power and protected freedom of speech. *(Ch. 16)*

Golden Bull of 1356 Edict of Holy Roman Emperor Charles IV establishing the method of electing a new emperor. It acknowledged the political autonomy of Germany's seven regional princes. *(Ch. 11)*

Gorbachev, Mikhail (b. 1931) The Soviet Communist Party secretary who, beginning in 1985, attempted to reform the Soviet communist system through arms reduction; liberalization in the satellite states; *glasnost,* or "openness" to discussion and criticism; and *perestroika,* or economic "restructuring." Though widely admired in the West, these measures failed, and Gorbachev ended up presiding over the end of the Soviet communist regime. *(Ch. 29)*

Gothic Period in European architecture, sculpture, and painting from the twelfth to early sixteenth centuries. Gothic architecture was distinguished by the pointed arch, ribbed vault, and point support, which produced a building characterized by verticality and translucency. Examples are the Cathedral of Notre-Dame of Paris and the royal portal at Chartres Cathedral. *(Ch. 10)*

Gracchi Ancient Roman faction led by Tiberius Sempronius Gracchus (163–133 B.C.) and later his brother, Gaius (153–121), both of whom were killed by their political opponents. They challenged the conservative **senate** on behalf of the poor. *(Ch. 5)*

"the Great Patriotic War" Term for World War II devised by **Joseph Stalin** to rally Soviet citizens against the German invasion. Stalin appealed to Russian nationalism and recalled past heroic defenses of Russia rather than communist themes. *(Ch. 28)*

Great Reform Bill (1832) British law that broadened the franchise and provided parliamentary seats for new urban areas that had not previously been represented. The bill was a major victory for the government and middle classes over the aristocracy. *(Ch. 21)*

Great Schism (1378–1417) Period during which two, then three, rival popes claimed to rule the Christian

Church in the West. The schism ended when the **Council of Constance** deposed all three competing previous popes and elected Martin V as the new pope. *(Ch. 11)*

guilds Merchant groups and associations of crafts and trades established in European cities and towns beginning in the thirteenth century. Guilds expanded greatly during the later Middle Ages. They provided economic benefits, fostered a sense of community, and served as mutual assistance societies. *(Ch. 9)*

gulag Network of 476 forced labor camps for political prisoners in the Soviet Union. The *gulag* (an acronym for "main camp administration") was first used by Lenin in 1918 but was greatly expanded by **Joseph Stalin** in the 1930s. *(Ch. 27)*

Gutenberg, Johann (ca. 1399–1468) German inventor of movable metal type. His innovations led to the publication of the first printed book in Europe, the Gutenberg Bible, in the 1450s. Printed books and broadsheets played a critical role in disseminating the ideas of the Renaissance and the Reformation. *(Ch. 12)*

Hagia Sophia Largest Christian church ever built, constructed in Constantinople from 532 to 537 for the Roman emperor **Justinian.** The church consists of two intersecting rectangular basilicas that incorporate arches; the whole is surmounted by a huge dome. *(Ch. 7)*

Hanseatic League Late medieval association of over a hundred trading cities, centered on the German city of Lübeck. The league dominated coastal trade in northern Europe from the fourteenth to the fifteenth centuries, until Dutch, English, and south German merchants finally gained shares of the wool, grain, and fur trades. *(Ch. 11)*

heliocentric theory Theory advanced by **Nicholas Copernicus** that the earth and other planets orbit the sun. Supported by the scientific and mathematical discoveries of **Johannes Kepler** and **Galileo Galilei,** heliocentrism, which means "sun-centered," won acceptance by the end of the seventeenth century. *(Ch. 17)*

Hellenism Term used to designate ancient Greece's language, culture, and civilization, especially after **Alexander the Great** spread them to other parts of the Mediterranean, western Asia, and North Africa. *(Ch. 4)*

Helsinki Accords (1975) Agreements signed by thirty-five countries in Helsinki, Finland, that committed the signatories to recognize existing borders, to increase economic and environmental cooperation, and to promote freedom of expression, religion, and travel. Dissidents in Soviet bloc countries soon fastened on these provisions to highlight the lack of human rights and to discredit the ruling communist governments. *(Ch. 29)*

Henry VIII (r. 1509–1547) King of England. Initially a defender of traditional Christianity, Henry broke with the papacy over the issue of his divorce. He needed a divorce, he argued, in order to marry a younger woman who might be able to produce a male heir to the kingdom. As a result of the dispute, Henry supported Reformers in the English Church. *(Ch. 14)*

Henry "the Navigator," Prince (1394–1460) Portuguese prince and director of Portugal's exploration and colonization of Africa's western coast. The Portuguese quickly established trading stations in the region, laying the foundations for their overseas empire. *(Ch. 13)*

heresy An opinion that goes against religious or political doctrine and beliefs. *(Ch. 7)*

Herodotus (ca. 485–425 B.C.) Ancient Greek historian; with **Thucydides,** a founder of history-writing in the West. The word *history* comes from a word used by Herodotus, *historiai,* meaning "inquiries" or "research." In his history of the Persian Wars, Herodotus saw the fall of the Persian Empire as part of a perpetual cycle of the rise and fall of empires. *(Ch. 3)*

Hildegard of Bingen (1098–1179) German abbess who was perhaps the most profound psychological thinker of her age. More than anyone before her, Hildegard opened up for discussion the feminine aspects of divinity. She was also adept in music and biblical studies. *(Ch. 10)*

Hitler, Adolf (1889–1945) The German dictator who, after being legally named chancellor in 1933, militarized Germany and started World War II in 1939, leading the country to defeat in 1945. His enforcement of state-sponsored **anti-Semitism** and racial purity among German people led to the murder of millions. *(Ch. 27)*

Hittites Builders of a great empire in Anatolia in the Late Bronze Age, the Hittites fought Egypt to a standstill and made history's first peace treaty between equals. Hittite is the oldest recorded Indo-European language, the language group to which English belongs. *(Ch. 1)*

Hobbes, Thomas (1588–1679) English philosopher. In his treatise *Leviathan,* Hobbes asserted that people are made up of mechanistic appetites and so need a strong ruler to hold them in check. However, he also envisioned citizens as potentially equal and constrained neither by morality nor by natural obedience to authority. *(Ch. 17)*

Homer Greatest ancient Greek poet, credited as the author of the epics the *Iliad* and the *Odyssey,* both written during the eighth century B.C. His dramatic stories inspired, moved, and educated the Greeks. *(Ch. 2)*

hominids The primate family *Hominidae,* which includes humans. The modern human being, *Homo sapiens sapiens,* is the only species of this family still in existence. *(Ch. 1)*

hoplite phalanx Battlefield tactic of **Archaic Greece** that relied on a tightly ordered unit of heavily armed, pike-bearing infantrymen. It was the dominant military force in western Asia and the Mediterranean region until 197 B.C. *(Ch. 3)*

Huguenots French Protestants, followers of the teachings of **John Calvin.** Huguenots battled Catholics throughout the sixteenth and seventeenth centuries. Many emigrated to other western European countries and England's American colonies, especially after the revocation of the **Edict of Nantes.** French Protestants gained full religious freedom in the nineteenth century. *(Ch. 15)*

humanism Western European literary and cultural movement of the fourteenth and fifteenth centuries. Humanists emphasized the superiority of ancient Greek and Roman literature, history, and politics, and focused on learning and personal and public duty. See also **Desiderius Erasmus; Francesco Petrarch; Thomas More.** *(Ch. 12)*

Hundred Years' War (1337–1453)   Series of conflicts between the ruling families of France and England over territory in France and the succession to the French crown. Sporadic raids and battles devastated the French countryside and checked population growth. The inspirational leadership of **Joan of Arc** contributed to France's eventual success in expelling the English from nearly all of the disputed land. *(Ch. 11)*

hunter-gatherers   Food-collecting society in which people live by hunting, fishing, and gathering fruits and nuts, with no crops or livestock being raised for food. During the **Neolithic Revolution,** some hunter-gatherers developed agriculture. *(Ch. 1)*

Hus, Jan (ca. 1370–1415)   Czech religious reformer who strongly attacked clerical power and privileges and advocated reform of church practice. His execution for heresy at the **Council of Constance** provoked a civil war in Prague and Bohemia. *(Ch. 11)*

iconoclasm   Rejection of, or even the destruction of, religious images in worship. Iconoclasm was the official policy of the Byzantine Empire from 726 to 843 and played a role in the continuing estrangement of Byzantium from the West. *(Ch. 8)*

impressionist   Late-nineteenth-century style of painting pioneered by the French artists Degas, Monet, Pissarro, Renoir, Sisley, and Morisot. Influenced by new theories that images were transmitted to the brain as small light particles, which the brain then reconstituted, the impressionists sought to capture what things looked like before they were "distorted" by the brain. *(Ch. 23)*

Inca   A flourishing sixteenth-century empire administered from the mountains of Peru and extending from modern Ecuador to Chile. It was conquered for Spain by Francisco Pizzaro (1470–1541), aided by a smallpox epidemic and native peoples seeking to end Inca domination. *(Ch. 13)*

Index of Prohibited Books   A list of books banned by the Roman Catholic Church because of moral or doctrinal error. First announced in 1559, it was only sporadically enforced and had little effect. The Index was suppressed in 1966. *(Ch. 14)*

industrialization   Beginning in Britain in the later eighteenth century, a system of **mass production** of goods in which specialization and mechanization made manufacturing efficient and profitable. Early industrialization enabled Britain to become the dominant world power in the nineteenth century. See also **factories.** *(Ch. 20)*

information technology   Term for the revolution in information availability and communications resulting from the late-twentieth-century development of personal computers and the Internet. See also **digital divide.** *(Ch. 30)*

"iron curtain"   Term used by Winston Churchill in a speech on March 5, 1946, to warn that, thanks to Soviet policy, a formidable de facto barrier was emerging in Europe, cutting the Soviet sphere off from the West and threatening the long-term division of the Continent. Though the term was not coined by Churchill, his phrasing dramatically affected public opinion in the West. The "iron curtain" suggested both the division of Europe and Soviet culpability throughout the cold war period. *(Ch. 28)*

Israelites   People who settled on the eastern shore of the Mediterranean around 1200 B.C., or perhaps earlier. Their belief in one God directly influenced the faith of Christians, Muslims, and modern Jews. See also **monotheism.** *(Ch. 2)*

Ivan IV, "the Terrible" (r. 1533–1584)   First Russian ruler routinely to use the title "tsar" (Russian for "Caesar"), he presided over the expansion and centralization of the Russian state. Ivan continued Moscow's expansion, begun by his grandfather Ivan III, south and east against Mongol-controlled states. Under Ivan IV, Russians moved east across Siberia for the first time. Within his expanding empire, Ivan ruled as an autocrat; he was able to bypass noble participation and intensify the centralization of government by creating ranks of officials loyal only to himself. *(Ch. 15)*

Jacobins   In revolutionary France, a political club named for a monastic order. One of the most radical of republican groups, the Jacobins purged the Girondins, originally fellow members of the club, from the National Convention in 1793. Leaders of the **Terror,** such as **Maximilien Robespierre,** came from their ranks. *(Ch. 19)*

Jesus of Nazareth (ca. 4 B.C.–A.D. 30)   Founder of **Christianity.** A forceful preacher and reformer who, to his followers, was Christ, "the anointed one" (from the Greek *Christos*), foretold in the Hebrew Bible as the redeemer of Israel who would initiate the Kingdom of Heaven. The dynamism and popularity of his teachings led to a clash with Jewish and Roman authorities in Jerusalem and to his crucifixion by the Romans. *(Ch. 6)*

Joan of Arc (d. 1431)   Charismatic French military leader during the **Hundred Years' War.** A late medieval mystic, Joan heard "voices" telling her to assist in driving the English from France. She was captured and burned as a heretic by the English. Later she was canonized as Saint Joan, patron saint of France. *(Ch. 11)*

Julio-Claudians   Dynasty of Roman emperors founded by **Augustus** and ruling from A.D. 14 to 68. The succession consisted of Augustus's stepson Tiberius, great-grandson Caligula, grandnephew Claudius, and great-great-grandson Nero. For elite Romans, this era was one of decadence and scandal; for ordinary people, it was a time of stability and peace. *(Ch. 6)*

July Revolution (1830)   Uprising in Paris in July 1830 that forced King Charles X to abdicate and signaled a victory for constitutional reform over an absolute monarchy. The liberal Louis Philippe was proclaimed "King of the French," with limited powers, by the Chamber of Deputies. The revolution sparked democratic uprisings in Belgium, Germany, Italy, and Russian Poland and helped persuade British peers to vote for the **Great Reform Bill.** *(Ch. 21)*

justification by faith   Doctrine professed by **Martin Luther** that Christians can be saved (justified) only by faith, a free gift of God, and not by penitential acts or good works. Luther's doctrine directly challenged the authority and fundamental practices of the Roman Catholic Church. *(Ch. 14)*

Justinian (r. 527–565)   One of the greatest of all Rome's emperors. His comprehensive collection of Roman law is the most influential legal collection in human history. He built **Hagia Sophia,** reformed the imperial administration, and fought constant wars to expand the empire. *(Ch. 7)*

Kepler, Johannes (1571–1630)   German astronomer. Kepler developed the three laws of planetary motion, known as Kepler's laws, which are still accepted, and mathematically confirmed the Copernican **heliocentric theory.** *(Ch. 17)*

Kriegsrohstoffabteilung (KRA)   The "War Raw Materials Office" that coordinated Germany's World War I economy. The KRA produced synthetic substitute products and created new mixed (private and government) companies to allocate raw materials. This body served as a model for later economic planning and coordination in Germany and elsewhere. *(Ch. 25)*

Kristallnacht   See **Crystal Night.**

laissez faire   French term meaning "to leave alone," it was applied to the economic doctrine put forward by **Adam Smith** in 1776. Smith advocated freeing national economies from the fetters of the state and allowing supply and demand to shape the marketplace. Laissez-faire ideas contributed to the drive to lower tariffs in the nineteenth century. See also **liberalism.** *(Ch. 21)*

Las Casas, Bartolomé de (1474–1566)   First bishop of Chiapas, in southern Mexico. A former *encomendero,* Las Casas passionately condemned the brutality of the Spanish conquests. In 1542 King Charles accepted Las Casas's criticisms, abolishing Indian slavery and greatly restricting the transfer of **encomiendas.** *(Ch. 13)*

Latin   Indo-European language of ancient Rome and its empire, from which today's Romance languages developed. *(Ch. 5)*

laws of motion   The natural laws of gravity, planetary motion, and inertia first laid out in the seventeenth century by **Isaac Newton.** Newton demonstrated that these laws apply to the solar system and could be used to predict the existence of an as-yet-unseen planet. *(Ch. 17)*

lay investiture   Control of church appointments by laymen. Emperor Henry IV (1066–1106) and Pope Gregory VII (1073–1085) disputed who should have this authority in the Christian world. The 1122 Concordat of Worms stipulated that bishops could be invested by kings only after a free church election. *(Ch. 9)*

League of Nations (1919–1946)   An international alliance established at the end of World War I without the membership of the United States. Though its covenant called for the peaceful settlement of disputes among member states and for sanctions against a member that went to war in violation of League provisions, it failed to prevent the escalating violence that culminated in World War II. *(Ch. 25)*

legion   Innovative and highly successful ancient Roman battle formation. The legion included many flexible, adaptable, and semi-independent groups that broke their enemies' order with javelins at long range, then charged with sword and shield. *(Ch. 5)*

Lend-Lease Act (1941)   Act by the U.S. Congress authorizing President **Franklin Delano Roosevelt** to lend or lease weapons or other aid to countries the president designated. A major declaration of American support for the threatened British, lend-lease was later extended to several other countries. *(Ch. 28)*

Lenin, Vladimir Ilyich (1870–1924)   Russian revolutionary. Leader of the **Bolsheviks** since 1903, he masterminded the November 1917 revolution that overthrew the **provisional government** and led to a communist regime in Russia. See also **New Economic Policy.** *(Ch. 25)*

Leonardo da Vinci (1452–1519)   A painter, engineer, and scientist, da Vinci rejected arguments and ideas based on imitation of the ancients. Rather, he advocated careful study of the natural world. *(Ch. 12)*

liberalism   Nineteenth-century economic and political theory that called for reducing government powers to a minimum. Liberals worked to impose constitutional limits on government, establish the rule of law, eliminate state regulation of the economy, and ensure a voice in government for men of property and education. *(Ch. 21)*

linear perspective   Revolutionary technique developed by early-fifteenth-century Florentine painters for representing three-dimensional objects on a two-dimensional plane. The technique is based in part on the observation that as parallel lines recede, they appear to converge. *(Ch. 12)*

Livia (58 B.C.–A.D. 29)   Wife of **Augustus** and mother of Tiberius, his successor. As one of Augustus's main advisers, she intrigued to secure the succession for Tiberius and was suspected of poisoning several family members, including Augustus himself. *(Ch. 6)*

Locarno, Treaty of (1925)   Treaty that introduced a new, more conciliatory spirit in international affairs. France and Germany accepted the postwar border between them, and Germany was again recognized as a diplomatic equal and entered the League of Nations in 1926. *(Ch. 26)*

Locke, John (1632–1704)   English philosopher. In his influential *Two Treatises of Government,* Locke asserted that the state arises from a contract that individuals freely accept. Thus, rebellion against abuse of power is justified. In addition, Locke theorized that human knowledge is largely the product of experience. See also **empirical method.** *(Ch. 17)*

Louis XIV (r. 1643–1715)   Longest-reigning ruler in European history, who imposed absolute rule on France and waged several wars attempting to dominate Europe. He was known as the Sun King, and his reign marked a great flowering of French culture. *(Ch. 16)*

Loyola, Ignatius (1491–1556)   Spanish nobleman and founder of the Society of Jesus, or Jesuits, which has been called the vanguard of the Catholic reform movement. After papal approval of the order, the Jesuits focused primarily on educating Catholics and reconverting Protestants. (*Ch. 14*)

Luddites   Organized groups of British workers formed in 1811–1812, who smashed machines and rioted to protest against industrialization, which they felt would threaten their livelihood. The name comes from their mythical leader, General Ned Ludd. (*Ch. 20*)

Luther, Martin (1483–1546)   German theologian and religious reformer. Luther began the Protestant Reformation in 1517 with the publication of his *Ninety-Five Theses,* which challenged indulgences and Catholic teachings on penitential acts. His translation of the Bible into German in 1522 standardized the modern German language. See also **Augsburg Confession; justification by faith;** *sola scriptura.* (*Ch. 14*)

Maastricht agreements (1991)   Agreements among twelve European Community countries at Maastricht, the Netherlands, to form the **European Union.** The member states agreed to expand cooperation on social, foreign, judicial, and security matters and adopted a timetable for a common policy on workers' rights, a common currency (the **euro**), and a common central banking structure. (*Ch. 30*)

Maccabees   Traditionalist Jews led by the Hasmonean family, who in 168 B.C. revolted against Hellenizing laws and influences. Their success is celebrated today during the Jewish holiday of Hanukkah. (*Ch. 4*)

Macedon   Weaker, less culturally advanced state on Greece's northern border. It was unified and led to power by **Philip II** and **Alexander the Great,** who became rulers of Greece. (*Ch. 4*)

Machiavelli, Niccolò (1469–1527)   Florentine politician and political theorist. His most famous work, *The Prince,* describes the methods a prince can use to acquire and maintain power. Often misunderstood as a defender of despotism, Machiavelli emphasized that a successful ruler needed to anticipate and consider the consequences of his actions. (*Ch. 12*)

Magellan, Ferdinand (1480?–1521)   Portuguese-born Spanish explorer who led the first expedition to sail around the world. After finding the South American passage to the Pacific Ocean, he sailed to the Philippines, where he was killed by natives. Survivors on one of his ships completed the circumnavigation. (*Ch. 13*)

Maginot Line   A 200-mile system of elaborate permanent fortifications on France's eastern border, named for war minister André Maginot, and built primarily during the 1930s. It was a defense against German frontal assault; in 1940 the Germans invaded by flanking the line. (*Ch. 26*)

Magna Carta (1215)   Momentous document that England's barons forced King John to sign. It required the king to respect the rights of feudal lords, not abuse his judicial powers, and consult the barons—in essence, it put the king under the law, not above it. (*Ch. 9*)

manifest destiny   Term coined in 1845 for the belief that the expanding United States was destined to occupy the North American continent from coast to coast. The rhetoric of manifest destiny was invoked to justify war with Mexico in 1846 and the acquisition of California and the Southwest from Mexico in 1848. (*Ch. 22*)

manor   In western Europe, a type of estate that developed under the Carolingians. One-quarter to one-half of the land was set aside as a reserve (or demesne), to be worked on behalf of the landlord; the remainder was divided into tenancies worked by individual peasants for their own support. (*Ch. 8*)

Maria Theresa (r. 1740–1780)   Habsburg archduchess of Austria and queen of Hungary and Bohemia. After successfully defending her right to the Austrian throne against attacks by **Frederick the Great** and others, she reformed and centralized the administration of her Austrian and Bohemian lands. (*Ch. 18*)

Marina, Doña (Malintzin) (1501–1550)   An Aztec by birth, she was sold to the Mayas and eventually became a translator and guide for the Spanish. After her critical role in the conquest, she married a Spaniard and lived as a Spanish noblewoman. (*Ch. 13*)

Marxism   Political and economic theories of the two German philosophers and revolutionaries, Karl Marx (1818–1883) and Friedrich Engels (1820–1895), which they called scientific **socialism** and which gave birth to modern communism. Marxism argued that the oppressed working class should and inevitably would rebel against the capitalist owners and build a communist society. (*Ch. 21*)

mass production   System in which great numbers of people work in centralized, mechanized **factories** to produce large quantities of goods; an essential feature of **industrialization.** A series of eighteenth-century inventions, culminating in the **steam engine,** enabled Britain to mass-produce textiles and benefit from the resulting increases in productivity. (*Ch. 20*)

Matteotti murder   The 1924 killing by fascist thugs of Italian moderate socialist Giacomo Matteotti after he denounced the fascist violence accompanying national elections. The public outcry following the murder eventually led **Mussolini** to commit to a more radical direction, which included the creation of a new, fascist form of state. (*Ch. 26*)

mechanistic worldview   Seventeenth-century philosophical view that saw the world as a machine that functions in strict obedience to physical laws, without purpose or will. Experience and reason were regarded as the standards of truth. (*Ch. 17*)

mercantilism   Economic policy pursued by western European states in the seventeenth and eighteenth centuries, stressing self-sufficiency in manufactured goods, tight government control of trade to foster the domestic economy, protectionist policies, and the absolute value of bullion. (*Ch. 16*)

Minoans   Society that flourished between 2000 and 1375 B.C. on the Aegean island of Crete, where Greece's first civilization appeared. Their sophisticated culture and economy were administered from their magnificent palaces. See also **Mycenaeans.** *(Ch. 2)*

mir   Russian peasant commune. After Tsar Alexander II freed the serfs in 1861, the mir determined land use and paid the government mortgages and taxes. Peasants could leave the land only with the mir's permission. *(Ch. 22)*

monasticism   Ascetic way of life. Christian monasticism was founded by an Egyptian layman, Anthony (d. 356), who renounced all worldliness and pursued a life of prayer in the desert. A more communal form of monasticism was created by Pachomius (290–346), who wrote the first monastic Rule—a code for daily living in a monastic community. Monasticism quickly spread throughout the Christian world. *(Ch. 7)*

monotheism   Belief that there is only one God. The Hebrew Bible places this belief as originating about 2000–1500 B.C., when God commanded Abraham to give up Mesopotamian polytheism for belief in one God. *(Ch. 2)*

More, Thomas (1478–1535)   Chancellor of England under Henry VIII. More's best-known work, *Utopia*, was highly critical of contemporary European kingdoms. It describes a fictional land of peace and harmony that has outlawed private property and all forms of wealth. More was executed when he refused to take an oath to support the **Act of Supremacy.** See also **humanism.** *(Ch. 12)*

Muhammad (570–632)   Prophet and founder of Islam. In 610 he began to receive revelations commanding him to teach all people a new faith that called for an unquestioned belief in one god, Allah, and a deep commitment to social justice for believers. Before his death, he had converted most of Arabia. See also **Five Pillars; Quran.** *(Ch. 8)*

Mussolini, Benito (1883–1945)   Italian fascist dictator. Mussolini founded the fascist movement in 1919 and took power in 1922. He replaced Italy's parliamentary democracy with a **corporative state** and pursued an expansionist foreign policy. He concluded the Pact of Steel with **Adolf Hitler** in 1939 and took Italy into World War II in 1940. Deposed in 1943, he was killed by partisans in 1945. *(Ch. 26)*

Mycenaeans   Militaristic people from the Greek mainland who conquered the **Minoans** around 1550–1375 B.C. Mycenaean civilization was a center of Bronze Age culture until its destruction around 1100 B.C. *(Ch. 2)*

mystery religions   Popular Hellenistic cults featuring the initiation of worshipers into secret doctrines. Mystery religions replaced the traditional Greek religion of the Olympian gods. Some ancient Egyptian cults were recast as mystery religions, influencing early Christianity. *(Ch. 4)*

Napoleon Bonaparte (1769–1821)   Emperor of the French (r. 1804–1815). A French general who took part in a coup in 1799 against the **Directory,** Napoleon consolidated power as first consul and proclaimed himself emperor with the approval of a national plebiscite in 1804. His military conquests exported French revolutionary reforms to the rest of Europe. He was finally defeated and exiled in 1815. *(Ch. 19)*

National Assembly (1789–1791)   Legislative body formed in France in 1789 after the Third Estate insisted on being certified as members of the Estates General as a whole. The National Assembly drafted the **Declaration of the Rights of Man and the Citizen** and a constitution that called for a constitutional (not absolute) monarchy. *(Ch. 19)*

National Socialist (Nazi) Party   The political party that grew from the movement that German dictator **Adolf Hitler** made his vehicle to power. Originating from the radical right in Munich in 1919, the Nazi Party won voting support during the early 1930s, paving the way for Hitler to be named German chancellor in 1933. *(Ch. 27)*

nationalism   Belief arising in the eighteenth century that people derive their identity from their nation and owe it their primary loyalty. The criteria for nationhood typically included a common language, religion, and political authority, as well as common traditions and shared historical experiences. Nationalism was a major force in most of the revolutions of 1848 and in the subsequent unification of Italy and of Germany. *(Ch. 21)*

Nazi Party   See **Nationalist Socialist (Nazi) Party.**

Nazi-Soviet Pact (1939)   Surprise agreement between the Soviet Union and Nazi Germany in August 1939 that each would remain neutral if the other went to war with some other nation. The pact freed Germany to attack Poland a few days later without fear of Soviet reprisal. *(Ch. 27)*

Neo-Babylonians   Rulers of western Asia between 612 and 539 B.C. who elaborately rebuilt Babylon, creating the famous Hanging Gardens. They destroyed Jerusalem, deporting many Judeans in what is known as the Babylonian Captivity. *(Ch. 2)*

Neolithic Revolution   Human discovery and spread of agriculture, between about 13,000 and 5000 B.C. People first domesticated dogs and other animals and then learned how to cultivate crops. *(Ch. 1)*

New Economic Policy (NEP) (1921–1928)   A Russian economic liberalization measure aimed at reviving an economy in crisis. The NEP restored considerable scope for private enterprise and allowed peasants to sell some of their harvest. After initial economic success, it was eventually considered a threat to the socialist state and was replaced by state-controlled central planning. *(Ch. 26)*

new imperialism   Era of European overseas expansion launched in the 1880s. In the following decades, Europeans subjugated 500 million people in Africa and Asia—one half of the world's non-European population. *(Ch. 24)*

Newton, Isaac (1643–1727)   English physicist, mathematician, and natural philosopher. Newton's mathematical computation of the laws of gravity and planetary motion, which he combined with a fully developed theory of inertia, completed the explanation for motion initiated by **Nicholas Copernicus.** See also **laws of motion.** *(Ch. 17)*

nongovernmental organizations (NGOs)   A network of organizations unaffiliated with governments but central to the international community, such as the Red Cross, Amnesty International, and Doctors Without Borders, that had gradually emerged by the early twenty-first century to deal with humanitarian relief and human rights issues. (Ch. 30)

North Atlantic Treaty Organization (NATO) An alliance for regional defense, created in 1949 by the United States, Canada, and western European nations, whose members agree to defend one another from attack by non-member countries. Its original aim was to contain the Soviet Union. (Ch. 29)

Nuremberg trials The war crimes trials conducted in Nuremberg, Germany. Most of the twenty-four defendants were convicted of war crimes and "crimes against humanity." (Ch. 28)

On the Donation of Constantine Work by Lorenzo Valla (1407–1457) proving that the *Donation of Constantine* was not written at the time of the emperor Constantine. The forged *Donation* purported to record Constantine's transfer to the pope of jurisdiction over Rome and the western half of the empire. Valla's work undermined the papacy's claim to political rule in central Italy. (Ch. 12)

Orthodox The Catholic Christian faith of Byzantium. It differed from Roman Catholicism by its use of Greek instead of Latin, the inclusion of icons in worship, an adherence to the Greek Church Fathers, some differences in basic theology, and many differences in customs and practices. (Ch. 8)

papacy Name for the institution ruled by the bishop of Rome who, in Roman Catholic tradition, is the successor to Peter, the most prominent apostle. Since Peter was believed to be the leader of the original followers of Christ, his successors, the popes (from *papa* by the fourth century), were believed to be the leaders of the whole church. (Ch. 7)

Papal Monarchy Period during the twelfth and thirteenth centuries when the power of the Catholic Church was increasingly expanded and centralized in the hands of the popes, as papal policy focused on recovering lost lands and rights in central Italy. (Ch. 9)

Papal States Beginning in the eighth century, territories held by the popes in central Italy under the protection of the Frankish kings. (Ch. 8)

papyrus Paperlike writing material used by the ancient Egyptians, Greeks, and Romans. Made primarily in Egypt from the papyrus plant, it was durable, flexible, and easy to write on. (Ch. 1)

Paris Commune (1871) Parisian workers' uprising intended to establish a workers' government under home rule. Stemming from labor discontent and the radicalization of workers during the siege of Paris in the Franco-Prussian War, the commune was suppressed by the army of the conservative French government. (Ch. 22)

Parliament English legislative institution, consisting of a House of Lords and a House of Commons, whose ancestors were the royal courts that met in 1265 and 1295. The king considered the courts a device to win support for royal agendas; the barons viewed them as opportunities to play a real policymaking role in government. In the late sixteenth and early seventeenth centuries, Parliament used control over monies to bargain with the Crown over foreign and domestic policies, leading to resistance to and eventual deposition of Charles I. The power of Parliament within the government was definitively established when it forced William and Mary to accept its role in government in the Glorious Revolution (1688). See also **Glorious Revolution.** (Ch. 16)

parliaments Initially expanded meetings of the royal court intended to secure consensus for royal policies. (Ch. 9)

paterfamilias Oldest living male in an ancient Roman family, who had supreme legal power within the household. Only the paterfamilias could own property free and clear. (Ch. 5)

Paul of Tarsus (d. ca. 67) Christian apostle and saint. A Jew from Anatolia and a Roman citizen, Paul first persecuted the Christians but became a believer around A.D. 36. Paul taught that the life and resurrection of **Jesus of Nazareth** offered all humanity the hope of salvation through faith. Under Paul, **Christianity** began its complete separation from Judaism. (Ch. 6)

pax Romana Latin for "Roman peace," the term refers to the period of peace and prosperity in the Roman Empire from A.D. 69 to 180. During this time the emperors emphasized extending citizenship and spreading prosperity throughout the provinces, and Italy was no longer the tyrant of the Mediterranean. See also **Flavians.** (Ch. 6)

Peace of Westphalia (1648) Treaty that ended the **Thirty Years' War.** The principalities within the Holy Roman Empire were recognized as virtually autonomous, severely weakening the power of the emperor. Calvinism joined Catholicism and Lutheranism as tolerated faiths within the empire, and the treaty closed the age of religious wars. (Ch. 15)

Pericles Leader of fifth-century-B.C. Athens when **demokratia** became entrenched as the government and way of life. Distinguished for his oratory and honesty, he established Athens as a great center of art and literature as well as a great empire. (Ch. 3)

Persian Empire Vast, prosperous, and law-abiding West Asian empire, from about 550 B.C. to its conquest by **Alexander the Great** around 330 B.C. The relatively tolerant rule of the Persian emperors represented the greatest success yet of a universal kingship. The Persians also built the first great navy. (Ch. 2)

Peter the Great (r. 1682–1725) Russian tsar. Brilliant, energetic, and tyrannical, Peter revolutionized Russian society by his determined efforts to westernize his nation culturally, economically, and politically. He modernized the army and navy, secured seaports, and made Russia into a great power. (Ch. 16)

Petrarch, Francesco (1304–1374) Influential Italian poet, biographer, and humanist during the Renaissance. Petrarch advocated imitating the actions, values, and culture of the ancient Romans to reform the excesses of the present world. (Ch. 12)

Petrograd Soviet   The *soviet* (council) of leaders of strike committees and army regiments elected in March 1917, when Petrograd's workers protested in response to severe wartime food and coal shortages. Central to the Bolshevik Revolution of 1917, the soviet eventually became the ruling power in the Russian capital—but only temporarily. (Ch. 25)

pharaoh   Ancient Egyptians' title for their king, an absolute, all-powerful, and all-providing ruler. It was believed that the ruler represented the ancestors and guaranteed the fertility of the soil. (Ch. 1)

Philip II (r. 359–336 B.C.)   King of **Macedon.** A brilliant soldier and statesman, Philip conquered the Greek world. He developed a well-trained, professional year-round army and mastered the technology of siegecraft. He was succeeded by his son, **Alexander the Great.** (Ch. 4)

Philip II (r. 1556–1598)   King of Spain, son of **Charles V.** An avid Roman Catholic, he ruled Spain at the height of its influence. Philip dispatched the ill-fated **Armada** to invade England and attempted to quash the revolt of the Netherlands. (Ch. 15)

philosophes   French term referring to thinkers and critics of the Enlightenment era, including **Voltaire** and Diderot. Philosophes applied to political and social thought the confidence in human reason and the intelligibility of natural law that **Isaac Newton** and other scientists had recently achieved. (Ch. 18)

Phoenicians   Canaanites whose civilization flourished about 1050–750 B.C. in present-day coastal Syria, where they established major trading ports. Master sailors, they planted colonies around the Mediterranean, many of which, including Carthage, became independent states. The Phoenicians exported the civilization of western Asia—including the Phoenician alphabet, derived from Ugarit—to the Mediterranean world. (Ch. 2)

plantation system   Agricultural practices developed by the fifteenth-century Portuguese to produce sugar on their island colonies in the Atlantic using involuntarily transported slaves from Africa. Portugal's prototype—wealthy absentee landlords and masses of forced labor producing cash crops on vast tracts of land—was the model for the New World plantation system. In seventeenth- and eighteenth-century French and English colonies in the Caribbean, large sugar plantations owned by wealthy, often absentee, landlords replaced smaller-scale independent farming. See also **slave trade.** (Ch. 16)

Plato (427–348 B.C.)   Ancient Greek philosopher, student of **Socrates.** One of Western philosophy's greatest exponents of idealism, Plato believed that the senses are misleading and that truth can therefore be attained only by training the mind to overcome commonsense evidence. In the *Republic,* Plato describes an ideal state in which philosophers rule as kings, benevolently and unselfishly. (Ch. 3)

polis   Term for an ancient Greek city-state, a system that reached its height around 700–300 B.C. The ideological and political organization of the polis emphasized equality and a shared community life for all citizens, not just the elite. (Ch. 3)

popular front   A term for antifascist electoral alliances and governing coalitions that Communists promoted from 1934 until 1939 to resist the further spread of fascism. Popular front coalitions won control of government in both Spain and France during 1936. (Ch. 27)

positivism   Philosophy of the French thinker Auguste Comte (1798–1857). Comte asserted that human history progressed through distinct and irreversible stages, leading inexorably upward to the final and highest stage of development, the positive—or scientific—stage. Positivism and its optimistic outlook for human progress were influential in both Europe and Latin America during the nineteenth century. (Ch. 23)

Potsdam conference   A July–August 1945 meeting held at Potsdam, Germany, between the USSR, the United States, and Great Britain to implement their earlier agreements concerning the treatment of defeated Germany. Many of the agreements reached were later abandoned amid growing hostility between the USSR and the Western democracies. (Ch. 28)

Prague Spring   The attempt by Czechoslovakian reformers in 1968 to gain freer cultural expression, democratization of Communist Party procedures, and broader participation in public life within the framework of a communist state. The forcible suppression of the movement by Soviet leaders seemed to signal the end of any hope for flexibility and openness within the Soviet sphere. (Ch. 29)

price revolution   Steady rise in prices in the sixteenth and seventeenth centuries, resulting from population growth and the influx of precious metals from Spain's New World territories. As wages lost one-tenth to one-fourth of their value, people sought new work, protested against taxes, and attacked scapegoats. The price revolution concentrated wealth in fewer hands and contributed to the rise of a new **gentry** class. (Ch. 15)

primogeniture   A legal inheritance system that provided the firstborn, usually the firstborn son, the right to inherit all the family land and farm. (Ch. 20)

Principate   The constitutional monarchy of the Early Roman Empire, from 31 B.C. to A.D. 192. The term comes from *Princeps,* or "first citizen," an old title of respect used in the **senate.** See also **Augustus; Flavians.** (Ch. 6)

professionalization   Establishment in the nineteenth century of common standards and requirements, especially in medicine, law, architecture, and engineering. Professionalization brought either government or self-regulation to vocations whose prestige rested on the claim of exclusive expertise in their fields. (Ch. 23)

proletariat   Term used by Karl Marx to describe the new class of industrial workers who owned none of the means of production and were totally dependent on factory owners for their livelihoods. In Marxist thought, capitalists were destined to be overthrown by the proletariat. See also **Marxism.** (Ch. 20)

provisional government   The body that ruled Russia from March to November 1917, in the wake of the revolution that overthrew the tsarist regime. Originally intended to be a temporary step to an elected constituent assembly, its policies caused discontents that the **Bolsheviks** were quick to exploit. (Ch. 25)

Ptolemies   Dynasty of Egyptian kings who ruled from 304 to 30 B.C., founded by Ptolemy I, a Macedonian general of **Alexander the Great.** It was the wealthiest, most sophisticated, and longest lasting of the Hellenistic kingdoms. See also **Alexandria.** (Ch. 4)

Punic Wars (264–146 B.C.)   Three wars during which the Roman Empire eventually destroyed Carthage. The Romans later adopted the Carthaginians' plantation system using massive numbers of slaves. (Ch. 5)

Puritans   Radical Protestants in late-sixteenth- and seventeenth-century England. Puritans emphasized Bible reading, preaching, private scrutiny of conscience, and de-emphasized institutional ritual and clerical authority. Puritans became a majority in Parliament during the reign of Charles I and led the campaign against the king during the English Civil War. (Ch. 15)

Putin, Vladimir   Elected president of Russia early in 2000, he had been director of Russia's secret police before coming to political prominence as prime minister in 1999. He cracked down on the insurgency in Chechnya and, as president, proved more energetic in dealing with Russia's problems than his predecessor, Boris Yeltsin. (Ch. 30)

putting-out system   The production in country homes of thread and cloth by spinners and weavers for an entrepreneur who bought raw materials and "put them out" to be finished by individual workers. This cottage industry system expanded in eighteenth-century Europe as increased numbers of agricultural laborers needed more nonfarm work in off-seasons. (Ch. 18)

Quran   Islamic sacred writings, which **Muhammad** communicated in the form of "recitations," insisting that he was transmitting a direct revelation from Allah. After Muhammad's death, his followers arranged the recitations into 114 *Suras,* or chapters, containing legal and wisdom literature and moral teaching. (Ch. 8)

rabbinic Judaism   Main form of Judaism, which emerged during the first century A.D. under the leadership of the rabbis, the spiritual descendants of the Pharisees. Rabbinic Judaism amplified and interpreted the Hebrew Bible to clarify Jewish practice, elevated the oral law to equal authority with the written **Torah,** and enabled Judaism to evolve flexibly. (Ch. 6)

Realpolitik   Style of governing that uses all means, including war, to expand the influence and power of a state. The best-known practitioner of Realpolitik was Prussian chancellor **Otto von Bismarck.** (Ch. 22)

Reconquista   Wars of reconquest in the Iberian Peninsula from the eleventh to fifteenth centuries. Spanish and Portuguese rulers seized territories from the weakening Muslim regime. By awarding reconquered lands to their nobles,

Christian kings enhanced their own status and power. (Ch. 9)

remilitarization of the Rhineland   The reoccupation of Germany's Rhineland territory by German troops in March 1936, in clear violation of the **Treaty of Versailles.** When the French and British did not resist the German move, **Adolf Hitler** was emboldened to additional acts of aggression elsewhere. (Ch. 27)

Renaissance   Term derived from the French word for "rebirth" used to describe a period of intense creativity between 1350 and 1500 when cultural values were based on imitation of classical Greek and Roman norms. (Ch. 12)

res publica   Romans' concept of their republic, which uniquely influenced Western political institutions. *Res publica* is Latin for "public thing," as opposed to *res privata,* "private thing," as the Romans characterized monarchy. (Ch. 5)

risorgimento   Italian term, beginning in the late eighteenth century, for the political and cultural renewal of Italy. It later came to describe the political and military events that led to the unification of Italy in 1861. (Ch. 22)

Robespierre, Maximilien (1758–1794)   French lawyer and revolutionary leader. A **Jacobin** who joined the Committee of Public Safety in 1793, Robespierre called for the **Terror** to suppress internal dissent. (Ch. 19)

Romanesque   Meaning "in the Roman style," this nineteenth-century term characterized the transitional architecture and painting of the period between the waning of Carolingian art and the full emergence of **Gothic** art in the twelfth century. Distinctive features of Romanesque churches are their exuberant decoration and ornament. (Ch. 10)

romanticism   Artistic movement, prevalent from the 1760s to 1840s, that rebelled against rationalism. Writers, painters, and composers rejected the Enlightenment and its rationalist values, instead praising emotion and sensitivity, and worshiping nature for its inherent beauty. (Ch. 21)

Rome-Berlin Axis   Alliance between Hitler's Nazi Germany and Mussolini's fascist Italy. Beginning as an informal understanding by 1936, it was cemented by an anti-Comintern agreement and eventually by an open-ended military alliance, the Pact of Steel, in 1939. (Ch. 27)

Roosevelt, Franklin Delano (1882–1945)   U.S. president who served from 1933 to 1945, through the Great Depression of the 1930s and most of World War II. His New Deal program, including large public works projects, was an innovative response to the Depression. (Ch. 28)

Rousseau, Jean-Jacques (1712–1778)   French writer and philosopher. In his 1762 work, *The Social Contract,* Rousseau depicted a hypothetical state with direct democracy in which citizens have inalienable rights to wide-ranging liberties. He was influential as a critic of an elite society still dominated by status, patronage, and privilege. (Ch. 18)

Sacred Union   An agreement made between French leaders of different political groups to cooperate during World

War I. The French government had initially feared that the Socialists might sabotage the war, when, in fact, they were eager to join the new government of national defense. *(Ch. 25)*

salons Regular gatherings in eighteenth-century Parisian private homes, where **Voltaire** and other **philosophes** read and discussed their works in progress, with the exchange of ideas facilitated by female *salonnières* (salon leaders). Anyone with appropriate manners could participate as an equal, enabling conversation to shift from maintaining the status quo to questioning it. *(Ch. 18)*

sans-culottes Ordinary citizens of revolutionary Paris, whose derisive nickname referred to their inability to afford fashionable knee pants ("culottes"). Because of their effective political organization, they were able to influence the direction of the French Revolution through pressure on the government as well as direct action, such as to overthrow the monarchy in August 1792. *(Ch. 19)*

Sappho (fl. ca. 625 B.C.) Ancient Greek poet from the island of Lesbos. Sappho wrote odes, wedding songs, and hymns expressing intimate feelings, including love for other women. She wrote of female sexuality in a male-dominated culture. *(Ch. 3)*

Schutzstaffel (SS) Nazi elite troops, led by Heinrich Himmler. Linked to the Gestapo, the secret political police, the SS specialized in institutionalized terror tactics and were responsible for some of the worst atrocities of the Nazi regime. *(Ch. 27)*

second industrial revolution Interrelated economic changes that resulted in a significant speedup in production in western Europe after 1850. Key factors were the introduction of new products, new methods of manufacture, and new materials such as mass-produced steel, synthetic dyes, and aluminum. *(Ch. 23)*

Second International International socialist organization founded in 1889 that met yearly to debate issues of broad concern. Beginning in 1907, it called for workers to strike and to refuse military service in case of international conflict. *(Ch. 24)*

Second Reform Bill (1867) British legislation that extended suffrage by lowering property qualifications and set equal population requirements for all parliamentary districts. The legislation bolstered the existing system, as the newly enfranchised clerks, artisans, and other skilled workers felt more a part of society. *(Ch. 22)*

Seleucids Dynasty of rulers of Asia Minor from 312 to 64 B.C. Founded by Seleucus (ca. 358–281 B.C.), a general of **Alexander the Great,** the kingdom spread **Hellenism** by establishing seventy colonies throughout the Near East. *(Ch. 4)*

senate In the ancient Roman Republic and Empire, the powerful council of elders that advised the monarchs (Latin: *senatus,* from *senex,* "old man"). Romans spoke of the senate's *auctoritas,* a quasi-religious prestige. *(Ch. 5)*

separate spheres Notion, especially prevalent in the mid-nineteenth century, of two distinct sets of roles—one male and public, the other female and private. While the man was out in the world advancing his career, the bourgeois woman was to run her home, providing her family with an orderly, comfortable shelter. *(Ch. 23)*

Seven Years' War (1756–1763) The first major war between European nations started and fought largely in their overseas empires, the Seven Years' War was in part a conflict between Britain and France for control of overseas possessions. Britain emerged the decisive winner, partly because France was simultaneously fighting on the European continent, where France and Austria tried to contain Prussia. *(Ch. 18)*

show trials Trials staged for ideological and propaganda reasons in the USSR. In the most famous, orchestrated by **Joseph Stalin** from 1936 to 1938, major communist figures were made to confess to trumped-up charges and executed. These trials helped persuade Soviet citizens that a high-level conspiracy was responsible for the USSR's economic woes. *(Ch. 27)*

Sistine Chapel Chapel at the Vatican Palace commissioned by Pope Sixtus IV in 1475, best known for Michelangelo's magnificent paintings of the Creation and Last Judgment. The monument vividly captures the cultural, religious, and ideological program of the papacy. *(Ch. 12)*

slave trade Europeans' trade with Africa in which involuntary laborers were bought and shipped to the Americas to be sold primarily to owners of plantations where sugar and other commodities were produced. The trade reached its peak in the eighteenth century, when approximately 7 million Africans were shipped across the Atlantic. The slave trade was an integral part of the "triangle trade" by which Europe, Africa, and the Americas were connected. See also **plantation system.** *(Ch. 18)*

Smith, Adam (1723–1790) Scottish economist who developed the doctrine of *laissez faire.* In his treatise *The Wealth of Nations* (1776), Smith argued that an economy regulates itself better without interference by government and without monopolies and other economic privileges. Smith suggested that people's economic activities are often "led by an invisible hand" to benefit society as a whole. *(Ch. 18)*

social Catholics Catholics in western Europe who believed that society bore responsibility for the well-being of the poor. They were following the ideas set out in 1891 by Pope Leo XIII (r. 1878–1903) in his encyclical *Rerum novarum* (Of New Things). *(Ch. 23)*

Social Darwinism Theory of social evolution first articulated by Herbert Spencer (1820–1902). According to Social Darwinists, human societies evolve in the same way as plants and animals, and the weak, poor, and improvident are not worthy of survival. Social Darwinism was used to justify callousness toward the poor at home and imperialist conquest abroad. See also **Darwinism.** *(Ch. 23)*

social market economy The late-twentieth-century socially oriented model of capitalism practiced in continental western Europe, providing a substantial safety net in health care and a commitment to public services such as transportation and day care. It competed with the U.S.

model, shared by Britain, which emphasized free enterprise. (*Ch. 30*)

socialism   Nineteenth-century economic and social doctrine and political movement that opposed private ownership and control of the means of production. Socialists believed that the "social" or state ownership of property, unlike private ownership, would benefit society as a whole, creating a more just system. (*Ch. 21*)

Society of Jesus (Jesuits)   Founded in 1534 by **Ignatius Loyola** (1491–1556), the Jesuits soon became leaders in the Catholic Counter-Reformation. The Jesuits were famed for their schools and work as spiritual advisers. (*Ch. 14*)

Society of Revolutionary Republican Women   In revolutionary France, a powerful political club that represented the interests of female **sans-culottes.** The society was included in a general ban on political participation by women that the Committee of Public Safety instituted in October 1793. (*Ch. 19*)

Socrates (469–399 B.C.)   Ancient Greek philosopher, a founder of the Western philosophical tradition. Socrates changed the emphasis of philosophy from the natural world to human ethics. He believed that no one who truly understood goodness would ever choose to do evil. Accused of being an atheist and corrupting the young, Socrates was executed in 399. Socrates' teachings were recorded and transmitted by his students, including **Plato.** (*Ch. 3*)

sola scriptura   Doctrine put forward by **Martin Luther** in *On the Babylonian Captivity of the Church* (1520) that church authority had to be based on biblical teachings. In particular he argued that the sacraments of the Catholic Church—other than baptism and communion—were not found in the Bible. (*Ch. 14*)

solidarism   Late-nineteenth-century policy of conservative and liberal parties to blunt the appeal of socialism. Solidarism emphasized the mutual responsibility of classes and individuals for one another's well-being and led to the passage of laws and benefits to improve the lot of the working class. (*Ch. 23*)

Solidarity   A trade union formed from a movement of shipyard workers in communist Poland in 1980. It became the nucleus of widespread demands for change—including independent labor organizations, the right to strike, and freedom of expression. Though forced underground in 1981, the movement eventually proved crucial to the downfall of the communist regime in Poland. (*Ch. 29*)

Solon (ca. 630–560 B.C.)   Statesman of early Athens. Appointed to a one-year term as sole archon in 594 B.C., Solon transformed Greek society through mediation, moderation, respect for law, and measures that liberated the poor and downtrodden. His economic reforms sparked a commercial boom. (*Ch. 3*)

Spanish Inquisition   Church court that began in 1478 when King Ferdinand and Queen Isabella obtained papal approval to control the grand inquisitor. The Spanish Inquisition investigated and condemned many former Jews and Muslims who were believed to have insincerely converted to Christianity. It became an important and lucrative instrument to expand state power. (*Ch. 11*)

"stab in the back" myth   The notion, widely held among Germans after their unexpected loss in World War I, that political intrigue and revolution at home had sabotaged the German military effort. It helped alienate Germans from their new democratic government. (*Ch. 25*)

Stalin, Joseph (1879–1953)   Soviet dictator. Secretary of the Communist Party since 1922, Stalin outmaneuvered his rivals after the death of Lenin to take control of the Soviet government by 1929. Stalin jettisoned the **New Economic Policy** and instituted a program of crash industrialization and agricultural **collectivization.** He concluded the **Nazi-Soviet Pact** in 1939 but joined the Allies after the German invasion of the Soviet Union in 1941. Victorious in World War II, Stalin sponsored the takeover of governments in eastern Europe by communist regimes, contributing to the development of the **cold war.** See also **"the Great Patriotic War"; gulag; Potsdam conference; show trials; Yalta conference.** (*Ch. 26*)

Stalingrad (1942–1943)   Decisive World War II battle. The Soviet Union, at immense cost in lives, launched repeated counterattacks on Germany's Sixth Army, stopping it from advancing farther and finally forcing it to surrender. The battle is often considered the turning point of World War II in Europe. (*Ch. 28*)

steam engine   Machine invented in England in its modern form by James Watt in 1777. The steam engine provided mechanized power for manufacturing and made **factories** and **mass production** possible. (*Ch. 20*)

Stoics   Believers in a philosophical system begun in Athens by Zeno (335–263 B.C.). Stoicism emphasized the pursuit of wisdom, the reliability of sensory experience, and freedom from all passion. Stoics focused on intentions as well as the results of actions. (*Ch. 4*)

Stresemann, Gustav (1878–1929)   German statesman of the Weimar Republic. Leader of the conservative German People's Party, Stresemann served briefly as chancellor in 1923, then as foreign secretary from 1923 to 1929. He secured a reduction of Germany's reparations payments and negotiated the **Treaty of Locarno,** paving the way for Germany's entry to the League of Nations in 1926. His death in 1929 was a blow to hopes for the development of democracy in Germany and peace in Europe. (*Ch. 26*)

Suez crisis (1956)   Crisis prompted by Egypt's nationalization of the British-owned Suez Canal. The effort of Britain, France, and Israel to seize the canal prompted a strong negative reaction in world opinion, forcing them to withdraw. The episode demonstrated the newly limited reach of the western European powers in world affairs. (*Ch. 29*)

suffragists   Activists who, beginning in the late nineteenth century, organized to win the vote for women. Adopting increasingly violent tactics, English suffragists (often referred to by contemporaries as "suffragettes") endured attacks by male thugs, were arrested, engaged in hunger strikes, and were force-fed. (*Ch. 24*)

Sumerians   Dominant inhabitants of Mesopotamia in the third millennium B.C. They established the world's first civilization, thirty flourishing city-states with a common culture, commerce, and tendency to make war on one another. *(Ch. 1)*

summa   An encyclopedic compendium of carefully arrayed knowledge on a particular subject. Examples are the two most famous works of **Thomas Aquinas**, the *Summa Contra Gentiles* and the *Summa Theologiae*. *(Ch. 10)*

surrealism   A movement in literature and the visual arts that emerged in Paris in the early 1920s. Though indebted to dada and its mocking defiance of convention, surrealism sought to find something positive by exploring the realm of the subconscious, partly by following some of **Sigmund Freud**'s insights about access to the subconscious. *(Ch. 26)*

Tacitus, Cornelius (ca. A.D. 55–120)   Roman historian of the "Silver Age." Tacitus lauded the simple virtues of the German tribes and expressed nostalgia for the Republic. His greatest works were *The Histories*, on the civil wars of A.D. 69, and *The Annals*, chronicling the emperors from Tiberius through Nero. *(Ch. 6)*

Tennis Court Oath (1789)   Pledge signed by all but one Third Estate deputy of the Estates General of France on June 20, 1789. The deputies swore to continue to meet until a constitution was drafted. *(Ch. 19)*

Terror (1793–1794)   Systematic repression of internal enemies undertaken by revolutionary tribunals across France at the urging of **Maximilien Robespierre**. Approximately fourteen thousand people were executed, including aristocrats, Girondins, and **sans-culottes**. The Terror ended with the arrest and execution of Robespierre in July 1794. *(Ch. 19)*

tetrarchy   Government ruled by four leaders. Emperor Diocletian established a tetrarchy in about 293 to address the Roman Empire's political instability, huge size, and complexity, as well as to promote experienced men and provide an orderly imperial succession. *(Ch. 7)*

Thatcher, Margaret (b. 1925)   As Conservative prime minister of Britain from 1979 to 1990, she spearheaded a number of measures to promote privatization and free enterprise at the expense of the welfare state and the British labor unions. So dramatic was the resulting change in direction that it is sometimes characterized as Thatcher's conservative revolution. *(Chs. 29, 30)*

third-century crisis   Period from A.D. 235 to 284, when the Roman Empire suffered barbarian invasions, domestic economic problems, plague, assassinations, and urban decline. Attempting to fend off invasions at opposite fronts, the emperors devalued the currency, leading to massive inflation. *(Ch. 6)*

Third Estate   In France, the common people, as distinct from the nobles (First Estate) and clergy (Second Estate). In the Estates General in 1789, it was presumed that the votes of the First and Second Estates would overrule those of the Third Estate, although the commoners vastly outnumbered the nobles and clergy. *(Ch. 19)*

Thirty Years' War (1618–1648)   Destructive war, involving most European countries but fought in Germany, resulting from sixteenth-century religious tensions, regionalism versus centralizing forces, and dynastic and strategic rivalries between rulers. See also **Peace of Westphalia**. *(Ch. 15)*

Thucydides (ca. 455–397 B.C.)   Ancient Greek historian; with **Herodotus**, a founder of history-writing in the West. A failed Athenian general, Thucydides made a careful study of the Peloponnesian War and prided himself on the accuracy of his account of the prolonged conflict. *(Ch. 3)*

Torah   First five books of the Bible. Accepted as sacred by the Hebrews around 425 B.C., it relates the working out of God's pact, or **covenant**, with the Hebrews, his chosen people. *(Ch. 2)*

Tordesillas, Treaty of (1494)   Treaty by which Pope Alexander VI divided the rights of colonization of the newly identified lands between Portugal and Spain. He had intended to give Africa to the Portuguese and the New World to Spain, but by a miscalculation Brazil remained in the Portuguese area. *(Ch. 13)*

total war   The concept, first associated with World War I, that war requires the mobilization of all a nation's resources and energies. The unexpected need to wage total war during World War I accelerated social and economic processes, from technological development to women's suffrage. *(Ch. 25)*

Toussaint-Louverture, François (1743–1803)   Former slave who governed the island of Saint Domingue (Haiti) as an independent state after the slave revolt of 1791. In 1802 French forces captured Toussaint-Louverture, who died in prison. *(Ch. 19)*

trading-post empire   Commercial system developed by Portugal in the sixteenth century to dominate trade in the Indian Ocean through fortified, strategically placed naval bases. All merchants were expected to acquire export licenses and ship products through Portuguese ports. *(Ch. 13)*

tragedy   Serious play with an unhappy ending. Greek tragedy emerged and reached its height in the fifth century B.C. in the works of Aeschylus, Sophocles, and Euripides. The essence of Greek tragedy is the nobility in the spectacle of a great man or woman failing because of a "fatal flaw," but learning from failure. *(Ch. 3)*

trasformismo   System of political manipulation used by Count Camillo di Cavour (1810–1861), Piedmont's prime minister, to create majorities in parliament to support his cabinet. The practice of using cajolery and bribery to transform foes into supporters would continue to characterize Italian government in the late nineteenth century. *(Ch. 22)*

Triple Alliance   Military alliance established in 1882 among Germany, Austria-Hungary, and Italy to counter the Franco-Russian Alliance (later the **Triple Entente**). The system of rival alliances contributed to the escalation of international tensions. *(Ch. 24)*

Triple Entente   Military alliance between Great Britain, France, and Russia, completed in 1907, countering the

Triple Alliance. The system of rival alliances eventually brought all of Europe into World War I. *(Ch. 24)*

triumph   Elaborate procession through the streets of ancient Rome. Triumphs were voted by the **senate** to salute a general's victory over a foreign army. *(Ch. 5)*

Truman Doctrine   The U.S. policy of containment, or limiting communist expansion, as outlined by President Harry Truman in 1947. Intended most immediately to deter any communist designs on Greece or Turkey, the doctrine was used thereafter to support any country that the United States considered threatened by communism during the **cold war.** *(Ch. 28)*

unilateralism   Term describing the increasing willingness of the United States to go its own way in world affairs after the end of the cold war, and especially after the terrorist attack on the United States in September 2001. In pursuing its own course, the United States was departing from the multilateral international system that it had sought to foster since World War II. This departure alienated many Europeans. *(Ch. 30)*

United Nations   International organization of nations founded in 1945 to encourage peace, cooperation, and recognition of human rights. The major powers—China, France, Great Britain, the Soviet Union, and the United States—were given a privileged position as permanent members of the Security Council, each with veto power. *(Ch. 28)*

urbanization   Term related to the growth of cities, largely connected to the **industrialization** of the late eighteenth and nineteenth centuries. Cities aided industry by providing markets for goods and a concentrated source of workers. However, with urbanization came a host of new problems such as urban slums, lack of sanitation, and pollution. *(Ch. 20)*

utilitarianism   Political theory of Jeremy Bentham (1748–1832). Bentham argued that the purpose of government is to provide "the greatest happiness of the greatest number" and that the test of government is its usefulness. Democracy was implicit in Bentham's philosophy: the greatest number could ensure its own happiness only by voting for its rulers. *(Ch. 21)*

Vasco da Gama (1460?–1524)   Pioneering Portuguese explorer and trader whose voyage from 1497 to 1499 around the Cape of Good Hope to Mozambique and India inaugurated a four-hundred-year-long Portuguese presence in the Indian Ocean region. *(Ch. 13)*

vassals   Drawing on both Roman and Germanic customs, vassalage linked two men—lord and vassal—in an honorable, reciprocal bond based on loyalty and service. Eventually leading nobles and their vassals formed a social and political elite. *(Ch. 8)*

Versailles, Treaty of (1919)   Peace treaty that the victors in World War I imposed on a defeated Germany in 1919. The harsh terms of this dictated peace produced a sense of bitterness and betrayal in Germany. *(Ch. 25)*

Vichy France   The term for the repressive French government that followed the Third Republic after France's defeat by Nazi Germany in 1940. Headquartered in the resort town of Vichy, the government collaborated with the victorious Germans, who occupied Paris. *(Ch. 28)*

Victorian morality   Nineteenth-century ethos wherein the values of the dominant middle class, which emphasized strict moral principles, especially regarding sex and drink, became the social norms. In Queen Victoria, who reigned for two-thirds of the century, the middle classes saw a reflection of their own values. *(Ch. 23)*

Virgil   Roman poet whose works contributed to the Augustan renewal. In the *Eclogues,* Virgil (Publius Vergilius Maro, 70–19 B.C.) describes the blessings of peace under **Augustus;** in the *Georgics,* he glorifies Italian agriculture. His *Aeneid* mythologizes Rome and describes both the burden and glory of empire. *(Ch. 6)*

Visigoths   Germanic people who served as allied troops for the Romans. When threatened by the Huns, the Visigoths crossed the Danube and settled in the Balkans. Eventually they sacked Rome in 410 and expanded their rule to parts of Spain and southern France. *(Ch. 7)*

Voltaire (François-Marie Arouet, 1694–1778)   Prolific French writer, critic, and reformer who embodied the spirit of eighteenth-century rationalism: its confidence, its increasingly practical bent, its wit and sophistication. His satires and philosophical critiques targeted Christianity, intolerance, and tyranny. See also **philosophes.** *(Ch. 18)*

Vulgate Bible   Latin version of new translations of the Hebrew Scriptures and Greek New Testament written by Jerome (331–420) for Pope Damasus. It was called the Vulgate because it was the Bible for the "people" (*vulgus*), whose language was Latin. *(Ch. 7)*

Warsaw Pact (1955–1991)   Military-diplomatic alliance of Soviet bloc countries, created to counter NATO. The pact established a joint military command and mutual military assistance, as well as a new basis for the continuing presence of Soviet troops in the satellite states. See also **cold war.** *(Ch. 29)*

welfare state   The concept, especially prevalent in Western countries after World War II, that government should adopt large-scale social welfare measures, while maintaining a primarily capitalistic economy. Among the welfare measures usually adopted were a national health service, old-age pensions, and insurance against unemployment, sickness, and disability. *(Ch. 29)*

Weltpolitik   Meaning "world politics," the term describes the policy pursued by Kaiser Wilhelm II (r. 1888–1918) to make Germany a world power, with colonies, a navy, and major influence among the Great Powers. The kaiser implemented his ambitious agenda with nationalistic appeals and bombastic threats. *(Ch. 24)*

World Health Organization (WHO)   Established as a specialized agency of the United Nations in 1948, it serves as the coordinating authority on international public health. It is headquartered in Geneva, Switzerland. *(Ch. 30)*

World Trade Organization (WTO)   Growing from a multilateral trade agreement in 1947, it sought, with mixed success, to promote freer trade throughout the world. By the end of the 1990s WTO meetings were drawing large demonstrations by anti-globalization activists, most notably in Seattle in 1999 and in Cancún, Mexico, in 2003. *(Ch. 30)*

Yalta conference   The meeting in February 1945 at Yalta, a Soviet Black Sea resort, between Stalin, Roosevelt, and Churchill. With Allied victory assured, they began outlining plans for the postwar order, including the military occupation of Germany. See also **Potsdam conference.** *(Ch. 28)*

Young Turks   Term describing the young intellectuals who wanted to transform the Ottoman Empire into a more modern, Westernized state. Self-exiled in the late 1860s in Paris and London, they overthrew the sultan and seized power in 1908. The expression has subsequently come to designate any group of activists pushing for political change. *(Ch. 22)*

Zionism   Nationalist Jewish movement. In the late nineteenth century, faced with growing **anti-Semitism,** some Jews argued that they would be safe only in their own nation. Zionism advocated establishing a Jewish state in the Jews' ancient homeland of Palestine, an idea that became reality with the creation of Israel in 1948. *(Ch. 24)*

Zoroastrianism   Religion founded about 1000–550 B.C. by the Persian prophet Zarathustra (*Zoroaster* in Greek). Zoroastrians believe in a supreme deity and a cosmic contest between good and evil within each individual. *(Ch. 2)*

Zwingli, Huldrych (1484–1531)   Town preacher of Zurich, Zwingli became a leader of the urban reformation in Switzerland and southwest Germany, emphasizing the importance of the community in the salvation of individuals. *(Ch. 14)*

Index

ing cold war, 908–913. *See also* Civilization(s); Religion(s)

Currency: standardization of British, 623; in Great Depression, 839. *See also* Money

Customs union: *Zollverein* as, 631, 690, 691; in EU, 950

Cuza, Alexander, 695

Czechoslovakia: independence of, 791; French alliance with, 794, 810; after World War I, 794; Hitler and, 862, 863–864; Nazi invasion of, 863–864; after World War II, 896; Prague Spring and, 922, 925–926, 926(illus.), 934; dissidence in, 934; Havel and Charter 77 in, 935; division of, 946

Czech people: German Confederation and, 675; nationalism of, 676

Czech Republic, 946; Iraq War and, 955. *See also* Bohemia

Dachau, 880

Dada movement, 832

Daguerre, Louis, 731, 734(box)

Daladier, Edouard, 860, 864

Dalmatia: Ottoman Empire in, 670

Danzig, *see* Gdansk

Darby family: Abraham and, 619, 627

Dardanelles, 783

Darwin, Charles, 727–729, 728(box)

David, Jacques-Louis, 605(illus.)

Davidson, Emily Wilding, 757

Dawes, Charles G., 828

Dawes Plan, 828, 829

Day care: in France, 969; subsidized, 969

Days of May uprising, 920, 963

DC, *see* Christian Democratic Party (DC, Italy)

D-Day landing, 888–889, 889(illus.)

Death camps, *see* Extermination camps (Nazi)

Death rates: decrease in, 621; in cities, 634, 722; in France, 634; in London, 725; in World War I, 779

Debt: following American Revolution, 590

Decembrist uprising (Russia), 669

Declaration of Pillnitz (1791), 597

Declaration of the Rights of Man and the Citizen (France), 594, 596–597

Declaration of the Rights of Woman (Gouges), 597

Decline of the West, The (Spengler), 830

Decolonization, 895, 929–932; after World War II, 928(illus.), 941

Deficit spending: in prerevolutionary France, 591; under Napoleon, 609

Deforestation, 639

Degas, Edgar, 732

De Gaulle, Charles, 897; Free French and, 873; West Germany and, 918(illus.); after World War II, 919; unrest under, 920; Algeria and, 930; Common Market and, 932

De Klerk, F. W., 970(box)

Delacroix, Eugène, 654, 655

Delic, Dzevad, 954(illus.)

Demilitarization: of Rhineland, 794, 810, 862

Democracy: liberals opposed to, 659; socialism and, 660–661; Chartism and, 667–668; in West, 701–708; World War I as crusade for, 786; in non-Western world, 807; after World

War I, 824–825; in east-central Europe, 826; after World War II, 826, 914–922; in Weimar Germany, 826–829; in Germany, 917–919; freedoms and, 948; in postcommunist countries, 957, 959–960; pluralism and, 977, 980. *See also* Communism; Fascism; Nazi Germany

Democratic capitalism, 957–964

Demonstrations, *see* Protest(s)

De-Nazification program, 894, 896

Denikin, Anton, 813(illus.)

Denmark: Napoleon and, 608; GNP in, 631(illus.); German Confederation and, 675; constitutional government in, 676(illus.); German-speaking provinces of, 690; parliamentary democracy in, 707; emigration from, 747(illus.); unemployment in, 841; welfare issues in, 915; protests against, 945; Iraq War and, 955. *See also* Scandinavia

Départements (France), 610

Department stores, 710(illus.), 711

Depression(s): in 1848, 672. *See also* Great Depression

Der Neue Zollhof, Düsseldorf, Germany (Gehry), 979(illus.)

Descent of Man, The (Darwin), 728

Desert Fox (Rommel), 875

De-Stalinization: in Soviet Union, 923–925

Détente, 926

"Deutschland, Deutschland über alles" (song), 668

Dialectical materialism: Marx on, 662

Dickens, Charles, 715–716, 733

Dictators: in Latin America, 665; Napoleon III as, 675

"Dictatorship of the proletariat," 662

Dien Bien Phu, 930

Diet (assembly): in Germany, 668; in Poland, 669

Diet (food): of industrial workers, 636; transportation of, 714

Digital divide, 972

Diplomacy in the Near and Middle East: A Documentary Record: 1914–1956 (Hurewitz), 795(box)

Directory (France), 601, 605

Disarmament: of Germany, 810

Disease: resistance to, 621; in urban areas, 634; venereal, 726; Pasteur and, 729; in World War I, 779; AIDS as, 972; global spread of, 972–973; pandemic, 973. *See also* Epidemics; Medicine

Disorienting Encounters: Travels of a Moroccan Scholar in France (Miller), 666(box)

Disraeli, Benjamin, 692, 702, 703(illus.)

Dissenters: as entrepreneurs, 624

Diversity: industrialization and, 620; in cities, 633

Divorce: in France, 600, 601, 607

Djugashvili, Josef, *see* Stalin, Joseph

Domestic servants, *see* Servants

Dominions: British, 929

Doré, Gustave, 697(illus.)

Dostoyevsky, Feodor, 733, 736

Dowry, 721

Draft (military), *see* Conscription

Dreadnought (ship), 765

Dresden: bombing of, 893

Dreyfus, Alfred, 758

Dreyfus affair, 753, 758–759

Drumont, Edouard, 753

Dry plate method: of photography, 734(box)

Dual monarchy, *see* Austria-Hungary

Du Bois, W. E. B., 793

Dubuffet, Jean, 911, 911(illus.)

Duce, Il: Mussolini as, 818

Duma (Russia): Nicholas II and, 763–764

Dunkirk: in World War II, 873

Dupin, Amandine-Aurore, *see* Sand, George (Amandine-Aurore Dupin)

Durham (Lord), 666, 700

Durham Report, 666

Durkheim, Emile, 730

Dutch: retreat from multiculturalism by, 964. *See also* Holland; Netherlands

Dutch East Indies: colonial officials in, 743(illus.); independence of, 929. *See also* Indonesia

Dynamite, 713

Dzerzhinsky, Felix, 814(illus.)

East Asian "tigers," 961

East-central Europe: France and, 794, 810; after World War I, 794, 796(illus.); democracies in, 806, 826; land reform in, 826; political movements in, 856; in World War II, 889; Yalta Conference and, 891; in 1990s, 957; globalization and, 961. *See also* Central Europe; Eastern Europe

Eastern Europe: industrialization and, 631–632; absolutism in, 668; agriculture in, 722; popular fronts in, 857; World War II and, 874–875, 899; Nazi plans for, 878; resettlement in, 878; communist bloc in, 922–926

Eastern front: in World War I, 776–777; Russian Revolution and, 777

Easter Rebellion, 779, 825

East Germany, 899, 906(illus.); protests in, 923; Soviet intervention in, 923; Ulbricht and, 925; emigration from, 938; reforms in, 938; merged into West Germany, 939. *See also* Berlin

East India Company, 614

Eastman, George, 731

Ebert, Friedrich, 789, 827

EC, *see* European Community (EC)

Economic Consequences of the Peace, The (Keynes), 798

Economic integration: in Europe, 932

Economics: laissez faire, 658. *See also* Marx, Karl; Marxism

Economy: of France, 591, 601, 609, 824–825; British, 614–615, 825; industrialization and, 620; classical, 658–659; revolutions of 1848 and, 671; in 1848, 672; of Ottoman Empire, 695; Second Industrial Revolution and, 712; African and Asian, 743; planning and, 780; peacetime, 791; of Soviet Union, 813, 814, 815, 933; of Italy, 816; after World War I, 819–820; Great Depression and, 838, 840–841; U.S. loans to Germany and, 839; government role in, 840–841, 841(box);

Fallada, Hans, 840
Families: of factory workers, 636–637; in Nazi Germany, 854; Swedish, 916; in Britain, 917; in France, 917, 969; gender roles and, 967–969; policies on, 969
Famines: in Ireland, 672; in Tsarist Russia, 762; in Soviet Union (1930s), 844
Fanon, Frantz, 930, 931(box)
Faraday, Michael, 729
Farben, IG: slave labor and, 880
Farms and farming, *see* Agriculture
Farrell, Thomas, F., 869
Fascism: in Italy, 811, 816–819, 817(illus.), 861–862; foundation of, 817; popular fronts and, 856; in Spain, 857–858, 859; in France, 859. *See also* Nazi Germany
Faust (Goethe), 655
February Patent (Austria-Hungary), 693
Federal Republic of Germany, *see* West Germany
Feminism: in 1848, 671; in France, 671; war and, 780; in Britain, 917; *Second Sex* and, 917; in 1970s, 920; expansion of, 969
Ferdinand VII (Spain), 650, 664
Ferry, Jules, 743
Fichte, Johann Gottlieb, 658
Fiction, *see* Literature; Novels
Fifth Republic (France), 919, 930
Films, *see* Movies
"Final solution," 878. *See also* Holocaust
Finances: in France, 596; in Ottoman Empire, 695. *See also* Taxation
Fini, Gianfranco, 962
Finland: Napoleon and, 608; independence of, 794; World War II and, 871
Fire at Sea (Turner), 654
First Estate (France), 592
First International (socialist), 752
First World War, *see* World War I
Five-Year Plan (Russia), 815
Flaubert, Gustave, 733, 736
Floor Burger (Oldenburg), 912(illus.)
Florida: U.S. acquisition of, 699
Flu, *see* Influenza
Flying shuttle, 625, 645
Foch, Ferdinand, 787–788, 797
Folies-Bergère, 821(illus.)
Folktales: nationalism and, 655
Food: in French Revolution, 595, 600, 601; prices for, 668; shortages in 1848, 672; transport of, 714. *See also* Diet (food)
Food riots, 779
Football, 824
Forced labor, *see* Labor; Slaves and slavery
Ford, Henry, 822(box)
Fordism, 820
Foreign Affairs (magazine): Kennan article in, 900(box)
Foreign aid, 972
Forge hammer, 627
"Fortress Truce," 773
Fortyn, Pim, 962
Foucault, Michel, 981
Foundling home, 636
Fourier, Charles, 660
Fourteen Points, 786–787, 789

Fourth Republic (France), 919
France: American war debt to, 590; *Ancien Régime* ("Old Regime") in, 590; Seven Years' War and, 590; fiscal crisis in, 590–592, 596, 601; reform in, 591–592; clubs in, 595–596; under Napoleon I, 604–610; Napoleonic Empire of, 606(illus.), 616; economy of, 609, 820; soldiers' pensions and, 610; monarchy in, 610–611; industrialization in, 629–630; GNP in, 631(illus.); labor in, 644, 759, 796; after Napoleonic Wars, 650, 651; nationalism in, 655, 658; July Revolution in, 663; freedom of the press in, 665, 666(box); revolutions of 1848 in, 671; in 1848, 673; republics in, 673, 674, 707, 919; Crimean War and, 682–683; parliamentary democracy in, 703, 706–707; under Napoleon III, 706–707; railroads in, 713; workers in, 720; public health and, 724; solidarism in, 726; Catholicism in, 730; religious toleration in, 731; colonies of, 740, 796; new imperialism and, 741, 743; anarchism in, 752; syndicalism in, 752–753; socialism in, 752(illus.); Third Republic in, 757–758; alliances of, 764; isolation of, 767; World War I and, 767, 772, 775, 775(illus.), 776, 787–788, 790, 805; army of, 773; Sacred Union in, 773, 787; Marne and, 788; in 1920s, 809–810, 825; east-central Europe and, 810; inflation in, 820; society and politics in 1920s, 824–825; industrial production in, 825; prosperity in, 825; Germany and, 828, 829–830; reparations owed to, 839; in Great Depression, 843; antidemocratic leagues in, 856; communism in, 859–860; popular fronts in, 859–860; Matignon Agreement in, 860; Mussolini and, 861; Czechoslovakia and, 864; World War II alliances and, 865; World War II and, 871–872, 889; in 1950s, 914–915; welfare issues in, 917; West Germany and, 918(illus.); in postwar period, 919; "Days of May" uprising in, 920; Mitterand and, 920–921; Suez Crisis and, 929; decolonization and, 929–930; Indochina and, 929–930; Algeria and, 930; EU and, 950, 951, 951(illus.); democratic capitalism in, 960; unemployment in, 961; Muslims in, 963, 980; day care in, 969; family policy in, 969
France, Battle of, 871–872, 874
Franchise, *see* Voting and voting rights
Francis I (Austrian Empire), 668
Franco, Francisco, 857, 858–859, 919
Franco-Prussian War, 688, 690, 706, 765
Franco-Russian Alliance, 764
Frankfurt: legislature in (1848), 675; Treaty of (1871), 692; European Central Bank in, 950
Frankfurt Assembly, 675
Frankfurt School, 831–832
Franklin, Benjamin, 590
Franz Ferdinand (Austria-Hungary): assassination of, 766, 766(illus.)
Franz Joseph (Austria-Hungary), 693, 761, 762
Free city: Danzig as, 864
Free Corps (Germany), 827

Freedom(s): in France, 594, 597, 665, 666(box); Hegel on, 662; in England, 664; political, 678; in Western cultures, 945; Mandela on, 970–971(box)
Free French, 873, 881, 889, 897
Free markets, 658; French distrust of, 591; government and, 841(box); in 1980s, 921(illus.); in postcommunist societies, 957
Freemasons: Russian, 669
Free trade, *see* Tariffs; Trade
French Communist Party, 813
French Congo, 744
French National Assembly, 963
French Revolution, 716; citizen army in, 586(illus.), 587; Estates General and, 592; National Assembly and, 592; Tennis Court Oath and, 592, 593(illus.); symbols and, 593, 598, 602–603(box); storming of Bastille in, 593–594; women in, 594–595, 594(illus.), 601, 602(illus.); phases of, 595–604; foreign war and, 597–599; capture of royal family in, 598; victory over Prussia and Austria, 598; political repression in, 599–600; Terror in, 599–600; Napoleon and, 604, 608; legacies of, 611; hereditary rule and, 615; Metternich on, 668
French Socialist Party, 813
French Worker, Autobiographies from the Early Industrial Era, The (Traugott), 626(box)
Freud, Sigmund, 754, 768, 830
Friedrich Wilhelm III (Germany), 681, 760
Friedrich Wilhelm IV (Germany), 673, 673(illus.), 675
Friendly societies, 640–641
Fronts: in World War I, 773, 774(illus.)
Führer (leader): Hitler as, 851
Fukuzawa Yukichi, 702(box)
Futurists, 754

Galápagos Islands, 727–728
Gandhi, Mohandas, 796, 807–808, 842(box), 843, 901, 901(illus.), 920, 977
Garibaldi, Giuseppe, 686–687, 688(illus.); unification of Italy and, 687(illus.)
Gas: poisonous, 776
Gaslights, 734(box)
Gatti de Gamond, Zoé, 660
Gauguin, Paul, 745, 754
Gay subculture, 821. *See also* Homosexuality
Gdansk: as "free city" Danzig, 864–865; Solidarity movement in, 935, 937(illus.)
GDP, *see* Gross domestic product (GDP)
Gehry, Frank, 978–979(box), 979(illus.)
G-8 (Group of 8), 947, 966, 973–974
Gender: roles, 638, 969; in unions, 644; bourgeois distinctions of, 719; social issues and, 915–917; in Britain, 916–917; in France, 917. *See also* Men; Women
General Government (Poland), 878
General Theory of Employment, Interest and Money, The (Keynes), 841(box)
Genocide: in Armenia, 762; in Sudan, 975. *See also* Ethnic cleansing; Holocaust
Geopolitics: Hitler and, 850
George III (England), 704(box)
George IV (England), 704(box)